THE ROUGH GUIDE TO THE
PHILIPPINES

**ROUGH
GUIDES**

This fifth edition updated by
**Nick Edwards, Esme Fox, Daniel Jacobs and
Mike MacEacheran**

Contents

Introduction to

The Philippines

Separated from its Southeast Asian neighbours by the South China Sea, the Philippines has always been a little different. As the only Asian nation colonized by the Spanish, this lush archipelago of dazzling beaches, year-round sun and warm, turquoise waters remains predominantly Roman Catholic, and culturally – a blend of Islamic, Malay, Spanish and American influences – it often feels light years away from its neighbours, with a string of elegant colonial towns that have more in common with Latin America than the rest of Asia. It's an enticing mix: all over the archipelago you'll discover tantalizing food, friendly people and exuberant festivals. And the variety is astonishing: you can surf, island-hop or dive pristine coral reefs in the morning, and in the same day visit mystical tribal villages, ancient rice terraces and jungle-smothered peaks.

Indeed, the Philippines is often underrated and misunderstood by travellers and its Asian neighbours, casually dismissed as a supplier of maids, tribute bands, mail-order brides and corrupt politicians, epitomized by the gaudy excesses of Imelda Marcos. Don't be put off: while poverty and corruption remain serious problems, the Philippines is far more complex – and culturally rich – than the stereotypes suggest.

The **Filipino people** are variously descended from early Malay settlers, Muslim Sufis from the Middle East, Spanish conquistadors and friars, and later, from Chinese traders. It's an old cliché, but largely true: Filipinos take pride in making visitors welcome, even in the most rustic barangay home. Equally important is the culture of entertaining, evident in the hundreds of colourful **fiestas** that are held throughout the country, many tied to the Roman Catholic calendar. Never far behind partying is eating: Filipino **food** is heavily influenced by Spanish and native traditions – expect plenty of fresh fish, roasted meats (pork and chicken) and, unlike in the rest of Asia, a plethora of addictive desserts, many utilizing the vast array of tropical fruits on offer.

ABOVE | ANZONES FESTIVAL, CAMIGUIN ISLAND

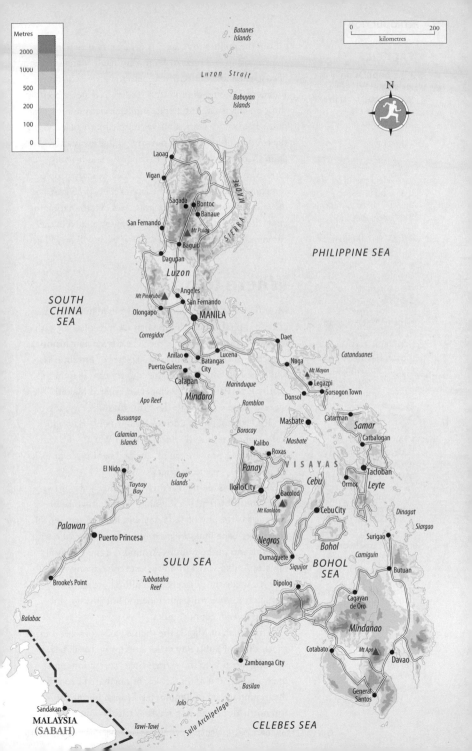

Metres
2000
1000
500
200
100
0

0   200
kilometres

N

Batanes Islands

Luzon Strait

Babuyan Islands

Laoag

Vigan

Sagada   Bontoc
     Banaue

San Fernando

▲ Mt Pulag

Baguio

Dagupan

Luzon

Mt Pinatubo ▲   Angeles
     San Fernando

Olongapo

MANILA

Corregidor

Daet

Anilao
Batangas City   Lucena

Puerto Galera

Calapan

Mindoro

Marinduque

Naga

Mt Mayon ▲   Legazpi
     Sorsogon Town

Donsol

Catanduanes

Apo Reef

Romblon

Masbate

Catarman

Samar

Catbalogan

Busuanga

Calamian Islands

Boracay

Kalibo

Roxas

Masbate

V I S A Y A S

El Nido

Cuyo Islands

Taytay Bay

Panay

Cebu

Tacloban

Iloilo City

Bacolod

Ormoc

Leyte

Mt Kanlaon ▲

Cebu City

Dinagat

Palawan

Puerto Princesa

Negros

Bohol

Surigao

Siargao

Dumaguete

Siquijor

BOHOL SEA

Camiguin

Butuan

Brooke's Point

SOUTH CHINA SEA

PHILIPPINE SEA

SULU SEA

Tubbataha Reef

Dipolog

Cagayan de Oro

Mindanao

Balabac

MALAYSIA (SABAH)

Sandakan

Tawi-Tawi

Jolo

Sulu Archipelago

Basilan

Zamboanga City

Cotabato

Mt Apo ▲

Davao

General Santos

CELEBES SEA

SIERRA MADRE

FACT FILE

- The **population** of the Philippines was estimated to be just over 102 million in 2016; half reside on the island of Luzon.

- The Philippines officially comprises 7107 islands, though the actual figure varies depending on the definition of "island"; reef tips and shoals number in the tens of thousands.

- The Philippines has the largest **diaspora** in the world; 11–12 million Filipinos live and work overseas, mostly as nurses, maids or on cruise ships.

- The richest individual in the Philippines is thought to be mall tycoon **Henry Sy** (SM Group), with a US$13.7 billion net worth – in a country where the average wage is less than US$300/month.

- **Tanduay rum** dates back to 1854, and today remains the nation's spirit of choice. Made with sugar cane milled in Negros, it's frequently cheaper than bottled water.

- Most Filipinos have at least one **uncle or aunt** named Boy, Girlie or Baby.

- Filipino and English are the **official languages** of the Philippines (Filipino is just a standardized version of Tagalog), but there are at least 171 languages spoken throughout the archipelago, with Cebuano following Filipino in popularity.

Even the **politics** in Asia's first democracy is rich in showmanship and pizzazz. From Ferdinand Marcos to the "housewife President" Cory Aquino to current controversial President Duterte, the country's leaders have never been short on charisma. But despite impressive economic gains in the last twenty years, all have conspicuously failed to rid the country of its grinding **poverty**, visible everywhere you go in shanty towns and rickety barangay, and brutally exposed by **Typhoon Yolanda** in 2013. Ordinary people somehow remain stoical in the face of these problems, infectiously optimistic and upbeat. This determination to enjoy life is a national characteristic, encapsulated in the common Tagalog phrase *bahala na* – "what will be will be".

Where to go

Most flights to the Philippines arrive in **Manila**, the crazy, chaotic capital which, despite first impressions, is worth at least a day or two of your time. The city's major historical attraction is the old Spanish walled city of **Intramuros**, while the best museums in the country can be found in nearby **Rizal Park** and skyscraper-smothered **Makati**. There are also some worthwhile day-trips from the city; top of the list is the island of **Corregidor** in Manila Bay, which was fought over bitterly during World War II and, with its now-silent guns and ruins, is a poignant place to soak up the history of the conflict.

Within easy striking distance of Manila – about two hours south by road – a highlight of the province of Batangas is the city of **Tagaytay** and its mesmerizing views over **Lake Taal**, the picture-perfect crater lake with **Taal Volcano** in the middle. Around the small coastal town of **Anilao** you'll find the best scuba diving near Manila, while the adjacent agricultural province of **Laguna** is known for its therapeutic hot springs and luscious *buko* (coconut) pies.

To the north of Manila the theme parks, beaches and wreck-dives of **Subic Bay** make a tempting break before the long bus ride to the extraordinary attractions and spell-binding mountain scenery of **northern Luzon**. From the mountain city of **Baguio**, it's a rough but memorable trip north along winding roads to tribal communities

JEEPNEYS

Millions of Filipinos depend on **jeepneys** – a kind of informal minibus service – to get to school and the office, or to transport livestock to market. Jeepneys are able to operate where roads are too narrow for regular buses, and as a result most travellers end up using them at least once. Despite the discomfort, for many it's one of the highlights of their trip – a genuine slice of Filipino life.

The original jeepneys, cannibalized from vehicles left behind by departing Americans at the end of World War II, have evolved over the past six decades into the mass-produced versions that you see on the streets today, decorated with chrome trinkets, blinking fairy lights and images of celebrities. Others sport religious mottos, crucifixes and images of saints, perhaps understandable given the high accident rates they rack up.

such as **Sagada**, known for its hanging coffins, and **Banaue**, where you can trek through awe-inspiring rice-terrace countryside. Off Luzon's northern tip are the alluring islands of **Batanes**, one of the country's greatest secrets, while along Luzon's west coast you can surf around **San Fernando** or explore the ravishing colonial town of **Vigan**, a UNESCO World Heritage Site.

Head south from Manila through the **Bicol** region and you'll reach perhaps the best-known of Philippine volcanoes, **Mayon**, an almost perfect cone that towers over the city of Legazpi and is a strenuous four- or five-day climb. Around **Donsol** you can swim with whale sharks, and in **Bulusan Volcano National Park** trek through lush rainforest to waterfalls, hot springs and volcanic craters. Even further off the tourist trail, **Catanduanes** offers excellent surfing, while **Marinduque** is a pastoral island backwater that only gets touristy for the annual **Moriones festival**, held at Easter.

For most visitors, the myriad islands and islets of the **Visayas**, right at the heart of the archipelago, are top of the agenda. In the Western Visayas, the captivating little island of **Boracay**, with its pristine beach, is on almost everyone's itinerary. If Boracay is too touristy for you, try laidback Siquijor or tiny Apo Island near Negros, a marine reserve where the only accommodation is in rustic cottages. For even less developed spots, head over to the Eastern Visayas for Panglao Island off Bohol, or the tantalizing beaches and waters of Malapascua off the northern tip of Cebu Island. For trekking and climbing make for **Mount Kanlaon National Park** on Negros, one of the country's finest wilderness areas. The largest city in the Visayas is **Cebu City**, the arrival point for a limited number of international flights – as well as

OPPOSITE FISHERMEN, MINDORO

a major hub for domestic airlines – making it a good alternative base to Manila. It's friendly, affordable and has a buzzing nightlife scene, with great restaurants and live music.

If you're looking for some serious diving, head for **Puerto Galera** on the northern coast of **Mindoro Island**. It also boasts some excellent beaches and trekking through the jungles of the interior to tribal communities. There's more world-class diving off the west coast of Mindoro at **Apo Reef**, although it can be pricey to get here.

To the west of the archipelago, out in the northern Sulu Sea, is the bewitching province of **Palawan**, most of it still wild and unspoilt. Many visitors come for the superb scuba diving, especially on the sunken World War II wrecks around **Coron Town** in the **Calamian Islands** to the north of Palawan proper. Palawan itself is home to the seaside town of **El Nido** and the **Bacuit archipelago**, hundreds of gem-like limestone islands with sugar-white beaches and lagoons. From **Puerto Princesa**, Palawan's likeable capital, strike out for the laidback beach town of **Port Barton** or the **Underground River**, an entrancing cavern system only accessible by boat.

In the far south, the vast island of **Mindanao** has long been the Muslim heartland of the Philippines, an enticing yet sadly troubled region (see box, p.405). The two offshore islands that are regarded as completely safe and still see large numbers of visitors are **Siargao**, which boasts surf beaches and secret lagoons, and wonderfully friendly and scenic **Camiguin**. You should check the security situation very carefully before considering a visit to the pristine waters of the **Enchanted River**, the durian capital and largest city of **Davao** or nearby **Mount Apo**. Note that western Mindanao, including the **Sulu archipelago**, at the time this book went to print was definitely too dangerous to visit due to continuing Muslim separatist unrest.

DIVE PARADISE

The Philippines is blessed by a dazzling richness and diversity of marine life and **diving** is one of the most popular activities in the archipelago. Under the waves lies an underwater wonderland of stupefying **coral gardens** teeming with brilliantly coloured reef fish, turtles, giant clams and starfish, while at depth there are giant rays and prowling sharks. Indeed, this vast tropical archipelago is at the heart of Southeast Asia's "coral triangle", the most biologically diverse marine ecosystem on earth, with over 300 types of coral and 350 fish species. Diving here is affordable and, thanks to warm waters, can be enjoyed year-round. If you're serious about your diving,

booking a trip on a **liveaboard** (see p.39) can be a memorable experience, giving you the opportunity to get away from the more popular dive resorts and explore the wilderness.

When to go

The Philippines has a hot and humid tropical climate with a **wet season** (southwest monsoon, or *habagat*) from May to October and a **dry season** (northeast monsoon, or *amihan*) from November to April. The **best time to visit** is during the dry season, although some regions get quite a lot of rain till February, and even the wet season sees many sunny days with short, intense downpours at dusk. January and February are the coolest months and good for travelling, while March, April and May are very hot: expect sunshine all day and temperatures to peak at a broiling 36°C. As well as higher humidity, the wet season also brings **typhoons** (see box, p.48), with flights sometimes cancelled and roads impassable. The first typhoon can hit as early as May, although typically it is June or July before the rains really start, with July to September the wettest (and stormiest) months. The Palawan, Mindanao and the southern Visayas are less prone to typhoons, and Mindanao sees less rain during the wet season.

AVERAGE TEMPERATURES AND RAINFALL

	Jan	Feb	Mar	Apr	May	Jun	Jul	Aug	Sep	Oct	Nov	Dec
MANILA												
°C	25	27	28.5	31.5	31	29	28.5	28	28	28.5	28	27
°F	77	81	83	89	88	84	83	82	82	83	82	81
Rainfall (mm)	0.74	0.46	0.58	1.1	4.2	8.5	13.9	13.6	11.8	6.2	4.8	2.1
BAGUIO (NORTHERN LUZON)												
°C	17	19	20.5	23.5	23	21	20.5	19.5	20	20.5	20	18.5
°F	63	66	69	74	73	70	69	67	68	69	68	65
Rainfall (mm)	0.74	1.2	1.1	1.4	4.8	10.2	14.8	14.2	12.6	8.4	6.6	3.2
SIARGAO (MINDANAO)												
°C	25.5	26	26	27	27	27	27	27	27	27	26	26.5
°F	78	79	79	81	81	81	81	81	81	81	79	80
Rainfall (mm)	17.5	13.4	16.3	8.4	5	4.2	5.7	4.1	5.6	8.8	14.2	20

Author picks

Scaling the heights of its awe-inspiring volcanoes, enduring sweltering jungle heat and traversing some of Asia's most isolated roads, our hard-travelling authors have visited every corner of this vast, magnificent archipelago – from the rice terraces of Luzon to the beaches of the Visayas. Here are their personal favourites:

Best beach hideaway You don't have to travel for days by bangka to find a slice of serenity in the Philippines; *Tuko Beach Resort* in Abra de Ilog, Mindoro (p.255) is just a couple of hours from Batangas but seems a million miles from anywhere, with dolphins off the beach and monkeys lounging in the trees.

Eat like a Filipino The best fried chicken in the Philippines? For purists, it's still knocked out by *Aristocrat* in Manila (p.89). The *halo-halo* here is amazing also, but *Aling Taleng's* (p.108) in Pagsanjan is sublime. For *buko* pie it's a close call, but *Orient* in Los Baños (p.107) is hard to beat.

Go wild Tackle the pristine jungle wilderness of Mindoro with an epic climb up Mount Halcon (p.247), or conquer Mount Kanlaon on Negros (p.295); trekking through the UNESCO World Heritage rice terraces in northern Luzon remains an enchanting experience (p.176), while seeing (or even snorkelling with) whale sharks, the world's largest fish, in Donsol (p.220) is truly magical.

Best stash of gold One of many reasons to resist the desire to flee Manila as soon as possible, the Ayala Museum (p.76) is an intriguing introduction to the history and lavish pre-Hispanic culture of the Philippines.

Go paddling Soak up the beauty of southern Luzon by taking a boat through the crystal-clear waters and exploring the awe-inspiring limestone cliffs of the Caramoan Peninsula (p.210).

> Our author recommendations don't end here. We've flagged up our favourite places – a perfectly sited hotel, an atmospheric café, a special restaurant – throughout the guide, highlighted with the ★ symbol.

FROM TOP JUVENILE MACAQUE, MINDORO; RICE TERRACES, BATAD; THE CARAMOAN PENINSULA

18

things not to miss

It's not possible to see everything the Philippines has to offer in one trip – and we don't suggest you try. What follows is a selective taste of the country's highlights: idyllic beaches, spectacular hikes, historic sites and fascinating wildlife. All highlights are colour-coded by chapter and have a page reference to take you straight into the Guide, where you can find out more.

1

1 BORACAY
Page 258

You'll never be short of things to do on picture-postcard Boracay Island, with its busy but stunning White Beach.

2 SURFING AT SIARGAO
Page 419

Avid surfers will find several locations where they can catch some decent waves, but Siargao, off the tip of Mindanao, is one of the best.

3 APO REEF MARINE NATURAL PARK
Page 254

The gin-clear waters of Apo Reef, off the west coast of Mindoro, are a scuba diver's dream.

4 CHOCOLATE HILLS
Page 349

Soak up the bizarre landscape of Bohol's iconic Chocolate Hills, conical brown-green mounds said to be the calcified tears of a broken-hearted giant.

5 VIGAN
Page 138

Wonderfully preserved slice of Spanish-era Philippines, with cobblestone streets and gorgeous Baroque architecture.

6 WHALE SHARKS
Page 220

Getting up close to these gentle giants off the coast of Donsol, in southern Luzon, is an unforgettable experience.

7 MOUNT MAYON
Page 215

The almost perfectly symmetrical cone of volcanic Mount Mayon makes for a challenging but thrilling climb.

8 ATI-ATIHAN FESTIVAL
Page 284

At this lively annual festival in Kalibo, on Panay Island, everyone wears indigenous dress and learns tribal dances.

9 BATANES
Page 181

Blissfully remote islands halfway between Luzon and Taiwan, home to rolling hills and wild stretches of coast.

10 MALAPASCUA
Page 334

Gorgeous and isolated island hideaway, with bone-white Bounty Beach and superb diving.

11 CORON ISLAND BY BANGKA
Page 397

Tour the jagged, gasp-inducing coast of Coron Island by bangka, taking in hidden coves, secret beaches and two pristine mountain lakes fed by springs.

12 MOUNT PINATUBO
Page 119

The lower slopes of Mount Pinatubo feature canyons formed after the massive 1991 eruption, while the crater is filled by a sulphuric mountain lake.

13 UNDERGROUND RIVER
Page 383

Near Puerto Princesa, Palawan, this is one of the longest subterranean rivers in the world, with eerie stalactites, vast caverns and hidden chambers.

14 RICE TERRACES
Page 176

The mind-boggling rice terraces around Banaue stand as one of Asia's greatest sights, and offer superb trekking.

15 TARSIERS
Page 349

Admire these tiny primates with the enormous, sorrowful eyes at their protected sanctuary in Bohol.

16 SAN AGUSTIN CHURCH
Page 62

This elegantly weathered Spanish pile in the heart of old Manila is the archipelago's oldest stone church.

17 HALO-HALO
Page 32

Nothing beats a tall glass of this icy Filipino treat on a hot day, a concoction of syrups, beans, fruits and ice cream.

18 EL NIDO
Page 388

The strikingly beautiful limestone islands around El Nido in Palawan offer exceptional exploring and adventure.

12

13

14

Itineraries

The following itineraries span the entire length of this incredibly diverse archipelago, from the historic cities of Luzon to the idyllic islands of the Visayas and the remote jungles of Mindanao. Given the time involved moving from place to place, you may not be able to cover everything, but even picking a few highlights will give you a deeper insight into the natural and cultural wonders of the Philippines.

THE GRAND TOUR

This three- to four-week tour gives a taster of the Philippines' iconic landscapes and islands from the nation's chaotic capital to the pristine sands of Boracay.

❶ Manila The nation's initially chaotic capital is a vast, boiling blend of history, high culture and wild nightlife. **See p.56**

❷ Banaue rice terraces It's worth taking the journey north to see one of the world's great man-made wonders. **See p.176**

❸ Sagada Extend your stay in northern Luzon with a trip to this rambling old town, home of the famed hanging coffins. **See p.170**

❹ Puerto Princesa Backtrack to Manila for the flight to Palawan's sleepy capital and the trip along the Underground River. **See p.375**

❺ El Nido Continue along the Palawan coast to the spectacular limestone scenery of the Bacuit archipelago. **See p.388**

❻ Coron Take the bangka across to Coron, where wreck-diving and dazzling coves await. See p.397

❼ Cebu City Fly to the nation's third city, home of Magellan's Cross and a host of historic attractions. **See p.315**

❽ Bohol Take the ferry to this historic island, home of the Chocolate Hills and the loveable tarsier. **See p.342**

❾ Boracay Backtrack to Cebu for the short flight to this famed resort island, where you can end your tour on a sugary white-sand beach. **See p.258**

ISLAND-HOPPING: THE WESTERN ROUTE

This tour takes in popular Mindoro en route to the western side of the Visayas, the physical and historic heart of the nation. This is perhaps the most alluring region of the Philippines, a sun-bleached concentration of islands littered with beaches, crumbling churches, sugar plantations and untouched reefs. This itinerary needs at least three weeks to complete in comfort, though you could race through it quicker.

❶ Puerto Galera Begin your tour at this accessible and congenial beach on the tip of Mindoro, which is also a prime dive resort. **See p.237**

❷ Romblon Ferries link Mindoro to the more remote Romblon archipelago, three main islands offering a laidback capital, challenging mountain and some splendid beaches. **See p.269**

ABOVE MOUNT MAYON

❸ Boracay A short boat ride south via Caticlan is the jewel of Philippine beach resorts, justly renowned for its mesmerizing (if crowded) white sands and its party scene. **See p.258**

❹ Guimaras Bus across from Caticlan to Iloilo City on the south side of Panay, from where it's another short boat ride to this island of mangoes, mountain bikes and handsome Spanish chapels. **See p.285**

❺ Silay After arriving on Negros by boat, connect via busy Bacolod to this delightful small town, where you can stay in the converted mansion of a sugar baron. **See p.293**

❻ Dumaguete Traverse Negros and spend some time in the pleasant city of Dumaguete, which has a lovely seafront promenade and is well placed for diving around Dauin and Apo Island. **See p.298**

❼ Siquijor Take another swift ferry ride across to the island of witches, rich in legend, culture and rugged beauty, as well as a growing number of relaxing resorts. **See p.303**

ISLAND HOPPING: THE EASTERN LOOP

Skip Manila altogether by beginning and ending your trip in Cebu City, taking in the wonderful variety of the Eastern Visayas. This route includes everything from urban nightlife, through remote islands and beaches with superb marine life, to inland natural wonders. This itinerary needs at least three weeks to do it justice.

❶ Cebu City Start off in the Philippines' surprisingly cosmopolitan second city, which has great dining, nightlife and shopping, as well as cultural sights and nearby Mactan Island for swimming. **See p.315**

❷ Moalboal Bus across to Cebu's west coast, where you can lounge on lovely Panagsama Beach, near the quiet town of Moalboal, or take a diving trip to tiny Pescador Island. **See p.339**

❸ Oslob Several hours south by bus from Moalboal is the small town of Oslob, famous for its friendly whale sharks. **See p.341**

❹ Bohol Travel by sea via Dumaguete to this fascinating island, which offers the charms of offshore Panglao Island, the Chocolate Hills and those adorable tarsiers. **See p.342**

THE GRAND TOUR

ISLAND-HOPPING: THE WESTERN ROUTE

ISLAND HOPPING: THE EASTERN LOOP

SOUTH CHINA SEA

PHILIPPINE SEA

SULU SEA

BOHOL SEA

MALAYSIA

CELEBES SEA

❺ Padre Burgos Take a boat from Ubay in eastern Bohol across to Bato on Leyte and on to the up-and-coming scuba centre of the southern Philippines. **See p.368**

❻ Sohoton Natural Bridge National Park Travel by bus north to Tacloban and nip across to the island of Samar to experience this jungle-clad, limestone wilderness. **See p.357**

❼ Camotes Islands Double-back to Leyte via Tacloban and take a ferry from Ormoc to this tranquil, picture-perfect island chain, with excellent diving and snorkelling. **See p.336**

❽ Siargao Island Return to Cebu for the short flight to Siargao, best known for surfing but also rich in empty, wild, sandy beaches and offshore islands. **See p.417**

THE DIVE MASTER

Millions of visitors come to the Philippines primarily for what's below sea level – the waters surrounding the island chain harbour some of the world's richest marine life. The following tour would ideally take at least three weeks – and lots of advance planning – to complete.

❶ **Puerto Galera** This easy-to-reach resort makes a great introduction to the local dive scene, with plenty of resorts and operators to choose from. **See p.237**

❷ **Apo Reef** Take a day or two to explore this protected reef off the west coast of Mindoro, home to sharks, turtles and rays. **See p.254**

❸ **Coron** Try to take the bangka across to Coron for some spectacular wreck-diving, primarily Japanese ships from World War II. **See p.394**

❹ **El Nido** Continue on to the Palawan mainland where the numerous dive schools at El Nido can help arrange trips to stunning Tubbataha. **See p.388**

❺ **Apo Island** From Puerto Princesa fly to Cebu City then head south to Dumaguete and Apo Island, another dive hot spot. **See p.303**

❻ **Panglao Island** From Dumaguete it's a short boat ride to this languid island, home to congenial resorts, beaches and dive sights. **See p.345**

❼ **Padre Burgos** Cross over to Leyte to experience this exciting dive location, home to whale sharks, dolphins and manta rays. **See p.368**

THE BEST OF THE BEACH

The appeal of hiking volcanoes or trudging city streets can wilt (especially in the tropical heat), when compared to the dazzling white beaches on offer in the Philippines. This itinerary takes in the best of the nation's strips of sand. This itinerary needs a minimum of three weeks, but given the focus on beaches, this route could obviously be extended into a much longer trip, especially as you will need to break up some of these journeys.

❶ **Marinduque** Take the short flight from Manila to this lesser-visited island and seek out some of the sandy beaches off its eastern coast. **See p.195**

❷ **Caramoan Peninsula** Hop on a ferry back to the Luzon mainland and head east to this rugged promontory, which harbours blue-water coves and enticing resorts. **See p.214**

❸ **Malapascua Island** Fly from Legazpi to Cebu City, where it's a four-hour bus and boat ride to this tiny islet ringed by chalky white sands. **See p.334**

❹ **Panglao Island** Double back the same way to Cebu City, then jump on a ferry to Taglibaran on Bohol, where the offshore Panglao Island boasts several glorious stretches of sand and great diving. **See p.345**

❺ **Camiguin Island** A sporadic bangka service from Jagna on Bohol connects with the compact, easy-to-explore Camiguin Island off the Mindanao coast, boasting gorgeous beaches, hot springs and hikes. **See p.410**

❻ **Sugar Beach** Travel back via Bohol to Dumaguete on Negros, then on via Sipalay to Sugar Beach, an ultra-laidback budget spot, close to idyllic Danjugan Island. **See p.296**

❼ **Boracay** After another long haul through Negros and across Panay to Caticlan, you'll be ready to flop out on legendary White Beach in Boracay, then join in the partying when you've got your energy back. **See p.258**

THE DIVE MASTER

THE BEST OF THE BEACH

THE TIME TRAVELLER

SOUTH CHINA SEA

PHILIPPINE SEA

SULU SEA

BOHOL SEA

MALAYSIA

CELEBES SEA

OPPOSITE HANGING COFFINS, ECHO VALLEY, SAGADA

THE TIME TRAVELLER

Evidence of the Philippines' long and complex history is sprinkled all over the archipelago, but northern Luzon is the most evocative of its tribal and colonial past, with handsome old cities and enigmatic remains. This itinerary could be completed in a fortnight, especially if you take some flights, but you'll get a lot more out of it over a good three weeks.

❶ **Intramuros, Manila** The oldest part of Manila drips with history, from Spanish churches and forts to illuminating museums. **See p.62**

❷ **Taal** Take a tour of this beautiful old town, home to the biggest church in Southeast Asia and *bahay na bato* architecture still redolent of colonial Spain. **See p.112**

❸ **Paete** The nation's woodcarving capital makes for an intriguing detour, sprinkled with the stores of local craftsmen. **See p.108**

❹ **Malolos** The oft-overlooked capital of Bulacan province is crammed with colonial remnants, from the elegant Barasoain Church to a smattering of sixteenth-century Spanish homes. **See p.117**

❺ **Vigan** The best-preserved colonial town in the Philippines is a treasure-trove of tiny museums, chapels and crumbling villas. **See p.138**

❻ **Laoag** The capital of Ilocos Norte boasts plenty of historic attractions of its own, while the Malacañang of the north, former holiday residence of the Marcoses, is a short ride away. **See p.143**

❼ **Sagada** Head into the mountainous heart of Luzon, where Sagada is a focus for the Igorots (Cordillera tribes) and the enigmatic hanging coffins. **See p.170**

❽ **Banaue and Batad** You'd be remiss to travel up here and not spend time among the legendary rice terraces, fantastical ridges in the mountains often shrouded in mist. **See p.176 & p.179**

BANGKA

Basics

Getting there

There are several options for non-stop flights to the Philippines from North America and from Australia; from Europe, the only non-stop flights are from London with Philippine Airlines. Otherwise, reaching the Philippines from outside Asia usually involves a stopover in Hong Kong, Singapore or Dubai. Most major airlines in the region have regular connecting flights to Manila; a few also fly direct to Cebu.

High season for Philippines travel is November to April, though airfares vary relatively little through the year. This is because the low season for the Philippines (May–Oct) is the peak season in Europe and the US, so flights heading out of these regions to various hub airports are often full.

If the Philippines is only one stop on a longer journey, you might want to consider buying a **Round-the-World** (RTW) ticket. Some agents and airline alliances also offer **Circle Pacific tickets**, which cover Australia, New Zealand, the west coast of North America and destinations in the Pacific; you can include Manila and/or Cebu on some itineraries.

From the UK and Ireland

Philippine Airlines (PAL) currently operates daily non-stop flights between **London** and Manila (14hr–14hr 30min). The second-fastest option is to fly via Hong Kong, from where there are numerous onward daily flights to Manila and Cebu. Plenty of airlines offer connecting flights to Manila from UK airports, such as KLM, via Amsterdam.

From Ireland, the speediest option is to take a budget airline to London and change there. London–Manila non-stop costs around £540–700, and from around £460 with stops. From the Republic of Ireland, the best fares are around €600–750 via the UK and the Middle East.

From the US and Canada

Philippine Airlines operates non-stop flights to Manila from **Los Angeles**, **San Francisco** and **Vancouver** (and direct flights from Toronto with a stop in Vancouver), charging around US$800–1000 for the round trip. However, other airlines offer alternative routes for as low as $500 return, such as **Korean Air** via Seoul and **Japan Airlines** via Tokyo. From New York and other east-coast cities, return flights cost around $600–1000. Note that in most cases, the longer you stay in the Philippines the cheaper your flight will be.

From Los Angeles or San Francisco, the flying time to Manila is around eleven hours. From the east coast of North America, flying via the Pacific, the journey will take around twenty hours excluding any layover (allow at least 2hr extra) along the way. If you choose to fly from New York via Paris, say, expect the journey to take around 24 hours altogether.

From Australia, New Zealand and South Africa

Philippine Airlines flies non-stop to Manila from **Sydney** (8–9hr) daily and from **Melbourne** (8–9hr) three times a week; it also flies from **Brisbane** (9–10hr), via **Darwin** (4hr 30min). Return fares online can be as low as Aus$700. **Qantas** also flies Sydney to Manila non-stop four times a week, but fares are usually much higher, starting around Aus$1000. If you want to get to **Cebu City**, you can fly via Hong Kong or Kuala Lumpur, although it's probably easiest simply to change in Manila.

From **New Zealand** there are no non-stop flights to the Philippines, so you'll have to go via Australia or a Southeast Asian hub such as Singapore or Hong Kong. Prices are in the NZ$1000–1300 range for Auckland–Manila via Hong Kong (15–20hr).

From **South Africa** you'll always make at least one stop en route to Manila, and often two. Depending on the length of the stop, the trip will take from 16 to 26 hours. Fares via the Gulf, Singapore or Hong Kong start around ZAR10,000 return in high season from Johannesburg.

A BETTER KIND OF TRAVEL

At Rough Guides we are passionately committed to travel. We believe it helps us understand the world we live in and the people we share it with – and of course tourism is vital to many developing economies. But the scale of modern tourism has also damaged some places irreparably, and climate change is accelerated by most forms of transport, especially flying. All Rough Guides' flights are carbon-offset, and every year we donate money to a variety of environmental charities.

From elsewhere in Asia

You can fly direct to the Philippines from almost every major city in Asia, with several budget airlines offering cheap fares. Many of these fly to **Clark International Airport** (see p.119), 80km northwest of Manila, so make sure you factor in additional travel time if necessary. Numerous flights make the two-hour trip **from Hong Kong** to Manila, with rates as low as HK$1400 (US$180).

AirAsia Zest zips between Manila and Kota Kinabalu, Kuala Lumpur, Macau and Seoul. **Cebu Pacific** also offers cheap flights from Bangkok, Jakarta, Kota Kinabalu, Kuala Lumpur, Shanghai, Seoul and Taipei to Manila, and several routes direct to Cebu City. The **Singapore–Manila** route (3hr 30min) is very competitive, served by Philippine Airlines, Singapore Airlines, Jetstar Asia Airways, Tigerair and Cebu Pacific from S$140 (US$100).

Handy **regional flights** include: Silk Air from Singapore to **Davao** on Mindanao (3 weekly; 3hr 50min); Malaysia Airlines from Kota Kinabalu (Sabah) to **Puerto Princesa** (3 weekly; 1hr 30min); and China Airlines from Taipei (Taiwan) to **Laoag** (northern Luzon). **Kalibo International Airport**, serving Boracay, has non-stop flights to Hong Kong, Seoul, Taipei and Singapore.

By boat

Many unlicensed boats ply back and forth between the Malaysian state of Sabah and the southern Philippines, but these are considered unsafe for tourists. At the time of writing even the primary licensed ferry route linking **Zamboanga City** with **Sandakan**, Sabah (non-stop) was not advised because of the security situation in Zamboaanga (see p.433).

AIRLINES

AirAsia Zest Ⓦ airasia.com
Cathay Pacific Ⓦ cathaypacific.com
Cebu Pacific Ⓦ cebupacificair.com
China Airlines Ⓦ china-airlines.com
Delta Airlines Ⓦ delta.com
Jetstar Asia Airways Ⓦ jetstar.com
KLM Ⓦ klm.com
Korean Air Ⓦ koreanair.com
Malaysia Airlines Ⓦ malaysiaairlines.com
Philippine Airlines Ⓦ philippineairlines.com
Qantas Ⓦ qantas.com.au
Silk Air Ⓦ silkair.com
Singapore Airlines Ⓦ singaporeair.com
Tigerair Ⓦ tigerair.com

AGENTS AND OPERATORS

Absolute Travel US ☎ 1800 736 8187, Ⓦ absolutetravel.com. Luxury tours to the Philippines that can be combined with other destinations in Southeast Asia. The fourteen-day Highlights of the Philippines tour includes Manila, Banaue, Sagada, Baguio, Bohol and Cebu City (US$5255, excluding international flights).

Allways Dive Expeditions Australia ☎ 1800 338 239 or ☎ 03 9885 8863, Ⓦ allwaysdive.com.au. All-inclusive dive packages to prime locations in the Philippines and Southeast Asia from around Aus$750 for seven nights (not including flights). Destinations in the Philippines include Coron, Dumaguete, Malapascua, Moalboal, Donsol and Puerto Galera. Also liveaboards to Cebu, Dauin, Tubbataha and Apo reefs, Coron wrecks and Anilao (from Aus$2400).

Bamboo Trails Taiwan ☎ 886 7 7354945, Ⓦ bambootrails.com. Small travel company offering some unique group itineraries in the Philippines, including the "Sugar Trail" through Negros and Siquijor.

Dive Worldwide UK ☎ 01962 302087, Ⓦ diveworldwide.com. Specialist dive operator offering trips to a number of destinations in the Philippines. A typical fourteen-day trip to Donsol to see the whale sharks including flights, domestic transfers and accommodation starts at £2145.

Grasshopper Adventures UK ☎ 020 8123 8144, US ☎ 818 921 7101, Australia ☎ 03 9016 3172; Ⓦ grasshopperadventures.com. Bicycle and guided tour specialists, with a variety of bike tours all over Asia and an eight-day guided tour of Bohol for US$2350.

North South Travel UK ☎ 01245 608291, Ⓦ northsouthtravel .co.uk. Friendly travel agency offering discounted fares worldwide. Profits are used to support projects in the developing world, especially the promotion of sustainable tourism.

Philippine Island Connections UK ☎ 020 7404 8877, Ⓦ pic-uk .com. Philippines specialist offering flights to the Philippines, plus hotel bookings, holiday packages and tours. They also offer domestic flight reservations, though it's often cheaper to book once you're in the Philippines.

STA Travel UK ☎ 0871 230 0040, US ☎ 1800 781 4040, Australia ☎ 13 47 82, New Zealand ☎ 0800 474 400, South Africa ☎ 0861 781 781; Ⓦ statravel.co.uk. Worldwide specialists in independent travel; also student IDs, travel insurance, car rental, rail passes and more. Good discounts for students and under-26s.

Trailfinders UK ☎ 0845 058 5858, Ireland ☎ 01 677 7888, Australia ☎ 1300 780 212; Ⓦ trailfinders.com. One of the best-informed and most efficient agents for independent travellers.

Getting around

The large number of budget airlines and ferry services between major destinations makes it easy to cover the Philippine archipelago, even on a tight budget, though the main drawback is that almost everything routes through Manila and Cebu. Long-distance road transport largely comprises buses and jeepneys – the utilitarian passenger

vehicles modelled on World War II American jeeps. Throughout the provinces, and in some areas of cities, tricycles – motorbikes with steel sidecars – are commonly used for short journeys.

Note that **holiday weekends** are bad times to travel, with buses full and roads jammed, particularly heading out of big cities to the provinces. Cities start to empty on Friday afternoon and the exodus continues into the night, with a mass return on Sunday evening and Monday morning; Metro Manila is especially gridlocked. Travelling is a particular hassle at Christmas, New Year and Easter with buses and ferries full (sometimes illegally overloaded), airports chaotic and resorts charging more than usual. If you have to travel at these times, book tickets in advance or turn up at bus stations and ferry piers early and be prepared to wait.

By plane

Air travel is a godsend for island-hoppers in the Philippines, with a number of airlines linking Manila with most of the country's major destinations; you will usually, however, have to backtrack to a major hub when jumping from one region to another. **Philippine Airlines** (PAL; ⓦ philippineairlines.com) has a comprehensive domestic schedule, while **Cebu Pacific** (ⓦ cebupacificair.com) offers even more routes and very cheap fares, particularly if you book some way in advance. There are several smaller budget airlines – **AirAsia Zest** and **Philippines AirAsia** (both ⓦ airasia.com) and **Tigerair** (ⓦ tigerair.com).

Cebu Pacific runs numerous flights out of its hub in **Cebu City**, saving you the effort of backtracking to Manila – you can, for instance, fly straight from Cebu City to Caticlan (for Boracay) and Siargao. **Davao** on Mindanao is a less developed third hub, with connections to Cebu City, Cagayan de Oro, Iloilo and Zamboanga, but you'll have to transfer in Manila and Cebu for other destinations.

Airfares

There's not a great deal of variation in **domestic airfares** offered by the main budget carriers, though PAL is usually the most expensive, being the only one offering traditional cabin service (snacks, drinks etc). Cebu Pacific has been known to sell seats for P1, and regularly offers fares of P499 one-way Manila to Coron (Busuanga) and P999 Manila to Zamboanga. But note that the low prices you see quoted on budget airline websites usually don't include taxes, and, unlike most PAL flights, you

can't change bookings once you've paid; there are also charges for bags and seat selection (P230 and P180 respectively on Cebu Pacific).

By ferry

Ferries and **bangkas** – wooden outrigger boats – were once the bread and butter of Philippine travel. Though still important, especially in the **Visayas**, most of the longer routes have been made redundant by the growth of budget air travel. Not only are flights faster and as cheap (or cheaper) than cabins on longer ferry routes (Manila to Mindanao for example), they are invariably safer. Indeed, despite some improvements in recent years, ferry accidents remain common in the Philippines and even in the dry season the open ocean can get surprisingly rough. The smaller bangkas are often poorly equipped, with little shelter from the elements, while even many of the larger vessels have been bought secondhand from Japan or Europe and are well past their prime. Ferries of all sizes are frequently crowded.

That said, for many shorter inter-island trips, ferries remain the only form of transport available, and – especially in the Visayas – island-hopping by boat can be an enjoyable and rewarding part of your trip.

There's a hierarchy of vessels, with proper ferries at the top; so-called big bangkas, taking around fifty passengers, in the middle; and ordinary bangkas at the bottom.

Filipino **ferry companies** (see below) operate ships of varying sizes on fixed schedules between major ports, while the timings of bangkas are usually more flexible. The major operator is **2GO**, with SuperCat part of the same group; the other key players are **Montenegro Shipping Lines**, **Cokaliong Shipping Lines**, **Oceanjet** and **TransAsia Shipping Lines**. These companies have regular sailings on routes between Manila, Batangas or Cebu and major cities throughout the Visayas and Mindanao, and on secondary routes within the Visayas.

FERRY COMPANIES

2GO ☎ 02 528 7000, ⓦ travel.2go.com.ph
Aleson Shipping ☎ 062 991 4258, ⓦ aleson-shipping.com
Besta Shipping Lines ☎ 02 345 5568
Cokaliong Shipping Lines ☎ 032 232 7211, ⓦ cokaliongshipping.com
CSGA ⓦ facebook.com/CSGAferrycorporation
E. B. Aznar Shipping ☎ 032 467 9447
F.J. Palacio Lines ☎ 032 255 4540
FastCat ☎ 02 842 9341, ⓦ fastcat.com.ph
George & Peter Lines ☎ 035 422 8431
Island Shipping Lines ☎ 032 422 6329

Jomalia Shipping ☎ 0905 399 8259
Kinswell Shipping Lines ☎ 032 255 7572
Lite Shipping ☎ 032 255 1721
Montenegro Shipping Lines ☎ 043 740 3201
Moreta Shipping ☎ 0917 844 2894, Ⓦ moretashipping.com
MV Star Crafts Pier 1 ☎ 0906 789 6363, Ⓦ mvstarcrafts.com
Navios Shipping Lines ☎ 0908 146 2243
Oceanjet ☎ 032 255 7560, Ⓦ oceanjet.net
Roble Shipping ☎ 032 416 6256
Si-Kat ☎ 02 708 9628, Ⓦ sikatferrybus.com
Starcraft ☎ 0906 789 6363
Starlite Ferries ☎ 02 724 3034, Ⓦ starliteferries.com
Super Shuttle ☎ 032 4127688, Ⓦ supershuttleroro.com
SuperCat ☎ 032 233 7000, Ⓦ supercat.com.ph
Trans-Asia Shipping Lines ☎ 032 254 6491,
Ⓦ transasiashipping.com
VG Shipping Lines ☎ 032 416 6226, Ⓦ vg-shipping.fi
Weesam Express ☎ 032 231 7737, Ⓦ weesam.ph

Fares and tickets

Ferry **fares** are very low by Western standards, especially if booked in advance, for example Manila–Cebu (P950), Manila–Puerto Princesa (P1450); add on around P500–1000 for a private cabin. **Tickets** can be bought at the pier up until departure, though it's often more convenient to avoid the long queues and buy in advance: **travel agents** sell ferry tickets, and the larger ferry companies have ticket offices in cities and towns. 2GO also offers online ticketing.

Accommodation and facilities

The cheapest ferry **accommodation** is in bunk beds in cavernous dorms either below deck or on a semi-open deck, with shared toilets and showers. Older ships might have just a handful of cramped cabins sharing a tiny shower and toilet. The major operators generally have newer ships with a range of accommodation that includes dorms, straw mats in an air-conditioned area and shared cabins (usually for four) with bathrooms. These ferries usually also have a bar, karaoke lounge and a canteen serving basic meals.

By bus

Bus travel can be relatively uncomfortable and slow, but you'll get a real glimpse of rural Philippines from the window, and meet Filipinos from all walks of life. Buses are also incredibly convenient: hundreds of routes spread out like a web from major cities and even the most isolated barangay will have a service of some sort. You won't go hungry either. At most stops local vendors will

jump on and offer you various snacks and drinks, while on the longer hauls, even express buses stop every three or four hours to give passengers a chance to stretch their legs and buy some food.

There are some downsides. Though the largest bus companies have fleets of reasonably new air-conditioned buses for longer routes, they rarely have toilets. On shorter routes buses can be dilapidated contraptions with no air conditioning and, in some cases, no glass in the windows. You'll also need to develop a high tolerance to loud music or Tagalog movies played at full blast throughout the trip.

Bus fares and frequencies

Fares are low: around P445 from Manila to Baguio and P647 to Tuguerarao. Beyond Manila roads can be poor, and even when the distances involved aren't great, the buses will make numerous stops along the way. Some bus companies advertise express services, but in reality a bus that goes from A to B without stopping is unheard of. Buses that have a "derecho" sign (meaning "straight" or "direct") in the window usually make the fewest stops.

Published **timetables** for most bus companies are non-existent, but departures on popular routes such as Manila to Baguio or Manila to Vigan usually happen every hour or half-hour. The larger operators – such as Victory Liner (Ⓦ victoryliner.com) and Philtranco (Ⓦ philtranco.com.ph) – allow you to book seats in advance on some routes, either online, by telephone (often engaged) or at the terminal. A list of bus destinations and the companies that cover them is given in the Manila chapter (see pp.81–83), and details of bus routes, with local contact details, appear throughout the Guide. Note, however, that there are so many bus companies (many of which go in and out of business on a regular basis, or have permits suspended), and so much variation in routes and journey times, that the information we give in the Guide is just a guideline and always subject to change.

By jeepney

The **jeepney** is the ultimate Philippine icon (see box, p.8), and remains an important form of transport, particularly in Manila, Cebu City, Davao and Baguio, where there are frequent services between key locations in each city. In the provinces, jeepneys connect isolated barangays to nearby towns and towns to cities, but they might run only two or three times a day, depending on demand (they often only leave when full), the weather and the mood of the driver. There are absolutely no timetables.

Routes are painted on the side or on a signboard in the window. Even so, using jeepneys takes a little local knowledge because they make numerous stops and deviations to drop off and pick up passengers. There's no such thing as a designated jeepney stop, so people wait in the shade at the side of the road and flag one down. The vehicles are cramped and incredibly uncomfortable, usually holding at least twenty passengers inside and any number of extras clinging to the back or sitting precariously on top. It can be a hassle to get luggage on and off – small items might end up on the floor, but larger items often go on the roof.

Fares are very low: in the provinces they start at P7 for a trip of a few kilometres, rising to P50 for two- or three-hour drives. In the cities, trips up to 4–5km cost P7, rising to P20 on longer routes. To pay, hand your money to the passenger next to you and say "*bayad po*" ("pay please"). If you're not sitting close to the driver, the fare will be passed down the line of passengers until it reaches him; he will then pass back any change; alternatively, you can run round to the front when you get off.

By FX taxi, city taxi and van

Not unlike jeepneys in the way they operate, **FX taxis** are air-conditioned Toyota Tamaraw vehicles (a bit like Range Rovers), with signs in the window indicating their destination. They made their debut in Manila in the late 1990s, and now operate in other cities and on some popular inter-city routes. However, routes are often not set, so it takes a little local knowledge to know where to catch the right vehicle. They can be a little claustrophobic – the driver won't even think about moving until he's got ten people on board, three more than the vehicle is designed for. In Manila most of these taxis charge P2–3 per kilometre.

Elsewhere in the Philippines you may encounter "**vans**" (often labelled "GT Express" meaning "Garage to Terminal"), which are generally cramped Isuzu, Suzuki and Nissan minivans (what would be called small passenger vans in the US) that follow fixed routes. They're usually a little more expensive than buses but they're much faster, as, unlike buses, they don't stop off every few hundred metres. In Luzon, vans often have their own terminals in major towns, and operate in competition with bus companies and jeepneys over long distances. Destinations are usually clearly marked on the windscreen.

City taxis generally fall into two categories: yellow airport taxis charge P60 base rate plus P4 per 500m; regular white taxis charge P30 plus P3.50 per 500m. The app-based taxi service **Uber** is available in Manila and Cebu, and is rapidly expanding to other parts of the country.

By tricycle and "habal-habal"

The cheapest form of shared transport, **tricycles** are ubiquitous in the provinces. In Manila and Cebu City they are prohibited from using certain roads, but almost everywhere else they go where they like, when they like and at speeds as high as their small engines are capable of. The sidecars are usually designed for four passengers – two facing forwards and two backwards – but it's not uncommon to see extras clinging on wherever they can, the only limiting factor being whether or not the machine can actually move under the weight of the extra bodies. Tricycles never follow fixed routes, so it's usually a question of flagging one down and telling the driver your destination.

Closely related but even more life-threatening is the motorcycle-for-hire, popularly known as "**habal-habal**" (the nickname is a sexual allusion – ask a Filipino friend). These motorcycles have two wooden platforms attached to each side, sometimes accommodating up to thirteen persons (believe it). Though there have been moves in Congress to change things, at the time of writing the habal-habal was still technically illegal; laughable when you consider how essential they have become in many parts of the country. In some rural areas, locals offer rides on ordinary motorbikes for negotiable rates.

Habal-habal **fares** typically start at P10 per person for a short trip of a few hundred metres on both forms of transport. Many tricycles charge a set rate per person for trips within town or city boundaries, usually around P10–25 (more in Manila). If you want to use the tricycle as a private taxi you'll have to negotiate a price – P25–30 is reasonable for a trip of up to 2km in the provinces. Anything further than that and the driver will ask for at least P50, though you can always try to bargain him down. Note, however, that tricycle drivers are notorious for ripping off foreigners, and especially in touristy areas you'll need expert bargaining skills to pay anything close to the local rate.

By car

It's possible to **rent a car** in the Philippines – a standard saloon car costs about P2000 per day – but you may not want to. Not only is traffic in cities often gridlocked, but most Filipino drivers have a very relaxed attitude towards the rules of the road.

Swerving is common, as is changing lanes suddenly and driving with one hand permanently on the horn, particularly if you're a bus or jeepney driver. That said, if you're used to driving in big cities this might not faze you too much, and in any case, once you reach more rural areas – northern Luzon for example – travelling by car can be incredibly convenient and open up a whole range of otherwise hard-to-reach destinations. Many travellers also rent **motorbikes**, but this is only recommended for experienced riders – the chances of having an accident are statistically fairly high. It's best to avoid driving at night altogether.

If you do drive, you'll need your **driving licence**; be prepared to show it if you get stopped. Rentals are allowed for up to ninety days – longer stays will require a Philippine licence. Vehicles in the Philippines drive on the right side of the road and distances and car speeds are in kilometres. The highways usually have a nominal speed limit of 100kph, but anywhere else you'll rarely be going faster than 30kph due to congestion.

Always **drive defensively** – cars, animals and pedestrians will pull out in front of you without warning (in many rural areas people are still not used to traffic), and always give way to jeepneys, which will happily drive you off the road. When passing anything, sound your horn twice as a warning (horns are rarely used in anger).

Note that **police** and "traffic enforcers" – uniformed men and women employed by local authorities to supplement the police – might try to elicit a bribe from you. If this happens it's best to play the dumb foreigner and hand over the "on-the-spot fine" of a few hundred pesos (make sure you have cash with you). If you take the moral high ground and refuse to play along, you'll probably end up having your licence confiscated or, in the worst case, your car towed away and impounded until you pay a fine to get it back.

CAR RENTAL AGENCIES

Avalon Transport Services Ⓦ avalonrentacar.com.
Avis Ⓦ avis.com.ph.
Budget Ⓦ budget.com.ph.
Europcar Ⓦ europcar.com.ph.
Hertz Ⓦ hertzphilippines.com.
JB Rent A Car Ⓦ jbrentacar.com.
Manila Rent a Car Ⓦ manilarentacar.org.
National Ⓦ nationalcar.com.
Nissan Rent-A-Car Ⓦ nissanrentacar.com.
Rent A Car Manila Ⓦ rentacarmanila.com.
Viajero Rent A Car Ⓦ viajerorentacar.com.
VIP Rent-A-Car Ⓦ viprentacar.com.ph.

Hiring a driver

For about P2000–2500 (plus fuel, driver's food and parking/toll fees) you can hire a small car and driver from some car rental agencies for up to eight hours, the extra expense more than justified by the peace of mind a local driver brings. Try Manila Rent a Car or the Chauffeur Drive packages at Europcar Philippines.

Beyond Metro Manila, it can be much cheaper to strike a private deal with a car or van owner looking for extra work. A typical rate for their services is P1500 a day (plus fuel and tolls), although you'll need to negotiate. A good way to find someone with a vehicle is to ask at your accommodation; alternatively, locals with cars wait at many airports and ferry ports in the hope of making a bit of money driving arriving passengers into town. You can ask these drivers if they're available to be hired by the day.

By bike

Given the volume of traffic (and driving standards) on most major roads, cycling around the Philippines can be a dangerous idea, but plenty of locals and travellers do use bikes in rural areas. Outfits such as **Bugoy Bikers** (Ⓦ bugoybikers.com) can help arrange guided or self-guided day-tours or longer excursions by mountain bike.

Accommodation

The Philippines has accommodation to suit everyone, from international five-star hotels and swanky beach resorts to simple rooms – sometimes no more than a bamboo hut on a beach – and budget hotels.

It's generally not necessary to book in advance unless you are visiting at the peak times of Easter, Christmas, New Year or during a major local festival (see pp.36–38). As always, you'll find the cheapest rates online, but if you do want to book by phone,

ACCOMMODATION ALTERNATIVES

The following websites are worth checking for useful alternatives to standard hotel and resort accommodation.
Airbnb Ⓦ airbnb.com.
CouchSurfing Ⓦ couchsurfing.org.
Vacation Rentals by Owner Ⓦ vrbo.com.

ACCOMMODATION PRICES

All accommodation prices published in the Guide represent the cost of the **cheapest room for two people sharing** – or beach hut sleeping two – **in high season**, namely November to April. Prices during the May–October rainy season are usually about twenty percent lower. Conversely, during Christmas, New Year and Easter, rates in the popular beach resorts such as Boracay can spike by around twenty percent. In some cases hotels will include **breakfast** in the price but it's worth asking about this when you book. You'll also find that as a "walk-in" guest you'll usually be able to get a cheaper rate than the rack rate listed on hotel websites, especially in the off-season and in less touristy areas.

Value Added Tax of twelve percent and an additional service charge is often included in the published rates, but not always. If you see a room advertised at P1000++ ("**plus plus**") it means you'll pay P1000 plus VAT plus service charge – always ask for clarification if you aren't sure which charge is which. These additional charges have been factored into all our rates.

Where **dormitory accommodation** is available, we've given the price of a dorm bed.

note that some hotels in out-of-the-way areas won't have a landline telephone on site, in which case they may have a mobile number and/or a booking office in a city (often Manila); details are given in the text as appropriate.

Hotels and beach resorts

The terms **hotel** and **beach resort** cover a multitude of options in the Philippines. A hotel can mean anything from the most luxurious five-star establishment down to dingy budget pensions or guesthouses with bars on the windows. Beach resorts in turn range from sybaritic affairs on private atolls, with butlers and health spas, to dirt-cheap, rickety one-room cottages on a deserted island. "Resort hotels" are a mid-range or top-range hybrid of the two, sometimes with their own area of private beach.

Many hotels and beach resorts accept credit cards, although there are exceptions, such as in rural areas where electricity supply is not dependable and also in the cheapest budget accommodation, where you must pay cash. It can be worth checking that the air conditioner, where available, isn't noisy. Rooms on lower floors overlooking main roads are best avoided as they can be hellishly noisy; always try to go for something high up or at the back (or both).

Note that in smaller towns and cities beyond Manila, hotels often use the English term "single" room to mean one double bed, and "double/twin" to mean a room with two double beds; in these cases "single" rooms will obviously be big enough for two people – you will rarely find a room that can only sleep one. In the Guide, prices quoted are always based on the **cheapest room for two people sharing** (a "double" in the Western sense), regardless of what the hotel calls it.

Budget

Budget hotels (typically P450–1000) offer little more than a bed, four walls and a fan or small air-conditioning unit, although if you're by the beach, with a pleasant sea breeze blowing and the windows open, air conditioning isn't really necessary. If you do get a private bathroom it will probably only have cold water, and the "shower" is sometimes little more than a tap sticking out of the wall producing a mere trickle of water. Breakfast is unlikely to be included in the rate, though there may be a canteen or coffee shop on the premises where you can buy food. At the higher end of the budget range, rooms are usually simple but can be reasonably spacious, perhaps – if they are on or near a beach – with a small balcony.

Mid-range

There are plenty of **mid-range hotels** (typically P1000–3000), mostly in towns and cities. The rooms typically have air conditioning and a private bathroom with hot water, and usually basic cable TV. Beach cottages in this bracket tend to be quite spacious and will often have a decent-sized veranda too. Most mid-range accommodation will feature a small coffee shop or restaurant with a choice of Filipino and Western breakfasts that may be included in the rate; if it's not, expect to pay around P100–150.

Top end

In Manila and Cebu, as well as the most popular beach destinations such as Boracay, you can splash out on extremely comfortable accommodation (from P3000). **Five-star comfort** is offered by some hotels and beach resorts, many of them owned and operated by international chains (well over P10,000). Cottages at the most expensive resorts are more like chic apartments, often with a separate living area. Many of these establishments include a lavish buffet breakfast in the rate, and sports facilities and outdoor activities are on offer, though you'll have to pay extra for those.

Campsites, hostels and homestays

Campsites are almost unknown in the Philippines. A small number of resorts allow you to pitch tents in their grounds for a negligible charge, but otherwise the only camping you're likely to do is if you go trekking or climbing and need to camp overnight in the wilderness or on a mountaintop. Note that rental outlets for equipment are few and far between, so you might need to bring your own gear from home.

There are very few **official youth hostels** in the country, most of them in university cities where they may be booked up by students throughout term time. A Hostelling International (HI) card can in theory give you a tiny saving of around P25 a night at the handful of YMCAs and YWCAs in the big cities. The problem is that few staff have any idea what an HI card is. On the other hand, **private hostels** can be found in many cities and touristic areas, plus it is quite common for budget hotels and resorts to have **dormitories**.

There's no official **homestay** programme in the Philippines, but in rural areas where there may be no formal accommodation, you'll often find people willing to put you up in their home for a small charge, usually no more than P200 a night, including some food. If you enjoy the stay, it's best to offer some sort of tip when you leave, or a gift of soft drinks and treats for the children. You can ask around at town halls if you're interested.

Food and drink

The high esteem in which Filipinos hold their food is encapsulated by the common greeting "Let's eat!" Though

Filipino food has a reputation for being one of Asia's less adventurous cuisines, there is a lot more to it than adobo (see box opposite), and young, entrepreneurial restaurateurs and chefs have started to give native dishes an increasingly sophisticated touch.

In the Philippines snacks – **merienda** – are eaten in between the three main meals, and not to partake when offered can be considered rude. It's not unusual for breakfast to be eaten early, followed by merienda at 10am, lunch as early as 11am (especially in the provinces where many people are up at sunrise), more merienda at 2pm and 4pm, and dinner at 7pm. Meals are substantial, and even busy office workers prefer to sit down at a table and make the meal last. Never be afraid to ask for a doggy bag – everyone does. At smarter restaurants, the final bill you get usually includes VAT of twelve percent and a service charge of ten percent, adding 22 percent to the price shown on the menu. Simple establishments do not add these surcharges.

Don't be confused by the absence of a knife from most table settings. It's normal to use just a fork and spoon, cutting any meat with the fork and using the spoon to put the food in your mouth. This isn't as eccentric as it first seems. Most meat is served in small chunks, not steak-like slabs, so you usually don't have to cut it at all. Fish can be skewered with your fork and cut with the side of your spoon. And a spoon is so much easier for the local staple, steamed rice, than a knife and fork. That said, in some "native-style" restaurants food is served on banana leaves and you're expected to eat with your hands, combining the rice and food into mouthful-sized balls with your fingers – if you don't feel up to this it's fine to ask for cutlery.

Filipino cuisine

Filipino food is a delicious and exotic blend of Malay, Spanish, Chinese and American traditions. Dishes range from the very simple, like grilled fish and rice, to more complex stews, paellas and artfully barbecued meats, many using local fruits such as calamansi, coconuts and mangoes. **Seafood** is especially rich – expect anything from meaty crabs and milkfish to grouper and stingray on the menu. Most meals are served with San Miguel, the local beer, and are followed by sumptuous tropical fruits and decadent desserts.

The staples

Rice is the key Filipino staple, often accompanied by little more than freshly caught fish with a vinegar sauce. **Lapu-lapu** (grouper) and **bangus** (milkfish) are commonly served, while squid, crab and prawns are especially good and cheap in the Philippines. **Chicken** is another key staple – competition for the best fried or barbecued chicken (*lechon manok*) is fierce. Popular dishes on virtually every menu include **sinigang**, a refreshing tamarind-based sour soup; **kare-kare**, a stew made from delicious peanut sauce with vegetables and usually beef; and sizzling **sisig**, fried pig's head and liver, seasoned with calamansi and chilli peppers. Filipino Chinese dishes such as **pancit** (noodles) and **lumpia** (spring rolls) are common. Probably the most popular meat is **pork**, transformed into dishes such as crispy *pata*, **adobo** (see box below) and **lechon**, roasted pig cooked whole on a spit over a charcoal or wood fire. In the Philippines, *lechon* is usually served with vinegar or special sauce (unique to each *lechon* shop but normally made from fruits or liver pâté, garlic and pepper). The meat is deliciously fragrant and juicy, but the real highlight is the crispy smoked skin, a fatty, sumptuous treat sold by the kilo. Pork is also the basis of **Bicol Express**, the best known of very few spicy local dishes, which consists of pork cooked in coconut milk, soy and vinegar, with chillies. Most of these dishes cost P100–250 in a typical restaurant.

Vegetables are not considered an integral part of Filipino meals, but may well be mixed in with the meat or offered as a side dish. In restaurants serving Filipino food, some of the most common vegetable dishes include *pinakbet*, an Ilocano dish (usually bitter melon, squash, okra, aubergine and string beans cooked in *bagoong*, a fermented fish sauce), and a version of Bicol Express with leafy vegetables such as *pechuy* (aka pak choy) and *camote* tops (sweet potato leaves) in place of pork.

Breakfast

At many hotels and resorts you'll be offered a Filipino breakfast, which typically consists of **longganisa** (garlic sausage), **tocino** (cured pork), fried *bangus* fish, corned beef or **beef tapa** (beef marinated in vinegar); you'll usually be offered **tapsilog**, a contraction formed from *tapa* (fried beef), *sinangag* (garlic fried rice) and *itlog* (egg), which is exactly what you get: a bowl of garlic rice with *tapa* and a fried egg on top. Other "combo" dishes include *tosilog* and *longsilog* (you get the idea).

If this sounds too much for you, there's usually fresh fruit and toast, though note that local **bread**, either of the sliced variety or in rolls known as *pan de sal*, is often slightly sweet (wholegrain or rye breads are unusual in all but a few big hotels). Another option is to ask for a couple of hot *pan de sal* with corned-beef filling; the beef takes away some of the bread's sweetness.

Street food

Though not as common as it is in Thailand or India, **street food** still has a special place in the hearts (and stomachs) of Filipinos as much for its plain weirdness as for its culinary virtues. Hawkers with portable stoves tend to appear towards the end of the working day from 5pm to 8pm and at lunchtime in bigger cities. Much of the food is grilled over charcoal and served on sticks kebab-style, or deep fried in a wok with oil that is poured into an old jam jar and re-used day after day. Highlights include deep-fried **fishballs** and **squid-balls** (mashed fish or squid blended with wheat flour), grilled **pig intestines** and *adidas* – **chicken's feet**, named after the sports-shoe manufacturer. Prices start from a few pesos a stick.

Street vendors also supply the king of Filipino aphrodisiacs, *balut*, a half-formed **duck embryo** eaten with beak, feathers and all; sellers advertise their proximity with a distinctive baying cry.

Carinderias and seafood buffets

Carinderias are usually humble eateries that allow you to choose from a number of dishes placed on a counter in big aluminium pots. Carinderia fare is usually a blend of Filipino and Asian dishes; typical choices might be adobo, pancit, *pinakbet*, chicken curry, grilled pork, sweet and sour fish, fried chicken and hotdogs. The only problem with carinderias is

---

ADOBO HEAVEN

It might seem simple – stewed pork and chicken – but it's hard to resist the justly revered national dish of the Philippines. **Adobo** originally meant "sauce" or "seasoning" in Spanish, but its use has morphed throughout Spain's former colonies – the Filipino version is actually indigenous to the islands, dating back to a dish cooked up here long before Magellan's arrival. Philippine adobo consists of pork, chicken or a combination of both slowly stewed in soy sauce, vinegar, crushed garlic, bay leaf and black peppercorns – it's the latter two ingredients that gives true adobo its distinctive flavour and bite. No two adobos are exactly alike however – you'll discover different versions all over the country.

that the food has usually been standing around a while and is often served lukewarm.

In urban areas and some beach resorts you'll also find **seafood** restaurants displaying a range of seafood on ice; order by pointing at what you want and telling the waiter how you would like it cooked.

Desserts and snacks

Filipinos adore **sweets** and **desserts**. Sold all over the Philippines, **halo-halo** (from the Tagalog word *halo*, meaning "mix") is a mouthwatering blend of shaved ice, evaporated milk and various toppings such as sweetened beans, fruits and taro, served in a tall glass or bowl – the "special" version usually has taro ice cream on top. A speciality of Laguna province (see p.107), **buko pie** is made by layering strips of young coconut and cake mix into a crispy pie crust – the addictive dessert has cult status in the Philippines and an intense rivalry exists between many pie-makers. The most popular traditional Filipino sweet is **polvorón**, a sort of short-bread made with flour, sugar and milk, and often sold in flavours such as cashew nut, chocolate and *pinipig* (crispy rice). Sold on every street corner, **turon** is a crispy deep-fried banana in a spring roll wrapper, while **leche flan** (caramel custard) is a staple on every restaurant menu. Filipinos also eat a huge amount of **ice cream** in an unorthodox range of flavours, including *ube* (purple yam), jackfruit, corn, avocado and even cheese.

For a snack in a packet, try salted dried fish like **dilis**, which can be bought in supermarkets and convenience stores. *Dilis* are a little like anchovies and are eaten whole, sometimes with a vinegar and garlic dip. They're often served along with other savouries (under the collective name *pulutan*) during drinking sessions. Salted dried **pusit** (squid) is also common.

Fast food

You'll find McDonald's in almost every big town, but the Philippines has its own successful **fast-food chains** fashioned after the US giant. There are hundreds of branches of Jollibee (chicken, burgers and spaghetti), Chowking (noodle soups, dim sum), Mang Inasal (barbecue and unlimited rice) and Max's (fried chicken) throughout the country – indeed, the corpulent "jolly bee" mascot is more ubiquitous than Ronald McDonald. Western-style **sandwich bars** have appeared in recent years too.

Most shopping malls also have **food courts**, indoor marketplaces that bring together dozens of small stalls serving Filipino, Japanese, Chinese, Thai and Korean food. Here you can easily get a decent lunch for under P200 including a soft drink.

In many provincial cities, look out also for **ihaw-ihaw** (grill) restaurants, usually native-style bamboo structures where meat and fish are cooked over charcoal and served with hot rice and soup.

International cuisine

There are some excellent French, Spanish and Italian restaurants in Manila and Cebu City, and dozens of **European** restaurants in Boracay. Prices depend on where you are. In areas of Manila, you can spend P2500 or more for a good three-course meal for two; in Boracay you could have a similar meal for half that. However, European cuisine on the coast tends to be a little less sophisticated, simply because it's hard to guarantee supplies of the necessary ingredients.

There are **Chinese** restaurants in every city and in many provincial towns. Don't expect modish Oriental cuisine though; most Chinese restaurants are inexpensive places offering straightforward, tasty food designed to be ordered in large portions and shared by a group. A filling Chinese meal for two often costs no more than P500. Another of the

---

VEGETARIAN FOOD

Committed **vegetarians and vegans** face a difficult mission to find suitable food in the Philippines. It's a poor country and many Filipinos have grown up on a diet of what's available locally, usually chicken and pork. If you ask for a plate of stir-fried vegetables it might come with slices of pork in it, or be served in meat gravy. Fried rice always contains egg and meat. That said, most Filipinos will be familiar with the concept of vegetarian food and will try to accommodate you where possible.

Chinese and Japanese restaurants offer the best range of vegetable-based dishes, though you'll have to emphasize that you want absolutely no bits of meat added. In Manila, and to some extent in other cities, and in Boracay, pizzas are an option, or you could head to an upmarket restaurant and ask the chef to prepare something special. At least breakfast is straightforward – even in the most rural resorts, you can ask for toast or pancakes and, if you're not vegan, an omelette or scrambled eggs.

FILIPINO FRUITS

The Philippines is justly celebrated for its variety and quality of fresh fruit, especially its mangoes, which are ubiquitous throughout the islands and always juicy and delicious. The list below is just a selection.

Atis (custard apple or sugar-apple) This fruit is pine-cone shaped, and about 10cm long with green scaly skin, and its ripe flesh is gloriously sweet and soft; it might look a bit like custard but it tastes like a combination of banana, papaya and strawberry or, more prosaically, bubble gum. With its black pips scattered throughout it can be messy to eat. The main season is late summer to October.

Balimbing (starfruit, aka *carambola*) Crunchy, juicy fruit, with a slightly sweet flavour that tastes a bit like a blend of apple, pear and grape.

Bayabas (guava) Fruit with a tough green skin and distinctive deep-pink pulp that has a sweet flavour, similar to passion fruit mixed with strawberry.

Buko (coconut) Another Philippine staple grown throughout the archipelago year-round, harvested casually by villagers as much as by commercial plantations for its refreshing juice and nutty white flesh. Used to make *buko* pie and a variety of desserts.

Calamansi Little green lime that is squeezed into juices, hot tea, over noodles, fish and *kinilaw* (raw fish salad) and into numerous dipping sauces.

Chico (sapodilla) Roughly the size of an egg, with brown skin and sticky, soft flesh that has a malty, exceedingly sweet flavour.

Durian The "king" of tropical fruit is spiky, heavy and smells like a drain blocked with rubbish – but its creamy inner flesh tastes like heaven. Rich in protein, minerals and fat, the durian is one of the more expensive fruits in the Philippines, though in Davao, the centre of production, you can buy whole ones for P50.

Guayabano (soursop) A large, oval fruit with knobbly spines outside and fragrant flesh inside.

Kaimito (star apple) Plum-coloured and round, about the size of a tennis ball, with leathery skin and soft white pulp inside that tastes a bit like grape.

Langka (jackfruit) The largest tree-borne fruit in the world (it can reach 40kg) is also one of the most delicious, with an interior of large, yellow bulbs of sweet flesh that tastes like flowery bananas.

Lanzones Small round fruit grown mostly on southern Luzon, especially in Laguna, and available October to December. It's also grown in northern Mindanao and especially Camiguin, where there is a festival in its honour (see p.410). It tastes a bit like a combination of grape and sweet grapefruit.

Mangga (mango) Eat as much mango as you can in the Philippines – you won't taste any better. Most grown on the islands turn from green to yellow as they ripen and are always very sweet. The main season runs June to August.

Mangosteen Nothing like a mango, this sumptuous fruit the size of a tangerine has a thick, purplish skin and creamy white flesh. The season runs June to August.

Marang If you travel in Mindanao look out for this special fruit. A bit like a breadfruit, it's a cross between jackfruit and *atis* but with a taste all its own.

Pakwan (watermelon) Usually available, but best between April and June.

Papaya You'll see papaya plants growing in gardens and along roadsides all over the Philippines and it's one of the cheapest fruits. Some 98 percent of the annual crop is consumed locally and it's extremely nutritious.

Piña (pineapple) The Spanish introduced the pineapple to the Philippines and, thanks to huge plantations run by Del Monte and Dole (both in Mindanao), it's one of the nation's biggest export earners.

Saging (banana) A staple crop in the Philippines, with a remarkable range of size and types grown in Mindanao and the Western Visayas throughout the year; the country is one of the largest exporters of bananas in the world.

Santol The *santol* is an apple-sized fruit, with a white juicy pulp often eaten sour with some salt. It's also popular as a jam or a bitter marmalade.

Philippines' favourite cuisines is **Japanese**, ranging from fast-food noodle parlours to expensive restaurants serving sushi and tempura.

Drinks

Bottled **water** is cheap; good local brands such as Nestlé Pure Life, Viva and Hidden Spring cost P20–30 for one litre in convenience stores. Note, however, that many hotels and restaurants have huge bottles of **mineral water** for guests and customers, which save you money and cut down on plastic waste. You can also purify your own water; chemical sterilization using chlorine is completely effective, fast and inexpensive, and you can remove the nasty taste it leaves with neutralizing tablets or lemon juice. Alternatively, you could invest in a purifying filter incorporating chemical sterilization to kill even the smallest viruses. Fizzy **soft drinks** such as Coca-Cola and Pepsi are available everywhere.

At resorts and hotels, the "**juice**" which usually comes with breakfast is – irritatingly, in a country rich in fresh fruit – often made from powder or concentrate. Good fresh juices, usually available only in the more expensive restaurants, include watermelon, ripe mango, sour mango and papaya. Fresh *buko* (coconut) juice is a refreshing choice, especially on a hot day. In general, sugar is added to fresh juices and shakes unless you specify otherwise, though you might well want sugar with the delightful drink made from calamansi, a small native lime.

Filipinos aren't big **tea** drinkers and, except in the best hotels, the only tea on offer is usually made from Lipton's tea bags. **Coffee** is popular and can be ordered anywhere, but the quality varies widely. It's usually instant, served in "three-in-one" packets, and dominated by Nescafé, although local, Malaysian and Indonesian brands are also available. Where real brewed coffee is served, it's often local and very good. Latte-addicts may be tempted by Starbucks which has scores of branches across Manila and is popping up in provincial towns such as Bacolod. Fresh milk is rare outside the cities so you'll often find yourself being offered tinned or powdered milk with coffee or tea.

Alcohol

The **beer** of choice in the Philippines is **San Miguel**, the local pilsner established in 1890 and still dominating ninety percent of the domestic market. San Miguel also produces Red Horse Extra Strong lager and a good apple-flavoured beer. The only major competition comes from Asia Brewery, which produces the uninspiring Beer na Beer and Colt 45 brands. Only a few foreign beers are available in bars and supermarkets, notably Heineken, Budweiser and Japanese brands. The worldwide fad for **craft ales** is gradually making its presence felt, however, with a number of decent Filipino microbreweries, especially in Metro Manila. For something stronger there are plenty of Philippine-made **spirits** such as Tanduay rum, San Miguel Ginebra (gin) and Fundador brandy. Wine can be found in liquor stores in the larger cities, though the range is usually limited to Australian or New Zealand mass-market brands and it tends to be pricey.

All restaurants, fast-food places excepted, serve alcohol, but **wine** is rarely drunk; a cold beer or fresh fruit juice is much preferred. European restaurants usually have a limited wine list. For an average bottle of Australian Chardonnay or Merlot expect to pay at least P750. For something authentically native, try the strong and pungent **tapuy** (rice wine) or a speciality called **lambanog**, made from almost anything that can be fermented, including fruit. In the provinces both can be difficult to find because they're usually brewed privately for local consumption, though *lambanog* is now being bottled and branded, and can be found on some supermarket shelves in Manila and other cities.

Health

As long as you're careful about what you eat and drink and how long you spend in the sun, you shouldn't have any major health problems in the Philippines. Hospitals in cities and even in small towns are generally of a good standard, although health care is rudimentary in the remotest barangays and anything potentially serious is best dealt with in Manila or Cebu. Doctors and nurses almost always speak English, and doctors in major cities are likely to have received some training in the US or the UK, where many attend medical school.

We've listed **hospitals** in the accounts of cities and major towns in the Guide; for a full list, plus a searchable database of doctors by location and area and expertise, check ⓦ rxpinoy.com.ourssite .com. There are **pharmacies** on almost every street corner where you can buy local and international brand medicines. Branches of Mercury Drug, the country's biggest chain of pharmacies, are listed on ⓦ mercurydrug.com.

If you are hospitalized, you'll have to pay a deposit on your way in and settle the bill – either in person or through your insurance company (see box, p.50).

We strongly recommend you are up to date with tetanus, typhoid and hepatitis A **vaccinations**.

Stomach upsets

Food- and waterborne diseases are the most likely cause of illness in the Philippines. Travellers' **diarrhoea** can be caused by viruses, bacteria or parasites, which can contaminate food or water. There's also a risk of typhoid or cholera – occasional cases are reported in the Philippines, mostly in poor areas without adequate sanitation. Another potential threat is that of hepatitis A. The authorities in Manila claim that **tap water** in the capital and most cities is safe for drinking, but it's not worth taking the chance – unless you filter it yourself, stick to bottled or mineral water (see opposite).

Mosquito-borne diseases

Dengue fever, a debilitating and occasionally fatal viral disease, is on the increase across tropical Asia. Many cases are reported in the Philippines each year, mostly during or just after the wet season when the day-biting mosquito that carries the disease is most active. There is no vaccine against dengue. Initial symptoms – which develop five to eight days after being bitten – include a fever that subsides after a few days, often leaving the patient with a bad rash all over their body, headaches and fierce joint pain. The only treatment is rest, liquids and paracetamol or any other acetaminophen painkiller (not aspirin). Dengue can result in death, usually among the very young or very old, and serious cases call for hospitalization.

In the Philippines, **malaria** is found only in isolated areas of southern Palawan and the Sulu archipelago (Basilan, Jolo and Tawi-Tawi), and few travellers bother with anti-malarials if they are sticking to the tourist trail. If you are unsure of your itinerary it's best to err on the safe side and consult your doctor about malaria medication. Anti-malarials must be taken before you enter a malarial zone. As resistance to chloroquin-based drugs increases, mefloquin, which goes under the brand name of Lariam, has become the recommended prophylactic for most travellers to the Philippines. This has very strong side effects, and its use is controversial; alternatives are atovaquone-proguanil (malarone) and doxycycline.

To avoid mosquito bites, wear long-sleeved shirts, long trousers and a hat. Use an insect repellent that contains DEET (diethylmethyltoluamide) and –

unless you are staying in air-conditioned or well-screened accommodation – you could even pick up a mosquito net treated with the insecticide permethrin or deltamethrin. Mosquito nets are hard to find In the Philippines, so buy one before you go. If you are unable to find a pre-treated mosquito net you can buy one and spray it yourself.

Leeches and rabies

If you're trekking through rainforest, especially in the rainy season, there's a good chance you'll encounter **leeches** (known locally as *limatik*), blood-sucking freshwater worms that attach themselves to your skin and can be tricky to remove (the bite doesn't hurt though). If you find a leech on your skin it's important not to pull it off, as the jaw could be left behind, leading to the risk of infection. Repeatedly flick its head end with your fingernail, or rub salt, tiger balm or tobacco juice onto the leech, then treat the wound with antiseptic. You can guard against leeches in the first place by securing cuffs and trouser bottoms. Climbers in the Philippines say that rubbing detergent soap with a little water on your skin and clothes helps keep leeches at bay. Though leeches might seem unpleasant, they actually present a negligible risk to healthy hikers, and it's fine to let them drop off of their own accord.

Stray and badly cared for dogs are everywhere in the Philippines are and far more dangerous than leeches: **rabies** claims about eight hundred lives a year. The stereotype of rabid animals being deranged and foaming at the mouth is just that; some infected animals become lethargic and sleepy, so don't presume that a docile dog is a safe one. If you are bitten or scratched, wash the wound immediately with soap and running water for five minutes and apply alcohol or iodine. Seek treatment immediately – rabies is fatal once symptoms appear. You should also consider getting a rabies shot before arrival in the Philippines.

MEDICAL RESOURCES

Canadian Society for International Health ⓦ csih.org.
Extensive list of travel health centres.
CDC ☎ 1877 394 8747, ⓦ cdc.gov/travel. Official US government travel health site.
Hospital for Tropical Diseases Travel Clinic ☎ 0845 155 5000 or 020 7387 4411, ⓦ www.thehtd.org.
International Society for Travel Medicine ☎ 1770 736 7060, ⓦ istm.org. Has a full list of travel health clinics worldwide.
MASTA (Medical Advisory Service for Travellers Abroad) ☎ 0870 606 2782, ⓦ masta-travel-health.com. For the nearest clinic in the UK.

South African Society of Travel Medicine ☎ 011 025 3297, 🅦 sastm.org.za. Offers latest medical advice for travellers and a directory of travel medicine practitioners in South Africa.
Travel Doctor ☎ 1300 658 844, 🅦 tmvc.com.au. Lists travel clinics in Australia.
Tropical Medical Bureau Republic of Ireland ☎ 1850 487 674, 🅦 tmb.ie.
Worldwise ☎ 09 522 9476, 🅦 worldwise.co.nz. Travel health advice and list of clinics in New Zealand.

The media

Filipinos are inordinately proud of their nation's historic status as the first democracy in Asia, a fact reflected in their love of a free press. Once Marcos was gone and martial law with him, the shackles truly came off, and the Philippine media became one of the most vociferous and freewheeling in the world.

There is a dark and apparently contradictory side to this, however – the Philippines is also one of the most dangerous places in the world to be a journalist, with many killed every year. Though **press freedoms** are enshrined in the Philippine constitution, paramilitary groups, privately owned militias and even politicians (especially in Mindanao) who have been targeted by the press often seek violent retribution. Due to corruption, few are brought to justice.

Newspapers

Major English-language daily broadsheet **newspapers** include the *Philippine Daily Inquirer* (🅦 inquirer.net), the *Philippine Star* (🅦 philstar.com), *Manila Bulletin* (🅦 mb.com.ph) and the *Manila Times* (🅦 manilatimes.net). There are dozens of tabloids on the market, all of them lurid and often gruesome. Most of these are in Tagalog, though *Journal Online* (🅦 journal.com.ph) is largely in English with some articles in Tagalog. Foreign news publications are harder to find. The best bet is to visit a five-star hotel, where lobby gift shops sometimes stock *New York Times The International Edition*, *Time* and *The Economist*.

Some of the most trusted reporting on the Philippines comes from the **Philippine Centre for Investigative Journalism** (🅦 pcij.org), founded in 1989 by nine Filipino journalists who wanted to go beyond the day-to-day razzmatazz and inanities of the mainstream press. Journalists working for the PCIJ were responsible for the exposé of former

President Joseph Estrada's unexplained wealth, which led to his eventual downfall. More recently, they have not shied away from publishing articles critical of controversial President Duterte.

Television and radio

Terrestrial **television networks** include GMA (🅦 gmanetwork.com) and ABS-CBN (🅦 abs-cbn.com), offering a diet of histrionic soaps, chat shows and daytime game shows with sexy dancers. Cable TV is now widely available in the Philippines, with the exception of some of the most undeveloped rural areas. Most providers carry BBC World, CNN and Australian ABC. During the season, there's American football, baseball and most of all basketball on various channels, though outside of Manila it's very hard to find the Be-in channel that carries Premier League football. Movie channels include HBO, Cinemax and Star Movies.

There are over 350 **radio** stations in the Philippines, and between them they present a mindboggling mix of news, sport, music and chitchat. Radio news channels such as DZBB and RMN News AM tend to broadcast in Filipino, but there are dozens of FM pop stations that use English with a smattering of Filipino. The music they play isn't anything special, mostly mellow jazz and pop ballads by mainstream artists. Among the most popular FM stations are Wow FM (103.5MHz) and Crossover (105.1 MHz). A shortwave radio also gives access to the BBC World Service (🅦 bbc.co.uk/worldservice), Radio Canada (🅦 rcinet.ca), Voice of America (🅦 voa.gov) and Radio Australia (🅦 abc.net.au/ra), among other international broadcasters.

Festivals

Every community in the Philippines – from small barangay to crammed metropolis – has at least a couple of festivals a year in honour of a patron saint, to give thanks for a good harvest, or to pay respects to a biblical character. It's well worth timing your visit to see one of the major events: the beer flows, pigs are roasted, and there's dancing in the streets for days on end.

The main fiesta months are from January to May; exact dates often vary. Major mardi-gras-style festivals include the **Ati-Atihan** in January in Kalibo (see box, p.284) and the **Sinulog** in January in Cebu (see box, p.317). One of the biggest nationwide festivals is the

Flores de Mayo, a religious parade held across the country throughout May in honour of the Virgin Mary.

A festival calendar

Listing all Filipino festivals is impossible. Those included here are larger ones that you might consider making a special trip for, at least if you happen to be in the area.

JANUARY AND FEBRUARY

Feast of the Black Nazarene (Jan 9) Quiapo, Manila
W quiapochurch.com. Devotees gather in the plaza outside Quiapo Church to touch a miraculous image of Christ. See p.73.

Ati-Atihan (variable, culminating on third Sun in Jan) Kalibo, Aklan. Street dancing and wild costumes at arguably the biggest festival in the country, held to celebrate an ancient land pact between settlers and indigenous Atis. See box, p.284.

Sinulog (third Sun in Jan) Cebu City, Cebu W sinulog.ph. Cebu's biggest annual event, in honour of the Santo Niño (an image of Jesus as a child). Huge street parade, live music and plenty of food and drink. See box, p.317.

Dinagyang (fourth week of Jan) Iloilo, Panay Island W facebook .com/DinagyangSalloiloFestival/. Relatively modern festival modelled after the Ati-Atihan; includes a parade on the Iloilo River.

Philippine Hot Air Balloon Fiesta (Feb) Clark, Pampanga
W philballoonfest.net. Balloon rides, microlight flying, skydiving and aerobatics displays.

Pamulinawen (first two weeks in Feb) Laoag City, Ilocos Norte. Citywide fiesta in honour of St William the Hermit. Events include street parties, beauty pageants, concerts and religious parades.

Panagbenga (Baguio Flower Festival; third week in Feb) Baguio City, Benguet W panagbengaflowerfestival.com. The summer capital's largest annual event includes parades of floats beautifully decorated with flowers from the Cordillera region. There are also flower-related lectures and exhibitions.

Suman Festival (third week in Feb) Baler, Aurora. Another mardi-gras-style extravaganza featuring street parades, dancing and floats decorated with the native delicacy *suman* – sticky rice cake rolled in banana leaves.

MARCH AND APRIL

Moriones (Easter weekend) Marinduque. A celebration of the life of the Roman centurion Longinus, who was blind in one eye. Legend says that when he pierced Christ's side with his spear, blood spurted into his eye and cured him. See box, p.197.

Arya! Abra (first or second week of March) Bangued, Abra. Highlights include hair-raising bamboo-raft races along the frisky Abra River and gatherings of northern tribes.

Bangkero Festival (first or second week of March) Pagsanjan, Laguna. Parade along the Pagsanjan River.

Kaamulan (first week of March) Malaybalay City, Bukidnon, Mindanao. Showcase of tribal culture and arts.

Pasayaw (third week of March) Canlaon City, Negros Oriental. Thanksgiving festival to God and St Joseph, with twelve barangays competing for honours in an outdoor dancing competition. The final "dance-off" is held in the city gym.

Boracay International Dragon Boat Festival (April) Boracay, Aklan. A local version of Hong Kong's dragon-boat races, featuring domestic and international teams competing in long wooden canoes on a course off White Beach.

Allaw Ta Apo Sandawa (second week of April) Kidapawan City, Cotabato. Gathering of highland tribes to pay respects to the sacred Mount Apo.

Turumba Festival (April & May) Pakil, Laguna. Religious festival commemorating the seven sorrows of the Virgin Mary. The festival consists of seven novenas, one for each sorrow, held at weekends.

MAY

Flores de Mayo (throughout May) Countrywide. Religious procession celebrating the coming of the rains, with girls dressed as the various "Accolades of our Lady", including Faith, Hope and Charity. Processions are sometimes held after dark and lit by candles – a lovely sight.

Carabao Carroza (May 3–4) Iloilo, Panay Island. Races held to celebrate the humble carabao (water buffalo), beast of burden for many a provincial farmer.

Pahiyas (May 15) Lucban, Quezon; also in the nearby towns of Candelaria, Tayabas, Sariaya, Tiaong and Lucena. Colourful harvest festival which sees houses gaily decorated with fruits and vegetables. It's held in honour of San Isidro Labrador, the patron saint of farmers.

ALL SAINTS' DAY

It's the day for Catholic Filipinos to honour their dead, but **All Saints' Day** on **November 1** is nothing to get maudlin about. Sometimes called All Souls' Day, it's when clans reunite at family graves and memorials, turning cemeteries throughout the country into fairgrounds. You don't pay your respects in the Philippines by being miserable, so All Saints' Day is a chance to show those who have gone before how much those who have been left behind are prospering. Filipinos approach All Saints' Day with the same gusto as Christmas, running from shop to shop at the last minute looking for candles to burn, food and offerings. The grave is painted, flowers are arranged and rosaries fervently prayed over, but once the ceremonial preliminaries are over, the fun begins. Guitars appear, capacious picnic hampers are opened and alcohol flows freely. Many families gather the night before and sleep in the cemetery. With many family graves in the provinces, Manila empties fast the day before All Saints' Day, as people leave the city by anything on wheels. Needless to say, it's a bad time to travel.

Obando Fertility Rites (May 17–19) Obando, Bulacan. On the feast day of San Pascual, women gather in the churchyard to chant prayers asking for children, an intriguing combination of traditional dance, Catholicism and far older animist beliefs.

AUGUST AND SEPTEMBER

Kadayawan sa Davao (third week of Aug) Davao City, Mindanao. Week-long harvest festival with civic and military parades and street dances.

Peñafrancia Fluvial Festival (third Sat in Sept) Naga, Camarines Sur. A sacred statue of Our Lady of Peñafrancia, the patron saint of Bicol, is paraded through the streets, then sailed down the Bicol River back to its shrine.

OCTOBER AND NOVEMBER

Kansilay (Oct 19 or closest weekend) Silay, Negros Occidental. Modern festival commemorating Silay's charter day. Eating and drinking contests, beauty pageants and an elaborate street parade.

Ibalong (third week of Oct) Legaspi, Albay and throughout Bicol region. Epic dances and street presentations portraying Bicol's mythical superheroes and gods.

Lanzones Festival (third week of Oct) Lambajao, Camiguin. Vibrant and good-natured outdoor party giving thanks for the island's crop of lanzones (a tropical fruit). See p.410.

Masskara Festival (third week of Oct) Bacolod, Negros Occidental. Festivities kick off with food fairs, mask-making contests, brass-band competitions and beauty pageants, followed by the climax – a mardi gras parade where revellers don elaborate masks and costumes and dance to Latin rhythms Rio de Janeiro-style. See p.289.

MIMAROPA Festival (November) Mindoro, Marinduque, Romblon and Palawan. An annual celebration of different Filipino cultures, featuring impressive street parades and dancing. Held in a different city each year.

DECEMBER

Christmas (December 25). The Christmas season officially starts Dec 16 and lasts until Epiphany on Jan 9. Churches are full for Midnight Mass on Christmas Eve, and some towns hold a Panunulúyan pageant in the days leading up to it, commemorating the journey of Joseph and the pregnant Virgin Mary to Bethlehem. Though Christmas is primarily a family festival, celebrated in the home, without the pageantry on show at other festivals, you'll still see groups of children singing carols all over the archipelago. Christmas Day itself is spent with family and friends – the country largely shuts down for the day.

Outdoor activities

For a sizeable proportion of the tourists who visit every year, the main attraction of the Philippines is the scuba diving. The abundance of exceptional dive sites and the high standard of diving instruction available have made the archipelago one of the world's foremost diving destinations.

It's not all about getting underwater though: there are some superb wilderness areas in the Philippines and dozens of volcanoes and mountains to be **climbed**, from the tallest in the country, Mount Apo (2954m), to more manageable peaks close to Manila in Batangas and Rizal provinces, some of which can be tackled in a day-trip. The country also offers opportunities for **caving, whitewater rafting, surfing** and **sailing**.

Scuba diving

Diving is possible **year-round** in the Philippines, with surface water temperatures in the 25–28°C range, the warmest conditions being from February to June. On deeper dives temperatures can drop to 22°C due to the upwelling of deeper, cooler water, so a light (3mm) wet suit is essential. During the typhoon season from June to November, be prepared for your plans to be disrupted if a major storm hits and dive boats are unable to venture out. **Visibility** depends on water temperature, the

---

DIVING DOS AND DON'TS

Divers can cause damage to reefs, sometimes inadvertently. Be aware of your fins as they can break off coral heads that take years to regrow. Don't grab coral to steady yourself, and always maintain good buoyancy control – colliding with a reef can be destructive. Don't kick up sediment, which can choke and kill corals. Below is a list of additional dos and don'ts:

- **Collecting aquatic life** Don't take home corals or shells, and never take souvenirs from wreck-dives or remove anything dead or alive – except rubbish – from the sea.
- **Touching and handling aquatic life** For many organisms this is a terrifying and injurious experience – it's best left to people who have experience with the creatures concerned.
- **Riding aquatic life** Hard to credit, but some divers still think it's a great lark to hang onto the back of a turtle or manta ray. Simply put, there are no circumstances in which this is right.
- **Spear-fishing** This has been outlawed in the Philippines, and environmental groups are increasingly reporting spear-fishers to the authorities for prosecution.

TOP 10 DIVE SITES

Anilao Closest dive site to Manila, teeming with soft coral and tropical fish. See box, p.116.

Apo Island Not to be confused with the reef (see below), this island off Negros is swamped with fish and forests of coral. See p.303.

Apo Reef Few divers and lots of big fish, two hours off the coast of Mindoro. See p.254.

Coron The best wreck-diving in the country, possibly in the world. There are 24 charted wrecks, Japanese ships sunk in one massive attack by US aircraft in 1944. See box, p.398.

Puerto Galera Unrivalled all-round destination with something for everyone, from novices to old hands. See box, p.242.

Padre Burgos Out of the way in undeveloped southern Leyte and a prime spot for discovering new dive sites. See p.368.

Panglao Island The dive sites close to the congenial Alona Beach resorts offer an exceptional range of marine life. See box, p.345.

Samal Island This sleepy island just off the coast of Davao, Mindanao, harbours numerous dive sites. See p.429.

Subic Bay The former US Navy base is an exceptional location for wreck-dives, with the USS *New York* one of the highlights. See box, p.124.

Tubbataha Reef You'll need to book a liveaboard trip but it's worth it, with guaranteed sightings of sharks and a good chance of mantas and whale sharks. See p.378.

strength of the current and wind direction, but generally lies in the 10–30m range.

There are currently seven **recompression chambers** (aka hyperbaric chambers) in the Philippines to treat recompression sickness (see p.40), including a mobile ship-based unit. All ostensibly offer a 24-hour emergency service, but note that facilities do close for maintenance and/or because there are no staff qualified to run them. You might want to check that your dive operator is aware of the nearest operational facility. If it's not, go somewhere else.

Dive trips

Most dives **cost around** P1300 to P1800 for certified divers, including rental of the boat and equipment such as mask, booties, wet suit, fins, weight belt and air tanks. For night dives and more demanding technical dives, expect to pay around P500 extra. If you've booked a package that includes accommodation at a dive resort, two dives a day will normally be included in the cost.

Courses

All PADI-accredited resorts offer a range of courses run by qualified professional instructors. If you haven't been diving before and aren't sure if you'll take to it, try a gentle twenty-minute "**discovery dive**", guided by an instructor for around P2000, or the longer PADI **Discover Scuba Diving** course for around P3000. The main course for beginners is the PADI **Open Water Diver Course** (from around P22,000) which will allow you to dive at depths up

to 18m. You might want to consider doing the pool sessions and written tests before you travel, then doing the check-out dives at a PADI resort in the Philippines. It saves time and means that you don't have to slave over homework in the tropical heat. If you choose this option, make sure that you bring your PADI referral documents with you.

Once you've passed the course and been given your certification card, you are free to dive anywhere in the world. You might also want to take another step up the diving ladder by enrolling in a more advanced course. There are many to choose from, including **Advanced Open Water Diver** (from P17,000), Emergency First Response (from P8000), which is also suitable for non-divers, and **Rescue Diver** (from around P24,000).

Liveaboards

There are two great advantages to diving from a **liveaboard** (a boat that acts as a mobile hotel) – you can get to places that are inaccessible by bangka and once you're there you can linger for a night or two. Liveaboards allow you to explore terrific destinations such as Apo Reef off the coast of Mindoro and Tubbataha in the Sulu Sea, arguably the best dive spot in the country. Packages include all meals and dives, but vary significantly according to destination; Tubbataha costs at least US\$1200–1600 per week, while trips around Coron start at around US\$130 per day. Most of the boats used have air-conditioned en-suite cabins for two. Packages often include unlimited diving and are always full board.

MARINE LIFE

The beauty of diving in the Philippines is that you don't have to dive deep to see some incredible marine life. Among the commonest are the exotic and brightly coloured **angelfish**, **damselfish** and eye-catching **humbugs**, striped black-and-white like the sweet. In shallow coral gardens you'll see inquisitive **clownfish** defending their coral nests either singly or in pairs, perhaps with minuscule juveniles at their sides. Also unmissable are the frenetic shoals of **dragonets** and **dottybacks**, with their psychedelic colouring. **Moray eels** take shelter in crevices in the reef and it's not unusual to see one, even in the shallows. Even **turtles** can be seen at this depth.

Where the coral plunges away steeply into an inky darkness, at depths of five or six metres, you'll see bright-green **parrot fish** and mesmerizing **batfish**, who patrol the reef edge in family shoals. These slopes and fore reefs are also home to **snappers**, **goatfish** and **wrasses**, the largest of which – the Napoleon wrasse – can dwarf a person. Deeper still, but usually in the more isolated dive sites such as Tubbataha, it's possible to see sharks, including **white tip reef sharks** and **grey reef sharks**, while if you're lucky an immense but gentle **manta ray** or **whale shark** might drift lazily past.

Poisonous species include the beautifully hypnotic **lionfish** (also called the flamefish), which hunts at night and has spines along its back that can deliver a nasty dose of venom, while shoals of **jellyfish** are common at certain times of year.

LIVEABOARD OPERATORS

Atlantis Dive Resorts Ⓦ atlantishotel.com. Operates the 32m-long *Atlantis Azores*, which has eight luxurious cabins with private bathrooms. Trips to Puerto Galera and Apo Reef (Oct–Dec), Tubbataha (mid-March to early June), Dumaguete (June–Sept) and southern Leyte for the whale sharks (Jan–March). Most trips US$3495–3995 for 6 days, 7 nights.
Expedition Fleet Ⓦ expeditionfleet.com. Trips to Tubbataha on the ten-cabin MV *Stella Maris Explorer* (from P97,000; 7 days, 6 nights).
Busuanga Seadive Resort Ⓦ seadiveresort.com. Trips to Apo Reef and the Coron wrecks with varying room rates and dive packages.
Discovery Fleet Ⓦ discoveryfleet.com. Various routes with two large ships, MV *Discovery Palawan* and MV *Discovery Adventure* (from US$2200; 6 nights, 7 days).

RECOMPRESSION CHAMBERS

Batangas City St Patrick's Hospital, Lopez Jaena St ☎ 043 723 8388, Ⓦ divemed.com.ph.
Cavite City Sangley Recompression Chamber, NSWG, Philippine Fleet Naval Base ☎ 046 524 2061.
Cebu City Cebu Recompression Chamber, Viscom Station Hospital, Military Camp Lapu-Lapu, Lahug ☎ 032 232 2464.
Makati City Makati Medical Center, 2 Amorsolo St, Makati City ☎ 02 817 5601.
Manila V. Luna Recompression Chamber, AFP Medical Center, V. Luna Rd, Quezon City ☎ 02 920 7183.
Roving Chamber Royal Coast Guard Action Center (two ships based in Cebu) ☎ 02 527 3880.
Subic Bay Subic Recompression Chamber, Olongapo City ☎ 047 252 7566.

DIVING RESOURCES

Asia Divers Ⓦ asiadivers.com. Thoroughly professional dive outfit with an office in Manila and a dive centre and accommodation in Puerto Galera. Good people to learn with.

Divephil Ⓦ divephil.com. Useful guide to scuba diving in the Philippines, plus information about destinations and accommodation.
SeaQuest Ⓦ seaquestdivecenter.net. Long-established operator with centres in Bohol and Cebu, offering general diving advice, safaris, courses and accommodation.
Underwater 360° Ⓦ uw360.asia. Online diving portal for several organizations, including *Asian Diver* diving magazine and Scuba Diver AustralAsia.

Trekking and climbing

The Philippines offers plenty of opportunities to explore pristine **wilderness** areas. Luzon, for example, has the Sierra Madre (see p.153), rarely visited by tourists and offering exhilarating trekking through dense rainforest and across dizzying peaks. In Bicol there are some terrific volcano climbs (Mt Mayon and Mt Isarog, for instance; see p.215 & p.209), while Mindoro, Palawan and the Visayas between them have dozens of national parks, heritage areas, wildlife sanctuaries and volcanoes. Mount Kanlaon (see p.295), an active volcano in Negros, is one of the country's more risky climbs, while Mount Halcon (see p.247) on Mindoro offers a raw, mesmerizing landscape of peaks, waterfalls and jungle, typical of wilderness areas throughout the archipelago.

The country actually has more than sixty **national parks** and protected areas, but because funds for their management are scarce, you won't find the kind of infrastructure that exists in national parks in the West. While the most popular climbs – Mount Apo in Mindanao (see p.432) and Mount Pulag in Mountain province (see p.165), for example – have trails that are relatively easy to find and follow, it's important to realize that for the most part trails are generally poorly maintained and hardly marked, if they're marked at all. There are seldom more than a few (badly paid) wardens or rangers responsible for huge tracts of land, and where accommodation exists, it will be extremely basic. Some national parks have administrative buildings where you might be able to get a bed in a dorm for the night, or where you can roll out a mattress or sleeping bag on the floor. They may also have basic cooking facilities, but the closest you'll get to a shower is filling a bucket and washing outside. Deep within park territory, the best you can hope for is a wooden shack to shelter in for the night.

This lack of facilities means you'll need to hire a reliable **guide**. Often, the place to make contact with guides is the municipal hall in the barangay or town closest to the trailhead. **Fees** range from P700–1500 per day depending where you are, plus food and water, which you'll have to bring with you as it's unlikely that you'll come across anywhere to buy anything once you're on the trail.

There are some **outdoor shops** in big cities – mainly Manila – where you can buy a basic frame-tent for P3000 and a sleeping bag for P1500. Other essentials such as cooking equipment, lanterns and backpacks are also available, and you may be able to rent some items, though the range of gear on offer is limited even in the best shops.

TREKKING AND CLIMBING RESOURCES

Metropolitan Mountaineering Society Ⓦ metropolitanms.org. Sociable trekking group running expeditions throughout the year. On the easier treks they may well be willing to take you along at short notice, though you might need to take a basic survival course to be allowed on the more challenging expeditions.
Mountaineering Federation of the Philippines Ⓦ mfpi .wordpress.com. An umbrella group that can offer general information about routes and practicalities.
Pinoy Mountaineer Ⓦ pinoymountaineer.com. This detailed and well-maintained site is a good place to read up about trekking and climbing, with sample itineraries for major climbs and a long list of climbing clubs in the country.

Caving

It's hardly surprising that **caving** – spelunking – is a growth industry, as there are huge caves to explore throughout the country. The largest cave systems are in northern Luzon – in Sagada (see p.171) and in Cagayan province near Tuguegarao, where the Peñablanca Protected Area (see p.152) has three hundred caves, many deep, dangerous and not yet

fully explored. The other exciting caving area is the Sohoton Natural Bridge National Park in Samar (see p.357).

Whitewater rafting and ziplining

Whitewater rafting is becoming more popular in the Philippines, notably along the Cagayan River and Chico River in northern Luzon (see p.174) and Cagayan de Oro River in Mindanao (see box, p.407). **Ziplines** have mushroomed all over the islands, but some are much tamer than others – some of the best are near Cagayan de Oro (see p.407) and Tibiao (see p.281).

Surfing and other watersports

Surfing is now well established in the Philippines in eastern Bicol (see box, p.202), Catanduanes (see p.229), eastern Mindanao (especially Siargao Island; see p.419), and around San Fernando in La Union (see p.136). There are also any number of hard-to-reach areas in the archipelago that are visited only by a handful of die-hard surfers, such as Baler in northern Luzon (see box, p.155), or around Borongan (see p.358) in eastern Samar. For general information visit Ⓦ surfingphilippines.com and Ⓦ surfingthephilippines.com.

Other sea-based watersports such as **kitesurfing, waterskiing, wakeboarding** and **ocean kayaking** are also growing in popularity, especially in major tourist destinations such as Boracay.

Spectator sports

When it comes to spectator sports, basketball and boxing are among the biggest passions in the Philippines. Pool – or what Filipinos call "billiards" – is also popular. Televised football (soccer) has some fans, though it is difficult to find in most of the country. Cockfighting is one of the few popular pastimes that harks back to the pre-Hispanic era.

Basketball

The Filipinos embraced **basketball** as they did everything else American, from pizza to popcorn. Every barangay and town has a basketball court, even if all it consists of are a couple of makeshift baskets nailed to wooden poles in the church plaza. The major league – the equivalent of the NBA – is the **Philippine Basketball Association** (PBA; ⓦpba.inquirer.net), founded in 1975. Twelve teams compete for honours, all of them sponsored by a major corporation and taking their sponsor's name. You might find yourself watching Meralco Bolts play San Miguel Beermen, or NLEX take on Rain or Shine. PBA games are all played in Manila (see box, p.97).

The San Miguel-Petron franchise (under the name Beermen) is the most successful, while Barangay Ginebra Kings is the most popular. The players are household names to most Filipinos: June Mar Fajardo (San Miguel Beermen), Ababou Dylan (TNT KaTropa) and Aguilar Raymond (Blackwater) command huge attention.

Boxing

Boxing has been big business in the Philippines since the Americans introduced the sport in the early twentieth century. In recent years, one name stands out in particular: **Manny "the Pacman" Pacquiao**, the poor boy from Mindanao who became world champion (see box, p.445). Fights are held almost every week, often at major venues in Caloocan (Manila), Cebu City, Mandaluyong (Manila), Tagaytay City, Victoria (Negros) and Taytay in the Luzon province of Rizal. Tickets are cheap and often sell out; whenever there's a bout of any significance Filipinos gather around every available television set. You can check schedules for fights at ⓦphilboxing.com.

Pool

Every town and city in the country has some sort of **billiards hall** (for **pool**, not traditional English billiards), even if it's just a few old tables on the pavement where games are played by kerosene lamps between locals for the price of a few San Miguels. The sport has always been popular – it's cheap and reasonably accessible – but has boomed over the last twenty years or so because of the success of **Efren Reyes** and **Francisco Bustamante**. Reyes, sometimes called "The Magician", is one of the pool world's great characters; a diminutive fellow with a toothy grin, he picked up the nickname "Bata" ("The Kid") while helping out in his uncle's pool halls in Manila as a child. He was born in Pampanga province, to the north of Manila, and can still occasionally be found on a Friday or Saturday night shooting pool in his hometown bars around Clark, good-naturedly scalping unsuspecting tourists' drinks. In 2006, Reyes and Francisco "Django" Bustamante represented their country as Team Philippines and won the inaugural **World Cup of Pool** by defeating Team USA – a victory of major significance for a country with few global sporting heroes. They repeated the feat in 2009, on home turf. Countrymen Dennis Orcollo and Roberto Gomez then won the title in London in 2013.

Cockfighting

Cockfighting is the Filipino passion few foreigners get to see – or understand, for obvious reasons. It's a brutal blood sport where fighting cocks literally peck and jab each other to death as onlookers make bets on the outcome. The fight begins when the two roosters are presented to each other in the pit. Both have a razor-sharp curved blade three inches long strapped to their leg. The fight is over in a burst of feathers in no more than a few minutes, when one rooster is too bloodied and wounded, or simply too dead, to peck back at its opponent when provoked. To make the evening last, most

---

COCKFIGHTING AND THE FILIPINO

Cockfighting has a long history in the Philippines. National hero José Rizal, martyred by the Spanish in 1896, once pointed out that the average Filipino loves his rooster more than he does his children.

Contrary to received wisdom, cockfighting was not introduced to the country by the Spanish. When conquistadors landed in Palawan shortly after the death of Magellan, they discovered native men already breeding domestic roosters to fight, putting them in shared cages and letting them scrap over small amounts of food.

Social scientists say cockfighting is popular in the Philippines because it reflects the national passion for brevity or a quick payoff, the trait of **ningas cogon** (*cogon* being a wild grass that burns ferociously and quickly). Part of the appeal is the **prize money**. For a P200 entrance fee, a struggling farmer from the backwoods could finish the day with P300,000 in his pocket, all thanks to a trusty rooster he has groomed and trained assiduously for months.

major cockfights feature seven contests. Anyone who likes animals should definitely stay well away.

If you do attend a cockfight (*sabong* in Tagalog), you'll be experiencing Filipino culture at its rawest – at the very least it might make you think again about how much "American influence" dominates the culture. It's best to start at one of the major cockpits in Manila (see box, p.97), or ask your hotel for the nearest place to see one. Entrance fees are minimal, but you'll rarely see women attending – the cockpit is the exclusive preserve of men, who see it as an egalitarian refuge from the world's woes, a place where class differences are temporarily put to one side and everyone wears flip-flops and vests. In Manila, foreign women should be OK at the main venues, but in the provinces you'll probably feel more comfortable with a male companion.

Culture and etiquette

For many travellers the Philippines seems less immediately "exotic" than other countries in Asia. English is spoken almost everywhere, people wear Western clothes and visit malls and the main religion is Catholicism. Combined with the approachability and sunny disposition of your average Filipino, this appears to make for a trouble-free assimilation into the ways and values of the Philippines.

However, this can lead to a false sense of security, which over time – as differences begin to surface – gives way to bewilderment and confusion. There are complex rules of engagement that govern behaviour among Filipinos, and failure to be sensitive to them can cast you unwittingly in the role of the ugly foreigner, ranting and raving with frustration at everyone you interact with.

Filipino etiquette

One of the major controlling elements in Filipino society – undetected by most visitors – is **hiya**, a difficult word to define, though essentially it means a sense of shame. *Hiya* is a factor in almost all social situations. It is a sense of *hiya* that prevents someone asking a question, for fear he may look foolish. It is *hiya* that sees many Filipinos refuse to disagree openly, for fear they may cause offence.

STREET KIDS

Despite the very real economic progress made in the last twenty years, millions of Filipinos still live in poverty. **Street children** (many orphaned) are one of the saddest consequences of this – some reports estimate that around 1.5 million kids are living rough. In Manila and other large cities you'll see very small children begging for money in the street or dancing in front of cars at dangerous interchanges for tips. You'll also come across kids aggressively begging for change; sometimes they are known as "**rugby boys**" – nothing to do with the sport, but a famous brand of glue that they sniff. Many locals refuse to give them money for fear of encouraging dangerous behaviour – others give a few pesos out of pity. If you want to help, a good place to start is the Cavite-based Life Child (@lifechild.org).

Not to have *hiya* is a grave social sin; to be accused of being *walang-hiya* (to be shameless) is the ultimate insult. *Hiya* goes hand in hand with the preservation of **amor-propio** (the term literally means "love of self"), in other words to avoid losing face. If you ever wonder why a Filipino fails to broach awkward subjects with you, or to point out that your flies are undone, it is because *hiya* and *amor-propio* are at work.

If you are ever in doubt about how to behave in the Philippines, bring to mind the value of **pakikisama**, which in rough translation means "to get along". For example, don't confront the waiter or bark insults if he gets your order wrong. This offends his sense of *amor-propio* and marks you out as being an obnoxious *walang-hiya* foreigner. Talk to him quietly and ask that the order be changed. The same rules apply with government officials, police, ticket agents, hotel receptionists and cashiers. If there's a problem, sort it out quietly and patiently. A sense of **delicadeza** is also important to Filipinos. This might be translated as "propriety", a simple sense of good behaviour, particularly in the presence of elders or women.

Yes, no, maybe...

One of the root causes of frustration during social intercourse is the use of the word **yes**. In their desire to please, many Filipinos find it difficult to say no. So they say yes instead. Yes (actually *oo* in

Tagalog, pronounced oh-oh, though most Filipinos would use the English word when talking to foreigners) can mean one of a great many things, from a plain and simple "yes" to "I'm not sure", "perhaps", "if you say so", or "sorry, I don't understand". A casual yes is never taken as binding.

The concepts of *hiya* and *amor-propio* also filter through to the language in the form of a great many euphemisms for the word no (*hindi* in Tagalog). Instead of replying in the negative, in order not to upset you a Filipino will typically say "maybe" (*siguro nga*), "whatever" (*bahala na*) or "if you say so" (*kung sinabi mo ba e*).

These subtleties of language are symptomatic of the unseen ebbs and flows of the tides that govern all social behaviour in the Philippines, few foreigners ever fully coming to terms with the eddies and whirls underneath.

Questions and greetings

Filipinos are outgoing people who don't consider it rude to ask **personal questions**. Prepare to be pleasantly interrogated by everyone you meet. Filipinos will want to know where you are from, why you are in the Philippines, how old you are, whether you are married, if not why not, and so on and so forth. They pride themselves on their hospitality and are always ready to share a meal or a few drinks. Don't offend them by refusing outright.

In rural areas it's still common for foreign men to be greeted by passers-by with calls of "Hey Joe!" This harks back to the GI Joes of World War II and American occupation.

Filipino time

Why do you never ask a Filipino to do something by the end of the week? He might think you're being pushy. That's an exaggeration of course, but beyond

---

PROSTITUTION AND SEX TOURISM

The Philippines, like some other Southeast Asian countries, has an unfortunate reputation for **prostitution** and **sex tourism**. It's a huge industry domestically with an estimated 800,000 men, women and, sadly, children working in the trade. The country's international image as a sex destination came about largely as a result of the US military presence here during and after World War II, when "go go" or "girlie" bars flourished around the bases at Clark and Subic Bay.

While it's illegal to sell or procure sex, the trade still operates under the guise of entertainment: sex workers are employed as singers, dancers, waitresses or "guest relations officers" in clubs and bars where they are expected to leave with any client who pays a fee (the "bar fine"). Then there's what are euphemistically dubbed "freelancers", prostitutes who independently cruise bars looking for paying customers. In the Philippines it's common (because it's so cheap) to hire these girls for several days or weeks to have what's called a GFE ("girlfriend experience").

According to the Coalition Against Trafficking in Women (Ⓦcatwinternational.org), some 15,000 Australian men a year visit Angeles, north of Manila, on sex tours; plenty of Americans, Brits and Europeans join them, while Koreans, Taiwanese and Chinese have developed their own networks, usually based in karaoke bars and restaurants. Manila, Cebu City, Subic Bay and Pasay City are also major sex destinations.

DATING WEBSITES

Though you will often see older Western men accompanied by young, attractive Filipina women all over the Philippines, don't assume that these women are prostitutes. The situation is confused by the legal and equally popular phenomenon of **online dating websites** that exclusively pair Filipinas with foreigners – plenty of the men you'll see have been matched with their Filipina "girlfriend" and intend to seriously date or even marry them (or already have), however dubious this might seem.

CHILD PROSTITUTION

The Philippine government estimates that almost half the sex workers in the country are **underage**, many of them street children lured from the provinces by the promise of work or simply food and water. In recent years, cyberporn has become a major problem – in 2014 the British-led Operation Endeavour uncovered a global network of paedophiles streaming live child abuse by video from the Philippines. If you suspect someone of being a paedophile or engaging in any abusive behaviour towards minors, call **hotline** ☏1-6-3 or visit Ⓦabs-cbnfoundation.com.

VIDEOKE CRAZY

"Videoke" = **video karaoke** is a major fad in the Philippines, with cheap videoke bars in almost every town and neighbourhood. While it can be fun to participate in a Filipino singing session, being regaled by drunken wailings wafting through your hotel window in the early hours isn't so amusing. Adding to the mix, most Filipino families own one or more karaoke machines that they use throughout the week, and always on special occasions, birthdays and weddings. Incidentally, a Filipino inventor (Roberto del Rosario) actually holds the patent for the karaoke machine.

the cities, the old joke still resonates for long-time residents of the Philippines.

In recent years, perhaps due to the number of young Filipinos returning home after an overseas education, the attitude towards **punctuality** has begun to change. For medical or work-related appointments you'll need to be on time, but for social gatherings turn up half an hour late: it is considered impolite to be on time for a party, for instance, simply because it makes you look like a glutton who wants to grab the food. The speed of service in restaurants in the Philippines has also improved, but you should still expect your patience to occasionally be tested.

Women travellers

Women travellers rarely experience problems in the Philippines, either travelling alone or as part of a group. The culture, however, is a **macho** one and, especially in the provinces, foreign women may experience being stared at or the occasional catcall or lewd comment in Tagalog. In the barangays, Filipino men hold dear the oft-regurgitated image of themselves in local movies as gifted romancers, able to reduce any lady to jelly with a few choice words and the wink of an eye.

Reacting to this attention is the worst thing you can do. If you smile and remain good-natured but distant, your potential suitors will get the message and leave you alone. To shout back or to poke fun, particularly if Romeo is with his friends, will cause him serious loss of face and lead to resentment and the possibility that they will try to get back at you.

Modesty is essential to the behaviour of young Filipinas, especially in the provinces, and this should also be the case with visitors. Shorts and T-shirts are fine for women anywhere (except for immigration offices), but bikinis are only for the beach, and even then it's considered bad form to wander through a resort's restaurant or souvenir shop without covering up first (a sarong is perfect for this). Topless sunbathing is unheard of among Filipinas, and tourists in popular resorts such as Boracay who remove their clothes are likely to attract an amazed, gossiping crowd of locals. For some Filipino men this reinforces the stereotype that foreign women on holiday are game for anything.

Shopping

The Philippines is a great place to buy indigenous art, woodwork, masks and religious artefacts, mostly at rock-bottom prices. Manila also contains a number of shiny malls with stores offering much the same designer gear you can find in London or New York. The country's two main department-store chains are Rustan's and SM. Both are good for clothes and shoes, at slightly lower prices than in Europe; children's clothes are especially inexpensive.

Souvenirs

Typical souvenirs include **models of jeepneys**, wooden **salad bowls**, cotton **linen** and small items such as **fridge magnets** made of coconut shell or carabao horn. In department stores you can find **cutlery sets** made from carabao horn and bamboo and costing less than P2000. **Woven place mats** and coasters are inexpensive and easy to pack to take home. Filipino **picture frames** are eye-catching and affordable. Made from raw materials such as carabao horn and Manila hemp, they are available in most department stores. All towns have markets that sell cheap local goods such as **sleeping mats** (*banig*) that make colourful wall hangings, and earthenware water jars or **cooking pots** that make attractive additions to a kitchen.

For serious souvenir-hunting, you'll have to rummage around in small **antique shops**. There aren't many of these, and they're often tucked away in low-rent areas. The better shops in big cities are listed in the Guide; elsewhere, ask around at your hotel. Many of the items in these shops are religious artefacts (see p.46), although you'll also find furniture, decorative vases, lamps, old paintings, mirrors and brassware.

BARGAINING

Prices are fixed in department stores and most retail outlets in malls, but in many antique shops and in markets, you're expected to **haggle**. Bargaining is always amicable and relaxed, never confrontational. Filipinos see it as something of a polite game, interjecting their offers and counter offers with friendly chitchat about the weather, the state of the nation or, if you're a foreigner, where you come from and what you're doing in the Philippines.

Never play hardball and make a brusque "take it or leave it" offer because that's likely to cause embarrassment and offence. Start by offering **fifty to sixty percent** of the initial asking price and work your way up from there. Note that foreigners tend to get less of a discount than Filipinos.

Some souvenir stores and antique shops will ship goods home for you for an extra charge. Otherwise you could send bulky items home by regular post (see p.51). Note that the trade in coral and seashells as souvenirs in beach areas is decidedly unsound environmentally, as is the manufacture of decorative objects and jewellery from seashells.

Tribal and religious artefacts

Not all tribal and religious artefacts are genuine, but even the imitations make good gifts. **Woven baskets and trays** of the kind used by Cordillera tribes are a bargain, starting from only a few hundred pesos. They come in a range of sizes and shapes, including circular trays woven from grass that are still used to sift rice, and baskets worn like a backpack for carrying provisions. The best are the original tribal baskets, which cost a little more than the reproductions, but have an appealing nut-brown tone as a result of the many times they have been oiled. You can find them in antique shops around the country and also in markets in Banaue and Sagada.

Rice gods (*bulol*; see p.97), carved wooden deities sometimes with nightmarish facial expressions, are available largely in Manila and the Cordilleras. In Manila, they cost anything from a few hundred pesos for a small reproduction to P20,000 for a genuine figurine of modest size; they're much cheaper if you haggle for them in Banaue or Sagada. At markets in the Cordilleras, look out also for **wooden bowls**, various wooden wall carvings and fabric **wall hangings**.

The best place to look for Catholic **religious art** is in Manila (see p.97), though antique shops in other towns also have a selection. Wooden Catholic statues called santos and large wooden crucifixes are common. Cheaper religious souvenirs such as rosaries and icons of saints are sold by street vendors outside many of the more high-profile pilgrimage cathedrals and churches such as Quiapo in Manila and Santo Niño in Cebu.

Textiles

In market areas such as Divisoria in Manila and Colon in Cebu you can find colourful raw cloth and finished **batik products**. Another native textile is **Manila hemp**, which comes from the trunk of a particular type of banana tree. Both *piña* and Manila hemp are used to make attractive home accessories sold in department stores, such as laundry baskets, lampshades and vases. The versatile and pliable native grass, **sikat**, is woven into everything from place mats to rugs.

SARI-SARI STORES

A Philippine institution, the humble **sari-sari store** – *sari-sari* means "various" or "a variety" – is often no more than a barangay shack or a hole in the wall selling an eclectic but practical range of goods. If you're short of shampoo, body lotion, cigarettes, rum, beer or you've got a headache and need a painkiller, the local sari-sari store is the answer, especially in areas without supermarkets. All items are sold in the smallest quantities possible: shampoo comes in packets half the size of a credit card, medicine can be bought by the pill and cigarettes are sold individually. Buy a soft drink or beer and you may be perplexed to see the store holder pour it into a plastic bag, from which you're expected to drink it through a straw. This is so that they can keep the bottle and return it for the deposit of a few centavos. Most sari-sari stores are fiercely **familial**, their names – the Three Sisters, the Four Brothers or Emily and Jon-Jon's – reflecting their ownership.

The sari-sari store is also held dear by Filipinos as an unofficial community centre. Many sari-sari stores, especially in the provinces, have crude sitting areas outside, encouraging folk to linger in the shade and gossip or talk basketball and cockfighting.

Department stores everywhere have a good selection of Philippine **linen products** with delicate embroidery and lace flourishes. Some of these are handmade in Taal (see p.114); a good set of pillowcases and bedsheets will cost about P2000 in Taal's market, half the price in Rustan's or SM. In beach areas you'll find a good range of cotton sarongs, cheap (from P200), colourful and versatile.

Jewellery

The malls are full of stalls selling cheap jewellery, but you'll also find silver-plated earrings, replica tribal-style jewellery made with tin or brass, and attractive necklaces made from bone or polished coconut shell. In Mindanao – as well as in some malls in Manila, Cebu City and at souvenir stalls in Boracay – **pearl jewellery** is a bargain. Most of the pearls are cultivated on pearl farms in Mindanao and Palawan. White pearls are the most common, but you can also find pink and dove grey. They are made into earrings, necklaces and bracelets; simple earrings cost around P500, while a necklace can range from P1000 for a single string up to P10,000 for something more elaborate.

Musical instruments

In Cebu, and increasingly on the streets of Manila and Davao, you can pick up a locally made handcrafted guitar, *bandurria* (mandolin) or ukelele. Though the acoustic quality is nothing special, the finish may include mother-of-pearl inlays, and prices are low – a steel-string acoustic guitar will set you back P2000. Mindanao's markets – such as Aldevinco in Davao – are a good place to rummage for decorative drums and Muslim gongs.

Travel essentials

Addresses

In the Philippines it is common to give an address as, for example, 122 Legaspi corner Velasco Streets, meaning the junction of Legaspi and Velasco streets (in the Guide this is written "122 Legaspi St at Velasco St"). G/F denotes street level, after which come 2/F, 3/F and so on; "first floor" or 1/F isn't used. Some addresses include the name of a **barangay**, which is officially an electoral division for local elections, but is generally used to mean a village or, when mentioned in connection with a town, a neighbourhood or suburb. The word barangay isn't always written out in the address, although it's sometimes included in official correspondence and

signposts, often abbreviated to "Brgy" or "Bgy". The term "**National Highway**" in an address doesn't necessarily refer to a vast motorway – on the smaller islands or in provincial areas, it just means the coastal road or the main street in town. When it comes to **islands**, Filipinos generally talk loosely in terms of the main island in the vicinity – so, for example, they would talk about visiting Panay when they actually mean offshore Pan de Azucar. We've adopted a similar approach in parts of the Guide, implicitly including small islands in coverage of the nearest large island.

Costs

While upmarket resorts in the Philippines can be as expensive as anywhere else in the world, for anyone with modest spending habits and tastes the country is inexpensive. Outside of Metro Manila you can get by on a frugal **budget** of around P1200 per person (£19.50/US$24/€22.50) a day, but you might need to avoid the most popular tourist destinations such as Boracay (or visit during the off-season), and you'll be limited to bare-bones cottages and pokey rooms in basic hotels, usually without air conditioning or hot water. On this budget you'd also have to confine your meals to local restaurants and carinderias, with little leeway for slap-up feasts in nice restaurants. You'd also have to plan any flights carefully, only buying the very cheapest tickets online or limiting yourself to buses and ferries.

A budget of P2000 (£32.50/US$40/€37.50) a day will take your standard of living up a few notches, allowing you to find reasonable beach cottage and hotel rooms and have enough left for modest eating out, drinking and budget flights. On P3500 (£57/US$70/€66) a day, you can afford to stay in solid, reasonably spacious cottages on the beach, usually with a veranda and air conditioning, and have plenty left over for domestic flights, good meals in local restaurants and some shopping.

Crime and personal safety

The Philippines has a reputation as a somewhat dangerous place to travel (at least in the US and UK), but if you exercise discretion and common sense this really isn't the case. Politically, the Philippines is a

---

EMERGENCY SERVICES
The 24-hour **emergency number** throughout the Philippines is ☎911.

volatile place, with secessionist movements present in Mindanao (see box, p.405) and communist guerrillas active in a number of areas. **Insurgency** rarely has an impact on tourists, but you should avoid trouble spots. Updated travel advisories are available on foreign office or state department websites including Ⓦstate.gov in the US and Ⓦfco .gov.uk in the UK.

There are occasional reports of **thieves** holding up vehicles at traffic lights and removing mobiles and cash from passengers. If you're in a taxi, keep the windows closed and the doors locked, just to be safe. In the Malate area of Manila and Angeles City, the so-called **Ativan Gang** has used the drug Lorazepam (Ativan is one of its proprietary names) to make their victims drowsy or put them to sleep – it's best to be on your guard in these areas if you're approached by people who seem unusually keen to offer you assistance, especially in bars.

Drug laws in the Philippines are stringent and the police are enthusiastic about catching offenders, especially under the Duterte regime. No one, foreigner or otherwise, caught in possession of hard or recreational drugs is likely to get much sympathy from the authorities. Carrying 500g or more of marijuana is deemed to be trafficking and carries the death penalty, while a lesser amount will usually result in a prison sentence.

Customs

Visitors are allowed to bring in four hundred cigarettes (or fifty cigars or 250g of pipe tobacco) and two bottles of wine and spirits not exceeding one litre each. If you arrive with more than US$10,000

in cash (unlikely) you are meant to declare it, and you won't be allowed to take out more than this sum in foreign currency on leaving. Note that not more than P10,000 in local currency may be taken out of the country, though this is rarely, if ever, enforced.

Electricity

Wall sockets in the Philippines usually operate at 220 volts (similar to Australia, Europe and most of Asia), although you may come across 110 volts in some rural areas – it's best to ask before plugging in appliances. Most mobile phones, cameras, MP3 players and laptops are dual voltage (older hair-dryers are the biggest problem for North American travellers). **Plugs** have two flat, rectangular pins, as in the US and Canada. **Power cuts** (known locally as "brown-outs") are less common than they used to be, but can still occur sometimes in the provinces. If you are worried about using valuable electrical equipment in the Philippines – a laptop computer, for instance – you should plug it into an automatic voltage regulator (AVR), a small appliance that ensures the voltage remains constant even if there is a sudden fluctuation or surge in the mains.

Entry requirements and visas

Most foreign nationals do not need a visa to stay in the Philippines for up to **thirty days**, though a passport valid for at least six months and an onward plane or ship ticket to another country are required.

Your thirty days can be extended by 29 days (giving a total stay of **59 days**) at **immigration offices** in Manila or around the country (see relevant

---

THE TYPHOON THREAT

Typhoons regularly rip across the Philippines – typically between July and November – and as **Typhoon Yolanda** (known internationally as Haiyan) proved in 2013, the effects can be catastrophic and deadly. Though you should always take typhoon warnings seriously (and check weather reports during typhoon season), there's no need to be unduly neurotic about for your own safety: the sad truth is that in the Philippines it's mainly poor neighbourhoods that bear the brunt of storms. Most modern hotels and buildings are built to withstand fierce typhoons, and you'll usually be given plenty of notice if a typhoon is heading your way – if it's a big one, go somewhere else and make sure you're nowhere near a ferry or boat when it hits. Though strong winds can be dangerous, flooding, ocean storm surges and landslides are the main cause of most damage and fatalities – if you are not in areas usually affected by any of these you should be fine. Note also that the aftermath of storms can dramatically affect transportation and the services in smaller villages and towns, though Filipinos are a resilient bunch and tourist services are often up and running remarkably quickly post-storm.

For **weather warnings** visit Ⓦpagasa.dost.gov.ph or Ⓦweatherph.org. If you want to volunteer or help in the aftermath of a typhoon, approach official charities such as Care (Ⓦcare.org), Save The Children (Ⓦsavethechildren.org) and the Philippine Red Cross (Ⓦredcross.org.ph).

chapters). The charge for this is around P3150, and you may be asked if you want to pay a P500 "express fee" that is supposed to guarantee that the application is dealt with within 24 hours. If you don't pay the fee, the process can take at least a week. Note that it pays to be presentably dressed at immigration offices, as staff might refuse to serve you if you turn up wearing a vest, shorts or flip-flops.

Many travel agents in tourist areas such as Malate in Manila and Boracay offer a **visa extension service**, saving you the hassle of visiting immigration centres but costing more, of course. Whatever you do, don't be tempted to use one of the fixers that hang around immigration offices, particularly in Manila. The "visa" they get you is often a dud and you run the risk of being detained and fined when you try to leave the country.

If you **overstay** your initial thirty days (but have not stayed beyond 59 days) you'll be fined at least P500, and the amount increases per day; overstay longer and you'll be sent to the nearest office of the Bureau of Immigration for a whole lot of trouble.

Temporary Visitor's Visa

If you know you want to spend longer than thirty days in the Philippines, apply for a 59-day **Temporary Visitor's Visa** at a Philippine embassy or consulate before you travel. A single-entry visa (with which you must enter the Philippines within three months of the issue date) costs £77/€91/US$96/Can$129/Aus$127/NZ$137/ZAR1250, while a multiple-entry visa, valid for one year from the date of issue (but with stays of a maximum 59 days within that year), is £134/€155/US$164/Can$220/Aus$216/NZ$234/ZAR2140. Apart from a valid passport and a completed application form (downloadable from some Philippine embassy websites), you will have to present proof that you have enough money for the duration of your stay in the Philippines.

Longer stays

Regardless of how you entered the Philippines, to stay longer than 59 days you must apply for **visa extensions** at immigration bureaus every two months (fees from P2900). There is now a new **Long Stay Visitor Visa Extension** (LSVVE) programme, which allows visitors to extend stays for six months in one go after their first thirty days, but this costs at least a hefty P11,500.

Note that if you have been in the Philippines continuously for six months, you must have an **Emigration Clearance Certificate** (P1210) to pass through immigration at the airport. After six months you must also apply for an **ACR-I card** or "Alien Certificate of Registration" for around P3000, and after sixteen months you need approval from the Chief of the Immigration Regulation Division. When you have been in the Philippines for **two years** you really will have to leave.

PHILIPPINE EMBASSIES AND CONSULATES ABROAD

For a full list of the Philippines' embassies and consulates, check the government's Department of Foreign Affairs website at Ⓦ dfa.gov.ph.
Australia Canberra Ⓣ 612 6273 2535, Ⓦ philembassy.org.au; Sydney Ⓣ 02 9262 7377, Ⓦ sydneypcg.dfa.gov.ph; Melbourne Ⓣ 03 9869 7182, Ⓦ philconsulate.com.au.
Canada Ottawa Ⓣ 613 233 1121, Ⓦ philippineembassy.ca; Toronto Ⓣ 416 922 7181, Ⓦ philcongen-toronto.com.
Ireland Dublin Ⓣ 01 437 6206, Ⓦ philippineconsulate.ie.
New Zealand Wellington Ⓣ 644 890 3741, Ⓦ philembassy.org.nz.
South Africa Pretoria Ⓣ 012 346 0451, Ⓦ pretoriape.dfa.gov.ph.
UK London Ⓣ 020 7451 1780, Ⓦ londonpe.dfa.gov.ph.
US Washington DC Ⓣ 202 467 9300, Ⓦ philippineembassy-usa.org; San Francisco Ⓣ 415 433 6666, Ⓦ philippinessanfrancisco.org; Los Angeles Ⓣ 213 639 0980, Ⓦ philippineslosangeles.org; New York Ⓣ 212 764 1330, Ⓦ philippinesnewyork.org; Chicago Ⓣ 312 583 0621, Ⓦ philippineschicago.org. Consulates also in Honolulu and Agada, Guam.

Gay and lesbian travellers

Few Filipinos, even the most pious, pay much heed to the Catholic Church regarding homosexuality, and the prevailing attitude is that people can carry on doing what's right for them. **Gay culture** in the Philippines is strong and largely unimpeded by narrow-mindedness, with the possible exceptions within politics and the military, where heterosexuality is still considered correct. Gays are respected as arbiters of fashion and art, and beauty parlours are often staffed by transsexuals.

The word **bakla** is used generically by many Filipinos and visitors to the Philippines to refer to gay people, but that would be inaccurate. A *bakla* considers himself a male with a female heart – a *pusong babae*. Most are not interested in a sex-change operation and consider themselves a "third sex", cross-dressing and becoming more "female" than many women. Another category of male homosexual is known as **tunay ne lalake**, men who identify themselves publicly as heterosexual but have sex with other men. Homosexuals who aren't out permeate every stratum of Philippine society; rumours circulate almost daily of this-or-that tycoon or politician who is *tunay ne lalake*.

Lesbians are much more reticent about outing themselves than gay men, no doubt because there is still societal pressure for young women to become the quintessential Filipina lady – gracious, alluring and fulfilled by motherhood and the home. Indeed, some Filipina lesbians complain that the more outspoken **tomboys** – lesbians are often referred to as tomboys – make the fight for women's rights even harder.

The **gay scene** is centred on the bars and clubs of Manila (see box, p.93), though there are also smaller scenes in other major cities such as Cebu, Davao and Cagayan de Oro. The websites Ⓦutopia-asia .com and Ⓦfridae.asia are useful sources of info on local gay life.

Insurance

A typical travel **insurance** policy usually provides cover for the loss of baggage, tickets and cash, as well as cancellation or curtailment of your journey. When securing baggage cover, make sure that the per-article limit will cover your most valuable posses-sion. Most policies exclude so-called dangerous sports unless an extra premium is paid: in the Philip-pines this can mean scuba diving, whitewater rafting, windsurfing, kitesurfing, trekking and kayaking. Note that at the time of writing, it was impossible to get coverage for visits to mainland Mindanao because of the security situation (see box, p.405).

If you need to make a claim, you should keep receipts for medicines and medical treatment, and in the event you have anything stolen, you must obtain an official statement from the police. In the Philippines this is sometimes a slow process that involves the police officer copying, by hand, the details of your loss into what is known as the police "blotter", or file. Once this has been signed by a superior officer you'll get an authorized copy.

Internet

Major cities have dozens of **internet cafés** and even in small towns and isolated resort areas you can usually find somewhere to log on. The cost of getting online at an internet café is around P10–40 per hour, depending where you are. Some rural and remote island destinations are still not connected at all, but in general **wi-fi** is becoming more common in cafés and hotels throughout the country. However, **connections** are often temperamental and speeds slow. Indeed, the Philippines has one of the lowest broadband ratings in the world. Hotels reviewed in the Guide will normally offer free wi-fi unless stated otherwise (see box, p.30).

Laundry

There are no coin-operated **launderettes** in the Philippines, but there are laundries all over the place offering serviced washes for about P50–150 for an average load (ranging between P20 and P60/kg). Most of these places will iron clothes for you for an extra charge. It's also possible to get clothes washed at pretty much any guesthouse, resort or hotel; the pricier the establishment the more it will cost.

Living and working in the Philippines

Opportunities to **work** in the Philippines are limited. Most jobs require specialist qualifications or experi-ence and, unlike other parts of Asia, there's not really a market for foreigners teaching English as a foreign language in paid posts. One possibility is to work for a diving outfit as a dive master or instructor. Rates of pay are low, but board and lodging may be provided if you work for a good operator or resort in a busy area (Boracay or Puerto Galera, for instance). Some international organizations also offer **voluntary placements** in the Philippines.

VOLUNTEERING ORGANIZATIONS

AVI Australia ☎ 03 9419 4280, Ⓦ avi.org.au. Well-established Australian organization (AVI is an abbreviation of its old name, Australian Volunteers International), offering short- and long-term postings for professionals interested in working in the developing world. Volunteers in the Philippines

---

ROUGH GUIDES TRAVEL INSURANCE

Rough Guides has teamed up with **WorldNomads.com** to offer great travel insurance deals. Policies are available to residents of over 150 countries, with cover for a wide range of adventure sports, 24hr emergency assistance, high levels of medical and evacuation cover and a stream of travel safety information. Roughguides.com users can take advantage of their policies online 24/7, from anywhere in the world – even if you're already travelling. And since plans often change when you're on the road, you can extend your policy and even claim online. Roughguides.com users who buy travel insurance with WorldNomads.com can also leave a positive footprint and donate to a community development project. For more information, go to Ⓦroughguides.com/travel-insurance.

have helped introduce sustainable fishing and marine conservation programmes and campaigned for the rights of minority groups.

Coral Cay Conservation UK ☎ 020 7620 1411, ⓦ coralcay.org. Non-profit organization that trains volunteers to collect scientific data to aid conservation in sensitive environments around the world, particularly coral reefs and tropical forests. Their Philippine base is in southern Leyte.

Peace Corps US ☎ 1 855 855 1961, ⓦ peacecorps.gov. Places people with specialist qualifications or skills in two-year postings in many developing countries, including the Philippines.

Projects Abroad US ☎ 1 888 839 3535, ⓦ projects-abroad.org. Worldwide organization that lodges people with host families while they work on projects from teaching English and building to jobs requiring more specialist knowledge such as medicine. Their programme in the Philippines is based on Cebu.

VSO (Voluntary Service Overseas) UK ☎ 020 8780 7200; Philippines ☎ 02 622 3812, ⓦ vso.org.uk. Charity that sends qualified professionals to work on projects beneficial to developing countries. At the time of writing, VSO was about to roll out a new programme of disaster risk reduction and peace-building initiatives.

Post

Airmail **letters** from the Philippines (ⓦ philpost.gov .ph) take at least five days to reach other countries, though in many cases it's a lot longer. International postcards cost P15 while letters up to 20g cost P34–51 depending on the destination. Ordinary domestic mail costs P12–17 for letters up to 20g. **Post offices** are generally open from 8am to 5pm, Monday to Friday.

If you have to post anything valuable, use registered mail or pay extra for a **courier**. DHL (ⓦ dhl .com.ph), Fedex (ⓦ fedex.com/ph) and the locally based LBC (ⓦ lbcexpress.com) and 2GO (ⓦ 2go .com.ph) have offices throughout the country (listed on their websites), and can deliver internationally.

Maps

If you want to seek out Philippines maps at home, you'll probably only find street maps of Manila and Cebu City, in addition to country maps. **Nelles Verlag** (ⓦ nelles-verlag.de) publishes two good maps – a country map with a scale of 1:1,500,000 and a Manila city map. They are sometimes available in Manila bookshops, but can be hard to track down. The 1:1,200,000 **Hema** map (ⓦ hemamaps.com.au) of the Philippines is another one to look out for before you arrive.

Road maps and country maps can be bought at branches of the National Book Store in all major cities and towns, although supply is unreliable. Many bookshops sell the **Accu-map** range of atlases (ⓦ accu-map.com), A–Z-like pocket books that cover

the whole of Metro Manila and detailed maps of Baguio, Subic Bay, Cavite, Angeles City, Puerto Galera, Boracay and other destinations. United Tourist Promotions publishes a range of decent maps called **EZ Maps** (ⓦ ezmaps.ph), covering Manila and the country's regions, with each sheet featuring a combination of area and town maps.

The best map offered by the **Philippine Department of Tourism (DoT)** locally is the free Tourist Map of the Philippines, which includes a street map of Manila, contact numbers for all overseas and domestic DoT offices and listings of hotels, embassies and bus companies. The **free maps** handed out at regional tourist offices vary greatly in quality and accuracy but are usually sufficient to prevent you getting lost.

For a more varied selection of area maps and sea charts of the Philippines, try the **National Mapping and Resources Information Authority** (☎ 02 810 5466, ⓦ namria.gov.ph) on Lawton Avenue, Fort Bonifacio, ten minutes by taxi from Makati, or download their maps online.

Money

The Philippine currency is the **peso**. One peso is divided into 100 centavos, with notes in denominations of P20, 50, 100, 200, 500 and 1000. Coins come in values of 25 centavos, P1, P5 and P10.

It's best to arrive with some local currency, though you can easily get cash from **ATMs** or **exchange booths** at the airport. ATMs are found in cities and tourist destinations all over the country, but not so much in less visited areas such as the interior of Mindanao, the northern mountains, parts of Palawan (outside Puerto Princesa and Coron Town), and in remote areas of the Visayas. It's best to use ATMs at major banks, and preferably in big cities, because these machines tend to be more reliable than provincial ones, which are often out of service. **Credit cards** are accepted by most hotels in cities and tourist areas, though the smaller hotels may levy a surcharge if you pay by card, and real budget places operate solely on cash. Only smarter, more international restaurants tend to accept cards.

Banks are normally open 9am–3pm Monday to Friday, and all major branches have ATMs and

> ### EXCHANGE RATES
> At the time of writing the **exchange rate** was around P50 to US$1, P61 to £1 and P53 to the €1.

currency exchange. The best-established local banks include BPI (Bank of the Philippine Islands), DBP (Development Bank of the Philippines), Metrobank and BDO (aka Banco de Oro); Citibank and HSBC also have branches in major cities. Most banks only change US dollars, and though many hotels will change other currencies, they offer poor rates. It's easy to change dollars in Manila, where there are dozens of small **moneychangers' kiosks** in Malate and P. Burgos Street, Makati, offering better rates than the banks; ask around at a few places and compare. In rural areas there are few moneychangers, and banks don't always change money, so if you're heading off the beaten track, be sure to take enough pesos to last the trip.

Opening hours and public holidays

Most **government offices** are open Monday to Friday 8.30am–5.30pm, but some close for an hour-long lunch break, usually starting at noon, so it's best to avoid the middle of the day. **Businesses** generally keep the same hours, with some also open on Saturday 9am–noon. **Banks** are open Monday to Friday 9am–3pm and do not close for lunch, except for some of the smallest branches in rural areas. **Shops** in major malls open daily 10am–8pm or 9pm, later during the Christmas rush or "Midnight Madness" sales; the latter take place every two weeks on the first Friday after each payday. **Churches** are almost always open most of the day for worshippers and tourists alike. Typically,

---

PUBLIC HOLIDAYS

January 1 New Year's Day
February 25 Anniversary of the EDSA Revolution
March/April (variable) Maundy Thursday, Good Friday
April 9 Bataan Day
May 1 Labor Day
May/June (June 25, 2018; June 4, 2019; May 24, 2020) Eid ul Fitr, the end of Ramadan
June 12 Independence Day
August 21 Ninoy Aquino Day
Last Monday in August National Heroes' Day
November 1 All Saints' Day (see box, p.37)
December 25 Christmas Day; the following day is also a holiday
December 30 Rizal Day, in honour of José Rizal (see p.437)

CALLING THE PHILIPPINES FROM ABROAD

The country code for the Philippines is **+63**. When calling the Philippines from abroad, dial 00 and then the country code, and remove the initial zero from the number.

---

the first Mass of the day is at around 6am, the last at 6pm or 7pm.

Government offices and private businesses close on **public holidays**, though shops and most restaurants remain open except on Good Friday and Christmas Day. Holidays are often moved to the closest Friday or Monday to their original date (see box below), so that people in the cities can use the long weekend to get back to the provinces to spend a few days with their families. This moving of public holidays is done on an ad hoc basis and is announced in the press just a few weeks – sometimes only a few days – beforehand.

Phones

If you want to use a **mobile phone** bought abroad in the Philippines, it will need to be GSM/Triband and to have global roaming activated. For local calls it will probably work out cheaper to buy a local **SIM card**, available at dozens of mobile-phone outlets in malls and convenience stores, for any of the country's four major mobile **networks**: Smart Communications, the best bet for iPhones (Ⓦ smart .com.ph), Globe Telecom (Ⓦ globe.com.ph), Talk 'N Text (Ⓦ talkntext.com.ph) and Sun Cellular (Ⓦ sun cellular.com.ph). Local SIMs start at just P40 (Globe and Smart) and you can top up your credit for P100 to P500. Note that your phone must be "unlocked" to use a foreign SIM card (this can usually be done at local electronics shops, for a fee). **Rates** depend on which pre-paid package you opt for – most come with unlimited domestic calls and texts to a certain limit. International call charges start at US$0.40 per minute, rising by US$0.04 every six seconds. When **phoning abroad**, it's usually cheaper to use a pre-paid phone card with a freephone access number from a landline – these can cost as little as just over P2/min. Of course, as long as you can get online, digital apps such as **Skype** and **WhatsApp** sidestep costs altogether.

Basic mobiles in the Philippines are very inexpensive, starting at around P600, so it can be worth buying one if you plan to stay for any length of time. You'll need to pay for your calls with pre-paid cards.

Time

The Philippines is eight hours ahead of Universal Time (GMT) all year round.

Tipping

Keep your purse or wallet well stocked with P10 coins and P20 notes for **tips**. In cafés, bars, hotel coffee shops and basic restaurants many Filipinos simply leave whatever coins they get in their change. For good service in average restaurants you should leave a tip of about **ten percent**. In more expensive restaurants where the bill could be a couple of thousand pesos, it's okay to leave a somewhat smaller tip in percentage terms – P100 is a reasonable amount. Bellhops and porters get about P20 each and taxi drivers usually expect to keep the loose change.

Tourist information

The **Philippine Department of Tourism** (DoT; ⓦtourism.gov.ph) has a small number of overseas offices where you can pick up glossy brochures and get answers to general pre-trip questions about destinations, major hotels and domestic travel. These offices are not so helpful, however, when it comes to information about places off the beaten track. The DoT has offices throughout the Philippines, but most of them have small budgets and very little in the way of reliable information or brochures. The best source of up-to-date information on travelling in the Philippines is guesthouses and hotels that cater to travellers, most of which have **notice boards** where you can swap tips and ideas.

Travelling with children

Filipinos are extravagant in their generosity towards **children**, but because so much of the country lacks infrastructure, specific attractions for them are often hard to find. Major hotels in big cities such as Manila and Cebu City have playrooms and babysitting services, but even in popular tourist destinations such as Boracay there are few special provisions in all but the most expensive resorts.

This doesn't mean that travelling with children in the Philippines is a nightmare – far from it. Filipinos are very tolerant of children, so you can take little ones almost anywhere without restriction, and they help to break the ice with strangers. They'll be fussed over, befriended and looked after every step of the way.

Supermarkets in towns and cities throughout the Philippines have well-stocked children's sections that sell fresh and formula milk, nappies and baby food. **Department stores** such as Rustan's and SM sell baby clothes, bottles, sterilizing equipment and toys. And travelling with children in the Philippines needn't be a burden on your budget. Domestic **airlines** give a discount of around fifty percent for children under twelve and hotels and resorts offer **family rooms**, extra beds for a minimal charge, or don't charge at all for a small child sharing the parents' bed. Most **restaurants** with buffet spreads will let a small child eat for free if he or she is simply taking nibbles from a parent's plate. Otherwise, try asking for a special portion – the staff are usually happy to oblige.

One potential problem for young ones is the **climate**. You'll need to go to extra lengths to protect them from the sun and to make sure they are hydrated. A hat and good sunblock are essential. As for **medical attention** in the Philippines, there are good paediatricians at most major hospitals, in five-star hotels and many resorts.

Travellers with disabilities

Facilities for the disabled are rare except in the major cities. Taxis are cramped, while bangkas are notoriously tricky even for the able-bodied. For wheelchair users the pavements represent a serious obstacle in themselves. Often dilapidated and potholed, they are frustrating at the best of times and simply impassable at the worst, when pedestrians are forced to pick their way along the gutter in the road, dodging cars and motorcycles.

In Manila, Cebu City, Davao and some other big cities, the most upmarket hotels cater to the disabled, as do malls, cinemas and some restaurants. Elsewhere, the good news for disabled travellers is that Filipinos are generous when it comes to offering assistance. Even in the remotest barangay, people will go out of their way to help you board a boat or lift you up the stairs of a rickety pier. However, once you're on board a ferry, for example, ramps and disabled toilets are almost certain to be non-existent.

The government-run **National Council on Disability Affairs** or NCDA (ⓣ02 932 6422, ⓦncda .gov.ph) is mandated to formulate policies and coordinate the activities of all agencies concerning disability issues, but it doesn't have much practical advice for disabled travellers. Staff at the group's Quezon City office can give general pointers on transport and where to stay.

Manila

MAKATI

1 Manila

If you like big cities you'll love Manila: it's a high-speed, frenetic place, where you can eat, drink and shop 24 hours a day and where the Filipino heritage of native, Spanish, Chinese and American cultures is at its most mixed up. Like many capital cities, Manila bears little resemblance to the rest of the country – something to remember if this is your first taste of the Philippines. With twelve million residents, much of it is chronically overcrowded, polluted and suffers from appalling traffic jams, yet in between the chaos lie tranquil gate-guarded "subdivisions" that resemble affluent parts of the US. There's extreme poverty here, with young children cleaning car windows, dancing or just begging for food at practically every interchange, while in enormous shopping malls thousands of wealthy, middle-class Manileños are as fashionable and hooked up with the latest iPhones as any of their contemporaries in London or New York.

Technically sixteen cities and one municipality make up what is officially known as **Metro Manila**, covering a vast 636 square kilometres. Travelling around the city takes some effort; its reputation as an intimidating place stems mainly from its size, apparent disorder and dispiriting levels of pollution, exacerbated by the equally fierce heat and humidity. To see the sights you will have to sweat it out in traffic and be prepared for delays, but the good news is that the main attractions are essentially confined to Manila proper: the old walled city of **Intramuros**; **Binondo** – Manila's Chinatown – north of the Pasig River; and the museums and parks grouped along the crescent sweep of **Manila Bay** and Roxas Boulevard. **Makati** and **Ortigas** to the east are glossy business districts best known for their malls and restaurants, though the **Ayala Museum** in Makati should not be missed. **Quezon City** on the city's northern edge is a little out of the way for most visitors, but it does boast some lively nightlife, most of it fuelled by students from the nearby **University of the Philippines**. Indeed, Manila prides itself on the quality of its restaurant, bar and club scene and the ability of its residents to whip up a good time – for many tourists, this will be their enduring memory of the place. The city is also a great place to pick up bargains, from the latest goods cranked out by Chinese factories to intricate native handicrafts.

Brief history
Malay settlements along the Pasig River delta go back at least one thousand years, with the **Kingdom of Tondo** most prominent, benefiting from a profitable trade with Ming-era China. After coming under the sway of the Sultanate of Brunei in the fifteenth century, the area was converted to Islam.

Spanish Manila
The village of **Maynila** fell under **Spanish rule** in 1571 when Miguel López de Legazpi defeated the local ruler Rajah Sulaiman II and established the colony of Manila. Spanish

FORT SANTIAGO, INTRAMUROS

Highlights

❶ **Intramuros** The atmospheric old Spanish city, with cobbled streets, the elegant San Agustin Church and poignant Rizal Shrine inside Fort Santiago. **See p.62**

❷ **The national museums** Two neighbouring museums housing the paintings of Filipino masters, relics from sunken ships and fascinating anthropology displays. **See p.66 & p.67**

❸ **Manila Hotel** The grand old dame of Philippine hotels. Even if you're not staying here, come to enjoy a drink in the sparkling *Lobby Lounge*. **See p.67, p.85 & p.93**

❹ **Ayala Museum** One of the best museums in the Philippines, an enlightening and

innovative introduction to the history of the islands. **See p.76**

❺ **Barbecue chicken** *Aristocrat*, Manila's most famous restaurant, still knocks out the best barbecue, along with a full roster of Filipino favourites. **See p.89**

❻ **Night out in Makati** From megaclubs to pubs, there's a good night out to suit everyone in Makati. **See p.93**

❼ **Manila markets** Whether you're looking for local crafts or pearl jewellery, Manila's vibrant and chaotic street markets offer the best bargains. **See p.98**

HIGHLIGHTS ARE MARKED ON THE MAP ON P.58

MANILA

MALABON

L Monumento   Balintawak   L Roosevelt

♦ University of the Philippines

North Avenue (Terminus)   M

L 5th Avenue

R. Papa   SAMPALOC   M Quezon Avenue

Chinese Cemetery   M GMA Kamuning

Abad Santos   QUEZON CITY   Katipunan

L Anonas

Blumentritt   L Laon Laan   L Anonas

P L Tayuman   L   M Araneta Center–Cubao

P Tutuban   L Bambang   P España   Betty Go-Belmonte

BINONDO   L D. José   L Gilmore   M Santolan

L Recto   Legarda   J. Ruiz

Carriedo   L   Pureza   V. Mapa

L Central Terminal Station   P Santa Mesa   ORTIGAS

Pandacan   M Ortigas

L UN Avenue   P   MANDALUYONG   M Shaw Boulevard

INTRAMUROS   P Paco   M Boni

Pedro Gil   L MALATE   FORT BONIFACIO

Quirino   San Andres   M Guadalupe   PASIG

Manila Bay   L Vito Cruz   P Vito Cruz

P Buendia   M Buendia

ERMITA   Gil Puyat   MAKATI

Cultural Center of the Philippines ♦   L Libertad   P Pasay Road

M Ayala

L EDSA   P EDSA

EDSA   Taft Avenue   M Magallanes

L M   ♦ Manila American Cemetery & Memorial

Baclaran   L

N

Mall of Asia ♦

PASAY   P Nichols

TAGUIG

Ninoy Aquino International Airport ✈   P FTI

Laguna de Bay

P Bicutan

0   2
kilometres

Pasig River

L —L	LRT-1 Green Line
L —L	MRT-2 (LRT-2) Purple Line
M —M	MRT-3 Yellow
P —P	Philippines National Railway (PNR)

1

Augustinian and Franciscan **missionaries** subsequently established themselves in villages around the city. The Jesuits arrived in 1581 and set up more missions, forming outlying centres of population – embryonic settlements that became the sixteen cities of today. Manila's central location on the nation's biggest island, Luzon, made it the obvious choice as the **colonial capital**, and it became the hub from which the Spaniards effected the political, cultural and religious transformation of Philippine society. From 1571 until 1815 (when it was ended by the Mexican War of Independence), Manila prospered from the **galleon trade** while the rest of the country remained economically stagnant. At 7pm on June 3, 1863, a catastrophic **earthquake** struck and large areas of the city crumbled, burying hundreds of people in the ruins. The new Manila that grew in its stead was thoroughly modern, with streetcars, steam trains and US-style public architecture, a trend that continued under **American rule** in the early twentieth century.

World War II

Manila suffered again during World War II. The **Japanese** occupied the city from 1942 until it was liberated by the US at the **Battle of Manila** in 1945. The battle lasted 29 days and claimed 1000 American lives, 16,000 Japanese soldiers and some 100,000 Filipinos, many of them civilians killed deliberately by the Japanese or accidentally by crossfire. Once again, Manila was a city in ruins, having undergone relentless shelling from American howitzers and been set alight by retreating Japanese troops. **Rebuilding** was slow and plagued by corruption and government inertia.

The Marcos era

In 1976, realizing that Manila was growing too rapidly for government to be contained in the old Manila area, **President Marcos** decreed that while the area around Intramuros would remain the capital city, the permanent seat of the national government would be Metro Manila – including new areas such as Makati and Quezon City. It was tacit recognition of the city's expansion and the problems it was bringing. **Imelda Marcos**, meanwhile, had been declared governor of Metro Manila in 1975 and was busy exercising her "edifice complex", building a golden-domed mosque in Quiapo, the Cultural Center of the Philippines on Manila Bay and a number of five-star hotels. Her spending spree was finally ended by the **EDSA Revolution** in 1986 (see p.442).

Manila today

In the 1990s, popular police officer **Alfredo Lim** won two terms as Manila mayor – his crime-fighting efforts certainly improved security in the city and he was elected a third time in 2007. He immediately and controversially set about undoing much of the work of his predecessor **Lito Atienza** (mayor 1998–2007), who had spent millions on city beautification projects. Though congestion and pollution remained huge and

---

MANILA ORIENTATION

The key tourist district is the area fronting **Manila Bay** along **Roxas Boulevard**, taking in the neighbourhoods of **Ermita** and **Malate**, and stretching north to the old walled city of **Intramuros** and over the Pasig River to **Chinatown**, also known as **Binondo**. **Makati**, 8km southeast of Manila Bay, is the city's central business district, built around the main thoroughfare of Ayala Avenue, and home to banks, insurance companies and five-star hotels. Just to the east of Makati (and almost an extension of it), lies the city's newest business and retail hub, **Fort Bonifacio**. The artery of Epifaño de los Santos Avenue, or just **EDSA**, stretches from major transport hub Pasay in the south to Caloocan in the north, curving around the eastern edge of Makati en route. Further along EDSA beyond Makati is the commercial district of **Ortigas**, which is trying to outdo Makati with its hotels, malls and air-conditioned, themed restaurants. Beyond that is **Quezon City**, where many bus routes from the north terminate, though otherwise it's largely off the tourist map.

1

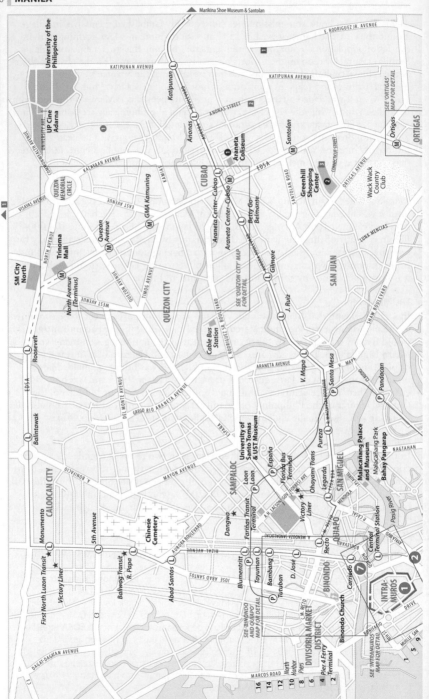

Marikina Shoe Museum & Santolan

University of the Philippines

UP Cine Adarna

KATIPUNAN AVENUE

E. RODRIGUEZ JR. AVENUE

KATIPUNAN AVENUE

Katipunan

Anonas

AÑONAS STREET

Santolan

Araneta Coliseum

CUBAO

EDSA

Santolan

Greenhill Shopping Center

Wack Wack Country Club

Ortigas

ORTIGAS

SEE 'ORTIGAS' MAP FOR DETAIL

QUEZON MEMORIAL CIRCLE

KALAYAAN AVENUE

GMA Kamuning

EAST AVENUE

Araneta Center-Cubao

Araneta Center-Cubao

Betty Go-Belmonte

SANTOLAN ROAD

ORTIGAS AVENUE

SAN JUAN

LUNA MENCIAS

SHAW BOULEVARD

CONNECTICUT STREET

SM City North

North Avenue Terminus

Trinoma Mall

North Avenue Terminus

Quezon Avenue

TIMOG AVENUE

QUEZON AVENUE

WEST AVENUE

QUEZON CITY

Cable Bus Station

E. RODRIGUEZ SR. BOULEVARD

SEE 'QUEZON CITY' MAP FOR DETAIL

Gilmore

J. Ruiz

Roosevelt

EDSA

Balintawak

DEL MONTE AVENUE

GREGO RIO ARANETA AVENUE

ESPAÑA

MAYON AVENUE

V. MAPA

ARANETA AVENUE

Santa Mesa

V. Mapa

V. MAPA

Pandacan

Monumento

CALOOCAN CITY

A. BONIFACIO

5th Avenue

Chinese Cemetery

AURORA BOULEVARD

SAMPALOC

University of Santo Tomas & UST Museum

España

Pureza

R. MAGSAYSAY BOULEVARD

Malacañang Palace and Museum

Malacañang Park

Bahay Pangarap

NAGTAHAN

First North Luzon Transit

Victory Liner

Baliwag Transit

R. Papa

Abad Santos

RIZAL AVENUE

JOSE ABAD SANTOS

Blumentritt

Tayuman

Bambang

Tutuban

D. José

Dangwa

Fariñas Transit

Laon Laan

Florida Bus Terminal

A.M. LACSON

FOREST AVE.

Ohayami Trans

Victory Liner

J.M. RECTO

A. MENDOZA (ANDALUCIA)

Legarda

SAN MIGUEL

MENDIOLA

F. CASAL

Recto

QUIAPO

Carriedo

BINONDO

Central Terminal Station

Central Terminal Station

Pasig River

AMPARO

BONIFACIO

INTRA-MUROS

BOULEVARD

Binondo Church

SEE BINONDO AND QUIAPO MAP FOR DETAIL

DIVISORIA MARKET DISTRICT

North Harbor Piers

Pier 4 Ferry Terminal

MARCOS ROAD

16 14 12 10 8 6 4 2

SEE INTRAMUROS MAP FOR DETAIL

MUELLE SAN

DRIVE

C3

C3

DAGAN-DAGHAN AVENUE

VISAYAS AVENUE

COMMONWEALTH AVENUE

UNIVERSITY AVE.

1

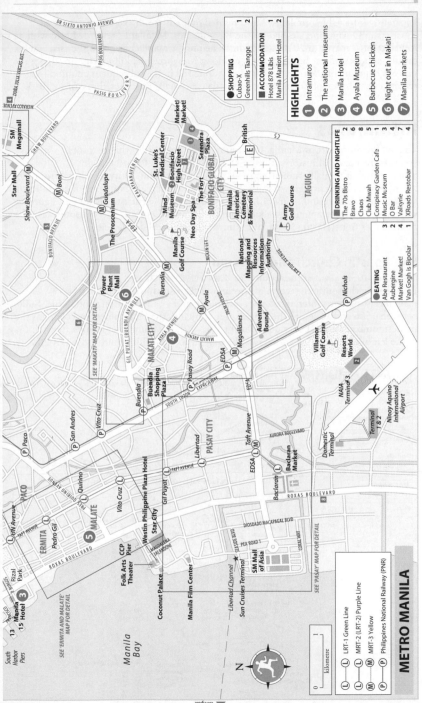

HIGHLIGHTS

1 Intramuros
2 The national museums
3 Manila Hotel
4 Ayala Museum
5 Barbecue chicken
6 Night out in Makati
7 Manila markets

● SHOPPING
Cubao-X 1
Greenhills Tiangge 2

■ ACCOMMODATION
Hotel 878 Libis 1
Manila Marriott Hotel 2

■ DRINKING AND NIGHTLIFE
The 70s Bistro 2
Bravo 6
Chaos 8
Club Mwah 5
Conspiracy Garden Café 1
Music Museum 3
O Bar 4
Valkyrie 7
XRoads Restobar 4

● EATING
Abe Restaurant 3
Aubergine 2
Market! Market! 4
Van Gogh Is Bipolar 1

METRO MANILA

Ⓛ—Ⓛ LRT-1 Green Line
Ⓛ—Ⓛ MRT-2 (LRT-2) Purple Line
Ⓜ MRT-3 Yellow
Ⓟ Philippines National Railway (PNR)

0 — kilometre — 1

N

Manila Bay

Corregidor

1

apparently intractable problems, Lim presided over a booming economy, removed squatters in Quiapo and cleaned up the Baywalk area. Manileños rewarded him with a fourth term as mayor in 2010, just months before the **Manila bus hostage crisis**, when a dismissed police officer hijacked a bus of Hong Kong tourists, killing eight of them; the mayor's handling of the tragedy was highly criticized in the subsequent enquiry. In a remarkable twist, ex-president **Joseph Estrada** (see p.443) was elected mayor in 2013.

Intramuros

The old Spanish heart of Manila, **Intramuros** is the one part of the metropolis where you get a real sense of history. It was established in the 1570s and remains a monumental, if partially ruined, colonial relic – a city within a city, separated from the rest of Manila by its overgrown walls. It's not a museum; plenty of government offices are still located here, and many of Manila's poorest call the backstreets home. A good way to see it is by arranging a **walking tour** with Carlos Celdran (see box opposite). The main drag is **General Luna Street**, also known as Calle Real del Palacio.

San Agustin Church and Museum

General Luna St • Church & museum daily 8am–noon & 1–5pm • P200 • ☎ 02 527 2746 • LRT to Central Terminal

Dominating the southern section of Intramuros, **San Agustin Church** boasts a magnificent Baroque interior, *trompe l'oeil* murals and a vaulted ceiling and dome. Built between 1586 and 1606, it's the oldest stone church in the Philippines, and contains the modest **tomb of Miguel López de Legazpi** (1502–72), the founder of Manila (see p.436), to the left of the altar. The church was the only structure in Intramuros to survive the

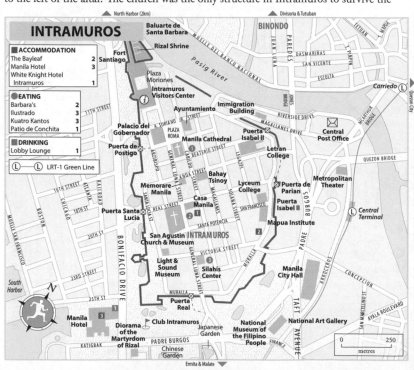

> **WALK WITH THE LOCALS**
>
> If sightseeing in Manila on your own seems a little intimidating, try **Walk This Way**, run by the highly entertaining Carlos Celdran (☎0920 909 2021 or ☎02 484 4945, ⓦcarlosceldran.com), who offers something between a history lesson and magical-mystery tour around the old city The "Classic Intramuros Walking Tour" (3hr; P1350, plus P75 Fort Santiago entry) runs roughly once a week. Also recommended is Ivan Man Dy of **Old Manila Walks** (☎0918 962 6452 or ☎02 711 3823, ⓦoldmanilawalks.com), who runs fun walking tours of Binondo and Intramuros.

devastation of World War II, an indication of just how badly the city suffered.

Access to the church is via the adjacent **San Agustin Museum**, a former Augustinian monastery that houses a surprisingly extensive collection of icons and artefacts, including rare porcelain, church vestments and a special exhibition on Fray Andrés Urdaneta (who led the second voyage to circumnavigate the world in 1528, and pioneered the Manila–Acapulco sea route), though the handsome two-storey building itself and the tranquil central cloisters are just as appealing. The old vestry is where Governor-General Fermín Jáudenes drafted the terms of Spanish surrender to the Americans in 1898, while the oratorio upstairs provides an alternative perspective of the church interior.

Light & Sound Museum

Victoria St at Santa Lucia St • The site opens on demand for a minimum of ten people Tues–Sat 9am–5pm, Sun 10am–6pm; smaller groups can enter but they must pay a total P1500 • P150/person • ☎02 524 2827, ⒺIsm.intramuros@yahoo.com • LRT to Central Terminal

One of the city's more unusual attractions, the **Light & Sound Museum** contains a series of dioramas enlivened by animatronic manikins acting out all the key moments in Philippine history (especially the heroic life of José Rizal) – it's a little cheesy, but fun nonetheless. The church-like museum building is a replica of the structure destroyed during World War II, originally the home of the Beaterio de la Compañía de Jesus, a religious school for girls founded in 1684.

Silahis Center

744 General Luna St • Daily 10am–7pm • Free • ☎02 527 2112, ⓦsilahis.com • LRT to Central Terminal

Established in 1966, the intriguing **Silahis Center** is a museum-like emporium selling arts, antiques and cultural publications from all over the Philippines. Across a pretty courtyard reached through the back door are the elegant *Ilustrado* restaurant (see p.88) and the atmospheric *Kuatro Kantos* café (see p.89).

Casa Manila

Plaza San Luis Complex, General Luna St at Real St • Tues–Sun 9am–5.45pm • P75 • ☎02 527 4084 • LRT to Central Terminal

The splendid **Casa Manila**, a sympathetic replica of an 1850s colonial mansion, offers a window into the lives of rich Filipinos in the nineteenth century. Redolent of a grander age, the house contains an impressive *sala* (living room) where *tertulias* (soirees) and *bailes* (dances) were held. The upstairs family latrine is a two-seater, which allowed husband and wife to gossip out of earshot of the servants while simultaneously going about their business. Though it's a faithful reproduction of period Spanish styles, Imelda Marcos commissioned the house in the early 1980s, during her "edifice complex".

Memorare Manila

Plazuela de Santa Isabel, General Luna and Anda streets • LRT to Central Terminal

Much of Intramuros was reduced to rubble during the Battle of Manila (1945) in World War II, a catastrophe commemorated by the **Memorare Manila**, a series of

1

moving sculptures surrounding a woman weeping as she cradles a dead child. Over a hundred thousand Filipinos are thought to have died in the fighting.

Bahay Tsinoy

32 Anda St at Cabildo St • Tues–Sun 1–5pm • P100 • ☎ 02 527 6083, ⓦ bahaytsinoy.org • LRT to Central Terminal

A small but enlightening museum, **Bahay Tsinoy** is a tribute to Manila's influential Chinese population. The name means "**house of the Filipino Chinese**", and the museum traces the crucial role of the Chinese in Philippine history from their first trade contact with the archipelago in the tenth century to the Spanish colonial period. Besides assorted artefacts and multimedia presentations, the displays include life-sized figures and authentic reproductions of objects related to Tsinoy (or "Chinoy") history. Among the items of interest are a large hologram representing the achievements of the Tsinoys and a charming diorama of the Parian ghetto, the area outside the city walls where Chinese were forced to live during Spanish rule. There's also a gallery of rare photographs and a Martyrs Hall dedicated to Tsinoys who formed guerrilla units against Japanese occupation.

Manila Cathedral

Plaza de Roma, Cabildo St at Beaterio St • Daily 6am–5.30pm, or 7.30pm for special event/mass • Free • ☎ 02 527 1796, ⓦ manilacathedral.ph • LRT to Central Terminal

Originally just a nipa and bamboo structure, **Manila Cathedral** was officially raised in 1581 but destroyed numerous times down the centuries by a combination of fire, typhoon, earthquake and war. The seventh version was comprehensively flattened during World War II but the Vatican contributed funds to have it rebuilt. The present Byzantine-Romanesque inspired structure was completed in 1958 from a design by Fernando Ocampo, one of the nation's finest architects, and is similar in style to the cathedral that stood here in the nineteenth century. A major two-year renovation was completed in 2014.

The cathedral lacks the rich historical ambience of San Agustin, but the interior is impressive in its simplicity, with a long aisle flanked by marble pillars, stained-glass rose windows and a soaring central dome. **Exhibitions** in chapels around the nave throw light on the tumultuous history of the cathedral, and even tackle weighty theological questions such as "what is a cathedral?" and the meaning of the Immaculate Conception (the cathedral was awarded the title of "Basilica of the Immaculate Conception" in 1981). Check out also the faithful reproduction of Michelangelo's *La Pietà* in a special chapel to the left of the entrance.

Fort Santiago

General Luna St at Santa Clara St • Daily 8am–6pm • P75 • ☎ 02 527 2961 • LRT to Central Terminal

The remains of **Fort Santiago** stand at the northwestern end of Intramuros. The first log fortress was built by Spanish conquistador Miguel López de Legazpi in 1571 on the ruins of Rajah Sulaiman's base, but was rebuilt in stone twenty years later. The seat of the colonial power of both Spain and the US, Fort Santiago was also a prison and torture chamber under the Spanish regime and the scene of countless military police atrocities during the Japanese occupation (1942–45).

Just past the entrance to the site, on the left, is the Baluartillo de San Francisco Javier, fortifications built in 1663 which now house the **Intramuros Visitors Center** (see opposite), a shop and a café. From here you can stroll through the gardens of **Plaza Moriones** to the fort proper, marked by a stone gate, walls and a moat – most of what you see today has been rebuilt in stages since the 1950s, after being virtually destroyed in 1945. Once through the walls, **Plaza de Armas** forms a pleasant green square inside the old fort, with a noble-looking **statue of José Rizal** in the middle.

Rizal Shrine
Mon 1–5pm, Tues–Sun 9am–6pm • Entry included with fort ticket

1

For most visitors the real highlight of Fort Santiago lies on the left side of Plaza de Armas, where the **Rizal Shrine** occupies a reconstruction of the old Spanish barracks (the brick ruins of the original are next door). The site is dedicated to **José Rizal** (see p.437), the writer and national hero who was imprisoned here before being executed in what became Rizal Park in 1896. On the ground floor, the Chamber of Texts preserves some original copies of Rizal's work, while excerpts are artfully displayed on iron girders. You can also peer into a reproduction of the room where he spent the hours before his execution. Upstairs the Reliquary Room displays some of Rizal's clothing and personal effects, while a larger hall houses the original copy of his valedictory poem, *Mi Último Adiós*, the greatest, most poignant work of Filipino literature. The poem was secreted in an oil lamp and smuggled out to his family; here it is displayed in various languages around the walls (the original was written in Spanish). While even the best English translations fail to capture the felicity of the original, they do give a sense of the sacrifice Rizal was about to make and of his love of the country:

Farewell, my adored country, region beloved of the sun,
Pearl of the Orient Sea, our Eden lost,
Departing in happiness, to you I give the sad, withered remains of my life;
And had it been a life more brilliant, more fine, more fulfilled
I would have given it, willingly to you.

Rizaliana Furniture Exhibition
Baluarte de Santa Barbara • Daily 8am–6pm • P10 donation

The eighteenth-century **Baluarte de Santa Barbara** overlooking the Pasig River now houses the mildly interesting **Rizaliana Furniture Exhibition**, showing off Rizal's Spanish colonial writing tables, four-poster bed and the like. More significantly, the exhibit lies above the infamous **dungeon** where around six hundred American and Filipino POWs were incarcerated and left to drown by the rising tide in 1945. There is a cross and **memorial** outside to mark their final resting place.

INFORMATION AND GETTING AROUND
Intramuros Visitors Center Baluartillo de San Francisco Javier, Fort Santiago (daily 8am–5pm; ☎02 527 2961, ⓦintramuros.gov.ph) offers information and maps, and can also arrange a guide if you need one.
Kalesas Inside Intramuros, for something a bit different you can hire a kalesa (horse-drawn carriage) – their drivers compete with Intramuros tricycles in pestering tourists for business. Rates depend on how hard you bargain. Fares for short journeys should only cost P50, while a 30min tour of the whole Intramuros area should cost no more than P350.

Rizal Park and around

The area south of Intramuros is dominated by **Rizal Park**, Manila's primary green space and the city's favourite meeting place since the Spanish era. On the fringes of the park lie two of the most important museums in the country, the **National Art Gallery** and the **National Museum of the Filipino People**, while on the other side of Roxas Boulevard, facing the bay, the **Manila Hotel** harks back to the city's golden age.

Rizal Park
Roxas Blvd • Daily 24hr • Free • **Nayong Pilipino** Mon–Fri 9am–7pm, Sat & Sun 9am–8pm • P40 • **Japanese garden** Daily 6am–10pm • P10 • **Chinese garden** Daily 6.30am–9.30pm • P10 • **Auditorium concerts** Fri, Sat & Sun at 6pm • Free • **Planetarium** Tues–Sun 8.30am–5pm; call or check Facebook page for show times • Free • ☎02 527 7889, ⓦfacebook.com/NationalMuseumPlanetarium • LRT to UN Avenue

Still referred to by its old Spanish name of "Luneta", **Rizal Park** is a ten-minute walk south of Intramuros. In a city notoriously short of greenery, the park was where the

1

colonial-era glitterati used to promenade after church every Sunday. These days, Rizal Park is an early morning jogging circuit, a weekend playground for children and a refuge for couples and families escaping the clamour of the city. **Hawkers** sell everything from balloons and mangoes to plastic bags full of *chicharon*, deep-fried pigskin served with a little container of vinegar and chilli for dipping. The park is often busy, with many distractions and activities, but few visitors report any problems with hustlers, pickpockets or what Filipinos generally refer to as "snatchers". The whole park is gradually being renovated under an ambitious plan that will take years to complete.

At the far eastern end of the park is an impressive Marcos-era giant **Relief Map of the Philippines**, though it could do with some renovation. In contrast, at the centre lies the lagoon, where the flashy "dancing fountain" entertains crowds every morning and evening. The park's other sundry attractions include: the **Nayong Pilipino**, a flower garden that's a tranquil haven from the hustle outside; a traditional **Chinese Garden**; a fairly bare **Japanese Garden**; the **Chess Plaza**, where amiable seniors challenge each other to board games; an open-air **auditorium** where free concerts are held at weekends; and a **Planetarium**, with regular shows.

Rizal memorials

Diorama of the Martyrdom of Rizal Daily 8am–5pm • P20 • **Light show** Wed–Sun 7pm (1hr) • P50/person, min 15 people (in English or Tagalog) • LRT to UN Avenue

The western end of Rizal Park is most associated with its namesake, **José Rizal**. The main focus is the stolid-looking **Rizal Memorial**, raised in 1912, where Rizal is entombed, and the 31m flagpole where Manuel Roxas, first President of the Republic, was sworn in on July 4, 1946. Just to the north is the site of **Rizal's execution** in 1896, marked by a memorial that also commemorates the execution of three priests garrotted by the Spanish for alleged complicity in the uprising in Cavite in 1872 – despite the carnival-like atmosphere around it, this is a very poignant site for most Filipinos.

Nearby is the **Diorama of the Martyrdom of Rizal**, containing a series of eight life-size sculptures dramatizing the hero's final days. If the gatekeeper is about you should be able to wander around, but to run the **light-and-sound presentation** they need at least fifteen people.

National Art Gallery

Taft Ave at Padre Burgos Ave • Tues–Sun 10am–5pm • Free • ☎ 02 527 1215, ⓦ nationalmuseum.gov.ph • LRT to UN Avenue

Just to the north of Rizal Park is the **National Art Gallery**, the foremost art museum in the Philippines, housed in the grand old Legislative Building (completed in 1926 and home of the Senate till 1996) on the northern edge of Rizal Park. Galleries are laid out thematically in rather desultory fashion over two floors, but each one is relatively small and easy to digest. The highlights are paintings by Filipino masters including **Juan Luna** (1859–99), **Félix Hidalgo** (1855–1913), **José Joya** (1931–95) and **Fernando Amorsolo** (1892–1972), with the most famous works displayed in the Hall of the Masters near the entrance; Luna's vast and magnificent *Spolarium* (1884) is here, a thinly veiled attack in oils on the atrocities of the Spanish regime, portraying fallen gladiators being dragged onto a pile of corpses.

Other galleries are dedicated to National Artist award winners (Amorsolo was the first in 1972), showcasing Joya's *Origins* and Amorsolo's *Portrait of President Manuel Roxas*. There's also a section on architect **Juan Arellano** (1888–1960), who designed the building, and a special gallery dedicated to the large Juan Luna collection; look out for his haunting *Mother in Bed* and the simple naturalism of *Study for Rice Harvesting*. The second floor contains mostly minor works from modern Filipino artists, and also a **Bones Gallery** where a huge sperm whale skeleton takes pride of place.

National Museum of the Filipino People

1

Finance Rd at Padre Burgos Ave • Tues–Sun 10am–5pm • Free • ☎ 02 527 1215, ⓦ nationalmuseum.gov.ph • LRT to UN Avenue

The absorbing **National Museum of the Filipino People** occupies what used to be the Department of Finance Building, a stately Greek Revival edifice completed in 1940. Much of the priceless collection of artefacts on display has been retrieved from **shipwrecks**, most notably the *San Diego*, a Spanish galleon that sank off Fortune Island in Batangas after a battle with the Dutch in 1600. Recovered in 1992, the ship yielded over five thousand objects, not all intrinsically valuable: you'll see chicken bones and hazelnuts from the ship's store, as well as tons of Chinese porcelain, storage jars, rosaries and silver goblets. Other rooms contain objects from wrecked Chinese junks going back to the early eleventh century – compelling evidence of trade links that existed long before the Spanish arrived.

The well-labelled **anthropology section** on the third floor is equally engrossing, with displays from almost every region and tribal group in the Philippines, including the enigmatic anthropomorphic jars discovered in Ayub Cave (Mindanao) that date back to 5 BC. These jars were used to hold the bones of ancestors.

Manila Hotel

1 Rizal Park, just east of Manila Ocean Park • ☎ 02 527 0011, ⓦ manila-hotel.com.ph • 1km north up Roxas Boulevard from Malate

The **Manila Hotel**, just northwest of Rizal Park, is the most historic of the city's luxury hotels, though now a little careworn. It's still the best place to get a sense of early twentieth-century Manila, those halcyon days when the city was at its cultural and social zenith; you can even stay (see p.85) in the **General Douglas MacArthur Suite**, residence from 1936 to 1941 of the man Filipinos called the Caesar of America. If staying the night is beyond your means, you can at least sip a martini in the lobby while listening to a string quartet and watching the capital's elite strut by.

When the hotel opened in 1912 it represented the epitome of colonial class and luxury. Lavish dances known as rigodon balls were held every month in the **Grand Ballroom**, with high-society guests dancing the quadrille in traditional *ternos* (formal evening dresses) and dinner jackets. Today staff glide around in similarly elegant attire.

The hotel has its own historical **archive**, containing signed photographs of illustrious guests, from Marlon Brando, looking young and slender in a native *barong* (formal shirt), to Ricky Martin and Jon Bon Jovi. The archive is available to guests only, but if you eat or drink at the hotel, one of the guest relations officers should be able to show it to you. South of the hotel is the **Quirino Grandstand** where various official functions take place, including a military parade on Independence Day.

Manila Ocean Park

Parade Ave, off Roxas Blvd (behind Quirino Grandstand) • Mon–Fri 10am–8pm, Sat & Sun 9am–8pm • Packages P580–990 • ☎ 02 567 7777, ⓦ manilaoceanpark.com • Taxi, bus or 15–20min walk from UN Avenue LRT station

At the far western end of Rizal Park, along the bayfront, lies **Manila Ocean Park**, one of the city's most popular attractions. The undoubted highlight is the **Oceanarium**, a huge saltwater tank viewed via a 25m-long walkway, packed with some twenty thousand sea creatures. Depending on what entry package you choose, it may include spectacular light shows, musical fountains, sea lion shows, a birds of prey exhibit, a trippy jellyfish installation and a penguin park.

Museo ng Pambata

Roxas Blvd at South Drive • Tues–Sat 9am–noon & 1–5pm, Sun 1–5pm; shadow puppet show first Sat of every month at 10am • Adults & children P250 • ☎ 02 523 1797, ⓦ museopambata.org • LRT to UN Avenue

The entertaining **Museo ng Pambata** (Children's Museum) has several hands-on exhibitions designed to excite young children; at the Maynila Noon exhibit they can

1

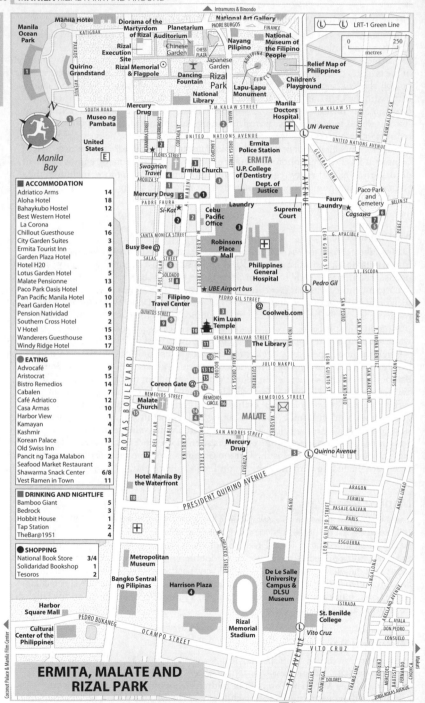

Intramuros & Binondo

National Art Gallery

LRT-1 Green Line

0   250
metres

ERMITA, MALATE AND RIZAL PARK

■ ACCOMMODATION

Adriatico Arms	14
Aloha Hotel	18
Bahaykubo Hostel	12
Best Western Hotel La Corona	4
Chillout Guesthouse	16
City Garden Suites	3
Ermita Tourist Inn	8
Garden Plaza Hotel	7
Hotel H20	1
Lotus Garden Hotel	5
Malate Pensionne	13
Paco Park Oasis Hotel	6
Pan Pacific Manila Hotel	10
Pearl Garden Hotel	11
Pension Natividad	9
Southern Cross Hotel	2
V Hotel	15
Wanderers Guesthouse	13
Windy Ridge Hotel	17

● EATING

Advocafé	9
Aristocrat	15
Bistro Remedios	14
Cabalen	7
Café Adriatico	12
Casa Armas	10
Harbor View	1
Kamayan	4
Kashmir	4
Korean Palace	13
Old Swiss Inn	2
Pancit ng Taga Malabon	2
Seafood Market Restaurant	3
Shawarma Snack Center	6/8
Vest Ramen in Town	11

■ DRINKING AND NIGHTLIFE

Bamboo Giant	5
Bedrock	3
Hobbit House	1
Tap Station	2
TheBar@1951	4

● SHOPPING

National Book Store	3/4
Solidaridad Bookshop	1
Tesoros	2

get a feel for history using interactive displays – replicas of ships, churches and native Filipino homes – and there's also a simulated rainforest and seabed. Once a month there's a shadow puppetry show.

Ermita and Malate

Two of the city's oldest neighbourhoods, **Ermita** and **Malate** nestle behind Roxas Boulevard, facing Manila Bay. Ermita was infamous for its go-go bars and massage parlours up until the late 1980s, when tough-guy mayor Alfredo Lim closed most of them, alleging that they were fronts for **prostitution**. But the massages and KTV hostess bars have gradually slipped back, this time to serve busloads of Japanese and Korean high-spenders, and there has been a resurgence of prostitution in Ermita; it is now the Philippines second-largest centre for paid sex after Angeles City.

Ermita and Malate otherwise remain in most part a ragbag of budget hotels, choked streets, fast-food outlets and bars, with street children all too prevalent on every corner, though the area does look to be changing; several high-end residential developments and hotels have already jazzed up some streets. Most of the sights in this area lie along Manila Bay in the form of the **Metropolitan Museum** and the **Cultural Center of the Philippines**, though **Paco Park**, to the east, is also worth a look if you have time.

Metropolitan Museum

Bangko Sentral ng Pilipinas Complex, Roxas Blvd • Mon–Sat 10am–5.30pm (Gold & Pottery Galleries Mon–Fri 10am–4.30pm) • P100 • ☎ 02 708 7829, ⓦ metmuseum.ph • LRT to Vito Cruz, then an orange CCP jeepney along Pablo Ocampo St to Roxas Bvd

The **Metropolitan Museum** is best known for the Central Bank's astounding collection of **pre-colonial gold and pottery**, which lies in the basement. Most of this stunning ensemble of magnificent jewellery, amulets, necklaces and intricate gold-work dates from between 200 BC and 900 AD, long before the Spanish Conquest. Look out for the extraordinary Kamagi necklaces (long threads of gold), Islamic art from Lake Maranao, ancestral death masks and items from the Surigao Treasure (see p.436). The pottery section is dull by comparison, though some of the pots here are very ancient. Note that the gold and pottery sections are closed on Saturdays. The museum also houses a fine permanent collection of contemporary and historic **artworks** from Asia, America, Europe and Africa (including Egypt), plus temporary displays from high-profile contemporary Filipino artists.

Cultural Center of the Philippines (CCP)

Pedro Bukaneg (off Roxas Blvd) • Tues–Sun 10am–6pm • Free; Museo ng Kalinangang Pilipino P40 • ☎ 02 833 2125, ⓦ culturalcenter .gov.ph • LRT to Vito Cruz, then an orange CCP jeepney along Pablo Ocampo St to Roxas Bvd

The monumental **Cultural Center of the Philippines (CCP)** was one of Imelda Marcos's grand plans for bringing world-class arts to the Philippines. Conceived during the early, promising years of her husband's presidency and opened on a night of great splendour in 1966, it's a slab-like construction typical of those built on Imelda's orders when she was

MANILA BAY BY BOAT

Sun Cruises (☎ 02 527 5555, ⓦ corregidorphilippines.com), CCP Terminal A, Pedro Bukaneg St, near the Cultural Center, runs daily jaunts around the **Manila Bay**, which can be fun despite the often distressing amounts of rubbish floating around. The views of the city at sunset, surrounded by the volcanoes of Bataan and Batangas, are magical. Most cruises (1hr 30min) include a meal on board and run Mon–Fri at 6pm and 8pm, Sat and Sun at 4.15pm, 6.15pm and 8.15pm (Mon–Thurs P550/person, Fri–Sun P650/person). Boats depart from the Sun Cruises terminal on Seaside Boulevard in Pasay, just north of SM Mall of Asia.

1

suffering from her so-called "edifice complex". Various productions by **Ballet Philippines** (see p.96) and Broadway-style **musicals** are staged in the **Main Theater**, and there is a decent **contemporary art gallery** on the third floor (free), showing temporary exhibits from Filipino artists. Upstairs on the fourth floor the **Museo ng Kalinangang Pilipino** holds small but engaging temporary exhibitions on various aspects of Filipino native cultures, as well as housing the permanent Asian traditional musical instruments collection.

The CCP also encompasses several other properties beyond the main complex, further along Pedro Bukaneg, such as the **Folk Arts Theater**, which is the venue for occasional pop concerts, jazz and drama (see p.96), and the **Manila Film Center** (see box below). Note that ferries to the island of Corregidor leave from near the CCP.

Coconut Palace

F. Ma. Guerrero St, next to CCP • Tours (no sandals or shorts allowed) are free but currently suspended • Get latest info on ☎ 02 832 6791 or ✉ drcomia@ovp.gov.ph

Built between 1978 and 1981 on the orders of Imelda Marcos for the visit of Pope John Paul II, the **Coconut Palace** is one of Manila's more bizarre monuments, an outrageous but strangely compelling edifice, seventy percent of it constructed from coconut materials. The pope rightly gave Imelda short shrift when he arrived, saying he wouldn't stay in such an egregious establishment while there was so much poverty on the streets of Manila, and suggested she spend taxpayers' money (the equivalent of some P37 million) more wisely. In 2011 the palace became the residence and office of the **vice president**. Guided tours were suspended at the time of writing, though they should resume in the future.

The Museum at De La Salle University

2401 Taft Ave • Mon–Fri 8am–6pm • P50; register at the main entrance first (bring photo ID), then pay at accounting before heading to the gallery in Yuchengco Hall • ☎ 02 524 4611, 🖥 themuseum.dlsu.edu.ph • LRT to Vito Cruz

Established in 1911, **De La Salle University**, at the southern end of Malate, remains one of the most prestigious private Catholic colleges in the Philippines. The **DLSU Museum** hosts rotating exhibitions showing work from its substantial collection of modern Filipino artists such as Diosdado Lorenzo and Araceli Dans. It's really just a small gallery but even if you're not an art fan, it's worth a quick look just to get a pass to wander the elegant neoclassical DLSU campus, far more redolent of classical Spain than the city outside.

THE MANILA FILM CENTER

If bricks could talk, those at the **Manila Film Center** in Pasay (see map, p.71) would have a sinister story to tell. Back in the 1970s, **Imelda Marcos** wanted to stage an annual film festival that would rival Cannes and put Manila on the international cultural map. But the centre she commissioned for the purpose was jerry-built and a floor collapsed in 1981, allegedly burying workers under rubble and killing many. No one knows exactly how many (some claim around 170) because most were poor labourers from the provinces, and records were not kept of their names. Police were told to throw a cordon round the building so the press couldn't get to it, and work continued round the clock. The centre was completed in 1982, some say with dead workers still entombed inside, in time for the opening night of the **Manila International Film Festival**. Imelda celebrated by walking onto the stage to greet the audience in a black and emerald green *terno* (a formal gown) thick with layer upon layer of peacock feathers that were shipped specially from India. The centre staged just one more film festival – some say it's haunted, and Imelda herself had it exorcized – and it soon had to make ends meet by showing *bomba* (soft porn) films for the masses. It was briefly rehabilitated in the late 1980s when it was used as a centre for experimental film-making, but after an earthquake hit Manila in 1990 it was abandoned. In 2001 it was partially renovated and now hosts transvestite song and dance extravaganzas dubbed the "Amazing Show" (see p.96).

1

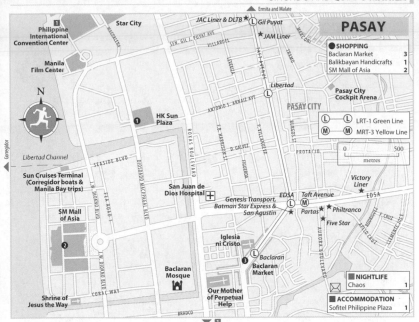

Paco Park and Cemetery

General Luna St at Padre Faura St • Tues–Sun 8am–5pm; open-air concerts Fri 6pm • P10; concerts free • ✆ 02 302 7182 • LRT to Pedro Gil or UN Avenue

A circular walled cemetery with an aged and beautiful garden dominated by a classical rotunda, **Paco Park and Cemetery** was built in 1820 just in time for victims of a cholera epidemic. After his execution in 1896, **José Rizal** (see p.437) was buried here in an unmarked grave. The story goes that his sister, Narcisa Rizal-Lopez, saw a group of guards standing beside a mound of freshly turned earth the length of a man; guessing this must be her brother's grave, she convinced the cemetery guardian to mark the site. Two years later Rizal's remains were exhumed and left in the custody of his family until 1912, when they were deposited beneath the Rizal Memorial (see p.66). A monument marks the location of the original grave.

The park's serenity has made it a favourite spot every Friday for "Paco Park Presents" – highly enjoyable **open-air concerts**, usually classical recitals by artists or students.

Binondo and Quiapo

Manila's Chinatown, **Binondo** exercises a curious, magnetic pull. This is city life *in extremis*, a rambunctious ghetto of people on the make, the streets full of merchants and middlemen flogging fake watches and herbs, sandalwood incense and gaudy jewellery. You can lose yourself for an afternoon wandering through its mercantile centre, snacking on dim sum at one of its many fan-cooled teahouses, and exploring the busiest thoroughfare, **Ongpin Street**. A visit to the sepulchral **Binondo Church** will give you some idea of the area's historical significance. Southeast of Binondo lies **Quiapo**, a labyrinth of crowded streets and cheap market stalls a universe away from the city's plush megamalls. The **Quiapo Church** here is said to be the most visited in the Philippines.

1

ARRIVAL AND DEPARTURE

On foot From Magellanes Drive in north Intramuros you can walk to Binondo in 15min across Jones Bridge.

By LRT The best LRT station for Quiapo and Binondo is Carriedo at Plaza Santa Cruz, only a short walk from the eastern end of Ongpin St.

BINONDO AND QUIAPO

By jeepney There are plenty of jeepneys to Binondo from M. Adriatico in Malate and Ermita, and also from Taft Ave marked for Divisoria. From Plaza Miranda, behind Quiapo Church, there are buses to Makati, and jeepneys and FX taxis to Quezon City, Ermita and Malate.

Binondo Church

Plaza San Lorenzo Ruiz, Ongpin St • Daily 5.30am–6.30pm • ☎ 02 242 4850 • LRT to Carriedo; Divisoria jeepneys go past the church

The always-buzzing Minor Basilica of San Lorenzo Ruiz is more commonly known as **Binondo Church**. It stands on the spot where Dominican priests established their church when they first came to Binondo in the late sixteenth century, though the original building was destroyed by shelling in 1762 when the British invaded Manila. The Dominicans promptly left, but returned in 1842 and completed the church you see today, a solid granite structure with an octagonal bell tower and elaborate retablo (altarpiece), in 1854.

The church was badly damaged by bombing during World War II and new features include the canopy at the entrance and the strikingly colourful murals on the ceilings. Depicting the life of Christ and the Assumption of the Virgin, these murals were not actually painted on the ceiling but were executed at ground level, then hoisted up.

The church is well known in the Philippines because it was where **Saint Lorenzo Ruiz**, the Philippines' first saint, served as a sacristan. Of Filipino and Chinese parentage, Ruiz was falsely accused of killing a Spaniard in 1636. It was probably because of this that he was encouraged to go to Japan, where he was arrested in Nagasaki in 1637 for spreading Christianity, and was executed for refusing to renounce his faith. The Vatican canonized him in 1987.

Ongpin Street

LRT to Carriedo

Ongpin Street, Binondo's principal thoroughfare, is about 2km long and runs eastwards through the heart of Chinatown to Santa Cruz Church. It was originally called Calle Sacristia but was renamed in 1915 after Roman Ongpin, a fervent nationalist who was said to be the first Chinese-Filipino to wear the *barong tagalog*, the formal shirt that became the national dress for men. Ongpin Street is now chock-full of restaurants, noodle parlours, apothecaries and shops selling goods imported from China, though it tends to shut down early these days; you'll find **Benavidez Street**, to the north of Ongpin, more lively at night.

Santa Cruz Church

Plaza Santa Cruz • Daily 6am–10pm • LRT to Carriedo

An immense white Baroque structure, **Santa Cruz Church** was originally completed in the seventeenth century for the swelling ranks of Chinese in the area, but was most recently rebuilt in 1957 after damage from earthquakes and war. The most revered image inside is a 250-year-old replica of the **Nuestra Señora del Pilar**, an apparition of Mary (the original of which is in Zaragoza, Spain), but the interior is otherwise unexceptional.

Escolta Street

LRT to Carriedo

The shopping thoroughfare **Escolta Street**, which leads southwest off Plaza Santa Cruz, was named after the horse-mounted military escorts of the British commander-in-chief during the British occupation of 1762. In the nineteenth century this was where Manila's elite promenaded and shopped, but its dizzy days as a Champs-Élysées of the Orient are long gone. Only a few examples of the street's former glory remain; just across the river on the right is the **First United Building**, a pink and white Art Deco gem designed in 1928 by Andres Luna de San Pedro, the son of painter Juan Luna. Opposite is another of his buildings, the all-white **Regina Building** of 1934, at 400–402 Escolta, with its Art Nouveau cupolas. Both buildings are occupied by shops and small businesses today.

Escolta Museum

2/F, Calvo Building, 266 Escolta St • Tues–Sun 9am–5pm • P50; ask the guard at the building entrance to let you in • ☎ 02 241 4762

The beaux-arts Calvo Building, completed in 1933, contains the quirky **Escolta Museum**. The main attraction is an extensive collection of multicoloured vintage bottles, but there are also scale models of Escolta's handsome buildings, old photos and paper advertisements from the 1930s.

Quiapo Church

910 Plaza Miranda • Daily 5am–9pm • ☎ 02 733 4434, ⓦ quiapochurch.com • LRT to Carriedo

Officially called the Minor Basilica of St John the Baptist, **Quiapo Church** – as everyone in Manila calls it – is the home of the **Black Nazarene**, a wooden icon, said to be

1

miraculous, that came to the country on board a galleon from Spain in 1606 and was enshrined here in 1787. The life-size image, bearing a cross, presides over the church from behind the altar.

The church burnt down in 1928, and the new building was expanded in the 1980s to accommodate the crowds that gather every year on January 9 for the **Feast of the Black Nazarene**, when 200,000 barefoot Catholic faithful from all over the Philippines come together to worship before the image.

Ilalim ng Tulay

LRT to Carriedo

The area around Quiapo Church is a good area for bargain-hunters (see p.99). Several stores that sell **handicrafts** at local prices are squeezed beneath the underpass leading to Quezon Bridge (aka Quiapo Bridge) on Quezon Boulevard, a place known as **Ilalim ng Tulay** ("under the bridge" or just Quiapo Ilalim).

University of Santo Tomas Museum

3rd floor, Main Building, University of Santo Tomas (UST), España Blvd • Mon 1–4.30pm, Tues–Fri 8.30am–4.30pm (closed university hols) • P50 • ☎ 02 781 1815, ⓦ ustmuseum.ust.edu.ph • 20min walk (or a short ride on any jeepney marked UST) from Recto LRT station

The **University of Santo Tomas Museum** is a marvellous throwback to the nineteenth century, an old-fashioned but fascinating private collection of historic documents, rare books and dusty displays on ethnology, natural history, archeology and arts. The collection dates back to 1871 and includes a stuffed orang-utan, a chair used by Pope John Paul II and a macabre two-headed calf. There are also some medieval coins, an assemblage of religious statues, a rather incongruous collection of Chinese porcelain, and some decent art, including *Pounding Rice* (1940) by Vicente Manansala, who also created the stunning, Cubist-influenced *History of Medicine* murals adorning the lobby of UST's medicine faculty in 1958.

UST itself has an interesting history. It was founded in Intramuros in 1611, making it the oldest university in Asia, with the current campus established in the 1920s. It served as an internment camp during World War II, and the old campus was virtually destroyed in 1944.

Today the university is much larger than it seems from the entrance, its **Main Building** an impressive Spanish Revival pile completed in 1927, and the elegant **Arch of the Centuries** above the main entrance on España Boulevard combining the ruins of the original arch of 1611 and its 1950s replica.

The Chinese Cemetery

South Gate entrance off Aurora Blvd, 4km north of Binondo • Daily 7.30am–7pm • Free • LRT to Abad Santos

The monumental **Chinese Cemetery** was established by affluent Chinese merchants in the 1850s because the Spanish would not allow foreigners to be buried in Spanish cemeteries. Entire streets are laid out to honour the dead and to underline the status of their surviving relatives. Several of the tombs resemble houses, with fountains, balconies and, in at least one case, a small swimming pool. Many even have air conditioning for the relatives who visit on All Saints' Day, when lavish feasts are laid on around the graves, with empty chairs for the departed. It has become a sobering joke in the Philippines that this "accommodation" is among the best in the city.

FROM TOP KALESA (P.65); SAN AGUSTIN CHURCH (P.62); BINONDO (P.71) >

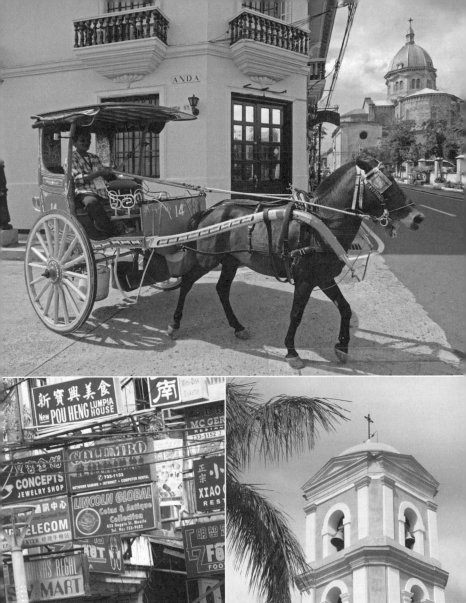

1 Malacañang Palace and Museum

1000 J.P. Laurel St, San Miguel • Mon–Fri 9am–noon & 1–3pm (closed public hols) • P50 • ☎ 02 784 4286, ⓦ malacanang.gov.ph •
Reservation requests including passport scan or photocopy must be emailed or posted to the palace to arrive at least 3 working days in advance
(see website) • No shorts, sleeveless tops or flip-flops; only one camera per group • The palace is a short taxi ride east of Intramuros and Quiapo

Home of the governor-generals and presidents of the Philippines since the 1860s, the
Malacañang Palace (also "Malacañan" Palace) is a fittingly grand and intriguing edifice,
well worth the minor hassle involved in arranging a visit (you can also join a tour).
Much of the palace is permanently off limits to the public, but you can visit the wing
that houses the **Malacañang Museum**. Housed in the beautifully restored Kalayaan
Hall, completed in 1921, the museum traces the history of the palace and of the
presidency from Emilio Aguinaldo to the present day. The origins of the Malacañang
go back to a smaller stone house dating from 1750, which was bought in 1825 by the
Spanish government and, in 1849, made into the summer residence of the governor-
general of the Philippines. After the governors' palace in Intramuros was destroyed in
the earthquake of 1863, the move to Malacañang was made permanent and the
property was extended several times over the years. The president actually resides in
Bahay Pangarap, across the river in **Malacañang Park**, and maintains his office in
Bonifacio Hall within the palace.

Makati

Some 5km east of Manila Bay, **Makati** was a vast expanse of malarial swampland until
the Ayala family, one of the country's most influential business dynasties, started
developing it in the 1950s. It is now Manila's premier business and financial district,
chock-full of plush hotels, international restaurant chains, expensive condominiums
and monolithic air-conditioned malls.

Opposite the station, the biggest mall is **Glorietta**, which has a central section and side
halls numbered 1–5, and heaves with people seeking refuge from the traffic and heat. A
short walk from Glorietta to the other side of Makati Avenue is **Greenbelt Park**, a
landscaped garden with the pleasant, modern, white-domed **Santo Niño de Paz Chapel** in
the centre. The park forms part of Makati's other main mall, **Greenbelt**, which, like
Glorietta, is divided into various numbered halls; on the north side is the excellent **Ayala
Museum** (see below). Just to the north is the pleasant green swathe of **Ayala Triangle**,
bordered by Ayala Avenue, Paseo de Roxas and Makati Avenue. Further along Ayala
Avenue, at the junction with Paseo de Roxas, is the **Ninoy Aquino Monument**, built in
honour of the senator who was assassinated in 1983, while a block further on is the
shimmering **PBCom Tower** (259m), at 6795 Ayala Avenue, the tallest building in the
Philippines (closed to the public).

Ayala Museum

Makati Ave at De La Rosa St • Tues–Sun 9am–6pm • P425 • ☎ 02 759 8288, ⓦ ayalamuseum.org • MRT to Ayala

Makati's one must-see attraction is the **Ayala Museum**, by far the best place in the
Philippines to get to grips with the nation's complex history. The mighty Ayala family
donated much of the initial collection in 1967, and this modern building was
completed in 2004. There are no dreary exhibits here, or ponderous chronological
approach – the permanent exhibitions just highlight the key aspects of Philippine
history beginning on the **fourth floor** with an extraordinary collection of pre-Hispanic
goldware, created by the islands' often overlooked indigenous cultures between the
tenth and thirteenth centuries. Over one thousand gold objects are on display, much of
it from the Butuan area in Mindanao, including the "**Surigao Treasure**" (see p.436).
Don't miss the astonishing Gold Regalia, a huge 4kg chain of pure gold thought to

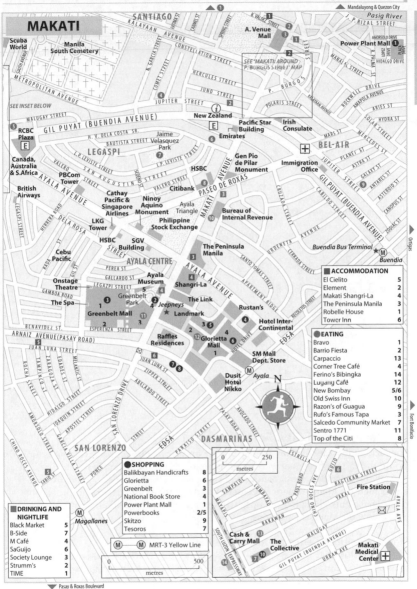

have been worn by a *datu* (chief). Other displays emphasize pre-Hispanic trade links with Asia, especially Song dynasty China, with a huge collection of porcelain and ceramics. On the **third floor** the "Pioneers of Philippine Art" showcases the museum's particularly strong collections of Juan Luna Realism, Fernando Amorsolo Impressionism and Fernando Zobel's more abstract work. On the **second floor** an extensive display of sixty dioramas dramatizes all the key events in Philippine history from prehistory to independence, while three audiovisual presentations tackle the postwar period, the Marcos years and People Power in 1986.

1

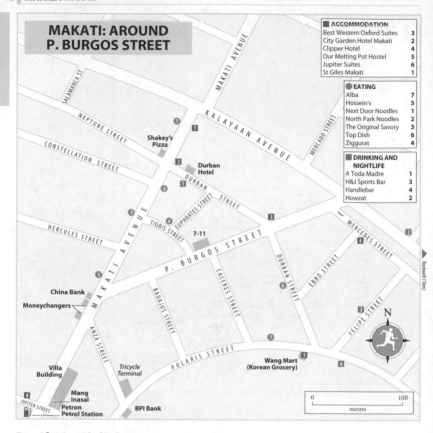

MAKATI: AROUND P. BURGOS STREET

■ ACCOMMODATION	
Best Western Oxford Suites	3
City Garden Hotel Makati	2
Clipper Hotel	4
Our Melting Pot Hostel	5
Jupiter Suites	6
St Giles Makati	1

● EATING	
Alba	7
Hossein's	5
Next Door Noodles	1
North Park Noodles	2
The Original Savory	3
Top Dish	6
Ziggurat	4

■ DRINKING AND NIGHTLIFE	
A Toda Madre	1
H&J Sports Bar	3
Handlebar	4
Howzat	2

Bonifacio Global City (Fort Bonifacio)

Bonifacio Global City (or **Fort Bonifacio**, after the army camp around which it is located) sits on the eastern fringes of Makati but is rapidly developing a separate identity of its own, with skyscrapers, posh condos and shopping malls developed by Ayala Corp. Other than the **Manila American Cemetery and Memorial**, there's little in the way of traditional sights, though the shops, bars and restaurants of Market! Market! (see box, p.89) show off Manila's ambitious, affluent side.

Manila American Cemetery and Memorial

McKinley Rd, Global City, Taguig • Daily 9am–5pm • Free • ☎ 02 844 0212, ⓦ abmc.gov • MRT to Ayala – walk across EDSA near its junction with Ayala Ave and then along McKinley Rd, passing Manila Polo Club on your right, and the cemetery entrance is at the roundabout 1km beyond the polo club; taxi from central Makati around P100

On the southeastern edge of Makati, 3km away from Glorietta mall, lies the serene **Manila American Cemetery and Memorial**, containing 17,201 graves of American military personnel killed in World War II, most of whom lost their lives in operations in New Guinea and the Philippines. The headstones are aligned in eleven plots forming a generally circular pattern, and set among a wide variety of tropical trees and shrubbery. There is also a chapel and two curved granite walkways whose walls contain mosaic maps depicting the battles fought in the Pacific, along with the names of the 36,285 American servicemen whose bodies were not recovered (rosettes mark the names of those since found and identified).

Ortigas and around

MRT to Shaw Blvd or Ortigas

A dense huddle of malls and offices, **Ortigas** lies 5km north of Makati on EDSA. The district began to come to life in the early 1980s, when a number of corporations left the bustle of Makati for its relatively open spaces; the Asian Development Bank moved here in 1991 and the Manila Stock Exchange followed one year later. Today its biggest draw for Manileños is the **SM Megamall**, one of Asia's largest shopping malls.

Lopez Memorial Museum

G/F Benpres Building, Exchange Rd at Meralco Ave • Mon–Sat 8am–5pm • P100 • ☎ 02 631 2417, ⓦ lopez-museum.com, ⓦ facebook.com/Lopez.Museum.Library • MRT to Ortigas (15min walk)

The one genuine cultural attraction in Ortigas is the **Lopez Memorial Museum**, founded in 1960 by tycoon Eugenio Lopez to provide scholars and students with access to his personal collection of rare books and since expanded to contain other treasures. The oldest is a priceless 1524 copy of the account of Magellan's circumnavigation of the world by one Maximilianus Transylvanus. The museum's art collection includes important paintings by nineteenth-century Filipino masters Juan Luna and Félix Hidalgo, as well as selected works by Fernando Amorsolo, who gained prominence during the early 1930s and 1940s for popularizing images of Philippine landscapes and beautiful rural Filipinas. The museum's Rizaliana includes some ninety letters written by José Rizal to his mother and sisters in the 1890s, along with the national hero's wallet and paintbrushes, his flute and his personal papers. Exhibits rotate every six months, as there's not enough space to display everything at once, but the library section always contains some of the best rare books, artwork and letters. Note that the museum is expected to move during 2017 or 2018, but no location has yet been fixed: check their website or Facebook page for latest information.

Marikina Shoe Museum

J.P. Rizal St, Marikina, 16km east of Rizal Park • Daily 8am–noon & 1–5pm • P50 • ☎ 02 646 2360, ⓦ marikina.gov.ph • LRT to Katipunan, then taxi

Nothing symbolizes the vanity of **Imelda Marcos** more than her collection of shoes, which numbered in the thousands on the eve of the EDSA revolution in 1986 (it's not known how many she owns today). This ghastly but admittedly stylish legacy is preserved at the **Marikina Shoe Museum** way out in the eastern suburbs, where 749 pairs belonging to the former first lady are displayed under her giant portrait, along with pairs owned by each president of the Philippines (the worn-out-looking shoes owned by Ferdinand Marcos make quite a contrast) and several other local celebrities. The history of shoemaking is explained upstairs. The museum is

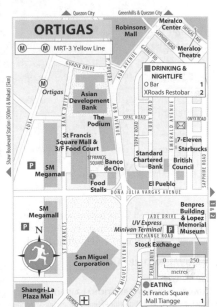

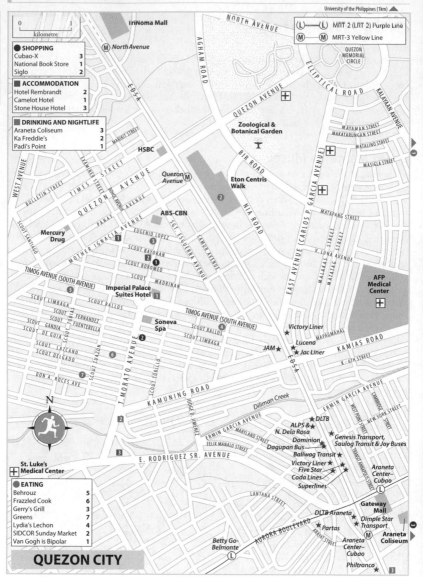

SHOPPING

Cubao-X	3
National Book Store	1
Siglo	2

ACCOMMODATION

Hotel Rembrandt	2
Camelot Hotel	1
Stone House Hotel	3

DRINKING AND NIGHTLIFE

Araneta Coliseum	3
Ka Freddie's	2
Padi's Point	1

L ⎯⎯ L	MRT 2 (LRT 2) Purple Line
M ⎯⎯ M	MRT-3 Yellow Line

EATING

Behrouz	5
Frazzled Cook	6
Gerry's Grill	3
Greens	7
Lydia's Lechon	4
SIDCOR Sunday Market	2
Van Gogh is Bipolar	1

QUEZON CITY

out in Marikina because the area was dubbed the "**shoe capital of the Philippines**" back in 1956; the industry's heyday was the 1970s and 1980s, though there are still several factories in the neighbourhood.

ARRIVAL AND DEPARTURE   MANILA

BY PLANE

NINOY AQUINO INTERNATIONAL AIRPORT (NAIA)
Almost everyone visiting the Philippines arrives at Ninoy

Aquino International Airport (NAIA; ☏02 877 7888, ⓦmanila-airport.net and ⓦwww.miaa.gov.ph), on the southern fringes of Manila, named after the anti-Marcos politician who was assassinated here in 1983.

Terminals The airport has four separate and unconnected terminals, making it seem, confusingly, as if there are several different airports (you may hear locals refer to them this way). Most international flights arrive at Terminal 1; Terminal 2, relatively nearby, serves only Philippine Airlines (international and domestic); the tiny Domestic Passenger Airport Terminal (aka Terminal 4) is 3km away on the other side of the airport and serves AirAsia Zest, SkyJet and Tigerair Philippines flights; further down Airport Rd is Terminal 3, served by Cebu Pacific, PAL Express, Cathay Pacific, ANA, KLM, Delta and Emirates; JAL may also move to Terminal 3 in the future. An "airport loop" shuttle bus (P20) connects all the terminals, running frequently throughout the day, but traffic congestion means transfers can take over an hour in some cases – leave plenty of time.

Tourist information Terminals 1, 2 and 3 have small Department of Tourism reception desks, open to meet all flights, where you can pick up maps and current information. Terminal 2 has an airport information desk that sometimes has city maps.

Services There are banks and ATMs at all terminals, but no left-luggage (baggage deposit) facilities. Free wi-fi is available inside the terminals.

GETTING INTO TOWN

The roads around the airport quickly become gridlocked in heavy rain or at rush hour; it can take anything from 20min to 1hr to travel the 7km to the main tourist and budget accommodation area of Manila Bay.

Airport taxis To head into the centre, the best thing to do is to take a cab. Yellow airport taxis charge slightly higher rates than normal white taxis (see p.84). The meter starts at P60 for the first 500m (though some drivers will still charge the old rate of P70) and adds P4 per additional 500m; reckon on P180–250 to Malate or Makati and P250–300 to Ermita, depending on traffic. Beware of scam artists – if the meter looks like it's going to hit P1000 anywhere inside the city you are being ripped off: take the taxi number and report the driver.

Pre-paid taxis The alternative to yellow taxis is to buy a ticket for a pre-paid "coupon" taxi at desks outside the terminals. Unless you have a large group, these big Toyota vans are expensive: P440 to Malate, P530 to Ermita, P330–440 to Makati and P610–940 to Quezon City.

Jeepneys It's possible to flag down a jeepney from the main roads near any of the terminals, but if you have bulky baggage it can be hard, sometimes impossible, to drag it on board.

Express bus UBE Express buses (📞 02 879 4497, 🌐 ubeexpress.com) run from terminals 1, 2 and 3 on three routes, to Pasay, Makati and Ermita (Robinsons Place mall on Pedro Gil St). However, departures are infrequent (every 2hr), and although the fare is P150, this is apparently an introductory offer – it's due to rise to P300, which will make it more expensive than a taxi.

Bus and LRT If you really want to do it on the cheap, take a P20 airport bus (not the one which serves the other terminals) from Terminal 3 to the San Agustin bus terminal in Pasay at the junction of Taft and EDSA (this can easily take an hour). You can then get an LRT train from EDSA station across the street or an MRT from nearby Taft station – so long as your baggage measures less than the LRT/MRT maximum of 90cm x 60cm. LRT/MRT "beep cards" (see p.83) are valid on this bus service.

DOMESTIC FLIGHTS DESTINATIONS

Domestic carriers are covered in Basics (see p.25).

Northern Luzon Batanes (1–2 daily; 1hr 45min); Laoag (1–3 daily; 1hr); Tuguegarao (1–3 daily; 1hr 10min).

Southern Luzon Legazpi (6–7 daily; 1hr 10min); Naga (3–4 daily; 1hr); Virac (1–3 daily; 1hr 10min).

Mindoro San José (1–2 daily; 1hr).

The Visayas Bacolod (12–14 daily; 1hr 15min); Caticlan (10–11 daily; 55min); Cebu City (28–30 daily; 1hr 15min); Dumaguete (4–7 daily; 1hr 25min); Iloilo (10–14 daily; 1hr 10min); Kalibo (11–13 daily; 1hr 10min); Tablas Island (2 weekly; 1hr); Tacloban (9–10 daily; 1hr 25min); Tagbilaran (8–9 daily; 1hr 25min).

Palawan Busuanga Island (8–9 daily; 1hr); Puerto Princesa (13–15 daily; 1hr 20min).

Mindanao Butuan (5 daily; 1hr 35min); Cagayan de Oro (11–13 daily; 1hr 30min); Cotabato (2–3 daily; 1hr 45min); Davao (21–24 daily; 1hr 50min); Dipolog (2 daily; 1hr 25min); General Santos (5–6 daily; 1hr 50min); Ozamiz (2 daily; 1hr 30min); Surigao (1 daily; 1hr 40min); Zamboanga (6–7 daily; 1hr 40min).

BY FERRY

2GO Travel ferries (incorporating Negros Navigation, SuperFerry, Cebu Ferries and SuperCat; 🌐 travel.2go.com .ph) use the passenger terminal at Pier 4, North Harbor (along Marcos Rd, a few kilometres north of Intramuros), from where a taxi to Ermita costs about P150.

Departures Bacolod (4 weekly; 20hr); Butuan (1 weekly; 23hr); Cagayan de Oro (4 weekly; 34hr); Cebu City (5 weekly; 23hr); Coron (2 weekly; 15hr); Dipolog (1 weekly; 32hr); Dumaguete (1 weekly; 26hr); Iligan (1 weekly; 42hr); Iloilo (4 weekly; 28hr); Ozamiz (1 weekly; 35hr); Puerto Princesa (2 weekly; 32hr); Zamboanga (1 weekly; 42hr).

BY BUS

Dozens of buses link Manila with the provinces. As a general rule (and to avoid extra time negotiating Manila's gridlock), for points south, you're best off going to or from Pasay, in the south of the city around the junction of Taft Ave with EDSA, while for the north you're better off using terminals in Cubao (Quezon City), towards the northern end of EDSA. From

1

Pasay you can take the LRT (see p.84) north to the Malate area or the MRT (see opposite) northeast to Makati and beyond. Alternatively, a taxi from the Pasay area to Malate costs less than P100. From most bus stations in Cubao it's a short walk to the Cubao MRT station; a taxi from Cubao to Makati costs around P150. Leaving Manila by bus can be confusing, however, as there's no central bus terminal – each company has its own station, albeit clumped together in Cubao and Pasay (a third cluster lies on Rizal Ave, known as "Avenida", in Quiapo). Usually, if you tell your taxi driver your destination, they will bring you to the right station. The list that follows includes some of the more popular operators. A useful website is ⓦphbus.com, where you can book buses and see timetables.

AROUND MANILA

Balanga (2–3hr). Bataan Transit ☎02 352 4727, ⓦbataantransit.com: Five Star Terminal, Epifanio de los Santos Ave, Cubao ☎02 911 7359 (every 15min midnight–10pm); Avenida Terminal, 1612 Doroteo Jose St, Santa Cruz (every 30min). Genesis Transport ☎02 709 0803, ⓦgenesistransport.com.ph: 101 A. Giselle, Park Plaza, EDSA at Rotonda, Pasay (every 15min 2.30am–7.30pm).

Batangas (express 1hr 30min; regular 2–3hr, depending on traffic). ALPS ☎0923 716 0472, ⓦalpsthebus.com: Araneta Center Bus Terminal, Cubao (every 30min). JAM ⓦjam.com.ph: 2124 Taft Ave, Pasay (by Gil Puyat/Buendia LRT station); 831 EDSA at Timog Ave, Cubao ☎0917 526 0008 (hourly 12.30am–11pm).

Clark/Angeles City/Dau (bus terminal) (1hr 30min–2hr). Five Star ☎02 853 4772, ⓦ5starbus.co: 2240 Aurora Blvd, Pasay Terminal (frequent departures). Philippine Rabbit ☎0922 867 7358: Rizal Ave at Recto (Avenida; every 30min 7am–8pm). Philtranco ☎02 851 8077, ⓦphiltranco.com.ph: EDSA at Apelo Cruz St, Pasay. Swagman Travel ☎02 523 8541, ⓦswaggy.com: *Swagman Hotel*, 411 A. Flores St, Ermita (small, expensive buses to Angeles City daily 8am, noon and 3pm).

Laguna JAC Liner ☎02 275 8245, ⓦjacliner.com: by Gil Puyat (Buendia) LRT station in Pasay; buses every 15min to Santa Cruz (for Pagsanjan; 2hr 30min) via Calamba (1hr 30min) and Los Baños (2hr).

Lemery/Tanauan (for Lake Taal; 2hr 30min). JAM ☎0917 526 0008, ⓦjam.com.ph: 2124 Taft Ave, Pasay (by Gil Puyat/Buendia LRT station); 831 EDSA at Timog Ave, Cubao (hourly 12.30am–11pm).

Malolos (1hr). First North Luzon Transit ☎0923 744 9253, ⓦfirstnorthluzontransit.com: Monumento LRT station; also vans and FX taxis from there and from SM City North mall, at the northern end of EDSA (400m north of North Avenue MRT station).

Mariveles (3–4hr). Bataan Transit ☎02 352 4727, ⓦbataantransit.com: Five Star Terminal, Cubao (every 20min midnight–9.30pm); Avenida Terminal, 1612

Doroteo Jose St, Santa Cruz (every 30min 3.30am–8pm). Genesis Transport ☎02 709 0803, ⓦgenesistransport.com.ph: 101 A. Giselle, Park Plaza, EDSA at Rotonda, Pasay (every 20min 1am–7.30pm).

Nasugbu (3hr). San Agustin Terminal from Park Plaza at the junction of Taft and EDSA in Pasay (every 10min 2.30am–11pm).

Subic Bay/Olongapo Victory Liner ⓦvictoryliner.com: Cubao Terminal, 683 EDSA ☎02 727 4688 (every 30min 2am–10pm; 3–4hr); Pasay Terminal, 651 EDSA ☎02 833 4403 (hourly; 4–5hr).

Tagaytay (1hr 30min). San Agustin from Park Plaza at the junction of Taft and EDSA in Pasay (every 10min 2.30am–11pm).

NORTHERN LUZON

Alaminos (6–8hr). Five Star ☎02 851 6614, ⓦ5starbus.co: 674 EDSA opposite Monte de Piedad St, Cubao (every 40min–1hr); Victory Liner ☎02 727 4534, ⓦvictoryliner.com: Cubao Terminal, 683 EDSA (hourly 3.30am–7.30pm).

Baguio (6–8hr). Genesis Transport ☎02 709 0803, ⓦgenesistransport.com.ph: 704 EDSA at New York St, Cubao (hourly 3am–7pm). Victory Liner ⓦvictoryliner.com: Cubao Terminal, 683 EDSA ☎02 727 4688 (hourly); Pasay Terminal, 651 EDSA ☎02 833 4403 (hourly). Joy Bus ☎02 853 3115, ⓦgenesistransport.com.ph: the Genesis Transport Terminals at 704 EDSA at New York St, Cubao ☎02 421 1413 (hourly); and 101 A. Giselle Park Plaza, EDSA at Rotunda, Pasay (hourly).

Baler (5–6hr). Genesis Transport and Joy Bus ☎02 421 1413, ⓦgenesistransport.com.ph: both from Genesis Transport Terminal, 704 EDSA at New York St, Cubao (5–8 nightly midnight–4am).

Banaue (8–9hr, all around 9pm daily). Ohayami Trans ☎02 516 0501, ⓦohayamitrans.com: J. Fajardo St at A.H. Lacson Ave, Sampaloc; Dangwa ☎02 731 2879: Carola St at Dimasalang Rd, Sampaloc. Coda Lines ☎0927 559 2197, ⓦcodalinesph.com: HM Terminal, Monte de Piedad St, Cubao.

Bontoc (12hr). Coda Lines ☎0927 559 219, ⓦcodalinesph.com: HM Terminal, Monte de Piedad St, Cubao (9pm nightly).

Kiangan/Lagawe (8hr). Ohayami Trans ☎02 516 0501, ⓦohayamitrans.com: J. Fajardo St at A.H. Lacson Ave, Sampaloc (daily 9.30pm).

Laoag (12–14hr). Fariñas Transit ☎02 731 4507, ⓦfarinastrans.com: Laon Laan St at M. de la Fuente St, Sampaloc (12 daily). Partas ☎02 727 8278, ⓦphbus.com: 816 Aurora Blvd at EDSA, Cubao Terminal (5 daily).

San Fernando (La Union; 6–8hr). Dominion Bus Lines ☎02 741 4146: EDSA at New York St, Cubao (hourly). Partas ☎02 727 8278, ⓦphbus.com: 816 Aurora Blvd at EDSA, Cubao Terminal (roughly hourly).

Sagada (12hr). Coda Lines ☎0927 559 219, ⓦcodalinesph.com: HM Terminal, Monte de Piedad St,

Cubao (9pm nightly).
Tuguegarao (10–12hr). Florida Liner ☎02 743 3809: Earnshaw St at A.H. Lacson Ave, Sampaloc (roughly hourly). Victory Liner ☎02 727 4688, ⓦvictoryliner.com: Cubao Terminal, 683 EDSA (10 daily). Five Star Terminal ☎02 911 7359, ⓦ5starbus.co: 674 EDSA opposite Monte de Piedad St, Cubao, Cubao (10 daily).
Vigan (8–10hr). Dominion Bus Lines ☎02 741 4146: EDSA at New York St, Cubao (roughly hourly). Partas ☎02 727 8278, ⓦphbus.com: 816 Aurora Blvd at EDSA, Cubao Terminal (roughly hourly).

SOUTHERN LUZON

Daet (7–8hr). DLTB ☎0916 123 4567: Taft Ave at Gil Puyat Ave, Gil Puyat/Buendia LRT (15 daily). Philtranco ☎02 851 8078, ⓦphiltranco.com.ph: EDSA at Apelo Cruz St, Pasay (6 daily). Superlines ☎02 414 3319: EDSA, Cubao, between New York St and Monte de Piedad St (5 daily).
Legazpi (8–10hr). DLTB ☎0916 123 4567: Taft Ave at Gil Puyat Ave, Gil Puyat/Buendia LRT (6 daily). Cagsawa ☎02 525 9756: 472 Padre Faura St at M.H. Del Pilar St (2 daily, plus 7 from Cubao). ALPS ☎0923 716 0472, ⓦalpsthebus .com: Araneta Center Bus Terminal, Cubao (6 daily).
Lucena (3hr 30min). JAC Liner ⓦjacliner.com: Donada St at Gil Puyat (Buendia), Pasay ☎02 404 2073 (hourly 8am–6pm). JAM Liner, ⓦjam.com.ph: 2124 Taft Ave, Pasay (Gil Puyat/Buendia LRT) ☎02 831 8264 (roughly hourly). Lucena Lines, 713 EDSA, Cubao ☎02 582 2362 (every 30–40min).
Naga (8–10hr). Philtranco, EDSA at Apelo Cruz St, Pasay ☎02 851 8078, ⓦphiltranco.com.ph (2 daily). DLTB ☎0916 123 4567: Taft Ave at Gil Puyat Ave, Gil Puyat/Buendia LRT (8

daily). ALPS ☎0923 716 0472, ⓦalpsthebus.com: from Araneta Center Bus Terminal, Cubao (4 daily).
Sorsogon City (10–12hr). DLTB ☎0916 123 4567: Taft Ave at Gil Puyat Ave, Gil Puyat/Buendia LRT (4 daily). Philtranco ☎02 851 8078, ⓦphiltranco.com.ph: EDSA at Apelo Cruz St, Pasay (10 daily).

MINDORO

Sabang & Muelle pier (Puerto Galera; 4hr). Si-Kat ☎02 708 9628, ⓦsikatferrybus.com: City State Tower, 1315 A. Mabini St, Ermita (daily 8.30am).
San José (10–12hr). Dimple Star Transport: Ali Mall, Cubao ☎02 517 4677; España Ave at Antipolo St, Sampaloc ☎02 985 1451: 1 daily via Abra de Ilog & Sablayan (10hr), 1 daily via Calapan and Roxas (12hr).

THE VISAYAS

Panay Philtranco ☎02 851 8077, ⓦphiltranco.com.ph: EDSA at Apelo Cruz St, Pasay; to Iloilo (2 daily; 17hr), via Mindoro.
Samar/Leyte Philtranco ☎02 851 8077, ⓦphiltranco .com.ph: EDSA at Apelo Cruz St, Pasay; to Ormoc (1 daily; 28hr) and Tacloban (1 daily; 26hr).

MINDANAO

Cagayan de Oro (2 days). Philtranco ☎02 851 8077, ⓦphiltranco.com.ph: EDSA at Apelo Cruz St, Pasay (via Surigao, 1 daily).
Davao (2–3 days). Philtranco ☎02 851 8077, ⓦphiltranco.com.ph: EDSA at Apelo Cruz St, Pasay (via Surigao, 3 daily).

GETTING AROUND

There are so many vehicles fighting for every inch of road space in Manila that at peak times it can be a sweaty battle of nerves just to move a few hundred metres. **Buses** and **jeepneys** belch smoke with impunity, turning the air around major thoroughfares into a poisonous miasma, but Manila's **taxis** are inexpensive and are mostly air-conditioned, and many visitors use them extensively. Manila's two light railway lines, the Manila Light Rail Transit (**LRT**) and the MetroStar Express (**MRT**) are cheap and reliable, but badly integrated – interchanges are poorly designed, and there are no through-fares, so you need to buy a new ticket (or tap your "beep card" again) when changing between LRT and MRT, and when changing between the LRT green and the LRT purple lines. Trains are best avoided during rush hour (Mon–Fri 7–9.30am & 5–8pm) when you may have to line up just to get into the stations, and carriages will be jam-packed.

METROSTAR EXPRESS (MRT)

The MetroStar Express (daily 5.30am–11pm, every 3–6min; ⓦdotcmrt3.gov.ph) is also known as MRT-3 (or yellow line, formerly the blue line). It runs for 17km along EDSA from Taft Ave in Pasay City in the south to North Ave, Quezon City in the north, connecting with LRT lines at the southern end and in the middle, and in the future at the northern end too.
Fares You can buy a single-journey ticket for P13–28, or purchase a stored-value "beep card" (ⓦbeeptopay.com) for P80 worth of travel plus a non-refundable P20 issue fee.

You can buy and top up "beep cards" from station ticket offices (though they sometimes run out), and from machines at the main entrances of stations. The cards are also valid on the LRT. If you plan to use the MRT and LRT a lot, you'll save a great deal of time by buying one; you'll still have to line up for a bag check before entering the station, but will avoid having to line up again for a ticket.
Safety Security guards patrol stations (and the first carriage is usually reserved for women), but watch out for pickpockets and the more brazen "snatchers", who rip phones, bags and wallets from your hand and make a run for it.

1

MANILA LIGHT RAIL TRANSIT (LRT)
The LRT (@lrta.gov.ph) has two elevated rail lines: the 17.2km Green Line (LRT-1); and the 13.8km Purple Line, which, confusingly, is known as MRT-2. The Green Line runs from Baclaran in the south to Roosevelt in the north, connecting with MRT-1 at Taft Ave/EDSA, and is due to connect at North Ave when the line on from Roosevelt is completed. The Purple Line runs from Santolan in Pasig City to Recto in Quiapo, close to the Green Line's Doroteo Jose station. Trains on both lines run frequently from 5am to 10pm, but there are no through-fares, and to change trains you have to exit one station and walk to the other.
Fares Tickets range from P15 to P30. "Beep cards" (see p.83) are valid on both the LRT and MRT.

PHILIPPINES NATIONAL RAILWAY
The vintage 1892 Philippines National Railway line (@pnr .gov.ph) is gradually being brought back into service and should eventually have trains from Tutuban station (see map, p.72) north to Malolos and south to Calamba. At present all it has are a few infrequent and not tremendously useful services down the South Luzon Expressway as far as Alabang.

JEEPNEYS AND FX TAXIS
While sometimes useful (linking SM Mall of Asia and Baclaran station, for example), jeepneys and FX taxis can be incredibly cramped, and traffic congestion can make even short journeys last hours.
Jeepneys are the cheapest way to get around, and they run back and forth all over the city. Fares are P7 for the first 4km, and increase by P1.50/km thereafter. Destinations are written on signboards at the front.
FX taxis You'll also see tiny minivans or "FX taxis", usually labelled UV Express, that zip between fixed points, usually without stopping, for around P20–30 per ride.

BUSES
Local buses in Manila bump and grind their way along all major thoroughfares, such as Taft, EDSA and Gil Puyat (Buendia) Avenue, but are not allowed on most side streets. The destination is written on a sign in the front window. Most vehicles are ageing contraptions bought secondhand from Japan or Taiwan, and feature no particular colour scheme; it's a matter of luck whether a bus has air conditioning.
Fares Most fares range P15–20 for the first 5km, and increase P2–2.20/km thereafter. As with jeepneys, traffic congestion will add travel time and even larger buses will often be packed.

TAXIS
Most Manila taxi drivers are honest these days and use the meter, though some may still try to set prices in advance or "forget" to switch it on (insist on the meter). Taxis come in a confusing mix of models, colours and shapes; most metered taxis are white (and often called "white taxis" to differentiate them from the yellow airport taxis that have higher fares).
Fares Fares are good value and you'll save time using white taxis over other road transport. The metered rate is an initial P30 for the first 500m, plus P3.50 for every 500m (or 2min waiting) thereafter. Uber also now operates in Manila (@uber.com/cities/manila).

INFORMATION

Tourist information The Tourist Information Center is in the Department of Tourism Building, 351 Sen Gil Puyat (Buendia) Ave, Makati (Mon–Fri 7am–6pm, Sat 8am–5pm; ☎02 959 5200 ext 101 or 102, @visitmyphilippines.com). There are also information desks in the airport arrivals sections.
Maps Many bookshops (see p.97) sell the Accu-map range of atlases (@accu-map.com), A–Z-like pocket-books that cover the whole of Metro Manila.

TOURS AND ACTIVITIES

Tours Filipino Travel Center, G/F *Palm Plaza Hotel*, 524 Pedro Gil St at M. Adriatico St, Ermita ☎02 528 4507, @filipinotravel .com.ph (Manila day-trips from P1565). Walk This Way and Old Manila Walks offer walking tours (see box, p.63).
Dive operators Asia Divers, 1741 Dian St, Abimir Place, Palanan, Makati ☎02 834 2974, @asiadivers.com; Scuba World, 1181 Pablo Ocampo St, Makati ☎02 895 3551, @scubaworld.com.ph.

ACCOMMODATION

Most of Manila's budget accommodation is in the Manila Bay area, specifically in **Ermita** and **Malate**, which also have a high density of cheap restaurants, bars and tourist services. In recent years a number of reasonably priced mid-range hotels have sprung up, as well as several five-star places along Manila Bay, joining the historic *Manila Hotel*. In the business district of **Makati**, there's some mid-range accommodation in and around P. Burgos St at the northern end of Makati Ave, beyond the *Mandarin Oriental Manila*. This is close to the red-light district, so if you want somewhere else in Makati try the somewhat anaemic but comfortable chain hotels In Arnaiz Ave (formerly Pasay Rd), behind the Greenbelt mall. The hotels in **Quezon City** are almost all around Timog Ave and Tomas Morato Ave, close to the nightlife; if you're planning to catch an early bus from Cubao, it might be worth staying here. If you have an early flight and a bit more cash to spend, try one of the convenient upmarket options close to the airport.

AIRPORT AREA (PASAY CITY)

Manila Marriott Hotel 10 Newport Blvd, Newport City Complex ☎ 02 988 9999, ⓦ marriott.com; map pp.60–61. Fabulous luxury hotel, right across from Terminal 3 (with free shuttle bus to all terminals). Stylish rooms come with flatscreen TVs and snazzy bathrooms with glass walls (with shades for the modest) and big tubs. The pool is a great place to chill out during the day. Price quoted here is the highest walk-in rate for a standard double; you should be able to get it for rather less if you book ahead or online. ☞ **P12,566**

INTRAMUROS AND RIZAL PARK

The Bayleaf Muralla St at Victoria St ☎ 02 318 5000, ⓦ thebayleaf.com.ph; map p.62. Swish boutique hotel in the historic heart of the city, with spacious, light, modern rooms, roof deck bar and restaurant with great views, and buffet breakfast included. ☞ **P7300**

Manila Hotel 1 Rizal Park ☎ 02 527 0011, ⓦ manila-hotel.com.ph; map p.62. Esteemed establishment that reeks of history (see p.67), at least in the old wing where General Douglas MacArthur stayed during World War II; if you've got P400,000 to spare you can stay a night in his suite. The lobby is a grand affair with black-and-white-tiled flooring and oxblood velvet sofas. The rooms, many in need of a revamp, remain stubbornly traditional, with dark wood and four-poster beds. ☞ **P8395**

White Knight Hotel Intramuros Cabildo St at Urdaneta St, Plaza San Luis Complex ☎ 02 526 6539, ⓦ whiteknighthotelintramuros.com; map p.62. Nineteenth-century building with heaps of character and 29 simple but spacious rooms tastefully furnished in period style, with bathroom, a/c and flatscreen TV. The cheapest option in Intramuros. ☞ **P1995**

ERMITA AND MALATE

Adriatico Arms 561 J. Nakpil St, Malate ☎ 02 521 0736, ⓦ aarmshotel.com; map p.68. A pleasant no-frills hotel in an unbeatable location. The 23 a/c rooms are smallish, but well kept and functional, and there's a good bar, but no breakfast. ☞ **P1450**

Aloha Hotel 2150 Roxas Blvd, Malate ☎ 02 526 8088, ⓦ alohahotel.ph; map p.68. A Manila Bay stalwart, the *Aloha* boasts a fine location with views of the bay from the front (5/F or above). The corridors are a bit scuffed, but the rooms are fine and spacious, and breakfast is included. There's a small café and a Chinese restaurant. ☞ **P4000**

Bahaykubo Hostel 1717 Maria Orosa St, Malate ☎ 02 243 7537, ⓦ facebook.com/BahaykuboHostel Philippines; map p.68. Very friendly, welcoming little hostel in a traditional Filipino house in a lively location, with use of the kitchen and a choice of a/c or fan-cooled dorms and rooms. ☞ Dorms **P350**, doubles **P800**

Best Western Hotel La Corona 1166 M.H. del Pilar St at Arquiza St, Ermita ☎ 02 524 2631, ⓦ bestwesternhotel manila.com; map p.68. Solid choice featuring stylish double a/c rooms with a modern Filipino theme and cable TV. Good location, and the rate includes a buffet breakfast. ☞ **P3000**

★ **Chillout Guesthouse** 612 Remedios St at Remedios Circle ☎ 02 218 7227, ⓦ facebook.com/Chillout.Manila; map p.68. This hostel, run by an enthusiastic young French crew, reopened in new digs in 2013, with a choice of fan or a/c en-suite rooms (P1450) and a/c dorms; the back rooms are quieter. There are lockers and a common kitchen area for self-caterers. ☞ Dorms **P350**, doubles **P650**

City Garden Suites 1158 A. Mabini St, Ermita ☎ 02 536 1451, ⓦ citygardensuites.com; map p.68. Standard hotel with sparsely furnished but clean a/c rooms and a reasonable coffee shop in the lobby. ☞ **P2464**

Ermita Tourist Inn 1549 A. Mabini St at Soldado St, Ermita ☎ 02 521 8770, ⓔ scenicviewtravel@yahoo .com; map p.68. Basic choice with thirty ageing a/c rooms (those with twin beds are bigger than those with double beds), including hot showers and simple breakfasts, but with wi-fi in the restaurant area only. There's a travel agent downstairs for flights and visas. ☞ **P1450**

Garden Plaza Hotel 1030 Belen St, Paco Park ☎ 02 522 4835, ⓔ gplazahotel@yahoo.com; map p.68. Congenial and well managed, the *Garden Plaza* is right next to Paco Park and has a/c rooms, a cute little mini swimming pool on the roof and a branch of the excellent *Old Swiss Inn* restaurant (see p.90). Breakfast is included but there's wi-fi in the lobby only, and standard rooms don't have windows. ☞ **P2196**

Hotel H2O Manila Ocean Park (behind the Quirino Grandstand), Ermita ☎ 02 238 6100, ⓦ hotelh2o.com; map p.68. The most original boutique hotel in Manila, with a chic "aqua" theme and fabulous views of the bay or Ocean World pool (for the nightly fountain shows). Rooms sport a trendy minimalist design and LCD TVs; some even have wall-sized in-room aquariums. The only (slight) downside is that the hotel is a bit cut off from the rest of the city. Rates include breakfast. ☞ **P5917**

Lotus Garden Hotel 1227 A. Mabini St at Padre Faura St, Ermita ☎ 02 522 1515 (free within Philippines ☎ 1800 1888 1515), ⓦ lotusgardenhotelmanila.com; map p.68. Snazzy modern rooms with cable TV and room service, as well as a gym, a spa, an excellent location and decent buffet breakfast (included) make this chain hotel a good deal – book online for the best rates. ☞ **P2464**

Malate Pensionne 1771 M. Adriatico St, Malate ☎ 02 523 8304, ⓦ malatepensionne.com; map p.68. Tucked away in an unbeatable position, this has been one of the area's most popular guesthouses for years. Rooms are furnished in Spanish-colonial style and book up quickly. Wi-fi in the lounge area only. ☞ Dorms **P490**, doubles **P950**

Paco Park Oasis Hotel 1032–1034 Belen St, Paco Park ☎ 02 521 2371; map p.68. Outside the walls of Paco Park, next door to the *Garden Plaza* (see above) and overall a

1

much better deal than its neighbour, this place offers a range of rooms, some with a whirlpool bath. There's a large swimming pool, pleasant terrace area, restaurant, and a travel agency in the lobby. ⬡ P3250

Pan Pacific Manila Hotel M. Adriatico St at General Malvar St, Malate ☏02 318 0788 (free within Philippines: ☏1800 8908 6362), ⬡panpacific.com/manila; map p.68. This is the top choice in Malate for superlative service (each room comes with 24hr butler facility), luxurious rooms and a buffet breakfast that could feed an army. Passing from the street chaos to the soothing outdoor swimming pool and jacuzzi is a surreal but pleasant experience. ⬡ P9102

Pearl Garden Hotel 1700 M. Adriatico St at General Malvar St, Malate ☏02 525 1000, ⬡pearlgardenhotel.net; map p.68. One of the best mid-range hotels on the block, with 83 small but clean and elegant boutique-style rooms. Note that the hotel is smoker friendly apart from one non-smoking floor, and the wi-fi can be a bit iffy. ⬡ P2600

★**Pension Natividad** 1690 M.H. del Pilar St, Malate ☏02 521 0524, ⬡pensionnatividad.com; map p.68. One of the best budget places to stay in the area, this place has spacious, impeccably clean rooms (some en suite and with a/c) in a large old family house. Popular with Peace Corps volunteers, it's safe, quiet and friendly; free wi-fi in the lobby only. ⬡ Dorms P400, doubles P1000

Sofitel Philippine Plaza CCP Complex, off Roxas Blvd, Malate ☏02 551 5555, ⬡sofitelmanila.com; map p.71. If you can afford it and want a luxurious room with a balcony and a view of the Manila Bay sunsets, this is the place to stay. The level of service is outstanding, and the hotel has a big choice of bars and restaurants as well as an excellent spa. ⬡ P14,712

Southern Cross Hotel 1125 M.H. del Pilar St, Ermita ☏02 521 2013, ✉thesoutherncrosshotel@gmail.com; map p.68. Friendly budget hotel with small but comfy rooms equipped with a/c, cable TV, bathroom and fridge. It's owned by an Australian national and there's an Aussie-style bar and food, large-screen TV and billiard table downstairs. ⬡ P1200

V Hotel 1766 M. Adriatico St, Malate ☏02 328 5553, ⬡vhotelmanila.com; map p.68. *V Hotel* offers sparkling rooms, though they are on the small side, and not all have windows. There's a small pool (often out of commission), and breakfast is included. ⬡ P1200

Wanderers Guesthouse 1750 M. Adriatico St at Nakpil St, Malate ☏02 474 0742, ⬡wanderersguesthouse.com; map p.68. The chilled-out balcony bar, bird's-eye view over Malate and low prices at this backpackers' hostel make it a firm favourite and a great place to hang out. Fan and a/c rooms are available, some with shared bathrooms. ⬡ Dorms P350, doubles P690

Windy Ridge Hotel 2033 M.H. del Pilar St, Malate ☏02

567 0741, ✉windyridgemanila@gmail.com; map p.68. Dwarfed by the surrounding high-rises, this six-floor hotel is a sweet little place to stay, with a/c, free breakfast, and discounts on three nights or more. ⬡ P2300

MAKATI

El Cielito 804 Arnaiz Ave (Pasay Rd) ☏02 815 8951, ⬡elcielitohotels.com; map p.77. Small but clean glass-fronted hotel close to Makati's malls, with modern, a/c rooms (some carpeted, some with wooden floors) and a coffee shop. Breakfast is included, and discounts are offered if you stay more than a couple of days. ⬡ P3500

★**Element** 4950 Guerrero St ☏02 805 1360, ⬡elementboutiquehotelmakati.com; map p.77. Run by an English-French couple, this lovely little place is everything a boutique hotel should be: beautifully designed, small and chic, with a super-modern, sparse elegance that's almost Japanese in its simplicity. The rooms range from simple standard to a sumptuous penthouse suite (P7500), but they're all an absolute pleasure to stay in. ⬡ P2600

Makati Shangri-La Ayala Ave at Makati Ave ☏02 813 8888, ⬡shangri-la.com; map p.77. Over-the-top opulence at this five-star establishment in the heart of Makati – chic rooms, fine service, waterfalls on every floor and a host of quality restaurants on site. ⬡ P18,390

The Peninsula Manila Ayala Ave at Makati Ave ☏02 887 2888, ⬡peninsula.com/Manila; map p.77. Ostentatious five-star that takes up a city block and has a superbly elegant lobby where people go to drink coffee and to see and be seen. There are no fewer than seven restaurants, running the gamut from Asian to French. Rooms are as you'd expect at this price, with luxurious furnishings and all mod cons. ⬡ P19,616

Robelle House 4402 Valdez St ☏02 899 8061, ⬡bit.ly/RobelleHouse; map p.77. This rambling family-run pension has been in business since 1977 and is still the most atmospheric budget accommodation in Makati, although located in a slightly desolate and remote backstreet. The rooms are large, with a/c and bathroom (but wi-fi in the lobby only), and the wooden staircases are authentically creaky. The best rooms are on the upper floor overlooking the hotel's pool. ⬡ P1750

Tower Inn 1002 Arnaiz Ave (Pasay Rd) ☏02 888 5170, ⬡towerinnmakati.com; map p.77. Mid-range hotel with 48 rooms, cable TV (but not many channels), wi-fi (only in the lobby), a business centre, a restaurant and a roof terrace, all within easy walking distance of Makati's shops and restaurants. Breakfast included. ⬡ P3050

AROUND P. BURGOS STREET

Best Western Oxford Suites Makati 518 P. Burgos St at Durban St ☏02 899 7988, ⬡oxfordsuitesmakati.com; map p.78. One of the best hotels on the P. Burgos

1

strip, with 232 spacious rooms and suites, gym, coffee shop and third-floor restaurant. Some rooms have kitchenette, living room and terrace. Buffet breakfast included. 🛜 P4400

City Garden Hotel Makati 7870 Makati Ave at Kalayaan Ave ☎02 899 1111, ⓦmakati.citygarden hotels.com; map p.78. A comfortable, modern boutique hotel with spacious and well-maintained a/c rooms, small rooftop swimming pool and giddy views from the rooftop café. Good location, the staff are efficient and you can negotiate a discount off season. 🛜 P3136

★**Clipper Hotel** 5766 Ebro St ☎02 890 8577, ⓦtheclipperhotel.com; map p.78. An atmospheric little gem, this Art Deco hotel is more South Beach than south Manila. Rooms are simple but spacious, and have cable TV. The only catch is its relative proximity to the main drag, which can be a little bit noisy at night. 🛜 P2688

Jupiter Suites 102 Jupiter St at Makati Ave ☎02 890 5044, ⓦjupitersuites.com.ph; map p.78. Offers spacious a/c singles and doubles, all en suite and with cable TV and internet. If you want quiet, ask for a room at the back – those at the front overlook the busy street and you'll wake to the sound of jeepneys honking their horns at 5am. Breakfast included. 🛜 P3980

Our Melting Pot Hostel 3/F Wang Mart Building, 37 Polaris St ☎028334736, Ⓔmymeltingpotbackpackers@ gmail.com; map p.78. In principle, two adjacent hostels (*Our Melting Pot* and *The Good Shepherd*), but in reality one large hostel with spic-and-span dorms and rooms, spacious public areas, breakfast included and free use of the gym downstairs. 🛜 Dorms P500, doubles P1450

St Giles Makati Makati Ave at Kalayaan Ave ☎02 988 9888, ⓦfacebook.com/StGilesMakatiPH; map p.78.

snazzy hotel, close to all the action. There's a pool and gym, and the rooms are elegantly furnished in light neutral tones. 🛜 P3923

QUEZON CITY

Camelot Hotel 35 Mother Ignacia Ave ☎02 373 2101, ⓦcamelothotel.com.ph; map p.80. You can't miss it: look for the mock-Arthurian spires. The rooms (all en suite with bathtubs) have a very slight medieval touch about their decor, but not as much as the public spaces, where there are suits of armour and Excalibur swords, a coffee shop called the *Winchester*, and a bar called the *Dungeon*. Breakfast and wi-fi cost extra. 🛜 P1695

Hotel 878 Libis 878 E. Rodriguez Jr. Ave ☎02 709 0154, ⓦhotel878libis.com; map pp.60–61. Fine mid-range option, with 29 stylish doubles all with verandas and cable TV. The super-cool lofts (P5500) and suites (P7500) are also worth considering. 🛜 P4500

Hotel Rembrandt 26 Tomas Morato Ave Extension ☎02 373 3333, ⓦhotelrembrandt.com.ph; map p.80. Medium-sized, modern hotel with a/c rooms, spa, cosy piano bar on the top floor with good views, and a *T.G.I. Friday's* on the ground floor. Breakfast included. 🛜 P3850

★**Stone House Hotel** 1315 E. Rodriguez Snr Ave ☎02 724 7551, ⓦstonehouse.com.ph; map p.80. A great-value, beautifully kept hotel – if in a slightly remote location – with cable TV, en-suite rooms and a tasty breakfast (included). The budget rooms are in the basement and lack windows, but are otherwise as comfortable as the standard rooms (P1300). Wi-fi is restricted to the ground-floor restaurant and roof terrace. Take a jeepney from Cubao MRT, heading west down E. Rodriguez Snr Ave. P600

EATING

Eating in Manila is a real treat; there's a full range of international and Filipino cuisine on offer, and budget eats available on every street corner and in every mall in the form of vast food courts. Everywhere you go, you'll see evidence of the Filipino love of fast-food franchises, with national chains such as *Jollibee*, *Chowking*, *Mang Inasal* (with unlimited rice) and *Max's* (for fried chicken) dotted all over the city. You should pay a visit to one of the ubiquitous Goldilocks (ⓦpadala .goldilocks.com.ph) stores, purveyors of the best *polvoron* (peanut candy) and cakes since 1966.

INTRAMUROS AND RIZAL PARK

The old walled city of Intramuros doesn't have many restaurants, but those it does have are mostly in old colonial buildings and are significantly more atmospheric than anything beyond the walls. For cheap eats, try the stalls (plates from P50) just within the walls on the eastern edge of Intramuros, or in nearby San Francisco St, in an area known as Puerta Isabel II.

Barbara's Plaza San Luis Complex, General Luna St ☎02 527 4083, ⓦfacebook.com/BarbarasHeritage Restaurant; map p.62. Elegant dining in a colonial setting, with woody interiors and rich Filipino and Spanish food pioneered by founder Barbara de los Reyes

in the 1970s. Best known for its touristy buffets (P549 for lunch; P699 for dinner) and the Kultura Filipina traditional music and dance show from 7.15pm. À la carte dishes go for P380–675. Daily 11.30am–2pm & 6.30–9pm.

★**Ilustrado** 744 General Luna St at the back of Silahis Center, facing Cabildo St ☎02 527 3674, ⓦilustrado restaurant.com.ph; map p.62. Nothing compares to *Ilustrado* if you're looking for the ambience of colonial Manila. The floors are polished wood, the tables are set with starched linen, ceiling fans whirr quietly and the cuisine is grand. Signature dishes include paella, creamy *bagnet* (deep-fried pork) and tender *lengua con setas* (ox tongue with brown sauce). Mains P420–590. Mon–Sat 11.30am–2.30pm & 6–10pm.

Kuatro Kantos 744 General Luna St ☎02 527 2345; map p.62. This charming little bar and café in the same old building (with same owners) as *Ilustrado* (see opposite) opens for breakfast – perfect for a good cup of coffee or a bite to eat while you're wandering around Intramuros. The hot *pan de sal* with corned beef or carabao cheese makes an excellent and very affordable snack, and their pesto is home-made and organic. Mains P250–450. Mon–Sat 8am–6pm, Sun 9am–6pm.

Patio de Conchita 681 Beaterio St ☎02 404 1122, ⓦbit.ly/PatioDeConchita; map p.62. This great find is off the beaten path but an excellent place to have lunch, with budget menus at P70–80. Food is served buffet style, with a range of top-notch Filipino dishes; try the *sinigang na baboy* (sour soup with pork; P75) and freshly barbecued squid (P280). Mon–Fri 7am–10pm, Sat 7am–9pm.

ERMITA AND MALATE

Advocafé G/F, Ramon Magsaysay Complex, Dr F. Quintos St ☎02 708 2366, ⓦadvocafe.com; map p.68. Excellent Filipino-grown arabica coffee, home-made cookies, and light meals at this cool little café, where you can also buy coffee beans and organic herbal teas. Profits go to the coffee-bean farmers and their indigenous communities up in the bundoks. Mon–Sat 6.30am–9pm.

★**Aristocrat** 432 San Andres St, facing Roxas Blvd ☎02 524 7671, ⓦaristocrat.com.ph; map p.68. Established out of an old van in 1936, *Aristocrat* is an institution among

Filipinos for its justly lauded barbecued chicken (P210) and pork (P175), as well as the whole spread of Filipino comfort food. The special *halo-halo* (P150) here is an extravagant concoction of taro ice cream, sliced banana, beans, *nata de coco*, ice and evaporated milk. Daily 24hr.

Bistro Remedios 1911 M. Adriatico St, just off Remedios Circle ☎02 523 9153; map p.68. Informal and homely restaurant with pretty Filipiniana interior and charming staff. The food is exclusively Filipino, with cholesterol-filled *pata* (fried pigs' knuckles) and *lechon kawali sa gata* (beef stew and fried pork in coconut milk; P190). There's also good fish and prawns, but not a great deal for vegetarians (mains P285–650). Daily 11am–3pm & 6–11pm (Sun till midnight).

Cabalen Robinsons Place (G/F, Padre Faura Wing), Pedro Gil St at M. Adriatico St ☎02 536 7987; map p.68. Hugely popular chain of restaurants famed for their gut-busting buffets (P398, plus P60 for drinks) of traditional dishes from the province of Pampanga, including *camaru* (rice-field crickets), *batute* (fried pig's trotters), *kuhol* (escargots), *sinigang tiyan ng bangus* (milkfish belly) and desserts such as *halayang ube* (purple yam pudding). Daily 10am–9pm.

Café Adriatico 1790 M. Adriatico St ☎02 738 8220; map p.68. This chic but casual stalwart of the Malate nightlife scene (it only closes for 2hr a day) opened a quarter of a century ago and was at the forefront of the area's revival. Light Spanish-Mediterranean themed meals include salads, omelettes and fondues (most mains P400–595). Try the authentic *chocolate-eh*, a thick chocolatey drink served as an anytime "snack". Daily 7am–5am.

TOP MANILA FOOD MARKETS

Food markets are scattered throughout the city, from no-frills street stalls to air-conditioned food courts in Manila's poshest malls – cuisine runs the gamut from Filipino snacks to high-end sushi. In general you'll be spending a lot less here than at sit-down restaurants, with small portions meaning plenty of scope for sampling different vendors.

Market! Market! Mabini Ave at McKinley Parkway, Bonifacio Global City ☎02 886 7519; map pp.60–61. This spotless high-end mall comes with tempting fresh-fruit stalls and a massive covered food court. Mon–Thurs & Sun 9am–9pm, Fri & Sat 10am–10pm.

Power Plant Mall Rockwell Drive at Estrella St, Makati ☎02 898 1702, ⓦpowerplantmall.com; map p.77. For a large and slightly upmarket selection of restaurants and stalls check out this plush mall on the edge of Makati. There's also a huge Rustan's supermarket (ⓦrustansfresh.com; same hours), a good choice for self-catering. Mon–Thurs 11am–9pm, Fri 11am–10pm, Sat 10am–10pm, Sun 10am–9pm.

St Francis Square Mall Tiangge Julia Vargas Ave at Bank Drive, Ortigas ⓦstfrancissquare.com.ph; map p.79. The alley along the east side of this budget

mall is cheap-eats paradise at lunchtime, with huge pots of delicious Filipino food dolled out for a few pesos. Inside St Francis Mall itself, the 3/F Food Court is another excellent place for local food (with a/c). Daily 10am–9pm.

★**Salcedo Community Market** Jaime Velasquez Park, Bel-Air, Makati ⓦfacebook.com/SalcedoCommunityMarket; map p.77. One of Manila's culinary highlights, featuring a dazzling display of gastronomic delights from all corners of the Philippines to take away or enjoy at one of the communal tables. Sat 7am–2pm.

SIDCOR Sunday Market Eton Centris parking lot, EDSA at Quezon Ave, Quezon City ⓦbit.ly/Sidcor; map p.80. Features 450 stalls selling a variety of fresh veg, fruit, meat and seafood. Sun 6am–2pm.

1

Casa Armas 573 J. Nakpil St at J. Bocobo St ☎02 536 1839; map p.68. This Spanish restaurant and tapas bar serves big plates of prawns sautéed in olive oil and garlic (P379) and Galician-style octopus (P289), as well as more substantial dishes such as a full paella (from P689 for 2–3 people). Mon–Sat 11am–midnight, Sun 6pm–midnight.

Harbor View South Gate A, Rizal Park ☎02 524 1532; map p.68. Located right on the harbour, between the US Embassy and *Manila Hotel*, this place is perfect for sunset viewing, with cool breezes, fresh seafood from the tank and all the classic Filipino dishes (from P270). It's a bit like a posh beach bar. Daily 11am–midnight.

Kamayan 523 Padre Faura St at Adriatico St ☎02 528 1723, ⓦkamayansaisakidads.com; map p.68. Excellent-value buffet restaurant with three sections: a traditional selection of Filipino dishes such as grilled fish, spicy crab, roast chicken and local vegetables; a Western section with more conventional roast beef and the like; and a Japanese area with sushi, tempura and noodles. The staff are dressed in elegant Filipino costumes and strolling minstrels work the tables doing requests. Mon–Fri lunch is P638–688, dinner P738–838; Fri–Sun it's P638–888 all day. Daily 11am–2.30pm & 6–10pm.

Kashmir 523 Padre Faura St (next to Kamayan) ☎02 524 6851, ⓦkashmirmanila.com; map p.68. Indian, Malay and Middle Eastern cuisine, with fiery curries and a mouthwatering selection of breads, set against wonderfully cheesy mock-Raj decor. Be warned: the chefs can be liberal with the spices, so think twice when the waiters ask if you want it very hot. Main dishes range P400–550. Daily 11am–11pm.

Korean Palace 1799 M. Adriatico St at Remedios St ☎02 521 6695; map p.68. One of a number of excellent Korean restaurants in the area, in part serving the growing numbers of Koreans here on nights out. The large menu includes some good dishes to share, such as fried beef, chicken or fish with piping-hot rice and various side dishes including tangy *kimchi* (pickled cabbage). Mains P320–490. Tues–Sun 11am–3pm & 5–11pm.

Old Swiss Inn Garden Plaza Hotel, 1030 Belen St, Pako Park ☎02 521 3002, ⓦoldswissinn.com; map p.68. A smaller branch of the Swiss restaurant in Makati (see opposite). Mon–Sat 6am–2pm & 6–10pm.

Pancit ng Taga Malabon 1025 Maria Orosa St ☎02 526 0755, ⓦpancitngtagamalabon.com; map p.68. The chain that claims descent from the original *Pancit Malabon* stall in the 1890s, when the addictive concoction of oysters, squid, shrimp, smoked fish (*tinapa*), deep-fried pigskin (*chicharon*), crab and duck eggs over thick rice noodles and golden sauce (P99) became known as *"pancit bame"*. Malabon was the location of the stall and the name has since been applied to noodle dishes nationwide. Mon–Fri 9am–8.45pm, Sat & Sun 11am–6.45pm.

Seafood Market Restaurant 1190 J. Bocobo St ☎02 521 4351, facebook.com/SeafoodMarketAnd Restaurant; map p.68. Here, the day's catch is laid out on ice and you pick from whatever the boat brought in. The choice typically includes giant prawns, lapu-lapu, lobster, fish lips (!) and sea slug, all cooked as you watch chefs work at flaming woks in a glass-fronted kitchen. It's not so cheap, though – a small meal for two might set you back around P800, a larger meal with drinks around P2500. Daily 11.30am–10.30pm.

Shawarma Snack Center 45 Salas St ☎02 525 4541; map p.68. Two branches of the *SSC* face each other across Salas St, so take your choice of plastic tables or a more rarefied atmosphere with tablecloths. The Middle Eastern dishes in both are superb and plentiful, with possibly the best falafels and kebabs in the city, and certainly the hottest chilli sauce. Mains mostly P300–400. Located in a small Muslim enclave in Malate, replete with halal food and a small mosque just off the road. Daily 24hr.

BINONDO AND QUIAPO

Binondo has no fancy restaurants and no bistros or wine bars; people come here for cheap, nourishing Chinese food in one of the area's countless Chinese restaurants or hole-in-the-wall noodle bars. Binondo and Quiapo also have a number of bakeries that are known in the Philippines for their *hopia*, a sweet cake-like snack with a soft pastry coating and thick yam paste in the middle.

Eng Bee Tin 628 Ongpin St ☎02 288 8888, ⓦengbeetin.com; map p.72. Filipinos often come to Binondo just to make a pilgrimage to this well-known bakery, which has specialized in various kinds of sweet, sticky mooncake and *hopia* since 1912. The bakers here invented *ube hopia* (P96), made with sweet purple yam and now imitated throughout the country, and you can also buy *tikoy* (P155), the sweet rice cake that is traditionally served during Chinese New Year. Daily 6am–10pm.

Ho-Land Hopia & Bakery 551 Yuchengco St at Carvajal St ☎02 242 9709; map p.72. Classic bakery (and *Eng Bee Tin* rival) serving *hopia* rolls for P40, but also savoury treats such as chicken, beef curry or mushroom pies (P40). Mon–Sat 7.30am–8pm, Sun 7.30am–5pm.

Mei Sum Tea House 965 Ongpin St ☎02 733 6495; map p.72. Despite its name, this is a restaurant rather than a teahouse. It's known for its excellent dim sums (P78–150), and in particular *siapao* (steamed stuffed buns), although they'll happily do you a full meal too (mains P210–520). Daily 5am–10pm.

President Grand Palace Restaurant 746–750 Ongpin St ☎02 244 5886; map p.72. Plush Cantonese restaurant with an extensive menu that includes excellent crab, lemon chicken, spicy pork with bean curd and a good selection of fresh vegetables. Best experienced with a group, so you can order multiple dishes to share, but single diners are also well catered for, with hearty noodle and rice dishes from P160. Note, however, that the menu offers shark's fin, which is extremely environmentally destructive – hunters cut off just the fin and leave the shark to die – so you may not wish to eat here. Daily 11am–10.30pm.

★ **Quick Snack** 637–639 Carvajal St ☎ 02 242 9572; map p.72. Tucked away down a side alley crammed with market stalls, it doesn't get better than this for a cheap, home-cooked Hokkien-style meal. It's best known for its *lumpia* (jumbo-size spring rolls; P75–85), but also does great soups, veg noodle dishes (P140) and more substantial treats such as crispy oyster rolls (P220). Mon–Sat 9.30am–5.40pm.

Salazar Bakery 783 Ongpin St ☎ 02 733 1392; map p.72. This bakery dates from 1947 and does a tasty *hopia* (P42), but is also great for savoury *asado* rolls (pork-stuffed buns) and small chicken pies – the hefty mooncakes (P130–160) are also worth a try. Daily 5am–10pm.

MAKATI

Makati is the best place in the city when it comes to quality and variety of restaurants, especially around P. Burgos St. Bonifacio Global City, to the east, is an emerging destination for mostly high-end restaurants.

Barrio Fiesta Makati Ave at Valdez St ☎ 02 899 4020; map p.77. There are various branches of this colourful Filipino chain restaurant dotted around the city, serving favourites such as crispy *pata* (from P690), *kare kare* (from P250), barbecued pork (P169) and *lechon* (roast pig; P350), with hefty portions of rice and daily buffet options. Mon–Wed 9am–midnight, Thurs–Sun 9am–2am.

★ **Carpaccio** 7431 Yakal St, San Antonio Village ☎ 02 867 3164, ⓦ carpaccio.com.ph; map p.77. Popular but never uncomfortably busy, this casual little restaurant tucked away down a side street behind Makati Fire Station serves excellent regional Italian food and has a good, affordable wine list. The speciality is carpaccio – the beef carpaccio (P465) is delicious – but almost everything is tasty (pasta and pizza P320–510), including the home-made ice creams and sorbets. Daily 11am–3pm & 6–11pm.

Corner Tree Café 150 Jupiter St ☎ 02 897 0295, ⓦ cornertreecafe.com; map p.77. A sweet little vegetarian restaurant, with a light, modern interior, where organic ingredients are used wherever possible. Needless to say, there are plenty of salads (P190) and tofu burgers (P335), but they'll also rustle up a veg Thai curry (P295) or a spinach and mushroom lasagne (P445). Daily 11am–10pm.

Ferino's Bibingka Cash & Carry Mall, South Luzon Expressway at Emilia St ☎ 0916 633 7298, ⓦ ferinos bibingka.com.ph; map p.77. This franchise hails back to a family business established in 1938. Look out for their small carts in malls, worth trying for the tasty charcoal-cooked *bibingka* (rice cakes; P115–125), daubed with

coconut and salted egg. Daily 10am–9pm.

Lugang Café G/F Glorietta 2, Ayala Center ☎ 02 542 0196, ⓦ lugangcafe.com.ph; map p.77. The original branch of this renowned Chinese restaurant was in Greenhills, between Ortigas and Quezon City, and is now closed, although there are plans to relocate and reopen it. In the meantime, if you want to check out its magnificent Taiwanese food, pork buns and *xiaolong bao* (pork dumplings; P268), you're confined to its branches in malls citywide, of which this is the most central; others can be found in SM Mall of Asia in Pasay and SM North EDSA at the northern end of Quezon. Daily 11am–10pm.

New Bombay G/F, Sagittarius Building III, 312 H.V. Dela Costa St ☎ 02 819 2892; G/F, Tower I, The Columns Condominium, Ayala Ave at Gil Puyat (Buendia) ☎ 02 901 3275; map p.77. Speak to Indian residents in Manila and most will tell you that this functional little restaurant is peerless for authentic Indian food. The menu is extensive and includes snacks such as mixed pakora, samosas, curries and freshly prepared naan, roti and chapati. Cheap, cheerful and very tasty (most mains P245–295). Daily 10.30am–11pm.

Old Swiss Inn 7912 Makati Ave at Olympia Towers ☎ 02 818 0098, ⓦ oldswissinn.com; map p.77. Traditional food (heavenly Gruyère fondue from P935), jolly alpine decor and waitresses in milkmaids' costumes – this place is as Swiss as it comes. The 24hr menu also includes the classic *gnagi* (pork knuckles; P698) and Zurich *geschnetzeltes* (shredded pork; P518). There's another branch in Paco Park (see opposite). Daily 24hr.

Razon's of Guagua 22 Jupiter St ☎ 02 899 7841; map p.77. Lauded Pampanga-style *halo-halo* (P110) and *pancit luglug* (fried noodles; P110) chain, with chicken or pork *asado* from P210. Daily 10am–10pm.

Rufo's Famous Tapa G/F, A. Venue Mall, Makati Ave ☎ 02 899 4207, ⓦ rufos.com.ph; map p.77. Chain best known for its *tapa* – tender Batangas beef, marinated and served in a rich, sweet sauce with a side order of fried egg and garlic rice (P119) for breakfast (served all day here). Their boneless *bangus* (milkfish; P132) and *tocino* (cured pork; P116) is also excellent. Daily 24hr.

Sentro 1771 Level 2, Greenbelt 3 ☎ 02 757 3940, ⓦ facebook.com/Sentro1771; map p.77. Modern Filipino restaurant that's packed with office workers at lunchtime and the pre-cinema crowd in the evenings. The menu (most dishes P190–530) includes modern variations of classics such as pork adobo, pancit and Bicol Express (spicy stew); the speciality is *sinigang na* corned beef (sour stew with corned beef; P595). Mon–Fri 11am–11pm, Sat & Sun 11am–midnight.

★ **Top of the Citi** 34/F Citibank Tower, 8741 Paseo de Roxas ☎ 02 750 5810, ⓦ chefjessie.com; map p.77. Mingle with Manila's upper class in this temple to fine dining with soaring views of the city. Top chef Jessie Sincioco crafts modern Filipino cuisine such as crunchy pork

1

sisig (pig's ear) with mayonnaise, Japanese dishes, pasta, steaks and her famous dessert soufflés (the chocolate flavour is hard to beat), while the trendy bar gets all the attention from 5pm with the best cocktails in the city. Fish and meat dishes are P800–950, except rib-eye steaks, which start at P1600. Mon–Fri 11am–11pm.

AROUND P. BURGOS STREET

Alba 38-B Polaris St, Bel-Air 📞02 896 6950, 🌐alba .com.ph; map p.78. Cosy Spanish restaurant with faux adobe walls and a wandering guitarist who croons at your table. Dishes include tasty tapas from P240, a large menu of paellas (from P580 for two), and plenty of fish and seafood from P450. There's also a deli counter selling Spanish-style cold cuts. Daily 11am–11pm.

Hossein's 2/F, 7857 LKV Building, Makati Ave 📞02 890 6137, 🌐hosseins.com; map p.78. This glitzy take on a kebab house has froufrou decor and prices to match. If you're not in the mood for a brain sandwich (P250), you can choose from dozens of Persian, Arabian and Indian dishes (with a huge range of curry and kebabs). Meze plates P160–471. Daily 11am–1am.

Next Door Noodles/North Park Noodles Next Door: 7876 Makati Ave 📞02 899 1893; North Park: 1200 Makati Ave 📞02 890 5952, 🌐northpark.com.ph; map p.78. Cheap-and-cheerful Chinese Next Door Noodles sits almost opposite its sister restaurant, North Park Noodles, which has a similar menu at the same low prices. Fantastic value – almost everything is under P200 (dim sum P58–213, noodles in soup P116–288 and fried rice P188–273). Mon–Thurs & Sun 10am–4pm, Fri & Sat 24hr.

The Original Savory 1 Constellation St at Makati Ave 📞02 899 9089, 🌐theoriginalsavory.com; map p.78. Legendary masters of fried chicken and sensational gravy since 1950 (half chicken P200, whole P380), whose original branch in Binondo (201 Escolta St) is currently being rebuilt from scratch. They also do superb bagoong (fermented shrimp sauce) rice for P195. Daily 9.30am–9.30pm.

Top Dish 4890 Durban St, near P. Burgos St 📞02 758 1122; map p.78. The best hole-in-the-wall Korean restaurant in town, open late and with reasonable prices (P220–250 for noodles), big portions and excellent kimchi (pickled cabbage). Mon–Sat 3pm–4am.

Ziggurat G/F Sunette Tower Building, Euphrates St at Tigris St 📞02 897 5179, 🌐bit.ly/ZigguratCuisine; map p.78. A seemingly endless menu featuring exotic dishes from the Middle East, Mediterranean and East Africa (try the P650 meze combos), with flavoured hookahs to round things off. Mains around P250–350. Daily 24hr.

BONIFACIO GLOBAL CITY (FORT BONIFACIO)

Abe Restaurant Serendra Plaza, Bonifacio Global City 📞02 856 0526; map pp.60–61. Most taxi drivers will know this much-loved Filipino restaurant (Pampanga-style),

where the two highlights are Abe's chicken supreme (chicken stuffed with galapong rice, chestnuts and raisins; P950 for two) and mutton adobo with popped garlic (P450). Other dishes utilize forest ferns, banana plant, tiny crabs and fabulous pork knuckle. Daily 11am–3pm & 6–11pm.

★**Aubergine** 32nd & 5th Building, 5th Ave at 32nd St 📞02 551 8392, 🌐aubergine.ph; map pp.60–61. The best reason to jump in a taxi and head over to Fort Bonifacio, this top-notch restaurant and patisserie delivers fresh ingredients and crisp flavours; the French-inspired international menu features slow-cooked Norwegian salmon (P1260), honey-glazed French duck breast (P1460) and Australian lamb rack (P1760). Daily 11.30am–2pm & 6–10pm.

QUEZON CITY

Quezon City is a burgeoning alternative to Makati and the Manila Bay area for restaurants and nightlife. To get to Quezon from the south of the city (Malate and Makati, for example), you can take the MRT to Kamuning or Quezon Avenue.

Behrouz 63 Scout Tobias St, off Timog Ave 📞02 374 3242; map p.80. Great late-night hole-in-the-wall snack place, run by a family of Iranians who cook authentic food. The lamb kebabs, beef kobideh (ground-beef kebabs; P210) and aubergine-based moutabal (baba ghanoush; P70) are all superb. Cash only; no alcohol. Daily 11am–5am.

Frazzled Cook 78 Gandia St at Tomas Morato 📞0917 633 3352, 🌐facebook.com/FrazzledCook; map p.80. A short taxi ride west of Ortigas proper, this shabby-chic purveyor of legendary paella negra (P375 for two people) serves an otherwise eclectic menu including squash soup (P145), spicy lamb stew (P395) and scampi pizza (P325). Mon–Thurs & Sun 11am–11pm, Fri & Sat 11pm–1am.

Gerry's Grill 24 Tomas Morato Ave at Eugenio Lopez Drive 📞02 415 9514, 🌐gerrysgrill.com; map p.80. This is the original outlet of the now popular chain, serving provincial Filipino dishes such as crispy pata (pig's knuckle; P495) and sisig (fried pig's ear and pig's face; P205). Mon–Thurs 10am–2am, Fri & Sat 10am–3am, Sun 10am–1am.

Greens 92 Scout Castor St off Tomas Morato Ave 📞02 415 4796; map p.80. Bargain-priced vegan and vegetarian food, from soups and salads to wraps, pasta and shepherd's pie with neither shepherd nor sheep (P120). Mon–Sat 11am–10pm, Sun noon–9pm.

★**Lydia's Lechon** 116 Timog Ave 📞02 921 1221, 🌐lydias-lechon.com; map p.80. The lechon at this local favourite is delicious (especially the boneless variety with paella), but the secret is the sauce – a sweet, barbecue concoction that will have you hooked. The meat is priced at P205 per quarter kilo. Daily 8am–9.30pm.

Van Gogh is Bipolar 154H Maginhawa St, Sikatuna Village 📞0922 824 3051, 🌐facebook.com/VGiBipolar; map pp.60–61. Cook and travel photographer Jetro lovingly prepares the dishes at this unique place by carefully selecting ingredients, such as honey and black mountain rice, that are supposed to enhance your mood by stimulating your seratonin and dopamine levels. "Daytime feast" set meal

(3–5pm) costs P555; a two-course meal is P777, four courses P999. Only twelve diners per night, so it's a good idea to book. Daily except Tues noon–3pm & 6–11pm.

DRINKING AND NIGHTLIFE

Few visitors to Manila are disappointed by the buoyant, gregarious nature of its **bars** and **clubs**. This is a city that rarely sleeps and one that offers a full range of fun, from the offbeat watering holes of Malate to the chic wine bars of Makati. Manila also has a thriving **live music** scene, with dozens of bars hosting very popular and accomplished local bands almost every night. Clubs are especially prone to open, close and change names with frequency, so check before you head out – websites such as ⓦ guestlist.ph are good places to get the latest information.

BARS
INTRAMUROS AND RIZAL PARK
Lobby Lounge Manila Hotel, 1 Rizal Park ☎ 02 527 0011, ⓦmanila-hotel.com.ph; map p.62. It's worth grabbing a coffee or artfully constructed cocktail in this elegant lobby bar, even if you're not staying at the *Manila Hotel* – it's one of the few places redolent of the city's golden age, with capiz chandeliers, *narra* wood ceiling and marble floors. Daily 24hr.

ERMITA AND MALATE
Nightlife in Ermita and Malate comprises a somewhat confusing mixture of budget restaurants, genuine pubs and a once again flourishing girlie-bar scene. Don't make the mistake of arriving early – most places don't even warm up until after 10pm and are still thumping when the sun comes up, with crowds in summer spilling out onto the streets. Friday, as always, is the big night; many places are closed on Sunday.

Hobbit House 1212 M. H. Del Pilar St at Arquiza St, Ermita ☎ 02 521 7604, ⓦfacebook.com/HobbitHouse Manila; map p.68. In 1973 entrepreneur Jim Turner

decided to open a bar that would pay homage to his favourite book, *The Lord of the Rings*. He staffed it with twenty people of restricted height, and a legend was born. *Hobbit House* has somehow endured, still employing short people, and offers a huge list of bottled beers, Tex-Mex food and nightly appearances at 9pm by a variety of local bands. It has also become a notorious tourist trap, with busloads of visitors brought in every night to have their photographs taken alongside the staff. Daily 5pm–1am.

Tap Station 1313 Adriatico St at Padre Faura St ☎ 0916 777 6373; map p.68. A microbrewery bar with a big selection of their own beers, including IPAs, brown ales and stouts. The brews are interesting, but a bit hit-and-miss; ask for a sample before you plump for one. They also show English football on the TV. Mon–Fri 5pm–2am, Sat 3pm–2am, Sun 3–11pm.

MAKATI
Makati nightlife used to revolve around office workers spilling out of the nearby banks and skyscrapers, but these days much of middle-class Manila parties in the bars and

LGBT NIGHTLIFE IN MANILA
The **LGBT scene** in Manila has been vibrant for many years. Even bars and clubs that aren't obviously gay are unreservedly welcoming and the LGBT community mixes easily and boisterously in the same nightclubs and bars. Traditionally, the gay nightlife scene centred on Malate, but that's no longer the case, although the shows at *The Library* (see p.96) are still worth checking out. Other LGBT resources are covered in Basics (see p.49).

Club Mwah 3/F The Venue Tower, 652 Bonifacio Ave, Mandaluyong City ☎02 535 7943, ⓦfacebook.com/ClubMwahOfficial; map pp.60–61. Club, bar and theatre featuring a burlesque transvestite show dubbed "Folliespiniana", based on traditional dances and "Las Vegas-Moulin Rouge" inspired acts. Thurs–Sat 7.30pm–1am.

Lipstick Mafia ⓦfacebook.com/LipstickMafia Manila. A very underground ladies-only lesbian party event put on monthly by invitation only. If you want to be in the loop, contact them via their Facebook page.

O Bar Ortigas Home Depot, Doña Julia Vargas Ave, Ortigas ☎02 584 1626, ⓦfacebook.com/

OBarPhilippines; map pp.60–61. Its claim to be the home of Asia's finest dancing drag queens may be a slight exaggeration, but you get the idea: drag shows, male go-go dancers and male pole dancers. It's very popular and always crowded, especially on weekends. Wed–Sun 10pm–6am.

XRoads Restobar Unit 108 Food St, Home Depot Complex, Julia Vargas at Meralco, Ortigas Center ☎02 631 0090; map pp.60–61. Pronounced "crossroads", this is Manila's coolest LGBT bar, open to all, with a dedicated Women on Top lesbian space, and a dancefloor, obviously, but intimate rather than thumping. Wed–Sun 10pm–6am.

1

clubs here, with plenty of expats and travellers thrown in – it's generally smarter, safer and more fashionable than Malate. The area around P. Burgos St is a bit seedier, though the girlie-bar scene here is being driven more by Korean and Japanese KTV-style joints these days, and there are several genuine pubs in between offering cheap beers and snacks.

A Toda Madre G/F Sunette Tower, Durban St ☎0998 985 5198; map p.78. A lively little tequila bar with proper, quality tequilas (such as Herradura and Don Julio), as well as, for your mixing-grade spirit, the promise of "not your typical margarita" (P400). In case that isn't enough, there are tacos and quesadillas too. ¡Ándele! Daily 5pm–2am.

★**Bravo** 1331 Angono St at JP Rizal Ave ☎02 899 5410; map pp.60–61. "Bravo!" indeed, if you're looking for an alternative to the usual flavourless industrial lager. This bar and restaurant out by Makati city hall makes its own Czech-style pilsner, and very good it is too – as indeed is their food and coffee. Top marks all round. Mon–Sat 11am–11pm.

H&J Sports Bar and Restaurant Felipe St ☎02 954 1130; map p.78. The old *Heckle & Jeckle* sports bar moved into these digs in 2013, where it boasts the same laidback vibe that's popular with expats, live blues and rock bands (nightly), Indian food, pool tables and TVs showing live English Premier League football. Happy hour Mon–Fri 2–10pm, Sat & Sun 2–7pm. Mon–Thurs 2pm–7am, Fri–Sun 24hr.

Handlebar 31 Polaris St ☎02 898 2189, ⓦfacebook .com/HandleBarBarAndGrill; map p.78. Hospitable biker bar owned by a group of Harley fanatics. It's primarily for drinkers (with lots of sport on the TVs) but the food also makes it worth a visit. The menu is nothing exotic, just solid, satisfying pizzas, burgers and pasta, or Big John's BBQ (P250–700). Daily 24hr.

Howzat 8471 Kalayaan Ave at Fermina St ☎02 897 3335, ⓦhowzat.ph; map p.78. Popular sports bar showing all major global sports events on wide TV screens via satellite. Very cheap all-you-can-drink specials run daily 5–8pm (San Miguel P310, local spirits P345), curry buffets on Fri (noon–3pm; P495 with beer) and a scrumptious Sunday roast (noon–3pm) for P695 including beer. Mon–Thurs 7am–2am, Fri–Sun 24hr.

M Café Ayala Museum, Greenbelt 4, Makati Ave ☎02 757 3000; map p.77. *Museum Café*, or M Café, as it's known, is a swish little place serving drinks and snacks all day, with draught beers and cocktails at night. Mains P275–750. On Thurs and Fri it's open till 2am with DJs spinning from 10pm. Sun–Wed 8am–11pm, Thurs–Sat 8am–2am.

Society Lounge G/F Atrium Building, Makati Ave at Paseo de Roxas ☎02 408 1852, ⓦsocietylounge .geoventuresconsulting.com; map p.77. Plush French-Asian fusion restaurant that morphs into trendy lounge bar every night, with plenty of fine wines and champagnes on offer. DJs spin house music at the weekends, when it

becomes more like a club. Mon–Wed 11am–midnight, Thurs & Fri 11am–2am, Sat & Sun 11am–4am (food 11am–3pm & 6–11pm).

QUEZON CITY

Quezon City's entertainment district is focused on Tomas Morato and Timog avenues, which intersect at the roundabout in front of *Imperial Palace Suites* hotel. The area has a growing reputation for quality live music (see opposite), while for more mainstream nightlife there are plenty of chic bars and franchised hangouts at the southern end of Tomas Morato Ave, near the junction with Don A. Roces Ave.

Padi's Point G/F Imperial Palace Suites, Tomas Morato Ave ☎02 920 7864, ⓦpadispoint.com; map p.80. Boisterous beer hall chain that serves very average Filipino food, although most guests are too drunk to care. Thurs and Sat are disco nights, and there's a happy hour daily 7–10pm. Several branches are scattered around the city, listed on the website. Daily 4pm–6am.

LIVE MUSIC BARS AND VENUES

Quezon City in particular has a reputation for live music, especially from up-and-coming bands formed by students from the nearby University of the Philippines, with an eclectic range of music, from pure Western pop to grunge, reggae and indigenous styles. Many of the venues in the area are dark, sweaty places that open late and don't close until the last guest leaves. Note that the venues listed here are known primarily for live music, but in Makati and Malate you're never far from a bar or club with a live band, especially at weekends.

ERMITA AND MALATE

Bamboo Giant 802a San Andres St at Quirino and Taft Ave ☎02 528 4558; map p.68. Acoustic bands play most nights in this beach-bar-style bamboo shack. It's easy going, with a chilled vibe, reasonably cold beers, and food if you want it. Mon–Sat 4pm–2am.

Bedrock Unit B, Bellagio Square, J Bacobo St ☎02 242 3347; map p.68. A rather nondescript little bar for most of the week, but on Fri and Sat evenings it takes over this little square, with live music on stage from around 8.30pm. Daily 3pm–3am.

TheBar@1951 (Penguin Café) 1951 M. Adriatico St, Malate ☎0939 634 6649, ⓦbar1951.weebly.com; map p.68. Legendary 1980s bohemian bar *Penguin Café* has been through several reincarnations since its heyday, but locals still refer to it by its old name. Live indie bands play most nights, and there's a P100 cover charge when they do. Beers P70–80. Tues–Sat 6pm–2am.

MAKATI

SaGuijo 7612 Guijo St, San Antonio, Makati ☎02 897 8629, ⓦfacebook.com/SaGuijo.Cafe.Bar.Events; map p.77. This hip, arty bar is the best indie venue in Manila, with both its live music (from 10.30pm nightly) and art gallery supporting up-and-coming talents. Effortlessly cool, but not pretentious with it. Tues–Thurs 8pm–2am, Fri & Sat 7pm–2am.

Strumm's 110 Jupiter St, Makati ☎02 895 4636; map p.77. A party-like atmosphere greets nightly bands at this Makati stalwart, which puts on mostly pop and indie but also old-school jazz on Tues. Cover P350 Mon–Thurs & Sun, P400 Fri & Sat. Daily 8pm–2am.

QUEZON CITY

The 70s Bistro 46 Anonas St, Quezon City ☎02 433 8070, ⊕facebook.com/The70sBistro; map pp.60–61. Legendary (in the Philippines) live music venue that plays host to some of the country's best-known bands as well as to impromptu jam sessions with big local names who happen to turn up – a great Manila experience. The only problem is it's a bit tricky to find: Anonas St is off Aurora Blvd on the eastern side of EDSA. Mon–Sat 6pm–3am.

Araneta Coliseum Gen. Araneta at Gen. McArthur, Quezon City ☎02 911 5555 ⊕aranetacoliseum.com; map p.80. This huge stadium (aka "Big Dome") is the usual venue for large-scale events and concerts, everything from Fall Out Boy and Ke$ha to Disney on Ice. Opens according to shows.

★**Conspiracy Garden Cafe** 59 Visayas Ave, Quezon City ☎02 453 2170; map pp.60–61. This wonderful little performance venue and café is a meeting place for artists, musicians, poets, songwriters and women's groups. *Conspiracy* was set up by the artists who perform there, among them luminaries of the independent Filipino music scene such as Joey Ayala, Cynthia Alexander and Noel Cabangon, who all perform regularly. Well worth the journey out here, but check first to see what's on. Mon–Sat 5pm–2am.

Ka Freddie's 120 Tomas Morato Ave at Kamuning St, Quezon City ☎0915 444 0241, ⊕facebook.com/KafreddiesMusicBarAndResto; map p.80. Music bar and restaurant, with pool tables and free wi-fi, opened by Filipino folk legend Freddie Aguilar, who still does weekly shows (Fri). Check their Facebook page to see who's playing. Cover P200–300. Daily 6pm–3am.

Music Museum Service Rd, Greenhills, San Juan ☎02 721 6726, ⊕facebook.com/MusicMuseumGroup; map pp.60–61. This "leisure-entertainment hub" hosts concerts, comedy shows, ballet, theatre and poetry readings, but the music is still the main attraction; performers are mostly popular Filipino pop and rock acts. Opens according to shows.

CLUBS

★**B-Side** The Collective, 7472 Malugay St, near Gil Puyat (Buendia) Ave, Makati ☎0922 998 9512, ⊕bit.ly/B-SideManila; map p.77. Bar/club venue for cutting-edge music with DJs from all over the world, especially known for its reggae sessions on "Irie Sundays". Free entrance and no dress code. Wed–Sun 9pm–4am.

Black Market Warehouse 5, La Fuerza Compound 2, Sabio St, Makati ☎0908 813 5622; map p.77. Warehousey club venue opened by the folks at *B-Side* in 2013, with talented resident DJs playing hip-hop, r'n'b and more, with a lot of bass and an eclectic range of guests. Cover usually P300. Wed–Sat 10pm–4am.

Chaos City of Dreams Manila, Asean Ave at Roxas Bvd, Tambo, just south of Pasay ☎0917 886 3678, ⊕chaosmanila.com; map pp.60–61. A luxury club in a prestigious mall, with confetti machines, LED curtains, laser light shows, table reservations, a VIP zone, cage dancers and all the paraphernalia. Sounds vary depending on the evening: Wed is band night, Thurs is hip-hop, weekends are party pop. Entry is usually P500 (one drink included), but can double for special events. Wed–Sat 10pm–6am.

TIME 7840 Makati Ave, Makati ☎02 519 8903; map p.77. The epicentre of the electronic music scene, with Filipino and international DJs performing live sets: this is the place for house and techno in Manila, with an easy-going vibe and a crowd who are into their music. Entry P500. Tues & Thurs–Sat 11pm–4am, Sun 7pm–2am.

Valkyrie The Palace, 11th Ave at 38th St, Fort Bonifacio ☎0917 680 8888, ⊕valkyrie.thepalacemanila.com; map pp.60–61. This huge dance club – the city's biggest and glitziest – is just one part of a huge clubbing complex that includes a more mature lounge club (⊕revel.thepalacemanila.com), a daytime pool club (⊕poolclub.thepalacemanila.com) and more. All of them aim for elegance and attract a well-heeled clientele, so leave your trainers at home and dress to impress, but don't forget your wallet. Cover (including two drinks) P800 weekdays, P1000 weekends. Wed–Sat 10.30pm–5am.

ENTERTAINMENT

For **listings**, try newspapers such as the *Philippine Daily Inquirer* (⊕inquirer.net) and the *Philippine Star* (⊕philstar.com), which have entertainment sections with details of movies, concerts and arts events in Manila. Daily shows of **traditional performing arts** (see box, p.96) are hosted at the Cultural Center of the Philippines and a handful of other venues. As for **films**, every mall seems to have half a dozen screens, and international movies are rarely dubbed. Good resources for checking upcoming events include Ticketworld (☎02 891 9999, ⊕ticketworld.com.ph) and TicketNet (☎02 911 5555, ⊕ticketnet.com.ph), on both of which you can buy tickets in advance, as well as listings websites such as ⊕clickthecity.com.

1

CABARET AND BURLESQUE

Amazing Show Manila Film Center, Jose W. Diokno Blvd, Pasay ☎02 834 8870, ⓦamazingshow.net. Fun transvestite musical variety show in the Manila Film Center (see box, p.70), involving singing, dancing and comedy skits, especially popular with Korean tourists. Tickets for foreigners P1500. Mon–Sat 8–9.10pm.

The Library 1739 Maria Orosa St, Malate ☎02 522 2484, ⓦthelibrary.com.ph. Nightly stand-up comedy/karaoke from veteran Manila drag queens where audience participation is very much part of the show – attracts a local straight and gay audience. Cover charge P200–500. Daily 8pm–3am (shows from 10pm).

THEATRE, DANCE AND CLASSICAL MUSIC

Cultural Center of the Philippines Roxas Blvd, Malate ☎02 832 1125, ⓦculturalcenter.gov.ph. Events here range from art exhibitions to Broadway musicals, pop concerts, classical concerts by the Philippine Philharmonic Orchestra, *tinikling* and *kundiman* (see box below). The CCP is also home to the Tanghalang Aurelio Tolentino (CCP Little Theater), where smaller dramatic productions are staged and films shown; Ballet Philippines (☎02 832 3689, ⓦballet.ph); Bayanihan, the National Folk Dance Company (☎02 516 3028, ⓦbayanihannationaldanceco.ph); and the CCP's resident theatre group, Tanghalang Pilipino, dedicated to the production of original Filipino plays (July–March; ⓦtanghalangpilipino.com). Nearby is the Folk Arts Theater (Tanghalang Francisco Balagtas), built for the Miss Universe Pageant in 1974 and now staging occasional rock concerts and drama.

Meralco Theater Meralco Ave, Ortigas ☎02 631 2222.

Stages everything from ballet and musicals by overseas companies to pantomimes with local celebs. Check websites such as ⓦticketworld.com.ph for the latest shows.

OnStage Theater Greenbelt 1, Makati ☎02 750 4180. Small venue mainly staging drama by local theatre groups, including Repertory Philippines (☎02 843 3570, ⓦrepertoryphilippines.ph), Manila's premier English-speaking theatre group.

Paco Park/Rizal Park "Paco Park Presents" hosts free classical concerts at 6pm every Fri, performed under the stars in the historic cemetery (see p.71); Rizal Park (p.65) stages similar free "Concerts at the Park" every Sun at 6pm.

CINEMAS

Arthouse cinema A venue for arthouse and independent films is the UP Cine Adarna (☎02 920 6863; ⓦfilminstitute .upd.edu.ph), UPFI Film Center building at Magsaysay and Osmeña avenues to the northeast of Quezon Memorial Circle, but screenings don't take place every day, so check before you head out there.

Multiplex cinemas Most shopping malls in Manila house multiplex cinemas that show all the Hollywood and Asian blockbusters in the original languages, including The Podium mall (12 ADB Ave, Ortigas; ☎02 633 8976), Greenbelt 3 in Makati (☎02 729 7777) and Power Plant Mall, Rockwell Drive, Makati (☎02 898 1440, ⓦcinema .powerplantmall.com). Tickets are usually around P150–250. In the Malate area, try Robinsons Place in M. Adriatico St (☎02 397 7020). Tickets for cinemas in the Greenbelt and Glorietta malls can be reserved online at ⓦsureseats .com for collection at the venue.

SPORTS

BOWLING

Coronado Lanes 4/F Star Mall, EDSA, Mandaluyong City ☎02 725 3965, ⓦpuyatsports.com. P100–140 per person (plus P35 for shoes). Daily 10am–midnight.

Paeng's Midtown Bowl Level 2, Robinsons Place, M. Adriatico St, Ermita ☎02 525 6442, ⓦpuyatsports .com. P140–165 per person (plus P35 for shoes).

Mon–Wed & Sun 10am–midnight, Thurs 10am–1am, Fri & Sat 10am–2am.

GOLF

There are three golf courses in Manila where non-members can turn up and pay for a round – it's usually first come, first served (which means waits of 1–2hr at weekends).

FILIPINO FOLK ARTS

The Philippines has a rich folk arts heritage, but a scarcity of funds and committed audiences with money to spend on tickets means it's in danger of being forgotten. Folk dances such as **tinikling**, which sees participants hopping at increasing speed between heavy bamboo poles that are struck together at shin height, are seen in cultural performances for tourists, but are only performed occasionally in theatres. The same goes for **kundiman**, a genre of music that reached its zenith at the beginning of the twentieth century, and combines elements of tribal music with contemporary lovelorn lyrics to produce epic songs of love and loss. To see if anything is on check out websites like ⓦticketworld.com.ph. The CCP sometimes puts on shows (see p.69); otherwise your best bet is to join the tourists at restaurants such as *Barbara's* (see p.88).

SPECTATOR SPORTS

Because the PBA (Philippine Basketball Association) teams are owned by corporations, and do not play in a home stadium, most **basketball** games are played at the Araneta Coliseum in Cubao (see p.95) and the Mall of Asia Arena at SM Mall of Asia in Pasay (ⓦmallofasia-arena .com); games usually run on Wednesday, Friday and Sunday from October to July. Tickets in the cheap seats, the "bleachers", cost as little as P100, while a ringside seat will set you back P200–600 or more. Tickets are available from ⓦticketnet.com.ph or ⓦpba.inquirer.net.

For cockfighting in Manila, the biggest venue is the huge air-conditioned Pasay City Cockpit Arena (168 Arnaiz Ave at Dolores St ☎02 816 6750), where fights are usually held Mon–Wed & Sun afternoons, noon–5pm.

You can book ahead on ☎02 832 8215 or ⓦgolfph.com.
Army Golf Club (Kagitingan) Bayani Rd, Fort Bonifacio, south of Makati ☎02 845 9555. Boasts some of the lowest green fees in the country (Mon–Fri P1150; Sat & Sun P1550).
Club Intramuros Bonifacio Drive at Soriano St (formerly Aduana St), Intramuros ☎02 527 6613,

ⓦfacebook.com/ClubIntramurosGolfCourse. This has basic facilities and a short eighteen-hole course that runs along the walls of the old city. Figure on around P3000 for green fees (P1800 daily), caddie hire and clubs.
Villamor Golf Course Jesus Villamor Air Base, Pasay ☎02 853 4977. Home of the Philippine Masters; green fees are P2000 (Mon–Fri) and P2500 (Sat & Sun).

SHOPPING

The combination of intense heat and dense traffic means many Manileños forsake the pleasures of the outdoors at weekends for the computer-controlled climate of their local **mall** – there can be few cities that have as many malls per head as this one. Note that the developers rarely pay as much attention to the surrounding roads as they do to their precious real estate, which means that traffic is especially gridlocked in these areas. Despite the growth of malls, there are still plenty of earthy outdoor **markets** in Manila, where you can buy food, antiques and gifts at rock-bottom prices, as well as some decent bookshops and fashion boutiques.

BOOKS
National Book Store (NBS) G/F Harrison Plaza, M. Adriatico St ☎02 525 8205, map p.68; Level 1 Robinsons Place, Ermita ☎02 536 7893, map p.68; Glorietta 1, Makati ☎02 625 5105, map p.77; Scout Borromeo at Quezon Ave, Quezon City ☎02 373 0852, map p.80; and in malls citywide; ⓦnationalbookstore.com. The country's major bookshop chain, concentrating on contemporary thrillers, literary classics and New York Times bestsellers, with much of what's on offer stocked specifically for students. Harrison Plaza daily 10am–8pm; Robinsons Place & Glorietta 1 Mon–Thurs & Sun 10am–9pm, Fri & Sat 10am–10pm; Quezon Ave daily 9am–9pm.
Powerbooks Level 2, Greenbelt 4, Makati ☎02 757 6428, ⓦpowerbooks.com.ph; map p.77. The best general bookshop in Manila, with eight branches around Metro Manila (the Makati one is the most central). It tends to have a more interesting range of books than NBS, although its prices are sometimes a bit higher for the same items. Daily 10am–10pm.
★**Solidaridad Bookshop** 531 Padre Faura St, Ermita ☎02 254 1086; map p.68. The bookshop with the best literary section in town. It's owned by the novelist F. Sionil José and, apart from stocking his own excellent novels, has a small selection of highbrow fiction and lots of material on the Philippines. Mon–Sat 9am–6pm.

BRIC-A-BRAC
Siglo 258 Tomas Morato St, Quezon ☎02 410 0241; map p.80. Mostly twentieth-century memorabilia, from old ashtrays to vintage toys, with a generally more interesting selection than in Ermita's antique stores, and usually at better prices too. Mon–Sat 10am–7pm.

FANCY DRESS
Skitzo Unit M, The Collective, 7274 Malugay St, San Antonio ☎0917 529 7548, ⓦfacebook.com/Skitzo .Costumes; map p.77. Designer costume shop crammed with garish outfits, glasses and accessories. Tues–Sat noon–9pm.

HANDICRAFTS AND SOUVENIRS
There are touristy shops all over Manila selling reproduction tribal art, especially bulol (sometimes spelt bulul) – depictions of rice gods, worshipped by northern tribespeople because they are said to keep evil spirits from the home and bless farmers with a good harvest. Genuine bulol are made from narra wood and are dark and stained from the soot of tribal fires and from blood poured over them during sacrifices. Good places to pick up souvenirs are markets (see p.98) and the Silahis Center (see p.63).
Balikbayan Handicrafts HK Sun Plaza, Macapagal Ave, Pasay (just south of the CCP) ☎02 832 7873, map

1

p.71; 1010 Arnaiz Ave (Pasay Rd), Makati ☎ 02 893 0775, map p.77; ⓦ balikbayanhandicrafts.com. The first stop for tourists looking for indigenous gifts and handicrafts are these justly popular stores (the Pasay branch is the bigger one). They sell a mind-boggling array of souvenirs, knick-knacks, home decorations, reproduction native-style carvings and jewellery, plus some larger items such as tribal chairs, drums and musical instruments. Staff can arrange to ship your purchases if requested. Pasay Mon–Sat 9am–9pm, Sun 10am–9pm; Makati Mon–Sat 9am–8pm, Sun 10am–8pm.

Tesoros 1325 A. Mabini St, Ermita ☎ 02 522 1580, map p.68; 1016 Arnaiz Ave (Pasay Rd), Makati ☎ 02 887 6285, map p.77; ⓦ tesoros.ph. A handicraft chain selling woven tablecloths, fabrics, *barongs* and reproduction tribal crafts such as *bulol*. Not as big as Balikbayan, but more convenient from budget hotels in Ermita. Both Mon–Sat 11am–8pm.

MALLS

Glorietta Ayala Center, Ayala Ave, Makati ☎ 02 752 7272, ⓦ www.ayalamalls.com.ph; map p.77. A maze of passageways spanning out from a central atrium, Glorietta has five sections, a large branch of Rustan's department store and heaps of clothes and household goods. At the Makati Ave end of the complex is Landmark, a big, functional department store that sells inexpensive clothes and has a whole floor dedicated to children's goods. There's a food court on the third floor. Mon–Thurs & Sun 10am–9pm, Fri & Sat 10am–10pm.

Greenbelt Ayala Center, Paseo de Roxas at Legaspi St, Makati ☎ 02 757 4853, ⓦ www.ayalamalls.com.ph; map p.77. A huge, sprawling mall with five sections: Greenbelt 3 and 4 on Makati Ave are the most comfortable for a stroll and a spot of people watching. Most of the stores are well-known chains – Greenbelt 3 has the affordable stuff (including Nike and Adidas) and Greenbelt 4 is full of expensive big names such as Armani and Jimmy Choo. There are some excellent restaurants in Greenbelt 3 for all budgets and more designers in Greenbelt 5 (DKNY, Hilfiger). Daily 11am–9pm.

SM Mall of Asia J.W. Diokno Blvd (facing Manila Bay) ☎ 02 556 0680, ⓦ smmallofasia.com; map p.71. This vast complex, the biggest in the Philippines, contains Manila's first IMAX, a seafront promenade, bowling alley, ice rink and hypermarket, as well as numerous restaurants and stores that appeal to a younger crowd. Any bus or minibus heading west on EDSA showing "MOA" or "Mall of Asia" will get you here. Daily 10am–10pm.

MARKETS

Taking a taxi from one of Manila's opulent malls to a more traditional market district such as Quiapo or Divisoria is like going from New York to Guatemala in thirty minutes – the difference between the two worlds is shocking. Needless to say, prices in Manila's markets are a lot cheaper than in the malls.

168 Shopping Mall Santa Elena and Soler sts, Binondo ⓦ 168shoppingmall.com; map p.72. Technically a two-section mall but more like a market, with over a thousand stalls flooded with mostly Chinese-made leather handbags, jackets, T-shirts, wallets, caps, toys, shoes and clothes for incredibly low prices. Forms part of the Divisoria market district (see below). Daily 8am–8pm.

Baclaran market Pasay City; map p.71. This labyrinthine street market is spread tentacle-like around the Baclaran LRT station; little stalls huddle under the LRT line as far as the EDSA station, and fill Dr Gabriel St as far west as Roxas Blvd. The focus throughout is cheap clothes and shoes of every hue, size and style, though you'll also come across fake designer watches and pirated CDs and DVDs. The market is a big, noisy, pungent place, and often incredibly crowded, but lots of fun. It's open all week but especially crowded every Wed, the so-called Baclaran Day, when devotees of Our Mother of Perpetual Help crowd into the Redemptorist Church on Dr Gabriel St for the weekly novena. Daily 24hr.

Divisoria Market District Claro M. Recto Ave, North Binondo; map p.72. For a range of bargain goods, from fabric and Christmas decorations to clothes, candles, bags and hair accessories, try fighting your way through the crowds at the immense market district. The pretty lanterns (*parols*) made from capiz seashells that you see all over the country at Christmas cost half what you would pay in a mall. The actual Divisoria Mall is at Tabora and Santo Cristo streets, but it's the warren of streets around it that are good

---

LIFE BEYOND THE MALL: INDIE RETAILERS

Megamalls haven't completely taken over Manila, and there are a couple of small shopping precincts where the outlets are strictly **independent**. In Makati, some of Manila's coolest artists and designers established **The Collective** at 7274 Malugay St (see map, p.77), which is now mostly given over to small cafés, but still hosts the shop Skitzo (see p.97) and club *B-Side* (see p.95). In Quezon City, **Cubao-X** (Cubao Expo) is a more active hub of independent retailers located on General Romulo Avenue, a short walk from Cubao MRT station (see map, pp.60–61), with a slew of interesting shops selling vintage toys, skateboarding gear, vinyl records, guitars and bric-a-brac.

DE-STRESSING MANILA: SPAS, STEAM AND SHIATSU

After a day sweating it out on Manila's congested streets, a couple of hours in a **spa** can be extremely tempting, especially now that there are plenty of reputable ones serving stressed-out locals rather than sex-starved tourists. Note also that most of the five-star hotels listed in "Accommodation" (see pp.84–88) have excellent spas.

Neo Day Spa G/F, Net One Center Building, 26th St at 3rd Ave, Bonifacio Global City ☎02 815 8233. Serene modern spa inspired by Zen minimalism, with elaborate Japanese-style massages from P1650 (90min), shiatsu for P1050 (1hr) and head and neck massages for P480 (20min). Mon–Thurs & Sun 1–11pm, Fri & Sat noon–11pm.

Soneva Spa 4th Forum Building, Tomas Morato Ave, Quezon City ☎02 926 6249, ⓦsonevaspa .com. Right on the main strip in Quezon City, this offers great value for your peso – come on a weekday afternoon and it's a dreamy, tranquil place with a huge roster of massages. Banana-leaf massages (warm leaves are swept over the body) from P716 for an hour, and back and feet combos from P697. Daily 1pm–midnight.

for bargains – especially Juan Luna, Ylaya, Tabora, Santo Cristo and Soler. Daily 24hr.

Greenhills Tiangge Greenhills Shopping Center, Ortigas Ave, San Juan ⓦgreenhills.com.ph; map pp.60–61. Sprawling market inside this mall north of Makati which is notorious for its illegal bargains: fake designer goods as well as pirated software and DVDs. There's also attractive costume jewellery on sale, and an area full of stalls selling jewellery made with pearls from China and Mindanao; a good-quality bracelet or necklace made with cultured pearls will cost from P1000, depending on the style and the number of pearls used. Other sections of the mall offer cheap mobile phones (some secondhand), household goods and home decor. Mon–Thurs 11am–9pm, Fri–Sun 10am–10pm.

Ilalim ng Tulay Quezon Blvd, Quiapo; map p.72. Hunt down the cheapest woodcarvings, capiz-shell items, *buri* bags and embroidery in Manila among the ramshackle stalls beneath the underpass leading to Quezon Bridge in Quiapo (literally "under the bridge"); tell drivers "Quiapo Ilalim". Daily 24hr.

DIRECTORY

Banks and exchange Most major bank branches have 24hr ATMs for Visa and MasterCard cash advances. The moneychangers around Mabini St in Ermita, P. Burgos St in Makati, and in some malls offer better rates than the banks (but shop around as rates vary; moneychangers that display their rates are likely to give better ones than those that don't).

Embassies and consulates Australia, Level 23, Tower 2, RCBC Plaza, 6819 Ayala Ave, Makati ☎02 757 8100, ⓦphilippines.embassy.gov.au; Canada, Levels 6–8, Tower 2, RCBC Plaza, 6819 Ayala Ave, Makati ☎02 857 9000, ⓦphilippines.gc.ca; Ireland, 3/F, 70 Jupiter St, Bel-Air 1, Makati ☎02 896 4668; New Zealand, 35/F, Zuellig Building, Makati Ave at Paseo de Roxas, Makati ☎02 234 3800, ⓦnzembassy.com/philippines; UK, 120 Upper McKinley Rd, McKinley Hill, Taguig City ☎02 858 2200; US, 1201 Roxas Blvd ☎02 301 2000, ⓦmanila.usembassy.gov.

Emergencies ☎911, police ☎117.

Hospitals and clinics Makati Medical Center, 2 Amorsolo St, Makati (☎02 888 8999, ⓦmakatimed.net.ph) is the largest and one of the most modern hospitals in Manila. Others include: Manila Doctors Hospital, 667 United Nations Ave, Ermita (☎02 558 0888, ⓦmaniladoctors .com.ph); St Luke's Medical Center, 279 E. Rodriguez Sr Blvd, Quezon City (☎02 723 0101, ⓦstluke.com.ph).

Immigration For visa extensions, the Immigration Building is on Magellanes Drive, Intramuros (Mon–Fri 8am–noon & 1–5pm; ☎02 527 3257). There's a smaller office (same hours) in Makati at 385 Gil Puyat Ave ☎02 899 3831, where it's often faster and easier.

Internet access Robinsons Place mall in Ermita is a free wi-fi zone, as is the square in front of Malate Church. Busy Bee, 1417 M.H. del Pilar St, Malate (☎02 256 4776) doubles as a Western Union office and is open 24hr (P35/ hr); Coolweb.com, 704 Pedro Gil St, Ermita (Mon–Fri 7am–9pm, Sat 8am–8pm, Sun 1–8pm) is cheaper (P20/ hr). Coreon Gate at 1774 M. Adriatico St, near *V Hotel* in Malata, is a cool a/c space with a coffee bar and fast internet connections, plus it's open 24hr (P40/hr or free for 6hr if you spend P100 or more on comestibles).

Laundry Faura Laundry, 570 Padre Faura St, Ermita, next to Robinsons Place, Ermita (Mon–Sat 9am–7pm, ☎02 526 7519) charges P33/kg.

Pharmacies You're never far from a Mercury Drug (ⓦmercurydrug.com) outlet in Metro Manila – at the last count there were two hundred of them.

Post Makati Central Post Office at Sen Gil Puyat Ave (Buendia) near Ayala Ave; Ermita Post Office at Pilar Hidalgo Lim St, Malate.

Around Manila

PAGSANJAN FALLS

Around Manila

Despite the proximity of the big city, the provinces that cluster around Metro Manila contain a surprisingly rich array of natural attractions. To the south lies stunning Lake Taal and its volcano, best approached from the refreshingly breezy city of Tagaytay, while further south, on the coast, Anilao offers outstanding scuba diving. North of Lake Taal, Los Baños is best known for its delicious *buko* pie, hot springs and mountain pools, and sits not far from the churning waters of the Pagsanjan Falls, where you can take a thrilling (and soaking) raft ride downriver across a series of rapids. North of Manila you can climb the lush slopes of Mount Pinatubo, explore remote Bataan province, or enjoy the beaches and activities on offer at Subic Bay.

The region was also the scene of some of the nation's most important historical events. The island of **Corregidor**, out in Manila Bay, is littered with thought-provoking monuments to World War II, while **Malolos**, north of Manila, was where the Revolutionary Congress was convened in 1898. National heroes **Emilio Aguinaldo** and **José Rizal** were both born in the region, and their family homes are preserved as museums.

Corregidor

The tadpole-shaped island of **CORREGIDOR**, less than 5km long and 3km wide at its broadest point, is a living museum to the horrors of war. Lying 40km southwest of Manila, it was originally used by the Spanish as a customs post. In 1942 it was defended bravely by an ill-equipped US and Filipino contingent under continual bombardment from **Japanese** guns and aircraft. Some nine hundred Japanese and eight hundred American and Filipino troops died in the fighting, and when the Americans retook the island in 1945, virtually the entire Japanese garrison of over six thousand men was annihilated: little wonder Corregidor is said to be haunted. The island was abandoned after the war, and was gradually reclaimed by thick jungle vegetation – it wasn't until the late 1980s that the Corregidor Foundation began to transform it into a national shrine.

If you visit Corregidor on a day-trip you'll be restricted to a **guided tour**. Perhaps understandably, the tours tend to focus on the heroism, bravery and sacrifice of the men who fought here, rather than the grisly nature of the fighting itself, but they are still a moving experience. Japanese tourists also come here in numbers to pay their respects to the dead of both sides.

Away from the reminders of one of the war's most horrific battles, Corregidor is unspoilt, peaceful and a great break from the city: you can walk marked **trails** that meander through the hilly interior (look out for the monkeys and monitor lizards), rent a kayak or circle the island in a bangka and do some fishing, organized through the ferry company or *Corregidor Inn*.

Highlights

❶ **Corregidor** Take the fast ferry to this idyllic, jungle-covered island at the mouth of Manila Bay, a poignant monument to World War II. **See p. 102**

❷ **Pagsanjan Falls** Home to rough rapids and a towering cascade, with the best *buko* pie in the Philippines in nearby Los Baños. **See p.108 & p.107**

❸ **Tagaytay** Clinging to a high volcanic ridge, this town offers mesmerizing views of Lake Taal and some of the tastiest food in Luzon. **See p.109**

❹ **Lake Taal** Take a bangka across this gorgeous lake and scramble up to the crater at the top of one of the world's smallest volcanoes. **See p.111**

❺ **Taal** Wonderfully preserved colonial town, with *bahay na bato* houses, ivy-clad churches and vibrant markets. **See p.112**

❻ **Anilao** A scenic stretch of coast with some choice resorts and excellent scuba diving. **See p.115**

❼ **Mount Pinatubo** Enticing volcanic peak, accessible by 4WD and on foot, with a beautiful crater lake at the summit. **See p.119**

HIGHLIGHTS ARE MARKED ON THE MAP ON P.104

The war memorials

Sound and light show P200

Tours begin near the ferry dock, with the statue of **General Douglas MacArthur**, who was reluctantly spirited away from the island before its capitulation in 1942. His famous words "I shall return" adorn the statue's base, though he actually made the pronouncement in Darwin, Australia. From here tours take in all the main sights on the island, including the **Filipino Heroes Monument**, commemorating Philippine struggles from the Battle of Mactan in 1521 to the EDSA Revolution of 1986, and the **Japanese Garden of Peace**, where the Japanese war dead were buried in 1945. Overgrown and lost, it was discovered in the 1980s, when the remains were cremated and brought back to Japan. A statue of the Buddhist bodhisattva Guanyin (or "Kannon" in Japanese) watches over the site. At some point you'll reach the **Malinta Tunnel**, a 253m-long

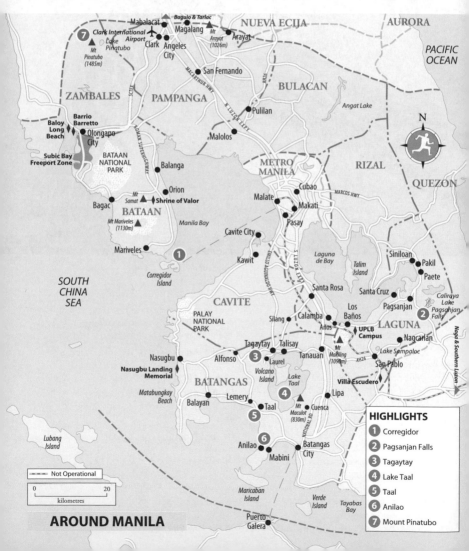

HIGHLIGHTS

1. Corregidor
2. Pagsanjan Falls
3. Tagaytay
4. Lake Taal
5. Taal
6. Anilao
7. Mount Pinatubo

AROUND MANILA

Not Operational

0 — 20 kilometres

chamber and network of damp underground bunkers where MacArthur (and President Manuel Quezon) set up temporary headquarters. You can only see the bunkers in an optional **sound and light show** that dramatizes the events of 1942.

Elsewhere you'll see the ruined concrete shells of the once vast barracks that dotted the island, and the remains of various gun batteries, peppered with bullet and shell holes. You can also visit the **Pacific War Memorial** and its small **museum** containing weapons, old photos and uniforms that were left behind. Finally, clamber the 57 steps to the top of the old **Spanish Lighthouse** at the island's highest point (191m), for stupendous views across to Bataan and Mount Mariveles.

2

ARRIVAL AND DEPARTURE   CORREGIDOR

By boat Sun Cruises (☎02 527 5555, ⓦcorregidor philippines.com) has a monopoly on transport to the island. It runs day-trips for P2350 (Sat, Sun & hols P2549). If you opt for a walking tour (easy) rather than the bus, the price drops to P1800 (per person, daily). Reservations must be made at least a day in advance; you will not be allowed to travel if pregnant. Check-in (and payment of the P30 terminal fee) is at the Sun Cruises terminal on Seaside Boulevard in Pasay, just north of SM Mall of Asia at 7am – for the 8am departure and ride to the island (1hr 15 min). Tours usually run on trolley cars that meet the ferries at around 9.30am, returning to the dock in time for the 2.30pm departure; lunch is included. You'll be back in Manila at around 3.45pm. Normally you can stay overnight on the island at the *Corregidor Inn* (☎0917 527 6350), which is owned by Sun Cruises, but the hotel is currently closed for refurbishment.

South of Manila

The provinces to the south of Manila – **Cavite**, **Laguna** and **Batangas** – are prime day-trip territory, easy to get to and rich in attractions. The star is **Lake Taal**, a mesmerizing volcanic lake with its own mini volcanic island in the centre, but there are plenty of less-visited natural wonders that provide a break from the city; you can ride down the river to the **Pagsanjan Falls**, soak in the **Laguna hot springs** or clamber up forested **Mount Makiling** for scintillating views. Divers should check out **Anilao** for the best reef action near the capital.

The region also serves up a healthy dose of history. **Paete** has retained its woodworking heritage and **Taal** itself is one of the most beautiful colonial towns in the Philippines. Lastly, many Manileños come here just to eat; *buko* **pie** is an especially prized treat made in Laguna.

GETTING AROUND   SOUTH OF MANILA

By bus and jeepney Without a car, the easiest places to reach by public transport are the attractions to the south of Laguna de Bay, though Batangas City and Tagaytay are also well served by buses. The lakeside town of Santa Cruz is the main transport hub for the area. All the attractions between Calamba and Santa Cruz are served by JAC Liner buses from Pasay in Manila (see p.82). Note that the Santa Cruz bus terminals line the National Highway outside the town itself, in the barangay of Pagsawitan. Jeepneys ply the Calamba–Santa Cruz route (P24). From Santa Cruz you can catch jeepneys on to Paete and Pagsanjan.

The Emilio Aguinaldo Shrine and Museum

Tirona Hwy, Kawit • Tues–Sun 8am–4pm • Free • ☎ 046 484 7643, ⓦ nhcp.gov.ph/museums/emilio-aguinaldo-shrine • Take a Cavite-bound jeepney or FX taxi from Baclaran LRT station in Manila, but make sure it will stop at Kawit

For most Filipinos, the province of Cavite ("ka-vee-tay") will forever be associated with the Philippine Revolution: in 1872 the Cavite Mutiny precipitated the national revolt against the colonial authorities (see p.438), and the province was the birthplace of independence hero **Emilio Aguinaldo**, the first President of the Republic. The **Emilio Aguinaldo Shrine and Museum** in **KAWIT**, 23km south of Manila, is the house in which he was born in 1869. He's also buried here, in a simple marble tomb in the back garden on the bank of the river. Philippine independence was proclaimed here and the Philippine flag first raised by Aguinaldo on June 12, 1898, is commemorated on that day every year, with the president waving the flag from the balcony.

With its secret passages and hidden compartments, the house is testimony to the revolutionary fervour that surrounded Aguinaldo and his men. A number of the original chairs and cabinets have secret compartments that were used to conceal documents and weapons, while the kitchen has a secret passage that he could use to escape if the Spanish came calling. In the general's bedroom, one of the floorboards opens up to reveal a staircase that led to his private one-lane bowling alley under the house and an adjoining hidden swimming pool. Downstairs, the museum displays various Aguinaldo memorabilia including clothes, journals and his sword, while upstairs there is the general's bedroom, a grand hall, a dining room and a conference room.

Calamba

The city of **CALAMBA**, just 54km from the capital, is best known today as the birthplace of national hero and revolutionary **José Rizal**. Once a rural backwater, Calamba is now the largest city in Laguna province and effectively a choked extension of Manila – there's nothing to see in the modern section, but the old barangay of **San Juan**, built in Spanish colonial style around the handsome **St John the Baptist Church** (1859), is worth a visit. A marker inside the church indicates that Rizal was baptized here by Fray Rufino Collantes on June 22, 1861. Commuter train services from Manila's Tutuban station are due to be extended down to Calamba in the future, but no date has as yet been announced.

Rizal Shrine

J.P. Rizal St at F. Mercado St • Tues–Sun 8am–4pm • Free • ☎ 049 834 1599, ⓦ bit.ly/rizal-shrine

The site where José Rizal was born in 1861 is now the **Rizal Shrine**, though the building here is a late 1940s replica of a typical nineteenth-century Philippine *bahay na bato* – it features lower walls of stone and upper walls of wood, *narra*-wood floors and windows made from capiz shell. All the rooms contain period furniture and the adjacent gallery has displays of Rizal's belongings, including the clothes in which he was christened and a fragment of the suit he was wearing when he was executed. In the garden is a *bahay kubo* (wooden) playhouse, a replica of the one in which Rizal used to spend his days as a child.

LAGUNA HOT SPRINGS

Just east of Calamba on the National Highway (accessible by the buses and jeepneys to Santa Cruz), the barangay of **Pansol** touts heavily for tourist custom on the health properties of its **hot springs**, which bubble from the lower slopes of Mount Makiling. There are dozens of resorts of varying quality that use the hot springs to fill their swimming pools, many catering to tour groups, day-trippers, company outings and conferences. It's best to visit on a weekday when the best ones can make for a relaxing few hours.

RESORTS AND SPAS

Makiling Highlands Resort Captain Mamon Rd, Pansol (just off the National Highway) ☎ 049 545 1259, ⓦ bit.ly/makiling. This lush resort has villas and rooms for overnight stays (from P1350) but the entrance fee is just P50. Hot pools spread out over many hectares of ground, and you can rent small wooden *kamaligs* (traditional huts) for P900 for 12hr, or just take a picnic

table for P300 weekdays, P450 weekends, and bring in food or order deliveries from local fast-food chains.

Monte Vista Hot Springs & Conference Resort National Highway, Pansol ☎ 049 545 1259. This sister resort to *Makiling Highlands* offers eighteen hot mineral pools, assorted giant slides and enough room for 1500 day visitors. The rate for a visit is P1350 for two people, which entitles you to a room and a 24hr stay.

Los Baños and around

The lakeside town of **LOS BAÑOS**, around 60km south of Manila, attracts a steady stream of domestic tourists who primarily come to gorge on its delectable **buko pies** (stuffed with young coconut), said to have first been cooked up here in the 1960s by a food technologist from the local university. Its campus has an interesting **Riceworld Museum**, while the looming volcano cone of **Mount Makiling** makes an enticing target for a day-hike.

Riceworld Museum

Pili Drive • Mon–Fri 8am–5pm • Free • ☎ 049 536 2701 ext 2675, ⊛ irri.org

The International Rice Research Institute, next to the university campus, is home to the unexpectedly absorbing **Riceworld Museum**, which showcases the importance of the staple that feeds half the world's population. Apart from an overview of the developing world's food shortages, the museum has a number of small but intriguing displays on the history, production and types of rice.

Mount Makiling

Trail begins at Makiling Center monitoring station, College of Forestry, Maliking Trail, southwestern end of UPLB campus (☎ 049 536 2577, ⊛ mountmakiling.org; P10 registration fee) • Jeepneys to the College of Forestry run from Lopez Ave at El Danda St (near Robinsons Mall, just off the National Highway)

The dormant volcano of **Mount Makiling** (1090m) is identifiable by its unusual shape, resembling a reclining woman. The mountain is named after Mariang Makiling (aka "Mary of Makiling"), a young woman whose spirit is said to protect the mountain. On quiet nights, so the legend goes, you can hear her playing the harp. The music is rarely heard any more, possibly because Makiling is angry about the scant regard paid to the environment by the authorities, but the University of the Philippines at Los Baños UPLB now manages the **Mount Makiling Forest Reserve** that blankets the mountain and is hoping to develop its ecotourism potential.

From the Makiling Center monitoring station, a well-established but strenuous 8.7km trail leads up to the summit (4–5hr). It's safe and easy to follow, but be prepared for leeches, sudden downpours and flash floods (the trail was closed for three months after two hikers drowned in 2012). **Guides** are not required. Most climbers start early and complete the hike in one day; you can pitch tents at the Malaboo and Tayabak campsites on the way up, but not near the summit.

ARRIVAL AND DEPARTURE
LOS BAÑOS AND AROUND

By bus and jeepney Los Baños is accessible via Green Star Express buses from Manila (p.82) or jeepneys from Calamba. To head back to Manila from Los Baños, note that the last bus departs around 8.30pm.

EATING

Numerous brands and stalls along the National Highway outside Los Baños sell *buko* pie, all at around P200 per pie (for the standard 9 inches). Note that shops will close early if they run out of pies. As well as those listed here, other specialist snack stores have set up to cash in on the crowds.

Lety's Buko Pie LBP Building, National Highway, Brgy Anos ☎ 049 536 1332, ⊛ letysbukopie.com. Established by Leticia "Lety" Belarmino in 1976, this is a local favourite (next door to *Orient*). Also sells cassava cake, pineapple pie and banana bread. Daily 8am–5pm.

Net's Cassava Cake National Highway, Brgy Anos ☎ 0921 722 5960, ⊛ bit.ly/nets-cassava. This popular little shop produces some of the most addictive cassava pudding in the Philippines (from P120 for a half-size one). They also have *buko* pie, pineapple pie and organic soursop juice. Daily 9am–7pm.

★Orient – the Original Buko Pie Bakeshop National Highway, Brgy Anos ☎ 049 536 3783. ⊛ bit.ly/original-buko. The best *buko* pies are still baked at this venerable store (note the double-parked cars and buses blocking the road), with young, tender coconut slices in a crispy, well-made crust. Be aware, however, that they do tend to sell out pretty much as as fast as they can bake them, although they'll take reservations on weekdays. From Calamba, the shop is on the left just before you reach the town centre; they have another branch at Silang on the Santa Rosa–Tagaytay road. Daily 8am–6pm.

2

Pagsanjan

Serving as the capital of Laguna province from 1688 to 1858, the town of **PAGSANJAN** lies 100km southeast of Manila and is home to a few old wooden houses, an unusually ornamental stone gate – or **Puerta Real** – and a pretty Romanesque church. The gate sits on the road to Santa Cruz (Rizal Street) and was completed in 1880, while **Our Lady of Guadalupe Church**, dating from 1690 but remodelled in the nineteenth century, is at the other end of Rizal. The town's main claim to fame these days is as the staging point for the dazzling **Pagsanjan Falls**, chosen by Francis Ford Coppola as the location for the final scenes in *Apocalypse Now* in 1975. Most tourists come not for the Hollywood nostalgia value, however, but to take one of the popular "**shooting the rapids**" trips along the Bumbungan River to the falls and back (see box below).

ARRIVAL AND INFORMATION   PAGSANJAN

By bus It can take up to 4hr to get to Pagsanjan from Manila if you hit bad traffic (around 2hr normally) – avoid weekends and public holidays. Jeepneys (P10) run frequently from Santa Cruz (see p.105) to Pagsanjan.

Tourist information The tourist office is in the municipal building (daily 8am–5pm; ☎049 501 3544, �🌐pagsanjan .gov.ph) in the centre of town, opposite the main church.

ACCOMMODATION AND EATING

★**Aling Taleng's** 169 General Luna St (just south of the Balanac Bridge) ☎0917 899 8484, �🌐bit.ly/talengs. This popular shop has been serving refreshing seven-ingredient *halo-halo* (P75) since 1933. Also serves all-day Filipino breakfast, burgers and great noodles. Daily 8.30am–6.30pm.
Calle Arco 57 Rizal St (National Hwy) ☎049 501 4584, �🌐bit.ly/calle-arco. This old-fashioned restaurant in a whimsical wooden house serves quality Filipino food such as *sinigang na baka sa langka* (beef tamarind soup with jackfruit, P270). Buy the sweet calamansi and tomatoes in jars (P250) to take away. Cash only. Daily 10am–10pm.
Pagsanjan Falls Lodge Pinagsanjan (Pagsanjan–

Cavinti Rd) ☎049 501 4251, �🌐pagsanjanfallslodge.com .ph. This resort has a decent family pool area, restaurant and a good range of very ordinary but clean and spacious rooms including fan rooms, a/c doubles plus fifteen rooms for up to three people. To get to the resort, take a jeepney from General Luna St (south of the river) in Pagsanjan. 📶 **P1500**
Tio Casio's Bibingka de Macapuno National Hwy, Sambat, Bubukal (5km west of Pagsanjan) ☎0926 888 6179, �🌐bit.ly/tio-casio. For a real treat make the trip out to this local stall for sumptuous slices of coconut-enriched *bibingka* (rice cake). Daily 8am–5pm (but may close earlier if stocks run out).

Paete

Sleepy **PAETE** ("pa-e-te"), is Luzon's **woodcarving capital**, packed with stores selling woodcarvings, oil paintings, wooden clogs (*bakya*) and gaily painted papier-mâché masks used in fiestas. Most of the stores (usually open daily 8am–6pm) are on **Quesada Street** in the centre of town. During the second week of January Paete holds its **Salibanda festival**, the feast of the Santo Niño (Holy Child), which includes a rowdy

SHOOTING THE RAPIDS AT PAGSANJAN

The fourteen **rapids** of the Bumbungan River (bangkas daily 7am–5pm; P1250 per person) are at their most thrilling in the wet season (June–Sept); during the dry season the "shooting the rapids" ride is more sedate. You don't need to be especially daring to do the trip, though you will get wet, so be prepared. **Ticket sales** are supervised by the local tourism office (see above), so go there first, and ignore touts offering tickets on the street. The trip includes a raft ride under the falls – make sure to protect your phone and camera. It's customary to tip the boatman, typically P100 per person.

It usually takes around an hour to climb just over 5km, up through the dramatic gorge in bangkas; when you get closer to the actual 30m-high **Pagsanjan Falls**, you can float on a bamboo raft (*balsa*) to go directly below the cascade into the cavern known as **Devil's Cave** for a swim, another thirty minutes or so. This is an additional P250 per head if not already negotiated as part of your boat trip.

procession along the main street in which participants and spectators splash water over each other. Paete is also well known for its sweet **lanzones** (harvested Oct–Dec). There is no accommodation, but you can visit the town easily in a day.

Santiago Apostol Parish Church

Quesada St at Roces St · Daily 7am–8pm · ☎ 049 557 0114

The town's crumbling but atmospheric Baroque **Santiago Apostol Parish Church** dates from 1646, but like many old Philippine churches it has been reduced to rubble by earthquakes on a number of occasions and rebuilt. The present structure dates from 1939, and has an ornate carved facade, weathered bell tower and a beautifully sculpted altar finished in gold leaf. The wonderfully vivid mural paintings near the main entrance date from the 1850s.

2

ARRIVAL AND DEPARTURE	PAETE
By jeepney Paete is 10km north of Pagsanjan, just off the main highway that hugs the east coast of Laguna de Bay.	It's best approached by jeepney (around P25) from Pagsanjan or Santa Cruz (take any one going to Siniloan).

EATING

★**Exotik** National Hwy, Longos (around 2km south of Paete). Enchanting restaurant modelled on a native village. The menu features typical Filipino dishes as well as frog, eel and stingray, but ask about seasonal dishes such as snake, wild boar and monitor lizard (which really does taste like chicken). Meats are cooked adobo-style, "sizzling" or in coconut milk. Most dishes range P200–300. Daily 7am–9pm.

Kape Kesada Art Gallery Quesada St ☎ 049 557 0013, ⓦ bit.ly/kapekesada. Café and gallery (selling paintings and books) that looks like a wooden Japanese house and serves brewed coffee (P65) and decent sandwiches. Tues–Sun 9am–8.30pm.

Tagaytay

The compact and breezy city of **TAGAYTAY**, 55km south of Manila, sits on a dramatic 600m-high ridge overlooking **Lake Taal** and its volcano, to which it serves as the gateway. The centre of town is a Rotunda (roundabout), where the ridge road, running east to west, meets the Aguinaldo Highway, running north towards Manila. The town's main transport hub is Olivarez Plaza, 200m north of the Rotunda. Tagaytay is very spread out and the views make it more expensive to stay here than in one of the barangays by the lake around Talisay (see p.112), which are quieter and more convenient if you intend to climb the volcano.

Tagaytay Picnic Grove

Tagaytay–Calamba Hwy, 5km east of the Rotunda · **Grove** Mon–Fri 7am–7pm, Sat & Sun 7am–8pm · P50 · **Zipline and cable car** P300 one-way, P400 return · ⓦ tagaytayzipline.com

You can take in the views from the **Tagaytay Picnic Grove**, a shabby ridgetop park, popular with day-trippers, that has huts available to rent. Inside the grove (but separately managed), the **Tagaytay Ridge Zipline & cable car** boasts a 250m-long zipline and a cable-car ride.

People's Park in the Sky

Tagaytay–Calamba Hwy, 7.5km east of the Rotunda · Daily 6am–6pm · P30 · ☎ 0916 832 8427

The **People's Park in the Sky** is the highest point in the area (750m) offering magnificent panoramas of the lake, the sea, Laguna de Bay – and the smog that hangs over Manila to the north. The other attraction up here is the modest **Shrine of our Lady, Mother of Fair Love**, constructed in 2003.

Sky Fun Amusement Park

Tagaytay–Nasugbu Hwy, 3km west of the Rotunda near *Taal Vista Hotel* · Daily 8am–10pm · P100, plus Sky Eye P150, Super Viking P100, Nessi Coaster P50, Wonder Flight P50 · ☎ 02 862 7704 or ☎ 046 831 7000, ⓦ bit.ly/sky-fun

Visitors with kids may enjoy the **Sky Fun Amusement Park**, which contains the "Sky Eye", the tallest Ferris wheel in the Philippines (at 63m), as well as thrill-filled rides

2

such as the "Super Viking" (a giant boat swing), the "Nessi Coaster" mini rollercoaster and "Wonder Flight", a roundabout for young kids.

ARRIVAL AND INFORMATION   TAGAYTAY

By bus Frequent San Agustin and BSC buses run every 15min from MRT-Taft (Pasay) on EDSA (see p.82) to Tagaytay (1hr 30min). Jeepneys from Olivarez Plaza (200m north of the Rotunda) head north, east and west to most points in Tagaytay for P8–11 depending on the journey.

Tourist information Tagaytay City Tourism Office is in the City Hall (3km west of Tagaytay's central Rotunda; daily 8am–5pm; ☎ 046 413 1220). The local police have a small tourist information post on the south side of the Rotunda.

ACCOMMODATION

Our Melting Pot 75 Smokey Hill (off Tagaytay–Nasugbu Hwy, 3km west of the Rotunda) ☎ 0915 774 0864, ☻ bit.ly/ourmeltingpot. Run by the same firm as its namesake in Manila (see p.88), this hostel is friendly, and its dorm beds are about the cheapest option in town if you're on a tight budget, although its private rooms are fan-cooled, and not such great value compared to places around the Tagaytay Picnic Grove, where you'd get an a/c room for the same price. ☞ Dorms P450, doubles P1100

Sonya's Garden Barangay Buck Estate, Alfonso (25km west of Tagaytay) ☎ 0917 532 9097, ☻ sonyasgarden .com. Romantic cottage accommodation in a blossom-filled garden. Cottages are *bahay na bato*-style, with antique beds, lots of carved wood and shuttered windows.

The rate includes a delicious breakfast and either lunch or supper. *Sonya's* is 12km beyond Tagaytay, so is tricky to reach without private transport: go past Splendido golf course and then look out for the signs on the right. ☞ P3000

★Theodore Hotel Tagaytay–Nasugbu Highway 500m west of the Rotunda ☎ 046 483 0350, ☻ thetheodorehotel.com. Very sleek centrally located boutique hotel with just ten stylish rooms each with its own design theme (from Pop Art to Japan), flatscreen TVs, spa, free 30min massage, and a tranquil garden and viewing deck. Note that prices jump by over a third at weekends, so come here Sun–Thurs for the best deals. ☞ P6100

EATING AND DRINKING

Adoration Convent of Divine Mercy (Pink Sister's) east off Aguinaldo Hwy (signposted), 1km north of the Rotunda. Tranquil religious institution (said to be popular with late president Cory Aquino), that sells home-baked food from a tiny gift shop to the left of the entrance. The nuns' home-made cookies – aka "angel cookies" (tasty oat biscuits; P120/box) – bring in the foodies. Daily 8am–4.30pm.

The Grill by Antonio's Tagaytay–Nasugbu Hwy, 1km west of the Rotunda ☎ 046 483 4847, ☻ antonios restaurant.ph/the-grill. The casual branch of a super-posh restaurant serving the best Filipino food in town. Highlights include the huge pots of richly stewed *bulalo* (P680) – a meal for two people – plates of fried *tawalis* (anchovy-sized lake fish, P200), a fine adobo (P290) and the barbecue chicken (P110). Daily 11am–9pm.

Josephine Tagaytay–Nasugbu Hwy, 3km west of the Rotunda ☎ 046 413 1801, ☻ bit.ly/josephine-tagaytay. An institution among Filipinos since the 1960s, serving good Filipino dishes such as *sinigang* (from P320 for four)

with mounds of steamed rice to go with those special views. They also do a weekend lunch buffet for P495. Mon–Fri 8am–9pm, Sat & Sun 7am–9pm.

Rowena's Hillcrest Plaza Tagaytay–Nasugbu Hwy, 200m west of the Rotunda ☎ 046 483 0717, ☻ bit.ly/ rowenas-hillcrest. Delicious pies and tarts: stop by for blueberry or strawberry cheese tarts (P55), or the classic *buko* pie (P200), plus excellent coffee (and decent meals, as it goes) at this town-centre branch of a café-restaurant whose original branch is out on the Santa Rosa road in Brgy San Francisco. Mon–Fri 8am–8.30pm, Sat & Sun 8am–9.30pm.

★Sonya's Garden Barangay Buck Estate, Alfonso (25km west of Tagaytay) ☎ 0917 532 9097, ☻ sonyasgarden.com. If you're not staying the night (see above), drop by for lunch or dinner: daily unlimited buffets cost P683 (breakfast is P560 for non-guests) and include delights such as pasta with sun-dried tomatoes and banana rolls with sesame and jackfruit for dessert. Book ahead.

THE TASTES OF LAKE TAAL

Lake Taal is famed for its delicious **fresh fish**, especially *tawilis* (a freshwater sardine only found here), tilapia and increasingly rare *maliputo* (a larger fish, also only found in Lake Taal, which is featured on the back of the P50 note). The other speciality is *bulalo* – rich beef **bone-marrow soup**. You'll find all of these in abundance in Tagaytay's restaurants.

Lake Taal and Talisay

The country's third-largest lake, awe-inspiring **Lake Taal** sits in a caldera below Tagaytay, and was formed by huge eruptions between 500,000 and 100,000 years ago. The active **Taal Volcano**, which is responsible for the lake's sulphuric content, lies in the centre of the lake, on **Volcano Island**. The volcano last erupted in 1965 without causing major damage, but when it blew its top in 1754, thousands died and the town of Taal was destroyed; it was rebuilt in a new location on safer ground an hour by road from Tagaytay to the southwest of the lake (see p.112). Before 1754 the lake was actually part of Balayan Bay, but the eruption sealed it from the sea, eventually leading to its waters becoming non-saline. Today it's still very active, and the island is occasionally closed – check the **Philippine Institute of Volcanology and Seismology** website (PHIVOLCS; ⓦ www.phivolcs.dost.gov.ph) for the latest updates.

The departure point for trips across the lake to the volcano (see box below) is the small town of **TALISAY** on the lake's northern shore, some 4km southeast of Tagaytay. This is a much more typical Filipino settlement, with a bustling market, fishermen doubling as tourist guides and nary a fast-food chain in sight.

2

ARRIVAL AND DEPARTURE   LAKE TAAL AND TALISAY

From Manila you can approach Lake Taal from two directions: from the north via Tagaytay, or via Tanauan, east of the lake. Once in Talisay **tricycles** should take you to nearby hotels or bangka operators for P8–10 per person, or P24–30 per ride.

Via Tagaytay From Tagaytay you can get a tricycle down to Talisay (P150–200), or get a "People's Park" jeepney to the Talisay turn-off (Tagaytay–Calamba Hwy, 5km east of the Rotunda; P11) and a tricycle or occasional jeepney from there.

Via Tanauan JAM buses from Manila (see p.82) to Batangas stop at Tanauan (P96). In Tanauan take a tricycle to the Talisay jeepney terminal (P10 per person); frequent jeepneys head to Talisay town from there (40min; P20).

VOLCANO ISLAND

Visitors to **Volcano Island** often get ripped off by local "guides" but it's easy to avoid making the same mistake; the only price you need to negotiate is the **bangka** to take you out to the island and back (plus the tricycle/taxi fare to the dock). They cost around P2000 (good for up to six people) if you arrange one independently, and can be arranged at the waterfront market in Talisay, or at any of the resorts (see p.112); *Taal Lake Yacht Club* (see below) is also a dependable choice. **Guides** will charge another P700 or so to take you up to the main crater (and even to cross on the boat with you), though the trail is easy to follow and you do not need one. On the island is a small information office where you must pay a tourist tax of P100 per person plus a P50 landing fee for the boat. There's a basic restaurant, with vendors selling overpriced drinks.

The principal highlight on the island is the walk up to the rim of the 1.9km-diameter **Main Crater Lake**, where you can look down onto tiny Vulcan Point island ("the island on an island"); the lake itself is usually off limits, depending on current PHIVOLCS warnings (see above). You can ride a **horse** up to the top of the crater for an additional P500 – most tourists do this because of the heat, but the trail is not difficult for anyone in reasonable fitness (and the condition of the horses is pretty appalling). The trail can be dusty, however, so bring a scarf for your mouth or buy a mask on arrival (P50). If you're staying the night by the lake, your hotel can arrange all this for you, with food and refreshments included, typically for P2000–3000 per person. There isn't much shade on the island, so don't go without sunblock, a good hat and plenty of water.

With an early start (boats usually run from 7am), you can climb to the Main Crater Lake and be back in Talisay in time for lunch (the hike takes around 30min depending on fitness level; the trail is around 2.3km with a height gain of 200m). If you want to spend more time on the water, make for the **Taal Lake Yacht Club**, about 1km east of Talisay (☎043 773 0192, ⓦtlyc .com), where you can rent sailing dinghies (Toppers from P1800/day) and kayaks (P1200/day).

ACCOMMODATION AND EATING

Most of the lakeside **resorts** are between Talisay and the village of Laurel a few kilometres to the south. **Hotels** are busiest from Sept to Feb (the coolest months) so book ahead if travelling at these times. Weekdays are always much cheaper year-round. Down by the lakeshore in and around Talisay, simple **eating places** sell barbecued meat and fish, but quality can be hit and miss; the numerous bakeries in Talisay are a safer bet for a snack.

★**Club Balai Isabel** Brgy Banga, Talisay ☎043 773 0004, ⓦbalaiisabel.com. This fashionable lakeside boutique resort is built around a century-old coconut and mango plantation just east of the town. Rates for the cosy hotel rooms and suites include breakfast, while the luxurious lakeshore suites and villas are self-catering (all have kitchens) and can accommodate up to six people. There's a swimming pool, and a variety of watersports and even a lake cruise can be laid on for guests. The *Terraza*

restaurant here is your best bet for a decent meal in Talisay. 📶 P5544

San Roque Beach Resort Talisay–Laurel Rd ☎043 773 0271, ✉sanroquebeachresort@yahoo.com. A welcoming place right on the lakeshore with startling views across to the volcano, owned by a lovely Dutch–Filipina couple, Leo and Lita. The spacious rooms have little extra touches such as flowering plants and reading lamps, and there are great fish meals. 📶 P1500

Taal

The town of **TAAL**, 130km south of Manila and a further 10km southwest of its namesake lake, is one of the best-preserved colonial enclaves in the Philippines and one of the few places you can get a real sense of its Spanish past. Founded in 1572 by Augustinians, it was moved to this location (and away from the deadly Taal volcano) in 1755 and today boasts a superb collection of endearingly weathered Spanish colonial architecture and *bahay na bato*-style homes, as well as one of the finest basilicas in Luzon. Several of the town's Spanish-era buildings are open to the public.

Basilica de St Martin de Tours

M. Agoncillo St • Daily 4am–6pm • Free; belfry tower P100

On the east side of Taal's central plaza lies the elegantly weathered bulk of the **Basilica de St Martin de Tours**, said to be the biggest church in Southeast Asia, its facade visibly cracked, peeling and studded with clumps of weeds. The present church, begun in 1856, has a magnificent interior and is often jam-packed for masses throughout the day. The church (and Taal) is a major pilgrimage site thanks to an aged pinewood image of the Virgin Mary known as **Our Lady of Caysasay**, only 20cm high, which is moved to a shrine on the edge of town each week (see p.114). The statue is said to have been fished out of the Pansipit River in 1603; it was lost then found again in a freshwater spring.

Galleria Taal

60 M. Agoncillo St • Tues–Sun 8am–5pm • P100 • ☎0906 763 2449, ⓦbit.ly/galleria-taal

This fine old house has been turned into the **Galleria Taal**, a museum of vintage cameras collected over the years by the president of the local camera club (whose family home this was). The cameras will only appeal to enthusiasts, but the house itself, and the collection of old photographs, both dating back to the 1870s, are of more general interest.

Leon Apacible Historic Landmark

59 M. Agoncillo St • Tues–Sun 8am–4pm • Free • ☎0917 852 1652

The **Leon Apacible Historic Landmark** is the ancestral home of **Leon Apacible** (1861–1901), lawyer and Filipino revolutionary. Built in the eighteenth century, it has the best-preserved interior in Taal: though it was renovated in 1870 and again in 1940, the wide, highly buffed *narra* floorboards, as well as the wide sweeping staircase (with its curved balustrade) are still original. The sliding doors and oriel windows betray American Art Deco influence while the transom filigree, featuring swirling chrysanthemums, is Chinese style.

CLOCKWISE FROM TOP MOUNT PINATUBO (P.119); CRATER LAKE, TAAL VOLCANO (P.111); *BAHAY NA BATO* (STONE-BUILT HOUSE), TAAL (P.112) >

Marcela Agoncillo Historical Landmark

14 M. Agoncillo St • Tues–Sun 8am–4pm • Free • ☎ 0929 530 5872

The **Marcela Agoncillo Historical Landmark** is the most evocative and visibly ageing house in Taal, with creaky wooden floors, a dusty library and old-fashioned *sala* upstairs. The eighteenth-century house is the ancestral home of **Marcela Mariño de Agoncillo** (1860–1946), creator of the first Philippine flag in 1898 (she was in exile in Hong Kong at the time). An exhibit of flags from the days of the Philippine Revolution adorns the lower half of the structure, and her statue (holding the flag) graces the garden.

Chapel of Caysasay

Calle Vicente Noble • Daily 7am–8pm • Free

The **Chapel of Caysasay**, located on the banks of the Pansipit River on the edge of town, is a beautiful coral-hewn chapel where the Our Lady of Caysasay image is transferred from its shrine in the basilica every Thursday and returned on Saturday afternoon. The ruined **Twin Wishing Wells of Santa Lucia**, a short walk from the chapel, are still reputed to have miraculous healing powers.

ARRIVAL AND INFORMATION   TAAL

By bus and jeepney Jeepneys between Lemery and Batangas (both accessible by bus from Manila) pass through Taal. To get here from Tagaytay involves taking a Nasugbu-bound bus to Boundry, just past Alfonso (15min), then a jeepney to Lemery (1hr) and a jeepney or tricycle from there to Taal.

Tourist information You can get a town map and basic information at the tourist information office in the square in front of the Basilica (daily 8am–5pm; ☎ 043 706 3368, ⍟ taal.gov.ph).

GETTING AROUND

By tricycle Taal's compact centre is easy to explore on foot, but if it's too hot you can easily hire a tricycle to whisk you around (P100–120 depending on how many sights and hours you take).

ACCOMMODATION AND EATING

Casa Cecilia Diversion Rd (just outside the centre) ☎ 043 408 0046, ⍟ bit.ly/casa-cecilia. Modern, cosy seven-room hotel sporting Spanish-style architecture and a patio overlooking the garden. Rooms are all en-suite doubles or twins, with parquet floors, tiled bathrooms and cable TV, and on the ground floor there's a good restaurant, *La Azotea*, serving typical Batangueño food (such as *bulalo*). Rates include breakfast. 🛜 **P3000**

Casa Punzalan C. Ilagan St at P. Gomez St ☎ 043 408 0084. This is the best budget option in the area, a beautiful and historic property in the town plaza overlooking the basilica. It contains three rather musty fan rooms and two a/c rooms, all with shared bathrooms. **P800**

My Kusina M. Agoncillo St at V. Ilustre St ☎ 0927 206 8588. A sweet little diner offering low-priced but well-presented staple dishes such as *pancit canton* (fried noodles; P65) and *sigsig* with rice (P75). The house upstairs, *Casa Emiliana*, is a smart two-room B&B. Daily 6am–7pm.

SHOPPING

Taal Public Market Calle Ananias Diokno. The market in the centre of Taal is a good place to eat and to look for local embroidery (*burdang Taal*), including cotton sheets, pillowcases, tablemats and *barong tagalog* and *saya*, the national costumes. Daily 5am–7pm.

Mount Maculot

P20, paid at the Registration Point • Guides can be organized at the trailhead (P400/day for up to five people, plus tips) • From Manila, take a Lemery-bound bus from Pasay (2hr 30min; P148) and get off in Cuenca, from where it's a 2km walk or tricycle ride (P15–20 per person) to the trailhead

Close to the town of **Cuenca**, on the southeastern side of Lake Taal, some 50km east of Taal itself, **Mount Maculot** (930m) affords mind-blowing views across the lake, surrounding jungle and puffy clouds to the horizon from its summit, yet is relatively undeveloped and (weekends excepted) tourist-free. If you set out from Manila very early – as most local climbers do – you can climb its lush slopes and be in Taal (or back in the capital) for dinner. One reason for Maculot's popularity is an area of sheer rock near the summit known as the **Rockies** (starting at 706m), which rises vertically up from the jungle and has a platform at the top, from where you can see across to Lake Taal. A steep but walkable path around the Rockies takes you to the platform.

The 2km walk or tricycle ride from Cuenca to the trailhead goes via the **Barangay No. 7 Outpost**, a small hut marked by a barrier across the road. Stop off along the way at the Registration Point near the Cuenca barangay administration hall, where you are supposed to register and pay. Though you can organize guides at the trailhead, they're not necessary – the trail is easy to follow (well marked by white arrows and signs), with steps and handrails most of the way. From the trailhead (behind the little sari-sari store known as the "mountaineer's store") it takes about two hours to reach the summit, depending on your fitness level, via the **Grotto of the Blessed Virgin Mary**, a small shrine.

Nasugbu and around

Some of the finest white-sand beaches near Manila lie along the Batangas coastline around **NASUGBU**, 37km west of Tagaytay. The coast here is pitted with resorts, mostly clearly signposted from the main road and grouped in three areas: to the north of Nasugbu on the chalky sands stretching to Fuego Point; around Nasugbu itself on Nasugbu Beach, which has darker sand and is more crowded; and about 12km south of Nasugbu by road along the similarly darker sands of **Matabungkay Beach**, which is often marred by the *balsas* (rafts rented by resorts) that line the shore. Other than the beach, the only real sight is the **Nasugbu Landing Memorial**, consisting of a steel landing craft and statues of soldiers coming ashore, which commemorates the second landing of American forces in the Philippines in 1945, at the end of World War II.

ARRIVAL AND DEPARTURE   NASUGBU AND AROUND

By bus From Manila, there are frequent Batman Star Express (BSC) buses to Nasugbu from the San Agustin terminal by EDSA LRT/Taft MRT station in Pasay. There are

jeepneys every few minutes between Nasugbu and Matabungkay (20min; P24).

ACCOMMODATION

Coral Beach Club Matabungkay Beach ☎ 0917 901 4635, ⓦ coralbeach.ph. A quiet, attractive hotel with restaurant (which is a bit overpriced), bar, pool tables, beachside pool and a/c rooms, all with cable TV and hot showers. Chauffeur-driven Manila transfers P4000–5000. ☞ **P2900**

Lago de Oro National Highway, Balibago, Calatagan (20km south of Nasugbu) ☎ 0917 504 2685, ⓦ lago-de-oro.com. Modern hacienda-style resort, notable for the cable wakeboard system in its lagoon; a cable drags you around the

lake rather than a boat. There's also good food in the European-style restaurant and a pool for lounging, and discounts are usually available outside public holidays. ☞ **P5500**

Twins Beach Club Matabungkay Beach ☎ 0917 824 3339, ⓦ twinsbc.de. Homely German-managed *pension* on the seafront, offering en-suite doubles with tiled floors. Small beach, swimming pool and alfresco bar. Some of the best-value accommodation in the area if you're content with the simple life. ☞ **P2000**

Anilao

Some 140km south of Manila, the resort of **ANILAO** (the name refers both to the village and the 13km peninsula beyond it) is primarily a diving destination, popular with city folk at weekends (when the area can get a little busy). During the week it's much more peaceful and you can often negotiate a discount on your accommodation, though there's little point in coming just for the beach.

ARRIVAL AND DEPARTURE   ANILAO

To reach Anilao by public transport, take a bus to Batangas City (see p.116) and then a jeepney west to Mabini or the wharf at Anilao village (1hr; P35), and continue by tricycle (fares depend on the resort, and may vary widely) along the coastal road to your resort.

2

DIVING AT ANILAO

The **reef** at Anilao is thriving, mainly because this is a protected marine sanctuary, with huge numbers of reef fish, small squid, cuttlefish, colourful nudibranchs (sea slugs) and all sorts of hard and soft coral. There are at least forty dive sites within thirty minutes of most resorts; the most highly rated are Twin Rocks, Basura, Mainit Muck (Secret Bay), Kirby's and Bethlehem. It's justly celebrated for Cathedral Rock, a marine park sanctuary at 20–30m; originally barren, the site comprises two large rock formations inside a natural amphitheatre, topped with a man-made cross and seeded with corals. The resorts are the easiest places to arrange dive trips. March to June is the best time for diving.

ACCOMMODATION

Aquaventure Reef Club Brgy Bagalangit ☏ 0917 587 7848, ⓦ aquareefclub.com. Comfortable, unpretentious resort 3km along the coastal road beyond Anilao. Operated by Manila-based dive outfit Aqua One, it's primarily a scuba resort, though it also offers island-hopping and snorkelling trips in rented bangkas. Double rooms come with fan or a/c and bath; buffet-style meals are served in a nice open restaurant overlooking the sea. ☞ P3320

Casita Ysabel Brgy San Teodoro ☏ 0908 172 3466, ⓦ casitaysabel.com. Preferred hideaway for non-divers (as well as divers), with its Tree Earth Spa and cosy cottages just off the beach (and local reef). Owner Linda Reyes-Romualdez has used Bali as inspiration for the best *casitas*, most of which have ocean views. Meals included. ☞ P6000

★ **Dive Solana** Brgy San Teodoro ☏ 0908 876 5262, ⓦ divesolana.com. Along the coastal road beyond the *Aquaventure Reef Club*, this is a slightly bohemian little retreat popular with divers and owned by Filipina film-maker Marilou Diaz-Abaya. All rooms (some right on the beach) come with a/c and cable TV, and the rate includes four buffet meals a day. It's always full at weekends, so book in advance. ☞ P7200

Vivere Azure Brgy Aguada Km 108, San Teodoro ☏ 02 771 7777, ⓦ vivereazure.com. Elegant boutique resort with the best views in Anilao and fourteen luxurious suites, each featuring earthy tones, stone and wood furnishings. Rates include all meals, use of the pool, kayaks and snorkelling gear, and promotional discounts are usually available. ☞ P20,300

Batangas City

Lying on the other side of Batangas Bay from Anilao, **BATANGAS CITY** has one of the fastest-growing populations in the Philippines but offers little to see. Its significance for most visitors is as a transit point on the journey to Puerto Galera on Mindoro.

ARRIVAL AND DEPARTURE   BATANGAS CITY

By ferry Batangas Port lies 2km west of the city centre. Ferries to Puerto Galera (around 2hr) depart Batangas Port Terminal 3, where Father n' Son Lines sell tickets to Muelle Pier (P230), Sabang (P230) and White Beach (P270) on large outriggers (daily 6.30am–5pm). Montenegro Lines and three other companies operate ferries to Calapan, 44km southeast of Galera (hourly; 2hr 30min; P240), and Fast Cat (8 daily; P190) do the same run in just 1hr 30min. Montenegro and Besta sail to Abra de Ilog, 30km west (16 daily; 2hr 30min; P260). Montenegro, Navios and CSGA also run ferries to Odiongan (1 daily; 7–10hr; P762) and Romblon (10 weekly; 11–13hr; P762), Navios sail to Cajidiocan (3 weekly; 16hr; P1000), and Super Shuttle have boats for Culasi (3 weekly; 14hr; P800). 2GO serve Caticlan

(1–2 daily; 10hr; P1014). You need to pay an additional terminal fee (P30) before boarding; departures for Galera also incur a P50 "Environmental User Fee".

By bus Batangas City is usually a 3–4hr bus ride from Manila (2hr via the STAR Tollway), depending on road congestion. You may find a jeepney at Batangas Port Terminal 3, with rides into Batangas City centre for P10; otherwise, tricycles will charge around P50. If you're heading to Nasugbu (2hr), Santa Cruz (3hr), Taal (1hr 30min) or Tagaytay (1hr 30min), take a jeepney or tricycle to one of the bus terminals in town. You'll find the JAM, ALPS and Ceres Transport terminals on P. Burgos St, a short ride from the port. Numerous buses wait at Terminal 2 for the frequent trip to Manila.

ACCOMMODATION AND EATING

★ **A&M Village Restaurant** Hilltop Ave, 400m off National Rd ☏ 043 723 1118. This restaurant near the University of Batangas is best known for sumptuous native

cuisine such as *bulalo*, *kare kare* and *leche* flan (mains P200–350). It's 3km from the port; most taxi or tricycle drivers should know it. Daily 8am–9pm.

Hungry Hippo UB Hilltop Arcade, National Rd ☎ 043 300 2323, ⓦ hungryhippo.com.ph. Another store with a cult following, right next to the University of Batangas, this local chain is beloved for its juicy hamburgers (from P105). Daily 8am–10pm.

RGR Traveler's Inn DJPMM Access Rd (off Rizal Ave between the city and the port) ☎ 043 723 6021, ⓦ bit.ly/rgr-travelers. A handy place if you need to spend the night in Batangas: nothing fancy, but clean and friendly, and conveniently located between the city centre and the port. ☎ **P700**

North of Manila

2

Most travellers zip through the provinces **north of Manila** – Pampanga, Bulacan and Bataan – to the justly famed attractions of northern Luzon, but there are a few reasons to break the journey. **Malolos** has some historic distractions, while **Mount Pintatubo** provides energetic hikes and gasp-inducing scenery. **Bataan** is a surprisingly wild province, with some excellent beaches and World War II monuments, while **Subic Bay** is turning into an appealing beach, dive and outdoor activity centre. Buses connect all the main attractions with Manila, though fast ferries would be much quicker to Bataan – if they are running (see p.121).

Malolos

The capital of Bulacan province, **MALOLOS** lies some 45km north of Manila, a relatively historic city of 250,000 best known as the location of the **Malolos Convention** of 1898, the meeting of patriots led by Emilio Aguinaldo that led to the establishment of the First Philippine Republic – the city served as the capital of the short-lived independent nation until 1899. Today, the location of the convention – **Barasoain Church** – is the city's biggest attraction.

Barasoain Church
Paseo del Congreso • Daily 5.30am–7pm • Free • ☎ 044 794 4340, ⓦ barasoainchurch.org

The current incarnation of **Barasoain Church** dates back to 1885, its handsome colonial facade and tower best known as the place where the Revolutionary Congress convened in 1898 (ever the showman, Joseph Estrada chose to be inaugurated president here in

---

SAN PEDRO CUTUD LENTEN RITES

Heading north through Pampanga province, you might be tempted by the rather voyeuristic prospect of watching a dozen or so Catholic devotees being voluntarily **crucified**, a gruesome tradition that started in 1962 and is euphemistically known as the **San Pedro Cutud Lenten Rites**. Every year on Good Friday at San Pedro Cutud, 3km west of **San Fernando**, a dozen or so penitents – mostly men but the occasional woman (and sometimes even the odd foreigner) – are taken to a rice field and nailed to a cross by men dressed as Roman soldiers, using 5cm stainless steel nails that have been soaked in alcohol to disinfect them. The penitents are taken down seconds later. In total some two thousand penitents walk to the site, flagellating themselves using bamboo sticks tied to a rope or shards of glass buried in wooden sticks. The blood – and the cries of pain – are real, but the motivation is questionable to some (one "regular" has been crucified at least 27 times). The Catholic Church does not approve of the crucifixions and does not endorse them, and the media have also turned against the rites, calling them pagan and barbaric – but always managing despite these reservations to allot copious front-page space to photographs of bloodied penitents.

In 2010 the local authorities banned tourists from attending for the first time, but in practice this is virtually impossible to enforce and every year some fifty thousand foreigners and locals attend the spectacle – you'll need to get here early to grab a good view (it's normal and accepted that folks jostle to get close-ups of the nails going in). Partas and Dominion Lines buses leave every hour for San Fernando from their terminals in Cubao.

1998). The church also houses the **Ecclesiastical Museum** on the upper floor, which displays religious relics such as antique prayer cards and a bone fragment of San Vicente Ferrer encased in glass, and puts on a light-and-sound presentation depicting events leading to the Philippine Revolution and the Philippine–American War.

Malolos Cathedral

Paseo del Congreso • Daily 7am–8pm • Free • ☎ 044 791 9352, ⓦ bit.ly/malolos-cathedral

In 1898, Aguinaldo made his headquarters at the grand **Malolos Cathedral**, also known as the Basilica Minore de la Nuestra Señora de Inmaculada Concepcion. The cathedral's Spanish origins lie in the sixteenth century, but Aguinaldo ordered its destruction in 1899, part of his "scorched-earth policy" to hamper the Americans. What you see today was primarily rebuilt in the 1930s, though work has continued to the present. Don't miss the venerable tree in front of the cathedral, known as the **Kalayaan Tree** (Tree of Freedom), said to have been planted by Aguinaldo himself.

Casa Real

Paseo del Congreso • Mon–Fri 9.30am–4.30pm • Free • ☎ 044 791 2716

A gorgeous Spanish house with origins in 1580 and serving many functions over the years, the **Casa Real** is primarily a small museum and shrine dedicated to the "**twenty women of Malolos**". These pioneers began a daring campaign for a school for women in 1888, and the museum has various displays on other barrier-breaking Filipinas from around the country.

ARRIVAL AND INFORMATION   MALOLOS

By van First North Luzon Transit (☎ 0923 744 9253, ⓦ firstnorthluzontransit.com) run buses from Monumento LRT station in Manila. Vans and FX taxis run to Malolos from Monumento and from SM City North, at the northern end of EDSA, 400m beyond North Avenue MRT station. A train service is planned from Manila's Tutuban station along the old Philippine National Rail line, but is not expected to be in operation for some years yet.

Tourist information The helpful provincial tourist office is in the Capitol Building (Mon–Fri 8am–5pm; ☎ 044 305 2023, ⓦ bulacan.gov.ph).

EATING

Enlin's Bakeshop 53 A. Mabini St ☎ 044 796 1029, ⓦ bit.ly/enlins-bakeshop. Malolos is famed throughout the Philippines for its *ensaymada*, a sweet, buttery bread treat, often crowned with grated cheese and sliced salted egg. *Enlin's*, opposite the church, sells boxes of the delicacy for P90 – they also sell *ube* (purple yam) flavour and popular *pastel de leche*. Daily 5am–9pm.

Clark and Angeles City

Some 80km north of Metro Manila, **CLARK** (or more formally Clark Freeport Zone; ⓦ www.clark.com.ph) is an odd mix of converted barracks, unappealing duty-free malls, IT industrial zones, golf courses and prostitution. Indeed, Clark and adjacent **ANGELES CITY** remain one of the Philippines' most notorious sun and sex destinations, with dozens of girlie bars catering to high-spending Western, Korean and Taiwanese men. Clark was the site of an American military base between 1903 and 1991, and like Subic Bay (see p.121) has been transformed into a "freeport zone" (a tax- and duty-free zone) since the departure of the US Air Force. It's been far less successful in shedding its sleazy image, however, though the **airport** has proved popular with budget airlines. If you are travelling to the airport or aiming to climb **Pinatubo** or **Arayat**, you may end up spending some time here, but otherwise there's little reason to linger. If you have to overnight in Clark, keep in mind that the hotels are almost universally geared to prostitution.

The name "Clark" is generally used to refer to the former base and the tourist area of Angeles City around it, particularly **Fields Avenue** on the south side where most of the bars are.

ARRIVAL AND DEPARTURE

CLARK AND ANGELES CITY

By plane Several budget carriers connect Clark International Airport (⊚crk.clarkairport.com), inside the former base area, with Singapore, Taipei, Seoul, Kuala Lumpur, Macau, Cebu and other regional destinations. Outside the terminal are a small convenience store and an ATM. Plenty of fixed-rate taxis meet each flight, but these are expensive (and drivers will try to charge more if they can): anywhere within Clark (including Fields Ave) is P300, the Dau bus terminal (see below) is P400 and Angeles City P500. Jeepneys (with a/c) run from the airport when full (minimum eight people) and charge P50 to anywhere in Clark or to the Dau bus terminal. Philtranco (☎02 851 8078, ⊚philtranco.com.ph) runs expensive (P300) but direct buses to Manila which stop at the airport at approximately 12.30am, 12.30pm and 5.30pm. Coming in the other direction, buses depart Manila at 6.30am, 11.30am and 8.30pm.

By bus For most destinations, head to the Dau bus terminal (pronounced "Da-oo") in nearby Mabalacat, served by almost continual buses from the capital and less frequently to and from Baguio, La Union, Aliminos and Vigan. An expensive but more convenient option for travelling between Manila and Clark is the Fly-the-Bus service operated by Swagman Travel (☎02 523 8541, ⊚swaggy.com). The bus leaves the *Swagman Hotel*, 411 A. Flores St, Ermita, at 11.30am, 3.30pm and 8.30pm daily and serves a number of hotels in Clark for P600 one-way (it heads back to Manila at 8am, noon and 3pm).

ACCOMMODATION AND EATING

Aling Lucing Sisig G. Valdez St ☎0906 305 0562, ⊚bit.ly/aling-lucing. Angeles City is known as the *sisig* capital of the Philippines, after the popular Filipino dish (made from pig's cheek and liver with calamansi and chilli), that was first cooked up at this unassuming restaurant in 1974. It's still the best place to sample it but ask how much it'll cost before you order; the restaurant notoriously does not publish prices (it was P185 at last check). The dish's inventor, *sisig* queen Lucia Cunanan, ran the place until 2008 when, at the age of 80, she was murdered by her gambling-addicted husband for refusing to give him money to bet with. Daily 8am–midnight.

Gill's Buko Sherbet & Ice Cream Booth 6, M&M's Lane, Nepo Mart ☎0998 570 9715, ⊚bit.ly/gills-buko. Much-loved local sweet treat supplier, where the signature *buko* sherbet (also served with lychees) comes at P20 per scoop. Daily 10am–6.30pm.

Red Planet Don Juico Ave, Angeles City ☎045 459 0888, ⊚redplanethotels.com. Your best bet for accommodation in Angeles is this generic but efficient, modern and reasonably priced chain hotel, located just off Roxas Highway between Clark and Angeles. 🛜 **P1500**

Mount Pinatubo

All visitors must pay a conservation fee (P500)

Nothing has quite been the same around **Mount Pinatubo** (1485m), 25km east of Clark, since 1991, when the volcano exploded in one of the largest eruptions of the twentieth century worldwide (see box, p.120). Today, visits to the resultant moon-like lahar landscape and lake is one of the country's top activities, though independent hikes to the top are not permitted. The local tribe, the **Aetas**, though devastated by the eruption, have legal ownership over the mountain.

Organized trips to the volcano leave from the small town of **Santa Juliana**, about 40km from Clark, where you register. From here, a 4WD takes you for an hour or so across flat lahar beds and over dusty foothills to the start of a gentle hike to **Lake Pinatubo** (around 5.5km, with a height gain of 300m; 2–3hr); some tour companies will take you closer (via the Korean-built "Skyway"), within ten minutes of the crater. The lake itself is stunning, with emerald-green waters and spectacular surrounding views. Bring a packed lunch. Swimming and boating on the lake are now banned.

ARRIVAL AND DEPARTURE

MOUNT PINATUBO

By bus and jeepney The North Luzon and SCTEX expressways make getting to Pinatubo easy enough, and it's feasible to visit as a day-trip from Manila. Coming from Manila or Clark on any Tarlac or Baguio bus, ask to be let off in Capas, where you can catch a jeepney or tricycle to Paitlin (P30), and then a tricycle to the barangay of Santa Juliana for around P60 (or go direct from Capas to Santa Juliana via tricycle; 1hr; at least P300 for the round trip). From Santa Juliana, the first 4WD trips (P3500 for up to five people, plus P500 for a guide) depart at around 5.30–6am from

2

PINATUBO BLOWS ITS TOP

On April 2, 1991, people from the village of Patal Pinto on the lower slopes of **Mount Pinatubo** witnessed small explosions followed by steaming, and smelt rotten egg fumes escaping from the upper slopes of the supposedly dormant volcano (the last-known eruption was six hundred years before). On June 12, the first of several major explosions took place. The eruption was so violent that shockwaves were felt in the Visayas and nearly twenty million tons of sulphur dioxide gas were blasted into the atmosphere, causing red skies to appear for months afterwards. A giant ash cloud rose 35km into the sky and red-hot blasts seared the countryside. Ash paralysed Manila, closing the airport for days and turning the capital's streets into an eerie, grey, post-apocalyptic landscape. By June 16, when the dust had settled, the top of the volcano was gone, replaced by a 2km-wide caldera containing a lake. Lava deposits had filled valleys, buildings had collapsed, and over eight hundred people were dead.

The eruption virtually destroyed the traditional way of life of the **Aeta people**, who had lived on the slopes of the volcano. Over twenty years later, many Aeta have re-established small villages near the mountain. Over seven hundred, however, live in poorly maintained bamboo houses on a special relocation site in Sitio Gala near Subic Bay dubbed the Aeta Resettlement and Rehabilitation Center, where they're almost entirely dependent on charitable organizations for their survival.

Capas Tourism Satellite Office (☎0999 356 5069, @capastourism@yahoo.com), and you won't be able to do the climb if you arrive in Santa Juliana later than 10am; it's best to arrive by 7am at the latest if possible.

TOURS

Several companies run Pinatubo trips, though none will volunteer the information that the longer treks are closed, so question them carefully about what's open to trekkers at present. Prices are dependent on group size. **Hiking** all the way is not really feasible, as it would take at least 8hr, and camping is not allowed.

Alvin's Mount Pinatubo Guesthouse Santa Juliana ☎0919 861 4102, ⓦmt-pinatubo.weebly.com. This little homestay run by a very friendly and welcoming couple offers accommodation, 4WD rental and trekking packages, as well as tours to local Aeta villages. The Mount Pinatubo trek (including Botolan Zambales mayor's fee) works out at P2350 per person in a group of five including packed lunch and use of toilet and shower facilities at the guesthouse; if there are just one or two of you, they can help you form a larger group to lower costs. ☎ Dorms P500, doubles P1200

Mount Pinatubo 4-Wheelers Club Santa Juliana ☎0919 608 4313, ⓦpinatubowendell.blogspot.com.

4WD trips are charged at P3000 for the jeep (for up to five), plus P500 for the guide, P500 conservation fee (per person) and P700 mayor's fee (per person): so P1900 each in a group of five, or P2950 each in a group of two.

Trekking Mt. Pinatubo ☎02 310 5036, ⓦtrekking pinatubo.com. Popular tours from Manila, beginning with a minibus ride to the Crow Valley (2hr 30min), where you transfer to 4WD jeep. Guides are good, but this is a long day-trip (pick up at 4am Sun–Fri, 3.30am Sat), and you won't get much time on the mountain. Trips from P13,000 for one person down to just P2650 per person in a group of ten or more.

Bataan

With 85 percent of it covered in mountainous jungle, the **Bataan** peninsula is one of the most rugged places in the country. The province, forming the western side of Manila Bay, will always be associated with one of the bloodiest episodes of World War II. For four months in 1942, 65,000 Filipinos and 15,000 Americans – "the battling bastards of Bataan" – held out here against the superior arms and equipment of the Japanese. After their surrender in April 1942, the Filipino and American soldiers, weakened by months of deprivation, were forced to walk to detention camps in Tarlac province. About 10,000 men died along the way. **Balanga** is the provincial capital, and there are some picturesque **beaches** on Bataan's southwest coast between **Mariveles**, some 50km south of Balanga, and **Bagac**.

Shrine of Valor

Daily 8am–5pm • P30, elevator up crucifix P10 (closed for repairs at time of writing) • Jeepneys between Balanga, Cabog and Bagac stop at the Mount Samat/Diwa intersection (20min); from here tricycles run to the top (30min each way; P200 round trip) or it's a sweaty 7km hike; hiring a van from Balanga should cost around P1500

A poignant memorial to the American and Filipino soldiers who fought and died here in World War II, the "Dambana ng Kagitingan" or **Shrine of Valor** occupies the summit of **Mount Samat** (564m), 16km inland from Balanga. The shrine has a chapel and a small museum of weapons captured from the Japanese, but the centrepiece is a 92m **crucifix** with an elevator inside (commissioned by Ferdinand Marcos in 1966); when functioning, it takes you to a gallery at the top with views across the peninsula and, on a clear day, to Manila.

Mount Mariveles

Take a tricycle from Mariveles to the barangay of Alasasin (P100), where you need to register at the barangay hall (P30) and can engage a guide

From Mariveles you can strike out for the ridge of dormant volcano, **Mount Mariveles** (1130m), a tricky overnight climb or a very long day for fit hikers. Apart from food and water, you'll need a good tent or bivouac, a sleeping bag and warm jacket – it can be surprisingly chilly when night falls. The caldera of Mariveles is huge; the ridge runs for 22km and includes several peaks – Tarak Ridge (the most accessible, from Alasasin), Banayan Peak and Mariveles Ridge.

ARRIVAL AND DEPARTURE — BATAAN

By bus Bataan Transit (ⓦ bataantransit.com) runs frequent a/c services from Manila, originating both at Five Star Terminal, Cubao (to Balanga every 15min midnight–10pm; 2–3hr; to Mariveles every 30min midnight–9.30pm; 3–4hr), and from Avenida Terminal (to Balanga and Mariveles every 30min). Genesis Transport (ⓦ genesistransport.com.ph) runs a similar service from Pasay to Balanga (every 15min 2.30am–7.30pm) and Mariveles (every 20min 1am–7.30pm), and between Mariveles and Baguio (every 2hr 2am–1pm).

Victory Liner (ⓦ victoryliner.com) connects Balanga with Olongapo for Subic Bay (every 30–60min; 1hr 15min). Jeepneys (6am–8pm; P19) ply the mountain highway between Balanga, Cabog and Bagac when full.

By boat From Manila, Baatan is a convenient 1hr zip across the bay to Mariveles or Orion (near Balanga), but at time of writing there was no service, although there has been in the past and may be again. Check with the Manila tourist office (see p.84).

ACCOMMODATION

Montemar Beach Club Brgy Pasinay, Bagac ☎ 02 811 5496, ⓦ montemar.com.ph. This large, well-established hotel is the best of a number of resorts along Bataan's southwest coast used mostly by Filipinos for weekend breaks. It's on a 500m stretch of clean sandy beach, and has watersports facilities and a swimming pool. The rooms have a/c and a private balcony overlooking either the beach or the gardens. ⓦ P6300

Subic Bay

Since the closure of US Naval Base Subic Bay in 1992, **SUBIC BAY** has been reinvented as a gate-guarded playground for the rich, with golf courses and plush hotels. For most foreign visitors, the main appeal is the wide range of watersports, diving and tranquil beaches.

The Subic Bay area is vast, most lying in Zambales province, an hour southwest of Clark via the SCTEX highway, and some 110km northwest of Manila. The old base itself is now the **Subic Bay Freeport Zone** (a tax- and duty-free zone), accessed by "gates" manned by security guards, and comprising two parts: most of the banks, restaurants, shops and hotels are located on a small island known as the **Central Business District (CBD)**, while on the **mainland** to the south lie the beaches and most of the outdoor activities, theme parks and attractions.

To the north of the CBD, linked by gates and bridges across the drainage channel (the main gate, at the end of Magsaysay Drive, is known as the **Magsaysay Gate**), **OLONGAPO CITY** – outside the Freeport Zone but considered part of the Subic Bay

2

area – is a typical Philippine provincial town, and is where the bus terminals are located. Around 5km north of Olongapo along the coast (also outside the Freeport Zone), **Barrio Barretto** is gradually shaking off its go-go bar days, though it still attracts its share of the ageing expat/Filipina "girlfriend" scene. Nearby **Baloy Long Beach**, a laidback row of bars and hotels right on the sand, is a better place to crash.

Most visitors come to Subic Bay for the **wreck diving**, which is superb (see box, p.124), but there are plenty of peaceful, clean **beaches** inside the former base if you just want to chill out (see box opposite).

Ocean Adventure

Camayan Wharf, Ilanin Rd, West Ilanin Forest Area • Daily 9am–6pm • P788; children under 12 P628; swim with dolphins (45min) P3700; beach encounter with dolphins (30min) P2400; dive with dolphins (30min) P4250 • ☎ 047 252 9000, ⓦ oceanadventure.ph • Free shuttle from the CBD 10.45am & 1.15pm (bus & taxi terminal on Aguinaldo St)

Next to Camayan Beach (see box opposite), **Ocean Adventure** is one of Subic's major tourist draws, comprising a small aquarium and arena for dolphin and sea lion shows. You can also swim, dive (includes dive gear; bring your certification), or have a brief encounter on the beach with the park's friendly dolphins.

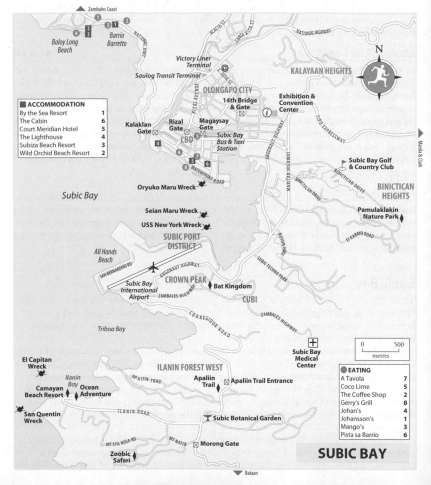

ACCOMMODATION
By the Sea Resort	1
The Cabin	6
Court Meridian Hotel	5
The Lighthouse	4
Subiza Beach Resort	3
Wild Orchid Beach Resort	2

EATING
A Tavola	7
Coco Lime	5
The Coffee Shop	2
Gerry's Grill	8
Johan's	4
Johansson's	1
Mango's	3
Pista sa Barrio	6

SUBIC BAY

SUBIC BAY BEACHES

All Hands Beach San Bernardino Rd ☎047 250 2270, ⓦallhandsbeach.com. On the north side of the airport and closest to the CBD, this is a tranquil stretch of sand and beach huts shaded by trees. Though it's being developed as a resort, during most weekdays you'll have it to yourself: P150, children under 3ft tall P100; beach package including use of huts P400. Daily 24hr (swimming till midnight).

Camayan Beach Ilanin Rd (off Corregidor Rd) ☎047 252 8000, ⓦcamayanbeachresort.ph. South of All Hands, the best beach in the Freeport Zone is Camayan Beach (formerly Miracle Beach) and now part of the *Camayan Beach Resort*; day visitors pay P500 (children under 12, P420), and you can rent snorkelling equipment (P300/2hr), or go diving (wreck dive including equipment rental P1500) or kayaking (P300/1hr). Daily 7.30am–8pm.

Baloy Long Beach After Barrio Barretto's scrappy beach, this is one of the better strips of sand in Luzon; locals charge a nominal entry fee (P50). Daily 24hr.

Zoobic Safari

Ilanin Rd, West Ilanin Forest Area • Daily 8am–4pm • P545, children 3–4ft (90–120cm) tall P445, under 3ft (90cm) free • ☎047 252 2272, ⓦzoobic.com.ph • Taxis from the CBD are P400–500

Subic Bay has its own zoo experience, the **Zoobic Safari**, which is popular with Manileños. However, though the animals are well treated, if you don't like zoos you're unlikely to enjoy this. Attractions include a tiger safari via jeep (where the guides feed chicken to the "wild" tigers); a serpentarium with iguanas, snakes and lizards; and "croco loco", where crocodiles leap for dangling chickens.

Bat Kingdom

Zambales Hwy, Crown Peak, Cubi • Taxi drivers should be able to take you to the right location for about P500 from Olopango or the CBD

Other than a few groups of monkeys, the most visible wildlife in the hills around Subic is a colony of around ten thousand bamboo bats, fruit bats and giant flying foxes – the so-called **Bat Kingdom**. The colony tends to move around within the Cubi, Crown Peak area, so ask locals where they are; during the day bats hang from trees asleep, but at dusk thousands take to the air to look for food.

ARRIVAL AND DEPARTURE   SUBIC BAY

By bus Most buses (see p.82) arrive in Olongapo City at the Victory Liner terminal (☎047 222 2241) or the Saulog terminal, off Rizal Ave either side of the junction with W 18th St (the Olangapo–Bugalon road).
Destinations Angeles City/Dau (Victory Liner: every 45min;1hr, via SCTEX); Baguio (Victory Liner: every 90min; 8hr); Manila Cubao (Victory Liner: every 30min; 2am–10pm; 3–4hr); Manila Pasay (Victory Liner and Saulog: each hourly; 4–5hr).

INFORMATION

Tourist information 2/F, Subic Bay Exhibition & Convention Center, 18 Efficiency Ave (just off the main Manila highway, at the edge of the Zone; daily 8am–5pm; ☎047 252 4655, ⓦmysubicbay.com.ph); staff can help book tours, hotels and arrange hikes (see box, p.125).
Internet access Twin Digistar, Magsaysay Drive (daily 8am–midnight; P25/hr). In Barrio Barretto, popular resorts and restaurants such as *Mango's* and *Johansson's* have reliable internet.
Banks and exchange There are a handful of moneychangers on Magsaysay Drive near the junction with Rizal Ave.

GETTING AROUND

SUBIC BAY FREEPORT ZONE

By taxi Jeepneys and tricycles are banned within Subic Bay Freeport Zone, so transport is provided by Megatsai taxis (24hr; ☎047 252 8102) and Winstar Transport buses; both have their terminals in the CBD in a car park (known as "park and shop") off the Rizal Highway, close to the Main Gate and a short walk from the Saulog Transit terminal over in Olongapo. Taxis charge fixed rates from here, with most fares P50 within the CBD. Elsewhere it's P120 to Pamulaklakin (see box, p.125) and Cubi, P300 to most beaches, and P400 to Zoobic Safari and Ocean Adventure.

OLONGAPO

By jeepney In Olongapo all jeepneys are colour-coded; from

West 18th St by the Victory Liner bus terminal you can take frequent blue jeepneys (direction "Castillejos") via Kalklan Gate (the western CBD entrance) to Barrio Barretto and Baloy (P12), or you can take a yellow jeepney to Magsaysay Gate.
By taxi and tricycle From the bus terminals to Magsaysay Gate, taxis will charge around P150, tricycles

around P50. From Olongapo to the Freeport, you'll have to walk across the Main Gate as the two systems are mutually exclusive (see p.123).
By car To rent a car contact Avis (daily 8am–5pm; ☎ 047 250 0357) at Unit 116, Charlie Building, Subic International Hotel Compound.

ACCOMMODATION

Places in the Freeport Zone tend to be plush and expensive. Barrio Barretto is dominated by resort complexes, but some of the bars (including *Johan's*, *Johansson's* and *Mango's*; see opposite) have low-priced rooms available.

SUBIC BAY FREEPORT ZONE

The Cabin Building 204, Schley Rd ☎ 047 250 3042, ⊛ thecabinsubic.com. This place is neat as a new pin and very welcome if you're looking for budget accommodation in the CBD, despite the rather silly false log cabin "look" on the outside. The rooms are small but immaculately clean; bathroom facilities are shared but also spotless. ⬥ Dorms P575, doubles P1150

Court Meridian Hotel Lot B, Waterfront Rd at Rojas St ☎ 047 252 2366, ⊛ courtmeridian.com. Modern hotel, very clean with comfortable rooms, flatscreen cable TV and breakfast included. The location is good, close to restaurants in the Central Business District. ⬥ P3267

★**The Lighthouse** Moonbay Marina Complex, Waterfront Rd ☎ 047 252 5000, ⊛ lighthousesubic .com. Lavish boutique hotel topped with a replica of a lighthouse (not working). The room theme is "aqua", with soothing blue and green tones, contemporary furnishings, DVD players, flatscreen TVs and a glass-walled bathroom, some with an old-fashioned tub. ⬥ P6700

BARRIO BARRETTO AND BALOY LONG BEACH

By the Sea Resort 99 National Hwy, Barrio Barretto ☎ 047 222 2895, ⊛ bythesea.com.ph. Fifty a/c rooms with cable TV either right on the beach or set back around a quiet garden. There's a convivial restaurant and bar overlooking the sea, and live music Fri. ⬥ P1200

Subiza Beach Resort Baloy Beach Rd, Baloy Long Beach ☎ 047 222 7909, ⊛ subizabeachresort.com. Big but peaceful resort-hotel in an unbeatable location right on the water. A wide range of immaculate rooms, good food (the menu includes Indian and Sri Lankan dishes) and a range of watersports. ⬥ P2750

Wild Orchid Beach Resort Subic Bay Baloy Beach Rd, Baloy Long Beach ☎ 047 223 1029, ⊛ wild orchidsubic.com. Justly popular choice, with standard "deluxe" rooms equipped with king-size beds, flatscreen TVs and DVD players. Welcome extras include *Captain Rob's Steakhouse* and *Barefoot Bar* on the beach, and an enormous pool (with jacuzzis and *Scalliwags* swim-up bar). ⬥ P4000

DIVE SUBIC BAY

Subic Bay is a popular **diving** site, boasting fifteen shipwrecks in still waters, all no more than fifteen minutes by speedboat from the shore. The **USS New York** is the star attraction of Subic's underwater world, a battle cruiser launched in the US in 1891. When World War II broke out, she was virtually retired, and when the Japanese swept the US Marines out of the Philippines, the Americans had no choice but to scuttle her as they departed from Subic in early 1942. The ship now lies on her port side in 27m of water between Alava Pier in the CBD and the northern end of Cubi Point runway at the airport. For experienced divers, the 120m-long hull presents excellent opportunities for what scuba divers call a "swim-through" – an exploration of the inside of the wreck from one end to the other.

The **El Capitan**, a Spanish-era wreck lying 20m down in a pretty inlet on the east coast of Subic Bay is a much easier wreck dive, suitable for novices. The **San Quentin** (16m) is the oldest-known wreck in Subic, a wooden gunboat scuttled by the Spanish in 1898 in a futile attempt to block the channel between Grande and Chiquita islands against invading Americans. Other Subic wrecks include the Japanese POW ship *Oryoku Maru* and the *Seian Maru*, a Japanese cargo vessel sunk by the American Navy in 1945.

One-dive packages with any of the operators start at around P2500.

DIVE OPERATORS

Johan's Adventure Dive Center Right on the shore at Baloy Long Beach ☎ 047 224 8915, ⊛ subicdive.com.

Boardwalk Dive Center Building 664, just off Waterfront Rd ☎ 047 252 5357, ⊛ boardwalkdive centre.com.

HIKING AROUND SUBIC

If you're feeling energetic, you can try numerous hiking trails around Subic Bay, though you'll need to contact the tourism department in advance (see p.123) to arrange mandatory guides; there's a standard fee of P50 per hike. The **Apaliin Trail** runs along the banks of the Apaliin River to the coast (2hr), while visits to the rainforest trails within the **Pamulaklakin Nature Park** (daily 9am–4.30pm) can include an optional three-hour tour from members of the **Aeta tribe** ("eye-ta") – for P250 they'll take you deep into the forest. The Aeta are "Negritos" (they have dark skin and look quite African), and their ancestors are thought to have been the first people to reach the Philippines. They get no cultural support or recognition from the government, but were generally well treated under US rule, and were one of the few groups sad to see the Americans leave. Aeta warriors later trained US Marines here for service in Vietnam. Taxis to Pamulaklakin from the CBD (15min) should cost around P400.

2

EATING

The best places to **eat** and **drink** line the CBD waterfront. Cheaper places are in Olongapo City on Magsaysay Drive and Rizal Ave. In Barrio Barretto, some of the **nightlife** still revolves around girlie bars, but certainly not all of it.

SUBIC BAY FREEPORT ZONE

A Tavola Building 299, Aguinaldo St (behind Venezia Hotel) ☎047 252 6556. The undisputed king of Italian restaurants in Subic, this gem is owned by an Italian chef, offering huge plates of home-made pasta (from P290), wood-fired pizza (from P360) and a good selection of affordable wines. Daily 11am–3pm & 6–10pm.

Coco Lime Harbor Point Mall, Rizal Hwy, CBD ☎047 252 2412. Decent Philippine, Thai and Malay dishes that taste good if not always totally authentic; great adobo rice (P200) and *pancit canton* (P190). Daily 11am–2pm & 5–10pm.

Gerry's Grill Waterfront Rd, near Labitan St ☎047 252 3021, ⓦgerrysgrill.com. Big, brash chain restaurant that sells local food in immense portions; think fried chicken (P265), *lechon kawali* (P275) and crab rice (P210). Daily 11am–11pm.

Pista sa Barrio Building 141, Waterfront Rd at Espiritu St ☎047 252 3187. Solid Filipino cuisine – *kare kare* for P330, half fried chicken (P200) and a huge range of *sinigang* (Filipino sour tamarind soup) from P275, plus especially good seafood – served inside or on the breezy covered deck. Free wi-fi. Daily 7am–midnight.

BARRIO BARRETTO AND BALOY LONG BEACH

The Coffee Shop 2 Rizal St at the National Hwy, Barrio Barretto ☎047 222 9350, ⓦbit.ly/the-coffee-shop. Late-night pit stop locally renowned since 1984 for its "jumbo tacos", packed with various meats and veggies in a soft taco shell (P95). Also does decent fried noodles (P160). Cash only. Daily 24hr.

Johan's Baloy Beach Rd, Baloy Long Beach ☎047 224 8915, ⓦsubicdive.com. Friendly pub and diner in Baloy, right on the beach (it also offers rooms from P700), with a range of excellent Belgian beers and decent food, as well as diving facilities (see box opposite). Daily 24hr.

Johansson's 128 National Hwy, Barrio Barretto ☎047 223 9293. Popular Swedish-owned hangout, with omelettes for breakfast, and a lunch and dinner menu that includes blue marlin steak and fries (P240), boiled veal with dill sauce (P290) or beef stroganoff (P220), with apple pie and ice cream (P120) for dessert. Daily 24hr.

Mango's 116A National Hwy, Barrio Barretto ☎047 223 4139, ⓦmangossubic.com. Beach bar, restaurant, cheap inn and local landmark (look out for the neon sign), serving both Filipino and Western cuisine. Breakfast from P225, and burgers from P325. Daily 24hr.

Northern Luzon

HIKING THROUGH RICE TERRACES, IFUGAO PROVINCE

Northern Luzon

North of Manila, Northern Luzon harbours some of the archipelago's least-visited wildernesses, and offers thrilling outdoor adventures including whitewater rafting, trekking, surfing, spelunking and mountain biking. As well as its wonderful mountainous areas and volcanic landscapes, the region is home to some of the country's best surf breaks, along with wild stretches of coast peppered with virgin beaches and emerald-green waters. It is also rich in culture, with a handful of beautifully preserved Spanish colonial towns lining the west coast. Inland are the tribal heartlands of the central Cordilleras mountain range, where spectacular rice terraces lie enveloped in clouds of mist. Further east is the Northern Sierra Madre National Park, the largest protected area in the country, offering exceptional trekking opportunities. More than 100km off the northern coast of Luzon, and closer to Taiwan than the Philippine mainland, lie the remote, scattered islands of Batanes province with their unforgettable hills and wild rugged cliffs.

Along the west coast north of Subic, the **Zambales coast** is dotted with laidback resorts, while the Lingayen Gulf is the location of the **Hundred Islands National Park** – a favourite weekend trip from Manila. The neighbouring stretch of coast at **Bolinao** offers wonderful virgin beaches at times flanked by dramatic rock formations. Further along the coast, the province of **La Union** draws visitors particularly for its surfing. North of here is Ilocos Sur, known primarily for the old colonial city of **Vigan**, where horse-drawn carriages bounce down narrow cobblestone streets. The area around the capital of Ilocos Norte province, **Laoag**, features a number of sites related to former dictator Ferdinand Marcos, who was born in the nearby village of Sarrat. On the northwestern edge of Luzon are excellent beaches around **Pagudpud**. Northern Luzon's east coast offers excellent surfing at **Baler**, while further north **Palanan** is the jump-off point for the barely explored **Northern Sierra Madre National Park**.

Despite the obvious appeal of the coast, for many visitors the prime attraction in Northern Luzon is the mountainous inland **Cordillera** region, where highlights include the mountain village of **Sagada** with its caves and hanging coffins, and the stunning rice terraces – designated by UNESCO as a World Heritage Site – around **Banaue**. In the village of **Kabayan** in Benguet province, it's possible to hike up to a couple of mountaintop caves to see ancient mummies. Kabayan also provides access to **Mount Pulag**, the highest mountain in Luzon.

VIVA VIGAN BINATBATAN FESTIVAL OF ARTS

Highlights

❶ Surfing in San Juan The sweeping beach in the surf capital of the north has big breakers, magical sunsets and resorts for every budget. See p.136

❷ Vigan Atmospheric old Spanish outpost with cobbled streets, horse-drawn carriages and lively festivals. See p.138

❸ Ilocos Norte A province full of appeal, from sleepy towns such as Sarrat to a number of important Marcos-related sites. See p.146

❹ Trekking in the Cordillera The Cordillera offers wonderful walks through tribal villages and UNESCO World Heritage rice terrace scenery. See p.156

❺ Kabayan A remote village home to centuries-old human mummies interred in caves and burial niches dug out of solid rock. See p.163

❻ Sagada Celebrated mountain Shangri-La with hanging coffins, caves to explore, whitewater rafting, exceptional trekking and very cheap lodgings. See p.170

❼ Batanes Enchanting group of little-visited rural islands off the northern tip of Luzon, offering unforgettable scenery and terrific trekking. See p.181

HIGHLIGHTS ARE MARKED ON THE MAP ON P.130

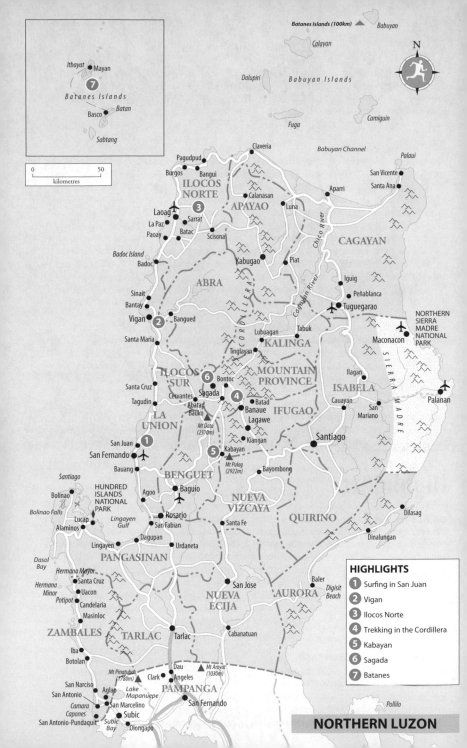

Batanes Islands (100km) Babuyan

Calayan

Dalupiri Babuyan Islands

Fuga Camiguin

Itbayat • Mayan

7

Batanes Islands

Basco • *Batan*

Sabtang

0 ———— 50

kilometres

N

Claveria *Babuyan Channel* Palaui

Pagudpud San Vicente
Burgos Bangui Santa Ana
ILOCOS Calanasan Aparri
NORTE Luna
Laoag **3** **APAYAO**
La Paz Sarrat **CAGAYAN**
Batac Scisona
Paoay

Badoc Island Kabugao Piat
Badoc **ABRA** Iguig
Sinait Peñablanca
Bantay Lubuagan Tuguegarao
Vigan **2** Bangued Tabuk Maconacon
Santa Maria Tinglayan **KALINGA**
  NORTHERN
  SIERRA
  MADRE
  NATIONAL
  PARK
ILOCOS **6** Bontoc Ilagan
SUR Sagada **MOUNTAIN** **ISABELA**
Santa Cruz Cervantes **4** **PROVINCE** Palanan
Tagudin Abatad Batad Cauayan
  Bauko Banaue San
  Mt Data Lagawe Mariano
  (2310m) **IFUGAO**
San Juan **1** Kiangan
San Fernando Kabayan
Bauang **5**
  Mt Pulag Bayombong
BENGUET *(2922m)*
Santiago Agoo **NUEVA**
Bolinao Baguio **VIZCAYA** Dilasag
HUNDRED **QUIRINO**
ISLANDS Rosario Santa Fe
Bolinao Falls **NATIONAL** San Fabian Dinalungan
Lucap **PARK** *Lingayen* Dagupan
Alaminos *Gulf* Urdaneta
Lingayen
Dasol **PANGASINAN**
Bay Baler
Hermana Mayor San Jose *Digisit*
Hermana Santa Cruz **NUEVA** *Beach*
Minor Uacon **ECIJA** **AURORA**
Potipot Candelaria
Masinloc Cabanatuan
ZAMBALES **TARLAC**
Iba Tarlac
Botolan *Mt Pinatubo* *Mt Arayat*
  (1780m) *(1030m)*
San Narciso Dau
San Antonio Aglap Clark Angeles
Camara San Marcelino *Lake* **PAMPANGA**
Capones Subic *Mapanuepe*
San Antonio-Pundaquit *Subic* San Fernando *Pollilo*
  Bay Olongapo

HIGHLIGHTS

1 Surfing in San Juan
2 Vigan
3 Ilocos Norte
4 Trekking in the Cordillera
5 Kabayan
6 Sagada
7 Batanes

NORTHERN LUZON

The Zambales coast

Zambales is an undeveloped rural province – known for its succulent mangoes – that is still largely undiscovered by foreign tourists. It is, however, worth a stop for its scenic **beaches**, good surfing and relaxing resorts. For a break from beaches you can head inland to **Lake Mapanuepe**, formed after Mount Pinatubo erupted in 1991.

Zambales beaches

The **beaches** along the Zambales coast benefit from wonderful sunsets and views of the South China Sea. One lovely long stretch of white sand lies close to the fishing village of **San Antonio** and its popular barangay of **Pundaquit** (sometimes spelled Pundakit), which is also the access point for **Camara** and **Capones islands** – the latter a great place to camp. If your passion is for surfing, make a beeline for *Crystal Beach Resort* just north of the town of **San Narciso**; the best surf is between September and February. Some 35km further north, **Botolan** offers a couple of sleepy but well-run resorts on a nice wide beach in the barangay of Binoclutan, and there's another attractive (brown sand) beach just 8km north of here in the provincial capital **Iba**; the tourist office can arrange tours focusing on mango production, or activities such as mangrove planting. Another 40km further north, the towns of **Candelaria** and **Santa Cruz** serve as jumping-off points to the **Islands** of **Potipot**, **Hermana Mayor** and **Hermana Menor**.

Potipot Island

You can hire a bangka from Candelaria's northern district of Uacón (5min; P400/boat, accommodating up to six people)

Tiny **Potipot Island** is an idyllic little white-sand getaway that you can walk around in just thirty minutes. At times you may have the island to yourself, although it can get busy at weekends and during school summer holidays (mid-March to early June).

The Hermana islands

SeaSun Beach Resort in Santa Cruz (see p.132) can arrange a day-trip to the Hermana islands (P1400/person)

Close to the border with Pangasinan province, **Santa Cruz** is the main access point for two privately owned islands in Dasol Bay: **Hermana Mayor** and **Hermana Menor**. Neither island has accommodation for visitors, but both have some picturesque coves of fine white sand and good snorkelling.

ARRIVAL AND INFORMATION   ZAMBALES BEACHES

By bus Victory Liner have services straight up the coast from Manila, stopping at major towns like Iba and Santa Cruz but able to drop you en route on request, and can often stop right by your resort – make sure to tell the driver where you're going. For Pundaquit, buses stop at San Antonio, a short tricycle ride away (10min), while to get to the Botolan resorts you'll have to catch a tricycle or jeepney (5min) from the spot on the main highway where buses drop you off. Regular local buses also connect all the towns along the coast.

By jeepney A number of jeepneys connect the towns along the coast.

By bangka Bangkas connect the Zambales towns with small islands off the coast – Pundaquit to Capones Island, for example (20min; P800). Hotels can often help organize bangka hire.

Tourist information Iba has a tourist office on the second floor of the town's Capitol building (Mon–Fri 8am–5pm; ☎047 307 2450, ⌨tourism.zambalesnow.com). Tours can be arranged from here.

ACCOMMODATION

SAN ANTONIO-PUNDAQUIT

Nora's Beach Resort ☎0918 278 8188, ✉norasbeachresort@yahoo.com. This basic, welcoming place has two little fan-cooled nipa huts on the beach and more comfortable a/c rooms set around a courtyard. The resort rents out bangkas (P1500/day), which are handy for

exploring nearby Camara and Capones islands, as well as Anawangin Cove where there's good snorkelling. 📶 **P2000**

Punta de Uian ☎0910 269 3858, ⌨puntadeuian.com.ph. The most upmarket place to stay along the Zambales coast, this large resort offers a selection of rooms from a/c doubles to family villas (P13,640). Facilities include two pools, basketball and tennis courts, and a playground. 🛜 **P4160**

SAN NARCISO

Crystal Beach Resort ☎ 047 222 2227, 🌐 crystalbeach .com.ph. Set on a pine tree-lined beach, this surfers' hangout is a large place with a few tiki huts and native houses along the sand, as well as a variety of neat a/c rooms, mostly built with native materials. The vibe is laidback, with hammocks slung between the trees and live acoustic bands playing by the bonfire on weekend nights. Surfboard rental (P400/half-day) and surfing lessons (P400/hr including board rental) are also on offer. Budget travellers can pitch a tent (P550/person). 🛜 **P1700**

BOTOLAN

Kawayan Farm Resort Brgy Santiago ☎ 0921 442 8573, ✉ georgehill_08@yahoo.com. Run by a friendly British-Filipino couple, this welcoming place has inexpensive bamboo huts (P900) and a handful of rooms, of which three are set around a fish pond, each with a balcony from where you can fish directly into the pond (the owners can provide rods). There's an inviting swimming pool, as well as videoke and a pool table. 🛜 **P2100**

Rama International Beach Resort Km 189, National Rd, Brgy Binoclutan ☎ 0917 523 7262, 🌐 ramabeach .com. This Aussie-run resort, with a nice stretch of beach right at the doorstep and a fish pond and chirping birds in the leafy

grounds, has a selection of family rooms as well as doubles a stone's throw away from the sea. They can also arrange trips to limestone caves near Santa Cruz, the old hilltop gold-mining town of Acoe or nearby Mount Binoclutan. 🛜 **P1869**

IBA

Palmera Garden ☎ 0908 503 1416, 🌐 palmera-garden.com. This shaded beachfront resort, around 2km north of Iba, has a selection of tiled rooms set around a leafy pool, and an open-fronted thatched restaurant; all have fridge, a/c and private bath. The free wi-fi, available in the public areas, reaches some of the bedrooms. 🛜 **P2200**

CANDELARIA

Dawal Brgy Uacón ☎ 0919 573 0952, 🌐 dawal.com.ph. Large concrete-block resort offering clean, good-value poolside accommodation; some of the rooms at the back are a bit dated. There's a barbecue area for guests, and a live band and disco (8pm–2am) on Sat nights. The resort arranges trips to Potipot but has no snorkelling equipment for rent. 🛜 **P1800**

SANTA CRUZ

SeaSun Beach Resort ☎ 0928 855 5125, 🌐 seasun.com .ph. Most of the rooms here have pretty blue tiles, private bath and a/c, while the five simple nipa rooms have fan and shared bath. There's a cluster of shaded open-fronted huts to while away the afternoon, an indoor bar with pool table and a coral reef perfect for snorkelling just 50m away. 🛜 **P600**

The Lingayen Gulf

Much of the western stretch of the **Lingayen Gulf**, between Bolinao and Dagupan, is taken up by working beaches where people fish in the gulf's rich waters and mend their nets. The gulf's primary attraction, the **Hundred Islands National Park** is home to some lovely beaches, while at the western end of the gulf around Bolinao you'll find wild stretches of coast and good **snorkelling**. At the northeastern end of the gulf, the capital of La Union province, **San Fernando**, provides access to more beaches and resorts as well as opportunities for trekking and climbing. There is also excellent **surfing** if you time it right, with surfers congregating in the resorts of **San Juan**.

Hundred Islands National Park

The tiny islands of **Hundred Islands National Park** – there are actually 123, but that doesn't have quite the same ring to it – cover almost twenty square kilometres. Some islands have beaches, but many are no more than coral outcrops crowned by scrub. Sadly, much of the underwater **coral** in the park has been damaged by a devastating combination of cyanide fishing (dripping cyanide in the water to stun the fish) and dynamite fishing (exploding dynamite in the water to kill the fish with shockwaves, then scooping them up when they float to the surface – of course this also kills the coral) along with typhoons and the El Niño weather phenomenon. The authorities are, however, going all out to protect what coral is left and help it regenerate, meaning you can only snorkel in approved areas.

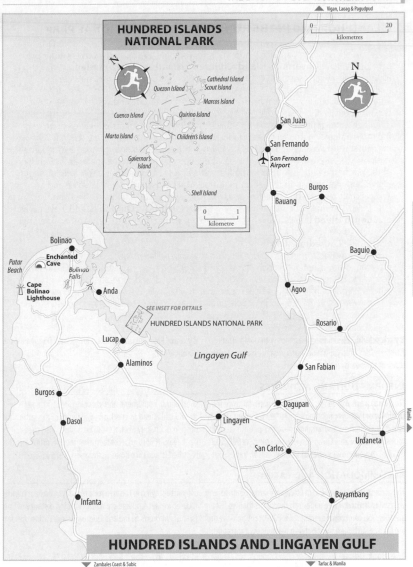

HUNDRED ISLANDS AND LINGAYEN GULF

Unless you want to camp, or stay at the one guesthouse on the islands, the closest base is the small town of **Lucap**, accessible from Alaminos, where day-trips set off; the town, however, is pretty dull and not recommended as a place to stay. It's far nicer to base yourself at one of the resorts near Bolinao (see pp.135–136).

ARRIVAL AND DEPARTURE

HUNDRED ISLANDS NATIONAL PARK

By bus The closest bus station to the Hundred Islands National Park is at Alaminos, 4km south of Lucap, accessible from Lucap by tricycle (see p.134). Victory Liner and Five Star serve Manila (roughly every 40min–1hr; 4–8hr) and Santa Cruz (every 30min; 2hr). Victory Liner buses from Manila continue to Bolinao (45min), and there are services to Dagupan (every 30min; 1hr 30min) from where you can change for Baguio or San Fernando La Union.

3

ISLAND-HOPPING IN THE HUNDRED ISLANDS NATIONAL PARK

The best way to visit the pretty cluster of islets that form part of the One Hundred Islands National Park is through an island-hopping trip. The only three islands with any form of development are **Governor's Island**, **Children's Island** and **Quezon Island**. A day-trip to all three from Lucap costs P1000 for a small boat for five people (larger boats are also available). You'll need to choose one island on which you will spend most of your time – the boatman will leave you there for a few hours then return, and you'll visit the other two more briefly.

A much more appealing option is to pay P1400 for a "service boat" allowing you to visit the more interesting undeveloped islands. Some of these dots of land are so small and rocky that it's impossible to land on them, while others are big enough to allow for some exploring on foot, with tiny, sandy coves where you can picnic in the shade and swim. One of the prettiest islands is **Marta**, actually two tiny islets connected by a thin strip of bright white sand that almost disappears at high tide. **Marcos Island** has a blowhole and a vertical shaft of rock; you can clamber to the top and then dive into a seawater pool about 20m below. A number of islands, including **Scout Island** and **Quirino Island**, have caves; on **Cuenco Island** there's a cave that goes right through the island to the other side. Shell Island has a lagoon in which you can swim at high tide, while birdwatchers should ask to stop beside **Cathedral Island**.

Boats are available from 6am and will return to Lucap no later than 5.30pm; if you are planning to stay overnight on one of the islands then you need to leave Lucap by 5pm, and you will be charged P3000 for a service boat to drop you off and pick you up next day. Whatever your plans, the park office (see below) may be able to arrange for you to join another group if you do not have enough people to fill a boat and want to save some money.

By tricycle Tricycles connect Alaminos with Lucap (15min; P100) and can drop you at your hotel or at the national park office at the nearby pier.

By van From Alaminos a/c vans serve Dagupan (1hr 30min; P65).

INFORMATION AND ACTIVITIES

National park office You can pay your park entrance fee (P40/day or P80/overnight, plus a P30 "environmental fee" and P10 insurance) and arrange camping permits at the tourist office by the Lucap jetty (daily 24hr; ☎075 205 0917, ⓦalaminoscity.gov.ph). They also rent out snorkelling equipment and camping gear, although you should call ahead to check on availability of the latter. The office has a handy ATM. It's also possible to visit the islands by kayak (P350/hr); contact the tourist office or the Hundred Islands Eco-Tours Association (T075 552 0773).

ACCOMMODATION AND EATING

The accommodation options in **Lucap** are largely uninspiring, so if you're staying in the area for a few days, consider basing yourself in **Bolinao** (see opposite). The hotels that we list are on Lucap's main strip and are within walking distance of one another. You can **camp** overnight for P200/tent on Governor's Island, Children's Island and Quezon Island. Eating options are limited, although most hotels have their own restaurant.

The Boat House Lucap ☎0921 642 8551, ⓦbit.ly/ boathouse-lucap. An unusual find among Lucap's unexciting eating places, this octagonal restaurant serves imported Hawaiian black angus steaks (P490) and fresh local fish including dorado (P290), plus about twenty wines from around the world. Fri–Sun 6–10pm.
Governor's Guesthouse Governor's Island ☎075 551 2505. The only permanent accommodation within the One Hundred Islands National Park, this guesthouse, sleeping ten, is a good choice for groups. You'll have the entire island to yourself once the day-trippers have gone. ☂ **P5000**

Maxine By the Sea Lucap ☎075 696 0964, ⓦmaxinebythesea.com. Simply furnished rooms with a/c, cable TV and private bath. There's wi-fi in the public areas and a popular open-fronted restaurant serving fresh seafood – try the calamari (P245). ☂ **P2950**
Villa Antolin Lucap ☎075 696 9227, ⓦvilla-antolin .com. Run by a welcoming retired Filipino couple, this is one of Lucap's best options, with clean rooms spread across two storeys and kitsch knick-knacks dotting the hallways. Not all rooms have hot water, so check first. ☂ **P1800**

Bolinao and around

The landscape around the town of BOLINAO is one of cascading waterfalls, rolling hills and white beaches, including the popular **Patar Beach** and the inviting **Bolinao Falls**. The **Church of St James** in the main square was built by the Augustinians in 1609 and boasts a good collection of wooden santos figures.

Patar Beach

The best-known beach in the Bolinao area is **Patar Beach**, 19km west of town, which has fine white sand and good surf. On the road to Patar there are a number of pleasant, relaxed beaches and resorts, which can arrange trips to a large **barrier reef** offshore, near **Santiago Island**, where there is some wonderful solitary snorkelling.

Bolinao Falls

21km south of Bolinao • P50 each waterfall (not always charged off-season), plus P50 to hire a lifejacket • The falls are not signposted; if driving, make sure to ask for directions, or catch a tricycle from Bolinao (around P500 return including waiting time; 45min)

The **Bolinao Falls** are two emerald waterfalls perfect for a refreshing dip. Bolinao Falls 1 has a cascading fall with a small pool, while the larger Bolinao Falls 2 has a series of inviting pools where you can easily while away an afternoon. You can rent open-fronted huts here for the day (P200) – there are only two basic stalls selling water and snacks so make sure to bring your own food for a picnic.

Enchanted Cave

Patar Rd • Daily 8am–6pm • P150

A popular attraction in the area is the **Enchanted Cave**, where you can descend a short flight of steep and slippery steps to swim in an underground pool of exceptionally clear water. It can get very busy on weekends; it's best to visit on a weekday.

Cape Bolinao Lighthouse

Close to Patar Beach, some 20km from Bolinao, stands the old **Cape Bolinao Lighthouse** (1905), which, sitting on a hill, rises 107m above sea level. There's an easy path to the base of the building; climbing up here from the main road is rewarded by great views across the South China Sea. Though you can't see them, not far offshore lie a number of submerged Spanish galleons and Chinese junks that, according to local lore, still contain treasure.

ARRIVAL AND INFORMATION

BOLINAO AND AROUND

By bus There are regular services from Manila to Bolinao with Victory Liner and Five Star (hourly; 6hr), with stops at Alaminos (45min from Bolinao). For Baguio or San Fernando La Union, take a bus to Dagupan (every 30min; 2hr) and change there.

By jeepney Jeepneys connect Bolinao with Alaminos, although they take much longer than the buses (leave when full; 1hr 30min).

By tricycle Tricycles connect Bolinao town to the resorts along the nearby beach (15min; P150) and to Patar Beach (25min; P200).

Tourist information The tourist office in Bolinao is on Rizal St (Alaminos–Bolinao Rd), opposite the High School (Mon–Fri 8am–5pm; ☎ 075 632 4479 or ☎ 0948 702 5629).

ACCOMMODATION AND EATING

There's only one recommendable **hotel** and no good **restaurants** in Bolinao proper; it's better to stay, and eat, at one of the nearby beach resorts.

BOLINAO

El Pescador San Andres St, Brgy Germinal ☎ 075 633 0527, ⓦ elpescadorbolinao.com. This large well-kept resort has more than fifty warm and welcoming rooms set in the "grand hotel" building by the beach, or in the less expensive "twin building" by the pool. There are also seven clean and cosy a/c kubo cottage huts, all with shared bath, decorated with pretty local materials, as well as a large inviting pool for adults, and a smaller one for children. 📶 Kubo cottage huts P1550, doubles P2350

THE ROAD FROM BOLINAO TO PATAR BEACH

Puerto del Sol Brgy Ilog Malino ☎075 710 7371, ⓦ puertodelsol.com.ph. Bolinao's most upmarket resort offers spacious, tastefully decorated a/c rooms in well-tended grounds, with dark wooden furniture, fridges, cable TV, private verandas and tea and coffee amenities. There's a pool, spa, open-air jacuzzi and a restaurant overlooking a pretty stretch of beach with shallow clear water. ☞ **P9000**

★Punta Riviera Resort Brgy Ilog Malino ☎075 696 1350, ⓦ puntarivieraresort.com. The best resort in the area, eco-friendly, with well-tended grounds, palm trees, infinity pool and a colourful dragon-fruit orchard. The tiled a/c rooms are clean and spacious, breakfast is included and the sauna and open-air jacuzzi are perfect spots to unwind after a kayaking trip through the resort's mangroves. Breakfast included. ☞ **P4704**

Rock View Beach Brgy Patar ☎0998 805 4878. The perfect choice for budget travellers, with closed nipa huts and simple a/c rooms (P2000), on a spectacular stretch of wild coastline overlooking rock formations. There isn't a restaurant, but guests can cook in the open-fronted kitchen. ☞ **P1500**

Villa Carolina y Juan Brgy Ilog Malino ☎0921 698 3340, ⓦ bit.ly/villa-carolina. Located just across the street from *Punta Riviera Resort*, this Belgian/Filipina-owned resort has simple rooms in its brown, mock-wood concrete buildings, which makes the place feel rather dark. There's a pool, kayaks for rent and cooked food upon request. ☞ **P3500**

Villa Soledad Brgy Ilog Malino ☎075 736 2239, ⓦ villasoledadbeachresort.com. Good-value rooms, although some of the family rooms can be a bit of a squeeze. Accommodation is set around a leafy tropical garden with basketball court and two palm-shaded pools. There's table tennis and billiards, too. Breakfast included. ☞ **P3000**

PATAR BEACH

Treasures of Bolinao Patar Beach ☎075 696 3266, ⓦ treasoookbolinao.com. Overloooking Patar Beach, this resort has a variety of a/c rooms, most with DVD players and private terraces, and you don't pay much more for the superior New Villa rooms (P4500, but no sea view) and Maharlika suites (P6800 for four). There's a pleasant pool area and a deck overlooking the beach. ☞ **P4000**

San Fernando and around

The capital of La Union province and site of a former US air base, **SAN FERNANDO** has little of interest to tourists. It is, however, the access point for the popular **San Juan** surfing beach, 8km north.

Chinese-Filipino Friendship Pagoda

Take Zigzag Rd or use the steps up Hero's Hill from Quezon Ave

If you have a few hours to spare in San Fernando, take a walk uphill to Freedom Park and the **Chinese-Filipino Friendship Pagoda**. The pagoda boasts great views across the rooftops and out to the South China Sea. There is more evidence of the Chinese influence in the area at the impressive **Ma-Cho temple**, along Quezon Avenue on the northern outskirts of the city.

San Juan

A dramatic crescent with big breakers that roll in from the South China Sea, the coast just north of **SAN JUAN** in the barangay of Urbiztondo is a prime **surfing beach**. Most of its resorts have surfboards to rent (P200/hr) and offer tuition (another P200). For experienced surfers there are two breaks in **Urbiztondo**, one a beach break in front of the main huddle of resorts and the other the **Monaliza** point break at the northern end of the beach. The best spot for beginners is the **Cement Factory** break in the nearby barangay of Bacnotan. The peak season is September to March; at other times there may be no waves but you can get significant discounts on accommodation.

ARRIVAL AND DEPARTURE

SAN FERNANDO AND AROUND

By bus The Partas terminal is north of San Fernando's plaza on Quezon Ave, while Dominion's is off Manila North Rd (a continuation of Quezon) at Don Flores St near *McDonald's*, just south of the city centre.

Destinations Baguio (Partas, and local buses from the

plaza: each hourly; 1hr 30min); Laoag (Partas: hourly; 6hr); Manila (Dominion & Partas: each roughly hourly; 6–8hr); Vigan (Dominion: 1–2 hourly; 3hr 30min; Partas: hourly; 3hr 30min).

Transport to San Juan Jeepneys (every 30min; 15min;

P14) run from the old market in San Fernando to San Juan, while a tricycle costs P100; alternatively, buses travelling between San Fernando and Laoag, Vigan or Abra province

pass through San Juan – ask the driver to let you off at one of the resorts.

INFORMATION AND ACTIVITIES

Tourist information San Fernando's city tourist office is in the city hall on F. Ortega Hwy, just north of the plaza (Mon–Fri 8am–5pm; ☎072 888 6922, ⓦbit.ly/san-fernando); the regional tourism office (Mon–Fri 8am–5pm; ☎072 888 2411, ⓦbit.ly/san-fernando-reg) is at *Oasis Country Resort*, 3km south of San Fernando.

Services Quezon Ave, San Fernando's main drag, has a number of banks with ATMs, as well as a police station in the city hall (☎072 888 6911).

Scuba diving Ocean Deep Diver Training Centre, on Poro Point just west of the airport (☎072 700 0493, ⓦoceandeep.biz).

ACCOMMODATION AND EATING

Unless you're staying the night in San Fernando before moving on, you're better off heading for the **San Juan resorts**. All the resorts listed are right on the beach and within walking distance of each other, and most of them have **restaurants**, but tend to get booked up in high season (Oct–March), so reserve ahead.

3

SAN FERNANDO

Halo Halo de Iloko 12 Balay Mercado, Zandueta St ☎072 700 2030. A restaurant and café with eclectic decor, including zebra-print walls and colourful window panes. The main draw here is the *halo-halo* (shaved ice with evaporated milk and toppings including fruit and purple yam; P99). Daily 9am–9pm.

Sunset Bay Brgy Canaoay ☎072 607 5907, ⓦsunsetbayphilippines.com. Just south of San Fernando, this welcoming resort overlooking the South China Sea has nicely decorated rooms giving onto a well-tended garden with potted plants and local crafts. There's a pool and a coral reef 90m off the shore where you can snorkel. 🛜 **P2300**

SAN JUAN

Angel and Marie's Place ☎0917 723 3253. The favourite surfers' restaurant in San Juan offers serious fish dishes such as tuna steak (P200) or squid adobo (P200), with banana chocolate crêpes for afters (P160), and Filipino breakfasts at the weekend. It also has rooms (P1000 with breakfast) and a smoothie shack on the beach. Mon–Fri 5–10pm, Sat, Sun & public holidays 6am–10pm.

The Circle Hostel ☎0917 505 4329, ⓦlaunion .thecirclehostel.com. Hip budget surf hostel, very sociable but with meagre breakfasts. You can stay in a dorm bed with your own mozzie net, or in a hammock. 🛜 Dorms **P550**, hammocks **P450**

Gefseis Greek Grill ☎072 603 0183. A great place for a Greek meal made with fresh local ingredients. Starters include succulent grilled octopus (P250); try with a souvlaki platter (P250–350) for main course. Daily 9am–midnight.

Kahuna Beach Resort and Spa ☎072 607 1040, ⓦkahunaresort.com. It may not be entirely in keeping with San Juan's laidback surfer vibe, but this upmarket resort certainly has verve. The rooms are stylish and comfortable, and the infinity pool is a great place to sip cocktails. 🛜 **P5265**

Little Surfmaid ☎072 888 5528, ⓦlittle surfmaidresort.com. At the northern end of the string of resorts, close to the Mona Liza point break, this Danish-owned place offers spacious a/c rooms with fridge, and there are nice touches such as colourful bedspreads from the Cordilleras. The more expensive rooms have little balconies, and there's a restaurant serving good food. 🛜 **P2500**

San Juan Surf Resort ☎072 687 9990, ⓦsanjuan surfresort.ph. Squarely aimed at surfers: there's a shop selling kit, and surf conditions are posted by the bar. It's worth paying a bit extra for a deluxe room with free breakfast and more reliable wi-fi. 🛜 **P1980**

Sebay Surf Resort ☎072 888 4075, ⓦsebaysurf central.com. The nicely decorated rooms here give onto a leafy pathway and are set in a thatched building adorned with nipa. There's also a larger wooden structure slightly further back from the beach that has more spacious family rooms. 🛜 **P2000**

Ilocos

Long and narrow, **Ilocos Sur** province is sandwiched by the sea on one side and the Cordillera Mountains on the other. For most tourists the highlight is undoubtedly the once important trading town of **Vigan**, one of the most atmospheric and enjoyable cities in the country. **Ilocos Norte**, meanwhile, is still strongly associated in Filipino minds with former president Ferdinand Marcos, and his family continues to wield considerable political power in the province. Sites related to the Marcos family include Ferdinand's **birthplace** in Sarrat, his **mausoleum** in Batac, and the mansion known as the **Malacañang of the North** beside Paoay Lake. On the northern coast, the town of **Pagudpud** draws visitors from across Luzon with some of the best beaches on the island.

Vigan

An unmissable part of any North Luzon itinerary, **VIGAN** is one of the oldest towns in the Philippines. Lying on the western bank of the Mestizo River, it was in Spanish times an important political, military, cultural and religious centre. The **old town** is characterized by its cobbled streets and some of the finest **colonial architecture** in the country, mixing Mexican, Chinese and Filipino features. Many of the old buildings are still lived in, others are used as curio shops, and a few have been converted into museums or hotels. The attractions are within walking distance of one another, with **Plaza Burgos** the most obvious reference point, and, adding to the old-world atmosphere, some streets are open only to pedestrians – unusual in the Philippines – and romantic horse-drawn **kalesas** (P150/hr).

Brief history

In pre-colonial times, long before Spanish galleons arrived, **Chinese** junks came to Vigan and helped it to become a major trading port. They arrived with silk and porcelain, and left with gold, beeswax and mountain products brought down by inhabitants of the Cordillera. Stories of Vigan's riches spread and before long immigrants from China arrived to settle and trade here, intermarrying with locals and beginning the multicultural bloodline that Biguenos – the people of Vigan – are known for.

Spanish domination

The **Spanish** arrived in 1572. Captain Juan de Salcedo conquered the town and named it Villa Fernandina de Vigan in honour of King Philip's son, Prince Ferdinand, who died at the age of 4. Salcedo then rounded the tip of Luzon and proceeded to pacify Camarines, Albay and Catanduanes. In January 1574 he returned to Vigan, bringing with him **Augustinian missionaries**, and setting about the task of creating a township his king would be proud of, with grand plazas, municipal buildings and mansions.

One of the potentially incendiary results of this Spanish political domination was the rise of a *mestizo* (mixed ethnicity) master class, whose wealth and stature began to cause resentment among landless natives. In 1763 things came to a head when revolutionary **Diego Silang** and his men assaulted and captured Vigan, proclaiming it capital of the free province of Ilocos. When Silang was assassinated by two traitors in the pay of the Spanish, his wife, Maria Josefa Gabriela Silang, assumed leadership of the uprising. She was captured and publicly hanged in the town square.

VIGAN'S FESTIVALS

The biggest secular festival is the week-long **Vigan Town Fiesta**, involving carnivals, parades, musical extravaganzas, beauty contests and nightly cultural shows. It culminates on January 25 with the celebration of the conversion of St Paul the Apostle, the town's patron saint. Almost straight after that, at the end of January, comes the **Kannawidan Ilocos**, a recent addition to the festival calendar celebrating the culture of Ilocos Sur. It includes a "battle of the bands" and a beauty contest.

The **Viva Vigan Binatbatan Festival of Arts**, held in the first week of May, includes dancing and music; the highlight is the religious celebration on **May 3** (Tres de Mayo), which starts with a Mass at Vigan's cemetery chapel and continues with dancing in Crisologo Street and a kalesa parade. **Holy Week** is also a special time in Vigan, with candlelit processions through the old streets and a *visita iglesia* that sees devotees doing the rounds of churches and cathedrals.

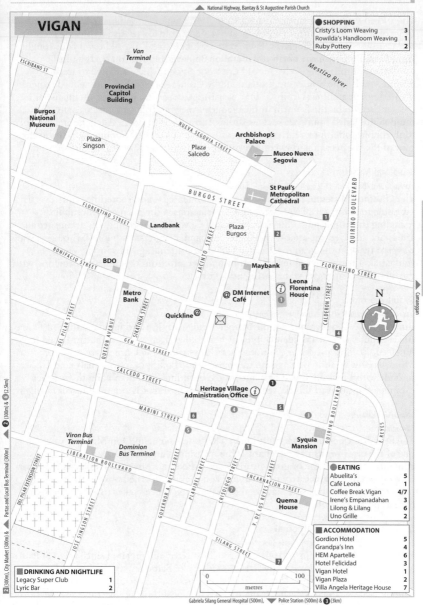

National Highway, Bantay & St Augustine Parish Church

VIGAN

Van Terminal

Provincial Capitol Building

Burgos National Museum

Plaza Singson

ESCRIBANO ST

Mestizo River

NUEVA SEGOVIA STREET

Archbishop's Palace

Plaza Salcedo

Museo Nueva Segovia

St Paul's Metropolitan Cathedral

BURGOS STREET

FLORENTINO STREET

Landbank

Plaza Burgos

JACINTO STREET

BONIFACIO STREET

BDO

Maybank

FLORENTINO STREET

QUIRINO BOULEVARD

CALDERON STREET

Metro Bank

SIKATUNA STREET

DM Internet Café

Leona Florentina House

Quickline

QUEZON AVENUE

DEL PILAR STREET

GEN. LUNA STREET

N

Cananganan

SALCEDO STREET

Heritage Village Administration Office

MABINI STREET

Viron Bus Terminal

Dominion Bus Terminal

LIBERATION BOULEVARD

QUIRINO BOULEVARD

E. REYES

Syquia Mansion

GOVERNOR A. REYES STREET

PLARIDEL STREET

CRISOLOGO STREET

ENCARNACION STREET

V. DE LOS REYES STREET

Quema House

JOSE SINGSON STREET

DEL PILAR EXTENSION STREET

SILANG STREET

3

Partas and Local Bus Terminal (300m) ◄

▲ 2 (300m) & ⑤ (2.5km)

◄ 2 (300m), City Market (300m) & ⑥ (3km)

0   100
metres

Gabriela Silang General Hospital (500m),   Police Station (500m) & ③ (3km)

The modern day

Unlike in Manila, many of Vigan's fine **old buildings** managed to survive World War II, though the humidity and their wooden construction makes preservation difficult. Many wealthy inhabitants left town in favour of a new life in Manila, allowing their ancestral homes to fall into partial ruin, though Vigan's 1999 inclusion on the **World Heritage Site** list at least guarantees it some level of protection and funding.

The old town

Most of the beautiful ancestral houses are in Vigan's **old town**. Also known as the Mestizo District or Kasanglayan ("where the Chinese live"), the old town runs roughly from Plaza Burgos in the north to **Liberation Boulevard** in the south. The most important thoroughfare is elegant old **Crisologo Street**, which is closed to traffic. Architecturally, the houses are fundamentally Chinese or Mexican, influenced either by the immigrant architects from China's eastern seaboard who prepared the plans, or by ideas picked up by the Spanish in their South American colony. Local artisans, meanwhile, added flourishes such as sliding capiz-shell windows. A few homes are open to the public, offering an intimate view of ilustrado (educated middle class) life at the turn of the nineteenth and twentieth centuries.

Crisologo Museum

Liberation Blvd • Daily 8.30–11.30am & 1.30–4.30pm • Donations welcome

The **Crisologo Museum**, former home of the influential – and sometimes controversial – Crisologo family, displays photographs, mementos and personal memorabilia, including the bright pink Chevrolet in which Governor Carmeling was ambushed in 1961. She survived the attack, unlike her husband, congressman Floro Crisologo, who was shot twice in the head in October 1970 while attending Mass inside Vigan Cathedral. There's a macabre selection of photographs from the death scene, along with the bloodied trousers he was wearing at the time.

Syquia Mansion

Quirino Blvd at Salcedo St • Daily except Tues 9am–5pm • P50 • ☎ 0915 663 3547

Built in 1830, **Syquia Mansion**, the former family mansion and holiday home of Doña Alicia Syquia, wife of President Elpidio Quirino, has been restored and furnished in nineteenth-century style. The various furnishings reflect the Chinese roots of the Syquia family, wealthy traders who migrated to the Philippines from mainland China to trade with the Spaniards. Look out for the beautiful 1910 piano and the wooden camphor chest that to this day emanates a strong smell that is a natural insect repellent.

Quema House

8 Encarnacion St

The beautiful **Quema House**, built in the 1820s, was home to Don Mariano Quema, one of the city's wealthiest merchants. The mansion is unique in Vigan in that it contains virtually all the original furnishings and decor, from the Vienna chairs in the living room to the intricately painted vines on the ceiling. The house is not regularly open to the public, but you may be able to persuade the caretaker to let you in if you have a special interest.

St Paul's Metropolitan Cathedral

Burgos St • Daily 6am till just after 6pm Mass (6.30pm Mass at weekends)

Built by the Augustinians in 1641, but much battered and repaired since then, **St Paul's Metropolitan Cathedral** was designed in "earthquake Baroque" style, with thick ramparts and a belfry built 15m away so that it stood a chance of surviving if the church itself collapsed. Given Vigan's history, it's not surprising that there's some Chinese influence; see, for example, the brass communion handrails.

Museo Nueva Segovia

Nueva Segovia St • Mon–Fri 9am–noon & 1–4pm (but often closed even at those times if the caretaker is away) • P20 • ☎ 077 722 2018

The **Archbishop's Palace** (*Arzobispado*), completed in 1783, is still the official residence of the Archbishop of Nueva Segovia (the old Spanish name for what is now Ilocos Sur). Inside, the **Museo Nueva Segovia** showcases ecclesiastical artefacts, antique portraits of bishops and religious paraphernalia from all over Ilocos Sur.

Burgos National Museum

6 Burgos St • Daily 9am–5pm • Free • ⓦ nationalmuseum.gov.ph

The **Burgos National Museum** was once home to one of the town's most famous residents, Padre José Burgos, whose martyrdom in 1872 galvanized the revolutionary movement. Between 1972 and 1975, the building became a branch of PNB bank – you can still see the teller windows on the ground floor. The first couple of rooms introduce Ilocano culture and traditions, with displays including farming and fishing tools, wooden coffins and a nose flute. The third room contains the chamber used to execute Burgos and his two companions, as well as an informative miniature model shedding light on the Spanish tobacco monopoly in the early eighteenth century. Furniture and other Burgos family memorabilia is displayed on the first floor.

ARRIVAL AND DEPARTURE   VIGAN

By plane Until Vigan's own airport is completed, the closest airport is in Laoag (see p.144).

By bus Dominion buses arrive at the terminal at the junction of Quezon and Liberation blvds, while the Partas terminal is by the city market about 300m south of the old town. From Laoag, local buses arrive at the local bus terminal near the city market, but will usually drop passengers in town on their way through. If travelling to Vigan from Lingayen, Dagupan or Alaminos in the Lingayen Gulf, head to Urdaneta and catch a

northbound bus from there (6hr). Buses from Vigan to Manila and Baguio stop in San Fernando (2hr).

Destinations Baguio (Dominion: hourly; 5hr); Laoag (local buses every 30min and Partas: every 30–60min; 2hr); Manila (Dominion, Partas, Viron: all roughly hourly, most departures in the afternoon; 9–10hr).

By van The van terminal is just by the Provincial Capitol Building. There are regular vans to Santa Maria throughout the day (leave when full; 45min; P50).

INFORMATION AND TOURS

Tourist office The provincial tourist office is at Leona Florentino House, 1 Crisologo St (daily 8am–5pm; ☎ 077 644 0315, ✉ sureilocossur@gmail.com). The municipal tourist office on Crisologo St ("Heritage Village Administration Office"; supposedly open daily 8am–5pm) is less helpful and often left unstaffed.

Tours A nice way to get around town, the kalesas, or horse-drawn carriages, also offer tours (P150/hr); you can find them on Burgos St by the cathedral, or on Salcedo St at

V. de los Reyes St. You can ask the *kutchero* (driver) to suggest a route that will take in the main sights; they normally include a visit to the pretty St Augustine Parish Church in the nearby town of Bantay. The grandiosely named "Vigan heritage river cruise" is a 45min boat trip with crackly recorded commentary (hourly 8.30–11.30am & 1.30–4.30pm; P100) that starts at Celedonia Garden in Beddeng Laud (P30 by tricycle from town).

ACCOMMODATION

Gordion Hotel V. de Los Reyes St at Salcedo St ☎ 077 674 0998, ⓦ vigangordionhotel.com. This brightly coloured place offers comfortable, old-fashioned, rooms. The large chintzy suite has a huge bathroom with a roll-top bath, although the room itself is a bit dark. There are occasional barbecues in the pleasant courtyard. 🛜 **P2800**

Grandpa's Inn 1 Bonifacio St ☎ 077 674 0686, ⓦ grandpas-inn.com. This ancestral house with bare brick walls and parquet flooring has been converted into a lovely inn full of old curios. There are a range of rooms, of which most are a/c and en suite, but the very cheapest are fan-cooled with a shared bathroom. Room 7 is a uniquely furnished twin room where you can sleep in a kalesa (carriage). 🛜 **P730**

HEM Apartelle 32 Gov. A. Reyes St ☎ 077 722 2173, ⓦ bit.ly/hem-apartelle. This small budget hotel is clean, affordable and very handy. All the six sparkling rooms have private bath, including singles (P600), staff are generally helpful and the location is perfect, but breakfast isn't included. **P1000**

Hotel Felicidad 9 V. de los Reyes St ☎ 077 722 0008, ⓦ hotelfelicidadvigan.com. A charming option in a beautiful colonial mansion offering tastefully decorated rooms with beautiful hardwood floors and high ceilings. The delightful maestro suite (P7500) features a solid ironwood king bed and a splendid antique dresser. 🛜 **P3000**

Vigan Hotel Burgos St at V. de los Reyes St ☎ 077 644 0169. A bit ramshackle but still with some character, this family-run hotel in a creaky old colonial building has en-suite a/c rooms (P995), but the cheapest are fan-cooled with shared bathrooms 🛜. **P595**

Vigan Plaza Plaza Burgos ☎ 077 722 8553, ⓦ bit.ly/vigan-plaza. In an excellent location on Plaza Burgos, and just a stone's throw away from the cathedral, this colonial hotel featuring beautiful tiled floors has rooms on three floors. The first- and second-floor options are in a better overall condition than those on the ground floor, most of which give onto a wall and are quite dark. Wi-fi in the lobby. 🛜 **P2800**

★**Villa Angela Heritage House** 26 Quirino Blvd ☎077 722 2914, ⓦbit.ly/villa-angela. The most charming of all the colonial hotels, this is a beautiful old museum of a place, wonderful value, and the top choice if you want to wallow in history. You can ask to be given the room Tom Cruise slept in: he stayed here for a few weeks when *Born on the Fourth of July* was being filmed on the sand dunes near Laoag. 🛜 **P1700**

EATING

Vigan doesn't offer much in terms of **restaurants**, although make sure to try some local specialities, including the town's famous crispy **empanada**.

3

Abuelita's 39 Governor A. Reyes St ☎077 722 2368. This popular restaurant has some interesting old curios up on its shelf, including radios, rusty number plates and an old sewing machine; the speciality is regional Ilocano cuisine. Food is displayed in pots at both lunch and dinner – just take your pick and pay accordingly. A meal will set you back about P100. Mon–Sat 7.30am–8pm.

Café Leona 1 Crisologo St ☎077 722 2212. Travellers are drawn to the outdoor tables that spill out on the street in the evening, although you can also dine in the tavern-style interior. The menu lists Ilocano and Japanese fusion dishes such as *longganisa maki* (P175), as well as pizza (P285) and Vigan specialities – try *daing na bangus*, marinated milkfish (P225). Daily 10.30am–midnight (Japanese dishes until 10pm only).

Coffee Break Vigan 3 Salcedo St ☎077 674 8998, ⓦbit.ly/coffee-break-vigan; Crisologo St at Liberation Blvd. Two branches, and both serve good espresso-based coffees (caffè latte P55), as well as ginger tea, and shakes including soursop and calamansi. There's fierce a/c and free high-speed wi-fi, but the only food they do is fettuccine-type pasta (pesto or carbonara; P120). Daily 9am–10pm.

Irene's Empanadahan 13 Salcedo St ☎077 674 0297. This fourth-generation empanada place has been going strong since the 1930s – locals say it's the best place in town to savour the Vigan speciality, which comes in several varieties, including pork, beef, chicken, (canned) tuna and, if you're lucky, crab (P35–60). Daily 7am–8pm.

Lilong & Lilang Brgy Bulala, 2.5km west of Vigan ☎077 604 0270, ⓦhiddengardenvigan.com. This leafy restaurant is located in a plant nursery and serves traditional Ilocano dishes, including *poqui poqui*, mashed grilled aubergine sautéed with onions and tomatoes with egg (P150). For dessert try the colourful *halo-halo* (P90), beautifully presented in a coconut husk bowl. A tricycle to get here will cost P40 (15min). Daily 6am–8pm.

Uno Grille 1 Bonifacio St ☎077 637 8299, ⓦgrandpas-inn.com. Courtyard restaurant with an open kitchen where you can tuck into Ilocano specialities such as bagnet *poqui poqui* (P115), Chinese dishes such as mandarin pork stew (P205), or an extensive selection of noodle and pasta dishes. Seasonal specials include wind-dried wild boar meat, elvers, and eggs scrambled with the roe of a local fish. Daily 10am–10pm.

DRINKING AND NIGHTLIFE

Nightlife is generally very low-key, with limited options – things quieten down substantially at 9pm, with the startling exception of *Legacy Super Club* in the town centre.

Legacy Super Club Crisologo St at Mabini St ☎077 722 7396. Owned by an influential local family, this one nightclub has been given permission to open within the old town. The music is an eclectic mix of local, Latin and electronic sounds. P100 entrance (includes one beer on Sat, two on other days). Mon–Fri 7pm–midnight, Sat 7pm–3am.

Lyric Bar Alcantara St, by Partas bus terminal ☎077 722 2988. Lively bar, in an old cinema south of the centre, with a dark interior featuring hexagonal mirrors and glitzy chandeliers. Live bands play weekly: acoustic on Mon–Wed, rock on Thurs–Fri. Daily 8.30am–3am.

SHOPPING

Cristy's Loom Weaving Camangaan, 3km southeast of the city centre ☎0916 491 9320, ⓦbit.ly/cristys. Here you can watch women weaving at old rickety looms (Mon–Sat 5am–5pm), and buy the finished products, including sheets, pillowcases, tablemats and runners, in the small nearby shop. To get here catch a tricycle from town (15min; P60) Daily 6am–9pm.

Rowilda's Handloom Weaving Crisologo St at General Luna St ☎0927 422 4127. This souvenir shop, with a workshop in nearby Camangaan, offers a selection of handwoven fabrics including place mats, table runners, napkins and blankets. Daily 8am–9pm.

Ruby Pottery 65 Liberation Blvd at Gomez St ☎077 674 0476. The massive wood-fired kilns here produce *burnay* – huge jars used by northerners for storing everything from vinegar to fish paste. Broken jars, called *gibak*, are used as a bed to dry salt. Carabao pound the wet clay under hoof, although you'll need to arrive between 8am and 11am to see them in action. Daily 8am–6pm.

VIGAN'S CRISPY EMPANADA

Don't leave Vigan without trying the local **empanada** – a crispy deep-fried tortilla of rice-flour dough containing cabbage and green papaya. Some empanadas – sometimes known as "special" – also contain an egg and longganisa (garlic sausage). Either way, eaten with sugar-cane vinegar and chopped shallots, they are delicious. The stalls on the western side of Plaza Burgos, known collectively as **empanadaan**, sell empanadas, okoy (egg, prawn, tomato and onion frittata, again eaten sprinkled with sugar-cane vinegar) and other street food.

DIRECTORY

Banks and exchange You'll find several banks with ATMs on Quezon Ave, including BDO and Metro Bank, a Landbank on Florentino St by Quezon Ave, and a Maybank at the corner of Plaridel and Florentino streets.

Hospital Gabriela Silang General Hospital (☎077 722 3362), south of the centre on Quirino Blvd.

Internet access Quickline, Bonifacio St (daily 8.30am–9pm; P15/hr); DM Internet Café, 13 Gov. A. Reyes St (daily 8.30am–7.30pm; P15/hr).

Police station Rivero St, Brgy 8, south of the city centre (☎077 722 0890).

Post office Governor A. Reyes St at Bonifacio St.

3

Santa Maria Church and around

38km south of Vigan • From Vigan, take any Manila-bound bus (1hr), or catch a van to Santa Maria (leave when full; 45min; P50); tricycles to Pinsal Falls leave from Santa Maria town (45min; P400 return)

The UNESCO World Heritage-listed **Santa Maria Church**, dating from 1769, is a solid structure with a brick facade, set on a hill and reached via 83 steps; unsurprisingly, it was used as a fortress during the Philippine Revolution. The interior is quite plain with the exception of its geometric floor tiles, and it's inhabited by birds and bats. While you're in the area it's worth travelling 8km to **Pinsal Falls**, a spectacular set of waterfalls with two large emerald-green pools. Make sure to bring snacks and refreshments, as there are no shops.

Badoc

The coastal road north of Vigan to Laoag is sealed all the way and the journey time is only two hours. If you do want to break the journey then you could stop at **BADOC**, the birthplace of the Filipino painter Juan Luna. His reconstructed house, known as the **Juan Luna Shrine** (Tues–Sun 8am–5pm; free; ☎0917 553 6084, ☻nhcp.gov.ph), stands in a side street close to the seventeenth-century Virgen Milagrosa de Badoc church. About 1km off the coast, **Badoc Island** is gaining a reputation for good surfing (late Oct to early March & late June to early Sept) – get there by renting a bangka from the little wharf in Badoc town.

Laoag

The congested streets of the Ilocos Norte provincial capital, **LAOAG**, can't compete with Vigan's historical core when it comes to aesthetic appeal, but there are a handful of things to do and see, and the city boasts one of the country's best museums. Laoag also makes an excellent base for exploring the beautiful coast at nearby **Suba** or touring sights associated with former dictator **Ferdinand Marcos**.

Museo Ilocos Norte

V. Llanes St at General Luna St • Mon–Sat 9am–noon & 1–5pm, Sun 10am–5pm • P50 • ☎077 770 45 87, ☻museoilocosnorte.com

Laoag's most interesting attraction, the **Museo Ilocos Norte**, provides an overview of the province's history and culture. Close to the main plaza, it's housed in a restored Spanish-era tobacco warehouse. Exhibits include vintage costumes, farming equipment and tribal artefacts, with a replica of an ilustrado ancestral home complete with antiques. The souvenir shop has some appealing books and gifts.

Sinking Bell Tower and St William's Cathedral
Bonifacio St

It's worth taking a look at the **Sinking Bell Tower**, built by Augustinian friars in 1612, which has a door big enough for a man on horseback to pass through. Today, however, the tower has sunk so much that you can only get through by stooping – although sadly the tower is closed to visitors.

In principle the bell tower belongs to **St William's Cathedral**, the large church across the street, with its magnificent white and gold two-storey facade and simple, matching interior. The church, which became a cathedral in 1961, was originally constructed at the beginning of the seventeenth century to replace a simpler wooden structure. Most of what you see today dates from the 1870s however, when it was rebuilt after a fire. The inside was redecorated in the 1970s with money donated by the public, the chandeliers being the gift of one Mr and Mrs Ferdinand E. Marcos.

Marcos Hall of Justice
V. Llanes St • Mon–Sat 8am–5pm • Free • ☎ 077 771 3768

The **Marcos Hall of Justice**, the square white building on the west side of Aurora Park, was where a young Ferdinand Marcos was detained in 1939 after being accused of the murder of one of his father's political opponents. Marcos wanted to graduate in law and used his time in detention wisely, swotting for the bar examination and successfully preparing his own defence.

ARRIVAL AND INFORMATION LAOAG

By plane The airport is 7km southwest of town (tricycle P100, jeepney from Gabu terminal on Balintawak St P30). PAL serves Manila (1hr).

By bus Partas buses from Manila (5 daily; 14hr) and Baguio (every 30–60min; 7–8hr) terminate at the Partas bus station on the western end of Rizal St. Viron (6 daily to Manila) have a terminal on Rizal St slightly closer to town at Peralta St; and Fariñas buses from Manila (12 daily) and Baguio (8 daily) drop passengers off at the corner of Fariñas and Castro streets. GMW buses from Tuguegarao (hourly; 6–7hr) arrive at the terminal at the corner of Gov. Agcaoli St and Primo Lazaro Ave. Local buses also connect Pagudpud (every 30min; 1hr 30min) and Vigan (every 30min; 3hr) to Laoag.

By jeepney Jeepneys to Paoay (every 30min; 40min; P34) and Batac (every 30min; 30min; P25) leave from the corner of Llanes St and Luna St, while those travelling to Sarrat leave east of town from F. Guerrero St (when full; 15min; P15).

Tourist information The helpful provincial tourist office kiosk is on Llanes St at General Luna St (daily 8am–5pm; ☎ 077 772 1213, ⊛ tourismilocosnorte.com), while the Laoag City tourist office (Mon–Fri 8am–5pm. ☎ 077 772 0467, ⊜ dotlaoagone@gmail.com) is on the second floor of the Pacific Building, Abadilla St.

ACCOMMODATION

Balay da Blas 10 Giron St ☎077 770 4389, ⦿bit.ly/balay-da-blas. A charming option, with superb-value warm and welcoming rooms decorated with antiques and colourful paintings. The larger family rooms also have a kitchenette, and there's a pleasant leafy seating area in the courtyard as well as an excellent restaurant attached (see below). Breakfast included but wi-fi in the lobby only. �🛜 P1200

Fort Ilocandia Brgy 37 Calayab (10km southwest of town) ☎077 670 9001, ⦿fortilocandia.com.ph. Built in 1983 and hastily completed for the wedding reception of Ferdinand and Imelda Marcos's youngest daughter (see below), this expansive resort aims for classic elegance rather than modern chic. It's set in 77 hectares amid sand dunes and pine forests; amenities include a golf course, swimming pool, paintballing, hot-air ballooning and a driving range. �🛜 P3400

Hotel del Norte 26 Fonacier St ☎077 772 1697, ⦿hoteldelnorte.weebly.com. This cheapo budget option has plain but perfectly decent rooms with private bathrooms. The very cheapest rooms are fan-cooled, but there are a/c rooms too (from P900), and singles (P380) for solo travellers. �🛜 P580

Hotel Tiffany General Segundo Ave at M.H. del Pilar St ☎077 770 3550, ⦿hoteltiffanylaoag.com. This motel-style place has tried for a 1960s US theme, with mellow polka dot and stripy themed rooms and an attached American-style diner serving cheeseburgers (P80) and milkshakes (P95). The lobby wi-fi reaches some of the rooms. �🛜 P1300

Java Hotel General Segundo Ave, 55-B Salet ☎077 770 5996, ⦿javahotel.com.ph. A pleasant option in a stone building with thatched roof, with tastefully furnished rooms featuring modern amenities. There's a swimming pool, tennis court and gym, and an airy restaurant serving good Filipino dishes. Rates include breakfast. �🛜 P2710

EATING

Food court Rizal St between Balintawak St and Llanes St. This little market hosts a handful of stalls selling empanadas, *bulalo*, *miki* (noodle soup) and other tasty Filipino staples, with tables to eat them at. Not all the stalls are open round the clock, but there's always something good to eat, whether it's a meal you're after or just a snack. Daily 24hr.

La Preciosa Rizal St ☎077 773 1162, ⦿lapreciosa-ilocos.com. Considered to be the best restaurant in town, with an emphasis on Ilocano cuisine. Bestsellers include *dinengdeng* (vegetable soup topped with grilled fish; P195) and crispy *dinardaraan* (pork meat cooked in blood sauce; P195). There's also a café displaying a selection of cakes (P100). Daily 10am–10pm.

★**Saramsam** Balay da Blas, 10 General Giron St ☎077 670 3219, ⦿balaydablas-laoag.com/dining.html. This cosy restaurant features two welcoming dining areas with clusters of lamps, wooden artefacts and shelves lined with beautiful oblong demijohns. The menu offers creative Ilocano dishes with Italian and Mexican influences; the *pinakbet* pizza (P220) is a burst of fresh flavours, while the *mungo* (spicy black lentils) with *chicharon* (P155) and the *poqui poqui* salad (mashed aubergine with onions and tomatoes; P150) are both exquisite. Daily 10am–10pm.

NIGHTLIFE

Cock House F.R. Castro Ave ☎077 772 3079. Laoag's only nightlife venue hosts bands from all over the Philippines, playing an eclectic mix from rock to R&B. The atmosphere is generally laidback, with customers enjoying the show as they sip a beer (P65). Daily 8pm–2.30am.

DIRECTORY

Banks and exchange There are plenty of banks along Rizal, including BDO and BPI.

Hospital Laoag General Hospital, Brgy 46 Nalbo, south of town (☎077 772 8828).

Internet access Print Hub, Bonifacio St, nearly opposite the Sinking Bell Tower (P25/hr; daily 8am–6pm).

Police Rizal St at Paco Roman St (☎077 771 1026).

Post office There's a small post office in the City Hall.

Sarrat

Some 8km east of Laoag is the sleepy, pretty village of **SARRAT**, where the eighteenth-century **Santa Monica Church** hosted the wedding of Marcos's youngest daughter Irene in 1983. Preparations for the wedding – costing US$10.3 million – involved thousands of men remodelling the town and 3500 contracted employees renovating the two-hundred-year-old church. Large parts of Sarrat were reconstructed, with houses torn down and rebuilt in the old Spanish style.

Marcos Birthplace Museum

National Highway • Mon & Tues and Thurs–Sun 9am–4pm • P50 • Jeepney from Laoag (leaving when full; 15min; P15)

Ferdinand Marcos was born in Sarrat on September 11, 1917, and his former home has been turned into the **Marcos Birthplace Museum**. The ground floor displays traditional Ilocano weaving instruments, while the first floor showcases Marcos memorabilia, including a set of his clothes worn during infancy; this place is really for Marcos completists only.

Ferdinand Marcos Museum

Batac, 15km south of Laoag • Wed–Mon 9am–noon & 2–4pm • P50 • ☎ 0917 772 6001 • Buses between Vigan and Laoag pass through Batac – ask the driver to let you off; Batac is also served by regular jeepneys from Laoag (every 30min; 40min; P25)

Marcos spent his childhood in the pretty town of **Batac** before moving to Manila to take up law. The **Ferdinand Marcos Museum**, or "presidential centre" showcases Marcos memorabilia and traces his political career in glowing terms; there's also a section dedicated to his romance with Imelda, who became his wife after only eleven days of courting. An adjacent building held his corpse until Imelda prevailed upon President Rodrigo Duterte to bury him in Manila's Libingan Ng Mga Bayani (Heroes' Cemetery) in 2016.

Paoay

A few kilometres west of Batac, **PAOAY** is the location of a UNESCO-listed **church** as well as the **Malacañang of the North**, the opulent mansion where **Ferdinand Marcos** stayed during presidential holidays.

St Augustine Church

Paoay Church Complex • Daily 6.30am–6pm • Buses between Vigan and Laoag pass through Paoay – ask the driver to let you off; there are also regular jeepneys (every 30min; 50min; P34) from Laoag via Batac

St Augustine church is perhaps the best-known "earthquake Baroque" church in the Philippines. Begun in 1804, it took ninety years to build and has 26 immense side buttresses designed to keep it standing. Nearby is a bell tower dating from 1793, which you can climb for views of the area, although you may have to find the caretaker to open it up for you.

Malacañang of the North

Suba, 10km from Paoay • Mon–Sat (except the first Mon of the month) 9am–4.30pm • P30 • ☎ 0906 521 1139 • Tricycles from Paoay's St Augustine Church (25min; P100) will then take you on to the Ilocos Norte Sand Dunes (see below) for P150 return

The **Malacañang of the North** is named after the presidential palace in Manila. The mansion, set on a five-hectare estate of gentle lawns giving onto the beautiful Paoay Lake, was the Marcoses' holiday residence between 1977 and the revolution in 1986. The property also comprised a golf course – Marcos was an avid golfer – which is now part of the *Fort Ilocandia* resort (see p.145). In 2012 part of the building was transformed into a **pro-Marcos museum**, with seven galleries highlighting some of the major reforms – but, naturally, none of the corruption or human rights abuses – implemented during his presidency. The Agriculture Room focuses on the building of waterways and dams – aiming for self-sufficiency, Marcos implemented irrigation programmes in order to supply water to the entire archipelago – while the Nation Building Room highlights the president's achievement in uniting his country by connecting the islands via a number of ambitious highways and bridges.

Ilocos Norte sand dunes

The Laoag Eco-Adventure Development (LEAD) Movement Inc (☎ 077 772 0538, ⓦ leadmovement.wordpress.com) arranges trips combining a 4WD ride and sandboarding (P2500/1hr for 4–6 people)

The coastline west of Laoag is a sight to behold. More like desert than beach, it measures almost 1km across at some points and reaches as far as the eye can see, fringed by huge **sand dunes**. The area has become a favourite among Manila film crews; the **Suba** dunes to the south – close to the *Fort Ilocandia* resort (see p.145) – are where Oliver Stone shot segments of *Born on the Fourth of July*.

Pagudpud and around

Seventy kilometres north of Laoag along the coastal road is **PAGUDPUD**, a typical provincial town providing access to several wonderfully picturesque **beaches**. The Pagudpud area is increasingly recognized as having all the beauty of Boracay, but just a fraction of the tourists and none of the nightlife.

Saud Beach
Tricycles from Pagudpud P70 (15min)

Saud Beach ("Sa-ud"), a few kilometres down a narrow road to the north of town, is a beautiful long arch of white sand backed by palm trees. Resorts on the beach rent out snorkelling equipment, and can provide bangkas (P400/hr) so that you can head to the best spots.

Kabigan Falls
Daily 7am–5pm • P20; compulsory guide P100 • Tricycle from Saud Beach P300 (35min), from Blue Lagoon P300 (25min)

About halfway between Saud Beach and Blue Lagoon are the **Kabigan Falls**, a beautiful cascade of water flowing down a steep incline of 34m and nestled in a pretty stretch of thick vegetation. There's a refreshing pool at the bottom of the falls, perfect for a swim. At the main road, where tricycles drop off, you'll have to register and hire a compulsory guide who will lead you to the falls – a beautiful 1.5km (30min) walk through picturesque rice paddies and lush mountain scenery.

Blue Lagoon
Tricycles from Pagudpud P500 (45min)

About 18km east of Saud is the glorious **Blue Lagoon** (also known as Maira-ira Beach). The setting is stunning, with dazzling water lapping a sugary crescent of sand; the breaks also attract surfers from July to January. One stretch of the beach has been overdeveloped with a large and incongruous resort, but it's possible to get away from that and still enjoy the sand and sea.

Kingfisher Beach
Tricycles from Pagudpud P300 (30min)

Kingfisher Beach, a gem of a place just 6km north of Saud Beach, is one of the country's best kitesurfing spots, its strong northwest or side shore winds making it an ideal spot for advanced surfers, especially between October and March. The waters are so clear that you're likely to spot flying fish, sea turtles, jackfish and even tuna as you surf. The 250m-wide reef with a flat lagoon is perfect for snorkelling, stand-up paddling and kayaking. You can rent equipment from the well-stocked *Kingfisher Resort* just on the beach.

Cape Bojeador Lighthouse and around
Daily 8am–6pm • Free • To get here from Pagudpud take a jeepney or local bus (both P35) towards Laoag and ask to be let off on the National Highway near the lighthouse; from here you can walk 900m up to the lighthouse (30min) or catch a tricycle (P10; 5min)

Some 36km west of Pagudpud is the **Cape Bojeador Lighthouse**, just outside the town of **Burgos**. Built in 1892, at 19.90m the lighthouse is the tallest in the country, and from the base there are unobstructed views of the coastline and across the South China Sea. It's still in use, but unfortunately you can't go inside it.

3

ARRIVAL AND INFORMATION

By bus Buses arrive on the main road in Pagudpud town. There are services from Manila (12hr), with local buses connecting the town to Laoag (every 15min; 2hr).
Tourist information In the town hall (Mon–Fri 8am–5pm; ☎ 0999 564 4678, ✉ ommpagudpud@yahoo. com).

PAGUDPUD AND AROUND

Services The Multi-Purpose Cooperative Bank has an ATM, and there is also one in the municipal hall, and another one in the nearby town of Bangui.
Tricycle tours Tricycles offer one-day tours taking in the area's major sights for around P800.

ACCOMMODATION AND EATING

Resorts around Pagudpud are a little pricier than similar establishments elsewhere, and many of them double their **prices** during high season (April & May, Holy Week & Christmas). It's always worth asking for a discount at other times. Budget travellers should consider a **homestay**. The tourist office has accredited more than a hundred, with fixed prices of P250 or P350/person for fan or a/c, and there are also unofficial homestays in the area. Contact the tourist office for details, or just wander along the road behind the main resorts on Saud Beach.

SAUD BEACH AND AROUND

Apo Idon ☎ 0917 510 0671, ⓦ apoidon.com.ph. Saud Beach's most upmarket resort offers a selection of comfortable rooms with dark wooden furniture. The more spacious suites (P9000) have private balconies with sea views; there's also a small pool, and a restaurant giving onto a beautiful stretch of beach. The downside is the deafeningly loud hum of the generator around the reception area. ☞ **P6000**
★BergBlick Brgy Burayoc ☎ 0939 458 1642, ⓦ bergblick-pagudpud.com. Halfway between Saud Beach and Blue Lagoon, this is an unusual find along the highway – a German-owned restaurant with waitresses in traditional Bavarian dress, offering excellent international and local dishes including home-made ravioli (P295) and *pinakbet* lasagne (P375). Try the BergBlick Pan (P480, serving 2–3), a platter with pork chop, pork roast, pan-fried potatoes, cabbage roll and fresh mixed salad, followed by the home-made crème brûlée (P180). Daily 9am–9pm.
★Evangeline Beach Resort Brgy Burayoc ☎ 0947 893 9648, ⓦ evangelinebeachresort.net. An excellent option comprising six comfortable rooms in a freshly painted thatched building with beautiful wooden interiors; there's also a spacious cottage with two double rooms, lounge area and fully equipped kitchenette. The beachside restaurant offers an extensive menu of Filipino and international dishes. ☞ **P3100**

BLUE LAGOON

Agua Seda ☎ 0920 969 9166, ⓦ aguasedabeach .pagudpodshore.com. Close to the hard-to-miss *Hannah's*

Beach Resort, this laidback family-run place offers nine a/c rooms with private bath. There's a pleasant restaurant in an open-fronted nipa and bamboo hut, and staff are often seen barbecuing fresh fish in the back yard with their guests. ☞ **P2612**
★Kapuluan Vista Sitio Banarian, Brgy Balaoi ☎ 0920 952 2528, ⓦ bit.ly/kapuluan. A gem of a place with a pleasant pool area and a great restaurant serving organic produce from the backyard, where free-range chickens also roam. Rooms are tastefully decorated with minimalist decor. Larger deluxe rooms sleeping four (P4750) have a loft and veranda, and there are also excellent-value rooms with shared bathroom sleeping two to six (P650/person). The bar and lounge, with it's cushioned seating and beanbags right on the beach, is the perfect spot for a sundowner. ☞ **P2700**
Wally's World Surf Homestay Sitio Banarian, Brgy Balaoi ☎ 0938 615 9568, ⓦ bit.ly/wallys-world. This friendly place is run by a family of keen surfers, and there's a surf break just outside the front door. There are three colourfully painted tiled a/c rooms, and a pleasant cottage with kitchenette sleeping four (P1400). ☞ **P700**

KINGFISHER BEACH

Kingfisher Resort ☎ 0927 525 8111, ⓦ kingfisher beach.com. Popular with kitesurfers, this is a particularly comfortable option, with tastefully decorated *casitas* with modern amenities, some with lofts. The cheapest rooms are little tiki huts with shared bath. The restaurant offers an extensive menu of Filipino and international dishes. ☞ **P3000**

The northeast

The **northeast** of Luzon, comprising the provinces of Nueva Vizcaya, Quirino, Aurora, Isabela and Cagayan, is one of the archipelago's least-explored regions, with kilometres of beautiful coastline and enormous tracts of tropical rainforest. Following the National Highway from Ilocos as it curves south brings you to the

biggest city in the region, **Tuguegarao**, the starting point for trips to the **Peñablanca Protected Landscape and Seascape**. Turning off the highway and following the north coast road brings you to **Santa Ana**, departure point for boat trips to the rugged and isolated **Babuyan Islands**.

The coast south of Santa Ana and east of Tuguegarao is cut off from the rest of Luzon by the **Sierra Madre** mountains. One of the only significant settlements is **Palanan**, jumping-off point for the barely explored **Northern Sierra Madre National Park**. The climbing and trekking possibilities here are exciting, but the area is so wild and remote that it's also potentially hazardous, with poor communications and areas of impenetrable forest. Further south on the coast – but unreachable by road from Palanan – is **Baler**, the best-known tourist destination in the northeast. This coastal town has become a popular surfing destination, but its location six hours from Manila means that it isn't swamped with weekenders.

3 Santa Ana and around

The northern coast of Luzon, part of Cagayan province, is skipped over by many visitors in their haste to head either west to Ilocos Norte or south to Tuguegarao. Yet the untouristy fishing town of **SANTA ANA** – on the northeastern point of Luzon – has much to offer, including some terrific white-sand beaches and a number of enticing offshore islands. **San Vicente,** 6km northeast of Santa Ana town centre, is the departure point for boats to the offshore islands and to Maconacon and the Northern Sierra Madre National Park (see p.153).

Anguib Beach

P100 • Bangkas from San Vicente (30min) cost P1500 return including waiting time

On the mainland, you can hire a bangka for the day to the lovely and secluded **Anguib Beach** on the eastern part of San Vicente. It is a beautiful 1.8km J-shaped stretch of beach with white sand and crystal-clear waters. While you won't find any accommodation here, it's a great place to pitch a tent. Make sure to bring water and food, as there are no shops or restaurants.

Palaui Island

P50 environmental fee plus P20 local tax (payable at San Vicente), plus compulsory guide (P300 for four people) • Bangkas from San Vicente to Punta Verde (15min; P1000 return) or Cape Engaño (45min; P1800 return)

The closest island to Santa Ana is **Palaui**, which has no roads or hotels and only limited electricity. From the main settlement of **Punta Verde** on the east of the island, two trails head north to **Cape Engaño** on the island's northern coast, a beautiful crescent lagoon watched over by an old Spanish lighthouse – the walk will take about three hours.

The Babuyan islands

Bangka from San Vicente (6hr; P7500 return) or negotiate passage on supply boat from Claveria

There's no longer a ferry, but fishing boats make the often rough crossing to the isolated and undeveloped **Babuyan islands**, a cluster of 24 volcanic and coralline islands 32km off the coast. Only five of the islands – Camiguin, Calayan, Fuga, Babuyan and Dalupiri – are inhabited and even **Calayan**, the most developed, has limited electricity. There are some beautiful beaches on several of the islands including Fuga and Dalupiri, and hot springs on the volcanic **Camiguin**.

ARRIVAL AND DEPARTURE   SANTA ANA AND AROUND

By plane Cagayan North International Airport opened in 2014 at Lal-lo, 77km west of Santa Ana, but is not yet served by scheduled passenger flights.

By boat Irregular boat departures from San Vicente pier

for Maconacon in the Northern Sierra Madre National Park (see p.153).

By bus Guardian Angels (commonly referred to as Everlasting) runs to Santa Ana from Manila (3 daily; 14hr), stopping opposite the main market, Centro Santa Ana, on the main highway. GMW Trans connects Vigan to Santa Ana (3 daily; 12hr).

By van There are regular vans from in front of the main market to Tuguegarao (every 30–40min 3am–3pm; 3hr; P180); change at Magapit (about halfway) for points west.

INFORMATION

Tourist information In Santa Ana's municipal building (Mon–Fri 8am–5pm). They can offer advice on island-hopping and arrange homestays.

ACCOMMODATION AND EATING

SANTA ANA

★ **Jotay Resort** ☏ 078 372 0560, ⊛ jotayresort.com. This small, eco-friendly resort facing the beach, run by an English-Filipino couple, offers a range of rooms with private bath, from small and basic to large and comfy (with one economy room at P600); a few face the pool, but most are set around the courtyard and parking area at the back. The restaurant specializes in excellent chilli crab – a must, but make sure you give at least a few hours' advance notice. 🛜 P1200

PALAUI ISLAND

Bayanihan Nature Village Punta Verde ☏ 0906 845 5472. Run by CEZA, this simple thatched place has dorm rooms, or you can pitch a tent in the grounds, just by a honey production centre (Feb–May). The local community's women's association prepares the food here, and also provides massages in the garden's open-fronted huts. Per person P250

BABUYAN ISLANDS

TPS Homestay Calayan Island. Run by the island's very hospitable head of tourism, this homestay is located in the centre of town near the sea. There are three simple rooms, two of which sleep four and have fan and communal bathroom; the other has a double bed, a/c and private bath. Travellers can also pitch a tent on the grounds, and make use of the kitchen; otherwise, staff can rustle up some food. Per person P250

Nomad Resort Philippines Camiguin Island ⊛ bit.ly/nomad-resort. A simple but comfortable lodge, with a choice of en-suite double rooms or a tent on the beach, and several excursions on offer, on foot or by boat. There's also a restaurant and a sunset bar. Tents (2 people) P250, doubles P1000

Tuguegarao

The capital of Cagayan province, **TUGUEGARAO** ("Too-GEG-er-rao") is a busy, tricycle-choked city with an airport that's convenient to fly to if you intend to explore the east coast around the Sierra Madre or the northernmost coast near Santa Ana, or head west into Kalinga province and its capital Tabuk. There are also small-aircraft flights from Tuguegarao to Batanes. The **city centre** is a kilometre south of **Tuguegarao Junction**, where the road from Santiago meets the National Highway that leads into town.

Tuguegarao is also the best starting point for a visit to a remarkable cave system at **Peñablanca**, and local travel agents offer **whitewater rafting** and **kayaking** trips on the Pinacanauan and Chico rivers, usually from August until February.

Tuguegarao Metropolitan Cathedral

Rizal Street at Luna St

The striking Baroque **Tuguegarao Metropolitan Cathedral**, dedicated to saints Peter and Paul, with its five-storey bell tower and striking red facade, is the region's biggest colonial church. Put up by the Dominicans in the 1760s, it survived quite serious damage in World War II. The facade is crowned with six little crests, and the windows and the columns are surrounded with moulded bricks adorned with crowns, stars and other symbols. Nor is this the town's only colonial church: the **San Jacinto Hermitage** at the western end of Legazpi Street is even older, dating from the seventeenth century.

Cagayan Provincial Museum

Provincial Capitol Compound, 3km north of Tuguegarao Junction • Mon–Fri 8am–5pm • Free • ☏ 078 304 1703 • Tricycle from city centre P50 (15min)

The small **Cagayan Provincial Museum** traces the history of Cagayan province; displays include fossilized bones of extinct animals that roamed the area during the Ice Age. The highlight is the replica (the original is on display in Manila's National Museum) of the toe bone of Callao Man, discovered by a team of archeologists in 2007 in nearby Callao Cave and dating back 67,000 years. Other displays feature intricately designed Chinese bowls and porcelain vessels, and heirloom pieces from the Spanish and American eras.

ARRIVAL AND DEPARTURE
TUGUEGARAO

By plane Tuguegarao airport is 2km north of Tuguegerao Junction, easily reached from town by tricycle (15min; P50). Cebu Pacific flies to Manila (daily; 1hr); SkyPasada (☎078 304 1054, ⌨skypasada.com) and NorthSkyAir (☎078 304 6148, ⌨northskyair.com) have flights to Basco in the Batanes Islands (3 weekly each; 1hr; P4800). For the Northern Sierra Madre National Park, NorthSkyAir serve Maconacan (roughly daily, depending on bookings; 30min; P2200), while SkyPasada fly to Palanan (3 weekly; P2200).

By bus Victory Liner buses stop on the National Highway, 300m north of Tuguegarao Junction; Five Star stop just north of the junction; Dangwa and Dalin arrive at Don Domingo Market, 100m southeast of the junction; GMW

and Florida are on Diversion Rd, west of the junction.
Destinations Baguio (Dangwa: daily 5pm; 11–12hr; Dalin: daily 4.30pm; 10–11hr); Laoag (GMW; 8 daily; 7hr); Manila (Florida, roughly hourly; Victory Liner, 10 daily; Five Star, 10 daily; 10–12hr); Vigan (GMW; 6 daily; 9hr).

By van Vans for Santa Ana (every 30–40min; 3hr; P180), Santiago (leaving when full; 3hr; P180), and Tabuk (leaving when full; 1hr 30min; P119) leave from a terminal on the National Highway, 300m south of Tuguegarao Junction. Vans for Santa Ana also leave from another terminal 200m further south. Vans for Santiago and Tabuk also leave from a terminal by Brickstone Mall, 100m north of the junction.

INFORMATION AND ACTIVITIES

Tourist information The regional tourist office (Mon–Fri 8am–5pm; ☎078 304 1499, ✉dotr2@yahoo.com) is in the Regional Government Center at 2 Dalan na Pavvurulun, off the National Highway about 500m east of the airport. You can ask here about permits and guides for the Peñablanca caves, or book trips in other parts of northeast Luzon including the Northern Sierra Madre National Park (see p.153). The provincial tourist office (Mon–Fri 8am–5pm; ☎078 844 0203, ✉cagayantourism@gmail.

com) is in the same building as the Cagayan Provincial Museum.

Activities For reliable first-hand information about caving, trekking, abseiling and climbing, contact the Sierra Madre Outdoor Club, aka SMOC (☎0917 272 6494, smoc1985@gmail.com). You can also contact Anton Carag at Adventure and Expeditions Philippines (☎0917 532 7480, ✉aepi@whitewater.ph), who heads kayaking and rafting trips locally and in Kalinga province.

ACCOMMODATION AND EATING

AdriNel's 29 Rizal St ☎078 844 1305. One of the city's few non-fast-food restaurants, offering a popular all-you-can-eat Filipino lunch (10am–2pm; P220). Other choices include the large family platter *familia sentenyal* (P800 for five people) that includes grilled and barbecued pork, vegetables, shrimp, crab and grilled fish. Daily 8am–8pm.
Hotel Carmelita 9 Diversion Rd (150m west of Tuguegerao Junction) ☎078 844 7027, ⌨bit.ly/hotel-carmelita. A handy budget hotel for lone travellers as it has cheap singles for just P350, and often promotional cheap rates on doubles too, although cheaper rooms tend to get taken up quite quickly, and the a/c can be quite noisy. There's a pool and a decent restaurant, but breakfast

isn't included. P1480
Hotel Roma Luna St at Bonifacio St ☎078 844 2222, ✉info_hotelroma@yahoo.com. The city's largest hotel offers comfortable private rooms, smoking and non-smoking (the former have balconies), but some give onto the interior patio and are consequently quite dark. It has a popular restaurant. 📶 P1600
Mango Suites Rizal St at Balzain St ☎078 304 1302, ⌨bit.ly/mango-suites. A good central option with modern, comfortable rooms and free airport transfers. A pleasant café-restaurant serves Filipino food and a smattering of Western dishes. 📶 P1200

Peñablanca caves

The major tourist attraction around Tuguegarao is the marvellous **cave system** at Peñablanca, 24km to the east. Peñablanca, officially known as the **Peñablanca Protected Landscape and Seascape**, is riddled with more than three hundred caves, many of them deep and dangerous, and a good number still largely unexplored. Most of the caves are protected, but it's possible to visit three – **Callao**, **Musang** and **Lattu-Lattuc** – without permission; all three can be done in a single day. Several other caves in the area can be visited with permission from SMOC in Tuguegarao (see opposite), but note that some of them are suitable only for experienced cavers. Also be aware that typhoons between August and November can flood the caves and make them impossible to visit.

Callao Cave

P20 (plus guide; typical donation P100) • Return boat trips to the bat cave (including waiting) cost P600 for up to fifteen people; from the pier close to the cave entrance; kayaks (in season) cost P200/hr

The easiest of the Peñablanca caves to visit is **Callao Cave**, which has seven immense chambers – previously nine but an earthquake in the 1980s cut off the last two. The main chamber has a natural skylight and a chapel inside where Mass is celebrated on special occasions. You'll need a guide – there are plenty at the entrance. Note that there are 184 steps to climb before you reach the entrance of the cave, and inside the rocks can be slippery during the wet season. It's also possible to rent **kayaks** – ask at the cave entrance.

Another attraction here is a short **boat trip** that takes you to the **bat cave**, where at dusk you can see great flocks of the creatures leaving to hunt.

ARRIVAL AND INFORMATION	PEÑABLANCA CAVES
By tricycle A tricycle from Tuguegarao to Callao Cave is around P700 (depending on your bargaining skills) including 30min waiting time. You can also hire a van (P2500/day plus petrol), which is particularly worth doing if you want to make a day of it and explore other caves nearby.	**Guides** Contact the SMOC (see opposite) for professional guides in caving and other outdoor activities including mountaineering and trekking. Rates for trekking guides are P1000/day plus food, and you'll need one guide per five people. Porters charge around P500/day plus food, depending on what they are carrying.

3

Northern Sierra Madre National Park

At almost 3600 square kilometres, the **Northern Sierra Madre National Park** remains one of the country's last frontiers and well worth the trouble of getting there. Said by conservationists to be the Philippines' richest protected area in terms of habitat and species, the park is eighty percent land and twenty percent coastal area along a spectacular, cliff-studded seashore.

One of the reasons for the health of the park's ecosystems is its inaccessibility. Though small aircraft connect the towns of **Palanan** and **Maconacon** to the outside world, to the east lies the Pacific, which is too rough for boats during much of the northeast monsoon (Dec–Feb) and typhoon (July–Oct) seasons. At present, no roads cross the park, but controversially – against opposition from environmentalists and the Church – a **road** is now being built from the provincial capital Ilagan across the park to Palanan on the coast; the project is scheduled for completion in 2018 or 2019.

The park has few wardens and no fences, so you can visit any time you want without restriction; it is essential, however, to take a **guide** if you are to visit safely. A guide can take you down the Palanan River to the village of **Sabang**, from where you can walk

---

THE DUMAGATS

The people known as the **Dumagats** are among the original inhabitants of the Philippines. The word Dumagat translates roughly as "those who moved to the ocean", and the area around **Palanan** is the last stronghold of their vanishing culture and way of life. Some have now settled but others remain nomadic, living in small camps on the beaches around Palanan, where they build temporary sloping shelters from bamboo and dried grass. Life for the Dumagats is simple in the extreme: they survive by hunting and gathering, using little modern equipment. The main threats to their existence are through the commercialization and exploitation of their homelands, along with exposure to diseases previously unknown to them. Every March members of the nomadic Dumagat community join with the settled inhabitants of Palanan for the **Sabutan festival**.

through farmland and forest to **Disadsad Falls**, a high cascade that crashes through dense forest into a deep pool. For some of the trip there's no trail, so you'll have to wade upriver through the water. Another memorable trip from Palanan takes you northwards along the coast to the sheltered inlets around the towns of Dimalansan and Maconacon. On the isolated beaches here the **Dumagat** people establish their temporary homes (see box, p.153).

ARRIVAL AND DEPARTURE   NORTHERN SIERRA MADRE NATIONAL PARK

By plane The small town of Palanan is the main gateway to the park, and it is also possible to enter via Maconacon. From Cauayan, Cyclone Airways (☎0915 387 6048 or ☎0929 875 6766) fly six-seater planes to Palanan (P2600) and Maconacon (P2400) depending on demand. From Tuguegarao, NorthSkyAir has flights to Maconacon (roughly daily, depending on demand, usually at 2.30pm; 30min; P2200), and SkyPasada fly to Palanan (Tues, Fri & Sun, 9am; 20min; P2200).

By boat and bus You can avoid flying by taking a long boat journey from San Vicente near Santa Ana (see p.150) to Maconacon (8–10hr; around P500), but it's basically a question of negotiating passage on a supply boat – check at the port for departures. Alternatively, take a local bus from either Baler (see opposite) or from Santiago City in

Isabela province (itself an 8hr trip from Manila) to Dilasag in Aurora province (daily, 1–2 departures 4–5am; 10–12hr), from where you can take a boat to Palanan (no fixed schedules; 6–8hr; around P300). There are also boats from Palanan to Maconacon (no fixed schedules; 4hr; around P500) or to Divilacan, which is connected to Maconacon by road.

On foot For hardy visitors, the most interesting option is to trek into the park from San Mariano. It's a five- to seven-day trek that requires a guide – contact the Palanan Wilderness Development Cooperative (see below). San Mariano is served by direct buses from Manila (Five Star: 6 daily; 8–10hr), and by local buses and vans from Ilagan and Cauayan (both served by vans on the Tuguegarao–Santiago route).

INFORMATION AND ACTIVITIES

Tourist information The park's tourism officer, Myrose B. Alvarez (☎0917 775 7526, ✉myrose0883@gmail.com), is based at the town hall in Palanan. Along with offering advice and information, she can help with arranging a homestay – there are no guesthouses or hotels in Palanan – and can inform the Department of Environment and Natural Resources (DENR) that you are planning to hike in the area.

Palanan Wilderness Development Cooperative A useful organization based in the town, which can help with guides (☎0928 341 5375, ✉amgpalanan@yahoo.com).
Cagayan Valley Programme on Environment and Development (CPVED) If you are interested in seeing the resident endangered Philippine crocodiles, or in birdwatching, this organization may be able to help (☎0920 974 2379, Mikaela_tess@yahoo.com).

Baler

The laidback east-coast town of **BALER** is known for its excellent, if intermittent, **surfing**. Surfing scenes in Francis Ford Coppola's *Apocalypse Now* were filmed at a break known as **Charlie's Point** at the mouth of the Aguang River, which is a 45-minute walk north of the main surfing beach of **Sabang**. When the film crew departed they left the surfboards behind, kick-starting local interest in the sport.

Dicasalarin Cove

P300 (P150 if arriving by boat) • Walkable from Digisit (2–3hr) which is 5km beyond Cemento Reef; also accessible from Baler by motorbike or 4WD, or by chartering a boat (40min)

If you're not after surf, then you could try the white beach at **Dicasalarin Cove**. You can snorkel here too, and there is a spot for shallow diving at the site of a reef rehabilitation programme. There are no shops or restaurants – only picnic cottages, so bring drinks and snacks.

Casiguran Sound

Genesis bus (every 2hr; 3–4hr) and vans (leave when full; 3–4hr) from Baler

The calm and picturesque inlet of **Casiguran Sound**, 120km northeast of Baler, is a lovely spot to while away a few hours. Protected from onshore winds and waves by a finger of

RIDING BALER'S WAVES

You can **surf** year-round at Baler, although the best waves usually come between September and March, especially early in the morning. The waves, averaging nearly 2m, are ideal for both amateur and experienced surfers. Lessons and kit rental are available at Sabang Beach.

Cemento Reef A strong world-class right-hand reef break, perfect for advanced surfers; competitions are held here.

Charlie's Point The most famous surf spot in Baler, gaining popularity in the late 1970s during the filming of *Apocalypse Now*.

Dalugan Bay, San Ildefonso This left-hand reef break peninsula offers good surf.

Dianed, Dipaculao North of Baler, this place has typhoon swells holding 1.2–1.8m waves.

Dicasalarin Point Right- and left-hand breaks, with reef breaks for the more experienced surfers and beach breaks for beginners.

Lobbot's Point, Dipaculao A left- and right-hand beach break holding 0.6–1.8m ground swells that break into the sandy gravel bottom.

Sabang Beach The sandy bottom beach break here is ideal for beginners; there are left and right breaks from September to March. You can rent surfboards and surfing lessons are available.

Secret Point, Castillo This surf spot breaks between two and four times a year and can offer a 140m ride.

hilly land, it makes perfect for **swimming** and is scarcely developed. You'll find little here in terms of restaurants and shops, apart from a few sari-sari stores around the fishing village.

ARRIVAL AND INFORMATION   BALER

By bus There are no road links north along the coast to the Northern Sierra Madre National Park, but you can catch a Danilo Express bus to Dilasag (2 daily; 4hr 30min) where you can get a boat to Palanan (no fixed schedule; 6–8hr; P300).

Destinations Baguio (Lizardo: 2 daily; 9hr); Manila

(Genesis and Joy Bus: 4–8 nightly; 5–6hr).

Tourist information The municipal tourist office is in the Municipal Building (Mon–Fri 8am–5pm; ☏ 0928 983 7668, ⓦ baler.gov.ph). The provincial government post some useful information on their website at ⓦ aurora.ph.

ACCOMMODATION AND EATING

All the best **accommodation** in Baler is on or around the beach at Sabang, which is a short tricycle ride (P20) from town. Apart from during the annual Aurora Cup in February, you won't have any problem finding somewhere to stay. The best eating options are in the hotels; all the options that we review have decent **restaurants**, some with lovely views.

Bay-Ler View Hotel ☏ 02 404 4784, ⓦ baylerview .com. Clean and comfortable accommodation right on the beachfront with lovely views over the ocean; the restaurant serves local and international dishes, staff are friendly and there's wi-fi in the communal areas. ⋙ **P1600**

Bay's Inn ☏ 02 404 4784, ⓦ baysinnbaler.com. One of the most popular resorts for budget tourists and out-of-town surfers, boasting panoramic views of Baler Bay, the Pacific Ocean and surrounding cliffs and beaches. It has clean fan or

a/c doubles with private showers and a popular restaurant with views. Surfboard rental available. ⋙ **P1000**

Costa Pacifica ☏ 0917 844 8371, ⓦ costapacificabaler .com. The plushest hotel in town and not a bad choice, with a pool and a variety of rooms available in the main hotel or its annexe across the way. Always agree the full net price in advance however, preferably in writing, and don't let them pull any stunts with sudden added service charges when you check out. ⋙ **P5313**

The Cordillera

To Filipino lowlanders brought up on sunshine and beaches, the tribal heartlands of the north and their spiny ridge of inhospitable mountains, the **Cordillera**, are seen almost as another country, inhabited by mysterious people who worship primitive gods. It's true that in some respects life for many tribal people has changed little in hundreds of years, with traditional ways and values still very much in evidence. If anything is likely to erode these traditions, it is the coming of tourists; already an increasing number of tribal people are making much more from the sale of handicrafts than they do from the production of rice.

The **weather** can have a major impact on a trip to the Cordillera, not least because landslides can cause travel delays during the rainy season (particularly May–Nov, but continuing until Jan or Feb). Since the rains come in from the northeast it's the places on the eastern side of the mountains – such as **Banaue** and **Batad** – that are usually worst hit, and fog can roll into those areas any time from October to February. Throughout the region it can get cold at night between December and February. Note that the rice terrace **planting seasons** vary significantly; the lower-lying areas typically have two plantings a year while the highlands have one. Terraces are at their greenest in the month or so before harvesting, although their barren appearance after a harvest can also be impressive.

Baguio and around

It's fair to say that its heyday as a rural retreat from Manila is far behind **BAGUIO**. The city centre is blighted by a polluted tangle of smoke-belching jeepneys and the large SM shopping mall hardly improves the scenery. Still, its position as a major hub for the Cordillera means that you're likely to pass through, and it does have some absorbing sights, plus, as a university city, a number of excellent restaurants and interesting nightlife. Baguio's municipal centre – the area around **Burnham Park** – was designed by renowned American architect Daniel Burnham in 1904, and based loosely on Washington DC. The main drag, **Session Road**, is lined with restaurants and shops, while the eye-catching **Baguio Cathedral** stands on a hill above.

Brief history

In the sixteenth century, intrepid **Spanish friars** had started to explore the region, finding a land of fertile valleys, pine-clad hills and mountains, lush vegetation and an abundance of minerals such as copper and gold. Soon more friars, soldiers and fortune-hunters were trekking north to convert the natives to Christianity and profit from the rich natural resources. In the nineteenth century, **colonizing Americans** took over and developed Baguio into a modern city, a showcase recreational and administrative centre from which they could preside over their precious tropical colony without working up too much of a sweat. In 1944, when American forces landed in Leyte, the head of the Japanese Imperial Army, **General Yamashita**, moved his headquarters to Baguio and helped establish a

---

TREKKING IN THE CORDILLERA

Since the road network is poor in many parts of the Cordillera, and there are so many jungle-clad peaks and hidden valleys, **trekking** is the only way to see some of the region's secrets: burial caves, tribal villages and hidden waterfalls. Gentle **day-hikes** are possible, particularly in the main tourist areas of Banaue and Sagada, but there are also plenty of **two- or three-day treks** that take you deep into backwaters. Don't be tempted to wander off into the wilderness without a guide: good maps are almost nonexistent and it's easy to become disoriented and lost. Medical facilities and rescue services are few and far between; if you get into trouble and no one knows where you are then you'll have a long wait for help to arrive.

Most of the **best trails** are around Sagada, Banaue, Bontoc, Tabuk and Tinglayan. In each of these towns you'll find a tourist office or town hall where someone will be able to help arrange **guides**. In smaller settlements a good place to look for a guide is at the barangay hall. Many guides won't have official certification, but will know the area exceptionally well. Your guide may also agree to carry equipment and supplies, but don't expect him to have any equipment himself. Most guides happily wander through inhospitable landscapes with only flip-flops on their feet – don't follow suit, as the going underfoot is often extremely rugged. Rates start from around P500 a day but they vary; ask in advance if the guide is expecting you to provide food for him. Certainly, the guide will expect a tip, even in the form of a few beers and a meal, for getting you home safely.

puppet Philippine government there under President José Laurel. In 1945 the city was destroyed and thousands lost their homes as liberating forces flushed out Yamashita and his army. The general quickly fled north into the interior.

The city is also etched on the Filipino consciousness as the site of one of the country's worst natural disasters, the earthquake of July 16, 1990, which measured 7.7 on the Richter Scale and killed hundreds, mostly in the city's vulnerable shanty towns, many of which cling precariously to the sides of steep valleys.

Burnham Park
Despite the efforts of the SM Mall, the city's centrepiece is still **Burnham Park**, a hilltop version of Rizal Park in Manila with a man-made boating lake at the centre. Even if it's a bit past its prime, the park is an interesting place to take a stroll and to watch the people of Baguio at play: there are boats for rent on the lake and tricycles for kids.

Baguio Cathedral
General Luna Rd • Mon–Sat 5am–7pm, Sun 4.30am–8pm • Free

Standing imperiously above Session Road, **Baguio Cathedral** is a striking example of "wedding cake Gothic" painted rose pink and with twin spires crowned by delicate minarets. Dating from 1936, it became an evacuation centre during World War II and withstood the US carpet-bombing of the city in 1945 – saving the lives of thousands who sheltered inside. There is a steep stairway to the cathedral from Session Road.

3

City Market
Magsaysay Ave, at the northern end of Session Rd • Daily 5am–8pm

The **City Market** is one of the liveliest and most colourful in the country, acting as a trading post for farmers and tribes not only from Baguio but also from many of the mountain communities to the north. Bargains include strawberries, which thrive in the temperate north, and you can also buy peanut brittle, sweet wine, honey, textiles, handicrafts and jewellery.

St Louis University Museum of Arts and Culture
St Louis University Campus, Bonifacio St • Mon–Sat 7.30–11.30am & 1–5pm • Free, but bring ID • ☎ 074 442 2793, ⓦ slu.edu.ph

The **St Louis University Museum of Arts and Culture** is a good place to get a general insight into the history of the north. It displays hundreds of artefacts from the Cordillera including tribal costumes, weapons and fascinating black-and-white photographs of sacrifices and other rituals.

Baguio Museum
DOT Complex, Governor Pack Rd • Tues–Sun 9am–5pm • P40 • ☎ 074 444 7541

The **Baguio Museum** showcases artefacts of indigenous tribes of the Cordilleras. There are separate displays about each of the major groups, including accessories, implements for rice farming, baskets, musical instruments, woodcarving and traditional dress. Upstairs is an exhibition on the history of Baguio. For an idea of how Baguio has changed, take a look at the set of three scale models of the city centre in 1909, 1928 and 2009.

Wright Park
Leonard Wood Rd, 4km east of the centre • Pony rides P200/30min, P300/hr • Taxi from city centre P90, "Mines View" jeepney from Mabini St P8.50

Wright Park is a popular public space where you can hire a sturdy mountain nag – optionally with a dyed-pink mane – for a quick trot around the perimeter beyond. On the other side of Leonard Wood Road, still within the park, is **The Mansion** (not open to the public). Built in 1908 for American governor-generals to the Philippines and damaged in 1945, it was rebuilt in 1947 as a holiday home for Philippine presidents.

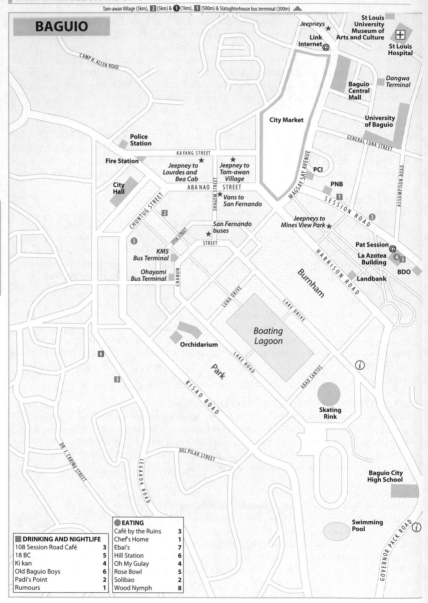

BAGUIO

CAMP H. ALLEN ROAD

St Louis
University
Museum of
Arts and Culture

Jeepneys ★
Link
Internet @

St Louis
Hospital

Dangwa
Terminal

Baguio
Central
Mall

University
of Baguio

City Market

GENERAL LUNA STREET

Police
Station

KAYANG STREET

Fire Station

MAGSAY SAY AVENUE

ASSUMPTION ROAD

★
Jeepney to
Lourdes and
Bea Cab

★
Jeepney to
Tam-awan
Village
STREET

PCI

City
Hall

SHAGEM STREET

ABANAO

CHUNTUG STREET

★ Vans to
San Fernando

PNB

SESSION ROAD

1

2

QISEK STREET

★
San Fernando
buses
STREET

Jeepneys to
Mines View Park ★

2

KMS
Bus Terminal

3

HARRISON ROAD

Pat Session @

La Azotea
Building

4 3

Ohayami
Bus Terminal

CHANUN

Burnham

Landbank

BDO

LUNA DRIVE

LAKE DRIVE

Boating
Lagoon

Orchidarium

LAKE ROAD

Park

ABAD SANTOS

6

KISAD ROAD

5

i

Skating
Rink

DR. J. CARINO STREET

LEGARDA ROAD

DEL PILAR STREET

Baguio City
High School

Swimming
Pool

GOVERNOR PACK ROAD

i

■ DRINKING AND NIGHTLIFE		● EATING	
108 Session Road Café	3	Café by the Ruins	3
18 BC	5	Chef's Home	1
Ki kan	4	Ebai's	7
Old Baguio Boys	6	Hill Station	6
Padi's Point	2	Oh My Gulay	4
Rumours	1	Rose Bowl	5
		Solibao	2
		Wood Nymph	8

Botanical Gardens

Leonard Wood Rd, 4km east of the centre • Daily 6am–6pm • Free • Taxi from city centre P70, Pacdal-bound jeepney from Magsaysay Ave P8.50

Travelling out of the city centre eastwards on Leonard Wood Road for 4km brings you to the **Botanical Gardens**, also known as the Centennial Park. You can wander through thick vegetation along winding concrete pathways, or join the locals relaxing and enjoying barbecued food at weekends.

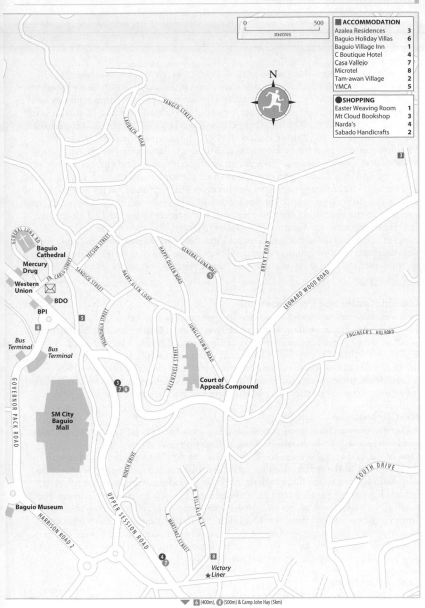

Mines View Park

6km east of the centre • Taxi from city centre P90, jeepney from Mabini St P12

Mines View Park has a viewing point overlooking an area that used to be the location of mining operations. To get there you have to make your way past countless souvenir stalls and hawkers – if you ever dreamed of having your photo taken with a sunglasses-wearing St Bernard dog then this is the place to do it. A short walk up the hill from the viewpoint is the **Good Shepherd Convent**, with a store inside the main gate where you can buy products made by the nuns, including strawberry, coconut or *ube* (purple yam) jam and cashew or peanut brittle.

Camp John Hay

Loakan Rd, 5km southeast of Baguio · **Historical Core** Daily 8am–5pm · ☎ 074 444 8358 · P60 · **Tree Top Adventure** Daily 8am–4.30pm · Canopy Ride P350 · ☎ 074 442 0800, ⓦ treetopadventureph.com · **Golf Course** ☎ 074 444 2131 · Taxi from city centre P75

Named after US president Theodore Roosevelt's secretary of war, **Camp John Hay** used to be a rest and recreational facility for employees of the US military and Department of Defense. During World War II the property was used by the Japanese as a concentration camp for American and British soldiers. In 1991 the camp was turned over to the Philippine government for development into an upmarket country club, with hotels, a **golf course**, private mountain lodges and sundry restaurants and clubhouses.

The expansive, undulating grounds have some pleasant walks through the pine trees and are also ideal for jogging. Jeepneys can't enter the park itself, so it's best to get a taxi. If you don't have a particular destination in mind then ask to be dropped at the entrance to the **Historical Core**. Here you can buy a ticket to see the Bell House, the holiday residence of the Commanding General of the Philippines, the Bell Amphitheatre and the site where General Yamashita formally surrendered to US forces. At weekends, Filipino families congregate close to the entrance to the Historical Core to enjoy picnics. Also close by is the **Tree Top Adventure**, where you can try a canopy ride or join guided walks.

Lourdes Grotto and Dominican Hill

Off Dominican Hill Rd · Taxi from city centre P65, Dominican-Mirador jeepney fromt Kayang St P8.50

High on a hill in the western part of the city is **Lourdes Grotto**, a Catholic shrine watched over by an image of Our Lady of Lourdes and reached by 252 steps. A kilometre further at the summit of the road is **Dominican Hill**, from where the views across the city are superlative. The crumbling Hotel Diplomat on the peak was built by a Dominican order, then later owned by a controversial entrepreneur and faith healer; it's abandoned and rather eerie today, but you can wander around inside.

BenCab Museum

6km west of the centre, Km 6 Asin Rd, Tadiangan, Tuba, Benguet · Tues–Sun 9am–6pm · P120 · ☎ 074 442 7165, ⓦ bencabmuseum.org · From central Baguio, take an Asin-bound jeepney from Kayang St (P11) or a taxi (around P120)

One of the best art galleries in the Philippines, the **BenCab Museum** is well worth the short trip out of the centre. Built to house the collection of local artist Ben Cabrera, who has a home and studio next door, it's an airy Modernist structure with lots of natural light and great views of the surrounding scenery. Two galleries house temporary exhibitions while the other seven contain permanent displays, including anything from Ifugao artefacts and old prints of the Philippines to paintings and sculptures by contemporary Filipino artists. Below the museum is an excellent **café** overlooking a duck pond and organic farm. The beautiful **garden** features cascading waterfalls and an eco-trail to a viewpoint on the hillside.

Tam-awan Village

366C Pinsao Proper · Daily 8am–6pm · P50 · ☎ 074 446 2949, ⓦ tam-awanvillage.com · Taxi from city centre P80, jeepney from Kayang St P11

On the northwest outskirts of Baguio, 5km from the centre, **Tam-awan Village** is a replica tribal village established in 1996 by a group of Filipino artists, including Ben Cabrera and Jordan Mang-osan. There is a small gallery with changing exhibitions, a gift shop and café, and a cultural show with dancing every Saturday afternoon – you can even stay the night here in a tribal hut (see opposite). Tam-awan means "vantage point" – on a clear evening, you'll see magnificent China Sea sunsets and even the Hundred Islands in the distance.

ARRIVAL AND DEPARTURE

By bus Though there are a number of terminals, most bus companies use Governor Pack Rd or the Slaughterhouse terminal on Magsaysay Ave. Victory Liner's Manila services use a terminal just off Upper Session Rd, KMS and Ohayami terminate on Chanum St, and local bus companies to La Union use a small terminal on Shagem St.

Destinations from Chanum St Banaue (KMS: 2 daily; 8hr; Ohayami: daily 9pm; 8hr); Kiangan (KMS: daily 9pm; 7hr).

Destinations from Governor Pack Rd Bolinao (Victory Liner: 4 daily; 5hr); Dagupan (Victory Liner: every 20min; 2hr 30min); Laoag (Partas: every 1–2hr; 7–8hr); Manila Cubao (North Genesis and Joy Liner both hourly; 6–8hr); Manila Pasay (Joy Liner hourly; 6–8hr); San Juan, stopping off at San Fernando (Partas: hourly; 2hr); Santa Cruz

(Victory Liner: 5 daily; 6hr); Tuguegarao (Dalin: 3 daily; 12hr); Vigan (Partas: hourly; 5–6hr).

Destinations from Shagem St San Fernando (various: hourly; 2hr 30min).

Destinations from Slaughterhouse Bontoc (D'Rising Sun: hourly 6am–4pm; GL Trans: 5 daily; 6hr); Kabayan (Norton Trans: 9am, 11am & noon; 3hr 30min); Sagada (GL Trans: 5 daily; 5–6hr).

Destinations from Victory Liner terminal Manila Cubao (Victory Liner: hourly; 6–7hr), Manila Pasay (Victory Liner: hourly; 6–7hr).

By van A/c vans travel from the Slaughterhouse terminal to Banaue (6 daily; 6hr) and Kabayan (leaving when full; 3hr; P150).

INFORMATION

Tourist information The department of tourism is in the Baguio Tourism Complex on Governor Pack Rd (Mon–Fri 8am–5pm; ☎074 442 7014, ✉dotregioncar@gmail.com),

and there's a smaller city information centre on Lake Drive in Burnham Park (Mon–Fri 8am–5pm; ☎074 446 3434).

ACCOMMODATION

Hotels in the centre can get quite noisy, so ask for a room away from the road; there are also a number of good choices **outside town** in peaceful pine forested areas – a much more pleasant way to experience Baguio than in its traffic-choked centre. You can also stay in traditional huts at the artist-run Tam-awan Village (see opposite).

Azalea Residences Leonard Wood Loop ☎074 424 8714, ⊛azaleabaguio.com. In a quiet location on the northeastern outskirts of the city, these upmarket serviced apartments in a log-cabin-inspired hotel include living area, dining room and kitchen facilities. The only downside is that the lower-floor accommodation looks onto a wall – ask for a room on the fourth floor with views across the countryside. ☎ **P6950**

Baguio Holiday Villas 10 Legarda Rd ☎074 442 6679, ⊛baguioholidayvillas.com.ph. The apartments here have two bedrooms and a kitchenette, making them a good choice for families. There are also clean doubles that are good value, despite being on the smallish side. ☎ **P2500**

Baguio Village Inn 355 Magsaysay Ave ☎074 442 3901. This spotless place, a 15min walk from the bottom of Session Road, is friendly and pretty homely, with wooden floors and wood panelling, although the single rooms in particular are rather small. Wi-fi in the restaurant area only. ☎ **P800**

C Boutique Hotel 5 Arellano at Moran, Brgy Gibraltar ☎074 619 0158, ⊛cboutiquehotel.com. A 15min walk from Mines View and Wright Park, this pleasant hotel in a peaceful location has seventeen small but well-appointed rooms with modern amenities. There are a couple of lounges, and a terrace where they light fires of an evening, as well as a restaurant and bar. ☎ **P4290**

★**Casa Vallejo** Upper Session Rd ☎074 424 3397,

✉casavallejo@gmail.com. Built in 1909 to house government employees, this Baguio landmark became the city's first hotel in the 1920s. It was one of very few buildings to survive World War II, but by the 1990s it had fallen into disrepair. It reopened in 2010 after extensive renovation and now has bags of US colonial-era charm; rooms are tasteful, modern and a bargain even in peak season. The windows are not double-glazed, so ask for one away from the road. ☎ **P2574**

Microtel Upper Session Rd ☎074 619 3333, ⊛microtelphilippines.com. Right above the Victory Liner terminal, this hotel, with a blue wooden facade, is a good option; it has neat and tidy rooms set on four floors. ☎ **P4250**

Tam-awan Village 366C Pinsao Proper ☎074 446 2949, ⊛tam-awanvillage.com. An unusual choice, featuring accommodation in traditional Ifugao and Kalinga huts that were acquired from the provinces and reassembled at this replica village (see opposite). The huts, all with shared bath, are simple but welcoming, and can sleep up to nine. Note that it can get surprisingly cold. ☎ **P1000**

YMCA Post Office Loop ☎074 442 4766. This large, central hostel has spotless twin rooms with flatscreen TVs and single-sex dorms with institutional rows of pine-wood beds crammed in every corner; the maze of echoing corridors gives the place a bit of a soulless feel. There's a large basketball court. ☎ Dorms **P385**, twins **P1420**

3

EATING

Baguio has some of the best **restaurants** in the country. There is also a good selection of street food, including a couple of places beside *Casa Vallejo* hotel serving *bulalo* (beef on the bone in a broth), and the usual fast-food outlets in the SM Mall.

★**Café by the Ruins** 25 Chuntug St ☎074 442 4010. Located in a breezy setting, with tables dotted around the World War II ruins of the residence of Baguio's first governor, this is one of the city's best restaurants, with excellent organic food prepared with home-grown herbs and served either indoors or in the shady yard. The duck *mami* (P200) is great, and there are home-made breads, pastries, muffins and scones (P88), too. Daily 7am–10pm.

★**Chef's Home** 13 Outlook Drive, Purok 3 ☎0916 444 5756, ⓦbit.ly/chefs-home. The Malaysian owner and chef rustles up exceptional Asian fusion dishes embracing Malay, Thai and Indian cuisine. Dishes are large enough to share, with most serving two to four; the crispy papaya salad is outstanding (P280). Mon–Sat 11am–2.30pm & 6–8.30pm.

Ebai's 151 Engineer's Hill, Upper Session Rd ☎074 446 9722. The exquisite carrot cake (P68) at this little café was originally baked for the wife of former president Ramos; it's a great little spot to refuel with a slice of carrot cake, or a dish of indigenous cuisine such as *bulalo* (P198) or pork adobo (P108). Daily 7am–9.30pm.

Hill Station Upper Session Rd ☎074 424 2734, ⓦhillstationbaguio.com. This place is within the *Casa Vallejo* hotel, with a smart but unpretentious dining room and waiting staff in military-style uniforms to reflect Baguio's history as a US hill station. The international menu exclusively features home-made dishes and includes stews from other famous hill stations in countries such as India. There is also a pleasant café/bar with delectable cakes, as well as dishes such as Thai seafood curry (P370) and lamb tagine (P400). Daily 6.30am–10pm.

Oh My Gulay 5/F La Azotea Building, 108 Session Rd ☎074 446 0108, ⓦbit.ly/oh-my-gulay. On the top floor of a little shopping precinct, this quirky veggie restaurant and art space was designed by renowned Baguio artist Kidlat Tahimik, and features stone walkways, mismatched furniture, a mock wooden boat and a little pond. Mains P130–155. Tues–Thurs 11am–8pm, Fri & Sat 11am–9pm, Sun 11am–7pm.

★**Rose Bowl** 88 Upper General Luna Rd ☎074 442 4213, ⓦrosebowlrestaurant.com. This highly acclaimed Cantonese restaurant follows family recipes brought over from China at the beginning of the twentieth century. Dishes use top-quality local vegetables, fish transported daily from the coast, and noodles from Manila's oldest noodle factory. Dishes serve three to four – try the roast bowl pancit (P400), and if you need the roast bowl veg chop suey (P259) to be meat-free, let them know when you order. Daily 10am–10pm.

Solibao Puso ng Baguio Building, Session Rd ☎074 442 3867, ⓦsolibao.com. This popular local restaurant may look like a fast-food franchise, but it's been dishing up solid Filipino food since 1972, no frills but reliably good, and it's an excellent place to check up the likes of *kare-kare* (stew of oxtail and banana flower in peanut sauce, P285 for two) or *lechon kawali* (crispy fried pork belly, P270 for two). Daily 8am–10pm.

Wood Nymph 36 Military Cut-off Rd (100m from the junction with Session Rd) ☎074 446 0272. One of Baguio's many Korean restaurants, this airy place has been serving the city's Korean community for nearly two decades. Seafood is the speciality here – try the *haemultung* (seafood stew, P700 for three people). The *galbichim* (braised short ribs, P290) are great too. Daily 10am–10pm.

DRINKING AND NIGHTLIFE

108 Session Rd Café 2/F La Azotea Building, 108 Session Rd. Packed at weekends, this place is a good spot to enjoy a few beers (P50) and live music (daily 5pm–midnight) – anything from country to classical. The American menu features burgers (P65). Happy hour 4.30–7pm. Daily 4.30pm–1am.

18 BC 16 Legarda Rd ☎074 304 2246, ⓦbit.ly/18-BC. A fun bar with nightly local bands, popular with students, especially at the weekend, but not to the extent of being overwhelmed with them. Acoustic rock is the mainstay here, but they sometimes have reggae or other sounds too. Daily 6.30pm–2.30am.

Ki kan beneath Baden Powell Inn, 26 Governor Pack Rd ☎074 244 4661. Popular with students and artists, this friendly bar often has live acoustic and reggae music in the evenings, with local bands on Fri nights (which is also barbecue night), open mike Mon–Thurs. There's also good cheap food (budget meals P70–75). Fri 6pm–2am, Sat–Thurs 7pm–midnight.

Old Baguio Boys Nevada Square, 2 Loakan Rd (50m from the junction with Session Rd) ☎074 422 9284. This place is all that's left of what used to be a whole collection of music bars in this little square, but it's keeping up the tradition anyway, with live bands every night and music till dawn. Cover charge P200. Daily 6pm–5am.

Padi's Point North Rd, Rizal Park ☎074 304 5105, ⓦpadispoint.com. Part of a chain with branches across Luzon, this bar has live and loud music until the wee hours. The menu includes a range of local dishes. Happy hour 1–9pm. Daily 1pm–4am.

Rumours 55 Session Rd ☎074 619 0152. A straightforward place to enjoy a drink, without intrusive music or other distractions. There's a better than usual choice of beers (P50) and snacks to enjoy with them. The signature secret-recipe cocktail "Power of Rumours" (P145) mixes eight varieties of spirits. Daily 11am–2am.

SHOPPING

Easter Weaving Room 2 Easter Rd, Guisad ☎074 442 4972, ⓦeasterweaving.com. Handwoven articles such as rugs, tablemats, wall hangings, textiles, cushion covers and bed linen. You can watch the weavers at work on old handlooms and, if you've got a few weeks to wait, place a personal order. It's on the northwestern outskirts of town; take a Guisad jeepney from Kayang St, north of Burnham Park (P8.50), or a taxi (around P80). Mon–Sat 8am–5pm.

★ **Mt Cloud Bookshop** Casa Vallejo, Upper Session Rd ☎074 424 4437, ⓦmtcloudbookshop.com. This small bookshop has an excellent selection of materials mainly on the Cordillera region, as well as works by local authors.

There are monthly book launches and author talks, too. Daily 10.30am–8pm.

Narda's 151 Upper Session Rd ☎074 422 4360, ⓦnardas.com. The traditional Cordillera Ikat style of weaving has been adapted to contemporary tastes at this shop – choose from a variety of handwoven arts and crafts, including attractive clothes, bags, rugs, linen and tablemats. Daily 8am–7pm.

Sabado Handicrafts 16 Outlook Drive. Local artist Greg Sabado displays a wide selection of handicrafts, including beautiful wooden artefacts, as well as furniture. Daily 8am–5pm.

DIRECTORY

Banks and exchange There are plenty of ATMs in the centre; you'll find moneychangers in the City Market at its southern end.

Internet access Link Internet, 168 Hora Building, Magsaysay Ave at Bonifacio St (daily 8am–midnight; P15/

hr); Pat Session Internet Café, 2/F 104 Session Rd (daily 24hr; P15/hr).

Police 24hr police station on Abanao St (☎074 442 4119).

Post office At the junction of Session Rd and Governor Pack Rd.

Kabayan and around

An isolated, one-road mountain village 85km northeast of Baguio, in Benguet province, **KABAYAN** makes a thrilling side trip – although because of the rough road you'll need to spend at least one night. There was no road here until 1960 and no electricity until 1978, and this extended isolation has left the place rural and unspoilt, a good place to experience the culture of the **Ibaloi**. The area around Kabayan is excellent **trekking** country, and climbers are also drawn here for the chance to ascend **Mount Pulag**, the highest peak in Luzon.

Kabayan came to the attention of the outside world in the early twentieth century when a group of **mummies**, possibly dating back as far as 2000 BC, was discovered in the surrounding caves. When the Americans arrived, mummification was discouraged as unhygienic and the practice is thought to have died out. Controversy still surrounds the Kabayan mummies, some of which have disappeared to overseas collectors, sold for

MAKING A MUMMY

The history of the Kabayan **mummies** is still largely oral. It is even uncertain when the last mummy was created; according to staff at the town's museum, mummification was attempted most recently in 1907 but the wrong combination of herbs was used. It's possible that the last successful mummification was in 1901, of the great-grandmother of former village mayor Florentino Merino.

What is known is the general procedure, which could take up to a year to complete. The body would have been bathed and dressed, then tied upright to a chair with a low fire burning underneath to start the drying process. Unlike in other mummification rituals around the world, the internal organs were not removed. A jar was placed under the corpse to catch the body fluids, which are considered sacred, while elders began the process of peeling off the skin and rubbing juices from native leaves into the muscles to aid preservation. Tobacco smoke was blown through the mouth to dry the internal tissues and drive out worms.

a quick buck by unscrupulous middlemen. One was said to have been stolen by a Christian pastor in 1920 and wound up as a sideshow in a Manila circus. Some remain, however, and some have been recovered. Officials know of dozens of mummies in the area, but will not give their locations for fear of desecration. You can, however, see several of them in designated mountaintop **caves**.

Opdas Cave

At the southern end of Kabayan village; follow the signs from the main road • P20 donation

Before heading on to the other burial sites, be sure to visit **Opdas Cave** at the southern end of Kabayan village. It contains around two hundred skulls and bones estimated to be up to a thousand years old, discovered in a pile but now arranged. Nobody knows why they were buried together, but one theory is that they died as a result of an epidemic. Call at the caretaker's house (the green corrugated iron building); a member of the family will open the gate and encourage you to pray to the spirits, asking them to allow you to enter and leave safely.

National Museum

At the western end of Kabayan beyond the bridge • Mon–Fri 9am–4pm • Free

Kabayan's small branch of the **National Museum** displays the costumes and traditions of the people of Kabayan; exhibits include traditional dress, wild boar skulls, rice wine jars and woven rattan baskets. There is an informative display on centuries-old rituals and beliefs, including burial practices – take a look at the mummy in foetal position inside the coffin.

Tinongchol Burial Rock

3km north of Kabayan • P30; guide P1000, including a visit to the National Museum (see above) and Opdas Cave (see above) • 4WDs can be arranged at the *Pinecone Lodge* (P700)

An hour's hike north of town is the **Tinongchol Burial Rock**, a large rock with deep niches that were carved to inter the mummified dead in coffins. Four of the seven man-made holes contain between five and ten coffins each – to this day it is unclear how the people of Kagayan hollowed these out.

Timbac Cave

1.2km above Kabayan • P30; Ibaloi accredited guide P1500 for up to seven people • Outside the wet seasons, 4WDs can be arranged at the *Pinecone Lodge* (see opposite)

When **Timbac Cave** is open, it's possible to hike up to see its mummies and return within the day. At last check the cave was closed for conservation work and no reopening date had been fixed. When visiting, it's essential to bring an Ibaloi guide not only to ensure that you don't get lost but also to respect local sensibilities: locals believe that unaccompanied outsiders will attract the wrath of the spirits. As one resident puts it, "If ever there is a curse, it will not be on you but on us." The tourist office (see opposite) can arrange an accredited guide.

It's a strenuous four- to five-hour climb to the cave. Take food and drink and aim to set off at around 6am. On the way ask your guide to point out the **Tinongchol Burial Rock**; you'll also see a number of **lakes** and **rice terraces** where farmers grow *kintoman*, an aromatic red rice. Your guide will retrieve the key to Timbac Cave from a caretaker who lives close by, and say the necessary prayers before you enter.

The walk back down to Kabayan takes three hours, or you can walk for an hour or so beyond the cave to the Halsema Highway and flag down a bus (the guide will charge extra for this) directly to Baguio, or head north to Bontoc and Sagada. Check the time of the last bus (usually late afternoon), and don't cut it too fine. It is not recommended that you do this in reverse and approach the cave from the highway, since you risk finding that the caretaker isn't there or offending locals by arriving without a guide.

Bangao Cave

Near Bangao village, 7km north of Kabayan • P30; guide P1000 • 4WDs can be arranged at *Pinecone Lodge* (see below)

If you don't have time to trek to Timbac Cave, or just want to see as much as possible while in the area, consider visiting the caves around Bangao village. The **Bangao Cave** has a handful of mummies in coffins, although they are in worse condition than those in Timbac. It's a two-hour walk from Kabayan, although you can reduce this to thirty minutes by hiring a 4WD to take you some of the way.

ARRIVAL AND INFORMATION   KABAYAN AND AROUND

By bus Norton Trans buses from Baguio's Slaughterhouse terminal stop along Kabayan's main road, departing from Baguio daily at 9am, 11am & noon (3–4hr) and returning to Baguio at 7am, 10am & 2pm.
By van Vans from Baguio's Slaughterhouse terminal serve Kabayan (7am–5pm every 2hr; 3hr; P150).

Tourist information The tourist information point is at the municipal hall (Mon–Fri 8am–5pm; ☎ 0917 521 5830, ✉ berrysangaojr@gmail.com).

ACCOMMODATION

3

Pinecone Lodge Main road, Kabayan ☎ 0929 327 7749. As the name suggests, this lodge is decked out in pine; the clean tiled rooms are spacious and all have private bath, and the living area with fireplace gives the place a cosy touch. It also has a restaurant, and great brewed coffee. **P550**

EATING

Brookside Café Main road, Kabayan. The friendly owner at this pleasant café with wooden benches rustles up simple dishes including soups, noodles and rice and meat, as well as sugary Benguet coffee that is just the thing on a cold Cordillera morning. Mon–Sat 6am–6pm, Sun 6–8am & noon–6pm.
Rockwood Café Main road, Kabayan ☎ 0927 654 2139. A chalet-like restaurant, popular with villagers and visitors alike, where you can try some locally grown organic arabica coffee, or get your teeth into some tasty Filipino pork, fish, chicken or vegetable dishes. Mon–Fri 8am–5pm, but earlier breakfasts and later suppers can be arranged by appointment.

Mount Pulag

Standing 2922m above sea level, **Mount Pulag**, located within Mount Pulag National Park, is the highest mountain in Luzon and even experienced climbers are required to take a guide to climb it. The terrain is steep, there are gorges and ravines, and in the heat of the valleys below, it's easy to forget that it can be bitterly cold and foggy on top. Despite what villagers may flippantly say, don't underestimate the difficulty of this mountain. It's essential to treat the area with respect: a number of indigenous communities including the Ibaloi, Kalanguya, Kankanay and Karaos live on Pulag's slopes and regard the mountain as a sacred place. They have a rich folklore about ancestral spirits inhabiting trees, lakes and mountains, and while they're friendly towards climbers you should stick to the trails.

The two best **trails** start from **Ambangeg** and **Kabayan**. Less used are the **Mountain Lakes Trail**, an hour's drive north of Kabayan, where you ascend Mount Tabayok and camp at the lakeside, and the **Enchanted Trail** starting in Tawangan, a two-hour drive north of Kabayan. Whichever way you choose to climb Pulag, the most exciting thing to do is to take a tent and expect to **spend the night** on top, but note that camping in the park is banned at weekends (Fri–Sun) and if weather conditions are bad. An alternative option to camping is accommodation in local homestays, which can be arranged by the Department of Environment and Natural Resources (DENR) Visitors' Center (see p.166). Two things to note before you set out are that visitor numbers may be restricted for conservation reasons, so it's wise to check ahead that you will indeed be able to visit on the date you have in mind; and that you'll need to bring a medical certificate stating that you're fit to do the trek (see p.166), or you won't be allowed to do it.

3

THE IGOROTS

The tribes of the Cordillera – often collectively known as the **Igorots** ("mountaineers") – resisted assimilation into the Spanish Empire for three centuries. Although the colonizers brought some material improvements, such as to the local diet, they also forced the poor to work to pay off debts, burned houses, cut down crops and introduced smallpox. The saddest long-term result of the attempts to subjugate the Igorots was subtler, however – the creation of a distinction between highland and lowland Filipinos. The peoples of the Cordillera became minorities in their own country, still struggling today for representation and recognition of a lifestyle that the Spanish tried to discredit as unchristian and depraved. The word Igorot was regarded as derogatory in some quarters, although in the twentieth century there were moves to "reclaim" the term and it is still commonly used.

Though some Igorots did convert to Christianity, many are still at least partly animists and pray to a hierarchy of **anitos**. These include deities that possess shamans and speak to them during seances, spirits that inhabit sacred groves or forests, personified forces of nature and generally any supernatural apparition. Offerings are made to benevolent *anitos* for fertility, good health, prosperity, fair weather and success in business (or, in the olden days, tribal war). Evil *anitos* are propitiated to avoid illness, crop failure, storms, accidents and death. Omens are also carefully observed: a particular bird seen upon leaving the house might herald sickness, for example, requiring that appropriate ceremonies are conducted to forestall its portent. If the bird returns, the house may be abandoned.

The Ambangeg trail

Ambangeg is a regular stop on the Baguio to Kabayan bus route; ask the driver to drop you at the visitor centre in the Bokod barangay of Ambangeg. It's a two- to three-hour walk from here to the **ranger station** where the hike officially begins, and where you can hire guides; you can also get a lift to the ranger station on a motorcycle (1hr; around P250). It's best to spend the night at the furthest campsite, about three hours from the ranger station, and ascend to the summit for dawn the next day. If you arrive in Ambangeg too late to ascend, staff at the visitors' centre can organize homestay accommodation.

The Kabayan trail

The trail from **Kabayan**, known as the **Akiki** or **Killer Trail**, starts 2km south of Kabayan on the Baguio–Kabayan road. As the name suggests this is a more difficult route than the Ambangeg trail, taking at least seven hours to reach the saddle camp near the summit. The next morning you will go to the peak, then descend.

INFORMATION

MOUNT PULAG

Trail information Before coming to Mount Pulag it's a good idea to contact Emerita Albas, the Protected Area's Superintendent, at the DENR Visitors' Center in the Bokod barangay of Ambangeg (☎ 0919 631 5402, ✉ ambangeg@gmail.com) for up-to-date information on which trails are most accessible at any given time of year. Be sure to check that you will be allowed to visit at the time you want to.

Medical certificate All climbers must present a medical certificate certifying that they are fit to climb the mountain, and giving the licence number and contact details of the doctor who issued it. You can find a blank form to print out at ⊕ bit.ly/pulag-certificate, but you'll need to visit a

doctor to get it filled out (at a pinch there's a health centre in Ambangeg where they'll do it for you).

Registration and fees You'll need to register and pay an entrance fee (US$15, or around P750), camping fee (P50) and local government heritage fee (P175). This can be done at the DENR Visitors' Center in Ambangeg or at the municipal hall in Kabayan (see p.165).

Guides You can hire a guide for the Ambangeg trail at the DENR Visitors' Center (P600 per group of up to five). The tourist office in Kabayan can arrange guides for the Kabayan trail (P1800 for a group of up to seven).

Bontoc and around

BONTOC lies on the Chico River, which divides Poblacion (the town centre) from the neighbourhood of Samoki. Primarily used by tourists as a transport hub, the town is also a good base for **trekking** and has easy access to the beautiful Maligcong rice terraces. The main road from Baguio to Bontoc (and through Poblacion) is the **Halsema Highway** or "Mountain Trail", a narrow, serpentine gash in the side of the Cordillera that's sometimes no more than a rocky track with vertical cliffs on one side and a sheer drop on the other. Although the road has been improved in recent years, it can still be an uncomfortable trip by public transport as some of the buses are crowded and not especially well maintained. The views, though, are marvellous, especially as you ascend out of Baguio beyond La Trinidad and pass through deep gorges lined with rice terraces.

Bontoc Museum

Uphill (west) from the market • Mon–Sat 8am–noon & 1–5pm • P60 • ☏ 0918 576 2170

Bontoc's one tourist sight is the **Bontoc Museum**, which includes wonderful artefacts and a collection of centuries-old Chinese porcelain and stoneware traded from different parts of the Cordillera region. Take a look at the disturbing photograph of a headhunting victim, whose corpse is being carried away for burial as his head is presented as a trophy around the village. There's a reconstruction of a traditional

3

HIKES AROUND BONTOC

Around Bontoc a number of **mountain trails** snake their way through beautiful rice paddy scenery. Most places are far off the tourist radar, and you probably won't see any Westerners in any of the towns; accommodation is basic, but it's worth heading this way if you want to really get a taster of life in Mountain Province.

MALIGCONG

Nearly 7km north of Bontoc, the stone-walled rice terraces around **Maligcong village** are at their best in June and July immediately before the harvest. From the point where public transport stops, a path descends into a valley and follows the contour of the terraces to Maligcong. There's a friendly homestay (see p.168) and a sari-sari store here, but no café so it's best to bring your own food. Jeepneys to Maligcong from Bontoc (8am, noon, 2.30pm, 4.30pm & 5.30pm; 30min; P25) leave from just above the market; the last return journey is at around 4pm.

MAINIT

From Maligcong it is a three-hour trek northwest through scenic rice paddies to **Mainit** ("Ma-i-nit"), a village known for its hot sulphurous springs, where you can also overnight (see p.168). Jeepneys to Mainit leave from just above the market in Bontoc (daily 1.30pm & 3pm; 1hr 15min; P35); the return trips are at 7.30am and 8am.

ALAB PETROGLYPH AND GANGA CAVE

A huge rock etched with drawings of humans with bows and arrows, the **Alab Petroglyph** is at the end of a two-hour hike uphill from the barangay of **Alab**, 9km south of Bontoc on the Halsema Highway. Although it was declared a national cultural treasure in 1975, little is known about who created these carvings or why. An hour further along is the **Ganga Cave**, a burial cave containing coffins and jars of bones. You'll need to find a guide in Alab for either destination – one reputable local guide is Ofelia Lopez (☏ 0948 435 2273). Regular jeepneys to Alab (hourly; 25min; P20) leave from in front of Bontoc's market.

BARLIG AND KADACLAN

Two villages east of Bontoc are well off the normal tourist route, but their wonderful rice terraces are certainly worth the trip. The closest village to Bontoc is **Barlig**, 40km east, which is also the starting point for a trek up Mount Amuyao (2702m). The trek can be done in a day (guides P1500 for up to five people), or you can continue to Batad (see p.179), 12km south, making it a two-day trip (guides P3000 for up to five people) – ask about guides at the Barlig town hall. There are no-frills lodges in town (see p.170). Rarely visited by tourists, **Kadaclan**, 44km east of Bontoc, is in a scenic location and ideal for getting away from it all for a day or two; it has basic accommodation (see p.170). Jeepneys to Barlig (daily 1pm & 3pm; 2hr; P120) and Kadaclan (daily 1pm & 2pm; 5hr; P180) leave from next to All Saints Cathedral in Bontoc.

Bontoc village on the grounds. The shop sells items that include handmade jewellery, books and CDs of traditional music.

ARRIVAL AND INFORMATION

By bus GL Trans buses arrive at Circle Station in Bontoc (the main junction, by the market), while D'Rising Sun buses stop by the police station near the Municipal Hall on Halsema Highway. Coda Lines will pick up and drop off on the Poblacion side of the bridge across the river, but their actual terminal is at the *Cable Café* in Samoki (see below). Local buses to and from Tabuk and Tinglayan stop at Lower Caluttit opposite Bontoc's Polytechnic College.

Destinations Baguio (GL Trans: 6 daily 8am–2.30pm; 5hr 30min; D'Rising Sun: hourly 6am–4pm; 5hr 30min); Manila (Coda Lines: 1 daily; 12hr); Tabuk (daily 9am; 6hr); Tinglayan (daily 9am; 3hr).

BONTOC AND AROUND

By jeepney Jeepneys for Sagada (hourly 8.30am–5.30pm; 45min; P50) leave from outside the *Walter Clapp Inn*, a block east of Bontoc's main drag.

By van Vans to Banaue (7.30am–1.30pm, leaving when full; 2hr; P150) leave from just off Halsema Highway beside Cooperative Bank.

Tourist information The municipal tourist office is by the Municipal Hall in Bontoc (Mon–Fri 8am–5pm; ☎0929 127 0892, ⓦbit.ly/bontoc-tourism), while the provincial tourist office is on the second floor of the Provincial Capitol Building (Mon–Fri 7.30am–5pm; ⓔmtprovtourismoffice@ yahoo.com).

ACCOMMODATION AND EATING

BONTOC

Archog's Hotel Samoki ☎0918 328 6908, ⓦbit.ly/ archogs-hotel. Each named after Bontoc's numerous neighbourhoods, the simple rooms here come with cable TV while the public spaces are brightened up with framed, handwoven textiles. The restaurant offers chicken (P120), beef (P160), seafood (P130–300) and noodles (P100). Wi-fi on the ground floor only. 🛜 **P600**

Cable Café Halfway up the main drag (Halsema Highway), with another branch across the river in Samoki ☎0918 521 6790. The Poblacion branch is Bontoc's main nightlife venue, where folk and country bands take centre stage daily at 8pm. Both branches serve food, but it tends to be better at the Samoki branch, where you can get a good-value Filipino meal deal including soup, meat, rice and coffee (from P120). Poblacion branch daily 24hr, Samoki branch daily 8am–11pm.

Churya-a Hotel Main St ☎0905 182 1606, ⓔpeckley3@gmail.com. Unremarkable doubles, mostly with attached bathrooms, right in the centre of town; there's a nice balcony eating area with a view over the mountains, which has wi-fi, although the rooms don't. 🛜 **P500**

Pines Kitchenette and Inn Above the market ☎0930 092 0994, ⓔjosephinekhayad@yahoo.com. This large family house was originally built to put up adopted World War II war orphans, as photographs in the lobby testify. Rooms are simple and the shared bathrooms (only one room has its own) just about pass muster, but the management is friendly and welcoming, and it's the most interesting place to stay in town. 🛜 **P400**

MALIGCONG

Maligcong Homestay (Suzette's) ☎0915 546 3557. Small homestay run by a friendly local woman that has three comfy little rooms with a couple of beds in each. The owner can also rustle up meals (P120) upon request, but let her know a few hours in advance. There are pretty views of the rice terraces from the breakfast table. **P700**

MAINIT

Geston Minerals Spring Resort ☎0920 454 0963. Run by a friendly woman, this green building has brightly painted rooms off a maze of narrow corridors. There are also two thatched cottages, built from stone and dried grass, giving onto four hot pools of varying temperatures – perfect for a soak after a long day's hike. **P1000**

KILLING ME SOFTLY

One Mountain Province delicacy, served in many restaurants, is **pinikpikan**, a chicken dish that translates as "killing me softly". The preparation involves beating the bird's wings and neck with a stick before it is killed in the belief that the beating brings blood to the surface, making the meat more tender and tasty. Once dead, the chicken is put on an open fire to burn off the feathers and is then mixed with cured pork; the burning of feathers and the blending of two types of meat adds to the flavour of the dish. When performing rituals, mountain tribes traditionally eat the head and the innards for good fortune and good health the day after the chicken is butchered.

BARLIG

Halfway Inn The seven tiny rooms at this simple place have wooden floorboards and spindly little desks; there's no hot water in the communal bathrooms (and no phone, either) but staff will happily boil a pot or two for you. There are pretty views from the terrace, and a restaurant serving very basic grub. **P400**

KADACLAN

Kadaclan Homestay ☎0910 411 0592, ⊛bit.ly/kadaclan-homestay. The owner boasts that his town is the "Shangri-La of the edge", and is hugely proud that the country's former president Gloria Macapagal-Arroyo visited this very homestay. Rooms are located in simple cottages, and guests have access to the kitchen. Per person **P100**

Sagada

The small town of **SAGADA**, 160km north of Baguio, has long attracted curious visitors. Part of the appeal derives from its famous **hanging coffins** and a labyrinth of **caves** used by the ancients as burial sites. But Sagada also has a reputation as a remote and idyllic hideaway where people live a simple life well away from civilization. The landscape here is almost alpine and the inhabitants are mountain people, their faces shaped not by the sun and sea of the lowlands, but by the thin air and sharp glare of altitude. Sagada only began to open up as a destination when it got electricity in the early 1970s, and intellectuals – internal refugees from the Marcos dictatorship – flocked here to write and paint. They didn't produce much of note, perhaps because they spent, it is said, much of their time drinking *tapuy* (the local rice wine). European hippies followed, as did the military, who thought the *turistas* were supplying funds for an insurgency.

While the town doesn't offer a lot to do, you'll find plenty of **activities** in the surrounding area. Other than that there's scope for just hanging out, settling down in the evenings by a log fire in one of the wooden cafés or restaurants. With so much fruit and vegetables grown nearby, the **food** in Sagada is among the best in the country, with lots of veggie choices – something of a rarity in the Philippines. A **curfew** means that you can't drink after 9pm, but almost everyone has gone to bed by then anyway.

SAGADA

■ ACCOMMODATION
George Guest House	6
Masferré	5
Rock Inn	1
St Joseph Resthouse	3
Sagada Guesthouse & Café	4
Sagada Homestay	2

● SHOPPING
| Sagada Pottery | 2 |
| Sagada Weaving | 1 |

● EATING
Gaia	6
Lemon Pie House	5
Log Cabin	1
Masferré	2
Sagada Brew	4
Yoghurt House	3

■ DRINKING
| Cellar Door | 1 |

Ganduyan Museum

Town centre • Roughly 1–6pm, depending on staff availability • P25; 20min guided tours may be available for a donation • ☎0949 800 4939

The wonderful little **Ganduyan Museum** displays a collection of Igorot artefacts, and it's worth asking for a guided tour, although this is not always possible. Among the objects on display are intricate strung-bead necklaces made with snake vertebrae, traditional kitchenware and a collection of spears used for defence. Plans are afoot for another branch by the Petron station 2km east of town, to house the heavier stone items.

Demang

If you have time then it's worth wandering 500m down to the village of **Demang**, reached from a turning on the right just beyond the *George Guest House*. The village is older than Sagada and remains practically untouched by tourism. It's a quiet residential area with several *dap-ay* (stone circles where community matters are resolved).

ACTIVITIES IN SAGADA

Sagada offers a host of thrilling outdoor **activities**, including **treks** through remote mountain villages and secluded valleys. The most reliable company for adventure sports is the American-run **Sagada Outdoors** (☎0919 698 8361, ⓦsagadaoutdoors.com).

TREKKING

One of the most popular hikes is to see the **hanging coffins** in **Echo Valley**. It's only a 25-minute walk from the centre of Sagada to the coffins, and it can be done alone with a map (souvenir shops sell sketch maps for around P25), but there are numerous paths and it isn't unknown for people to get lost. On the whole, it's better to take a guide (P200/group of up to ten) who can also fill you in on local history and traditions. The coffins can also be visited as part of the popular three-hour Central Sagada Eco-Tour (P600/group of up to ten) – ask at the Sagada tourist information centre (see p.172). After the coffins, the path takes you along a short stretch of an underground river at Latang Cave and ends at the **Bokong Waterfall** on the eastern edge of Sagada, where you can swim. The waterfall can also be reached from town without a guide in about half an hour, although it's easy to miss the steps on the left about 500m beyond Sagada Weaving. Other guided hikes offered by the tourist office and Sagada Genuine Guides (see p.172) include a walk to the **Bomod-ok Waterfall**, rice terraces and villages north of Sagada (3hr); a dawn trip to a scenic area of rice terraces known as **Kiltepan** (1hr 30min); and a trek on **Mount Ampacao** (3–4hr).

CAVING

Caving in Sagada's deep network of limestone channels and caverns is exhilarating but potentially dangerous. Many caves are slippery and have deep ravines. A small number of tourists have been killed in them, so it's essential to hire a reliable, accredited **guide**.

The most commonly visited cave is **Sumaging** (P500 per four visitors, plus P350 for transport), also known as Big Cave, a 45-minute walk south of Sagada. The chambers and rock formations inside are eerie and immense, named after things they resemble – the Cauliflower, the Rice Granary and such like. Guides with lanterns will take you on a descent through a series of tunnels you'll only be able to get through by crawling, ending in a pool of clear water where you can swim. Ideally you should wear trekking sandals, but otherwise shoes can be left at an appropriate point and the final sections negotiated barefoot.

Like many caves in the area, Sumaging was once a burial cave, although there are no coffins or human remains there now. However, a standard caving itinerary will also include a visit to the entrance of **Lumiang Burial Cave**, a short walk south of Sagada and then down a steep trail into the valley. Around a hundred old coffins are stacked in the entrance. Pointing at them is considered the worst kind of bad luck; lizards, on the other hand, are auspicious – you'll see their images carved onto some of the coffins.

Lumiang is also the starting point for the **Cave Connection** trip (P800 for one or two people, P400 for each additional person; transport P400), which heads through passages linking it to Sumaging. It's a three- to four-hour excursion and not for the faint-hearted; it might be best to try Sumaging first. At points you'll need to descend a few metres without ropes, jamming your limbs against the rock walls and edging your way down.

RAFTING

Rafting is possible on the **Chico River** from June until December, although at the beginning of the season it may only be possible to raft the upper sections. October and November see the most pleasant weather, but the highest water is in December and early January, making it possible to go further downstream. The main operator is Sagada Outdoors (see above). You normally spend around 2hr in the water (P3500/person for three or four, P3000 for five to seven; if there are just one or two of you, they may possibly be able to hook you up with a larger group).

MOUNTAIN BIKING

The mountainous landscape around Sagada offers rough terrain and remote trails that are ideal for **mountain biking**. Most tracts are steep and technical, and mainly suited to experienced individuals. Some back roads provide less technical riding, but there are still extended climbs. The cool mountain temperatures, fresh clean air and scenic beauty make this one of the country's best spots to explore on two wheels.

3

ARRIVAL AND INFORMATION

By bus and jeepney Transport operates from the main junction, opposite the commercial centre. Coda Lines run a daily bus to Manila (13hr). GL Trans buses serve Baguio (5 daily; 5–6hr). Jeepneys run to and from Bontoc (every 30min 6.30–9am, then hourly 9am–1pm; 40min; P50). For Banaue, take a jeepney to Bontoc and change there. Getting to Sagada or Bontoc from the coast involves taking vans in stages from Bitalag (just north of Tagudin on the San Fernando–Vigan road), via Cervantes and Abatan Bauko; set off early from Vigan or San Fernando if you aim to do this in a day.

Environmental fee All visitors to Sagada must register and pay an environmental fee (P35), payable at the tourist information centre. Keep the receipt with you as you'll need to show it when visiting the main sights.

Tourist information There's a small tourist information centre in the old town hall (7am–5pm; **☎** 0905 513 7626, **ⓦ** bit.ly/sagada-tourism).

Tours The tourist information centre has a list of guided tours with fixed prices, as does the privately owned Sagada Genuine Guides (daily 6am–7pm; **☎** 0929 556 9553, **ⓦ** saggas.org) near *Yoghurt House* (see opposite). In addition to adventure activities, Sagada Outdoors (see box, p.171) offers custom-made and off-the-beaten-track tours in the region.

SAGADA

ACCOMMODATION

The town gets packed out at Christmas and Easter, so if you're planning to visit at these times try to book ahead.

George Guest House ☎ 0920 948 3133, **ⓔ** george_inn05@yahoo.com. A popular choice among travellers, with clean rooms with private showers and hot water; rooms in the annexe up the hill are more spacious but the same price; they also have another annexe down the hill with cottages sleeping six (P1800) to twelve (P3600), all with kitchen, living area, TV and fireplace. **⏦** **P600**

★Masferré ☎ 0918 341 6164, **ⓦ** masferre.blogspot.com. One of Sagada's best options right in the centre, offering spotless cosy rooms with pine-wood furniture and private bath. It's owned by the family of early twentieth-century photographer Eduardo Masferré, whose historical pictures of local indigenous people decorate the (excellent) restaurant. **⏦** **P1800**

★Rock Inn Just over 2km east of town **☎** 0905 554 5950, **ⓦ** rockinnsagada.com. Set on four verdant hectares with an orange grove, this place allows guests to pick their own fruit (P50/30min). The cosy rooms are in a large building with wooden furnishings, and there's a spacious attic dorm, too. Aptly enough, the airy restaurant serves dishes using fresh local produce. **⏦** Dorms **P500**, doubles **P1300**

St Joseph Resthouse ☎ 0918 559 5934, **ⓦ** saintjoseph resthousesagada.blogspot.com. Converted from a convent and owned by the Anglican church, this guesthouse has cheap, basic rooms in a separate block, while those in the main building have more character and offer private bath, with wi-fi in the reception area. There are also some cottages (P1700) sprinkled along a grassy slope, the largest of which sleeps eight (P3500). **⏦** **P500**

Sagada Guesthouse and Café ☎ 0906 190 9661. Not to be confused with the much cosier *Sagada Homestay*, this place, a stone's throw away from the bus terminal, has simple economy rooms with spongy beds and shared bathroom, as well as more comfortable doubles. There's a little terrace overlooking the road. **⏦** **P600**

★Sagada Homestay ☎ 0919 702 8380, **ⓔ** sagadahomestay@yahoo.com.ph. This friendly, welcoming homestay offers neat and tidy rooms with or without private bath. It includes a couple of lounge areas that are perfect for meeting other travellers, as well as a guest kitchen. There's wi-fi in the main building, and a laundry service. **⏦** **P600**

EATING

★Gaia Café ☎ 0929 597 9451, **ⓦ** bit.ly/gaia-cafe. Near the entrance to Lumiang Burial Cave, this wonderful eco-friendly restaurant offers inventive dishes, using largely organic ingredients and mostly vegan, including *miki mi na* – squash noodles sautéed with green beans, carrots and mushrooms (P125), all served on a covered patio with terrific views over the rice terraces. Daily 7am–7pm.

Lemon Pie House ☎ 0907 782 0360, **ⓦ** sagada lemonpiehouse.blogspot.com. On the southern side of town, this place is renowned for its lemon meringue pie (P30) that customers enjoy at low wooden tables, all designed and assembled by the owner-cum-carpenter.

Between March and May they also bake a great blueberry pie using local fresh fruits. Daily 6am–8pm.

Masferré ☎ 0918 341 6164, **ⓦ** masferre.blogspot.com. It's worth coming here to take a look at the wonderful set of black-and-white photographs of Sagada and various indigenous mountain cultures taken by Eduardo Masferré in the late 1930s and early 1950s. The Western menu includes popular super-subs (P200) and sandwiches (P180), as well as burgers and steaks (both P205). Daily 7am–8pm.

★Log Cabin ☎ 0920 520 0463. Up the hill beyond the *Sagada Guesthouse*, the *Log Cabin* does some of the best food in town. The welcoming wooden interior is warm and cosy, and the crackling fireplace further adds to the homely atmosphere. Sat evenings see a popular buffet (P390) with fresh ingredients bought from the market, while on other days there's an à la carte menu with a focus on French dishes. Reserve by 3pm if you plan to dine in the evening, and preferably a day or two ahead for the buffet. Daily 6–9pm.

Sagada Brew 0917 808 7833. This Italian-influenced café offers scrumptious home-made brownies (P20) and Italian-style coffee, as well as such un-Italian confections

as a Starbucks-style caramel "macchiato" (P120). The menu includes soups (P100), sandwiches made with freshly baked focaccia (P150) and tasty pasta dishes (P150). Daily 7.30am–9.30pm.

Yoghurt House 0908 112 8430. A popular place with travellers, this wood cabin offers hearty breakfasts and home-made yoghurt – try the fruit salad with yoghurt and honey (P150). Main dishes (P180–240) are pretty good too; enjoy your meal on the narrow balcony as you watch life go by. Daily 8am–8.30pm.

DRINKING

Cellar Door 0918 842 8506, bit.ly/sagada-cellar. A 15min walk west of town, this outdoor bar set among fragrant pine trees brews its own ales and stouts (P180 for 430ml), some with odd ingredients (the coffee stout really does have coffee in it, for example). The amber ale in

particular really hits the spot, the location's beautiful and they get a fire going after dark to sit round. There's a restaurant too, but by 10hr prior reservation only. Daily 6–9pm.

SHOPPING

Sagada Pottery A 15min walk west of the centre 0975 008 4800. High-quality stoneware, made on the premises. One of the potters will demonstrate their craft for P100, and for P100 per person you can have a go yourself. Daily 10am–6pm.

Sagada Weaving Nangonogan 0917 506 9184, bit.ly/sagada-weave. A short walk east of the centre. Here you can buy fabrics and accessories produced using

traditional tribal designs. More than half a dozen people work at sewing machines in the shop itself, while next door you can see the weaving being done on wooden looms. It's a good place to pick up a gift such as a *bahag* (loincloth), an exquisitely hand-loomed piece of long cloth wrapped around a man's middle but increasingly bought by tourists as a throw or table runner. Daily 7am–6pm.

DIRECTORY

Banks and exchange The best ATM is by the tourist office in the old town hall. There are others in the Sagada Rural Bank (Tues–Sat 8.30am–4.30pm), downstairs from the old town hall, and in the Treasure Link Cooperative Society on the top floor of the Commercial Centre (Mon–Sat 8.30am–3pm), but only accessible when those are open.

Hospital For minor ailments you can visit the Municipal Health Office (Mon–Fri 8am–5pm); there's also a small

hospital, St Theodore's, on the northeastern edge of the village.

Internet access In town are a few small internet cafés, such as 5-11-Ten by *Yoghurt House* (daily 8.30am–8pm; P20/hr) and Golinsan on the other side of the road from the tourist office (Mon–Sat 8am–4pm; P30/hr).

Police Next to the Old Municipal Hall (24hr; 0998 967 4396).

Post office In the Old Municipal Hall.

Kalinga province

The mountains, rice fields and villages in **Kalinga province** rarely see visitors, never mind foreign tourists. This is real frontier travel, with massive potential for hiking and climbing. Outside the towns of **Tinglayan** and **Tabuk**, the only accommodation is in simple lodges or local homes, the only shops are roadside stores, and electricity is a rarity so bring a flashlight.

The Kalinga, once fierce **headhunters**, are remembered for their indomitable spirit and their refusal to be colonized. Most Kalinga communities live on levelled parts of steep mountain slopes, where a small shrine called a *bodayan* guards the entrance to the village. You could also ask your guide (see box, p.174) about visiting a **tattoo artist**, many of whom still work using traditional materials and designs; it is possible to have a tattoo yourself (around P500), but if you do this, make sure that the thorn used to insert the ink is a fresh one.

HIKING IN KALINGA: GUIDES

Wherever you go hiking in Kalinga you'll need a **guide**; essential not only to avoid getting lost but also to ensure that you respect local sensibilities. Occasionally there are disputes – over water rights, for instance – that result in violence, and a guide will stop you stumbling into any areas where tensions might be high. Law and order in the province still relies very much on tribal pacts (*bodong*) brokered by elders. The best-known local guide is Victor Baculi, the *pangat* (tribal leader) of Luplupa of nearby Luplupa (🅦 bit.ly/ victor-baculi); he can usually be contacted through *Luplupa Riverside Inn*, who can put you on to other guides if he is not around. Rates are not fixed and could be anything from P500 to P1000 per day.

Tinglayan

The town of **TINGLAYAN**, about 50km from Bontoc and 60km from Tabuk, is well placed if you want to explore Kalinga province. From here you can strike out on **mountain trails** carved by the Spanish when they tried, and failed, to bring the Kalinga people into the Catholic fold. Trails pass through tribal villages and rice terraces at Lubo and Mangali, to the crater of the extinct volcano Mount Sukuok, and to a number of mountain lakes including Bonnong and Padcharao. Rice is planted twice a year around Tinglayan, and the fields are at their greenest from March to April and September to October.

Lubuagan

They don't see many tourists in **LUBUAGAN**, 18km north of Tinglayan on the road to Tabuk, but it makes for a worthwhile stop. The town itself has a makeshift air, lined with grey concrete buildings and with livestock wandering in the street, but it's beautifully located amid rice terraces. Remarkably, it was the capital of the free Philippines for 35 days in 1900, when the revolutionary President Aguinaldo established his headquarters in the town before being forced to flee the US army.

The barangay of Mabilong, east of the centre, is known for its **textiles** and you can arrange to visit one of the women who weave at home, sitting on the floor using rudimentary handlooms. Ask at the **town hall** to arrange a visit, or for advice about hiking routes and **guides**. You might also ask about the **cultural village**, around thirty minutes from the town, where traditional dance performances occasionally take place.

Tabuk

While it has little to see, the agricultural town and provincial capital of **TABUK**, 50km north of Tinglayan, offers a surprisingly decent choice of accommodation and the

RAFTING THROUGH THE RICE TERRACES

The area around Tabuk offers excellent **rafting** opportunities on the Chico River, which snakes its way through spectacular rice terrace scenery. The most reliable company is **Chico River Quest** (☎ 0917 750 2913, 🅦 chicoriverquest.com), which runs trips for all levels – they have seven rafts and use one or two guides per raft. The prime rafting season is July through to October; trips between October and December are dependent on rainfall.

The best run for **beginners** starts at the confluence of the Pasil and Chico rivers, and lasts about two hours (P4000/person for a minimum of five people, including transport and food). More experienced rafters should ask about a longer run which starts upriver in Tinglayan (4–6hr; P7000/person for a minimum of five). This trip also allows you to stop off halfway down for a one-hour canyon hike.

region's only internet access and banks. The town serves as a base and jumping-off point for trekking excursions, visits to tribal tattoo artists and **rafting** on the nearby Chico River.

Ryan's Farm
Mapaoay, Ipil, 6km north of Tabuk • Daily 8am–5pm • P50 • ☎ 0916 755 7078 • A tricycle from Tabuk costs around P70–90

While in Tabuk, take the time to visit **Ryan's Farm**, owned by Corazon and Jeremy Ryan. They have an orchard and fish ponds, and experiment with vermiculture (worm composting) and organic agriculture, but most of all it's just pleasant to enjoy their conversation – possibly over a glass of home-made *bugnay* (local berry) wine. They may also be able to prepare a meal (P250) and even let you camp overnight (P200) if you call in advance to arrange it.

ARRIVAL AND INFORMATION

KALINGA PROVINCE

In the **dry season** Tinglayan, Tabuk and Lubuagan can be reached by jeepneys from Bontoc, although services in this area are anything but regular and it's a bumpy road, so the trip can take many hours. In the **rainy season** (particularly July–Oct) it may be impossible to travel between Tinglayan and Tabuk due to the road conditions, in which case Tinglayan is best approached from Bontoc while Tabuk is reached via Tuguegarao.

TINGLAYAN
By bus There are two daily buses each way between Bontoc and Tabuk that stop in Tinglayan.
By jeepney A couple of jeepneys run from Bontoc to Tinglayan daily (2hr 30min; P130) and a handful of jeepneys run between Tabuk and Tingalayan (3hr 30min; P100).

LUBUAGAN
By bus There are two daily buses each way between Bontoc and Tabuk that stop in Lubuagan.
By jeepney A handful of jeepneys pass through Lubuagan on their way between Tabuk (2hr 30min) and Tingalayan (1hr 30min).

TABUK
By bus From Manila, Victory Liner and Dangwa buses run to Tabuk (1 daily each; 12hr). From Baguio (10hr) you can take a GL Trans (6 daily) or Dangwa (1 daily). There are two daily buses connecting Bontoc to Tabuk (4hr) via Lubuagan and Tinglayan.
By jeepney Jeepneys from Bontoc stop off in Tinglayan and Lubuagan on their way to Tabuk.
By van Vans from Tuguegarao (leaving when full; 1hr 30min; P119) leave from the Santa Ana terminal on the National Highway and from Brickstone Mall terminal.
Banks You can withdraw cash at the PNB and DBP banks in the barangay of Dagupan, and Land Bank and Rural Bank in the barangay of Bulanao.

ACCOMMODATION AND EATING

TINGLAYAN
Luplupa Riverside Inn Luplupa ☎ 0915 283 7885. Easily the best place to stay in town, with rustic parquet floors and simple rooms with wooden shelves, a stool and table. On the first floor you can relax in a little lounge area, which displays a collection of local artefacts. No hot water, but staff can boil some for you. **P600**
Sleeping Beauty Inn Poblacion ☎ 0927 943 2163. Named after the nearby mountain, which is shaped like a female figure, this place has five colourfully painted rooms with cherry-red tiled floors. There's a small communal area and a restaurant upstairs. The owners also rent out a few rooms on the other side of the bridge in Luplupa. **P400**

TABUK
Davidson Hotel Provincial Rd, Bulanao ☎ 0917 579 7110. One of Tabuk's better-equipped hotels, with a pool, gym and a good restaurant serving local and international

dishes. Rooms vary considerably – some are spacious, clean and tidy while others are in disrepair – make sure to take a look at a few before settling in. 🛜 **P1300**
Golden Berries San Juan ☎ 0915 844 4119, ⍟ goldenberrieshotel.com. The owners here process, grind and package locally grown coffee beans on the premises – you can buy the finished product at the hotel's little shop. The rooms in the "old" building are a bit tired; those in the "new" block at the back are more comfortable with modern amenities. There's also a restaurant, although the food is less than average. 🛜 **P1000**
Grand Zion National Highway, Purok 7, Bulanao ☎ 0916 373 4366, ⍟ bit.ly/grand-zion. Tabuk's most upmarket hotel features spacious, tastefully decorated rooms in an airy building resembling an alpine lodge. There are pleasant gardens at the back with an inviting swimming pool, and a restaurant serving an array of dishes. 🛜 **P1350**

3

Ifugao province

Landlocked Ifugao **province** is characterized by spectacular rugged terrain, lush forests and verdant river valleys dotted with tribal villages. A number of Ifugao communities still wear traditional dress, although you'll have to trek to remote villages to experience authentic tribal life. The Ifugaos are a proud people who have preserved their ancestral past, largely because they managed to sustain resistance during the Spanish colonial regime, which, as in Kalinga, failed in subduing the highlanders. The highlights of the region are the spectacular **rice terraces**, handcarved in the mountainside more than two thousand years ago and now designated by UNESCO as a **World Heritage Site**.

Banaue

It may only be 300km north of Manila, but **BANAUE** might as well be a world away, 1300m above sea level and far removed in spirit and topography from the beaches and palm trees of the south. The town itself is small and not hugely impressive, centred on a marketplace, with a few guesthouses, some souvenir shops and a couple of good **museums**, but its location is superb. This is the heart of **rice terrace** country: the terraces in Banaue itself are some of the most impressive and well known, and there are hundreds of others in valleys and gorges throughout the area, most of which can be reached on foot. There is rustic accommodation at nearby **Batad** (see p.179), so you could stay overnight and hike back the next morning.

Museum of Cordillera Sculpture

Bissang Tam-an • Daily 8am–5pm • P100 • ☎ 0919 774 8507, ✆ cordilleranmuseum.weebly.com • P15 tricycle ride from town

The private collection of American expat George Schenk, the wonderful **Museum of Cordillera Sculpture** displays a fine array of Ifugao cultural objects. Highlights include *bulol* rice deities – guardian figures placed in the rice paddies in order to protect them from malevolent spirits and bring abundant harvests – and wooden statuettes of pregnant wives, carved by husbands who would devoutly pray to them believing that this would ease their spouse's pregnancy.

Banaue Museum

Poblacion • Daily 8am–4pm • P50 • ☎ 0916 694 4511

The family-run **Banaue Museum** houses part of the collection of American anthropologist Henry Otley Beyer, the grandfather of the current owner. The objects were acquired from Ifugao province and the adjoining areas, and include ceremonial necklaces, black-and-white photographs of tattooed Ifugao ancestors, and wooden gods that were placed in rice granaries, serving as guardians of the harvest and the fields.

BANAUE'S STAIRWAYS TO HEAVEN

The **rice terraces** around Banaue are among the great icons of the Philippines, and were hewn from the land two thousand years ago by Ifugao tribespeople using primitive tools, an achievement in engineering terms that ranks alongside the building of the pyramids. Called the "Stairway to Heaven" by the Ifugaos, the terraces would stretch 20,000km if laid out end to end. Not only are they an extraordinary sight, but they are also an object lesson in **sustainability**.

The terraces are on the UNESCO World Heritage list, and they will not last forever if they are not protected. They have always been subject to constant deterioration, due to erosion, imperfect irrigation systems and the actions of earthworms. Following a shortage of young people to help carry out repairs – rice farming held little allure for many of them, understandably tired of the subsistence livelihood their parents eked from the land – strict measures have been taken in recent years to protect and revive the paddies, and young farmers are slowly returning to work in the fields.

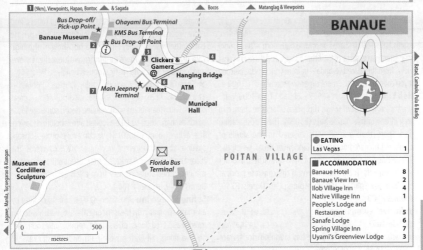

Don't miss the Ifugao coffin – tradition dictates that the dead had to be sealed inside and kept under the house, with the top of the coffin serving as a bench. If the museum is closed during opening hours, ask at the neighbouring *Banaue View Inn* for the key.

Lookout points

Tricycle P200 return

Two kilometres north of town is a series of five **lookout points** for the rice terraces, where Ifugao elders in traditional costume hang out and ask for a small fee if you want to take their photograph. The third lookout point has the view depicted on the P1000 banknote; you'll get the best vista from the fifth lookout.

ARRIVAL AND DEPARTURE   BANAUE

By bus Buses from Manila and Baguio drop passengers off outside the municipal tourist centre, but depart from their respective terminals. Coda Lines, Ohayami and Dangwa all have evening services to Manila (8–9hr); Ohayami and KMS have early-evening departures for Baguio (8hr).

By van Vans from Bontoc stop outside the municipal tourist centre (leaving when full, 11am–1pm; 1hr 30min; P150). There are six daily departures for Baguio, best booked a day in advance at the office just below the municipal tourist centre (6hr; P360).

INFORMATION

Environmental fee All visitors must register and pay the environmental fee (P20) at the municipal tourist centre.
Tourist information The municipal tourist centre is on the western end of the main drag, where the buses stop (daily 5.30am–5pm; ☎ 0906 770 7969, ✉ elahd_ban@ yahoo.com).

Tours You can hire an accredited guide to explore the surrounding area; rates vary depending on where you go – ask at the municipal tourist centre for a list of destinations with fixed rates. Guesthouses can enquire about motorbike rental, or call local guide Elvis who rents out his bike (P1200/day; ☎ 0935 292 2982).

ACCOMMODATION

Banaue's **accommodation** is generally simple but clean and friendly, and many places have restaurants attached. Finding somewhere without a reservation is not a problem, except at Christmas and Easter.

Banaue Hotel Ilogui Tam-an ☎ 0908 400 7596, ✉ pta_banauehotel@yahoo.com. This vast, rambling hotel hasn't changed its decor much since opening in the 1970s. Rooms are comfortable and spacious nonetheless,

and there are deluxe options (P3000) and suites (P7000) with nice views, plus a pleasant swimming pool and a bar with pool table. Wi-fi is available in the lobby, and there's a youth hostel attached. 🛜 **P2300**

Banaue View Inn Poblacion ☎0916 694 4511, ✉banaueviewinn_1984@yahoo.com. The tiled-floor rooms here – with shared or private bathroom – have more character than in some of the other lodges, and there are great views from the shared veranda – or from your private balcony if you choose one of the more expensive rooms. 🛜 **P1000**

Ilob Village Inn Bocos ☎0995 283 8111, ✉ilobvillage @gmail.com. East of town, this place offers the chance to stay in one of five native huts (P1000). The oldest, dating back more than a century, is covered in the skulls of carabao, butchered during the *binogwah* ritual, when the Ifugao bring out the skeletons of their forefathers in order to pay respects. The private rooms in the concrete block at the back are spartan and uninspiring. 🛜 Dorms **P250**, doubles **P600**

★Native Village Inn Uhaj, 9km west of Banaue ☎0916 405 6743, 🌐nativevillage-inn.com. On the road to Hapao, this wonderful place has stunning rice terrace views – there are two lookout points where guests are encouraged to take their breakfast, and where you can easily while away a few hours just soaking in the scenery. The food is another highlight, and includes fresh home-baked bread. Accommodation is in seven comfortable native huts dotted around the verdant grounds. Call Elvis (☎0935 292 2982) for a free pick-up from Banaue. 🛜 **P2200**

People's Lodge and Restaurant Poblacion ☎074 386 4014, Ejerwin_t@yahoo.com. This lodge offers simple rooms, some of which share cold showers and toilets, and more expensive, slightly more spacious rooms with private bath (otherwise, you pay P100 for a hot shower, although cold ones are free). There's a terrace with excellent views and a lounge area with rustic wooden benches. 🛜 **P500**

★Sanafe Lodge Banaue Trade Centre, Poblacion ☎0918 947 7226, ✉susanmparades@gmail.com. A great option, with clean rooms with wooden decor; some are more spacious than others so take a look at a few before choosing. The deluxe room (P1600) is worth every peso – clean, spacious and with excellent views over the rice terraces. The place also has one of Banaue's better restaurants, where you can enjoy spectacular scenery from the breakfast table. 🛜 Dorms **P200**, doubles **P1000**

Spring Village Inn Poblacion ☎074 386 4037. Run by an affable woman, this pleasant guesthouse, with a wooden interior and tiled floors, offers clean, comfortable rooms set on two floors, all with private bath and hot shower. 🛜 **P1500**

Uyami's Greenview Lodge Poblacion ☎0920 540 4225, 🌐ugreenview.wordpress.com. The homely doubles here have wooden floors and pine interiors, although the cheaper concrete rooms on the bottom floor aren't as snug, with common bathrooms and cold showers (hot water is an additional P50). The restaurant has wonderful rice-terrace views and wi-fi, and rustles up appetizing local dishes. 🛜 **P500**

EATING

Most of the best food is served in **lodges**. *People's Lodge and Restaurant*, *Uyami's Greenview Lodge* and *Sanafe Lodge* have some good dishes, while *Banaue Hotel* is the most upmarket choice.

Las Vegas Poblacion ☎0918 440 9932. This popular restaurant serving mainly Filipino food has a smattering of American and international memorabilia sitting alongside wooden Ifugao statuettes, and offers healthy salads (P70) as well as dishes such as beef *tapa* (P99). Daily 6am–10pm.

DIRECTORY

Banks and exchange W&L moneychangers, 3/F Banaue Building in the main square (daily 8am–5.30pm) don't offer great rates. The ATM by the municipal hall accepts foreign cards, but has been known to swallow them.
Internet access Clickers (daily 7am–7pm; P20/hr) and Gamerz (daily 8am–7pm; P20/hr) are both on the third floor of the Banaue Building in the main square.
Post office South of town near the *Banaue Hotel* (Mon–Fri 8am–5pm).

Around Banaue

The area around Banaue offers spectacular **rice terrace** scenery, with five areas designated UNESCO World Heritage Sites. **Trekking** through the stone-walled terraces and overnighting in typical Ifugao huts in rural villages is a major highlight. The most popular trek is to the remote little village of **Batad**, which has become something of a pilgrimage in recent years for visitors looking for rural isolation and unforgettable scenery. Other nearby villages include **Cambulo**, **Pula** and **Banga-an**. While less explored, the barangay of **Hapao** 16km southwest from Banaue, offers stunning terrace scenery that easily rivals that of Batad; 7km farther in the same direction is **Hungduan**, home to spectacular spider web terraces, mainly serving as a base for trekkers climbing Mount Napulawan (2600m).

Batad and around

BATAD nestles in a natural amphitheatre, close to the glorious **Tappia Waterfall**, which is 40m high and has a deep, bracing pool for swimming. There are signs that life here is beginning to change – the village now has electricity and a dozen simple **guesthouses** have sprung up – but it remains peaceful. There are several good hikes, including to **Banga-an**; ask around at the lodges for a guide, or try Robert's Trekking Adventure (T 0975 450 5609, E robert.immotna@yahoo.com). One way to head back to Banaue from Batad is to backtrack south for about 16km to the tiny village of **Banga-an**, no more than a few dozen Ifugao homes perched between rice terraces close to the National Highway. You can **stay** here (see below), but it's a good idea to book ahead if you're relying on this after a hike – your guide will probably be able to do this for you.

ARRIVAL AND DEPARTURE — BATAD AND AROUND

On foot It is possible to walk the 16km to Batad from Banaue.

By jeepney Most people cut out the first 14km of the walk from Banaue to Batad by taking a jeepney to just past Saddle (daily 8.30am; 1hr; P150), from where it is a 30min walk downhill to Batad.

ACCOMMODATION AND EATING

BATAD

Batad Pension T 0918 964 3368, W bit.ly/batad-pension. A pleasant *pension* decorated with wooden furniture made by the owner-cum-sculptor, whose little workshop is in the back yard. The simple rooms are brightened up with a thin layer of paint and colourful blankets – those upstairs have great views. Guests can also sleep in a native hut. P500

Hillside Inn T 0917 811 8642, W bit.ly/hillside-batad. The basic rooms here are pretty poky, with spindly furniture and thin plywood walls, although the restaurant does have great views over the terraces. The menu offers an eclectic mix of international and local dishes, including Middle Eastern *malawach*, a thick pancake of thin layers of puff pastry (P80). P500

Simon's Viewpoint Inn T 0930 507 7467, W bit.ly/simons-view. This popular guesthouse with walls covered in travellers' notes has a selection of clean simple rooms, some with excellent views over the terraces. There's a good restaurant serving a variety of international dishes including freshly baked pita bread, Israeli-style *shakshuka* (P90), and pizza (P150). P500

BANGA-AN

Banga-an Family Inn & Canteen T 0909 101 9068. Overlooking the village from the highway, this is where most hikers stop off for the night on the way back to Banaue. Rooms are basic and spartan, with cold showers – you can ask the staff to boil some hot water for you. You can also overnight in traditional huts that sleep four to six people (P600). The restaurant serves simple Filipino dishes. P350

Pula and Cambulo

From the Banaue Awan-Igid viewpoint, 9km outside Banaue, you can trek east through fields and terraces to the villages of **PULA** and **CAMBULO**. There are some unforgettable sights along this route, including waterfalls, steep gorges and a hanging bridge near Pula that requires a bit of nerve to cross. The journey from Banaue viewpoint to Pula takes about four hours, and from Pula to Cambulo it's another two hours. You can camp or spend the night at one of the small **inns** or homestays in Cambulo. From here it's two hours to Batad, from where you can walk up to Batad Saddle and hop on a jeepney back to your hotel.

Pula is also the start of a hike up **Mount Amuyao** (2702m), a full day's walk and not something to be attempted without a guide and plenty of stamina. You'll need to sleep at the top and return next day, or you can continue to Barlig (see p.167) and eventually Bontoc.

ACCOMMODATION — PULA AND CAMBULO

Cambulo Country Cabin Cambulo T 0939 932 1009, W bit.ly/cambulo. This family-run place has five simple rooms with shared bathroom facilities. Food is available and they give out local maps and information leaflets. P600

Hapao and Hungduan

The rice terraces in the barangay of **HAPAO**, around 16km from Banaue, are spectacular. Hapao has a couple of homestays and is home to the **Hapao hot springs**, where you can take a dip in two natural pools. Further on, the small town of **HUNGDUAN**, less than 10km from Banaue as the crow flies but reached by a protracted looped road, is the location of the **Bacung spider web terraces**, at their best in April and May. The trip is well worth it, and you can overnight in the town itself. Hungduan is also the start of a hike up **Mount Napulawan** (2600m) for which you will need a guide.

ARRIVAL AND INFORMATION   HAPAO AND HUNGDUAN

By jeepney Jeepneys from Banaue run to Hapao (noon–5pm; 1hr; P30) and Hungduan (noon–5pm; 1hr 30min; P50).

By tricycle You can travel by tricycle from Banaue to Hapao (1hr; P550) and Hungduan (1hr 30min; P700).

Guides It is possible to organize guides to both Hapao and Hungduan at the tourist information point at Bokikwan on the way to Hapao; this is where all visitors must register and pay an environmental fee of P20.

ACCOMMODATION

Base Camp Hapao ☏ 0935 292 2982, ✉ guitrek_v@ hotmail.com. A pleasant place to stay with just two native huts with communal bathrooms. Guests are encouraged to have a go at pounding rice with pestle and mortar before consuming the finished product. You can also plant rice with the locals in harvest season. **P500**

Coop Lodge Hungduan. Set within a building that includes a sari-sari store selling snacks and other basic necessities, this simple lodge is popular among climbers heading to Mount Napulawan who overnight here before leaving at sunrise or on their way back to Banaue. Staff can heat up hot water for a quick wash. **P500**

Mayoyao

There are buses to Mayoyao from Banaue (1 daily; 3hr) and Santiago (3 daily; 4–5hr)

Home to some arrestingly beautiful rice terraces listed as a UNESCO World Heritage Site, **MAYOYAO** is rarely visited due to the poor road condition, although it's well worth taking the time to travel here. The terraces are punctuated by distinctive pyramid-roofed local houses, and by stone burial mounds called Apfo'or. They are at their greenest from April to May and October to November.

ACCOMMODATION   MAYOYAO

Milcah Lodge ☏ 0935 208 7698. A cosy little place, conveniently located right in the middle of town, spotless

and friendly, with great views. One room has its own bathroom; the others share. **P500**

Kiangan and around

On September 2, 1945, General Yamashita of the Japanese Imperial Army surrendered to US and Filipino troops in the town of **KIANGAN**, 10km from the provincial capital Lagawe (which is itself 24km south of Banaue). The event is commemorated with a large **shrine** although the actual site of the surrender (marked with a plaque) is now occupied by the library of the nearby Kiangan Elementary School. The hill on the right as you look out from the front of the shrine is where the Japanese holed up for their last stand; it's known as the **Million Dollar Hill** for the supposed cost of the artillery with which the US shelled it. Across from the shrine, the **Ifugao Museum** (Mon–Fri 9am–4pm; free) displays everyday local artefacts including men's hip bags used to store betel nut, and a mouth harp, considered to be a courtship instrument played to express intimate love.

The **rice terraces** around Kiangan are at their best in April and May. You can take a jeepney to the terraces at either **Nagacadan** (20min; P15) or **Julungan** ("Hul-ungan"; 1hr; P50). Tricycles also make it to Nagacadan (15min; P75 each way). Ask at Kiangan tourist office if you need a guide.

ARRIVAL AND INFORMATION

By bus The nearest bus station to Kiangan is in Lagawe, 14km away, served by Ohayami buses from Manila (1 daily; 8hr) and Baguio (1 daily; 6hr).

By jeepney Jeepneys connect Kiangan and Lagawe (15min; P15), from where there are regular jeepneys to Banaue (1hr; P37).

KIANGAN AND AROUND

By tricycle There are tricycles from Lagawe to Kiangan (20min; P100).

Tourist offices The tourist office is next to the municipal hall (Mon–Fri 8am–5pm; ☎ 0915 811 8500, ⓦ bit.ly/visit).

ACCOMMODATION

★**Ibulao, Ibulao** Ibulao ☎ 0917 553 3299, ✉ totokalug@yahoo.com.ph. This highly acclaimed eco-lodge and B&B, set in one hectare of land midway between Lagawe and Kiangan, has a selection of creatively presented rooms mostly decorated with Ifugao woodcarvings. The family room for six (P3000) with stone floors is particularly impressive, built around exposed rocks. Owner and doctor Roberto Kalungan also arranges rafting trips. He is rather selective with his guests, asking them to introduce themselves in detail via email before offering the possibility of overnighting. Bookings are essential; no walk-ins are accepted. ☞ P1800

Kiangan Youth Hostel Poblacion ☎ 0915 704 8398, ⓦ kiangan-hostel. A basic option in the centre of Kiangan, with three simple private rooms with private bath (cold showers only) and two single-sex dorms. ☞ Dorms P150, doubles P500

Batanes province

Almost 150km off the northern coast of Luzon, **Batanes** is the smallest, most isolated province in the country – the islands are closer to Taiwan than to the northernmost tip of Luzon. This is a memorable place with otherworldly scenery, where doors are rarely locked and welcomes are warm even by Filipino standards. The people are different, the language is different, even the weather is different. The coolest months (Jan–March) can get chilly, with temperatures as low as 10°C, while the hottest months (May and June) are searing. For visitors, the islands are at their best from February to June. Just three of the ten islands in the Batanes group are inhabited: **Batan** – the location of the capital **Basco** – **Sabtang** and **Itbayat**.

Batanes can be idyllic, but it would be wrong to portray it as a tropical utopia. Realities of life this far away from the rest of the world can sometimes be harsh. Petrol and provisions are brought in by ship, which means that they cost more, and when **typhoons** roar in from the east (July–Sept) it may be impossible for ships or aircraft to reach the islands. Boredom can set in and locals joke that during the typhoon season the cargo ship brings fifty thousand sacks of rice but sixty thousand crates of gin.

The native inhabitants of Batanes, the **Ivatan**, trace their roots to prehistoric Formosan immigrants. Most still make a living by cultivating yams and garlic or raising goats and cows; if you visit a village during the daytime, be prepared to find that almost everyone is out in the fields. Some women still wear rain capes called *vakul*, made from the stripped leaves of the *voyavoy* palm. The main **dialect**, Ivatan, includes some pidgin Spanish: "thank you" is *dios mamajes* and "goodbye" is *dios mavidin* (if you are the person leaving) or *dios machivan* (if you are staying behind).

Batan Island

Batan Island is the biggest in the group and site of the tiny capital, **BASCO**. The town boasts a spectacular location on the lower slopes of **Mount Iraya**, a volcano that hasn't erupted since the fifteenth century but is still officially active. You can walk around the town in half an hour, and there are no specific attractions, but it's a pleasant and friendly place, built around a rectangular plaza with the municipal buildings and church on the north side and the sea to the south.

3

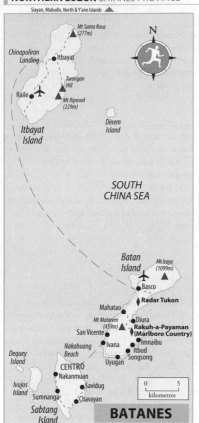

Siayan, Mabudis, North & Y'ami Islands

Mt Santa Rosa (277m)
Chinapoliran Landing
Itbayat
Torongan Hill
Raile
Mt Riposed (229m)
Itbayat Island
Dinem Island

SOUTH CHINA SEA

N

Batan Island
Mt Iraya (1099m)
Basco
Radar Tukon
Mahatao
Mt Matarem (459m)
Diura
Rakuh-a-Payaman (Marlboro Country)
San Vicente
Imnaibu
Nakabuang Beach
Ivana
Itbud
Songsong
Dequey Island
Uyugan
CENTRO
Nakanmuan
Ivujos Island
Savidug
Sumnanga
Chavayan
Sabtang Island

0 — 5
kilometres

BATANES

Around the island

Most organized tours start by heading south from Basco along the coastal road to the *Batanes Resort* (see p.184), before turning left up a narrow road to an abandoned weather station called **Radar Tukon**. This can also be done on foot as a day-hike: it's about an hour from Basco and from here the whole island is spread at your feet. Beyond the weather station is the swanky *Fundacion Pacita* hotel (see p.184), and some tunnels nearby created by the Japanese army during World War II.

After heading back to the coastal road you can return to Basco, or continue south through the pretty old Spanish village of **Mahatao** and on to **Ivana** ("Ih-va-na"), with its eye-catching yellow church, where ferries set off to Sabtang. Just opposite the church is the pier for ferries to Sabtang Island. In Ivana you will also find **Dakay's House**, the oldest stone house in Batanes, built in 1887. Although it is inhabited, you are welcome to poke your head in to take a look at the interior, which has wooden floors traditionally polished with banana leaves.

The coastal road round the southern end of the island brings you to the village of **Uyugan** before turning north to **Song Song**, where you can see the remains of stone houses that were washed away by a tidal wave. After Itbud there is a turning inland and uphill taking you through **Rakuh-a-Payaman** (known to tourists as "Marlboro Country"), elevated pastures inhabited by Ivatan bulls and horses, grazing against the backdrop of Mount Iraya and the Pacific Ocean.

After passing through the pastures you can either return to Mahatao (and from there to Basco) or continue to **Diura**, a small fishing village and the nearby Spring of Youth, a twenty-minute walk away. Here there's a wonderful stone pool perfect for a refreshing dip, with spectacular views over the ocean and Mount Iraya. There's no route for vehicles up the coast from Diura so unless you're hiking you'll need to head back to Basco via Mahatao.

Sabtang Island

Don't miss the opportunity to spend at least a day exploring **Sabtang Island**, a peaceful place dotted with Ivatan stone villages where life seems to have altered little in a hundred years. Ferries arrive in the port on the island's northeast coast, in the **Centro** area, where there's a Spanish church, a school and a few houses.

You can do a circuit of the island on foot, but with a vehicle it's necessary to double back and visit the eastern and western parts of the island separately. You could start by heading south from the port to **Chavayan**, about 10km away. On the way there are the remains of a fortress (*idjang*) that stands high on a hill; it served as a lookout point for the Ivatan to defend themselves from approaching invaders, as well as to monitor marine migration patterns. The path is steep in places, so take it slowly. Chavayan itself has some of the island's best-preserved traditional homes and a small chapel, as well as the Sabtang Weavers' Association, where you can purchase artefacts as well as enjoy fresh coconut and home-made biscuits prepared by members of the association.

From Centro you can also walk 9km to **Sumnanga**, passing through the tiny village of **Nakanmuan**, with a few traditional houses. About 3km further along is the fishing village of Sumnanga, home to the lovely Devuk Bay. From here you may be able to rent a boat (around P500) to visit Ivujos Island – it's inhabited only by grazing cows. From Sumnanga you can hop on a scooter or tricycle (P250) to return to Centro.

Itbayat Island

Of the three inhabited islands in the Batanes group, **Itbayat Island** is the least accessible. There's no public transport, either, so you'll have to get around on foot or by asking one of the residents who owns a motorbike to give you a lift. It's crisscrossed by trails made by farmers and fishermen, making for superb trekking in good weather.

The ferry lands at the west coast harbour of Chinapoliran, from where you can walk or hitch a lift to the pretty little capital, **ITBAYAT**. There are great views of the island, and the others nearby, from the viewpoint of Mount Karaboboan, also known as **Mount Santa Rosa** (277m), on the northern side of the island. Alternatively, go looking for the stone boat-shaped burial markers at Torongan Hill, above a cave where the first inhabitants of the island are believed to have lived.

ARRIVAL AND DEPARTURE   BATANES PROVINCE

By plane The only way to get to the Batanes islands is by air, with all flights landing in Basco. You can fly from Tuguegarao with Sky Pasada and North Sky Air (each 3 weekly; 1hr 30min; P4800), and from Manila with PAL (1 daily; 1hr 45min; P6104) and Skyjet (6 weekly; 1hr 10min; P6613). Basco is also connected to Itbayat (see below). A tricycle from the airport into Basco is P40 (5min); many hotels offer free airport transfers.

GETTING AROUND

By plane North Sky has flights from Basco to Itbayat (no fixed schedule, but flying whenever they get eight bookings; 20min; P1800).

By ferry Ferries leave Ivana pier in Batan for Sabtang daily at 7.30am, returning around 12.30pm (30min; P75 each way). A jeepney for Ivana leaves Basco around 6.30am to connect with the ferry, or you can take a tricycle. The channel between Batan and Sabtang is known for its strong currents and big waves – avoid the crossing in rough weather. For Itbayat, ferries leave Basco at 6am daily (3hr; P450), returning around 11am, but be warned that it can be a very rough and uncomfortable crossing, and may be cancelled for days in a row if sea conditions are particularly poor.

INFORMATION

Credit cards are not accepted in Batanes, so make sure that you have enough cash. You should be able to change dollars at PNB in Basco, but not at a favourable rate. PNB and Land Bank in Basco have ATMs, but it's probably best not to rely solely on them.

BATAN ISLAND

Registration fee There is a "sustainable ecotourism fee" of P350 payable on arrival; keep your receipt on you as you may be asked to show it at places around the island. Leaving by air, you are charged a P100 "terminal fee".

Tourist Information The heritage and tourism section of the governor's office is on National Rd (Mon–Fri 8am–5pm; ☎ 0929 230 5934, ⓦ batanes.gov.ph).

Tours Ivatan Travel & Tours (☎ 0916 228 6883, wbit.ly/ ivatan-travel) and Batanes Tours and Travel (☎ 0920 217 9031, ⓦ amazingbatanes.com) organize island tours, as well as biking and trekking. For scuba diving contact Dive Batanes (☎ 0939 922 4609, ⓦ divebatanes.com).

SABTANG ISLAND

Registration fee There is a registration fee of P200 payable at the tourist centre on arrival.

Tourist information The tourist centre (daily 8am–5pm; ☎ 0918 488 2424) is to the left as you leave the port. They have no maps or brochures but can provide advice on routes, and will collect your registration fee. If you want a tour of the island, call the tourist centre in advance or organize it in Basco.

GETTING AROUND

BATAN ISLAND

By jeepney If you are in a group then the easiest way to get a quick overall picture of the beauty of Batan is to hire a jeepney with driver for the day (around P2000) through your accommodation. It's also possible to travel in public jeepneys that connect settlements along the coastal road, but you'll have to be prepared to wait and probably to do some walking and hitching.

By tricycle To charter a tricycle with driver, contact BATODA (Batanes Tricycle Operators & Drivers Association; ☎ 0929 703 8404).

By bike Most lodges rent out bicycles (P300/day for regular bikes, P500–1000/day for mountain bikes), as do shops such as DLMV in Basco (☎ 0909 724 8476) and travel agencies such as Batanes Grand Holidays (☎ 078 844 2880, ⓦ bghtraveltours.wordpress.com). The Petron filling station rents out motorcycles (P800/day). While the roads are very quiet, there are a number of blind bends, so take it easy and be sure to observe the speed limit of 20km/hr in towns.

SABTANG ISLAND

By tricycle You can charter a tricycle to tour the island for around P1500 for two to three people.

ACCOMMODATION

BATAN ISLAND

The potential for trekking and camping on Batan is enticing. There are no campsites, but as long as you respect the landscape no one minds if you pitch a tent for the night near a beach. Whatever you do, take food and water, because there are few places to get provisions. All the accommodation listed below is in or around Basco; don't expect fast internet or strong water pressure anywhere.

Amboy Hometel 3km south of Basco, Brgy Chanarian ☎ 0920 910 3492, ⓦ batanesamboyhometel.com. This B&B has twelve a/c rooms with private bath, all painted in different colours. There's a TV with DVD player in each, while a restaurant by the little garden area serves seasonal dishes. 🛜 P2200

Batanes Resort 2km south of Basco, Brgy Kaychanarianan ☎ 0918 553 3734, ⓔ batanesresort_ ivatanlodge@yahoo.com. Tidy little stone duplex cottages, with hot showers, sitting on a breezy hillside with steps leading down to a marvellous black-sand cove. The restaurant has good food and a pleasant terrace. P1800

Batanes Seaside Lodge National Rd, Brgy Kaychanarianan ☎ 0927 788 5508, ⓦ batanesseaside lodge.com. Right on the seafront, this lodge has fifteen decent-sized rooms and is very handy for the airport. There's a large restaurant serving Ivatan dishes and a couple of lounge areas with armchairs. 🛜 P2400

★ **Fundacion Pacita** Brgy Chanarian ☎ 0939 901 6353, ⓦ fundacionpacita.ph. The island's most upmarket accommodation option was the former home of artist Pacita Abad until her death in 2004; the common area exhibits Abad's art while the rooms, all with balconies and exceptional views, are tastefully decorated with works of Filipino artists. A portion of the proceeds goes to heritage conservation in Batanes, and provides art scholarships for Ivatan students and supplies for local schools. The restaurant serves wonderful Ivatan cuisine. 🛜 P11,700

Midtown Inn Abad St at Lizardo St, Brgy Kayhuvokan ☎ 0921 367 7933, ⓦ midtowninnbatanes.com. The decor's a little bit lurid, but this is a good choice, reasonably spacious and centrally located, right in the middle of town, with breakfast included, and decent wi-fi, though only in the lobby area. 🛜 P2600

Octagon Bed & Dine Brgy Kaychanarianan ☎ 0999 180 2944, ⓦ batanesoctagon.weebly.com. The three spacious rooms here are jam-packed with furniture and knick-knacks, including wooden trunks, vases, armchairs and chintzy bedspreads. Accommodation gives onto a balcony from where there are wonderful views of the ocean. 🛜 P3000

SABTANG ISLAND

Harold Gabotero's Vernacular House Brgy Chavayan ☎ 0998 553 9098. This small homestay, in a traditional old house, is the top choice for a place to stay in Sabtang. Per person P150

ITBAYAT ISLAND

Cano's Lodging Services Itbayat ☎ 0919 300 4787, ⓦ bit.ly/canos-lodging. A homestay run by former history teacher and municipal tourism officer Nanay Cano, who'll happily gen you up on the island and its ways, cook meals to order and generally make you feel right at home. Per person P250

EATING

BATAN ISLAND

Several of the lodges in Basco have restaurants or can make food to order, while elsewhere on the island you'll be reliant on the occasional small canteen so it's best to travel with at least a snack and some water.

Octagon Bed & Dine Brgy Kaychanarianan ☎ 0999 180 2944, ⓦ batanesoctagon.weebly.com. This octagonal restaurant, decorated with colourful paintings, wooden masks and other artefacts, offers what is probably the most extensive menu on the island, with most dishes at around P200 but good for two or three people. Daily 7am–11pm.

Pension Ivatan Brgy Kayvalugan ☎ 078 373 0587, ⓦ bit.ly/pension-ivatan. This friendly restaurant (which is also an excellent *pension*) is decorated with beautiful glass buoys that were washed up ashore from nearby Taiwan. The menu focuses on traditional Ivatan cuisine – the large Ivatan platter (P1700) will easily feed four to five; it includes coconut crab, lobster, cuttlefish, local salad and *uved*, a Batan delicacy of fish and pork sautéed with coconut. Daily 7am–9pm.

St Dominic College Canteen National Rd. This self-service canteen is used by students of the attached St Dominic College, but open to all. There are a variety of inexpensive dishes on offer, including *mami* (noodle soup), super-fresh local fish, and *halo-halo*, almost all priced at P50–100. Mon–Sat 8am–9pm, Sun 8am–8.30pm.

SHOPPING

BATAN ISLAND

Yaru National Rd, Brgy Kaychanarianan ☎ 0949 985 7037, ⓦ bit.ly/yaru-gallery. Run by an association of artists who aim to make the arts a sustainable source of income on the islands, this small gallery and shop sells paintings as well as a few souvenirs, including lovely painted cards of Batanes sights. Daily 2–7pm.

3

Southern Luzon

MOUNT MAYON

Southern Luzon

Southeast of Manila, the provinces that make up Southern Luzon are home to some of the country's most popular attractions, particularly favoured by local tourists. The region is not yet on the backpacker trail, which can mean few budget accommodation options; however, it's blessed with some extraordinarily diverse natural phenomena. One of the area's top draws is the picturesque Mount Mayon volcano, whose cone is reputedly the most perfectly symmetrical in the world. Southern Luzon is also one of the few places on earth where you can swim with the world's largest fish, the gentle whale shark. It is also blessed with underground rivers, glorious white-sand beaches, limestone cliffs, spectacular surfing waves, hot and cold springs and historic buildings dating back to the Spanish colonial era.

The National Highway south from Manila takes you down to **Quezon province**, home to **Mount Banahaw**, a revered dormant volcano that presents one of the most rewarding climbs in the country. Quezon is linked by ferry to the beautiful island province of **Marinduque**, still largely untouched by mass tourism and best known for its Easter festival, the **Moriones**.

Beyond Quezon is the **Bicol** region, which encompasses the remainder of Southern Luzon and includes the mainland provinces of **Camarines Norte**, **Camarines Sur**, **Albay** and **Sorsogon** and the island provinces of **Catanduanes** and **Masbate**. Known throughout the Philippines as an area of great natural beauty – and for its delicious **cuisine**, characterized by the use of chillies and coconut milk – Bicol is studded with volcanoes, including **Mount Bulusan** and **Mount Mayon**, and offers superb coastline with some great beaches and island-hopping opportunities, particularly around **Legazpi** and **Sorsogon City**. Best of all is the **Caramoan Peninsula**, where tourism is developing apace but where it's still possible to find deserted hideaways. There are also attractions offshore, and although it can't rival the Visayas for scuba diving, Bicol does have an ace up its sleeve in the form of **Donsol**, home to huge whale sharks. Other water-based activities include surfing in **Daet** and wakeboarding at **CamSur Watersports Complex** near Naga. Two island provinces add further variety to Bicol's fabulous mix: **Masbate** is the Philippines' wild east, cattle country where the biggest tourist draw is the annual rodeo in April. **Catanduanes**, meanwhile, is infamous for its exposure to passing typhoons – ironically it's this extreme weather, however, that attracts surfers to its beaches.

ARRIVAL AND DEPARTURE

By plane There are commercial airports in Naga, Legazpi, Virac (Catanduanes) and Masbate City.

By train There is a train line between Manila and Legazpi via Naga, but at the time of writing, the only operational part of the route was between Sipocot (approximately 44km northeast of Naga) and Naga. The Philippine

MORIONES FESTIVAL

Highlights

❶ Moriones festival Every Easter the beautiful little island of Marinduque lays on a boisterous religious pageant celebrating the life of Longinus, the Roman soldier who pierced Christ's side at the Crucifixion. **See p.197**

❷ Caramoan Peninsula Limestone cliffs, remote islands and beautiful secluded beaches much beloved by international TV companies – especially since the *Survivor* series was filmed here. **See p.209**

❸ Bicolano cuisine Savour spicy Bicolano cuisine, some of the country's best, prepared with chillies and plenty of coconut milk. **See box, p.214**

❹ Mount Mayon Even if you don't climb it, you can't miss its almost symmetrical cone standing imperiously above Legazpi. **See p.215**

❺ Swimming with whale sharks, Donsol Snorkel with the gentle giants of the sea, the world's largest fish. **See p.220**

❻ Ticao Island This small island in the Masbate province is well worth the extra boat ride, with deserted beaches, cascading waterfalls, native villages and excellent diving. **See p.228**

HIGHLIGHTS ARE MARKED ON THE MAP ON PP.190–191

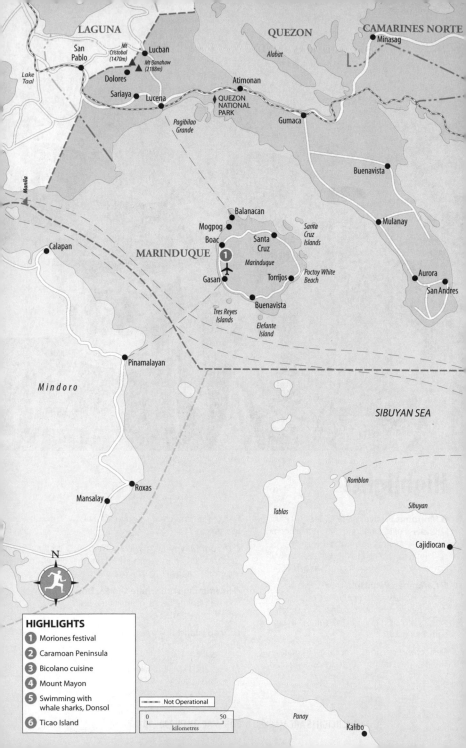

LAGUNA

San Pablo

Mt Cristobal (1470m)

Lucban

Mt Banahaw (2188m)

Dolores

Sariaya

Lucena

Lake Taal

QUEZON

Alabat

Atimonan

QUEZON NATIONAL PARK

Pagibilao Grande

Gumaca

Manila

CAMARINES NORTE

Minasag

Buenavista

Mulanay

Aurora

San Andres

Balanacan

Mogpog

Boac

Santa Cruz

Marinduque

MARINDUQUE

Santa Cruz Islands

Poctoy White Beach

Gasan

Torrijos

Buenavista

Tres Reyes Islands

Elefante Island

Calapan

Pinamalayan

Mindoro

SIBUYAN SEA

Roxas

Mansalay

Romblon

Sibuyan

Tablas

Cajidiocan

N

HIGHLIGHTS

1 Moriones festival
2 Caramoan Peninsula
3 Bicolano cuisine
4 Mount Mayon
5 Swimming with whale sharks, Donsol
6 Ticao Island

Not Operational

0 — 50
kilometres

Panay

Kalibo

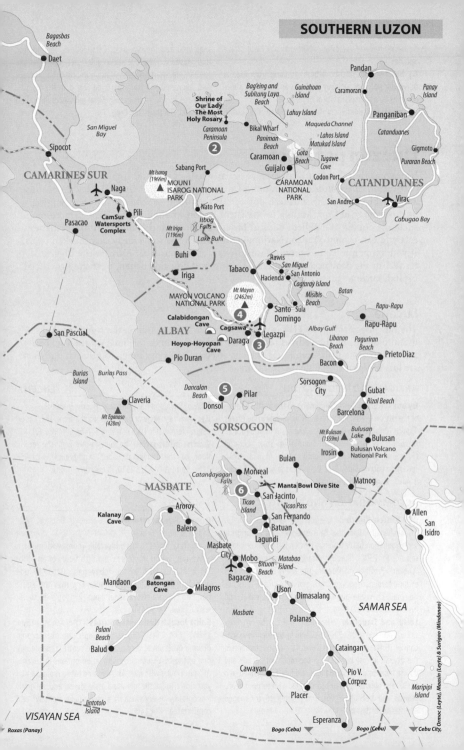

SOUTHERN LUZON

Bagasbas Beach
Daet

Sipocot

San Miguel Bay

CAMARINES SUR

Naga
Pili
CamSur Watersports Complex
Pasacao
Pili

Mt Isarog (1966m)
MOUNT ISAROG NATIONAL PARK

Shrine of Our Lady The Most Holy Rosary
2
Caramoan Peninsula
Bikal Wharf

Bag'eing and Subitang Laya Beach
Guinahoan Island

Pandan
Caramoran

Panay Island
Panganiban

Lahuy Island

Maqueda Channel
Lahos Island
Matukad Island

Catanduanes
Gigmoto
Puraran Beach

Sabang Port

Caramoan
Guijalo
Paniman Beach
Gota Beach
CARAMOAN NATIONAL PARK
Tugawe Cove
Codon Port

CATANDUANES

Nato Port
Itbog Falls
Mt Iriga (1196m)
Lake Buhi
Buhi

San Andres
Virac

Cabugao Bay

Iriga

Tabaco
Rawis
San Miguel
San Antonio
Hacienda

Cagraray Island
Misibis Beach
Batan

MAYON VOLCANO NATIONAL PARK
Mt Mayon (2462m)
4
Santo Sula Domingo

Rapu-Rapu
Rapu-Rapu

ALBAY
Calabidongan Cave
Cagsawa
Daraga
3
Legazpi

Albay Gulf
Libanon Beach
Paguriran Beach

San Pascual

Hoyop-Hoyopan Cave
Pio Duran

Bacon
Prieto Diaz

Burias Island
Burias Pass
Claveria
Mt Eganoso (428m)

Dancalan Beach
5
Pilar
Donsol

Sorsogon City
Gubat
Rizal Beach
Barcelona

SORSOGON

Mt Bulasan (1559m)
Bulusan Lake
Bulusan

Bulan
Irosin
Bulusan Volcano National Park

Catandayagan Falls
Monreal
6
Manta Bowl Dive Site
San Jacinto
Ticao Island
Ticao Pass
Matnog

MASBATE
Aroroy
San Fernando

Allen
San Isidro

Kalanay Cave
Baleno
Batuan
Lagundi

Masbate City
Mobo
Bagacay
Matabao Island
Bituon Beach

Mandaon
Batongan Cave
Milagros

Uson
Dimasalang

Masbate
Palanas

SAMAR SEA

Palani Beach
Balud

Cataingan

Mariripi Island

Pio V. Corpuz

Cawayan
Placer

Jintotolo Island
Esperanza

VISAYAN SEA

Roxas (Panay)
Bogo (Cebu)
Bogo (Cebu)
Cebu City,

Ormoc (Leyte), Maasin (Leyte) & Surigao (Mindanao)

National Railway website (@pnr.gov.ph) will have updates.

By bus There are plenty of buses running from Manila down the National Highway via Naga and Legazpi, some going as far as Sorsogon City or beyond.

By boat In addition to ferries between the Luzon mainland and the Islands of Catanduanes, Marinduque and Masbate, there are also regular services across the Bernardino Strait between Matnog in Sorsogon province and Allen and San Isidro ports on Samar in the Visayas. Masbate has ferry links to several provinces including Romblon, Batangas and Cebu.

Quezon province

Known as the "Coconut Province", as nearly half of the land is given over to cultivation of coconut palms, much of the northern part of **Quezon** is mountainous and hard to reach. The southern portion of the province serves mainly as a staging post on the road from Manila to the Bicol region, though it does have attractions such as a couple of excellent climbs, **Mount Banahaw** and **Mount Cristobal**. Further east you can explore **Quezon National Park**, which has some fairly easy marked trails. If you happen to be in Quezon in mid-May, check out what is by far the biggest festival in the province, the **Pahiyas**, held in and around **Lucban**, near the provincial capital, **Lucena**.

Lucena

The bustling town of **LUCENA** is worth considering for a stop on the route south, as a useful base during the **Pahiyas** festival in nearby Lucban or for those on their way to Marinduque via Dalahican port. The city itself doesn't offer much to visitors, but there are lots of sights in the surrounding area.

ARRIVAL AND INFORMATION   LUCENA

By bus The Grand Central Terminal is on the northern edge of the city on Diversion Rd. It's a 15min jeepney ride (every 15min; 10min; P8) to Quezon Ave, the main thoroughfare. Destinations Daet (DLTB: hourly; 4–5hr); Legazpi (Raymond Transportation: hourly; 8hr); Manila (JAM, Jac Liner, Lucena Lines & N. Dela Rosa: every 30–40min; 3–4hr); Naga (Raymond Transportation: hourly; 5–6hr);

Tabaco (Raymond Transportation: hourly; 9–10hr).

By jeepney Regular jeepneys travel from the Grand Central Terminal to Lucban (every 15min; 60min; P40).

Tourist information The tourist office is on the second floor of the Provincial Capital Compound (Mon–Fri 8am–5pm; ☎042 373 7510, @quezon.gov.ph).

ACCOMMODATION AND EATING

ADV Koffee Klatch 88 Quezon Ave ☎042 373 0053. Established in 1958, this café is owned by a sprightly septuagenarian baker who has written her own cookbook (on sale for P500), filled with traditional recipes from the "Coconut Province" of Quezon. The many savoury dishes include *hardinera*, pork cooked in tomato sauce (P130), but the main draw are the excellent home-made cakes and biscuits. Daily 7am–8pm.

Luisa and Daughter Quezon Avenue Extension, Brgy Gulang-Gulang ☎042 710 7543. Run by the friendly Maria-Carmen (Luisa's daughter), this is one of the best restaurants in the city. Sit in cosy booths or in the courtyard outside and choose from dishes such as Bangus sardines (P200), filled crab (P330) and *ubod lumpia* (an egg roll filled with coconut heart, prawns and peanuts; P105). Don't forget to try mango cheesecake for dessert (P115). Daily 10am–10pm.

Queen Margarette Hotel 1 People Square, M.L. Tagarao St at Granja St ☎042 373 7171, @queen margarettehotel.com. Comfortable rooms with modern amenities, set on the fourth and fifth floors of an office block; there's wi-fi in the lobby only. Rates include breakfast at the Chinese restaurant within the same building. There's also a sister hotel just outside town, with a pool. ☎ **P2650**

Saint Joseph Residential Suites 7 Trinidad St, Brgy 1 ☎042 717 1145, @thesaintjoseph.com.ph. Located down a quiet street very close to the centre, this is easily one of the best-value accommodation options in Lucena. All suites come with mini-kitchens and living rooms, and if you don't mind the grandma-style decor and religious iconography everywhere, it's extremely homely and comfortable. ☎ **P1400**

Lucban

Quezon province's major tourist draw is the **Pahiyas thanksgiving festival**, held every year on May 15 in **LUCBAN**, which sits at the foot of Mount Banahaw, 26km north of Lucena. It's a quaint little town and a pleasant spot to have a stroll, but there's not too much to see; it's worth taking a moment to visit the **St Louis Church**, which dates from the 1730s.

Kamay ni Hesus

Tricycle P10 (10min), jeepney P8 (every 15min; 10min)

You could join the faithful as they climb **Kamay ni Hesus** – a hill on the edge of Lucban peppered with tableaux depicting the stations of the cross and topped with a large, open-armed statue of Christ – in the hope of being cured of various ailments. The route up is exposed, and can be tiring on a hot day, but it's worth it for the wonderful views. Although a church stands at the base of the hill and masses are regularly held, the whole site has something of a theme-park feel, with a children's playground and replica Noah's ark.

ARRIVAL AND DEPARTURE   LUCBAN

By jeepney Regular jeepneys connect Lucban with Lucena (every 15min; 60min; P40).

By van Regular vans run between Lucban and Lucena (P50)

and are slightly quicker than jeepneys. To get to Manila, you'll need to catch a van to Calamba (hourly; 2hr; P120) and change there for an onward bus (every 15min; 40min).

ACCOMMODATION AND EATING

If you're coming to Lucban during the **Pahiyas festival** you should book **accommodation** well in advance – some places get their first reservations a year ahead. Expect the prices to be inflated. There are surprisingly very few good options in the centre, although staying in the colourful heart of town during festival time makes for a wonderful experience. Note that most accommodation options listed here do not have reliable **wi-fi**, and where available it's usually only in public areas such as the lobby. In terms of **eating**, be sure to try the famous garlicky **Lucban longganisa** (sausage) – particularly delicious when served with *achara* (pickled papaya) – and for dessert try **budin** (cassava cake). Cheap food stalls by the church sell **pancit habhab**, a local noodle dish served on a banana leaf and traditionally eaten with your hands.

Batis Aramin Resort ☎ 042 540 4401, ⟨w⟩ aramin.ph. About 1km from the town proper, this large resort offers a range of spacious, plush rooms connected by a hanging bridge. There's a large pool with an artificial waterfall and slide, a basketball court, a lagoon, and an adventure camp with ziplines and rope courses. <u>P2500</u>

Buddy's Restaurant Rizal Park ☎ 042 540 3394. Located on the town's main square, this place may be a chain, but it's laidback and has colourful Pahiyas festival

kiping (rice paper) decorations dangling from the ceiling. Seating is on small wooden benches, and the menu includes pancit Lucban (noodles with pork; P175) and longganisa (P115). Daily 9am–10pm.

★ **Isabelito's Garden Resto** Deveza Farm, Arellano St at Placencia St ☎ 0915 847 9380. Located in a garden centre, surrounded by plants and ponds, this lovely, airy restaurant has chunky wooden tables and bamboo partitions. Bestsellers include crunchy Bicol Express (P285),

---

PAHIYAS FESTIVAL

Each May during the **Pahiyas festival**, Lucban is transformed into something from a fairy tale, the houses decorated in the most imaginative fashion with fruit, vegetables and brightly coloured *kiping* (rice paper), which is formed into enormous chandeliers that cascade like flames from the eaves. The winner of the **best-decorated house** wins a cash prize and is blessed for twelve months by San Isidore (the patron saint of farmers). It's open house for visitors during Pahiyas, and people are especially honoured to have foreigners come in to admire their decorations.

The festival itself starts with a solemn Mass at dawn and goes on well into the night, with much drinking and dancing in the streets. There is a parade, a beauty contest, a marching band and a carabao parade in which enormous water buffalo, more used to rice fields and mud holes, are led through the streets in outrageous costumes.

4

crispy *kare kare* (a Filipino curry made from stewed meats, vegetables and peanut sauce; P320) and *papel de liempo* (bacon strips with smoky barbecue sauce; P205). Daily 9am–9pm.

Patio Rizal 77 Quezon Ave ☎ 042 540 2112, ✉ patiorizal@ yahoo.com. This centrally located hotel is one of the most comfortable in town, offering decent rooms with carpet; the deluxe (P3000) and premier suite (P3200) are substantially larger and more welcoming. Each floor has a small seating area with wooden chairs and old paintings of the town centre, and there's a good restaurant on the ground floor serving a selection of Filipino dishes. Rates include breakfast. P1800

Mount Banahaw and around

Northwest of Lucena, the town of **DOLORES** is the starting point for treks up **Mount Banahaw** and **Mount Cristobal**, which stand on either side of the town. Both mountains are protected areas and some of their hiking trails have been closed for the past few years to reduce human impact on the environment.

Considered sacred, 2188m Mount Banahaw has spawned a huge number of **legends** and superstitions: one says that every time a foreigner sets foot on the mountain it will rain. Members of various sects still live around the base of the mountain, claiming that it imbues them with supernatural and psychic powers. Its slopes thick with jungle, Banahaw is a challenging but rewarding **climb**, with panoramic views of the surrounding country from the crater rim. Treat this mountain seriously, because although the trail looks wide and well-trodden, it soon peters out into inhospitable rainforest – even experienced climbers allow three days to reach the summit and get back down, while a crater descent should only be attempted by experts.

If you haven't time to reach the summit, you might prefer simply to trek to **Kristalino Falls** (Crystalline Falls) and back, which can be done in a day. One and a half hours further on is a second waterfall, whose surroundings make an ideal **campsite**.

Mount Cristobal

Mount Cristobal is seen as the negative counterpart to the positive spiritual energy of Mount Banahaw. It takes up to six hours of serious trekking along an awkward trail to reach Jones Peak, which is 50m lower than the inaccessible summit. The climb isn't recommended for beginners or unaccompanied trekkers.

ARRIVAL AND INFORMATION   MOUNT BANAHAW AND AROUND

By bus, jeepney and tricycle To reach the access town of Dolores, take one of the Jac Liner, JAM, Lucena Lines or N. Dela Rosa buses that run hourly between Manila (Buendia or Cubao) and Lucena, and get off at San Pablo (a 2hr journey), from where there are jeepneys to Dolores (hourly; 25min; P20) from the market. From Dolores, take a tricycle to the barangay of Kinabuyahan (20min; P250).

Guides The municipal tourist office, in the Municipal Hall, National Rd, Dolores (Mon–Fri 9am–5pm), can help

organize guides (from P250 for six to ten people/day), although you will need to inform the Tourism Officer, Laarni Alilio, a few days in advance (☎ 042 565 6515, ✉ laarni _alilio@yahoo.com).

Permits To reach the summit of Banahaw you need a special permit issued by the Protected Area Management Board; the Municipal Environment and Natural Resources Department can help (☎ 042 565 6515).

ACCOMMODATION AND EATING

Kinabuhayan Kafe Dolores ☎ 0916 221 5791. Owned by artist Jay Herrera, this quirky café and B&B offers accommodation in two cosy native huts that are filled with knick-knacks; there's also a small swimming

pool. Hearty mains are made to order – the cuisine is mainly international with a Filipino twist – and overnight rates include three daily meals. Wi-fi available in the café only. Rates are per person. 🛜 P3000

Quezon National Park

Quezon National Park, about 25km east of Lucena near the town of **ATIMONAN**, is off the well-beaten trail, far from the picture-postcard beaches of the Visayas and too distant from Manila to make it a viable weekend trip. Though relatively small at just ten square kilometres, the park is so dense with flora and fauna that you have a good chance of seeing anything and everything from giant monitor lizards to monkeys, deer and wild pigs. The park is also home to the *kalaw*, a species of hornbill.

It takes about an hour to walk along the paved trail to the highest point, 366m above sea level, which has a viewing deck from where you can see both sides of the Bicol peninsula. The summit is known as **Pinagbanderahan**, meaning "where the flag is hoisted", because both Japanese and American flags were flown there before the Philippine flag was raised in 1946. There are also numerous **caves** in the park that can be explored with guides, experience and the right equipment.

ARRIVAL AND INFORMATION — QUEZON NATIONAL PARK

By bus The turning for the park is on the Maharlika Highway, which runs from Lucena to Atimonan. The winding approach road to the park, known locally as *bituka ng manok* (chicken's intestine), is a challenge for buses: from Lucena's Grand Central station, you can get any bus heading east through Bicol (to Daet, for instance) or an Atimonan-bound bus, as all these vehicles pass the park entrance (every 15min; 1hr).

Guides Enquire at the Atimonan Municipal Tourism Council, Aitmonan Old Municipal Hall Compound (T 0917 5605 647, E konjohn10 @yahoo.com; P300/day for a group of eight).

ACCOMMODATION AND EATING

Tamarind Tree Resort Padre Burgos T 0917 853 8062, W thetamarindtreeresort.com. Located along the coast, just a 20min drive from the park entrance, this resort has a range of different-sized nipa huts with fans (or with a/c, for P1800) scattered along the beach, and up on the hilltop, as well as small tents for those on a budget. There's also an outdoor pool, and island-hopping and caving tours are available. Limited wi-fi in the restaurant only. Camping (2-man tent) **P600**, nipa hut **P1000**

4

Marinduque

With its numerous caves and pretty beaches, tiny **MARINDUQUE** ("mar-in-DOO-kay") island, where most of the 230,000 residents lead a life of subsistence coconut farming and fishing, is a great place to get away from it all for a few days. The island is known as the "Heart of the Philippines" both due to its shape and location within the country. Work your way slowly around the coastal road south of **Boac**, then across the island to **Torrijos** and **Poctoy White Beach**, where you can live cheaply in the shadow of majestic **Mount Malinding**. There's some excellent island-hopping too, with spectacular beaches and coves to explore around the **Tres Reyes Islands** off the southwest coast and the **Santa Cruz Islands** off the northeast. Marinduque is known for its **Moriones festival**, an animated Easter tradition featuring masked men dressed like Roman soldiers (see box, p.197). If you plan to visit during Holy Week then you should book ahead.

Marinduque has had its share of problems. When copper mining was begun here in 1969, many thought it was the dawn of a new era. Sadly, the dream ended in disaster and recrimination as waste from disused pits flowed into the island's rivers on two separate occasions, destroying agricultural land, the livelihood of the locals and marine life – which is still trying to recover.

Boac

BOAC ("bow-ak") is an orderly, compact town with neat streets and low-rise buildings laid out around a central plaza. The area around the cathedral has numerous typical Filipino *bahay na buto* (wooden houses), the windows boasting carved wooden shutters instead of glass and the balconies exploding with bougainvillea and frangipani. Many of these houses were built in the nineteenth century and are now a photogenic, if faded, reminder of a style of architecture that is rapidly disappearing.

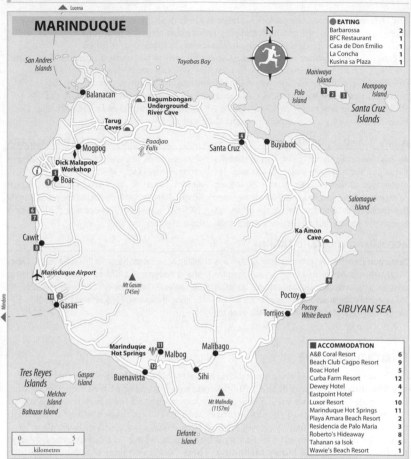

▲ Lucena

MARINDUQUE

N

San Andres Islands

Tayabas Bay

● Balanacan

Bagumbongan Underground River Cave

Tarug Caves

Mogpog

Paadjao Falls

Dick Malapote Workshop

ⓘ

● Boac

6
7

Cawit

8

✈ Marinduque Airport

Mt Gasan (745m)

Gasan

10 2

Tres Reyes Islands

Gaspar Island

Buenavista

Melchor Island

Baltazar Island

Marinduque Hot Springs

13 ● Malbog

12

Sihi

Mt Malindig (1157m)

Elefante Island

Maniwaya Island

Polo Island

1 2 3

Mompong Island

Santa Cruz Islands

Santa Cruz ● Buyabod

4

Salomague Island

Ka Amon Cave

9

Poctoy

Torrijos ●

Poctoy White Beach

SIBUYAN SEA

Malibago

0   5
kilometres

The cathedral

High Town • Daily 5am–6pm

Construction of Boac's atmospheric Spanish Gothic **cathedral** started in 1580 in honour of the Blessed Virgin of Immediate Succour, and was used in its early years as a refuge from pirate attacks. Most of the original main structure, including the red-brick facade and the belfry, is well preserved and there's a pleasant garden outside. Look out above the main doors for a stone niche containing a statue of the Blessed Virgin, enshrined here in 1792. Devotees say it is the most miraculous statue in the country and tell of blind people who have regained their sight after praying fervently beneath it day and night.

Marinduque National Museum

Boac Plaza • Mon–Fri 9am–4pm • P20 • ☎ 0926 122 3555

The small **Marinduque National Museum** is located in a lovely Spanish colonial building that previously served as a prison, a boys' school and a courthouse. The museum briefly charts the island's geological history, before introducing more recent history including evidence of pre-Spanish trade with China. Displays include sixteenth-century Chinese storage stoneware jars with dragon designs that were found on the seabed by Gaspar Island, as well as early musical instruments used during special events and celebrations. There is also a collection of Moriones masks, along with descriptive captions tracing the festival's roots.

Marinduque's west coast

The **west coast** from Boac south to **Gasan** and a little beyond boasts a number of **resorts**. The beaches are pebbly but they do offer fine views of the sunset and across the sea towards Mindoro in the distance. The resorts are often full for the Moriones festival (see box below) and at Christmas, but at any other time you might find that you are the only guest. South of Gasan lies the sleepy town of **Buenavista**, where jeepneys usually terminate – so you'll have to wait here for onward transport.

Gasan

It's much better to stay in the nearby resorts than in **GASAN** itself, though the modern **St Joseph Catholic Church** is worth a look for its views, and the town has a few small souvenir shops selling Moriones-themed products and tasty arrowroot biscuits (which, along with *bibingka* rice cakes, are a Marinduque speciality).

St Joseph Catholic Church
Quezon Ave, Brgy 1, Gasan Poblacion

Perched on a hillside, **St Joseph Catholic Church** offers wonderful **bay views** from its leafy back terrace, especially at sunset. Built in the first decade of the new millennium, the church features a beautiful thick wooden door carved by a renowned Mogpog sculptor. The intricate ceiling was designed to resemble a palm leaf, while the inner side walls are lined with coconut shell dividers. At the back are the remnants of the old church, from 1609.

Tres Reyes Islands
Boat from Sitio Castillo, Gasan P40 (15min); or arrange a private island-hopping trip with your resort (P1500)

The beautiful **Tres Reyes Islands** – popularly known as **Baltazar**, **Melchor** and **Gaspar** after the biblical Three Kings – lie a few kilometres offshore of Gasan. There is some good **scuba diving** here, which can be arranged (see p.200) or at one of the resorts. On the far side of Gaspar Island there's a white-sand beach with good coral for **snorkelling**; a small fishing community is located on the eastern tip of the island, but there's no formal accommodation.

Marinduque hot springs
Sitio Mainit, Brgy Malbog, Km3 • Daily 8am–10pm • Day rate P50, overnight P1600 • ☎ 0917 382 9416 • Tricycle from Buenavista P40 (10min)

Located in spacious grounds, the inviting **Marinduque hot spring** pools are a pleasant spot to while away a few hours. There are a couple of large pools, as well as three smaller pools that can be rented out privately (P1000/5hr – call in advance). There are picnic huts, too.

MORIONES FESTIVAL

The **Moriones festival** celebrates the life of Longinus, the Roman soldier who pierced Christ's side during the Crucifixion. Blood from the wound spattered Longinus's blind eye, which was immediately healed. Converted on the spot, he later attested to the Resurrection and, refusing to recant, was executed. The Marinduqueyo version of this tale is colourful and bizarre, involving fanciful masked figures dressed as centurions chasing Longinus around town and through nearby fields. Several Moriones pageants are staged in Marinduque during **Holy Week**, with extra events added in recent years for the benefit of tourists (see ⓦ marinduque.gov.ph for more information). Although the festival originated in Mogpog, and other towns including Santa Cruz have their own versions, these days the major Moriones celebrations are in **Boac**.

4

Mount Malindig

Enquire at the tourist office in Boac or at the barangay hall in Sihi, Buenavista to organize a compulsory guide (P500/day)

The highest peak of Marinduque is **Mount Malindig**, a 1157m volcano that's considered dormant. It's possible to climb to the summit; the hike can be done in a day starting from the barangay of Sihi in Buenavista, with the ascent taking about three and a half hours and the descent significantly less.

Marinduque's east coast

Marinduque's **east coast** offers a number of wonderful secluded beaches, the nicest of which is **Poctoy White Beach**. There are fewer resorts on this stretch of coast than on the west, and it's well worth spending a couple of days.

Poctoy White Beach

P25 environmental fee • Jeepneys between Santa Cruz and Torrijos stop off at Poctoy (hourly; 1hr 30min; P40)

Just 2km from the barangay of Torrijos is **Poctoy White Beach**, where the sand is not as pale as the name suggests but is still much better than the pebbles on the west coast. The views across the bay to Mount Malindig can also be spectacular. The stretch of beach is packed with huts which can be rented for the day, and it has a small market where you can buy the catch of the day by weight; pay a little more and you can have it cooked.

Ka Amon Cave

Brgy Bonliw • Compulsory guides (P150) can be organized at Bonliw Barangay Hall • ☎ 0926 648 7033 • Jeepneys from Torrijos to Brgy Bonliw (hourly; 20min; P20)

Eleven kilometres north of Torrijos is the **Ka Amon Cave**, a series of seven chambers that were once pre-Hispanic funeral grottoes – you can still see skeletal remains and broken pottery as you enter the first chamber. Chambers six and seven are off limits to visitors in order to preserve the cave habitat and fauna, which includes bats and birds. You'll still be able to see about one hundred bats (more during the rainy season) in chamber five, where tours end.

Santa Cruz and around

If you're interested in exploring the caves and islands in the northeast of Marinduque, **SANTA CRUZ** is the best base for a day or two. That said, the town is unmemorable – the only sights a whitewashed Spanish-era church and the dilapidated wooden convent next to it – and the narrow streets in the centre are choked with tricycles and jeepneys from dawn to dusk. Be prepared for noise.

Santa Cruz Islands

Boats leave from Buyabod port, 5km east of Santa Cruz by tricycle (P120; 15min); contact Edwin Romasanta to organize a boat (☎ 0920 609 9279) for island-hopping (P2000–3500)

The islands of Maniwaya, Mompong and Polo, collectively known as the **Santa Cruz Islands**, make for a wonderful day-trip. The closest to the mainland is **Polo**, which is rich in wetland forests and transient birds, local macaque monkeys and fruit bats. While the island is dotted with a few pleasant beaches, it's a good idea to head further on to **Maniwaya**, which boasts a long stretch of fine sand lined with a few accommodation options.

On the northeastern side of the island is the spectacular **Palad Sandbar**, a stretch of coral sands with crystal-clear waters that appears only during low tide. The furthest of the islands is **Mompong**, with its distinctive Ungab sedimentary rock formation that acts as a natural bridge – the waters here are emerald green, and it's a wonderful spot for a swim.

Bagumbongan Underground River Cave

Brgy San Isidro • P300 • Entry fee includes compulsory guides, who can be arranged at the tourist information centre on the way to the cave • Jeepneys from Santa Cruz (daily 11am & 4pm; 1hr; P28); tricycles from Santa Cruz (45min; P800 including waiting time)

About 24km west of Santa Cruz, the 2km-long **Bagumbongan Underground River Cave** is the longest underground river in the province. There are some fixed ropes and spots where water reaches chest height. Helmets, lights and gloves are provided. Guides will lead you inside the cave for about 1km, ending up at a cascading waterfall of about 10m before turning back; they can also take experienced cavers all the way to the other side. Note that you won't be able to explore the cave during heavy rains.

Mogpog

In the northwest corner of the island, the little town of **MOGPOG** doesn't offer much for visitors, although it is renowned across the island for being the birthplace of the **Moriones festival** (see box, p.197) and holds its own festivities – smaller in scale than those in Boac – during Holy Week. The word Mogpog comes from the tagalog word *mag-aapog*, which roughly translates as "abundance of lime" and the area around town is indeed rich in limestone, with a number of **caves** to explore.

Dick Malapote workshop

Brgy Janagdong, 1km west of Mogpog • ☎ 0939 468 2365 • Tricycle from Mogpog P40 (10min), then ask around – locals know where Dick Malapote lives

One of the most famous Moriones **costume makers**, Dick Malapote has been creating centurion outfits for more than 25 years, selling whole sets of armour for as much as P15,000. He welcomes visitors at his workshop but doesn't speak much English, so the best bet, if you are interested, is to enquire at the provincial tourist office near Boac (see p.200), who can arrange for someone to accompany you.

Tarug Caves

Brgy Tarug, Bocboc • By donation to local guides (P50) – ask around at the village you pass through on the way to the cave • Jeepney from Mogpog towards Santa Cruz (every 30min; 30min; P20), followed by a 1.5km (45min) trek; ask the driver where to get off

The **Tarug Caves** are actually one enormous cave with three chambers set inside a 300m-tall limestone spire that's barely 3m wide at the top. You can climb to the top, where the reward is a panoramic view of the Bondoc peninsula to the east and the Tablas Strait to the west.

Paadjao Falls

Brgy Bocboc, 10km from Mogpog • Jeepney from Mogpog (daily 9am & 3pm; 30min; P20); tricycle P400 return including waiting time (30min)

About ten minutes' uphill walk from the main road, nestled within coconut groves, are the gently cascading **Paadjao Falls**. There are a series of pools here, perfect for a little dip – the largest is at the foot of the uppermost fall. Join the locals sitting on the rocks, letting the strong jet stream of water massage your back and shoulders.

| **ARRIVAL AND DEPARTURE** | **MARINDUQUE** |

By plane At the time of writing Marinduque airport was closed for renovations; flights to Manila (45min) are due to resume when it reopens.

By boat There are ferries from Lucena to Balanacan port with Montenegro Lines (departures 4am, noon, 4pm & midnight; 3hr; P280); and with Starhorse (departures 2.30am, 3.30am, 7.30am, 10.30am, 11.30pm, 3.30pm, 9.30pm and 11.30pm; 3hr; P260). Jeepneys from Boac meet incoming ferries to Balanacan (1hr; P50). Heading back to

Lucena, Starhorse ferries depart at 5am, 7.30am, 11.30am, noon, 2.30pm, 3.30pm and 7.30pm, while Montenegro Lines returns at 8am, 10am, 12pm and 8pm. There are outrigger services between Gasan on Marinduque and Pinamalayan in Mindoro (daily 8am; 3–4hr; P265). Daily bangkas connect Buyabod port, which lies east of Santa Cruz, to Catanauan in Quezon province (daily 11am; 3hr; P200).

By bus Jack Liner travels between Boac and Manila using the roll-on-roll-off ferry (daily 8pm; 8–9hr).

4

GETTING AROUND

By jeepney No jeepneys loop the entire island; if you're planning on travelling to multiple destinations you'll have to change. On the west and north coasts they run from Boac–Gasan–Buenavista, and Boac–Mogpog–Santa Cruz, while on the east coast there are services from Santa Cruz–Torrijos. To get to Buenavista from Torrijos you'll have to take a jeepney to Malibago and change there. It is possible to travel around the entire island by jeepney in two days, but four or five would be more comfortable, particularly since if you miss the last jeepney (most services stop at 4–5pm), you can easily find yourself stranded.

By van Easier than travelling by jeepney is renting a van for around P3500/day. Most accommodation options can help organize this, or enquire at the provincial tourist office near Boac (see below).

INFORMATION AND ACTIVITIES

Tourist information The helpful provincial tourist office (Mon–Fri 9am–5pm; ☎042 332 1177), in the Capitol Building complex on the road between Boac and the airport, has a handful of leaflets, but once on the road be prepared for a lack of reliable information.

Banks and exchange There are banks with ATMs in Boac, including Land Bank, RCBC and PNB, all along Reyes St. RCBC and PNB also have branches in Santa Cruz.

Scuba diving There are no dive shops on the island, but keen scuba divers should contact Freedom Dellosa (☎0920 223 0904, ✉coraldiver@hotmail.com). He can arrange equipment rental, as well as open-water courses (P14,000).

ACCOMMODATION

BOAC

Boac Hotel Deogracias St at Nepomuceno St ☎042 332 1121, ✉theboachotel@yahoo.com. This big yellow building is the oldest hotel in town, and its antiques and wooden furniture lend it an appealing atmosphere. The single rooms with just one single bed allegedly sleep two, although they are tiny, even just for one; you're better off going for a deluxe (P1200) with a double bed. The cheapest rooms are fan only, while standard rooms and above have a/c. Limited wi-fi. 📶 P500

Tahanan sa Isok Canovas St ☎042 332 1231, 🌐tahanansaisok.com. The entrance of this welcoming hotel has a homely feel, with a glass cabinet with books, a piano and a few religious knick-knacks. The staircase leading up to the accommodation is lined with potted plants, and the rooms are great value, with chocolate-coloured furniture, although some of the single beds are tiny. There's also a pleasant pool. Limited wi-fi. 📶 P1000

THE WEST COAST

★**A&B Coral Resort** Brgy Balaring ☎042 332 0121 or ☎0947 556 8986, 🌐abcoralresort.webnode.fr. This lovely little place has warm and welcoming a/c rooms with private bath in a building overlooking the sea. The plant-festooned garden with a large pomelo tree is dotted with knick-knacks, including old carriage wheels, while the lounge area features fibre deck chairs and wicker sofas. There are also two outdoor jacuzzis. 📶 P1800

Eastpoint Hotel Brgy Balaring ☎042 332 2229, 🌐eastpointhotel.com. This small, modern-looking hotel by the beachfront offers a range of clean and comfortable rooms, including family ones (P2000). It's worth upgrading to a twin (P1200) or executive (P1500) room, as standards are the only ones without a/c, hot showers and cable TV. P1000

Luxor Resort Brgy Pangi ☎042 332 0562. Some 1.5km north of Gasan, with simple, bright-yellow concrete cottages set along a leafy pathway. All have a/c, flatscreen TV and private bathroom. The welcoming shaded area by the sea is the perfect spot to enjoy a sundowner, and there's a restaurant serving excellent artisan Italian pizzas. Limited wi-fi. 📶 P1500

Roberto's Hideaway Cawit ☎0917 832 3148 or ☎0915 285 2643, 🌐robertoshideawaybeachresort.com. This charming palm-shaded resort has a range of a/c cottages sleeping from two to four people, decorated in varying styles from native Filipino to Mediterranean and Asian fusion. There's also a beachfront bar area and karaoke room. P1800

BUENAVISTA AND AROUND

Curba Farm Resort Brgy Uno ☎0948 714 3488, 🌐facebook.com/CurbaFarmResort. There's a cowboy theme going on here, with framed guns and Wild West memorabilia decorating the premises. The four rooms are on a grassy slope overlooking an inviting pool with an artificial waterfall; there's also a billiards table, and an attached restaurant/bar with outdoor seating serving local and international dishes, including mixed seafood (P185) and T-bone steaks (P349). Rates include breakfast. Wi-fi in public areas. 📶 P1200

Marinduque Hot Springs Sitio Mainit, Malbog, Km3 ☎0917 382 9416. Set in lovely verdant grounds, this resort offers a series of rooms connected by a pebbly pathway dotted with wooden statuettes; the spacious family rooms (P2600) with two double beds are great value, though the cheaper a/c doubles and twins (P1600) are not as appealing. You can also camp, though you'll need to pay the P70 entrance fee to the springs. Camping P300, doubles P1300

POCTOY

★**Beach Club Cagpo Resort** Brgy Cagpo ☎0921 993

2537, ⓦ beachclubcagpo.com. Located on a lovely stretch of sand, the blue and white rooms take their inspiration from Greece, with rough whitewashed walls and paintings of Greek islands. There's a welcoming a/c cottage (P1500), as well as one standard double with fan and a deluxe fan room (P1250). The restaurant serves international dishes prepared with fresh herbs from the garden, including great home-made burgers (P165), vegetable curry (P140) and wood-fired pizzas (P330). There's also an eight-bed dorm with lockers; blankets and pillows are not supplied. Dorms P350, doubles P1100

SANTA CRUZ

Dewey Hotel Brgy Maharlika ⓣ 042 660 7904. This hotel is set in two green and yellow buildings, and offers clean rooms with mustard-yellow tiles; there are also spacious suites (P2500) with two double beds, and a little rooftop pool with a couple of sunloungers. Meals are available on request. P1400

SANTA CRUZ ISLANDS

Playa Amara Beach Resort Maniwaya Island ⓣ 0928 507 0362, ⓦ bit.ly/PlayaAmara. One of the newer options on the island, this relaxed resort offers doubles with fan (and some with a/c; P2500) in the main building, plus large family rooms (P3500) and beachfront nipa huts with balconies (P1500). There's also a bar and restaurant. Electricity is only from 3–8pm. P1200

★**Residencia De Palo Maria** Maniwaya Island ⓣ 0998 539 4726, ⓔ residenciadepalomaria@yahoo .com. One of the best accommodation options on the island, offering comfortable a/c rooms with cable TV (P2300), as well as cheaper native cottages that are equally welcoming, and even feature their own little outdoor patio with flatscreen TV. There's a breezy restaurant by the swimming pool serving local dishes (P160–250), and the resort offers all manner of watersports, including banana boats, diving, waterskiing and kayaking. P1500

Wawie's Beach Resort Maniwaya Island ⓣ 0906 751 2497, ⓦ bit.ly/WawiesResort. Set on a lovely stretch of white-sand beach, backed by shady palms, *Wawie's* offers a range of native rooms with fans, as well as larger family rooms (P1500). Those on a budget can opt for 12-hr native-style *kubo* huts (P500) or tents on the beach. Can get very crowded. Camping P300, doubles P1000

EATING AND DRINKING

4

BOAC

BFC Restaurant Brgy Malusak ⓣ 0921 298 4688. This cosy little restaurant features dark brick walls and wooden tables, and gets particularly busy at lunchtime. The menu includes the usual Filipino staples, including beef steak (P120), chicken dishes (P60) and chop suey (P75). Daily 7am–7pm.

★**Casa de Don Emilio** Mercader St ⓣ 042 332 1699. The best restaurant in town, set in a beautiful Spanish colonial building with polished hardwood floors. The owner, a keen musician, has a fascinating collection of old instruments, including an antique double bass, trombone, trumpet and sax – all displayed along the restaurant's walls. The restaurant specializes in coconut dishes – try the native chicken cooked in coconut milk (P225). Daily 10am–9pm.

La Concha Brgy Malusak ⓣ 042 332 2854. This no-frills self-service joint with menus plastered over the walls offers standard local food for about P75 per dish, as well as pizzas (P70); there's also a Japanese section featuring vegetable tempura (P60). Daily 6am–9pm.

Kusina sa Plaza Mercader St ⓣ 042 332 1699. Popular restaurant on Boac's main square, displaying a range of Filipino dishes that will cost about P100 per meal. The attached coffee shop (with free wi-fi) serves pizzas (P350) and pasta (P75). Daily 7am–8pm.

GASAN

Barbarossa San José St ⓣ 0908 377 6656. This German-owned place is where the island's handful of expats regularly meet, gathering over refreshing ice-cold beer in frozen mugs (P88). The menu features a range of international dishes including bockwurst sausage (P250), pizza (P300) and spaghetti bolognaise (P175). There are occasional live bands. Daily 10am–9pm.

Daet and around

The capital of Camarines Norte, **DAET**, 200km southeast of Manila, is overrun with tricycles, but the nearby coastline has more than its fair share of unspoilt beaches and islands; the fickle waves at **Bagasbas Beach** and **San Miguel Bay** are a particular attraction for surfers.

Daet's busy little central plaza is a popular meeting place in the evenings. One block north is the 1950s **Provincial Capitol**, in front of which Kalayaan (Freedom) Park features the tallest statue of **José Rizal** outside Manila. Erected in 1899, this was the first monument to Rizal in the country and set the trend for thousands of others in plazas across the archipelago.

Bagasbas Beach

Tricycle from Daet P40 (20min)

The waves that crash in from the Pacific onto wild and windswept **Bagasbas Beach**, 4km northeast of Daet, are sometimes big enough for **surfing** (see box below), particularly between November and March. In fact, the whole area of coast east of Daet has become something of a surfers' hangout, though the shore can be pretty much deserted by all but stray dogs on weekdays. Despite its reputation, the area is a little run-down and strong winds have ripped through most of the hotel and restaurant signs. Though not in surfing season, the beach gets more lively during the summer months of June and July, when the locals are on holiday.

ARRIVAL AND INFORMATION

By bus Buses arriving in Daet stop at the edge of the city on the National Highway, from where it's less than 2km into town; plenty of tricycles travel the route for P30. Philtranco, DLTB and Superlines travel to Manila (roughly hourly; 7–8hr), stopping off in Altimoan (4–5hr) and Lucena (5–6hr).

By van Regular vans connect Naga to Daet (every 30min;

DAET AND AROUND

2hr; P180).

Information The municipal and provincial tourist offices are both in Daet on J. Pimentel St at Magallanes Iraya St (both Mon–Fri 8am–5pm; provincial ☎054 721 3087; municipal ☎054 441 6163). There's also a tourist information centre on Magallanes Iraya St (Mon–Fri 8am–5pm, Sat 8am–noon; no phone).

ACCOMMODATION

DAET

Francesco's Suzara St at Dimasalang ☎054 440 0031, ✉francescoinn@yahoo.com. This small hotel, situated above a Japanese-style restaurant, has just four spacious, modern and comfortable rooms that all come with tea-making facilities. King (P3000) and queen (P2500) rooms are larger than the regular twins and have double beds. Rates include breakfast. Wi-fi is available in public areas. There's also a restaurant serving typical Filipino dishes. Wi-fi in public areas. 🛜 **P2000**

Hotel Formosa Vinzons Ave, Brgy Lag-On ☎054 571 3566, ✉hotelformosa@yahoo.com. This is one of the city's best options, offering neat and tidy tiled rooms with flat-screen TV and wooden furniture. Some rooms face the interior and as a result may be a bit dark, but the premises are kept spick-and-span and there's free welcome tea upon arrival. 🛜 **P2000**

BAGASBAS BEACH

Bagasbas Lighthouse Hotel Resort ☎054 731 0355, 🌐bagasbaslighthouse.ph. On the seafront, this is by far the area's best option, with stylish accommodation in deluxe rooms (P2750) or cheaper converted trailer rooms. There are also "backpacker rooms" with bunks. The poolside restaurant serves Filipino favourites and Bicol specialities (see box, p.214) including Bicol Express and *laing*. Mains P155. Wi-fi in lobby only. 🛜 Dorms **P550**, doubles **P1750**

Surfer's Dine-Inn ☎0916 475 9053, ✉surfers dineinn@yahoo.com. This laidback place offers a few simple rooms off a paved walkway; the concrete rooms (P700) are acceptable if you're just here to catch a few waves, although you'll probably have to fend your way through a cobweb or two. There are also a couple of fan-cooled nipa huts. The restaurant serves inexpensive sharing dishes (around P200). Wi-fi in public areas. 🛜 **P500**

EATING

DAET

KFisher 1101 V. Basit St ☎0917 529 0357. Though the

decor screams cheap American diner, this places serves tasty local food. The speciality is seafood, ranging from

---

SURFING AND KITESURFING ON BAGASBAS

Several places on **Bagasbas Beach** rent out surfboards and offer tuition. **Experienced surfers** who want to look beyond Bagasbas should ask about the breaks in nearby **San Miguel Bay**, which often has very good waves close to the town of Mercedes and around the seven islands known as the Siete Pecados.

Hang Loose ☎0921 251 8748. Friendly outfit. The owners are a wealth of local info and offer surfboard rental for P200/hr and lessons for P200/hr. Daily 6am–7pm.
Mike's Kites ☎6399 5458 9995, 🌐mikes-kites.com.

kitesurfing, starting at US$65 for a day's equipment rental or US$60 for a 2hr introductory session. If the wind and waves are not cooperating, they also rent out sea kayaks and organize island-hopping trips. Daily 5am–2am.

pusit (squid; P75) to sushi (P298) and sashimi (P175); there's wi-fi too. Daily 10am–10pm.

Ksarap Vinzons Ave 📞 054 440 5151. This very atmospheric bamboo-built restaurant, surrounded by leafy plants, fountains and colourful lanterns, is one of the best in Daet. Savoury dishes include empanadas (P20), sizzling tofu with mushrooms (P140) or fish steaks (P80); most people round things off with the ubiquitous *halo-halo* (P70). Daily 9am–10pm.

BAGASBAS BEACH

Kusina ni Angel Run by the well-spoken Angel, this no-frills restaurant has a nipa roof and tables clustered together both indoors and out. It's great for breakfasts (P220), and also has a good range of typical Filipino meat, poultry (P260) and seafood dishes (P280) to share. Daily 8am–10pm.

Leo's Cuisine 📞 0917 315 5531. Good option right on the beachfront, with tables facing the ocean as well as an indoor area decorated with the owner's surfboards and surfing awards and a glass cabinet displaying all manner of knick-knacks. The fish- and seafood-based menu includes sizzling Thai squid (P240) and calamari (P240). Daily 9am–10pm.

Camarines Sur province

Lying at the heart of Bicol, the laidback province of **Camarines Sur**, with a spectacular stretch of rugged coastline to the east, is rich in natural beauty, with secluded beaches and peaceful lakeside spots. The region is fast becoming a prime destination for young adventure sports enthusiasts, many of whom flock here from Manila to wakeboard at the **CamSur Watersports Complex**.

Naga

Centrally located in Camarines Sur, the lively university city of **NAGA** was established in 1578 by Spanish conquistador Pedro de Chavez. Although there are a couple of sights in the city itself, its place on the tourist map is due mainly to the success of the **CamSur Watersports Complex**, or CWC, in nearby Pili (see p.206). Naga offers an alternative base, with a fun nightlife scene thanks in part to its large student population. Things are particularly lively during the nine-day **Peñafrancia festival** in September, held in honour of Our Lady of Peñafrancia, when as many as a million devotees and tourists flood the streets. The city is also home to three impressive holy sites – the **Peñafrancia Basilica Minore**, **Our Lady of Peñafrancia Shrine** and the **Naga Metropolitan Cathedral**.

Naga centre is focused on two main squares, **Plaza Rizal** and **Plaza Quince Martires**, surrounded by fast-food restaurants, banks, convenience stores and pharmacies. The main drag, **Elias Angeles Street**, runs north to south; to the east, along Panganiban Drive, is the Naga River. Swish **Magsaysay Avenue**, to the northeast, running from Avenue Square mall to City Hall, has many of Naga's best bars and restaurants, as well as a handful of hotels.

University of Nueva Caceres Museum

J. Hernandez Ave • Mon–Fri 8am–noon & 2–5pm, Sat 8am–noon • Free • 📞 054 472 6100

Run by an enthusiastic curator who will willingly talk you through the displays, the **University of Nueva Caceres Museum** gives an overview on the city's history from the ancient period to the present day. There is a very concise section on the Arab and Muslim influence in the southern Philippines, and details on Chinese trade. Highlights include Chinese porcelain and earthenware dishes that were bartered for local items, as well as local dresses showing how three hundred years of Spanish rule influenced the attire of Bicolanos.

Holy Rosary Minor Seminary

Elias Angeles St • **Archeological Museum** Mon–Fri 8am–5pm, Sat & Sun by appointment only with the curator (📞 0919 592 0724) • P20 • 📞 054 473 8297

One of the country's oldest institutes for higher learning, the beautiful red-brick complex of the **Holy Rosary Minor Seminary** was built in 1785 as a vocation house. It was declared

4

a National Historical Landmark in 1988, and still houses the dormitories of priests and active seminaries. It also holds the small, privately owned **Archeological Museum**, which displays a lovely collection of trade wares from China, Vietnam and Thailand, along with ancient relics – including the country's most extensive collection of primary burial jars from the Bicol region, dating back to 200 AD. By far the most unusual displays are dinosaur eggs from the Mongolian Gobi Desert, dating back 146–165 million years.

Metropolitan Cathedral

Elias Angeles St • Daily 7am–5pm

The **Metropolitan Cathedral** is the largest church in Southern Luzon and the seat of the Archdiocese of Caceres. The original structure was built in 1595 near the Naga River; after being destroyed by fire in 1758, it was rebuilt on this site, only to be damaged by a typhoon in 1856, and subsequently an earthquake in 1887. The church was built in Romanesque Baroque style using Spanish Royal funds – note the Spanish royal seal above the door.

At daybreak on the opening day of the **Peñafrancia festival**, an image of the Virgin – known as "Ina" (Bicolano for mother) – is taken from its permanent home at the Peñafrancia Basilica Minore, east of town, and carried to the cathedral by barefoot devotees (*voyadores*); she then spends the nine days of the novena at the cathedral before being returned to her permanent home.

Our Lady of Peñafrancia Shrine

Peñafrancia Ave • Daily 7am–5pm

Originally built by Spanish expat Miguel de Covarrubias from nipa and bamboo, **Our Lady of Peñafrancia Shrine** was reconstructed in stone around 1710, and reworked again by Bishop Isrido Arevalo around 1750. Today it boasts a charming Spanish-style

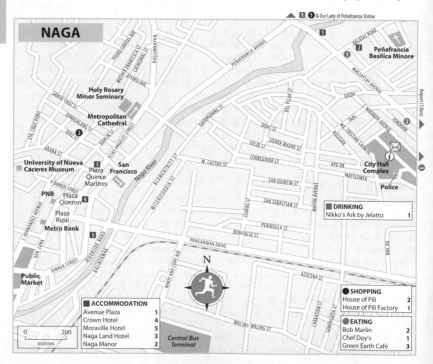

red-brick and yellow-painted exterior with wide archways. The church used to be the home of the "Ina" Peñafrancia Virgin statue before the new Peñafrancia Basilica Minore (see below) was built.

Peñafrancia Basilica Minore

Balatas Rd • Daily 7am–5pm

The **Peñafrancia Basilica Minore** is the newest of Naga's three religious sites: construction began in 1976 and wasn't completed until 1981. It was built as the new home for the "Ina" Peñafrancia statue of the Virgin Mary, which dates from 1710 and was commissioned by Miguel de Covarrubias, who also built the Our Lady of Peñafrancia Shrine (see opposite). A huge green- and yellow-painted structure, surrounded by sculpted gardens and palm trees, the basilica's facade is covered by a huge stained-glass window, said to be the largest in the Philippines. Created by stained-glass artist and mural painter Pancho Piano, it depicts the Peñafrancia Virgin surrounded by clouds, angels and religious figures. Inside, you'll find more stained-glass windows, as well as a stained-glass central dome and a beautiful altarpiece.

ARRIVAL AND INFORMATION NAGA

By plane Naga airport is 12km east of town, in the provincial capital Pili; taxis connect the city to the airport (P350; 15min).

By bus Buses to Naga arrive at the Central Bus Terminal in Central Business District 2 (CB2) on Ninoy and Cory Ave, which is across the river to the south of the town centre, close to the SM Mall; you'll have to take a tricycle from here (10min; P8) to the centre. Many companies run the route to Manila, including DLTB (6 daily; 8–10hr), stopping off in Atimonan (for Quezon National Park; 6hr) and Lucena (6hr). Most buses to Manila depart between 6 and 10pm. There are also local buses to Legazpi (every 30min; 3hr) and Daraga (every 15min; 3hr), although for both these destinations it's quicker to catch a van.

By van Vans arrive and leave from opposite the Central Bus Terminal in Central Business District 2.

Departures Daraga (hourly; 2hr; P130); Legazpi (every 30min; 2hr; P140); San José (for Sabang port on the Caramoan Peninsula; hourly; 1hr 30min; P150); Tabaco (every 30min; 2hr; P180).

Tourist information The Naga City Arts, Culture and Tourism Office is in the DOLE Building, City Hall Complex, J. Miranda Ave (Mon–Fri 8am–5pm; ☎054 478 3987, ⓦnagax.com). Staff can provide city maps and organize traditional Bicolano cooking courses (P1000/day), as well as help organize guides for Mt Isarog (see p.208).

ACCOMMODATION

Many hotels, particularly the budget ones, are fully booked during the **Peñafrancia festival** so make sure to plan ahead if you're coming at this time. For the rest of the year, finding a room shouldn't be a problem. Unless otherwise stated, the **wi-fi** at most of the hotels listed here can be pretty unreliable, and may only be available in public areas.

Avenue Plaza Magsaysay Ave ☎054 473 9999, ⓦtheavenueplazahotel.com. In a class of its own in Naga, with rooms of an international standard, along with a swimming pool, gym and sauna, and an excellent restaurant, featuring fusion and international cuisine. The hotel is on Naga's entertainment strip, with plenty of restaurants and bars on its doorstep, and there's low-key piano music in the lobby in the evenings. ≈ **P3990**

Crown Hotel P. Burgos St ☎054 473 1845. A decent option right in the centre of Naga, with a range of different rooms. Standards (with a double bed) are spacious and simple, while the deluxe rooms (P2250) have better furniture. Suite A (P5400) is a big jump up, featuring a comfortable living area and a king-size bed. There are a couple of 24hr restaurants offering a range of Chinese dishes. ≈ **P1350**

Moraville Hotel Dinaga St ☎054 473 1247, ⓦmoraville.com.ph. A very reasonable option with appealing rooms at bargain prices, this place has a few different branches throughout the city. The rock walls and chintz may be a bit too much in some rooms, but overall the accommodation is clean and comfortable. Expect to pay a bit more for a/c rooms (P1100). If you're on a budget and only in town for a night, you might want to opt for the 12hr rate (P350). **P800**

Naga Land Hotel Elias Angeles St ☎054 473 2111, ⓦthenagalandhotel.com. With its refined lobby, fancy cake shop and grand staircase, this place seems like a very upmarket hotel, but the upper floors and rooms don't quite match up. Standard rooms are simple and comfortable, but have tired furniture, while the deluxe rooms (P1700) have nicer decor. **P1200**

Naga Manor Balatas Rd 054 881 0426, thenagamanor@gmail.com. Housed in a lovely cream mansion, this place is well worth the extra spend. An elegant marble staircase takes you up to a handful of spacious, beautifully decorated rooms, some with private balconies. P2243

EATING

Naga's local specialities include **log-log kinalas** (noodle soup with pork, liver sauce and roasted garlic) often served with toasted **siopao** (pork buns), and anything made with pili nuts. The town's restaurants are mostly along Magsaysay Ave, but there are also plenty of fast-food chain places in the centre.

★**Bob Marlin** Magsaysay Ave 054 473 1339, bobmarlin.ph. This popular restaurant has an atmospheric outdoor seating area with colourful low lighting and a roof of native reed and reclaimed wooden pallets; there's also an indoor area with wall-mounted plates signed by famous visitors, praising the restaurant's award-winning crispy *pata* (deep-fried pork leg; P429 for five people). As the name suggests, the music is laidback, with lots of reggae and ska. Daily 11am–midnight.

Chef Doy's Cereza Compound, Magsaysay Ave 054 478 2519. Doy rustles up imaginative Filipino fusion dishes that include sautéed baby squid with garlic, bay leaves and black pepper (P199) and boneless milkfish with vegetables in guava broth (P212). Dishes are large enough to share, and you can either eat alfresco on the patio or in the dark interior, where the walls are plastered with customers' notes and scribbles. Daily 10am–10.30pm.

★**Green Earth Café** Villa Sorabella Subdivision, Concepcion Grande 054 475 5018. A truly unusual find in this country of meat-lovers, this excellent vegetarian health-food café serves creative dishes prepared with fresh local ingredients; the bread (P40) is home-made, as is the excellent dairy-free banana mango ice cream (P55). The wide menu includes veggie burgers, rice-noodle pad Thai (P185), *pako* salad (a type of fern mixed with salted eggs and tangy vinegar; P165) and the bestselling club sandwich of home-made tofu and grilled vegetables (P175). It's 4km east of Naga; to get here catch a jeepney heading for "Centro Concepcion" (every 30min; 20min; P8), and its the third turning on the right off Soriano Ave. Mon–Thurs & Sun 10am–9pm.

4

DRINKING AND NIGHTLIFE

Magsaysay Ave is the centre of the city's nightlife, with many of the more expensive restaurants and a few bars. The *Bob Marlin* restaurant (see above) is also a great drinking spot.

Nikko's Ark by Jelatto Peñafrancia Ave at Magsaysay Ave 054 472 5111. Turn the corner just after Magsaysay Ave bridge and you'll see a huge white ship. Climb up to the top and you'll find a busy bar with live music on weekends. They have a good range of cocktails (P150) and also serve food such as pizzas (P230) and chicken satay (P160). Downstairs are a range of karaoke rooms. Daily 5pm–2am.

SHOPPING

House of Pili T. Enrile Building, P. Diaz St 054 811 2520. More conveniently located than the factory, this small shop is located right in the centre of town and is the best place to pick up all manner of pili nut products, from tarts and sweets to cookies. Daily 9am–8pm.

House of Pili Factory 178 Jacana St, RJ Village, Haring, Canaman 054 474 5160, jempastries.com. Some 3km north of town, this is a family-run pili production factory where, during working hours (Mon–Fri 8am–5pm), it's possible to watch staff coating, glazing and packaging all manner of pili products – which you can then buy at the attached shop. If you can't make it out to the factory, note that there's also a shop in town. Daily 7am–8pm.

DIRECTORY

Banks There are plenty of banks, including Metro Bank, BPI and PNB on Plaza Rizal.

Police City Hall Complex, Miranda Ave (24hr hotline 054 472 3000).

Post City Hall Complex, Miranda Ave (Mon–Fri 8am–5pm).

CamSur Watersports Complex (CWC)

Provincial Capitol Complex, Brgy Cadlan, Pili • Mon 8am–9pm, Tues–Sun 8.30am–9pm • Prices vary – P370 for a half-day on the main course, plus P750 for wakeboard rental and P90 for helmet and life-vest rental • Swimming pool P200 per half-day • 054 477 3344, cwcwake.com

Located just under 10km southeast of Naga, **CamSur Watersports Complex (CWC)** is an international-standard wakeboarding course. There is a beginners' winch park, where

FROM TOP CAGSAWA RUINS IN FRONT OF MOUNT MAYON (P.216); TICAO ISLAND (P.228) >

you can practise standing up on a straight run, and it's also possible to use a kneeboard on the main course, which involves six turns and an assortment of ramps and rails for those who know what they're doing. The complex also has a swimming lagoon and a pool.

ARRIVAL AND DEPARTURE
CAMSUR WATERSPORTS COMPLEX (CWC)

By shuttle The easiest way to get to CWC is to take a free shuttle, departing from Naga's SM Mall and along Magsaysay Ave – contact CWC for the current timetable. There is also a free shuttle service that meets incoming flights at Naga airport.

By bus and jeepney From the bus terminal in Naga you can take a bus towards Legazpi (20min) or a jeepney to Bula or Partido (every 30min; 25min; P12); ask the driver to let you off by the CWC entrance by the highway. At the entrance, you can take a tricycle (10min; P50) or habal-habal (5min; P10) to get into the complex itself.

ACCOMMODATION AND EATING

Villa del Rey Hotel 🖀 054 477 3349, 🌐 cwcwake.com. A huge range of accommodation options, from simple tiki huts to cute cabanas (P2750), converted containers (P1950) and cosy wood cabins (P2725). There are also private villas (P4950) with small gardens and breezy outdoor bathtubs surrounded by greenery and bamboo shoots. The wi-fi reaches some of the rooms, and there are a couple of restaurants and bars. 🛜 **P1750**

Lake Buhi

Regular vans connect Naga to Buhi (hourly; 1hr 30min; P85)

Mostly enclosed by hills – some of which rise as high as 300m – **Lake Buhi** lies 52km southeast of Naga. From the lakeside market in the surprisingly busy town of **BUHI**, on the south shore, you can charter a **bangka** to take you across the water (20min; P100); once you're across, it's a fifteen-minute walk to the wonderful twin **Itbog Falls** in the barangay of Santa Cruz, 5km from Buhi. The falls crash through thick rainforest into deep pools that are perfect for swimming. You can also trek to the falls from Buhi, a terrific hour-long hike through rice paddies and along rocky trails. You'll have to organize a guide with Mary Grace Oafallas, the Executive Director for Culture and the Arts (🖀 0947 187 0457, 📧 dj.graceangel20@yahoo.com).

ACCOMMODATION

★**Lake Buhi Resort** Brgy Cabatuan 🖀 0926 616 2131, 🌐 lakebuhiresort.ph. Owned and run by affable Cyrus Obsuna, this wonderful resort, 4km northwest of Buhi, has tastefully furnished accommodation in well-manicured grounds; a spiral staircase leads up to a series of spacious rooms in the main building – the cosy attic room (P3000) is probably the most inviting, with a living area and terrace. There's also a swimming pool. Rates include breakfast. **P2200**

Mount Isarog National Park

One of the Philippines' most spectacular and least trampled areas, **Mount Isarog National Park** covers forty square kilometres in the heart of Camarines Sur, about 40km east of Naga. At its centre stands **Mount Isarog** (1966m), the second-highest peak in Southern Luzon and part of the Bicol volcanic chain that also includes Mayon. Isarog is considered potentially active, although it is not known when it last erupted.

The jungle is thick and steamy, and the **flora and fauna** are among the most varied in the archipelago. Long-tailed macaques and monitor lizards are a pretty common sight, while with a little luck you may also spot the indigenous shrew rats, reticulated pythons and rare birds such as the bleeding-heart pigeon, red-breasted pitta and blue-nape fantail. Reaching the summit (see box opposite) takes two days of strenuous climbing. At the top is a large crater with a couple of sulphuric rivers that meet here and stream down the southeastern part of the mountain.

CLIMBING MOUNT ISAROG

The easiest and most commonly used route to the summit of **Mount Isarog** is the **Panicuason trail**, which starts at the barangay of Panicuason and takes two days. There are two other recognized routes on the mountain – the PLDT trail and the more challenging Patag-Patag trail – both of which also take two days.

You will need a climbing **permit** (P10/day) and a local **guide** (P550/day) to climb Mount Isarog – Kadlagan Outdoor Shop at 16 Damasalang St, Naga (☎0919 800 6299, ✉kadlagan @yahoo.com) can process applications and help with guides; for the latter you can also contact the Naga City Arts, Culture and Tourism Office in the DOLE Building, City Hall Complex, J. Miranda Ave (Mon–Fri 8am–5pm; ☎054 478 3987, ✇nagax.com).

The **best time** to trek is between March and May, but it is possible at other times, weather allowing; September to December is particularly wet.

A number of paths on Isarog's lower slopes lead to **waterfalls** – including Mina-Ati, Nabuntulan and Tumaguiti – all of which are surrounded by thick rainforest and have deep, cool pools for swimming. The easiest to reach is beautiful **Malabsay**, a powerful ribbon of water that plunges into a deep pool surrounded by forest greenery. It's a delightful place for a dip. There are also hot springs in the barangay of **Panicuason** (P200), the most popular starting point for climbing the mountain.

ARRIVAL AND DEPARTURE   MOUNT ISAROG NATIONAL PARK

By jeepney To get to the barangay of Panicuason, starting point for the Panicuason trail (see box above), take a jeepney (hourly; 40min; P30) from close to the market in Naga. There are no jeepneys from Panicuason back to Naga after 3pm (4pm in summer), so keep an eye on the time. If you get stuck you can catch a habal-habal (15min; P100).

ACCOMMODATION

Panicuason Hotspring Resort ☎0906 252 7344, ✉hotspring.resort@yahoo.com. The closest accommodation to the national park, offering simple rooms in the "old" building along with much more appealing doubles with modern bathrooms in a newer block (P1600). There is no hot water, but the four hot spring pools are just at your feet. Adventure activities include two ziplines (P200–300) and a waterball (P100/5min), and there's a restaurant. There's wi-fi in the restaurant only. 🛜 **P1300**

Caramoan Peninsula

The wild and sometimes windswept **Caramoan Peninsula**, 50km east of Naga, is blessed with limestone cliffs and blue-water coves to rival the Visayas or Palawan. Until recently its relative isolation and lack of infrastructure meant that it attracted only a handful of tourists. Then in 2008 the French production of the *Survivor* TV show was filmed here, and other international productions swiftly followed suit. While the area hardly rivals somewhere like Boracay in terms of development, it is attracting increasing numbers to its rugged, scenic landscape. The **dry season** runs from February to September, while October to December sees the most rain.

Caramoan

There isn't much to delay you in the town of **CARAMOAN** other than a few souvenir shops, a couple of simple restaurants and some decent enough accommodation options. If you have a bit of time to kill, it's worth taking a stroll to the **Michael the Archangel Parish Church** on National Road, a pretty red-brick building constructed in the 1600s. The church was originally built with light materials such as bamboo, wood and nipa, but in the 1800s it was renovated using clay, stone and adobe. Opposite is the covered produce **market**.

ISLAND-HOPPING FROM THE CARAMOAN PENINSULA

Island-hopping tours are a good way to visit Guinahoan, Lahos, Matukad and Lahuy islands as well as Bag'eing and Sabitang Laya beaches. Trips can be arranged through most accommodation or tour operators in Caramoan town; Solmairena Travel Services at 28 Valencia St, Brgy Binanuahan (☎0908 163 7726, ✉solmairena@gmail.com), are recommended. Alternatively you can hire a bangka direct from Bikal Wharf or from Paniman Beach, both around 5km north of Caramoan town, at P1500–2500 for the day, depending on the distances covered. Be prepared to haggle quite a bit to get these prices.

Gota Beach

6km northeast of Caramoan town • P300 • Tricycle from Caramoan town P150 (20min)

Part of the **Caramoan National Park**, the government-owned **Gota Beach** became a tourist attraction when accommodation for the filming crew of the *Survivor* series was built here. Reachable from Caramoan town along a surfaced but damaged road, the beach itself is a bit of a let-down, although it continues to attract tourists who head to the resort intrigued to see what put this place on the map.

Guinahoan Island

With its grassy terrain and grazing cows, the inhabited **Guinahoan Island** is an unusual sight among the Caramoan Peninsula's jagged limestone cliffs. The island has some lovely **beaches** with white and pink sand; it's a 45-minute trek from the shore to the **Guinahoan Lighthouse**, which still functions as a beacon for fishermen at night and offers wonderful views of the nearby islands.

Lahos Island

Also known as Bichara, the small **Lahos Island** consists of two stunning limestone formations connected by a short stretch of sand. Except during high tide, you can spend some time on the beach that cuts through from one side of the island to the other, which has deep, clear water.

Matukad Island

One of the smallest islands in Caramoan, **Matukad Island** is a pretty spot with some of the whitest sand in the area. Within the island there's a hidden lagoon; you'll have to scramble to the top of rugged limestone cliffs to find it, and you shouldn't attempt to do so without a guide – contact the Caramoan tourist office (see opposite). The lagoon is allegedly inhabited by one milkfish; legend says that the little creature protects the island, and brings ill fortune to those who harm it.

Lahuy Island

At 10km long and 3.5km wide, **Lahuy** is the largest island in the northern part of the Caramoan Peninsula; it is also known as "Treasure Island" because of its history of gold mining. There is still small-scale gold panning in the barangay of **Gata**, and visitors can try their hand for a minimal fee. The island is wonderful at low tide when you can see the beautiful white sandbar of **Manlawe** covered in a thin layer of crystal-clear water. There are floating cottages (P200) where you can have a snack, although make sure to bring your own food.

Bag'eing and Sabitang Laya beaches

Located on a triangular-shaped island of the Lucsuhin group of islands, the lovely **Bag'eing and Sabitang Laya beaches** are among the filming locations of the *Survivor* series. Both have coral-yellow sand dotted with rock formations and shallow emerald-green waters that are perfect for swimming and snorkelling.

Paniman Beach

Paniman Beach is one of the jumping-off points for island-hopping tours. The black sand is nothing to write home about, but there are a few accommodation options, so if you don't want to head inland to Caramoan town, you may want to consider overnighting here.

The Shrine of Our Lady The Most Holy Rosary

From the main road in the barangay of Tabgon, 9.5km northwest of Caramoan town, you can climb 524 steps to the top of Caglago Mountain to reach the **Shrine of Our Lady The Most Holy Rosary**, a white concrete statue of the Virgin Mary spreading her arms in benediction; from the 213m summit, you will be rewarded with wonderful views over the peninsula and the surrounding islands. It's a great spot to watch the sun rise over the bay.

ARRIVAL AND DEPARTURE   CARAMOAN PENINSULA

By plane The closest airport is in Virac, on Catanduanes (see p.230), from where you can catch a tricycle to Codon port (1hr; P500), and then hire a private bangka to Guijalo ("Gee-ahlo") port (45min; P1500).

By boat The easiest way to reach the peninsula is by taking a bangka to Guijalo (daily 5.30am, 7am, 8.30am, 11am; 2hr; P120) from the small port of Sabang, east of Naga by van (hourly; 2hr; P100). If you miss the last bangka at 11am, you can hire a boat for P4000 (for six people). From Guijalo it's a 15–20min hop by tricycle (P150) to Caramoan town. From Nato Port, connected by

bus to Naga (leaving Naga daily 4.30am, returning to Naga 1pm; 2hr), there are ferries to Guijalo (daily 6.30am, returning from Guijalo to Nato port 10.30am; 3hr 30min; P150).

By bus Visitors coming direct from Manila can take a Raymond Transport bus from Cubao to Sabang Port (daily noon, 2pm, 3.30pm & 7pm; 12hr) or to Caramoan town (daily 4pm; 18hr). Both buses pick up passengers in Naga. The road, however, is poor – until it is eventually upgraded, on the whole the sea route is a better option.

INFORMATION AND ACTIVITIES

Tourist information The tourist office is in the Municipal Compound in Caramoan town (Mon–Fri 8am–5pm; ☎0928 407 9960, ✉caramoan.tourism@gmail.com).
Banks and exchange There is a UCPB bank with ATM on

Real St in Caramoan town, although it only accepts MasterCard (not Visa), and it's probably unwise to rely upon it – make sure to bring enough pesos.

ACCOMMODATION

The two jumping-off points for island-hopping tours, **Paniman Beach** and **Bikal Wharf**, make good bases if you have limited time in the area. It's possible to **camp** on some of the islands, including Matukad, Lahuy and Bag'eing Beach; the inhabited Lahuy Island is probably the most recommendable as there is a fresh water source. Unless otherwise stated, all accommodation options listed here have **limited wi-fi**.

BIKAL WHARF

Rex Tourist Inn Tawog ☎0939 204 3692, ⊛rex touristinn.com. Nearly 1km from Bikal Wharf, this pleasant resort has twenty rooms in well-tended grounds, all with cable TV and a/c. There's a good-sized pool, climbing wall and a rustic bamboo bar looking over the Lubok River, which is a tranquil spot for a few hours' kayaking (P800/day). In busier months, bands play at the restaurant in the evenings. ☎ **P1500**

CARAMOAN TOWN

La Casa Roa Teoxon St ☎0917 596 5881, ⊛lacasaroa .wordpress.com. The most atmospheric hotel in town, this welcoming place offers comfortable, private

colour-coded rooms with mock-period furniture. The spacious rooms on the first floor (P1850) have beautiful parquet floors; no.1 is the nicest. There's also a communal lounge with wicker furniture and a large sunny terrace. The annexe is not as inspiring, with small bare rooms. ☎ **P950**
Istaran Budget Hotel Teoxon St ☎0948 229 0915, ⊛istaran.wordpress.com. This is a reliable budget choice, with simple cabins as well as standard double (P1000) and triple rooms (P1200). Overall the premises are very clean, neat and tidy. There's a small restaurant downstairs, and in-room massage at P350. The hotel offers island-hopping packages, starting at P3000 for two people for two days and one night. ☎ **P800**

4

GOTA BEACH

Gota Village Resort ☎ 0920 965 0390, ⓦ caramoan islands.com. This resort, built to house the crew of the *Survivor* TV series, has more than 130 cabañas cluttered together on a grassy slope, which come in small, medium (P2750) and large (P3000), and are much more appealing inside than out, with rustic cosy interiors more suited to an alpine lodge than a beach resort. There is also pricier VIP accommodation (P5000) on nearby Hunongan Cove. Between Feb and June it's often block-booked for filming, but there's a bit of an eerie feel when the place is empty. 🛜 **P2500**

PANIMAN BEACH

Breeze and Waves ☎ 0918 913 9623, ⓦ caramoan -breezeandwaves.weebly.com. Sea-facing concrete block offering a/c rooms with salmon-pink furnishings; the bare walls could do with a bit of brightening up, but overall the accommodation is clean, and there are hot showers. If you're after something with a bit less concrete, you can try the attached *Daniel's Resort* owned by the same family –

where the walls are plastic faux-wood. 🛜 **P1500**

La Playa Puerto Merced ☎ 0920 281 6362. This resort has a few little fan-cooled bamboo huts with shared bath that are perfect if you're on a budget; there are also a/c rooms (P2500) in a concrete building – some are better than others, and make more use of native materials. There's also a large bungalow sleeping eight (P7000). 🛜 **P800**

TUGAWE COVE

Tugawe Cove Resort ☎ 0917 501 6711, ⓦ tugawe coveresort.com. One of the nicest places to stay on the Caramoan Peninsula – and offering the only way to get to see the private Tugawe Cove – this lovely resort is located on a wonderful stretch of private beach with crystal-clear waters. Accommodation is in 27 comfortable cabañas with modern amenities, set around a lake and dotted along the hillside. On the hilltop are the restaurant and an inviting infinity pool with incredible views over the coast and surrounding islands. In the evenings, it's worth heading out on a trip to see bioluminescent plankton within the cove. 🛜 **P8000**

Albay province

Thanks to its central location, **Albay province** is considered to be the gateway to the Bicol region. At the heart of Albay is **Mount Mayon**, with its almost perfect cone-shaped bulk rising from paddy fields to the north and majestically looming over the city of **Legazpi**. Legazpi is the jumping-off point for the rest of the region, where highlights in the lovely countryside include quiet beaches around the town of **Santo Domingo**, the eerie remains of a church at **Cagsawa**, and the **Hyop-Hoyopan** and **Calabidongan caves**. Northwest of Legazpi is the little port of **Tabaco**, from where there are regular ferries across to Catanduanes.

Legazpi

About 100km south of Naga, the busy port city of **LEGAZPI** (sometimes spelt Legaspi) is the jumping-off point for climbing **Mount Mayon** and makes a convenient base to explore the surrounding area. The city centre is divided into two parts at either end of the National Highway. The **old town**, where you'll find the City Hall and most of the top-end hotels, is centred on Peñaranda Park and known as the **Albay district**. A couple of kilometres to the northeast is the new town, or **City Proper**, a muddle of small businesses, banks, cinemas and market stalls where the rest of the hotels are located, along with the waterfront **Embarcadero de Legazpi**, a large mall that also offers go-karting, arcade games, watersports and live music. It's a 25-minute walk between Albay and City Proper, along a busy, polluted road lacking a decent pavement – a tricycle or jeepney is a better option.

Lignon Hill

Daily 8am–10pm • P25 • ☎ 0922 883 6722 • Jeepney Loop 1 or 2 (every 20min; 10min; P8), then 2km uphill walk (30min)

Northwest of the city centre, **Lignon Hill** is popular with local families and is not only a great viewpoint for Mayon but also a destination in its own right. Attractions include a zipline, hanging bridge, Japanese war tunnels and quad bikes that can be rented at the base of the hill for tours to see volcanic rock formations. The hill is also the location of

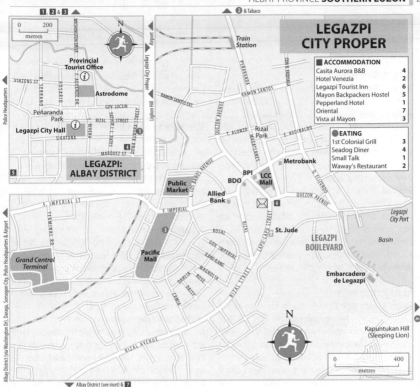

the **Philippine Institute of Volcanology and Seismology** (PHIVOLCS) research station (ⓦphivolcs.dost.gov.ph).

ARRIVAL AND DEPARTURE

LEGAZPI

By plane The airport is 2km northwest of City Proper; incoming flights are met by tricycles at the airport (5min; P50). PAL and Cebu Pacific serve Manila (3 daily; 1hr 10min).

By bus All buses arrive at the Grand Central Terminal on the western edge of City Proper. Dozens of a/c buses ply the route to Manila, including Philtranco, and there are plenty of local buses.

Destinations Manila (dozens daily; 8–10hr); Naga (every 15min; 2hr); Sorsogon City (every 15min; 1hr 30min); Tabaco (every 20min; 1hr).

By jeepney Regular jeepneys make the trip to Santo Domingo (hourly; 30min; P20).

By van Vans arrive at and leave from the Grand Central Terminal.

Destinations Bulan (hourly; 2hr 30min; P180); Donsol (hourly; 1hr 30min; P75); Naga (every 30min; 2hr; P140); Pio Duran (hourly; 2hr; P135); Sorsogon City (every 30min; 1hr 20min; P90); Tabaco (every 30min; 45min; P50).

By boat The wharf is at the eastern end of Quezon Ave in City Proper. Outrigger boats travel to Rapu-Rapu, Albay (daily 7am & noon; 3hr; P150).

INFORMATION AND TOURS

Tourist information The city tourist office is in the City Hall Building on Rizal St in Albay district (Mon–Fri 8am–5pm; ☎052 480 2698, ⓦlegazpi.gov.ph), while the provincial tourist office is on F. Aquende Drive, also in Albay district (Mon–Fri 8am–5pm; ☎052 481 0250, ⓦalbay.gov.ph); there is also an info kiosk at the airport that opens when flights arrive.

Tours For private tours, car rental, trekking (including Mount Mayon), ATV rides and other adventure tourism, try Your Brother Travel & Tours (☎052 742 9871, ⓦmayonatvtour.com) or Bicol Adventures and Tours (☎0917 571 4357, ⓦbicoladventureatv.com). You can also ask at the tourist offices about arranging a guide for Mount Mayon (see p.215).

ACCOMMODATION

Unless otherwise stated, all accommodation options listed here have limited **wi-fi**, and where available it's often only in public areas or the restaurant.

CITY PROPER

Legazpi Tourist Inn 3rd Floor, V&O Building, Lapu-Lapu St at Quezon Ave ☎052 480 6147, ✉legazpitouristinn@yahoo.com.ph. On the second floor of an office block, this simple place offers plain rooms, some with fan. The more expensive standard rooms (P1200) have a/c and TV, but the deluxe rooms (P1600) with cable TV are worth the extra – they're much larger and in better condition than the standards. 🛜 **P700**

Oriental Taysan Hill, Santo Niño Village ☎052 742 8888, ⓦtheorientalhotels.com. This upmarket hotel sits on Taysan Hill, overlooking the city, and offers some of the best views of Mount Mayon and the Gulf of Albay. Comfortable rooms feature amenities such as rain showers and high-speed internet; facilities include spa, infinity pool, children's pool, gym and babysitting services. 🛜 **P4888**

ALBAY DISTRICT

Casita Aurora B&B Doña Aurora St, Old Albay ☎052 742 2169. Owners Martin and Elizabeth offer just four rooms in their cosy home, which is decorated with stained glass, small trinkets, and with vintage wooden and wicker furniture. The tasty breakfasts (included in rates) are served in the country-kitchen-style dining room. There's also a large leafy garden and rooftop patio offering spectacular Mayon views. 🛜 **P2000**

Hotel Venezia Renaissance Gardens, Washington Drive ☎052 481 0888, ⓦhotelvenezia.com.ph. Close to the airport, this upmarket hotel oozes minimalist chic, with rooms set on three floors. Standard rooms are tiny, while the much more spacious junior suites (P4270) with king-size beds, sacrifice a little style for a lot more space. There's a café in the lobby serving delectable cakes. 🛜 **P3500**

Mayon Backpackers Hostel Brgy Maoyod ☎052 480 0365 or ☎0905 518 6076, ⓦmayonbackpackers.wordpress.com. Legazpi's only hostel has a series of tiled four- and six-bed dorms, each with its own bathroom and wooden bunks and lockers. There's one double room with a/c and private bath, a communal guest kitchen and all-day tea and coffee; rates include a light breakfast of toast and fruit. 🛜 Dorms **P250**, doubles **P1000**

Pepperland Hotel Airport Rd, Washington Drive ☎052 481 8000, ⓦthepepperlandhotel.com. Not far from the airport, this stylish Spanish colonial-style hotel is named after the Bicol favourite, the chilli pepper – evident from the giant chilli sculpture which adorns the front of the building. Rooms are plush and colourful, and there's also an excellent restaurant and trendy café. 🛜 **P3300**

★**Vista al Mayon** Washington Drive ☎052 481 0308, ✉vistaalmayon@yahoo.com. In a good location close to the airport and restaurants, this is a good choice among the city's inexpensive options, with knick-knacks dotted about the entrance hall and comfortable rooms with little wicker details; there's also a piano, billiards table and a small swimming pool in the courtyard (the pool is used for children's lessons at the weekend, when it can get a bit noisy and crowded). Rooms upstairs in the annex (P2000) offer those sought-after Mayon views, as well as kitchenettes. 🛜 **P1450**

EATING

1st Colonial Grill Pacific Mall, City Proper ☎052 481 1213. This popular restaurant within Pacific Mall is renowned for its unique pink chilli ice cream (P89) that gives quite a kick; other flavours include roasted rice (*tinutong*) and pili nut. The menu features fish and seafood dishes such as grilled mussels (P249) and barbecue pork (P200) that are large enough to share. Daily 9am–8pm.

★**Seadog Diner** Legazpi Boulevard, Barangay Puro ☎0918 952 2996. Cosy little restaurant right on the waterfront, offering brick-oven-baked pizza (from P280) and Bicolano classics. Try the lunchtime set menu (P200) of Bicol Express with *pinangat* and a drink. Daily 7am–midnight.

SPICING IT UP IN BICOL

Bicolano **cuisine** is unusual in the Philippines, and is noted for its use of coconut and chillies. Most Bicolano dishes are prepared by sautéeing or simmering ingredients in coconut cream – traditionally minced, diced or ground pork, smoked fish (*tinapa*) or small shrimps. Among the most common dishes are **Bicol Express**, named after a famous train service, made with coconut cream, diced pork, small shrimps, chilli and garlic, and sometimes pineapple; **laing**, a spicy dish of delicious taro leaves, coconut cream, ground pork and minced small shrimps; and **pinangat**, which uses the same ingredients as *laing*, although the taro leaves here are tied together and wrapped around the ground pork and small shrimps, before being submerged in coconut cream. To sample some of the best Bicolano cuisine, head for *Seadog Diner* or *Waway's* (see above) *Restaurant* in Legazpi (see opposite).

Small Talk 51 Doña Aurora St, Albay district ☎ 052 480 1393. The most atmospheric dining experience in the city, located in an ancestral home complete with family pictures and old photographs of Mayon. The menu covers all the Filipino standards, with some twists on Bicolano cuisine (see box opposite) including pasta with Bicol Express (P105) and the fiery Mayon stuffed pizza, with *laing*,

longganisa sausage and Bicol Express (P265). Daily 11am–10pm.

Waway's Restaurant Peñaranda St, Bonot ☎ 052 480 8415. Join the local working crowd for an all-you-can-eat buffet lunch (P250) of native Bicolano specialities in a large and airy restaurant. The evening menu (mains P150–200) is not so good. Daily 7am–8pm.

DIRECTORY

Banks There are numerous banks on Rizal Ave as well as ATMs in the shopping malls. In the Albay district, you'll find a Land Bank ATM in the Provincial Capitol Annex.

Police The Albay police provincial office is at Camp Gen. Simeon A. Ola (☎ 052 820 6440), west of the Albay district.
Post office Lapu-Lapu St at Quezon Ave in City Proper.

Mount Mayon

The elegantly smooth cone of **MOUNT MAYON** (2460m) may look benign from a distance, but don't be deceived. The most active volcano in the country, Mayon has **erupted** more than forty times since 1616, the date of its first recorded eruption. The most deadly single eruption was in 1814 when around 1200 people were killed and the church at Cagsawa (see p.216) was destroyed; 77 people, including American volcanologists, were killed in a 1993 eruption. In August 2006, an "extended danger zone" was enforced but the expected eruption did not occur. Three months later, however, Typhoon Durian caused mudslides of volcanic ash and boulders on Mayon that killed hundreds. Further eruptions and ash ejections have occurred since.

The presence of Mayon results in strange **weather conditions** in and around Legazpi, with the volcano and the surrounding area often soaked in rain when the rest of the country is basking in unbroken sunshine.

4

Daraga

Jeepney from Legazpi (every 5min; 15min; P10)

Five kilometres west of Legazpi, the busy market town of **DARAGA** is home to **Daraga Church**, an imposing eighteenth-century Baroque structure built by Franciscan

CLIMBING MOUNT MAYON

The traditional window of opportunity for an ascent of Mount Mayon is **February to April**, and even then you'll have to be well prepared for cold nights at altitude and the possibility of showers. At any other time of year you could be hanging around for days waiting for a break in the weather. Though the slopes look smooth, it takes at least two days to reach the highest point of the trail, working your way slowly through forest, grassland and deserts of boulders. Above 1800m there's the possibility of being affected by poisonous gases, and climbers are not allowed past 2000m even if there's no imminent threat of eruption.

There are various approaches to Mayon, although the accredited and authorized jump-off point is at **Lidong**, Santo Domingo, where the **Mayon Volcano National Park** is located. You'll have to bring all your food with you from Legazpi; there are sources of water on the volcano, but you'll need purifying tablets.

INFORMATION AND GUIDES

Whatever you do, don't attempt the climb without a **guide**. Guides are mandatory and setting out without one would be foolhardy in the extreme. Local guides at Lidong, Santo Domingo, can assist tourists, although it's probably wise to arrange one in advance at the tourist offices in Legazpi (see p.213), where you can also check to see whether conditions are suitable for an ascent. Another good source of information is the Institute Of Volcanology And Seismology (Ⓦphivolcs.dost.gov.ph), in Legazpi on Lignon Hill (see p.213).

missionaries from blocks of volcanic lava. The exterior was decorated by skilled stonemasons with statuary, carvings, alcoves and niches, but until recently had been falling into disrepair. It was declared a national cultural treasure in 2008 and has now been restored to its former glory.

ACCOMMODATION AND EATING   **DARAGA**

Daraga offers a couple of surprisingly good **dining** options in pleasant surroundings, while **staying** here provides a good alternative to the hustle and bustle of central Legazpi.

Balay Cena Una F. Lotivio at P. Gomez St ☎0917 827 9520, ⟁balaycenauna.com. Located in a beautifully restored ancestral home with lovely parquet floors, this excellent restaurant serves tasty international dishes, such as the signature fillet of lapu-lapu (grouper) in butter and garlic sauce (P265) or Wagyu beef steak (P1512) flown over directly from Japan, plus excellent butterflied king prawns with *pinangat* (taro leaves wrapped around ground pork and prawns, cooked in coconut milk; P302). There's a Sunday buffet (11am–3pm; P350). Mon–Sat 10am–10pm, Sun 11.30am–9pm.

Balay de la Rama Daang Maharlika Hwy ☎0918 385 7939, ⟁balaydelarama.com. This cosy family-run B&B has just six rooms with a/c. Decorated in native Filipino woods and *abacá* fibres, each room has an individual feel, and some have private balconies with fantastic views. There's also a lovely garden with hammocks and a mango tree. Breakfast is included. Limited wi-fi. ⟁ P1800

Cagsawa ruins

Ruins Daily 6am–10pm • P10 • **Swimming Pool** Daily 6am–10pm • P50 • **Galeria de Cagsawa** Daily 7am–6pm • P20 • Take a jeepney (P10) from Legazpi in the direction of Malabog or Polangui; make sure to tell the driver where you want to get off

Eight kilometres northwest of Legazpi, beyond Daraga, the **Cagsawa ruins** are the remains of a Spanish church, dating back to 1773. Much speculation surrounds the church as some claim that it was destroyed by the 1814 eruption of Mayon, while others say it was by earthquakes and typhoons. The ruins are small and there's not much to explore, but they are picturesque, standing in gardens close to paddy fields with marvellous views across the plain to Mount Mayon. This is a popular spot, so if you want peace and quiet – or if you want to take photographs before the cumulus roll in to obscure the volcano's tip – take an early jeepney. You can buy drinks and snacks from the souvenir stalls and sari-sari stores outside the ruins.

There's a **swimming pool** just by the ruins, along with the **Galeria de Cagsawa**, a small gallery with photos and paintings by local artists depicting Mount Mayon's eruption.

Hoyop-Hoyopan Cave

17km west of Legazpi • Daily 7am–7pm • 1hr guided tour P300/group of six; guides only receive 20 percent of the entrance fee so tips are appreciated • Jeepney from Legazpi to Camalig (every 20min; 45min; P20), then change to another jeepney towards Cotmon (P10) or catch a habal-habal (15min; P100)

Hoyop-Hoyopan – meaning "Blowing Wind" due to the breeze inside – is the most easily accessible of fourteen limestone **caves** near Legazpi. It's a well-established attraction, privately owned, and guides are available at the entrance, although you could try local guide Bam Nuylan (☎0927 969 9855) if nobody is there. Guides will point out fragments of burial jars dating back two thousand years; incongruously, there is also a concrete dancefloor built in 1972, when parties were held in secret to avoid the curfew of the martial law era.

Calabidongan Cave

24km west of Legazpi, 7km from Hoyop-Hoyopan • 3hr tour (compulsory) with guide P550 per person

Calabidongan (Cave of the Bats) is a more difficult cave to explore than Hoyop-Hoyopan as it is always partly flooded and at one point requires a very short swim. It is best visited in April and May, as at other times the water level can be too high. Make sure to bring a torch and wear rubber shoes or sandals; don't take a camera unless you have a waterproof bag. Hoyop-Hoyopan is the jumping-off point for Calabidongan; guides there can arrange a habal-habal (15min; P100) for those who don't want to walk (7km; 1hr).

Santo Domingo and around

About 13km northeast of Legazpi along the coastal road, the small town of **SANTO DOMINGO** is a tidy, friendly little settlement with an atmospheric old Spanish church on the north side of the narrow main street. In the barangay of **Buyuan** is a signposted turning for a nine-hole golf course and stables offering horseriding (P500 to ride to the lowest camp on Mount Mayon).

Calayucay Beach

East of Santo Domingo, a concrete road winds its way up and down through some delightful, pristine countryside, with the main destination being **Calayucay Beach**, 2.5km east of the town. It's pretty but not spectacular, though the views across Albay Gulf are attractive and its resorts are good places to relax.

Sogod Beach

About 10km north of Santo Domingo, near Bacacay, is **Sogod Beach** – a pleasantly rustic stretch of black volcanic sand sometimes known as the Mayon Riviera. As well as day-cottages for picnickers, there are a couple of resorts with accommodation.

Cagraray

You can reach Cagraray by boat from Tabaco (the island's resort organizes boats for their guests), or by taking the bridge from the peninsula east of Santo Domingo – more reliable than a boat during typhoon season, but not used by public transport, so you'll have to rely on a private transfer

The island of **Cagraray**, 26km east of Santo Domingo, connected to the mainland by bridge, has some wonderful white-sand beaches in **Sula** and **Misibis** on the southeast coast. The sand here is naturally black thanks to Mount Mayon's volcanic activity, but the white sand that covers the beaches now was brought over from nearby Masbate. There is only one resort here, on Misibis beach (see below), although you can camp out. Hiring a bangka should cost P500–P1000 for a full day.

ARRIVAL AND DEPARTURE   SANTO DOMINGO

By jeepney Jeepneys connect Legazpi to Santo Domingo (hourly; 30min; P20) from where there are services to Calayucay Beach (hourly; 30min; P40). Jeepneys also connect Sogod Beach to Tabaco (every 30min; 30min; P23).
By van From Legazpi there are vans to Bacacay (for Sogod

Beach; hourly; 45min; P35).
By tricycle You can get a tricycle from Santo Domingo to Calayucay Beach (10min; P8) or Sogod Beach (30min; P100). A tricycle from Bacacay to Sogod Beach is P60 (10min).

ACCOMMODATION

Unless otherwise stated, all accommodation options listed here have limited **wi-fi**, and where available it's often only in public areas or the restaurant.

Coastal View Beach Resort Calayucay Beach ✆0999 994 1099, ✉coastalviewb@yahoo.com. The first resort you come to on Calayucay Beach is also one of the best on this strip, albeit on slightly overbuilt grounds with a concrete promenade by the sea. The standard rooms are spacious, with poolside or Mount Mayon views, while the executive rooms have more attractive decor. ☎ P2000
Costa Palmera Resort Calayucay Beach ✆0932 843 4998 or ✆0917 552 8871. This is a decent option with a range of a/c economy rooms as well as suites (P2060). Best

of all are probably the two poolside rooms (P3080). P1250
Misibis Bay Misibis Bay, Cagaray ✆02 661 8888, ⓦmisibisbay.com. This large high-end resort, set in generous grounds, offers 37 luxurious villas with prices to match. Facilities include seven swimming pools, a spa, restaurant and a range of watersports. At the time of research, a separate complex nearby with more rooms was under construction. ☎ US$570
Mullner Beach Resort Sogod Beach ✆0928 450 3185, ✉johnrojero@yahoo.com. Set in pleasant grounds

4

dotted with palm trees, this resort offers simply furnished cottages and more spacious family rooms; the "private room" sleeping three (P2500) is the best value, with a living area and chintzy bedroom. There's cold water only, and no restaurant so you'll have to bring your own food or eat at one of the other resorts. 📶 **P1500**

Tabaco

TABACO, 26km northeast of Legazpi, is a busy little port that functions as the gateway to **Catanduanes** (see p.229). The town itself doesn't offer much to visitors, although it's worth knowing that it has a couple of surprisingly decent hotels, should you happen to get stuck here for the night to catch the early ferry to Catanduanes.

ARRIVAL AND DEPARTURE   TABACO

By bus Buses arrive at the bus terminal 1.5km outside the centre; a pedicab to the centre of Tabaco is P10 (10min), while a tricycle costs P25 (5min). A/c PLTB buses travel to Manila (daily 7.30am & 5.30pm; 10–12hr); plenty of local buses also make the journey, with most leaving around 5pm (15 daily; 10–12hr).
By jeepney The jeepney terminal is on the main street just by the Tabaco City mall and market.
Destinations Bacacay (for Sogod Beach; every 30min; 30min; P21); Legazpi (every 15min; 40min; P25); Santo

Domingo (every 30min; 30min; P24).
By boat The port is a 10min walk from the jeepney terminal down the road running next to the market. There are ferries to Virac (daily 6.30am) and San Andres (fast craft; daily 7am & 12pm; P320) on the southwest coast of Catanduanes, which can be a rough crossing, particularly from October to December.
By van Vans to and from Legazpi (every 30min; 40min; P50) and Naga (every 1–2hr; 2hr 30min; P180) use the bus terminal.

ACCOMMODATION AND EATING

Amore Coffee Arellano St ☎0998 978 7986. This little café with wooden stools, a couple of armchairs and a sofa offers eight varieties of coffee beans including the prized civet coffee (P180); desserts include Belgian waffles (P65) and coffee brownies (P20), and there are savoury snacks too, such as sandwiches (P315) and nachos (P85). Free wi-fi. Mon–Sat 11am–11pm, Sun 9am–9pm.
HCG Residence Mansion Ziga Ave ☎052 487 7333. Located in the centre of town, opposite the Jeepney terminal, this is a good, safe option with clean, tiled a/c rooms. Those on a tight budget may want to opt for the 12hr option (6pm–10am; P1800). There's also an in-house restaurant serving Japanese dishes. 📶 **P2300**
Isiaya's Garden Bistro Villaruel St ☎052 203 0071,

🌐 bit.ly/Isiayas. Owned and run by Filipina celebrity Aya Medel, former actress and sex symbol, this lovely restaurant serves up Japanese and Bicolano fusion dishes in a leafy garden filled with fountains and fish ponds. Plates include pili-crusted fish fillet (P215), yakisoba noodles (P180) and various types of sushi (P150–P210). Daily 11am–2pm and 5–10pm.
JJ Midcity Inn Herrera St ☎052 487 4158, 🌐 jjmidcityinn.com. Above a small shopping complex, this place is a pleasant surprise – rooms are clean and modern, although the standard single with bunk bed (P750) is a bit of a squeeze. There's a karaoke bar within the hotel, so it can be quite noisy until it closes at midnight. Rates are cheaper for stays of up to 12hr. 📶 **P2500**

Sorsogon province

A toe of land with a striking volcanic topography and some little-known beaches, lakes, hot springs and waterfalls, **Sorsogon province**, south of Albay, is the easternmost part of mainland Bicol. The province is best known to tourists for the chance to snorkel with whale sharks off the coast near **Donsol**, but it's also a great area for activities such as hiking and caving. **Sorsogon City** makes a good base for exploring the area's many lovely beaches – the nicest stretch of sand being **Rizal Beach**, in the barangay of Gubat to the east of Sorsogon City. There are many pristine coves to explore along the coast around **Bacon**, while south of Sorsogon City **Mount Bulusan** is a climbable, active volcano.

Driving through Sorsogon province you will pass many stalls selling items made from **abacá**, the fibre of a species of banana tree and one of the major products of the province. Sometimes known as Manila hemp, although it also grows in Malaysia and Indonesia, it is processed to make everything from banknotes to teabags.

SORSOGON OUTDOOR ACTIVITIES

Although Donsol is famous for its whale shark watching, there are plenty of other activities elsewhere in Sorsogon for nature lovers and outdoor enthusiasts.

SCUBA DIVING

There's scuba diving at the infamous **Manta Bowl** (see p.228); though it's actually closer to Ticao Island (see p.228), it is best reached from the dive shops attached to several of the resorts in Donsol. The site is far from shore, and requires divers to descend rapidly and cling onto rocks – try to get a reef hook or gloves. You then use the strong drift to move towards the Manta Bowl, and if you're lucky you will be rewarded with close-up views of mantas or even whale sharks. This is not a dive for beginners, whatever the dive shops may tell you when trying to get your business. Also, be on the lookout for shoddy equipment. Donsol EcoTour (☎0632 576 5934, ⊛donsolecotour.com) are a reputable choice for Manta Bowl dives.

OTHER ACTIVITIES

The Sorgoson area is home to a large number of fireflies, and in certain conditions they create a huge spectacle along the riversides. **Firefly-watching** has become a popular attraction; one of the best companies to do this with is **Buhatan River Eco Adventure** (☎0939 938 1215, ⊛bit.ly/buhatan). As well as the fireflies, they offer **birdwatching**, sunset **cruises** with dinner, kayaking and **mangrove tours**. A cruise down the river in a floating cabana, combining firefly-watching, birding, local snacks and live music costs P2000 per person, or P4500 per person with dinner.

A day of **island-hopping** near the island of Ticao in Masbate province (P7000 for up to ten people; plus registration fee P100/person) can be arranged through the visitor centre in Donsol (see below). *Giddy's Place* (see p.220) can also sort out **kayaking** trips on the Ugod River (P1500/person).

4

Donsol

The area around the sleepy town of **DONSOL** is best known for one of the greatest concentrations of **whale sharks** in the world. The number of sightings varies: during the **peak months** of January to April there's a very good chance of encountering these gentle creatures, but on some days (particularly early or late in the season, which stretches from December to early June) you might see none. **Swimming** with these colossal sharks as they sedately glide through the clear waters, their enormous mouths opening more than 1m wide to gulp down huge quantities of plankton, is a truly unforgettable experience, but remember that you need to be a good swimmer and a decent snorkeller to get into the water with them. Outside of whale shark season, there's not much here for travellers, and most of the accommodation options and even some restaurants are **closed**.

ARRIVAL AND DEPARTURE   DONSOL

By bus Philtranco has a daily bus from Manila (12hr). Buses travelling between Sorsogon City and Donsol (every 15min; 1hr) arrive at Junction Putiao (see below).

By jeepney Jeepneys and a/c minivans arrive at a terminal on the southern edge of town. For Sorsogon City, catch a jeepney towards Daraga and ask the driver to let you get off at Junction Putiao (every 30min; 1hr; P60), from where the buses leave.

By van There are regular vans to Legazpi (hourly; 1hr 30min; P75).

By boat Ferries from Masbate City arrive at Pilar port, 15km south of Donsol by jeepney (every 30min; P15) or tricycle (30min; P250). There is one daily roll-on-roll-off ferry (departs Pilar 4–5am depending on the tide; 4hr; P230) and three fast crafts (daily 8am, noon & 4pm; 2hr; P396).

INFORMATION

Tourist information The Visitor Centre (daily 7am–6pm; ☎0927 483 6735) is northwest of Donsol among the resorts in the barangay of Dancalan, P40 away by tricycle from the centre of town. You'll need to check in here if you want to swim with the whale sharks (see box, p.220).

WHALE SHARKS IN DONSOL

Known locally as the *butanding*, the **whale shark** is a timid titan resembling a whale more than the shark that it is. It can grow up to 20m in length, making it the largest fish in existence. These gentle giants gather around Donsol every year, around the time of the northeastern monsoon, to feed on the rich shrimp and plankton streams that flow from the Donsol River into the sea, sucking their food through their gills via an enormous vacuum of a mouth.

Whale sharks were rarely hunted in the Philippines until the 1990s, when demand for their meat from countries such as Taiwan and Japan escalated. Cooks have dubbed it the "tofu shark" because of the meat's resemblance to soybean curd. Its fins are also coveted as a soup extender. Tragically, this has led to its near extinction in the Visayas and further south in Mindanao. In Donsol, however, where the creatures are protected, attitudes seem to be changing, with locals realizing that whale sharks can be worth more alive than dead, attracting tourists and thus investment and jobs.

WHALE-SHARK-WATCHING

At the Donsol Visitor Centre (see p.219) you can complete all the formalities for **renting a boat** for a whale-shark-watching trip. Boats cost P3500 for up to six people, and there's a registration fee of P300 for foreigners (P100 for Filipinos). In peak season, especially at weekends, queues can start to form before the centre opens, so arrive early.

Before boarding you will need to watch a video briefing in which a **Butanding Interaction Officer** (BIO) explains how to behave in the water near a whale shark. The number of snorkellers around any one shark is limited to six; flash photography is not allowed, nor is scuba gear; and the animal's tail should be avoided as it can do serious damage. Some boatmen flout these rules in order to keep their passengers happy, but this risks distressing the whale sharks and should not be encouraged. Check, too, that your boat has one of the mandatory propeller guards.

Snorkelling equipment can be rented from outside the visitor centre (P150 for mask and snorkel, plus P150 for flippers). Each boat has a crew of three, the captain, the BIO and the spotter, each of whom would welcome a token of your appreciation. All this makes it an expensive day out by Philippine standards, but your money is helping the conservation effort. Take plenty of protection against the sun and a good book. Once a whale shark has been sighted you'll need to get your mask, snorkel and flippers on and get in the water before it dives too deep to be seen.

ACCOMMODATION

The **resorts** are about 2km northwest of the town centre, on **Dancalan Beach**, and most are closed outside of the whale-shark-watching **season** (Dec–June). Donsol itself is becoming more tourist-oriented as locals aim to capitalize on growing visitor numbers; although there are few hotels, there are numerous **homestays**. Contact the Visitor Centre (see p.219) for an up-to-date list. Most of the accommodation options listed here have only limited **wi-fi**, usually only available in the public areas, lobby or restaurant.

DONSOL TOWN

Aguluz San Jose St ☎ 0918 942 0897. Run by the lovely Pepé and his wife, and open year-round, this welcoming homestay has beautiful *narra* wood floors and spacious, clean rooms, which once belonged to their six children. Guests can also use the lounge and kitchen, as well as request home-cooked meals. 📶 **P1700**

Giddy's Place 54 Clemente St ☎ 0917 848 8851, ⓦ giddysplace.com. This place offers standard rooms at the back by the pool, and deluxe rooms (P3360) at the front. All have kettle, fridge and TV, and there's a dive shop and restaurant (see opposite). Limited wi-fi. 📶 **P2800**

DANCALAN BEACH

AGM ☎ 0919 688 2264 or ☎ 0906 368 7805, ⓦ agmresort.com. This is the first resort on the strip if you're coming from Donsol town, and it has rows of thatched bamboo-fronted cottages and clean and tidy a/c concrete rooms with hot and cold showers. There's also a pool overlooking the sea. Limited wi-fi. 📶 **P2200**

Dancalan Beach Resort ☎ 0915 420 3285, ⓦ bit.ly/dancalan. As well as a simple, small concrete room with a double bed and shared bathroom, this spacious seafront resort offers thatched nipa huts and simple budget fan rooms (both P800), as well as concrete cottages (P1500) set around a large lawn area. There's also a restaurant, billiard room and massage hut. Limited wi-fi. 📶 **P500**

Elysia ☎ 0917 547 4466 or ☎ 0926 475 9762, ⓦ elysia-donsol.com. This Korean-owned resort is the most upmarket choice along the strip, with minimalist decor, bamboo beds and wooden loungers by the pool. There are a few hammocks slung along the beach and a restaurant serving Filipino and Italian dishes. The resort accepts credit cards. Wi-fi in the restaurant. 📶 **P3150**

Vitton ☎0917 544 4089, ⓦbicoldivecenter.com. One of the area's best resorts, with clean and spacious rooms, most with private veranda. The restaurant serves good international food. The *Woodland Beach Resort* next door, owned by the same people, offers "backpacker rooms" sleeping three for P500/person. Limited wi-fi. 📶 **P2300**

EATING AND DRINKING

★**Baracuda** Dancalan Beach ☎0917 624 0163. Sprightly owner Juliet shakes up potent margaritas, daiquiris and piña coladas (P150) at this lovely bamboo restaurant with cushioned seating. Her food is delicious, too, including mouthwatering sashimi (P305), squid salad (P205) and prawns with garlic and olive oil (P180). Lunch is available upon request. Dec–June daily 6pm–midnight.

Butanding Bar & Resto 54 Clemente St ☎0917 848 8851, ⓦgiddysplace.com. Part of *Giddy's Place* hotel (see opposite), this is one of the town centre's better options.

The menu is international, with dishes including pork schnitzel (P280), Hungarian sausage (P300) and blue marlin tandoori (P300); they also serve cocktails (P135) and there's wi-fi. Daily 6am–midnight.

Shanley's E. Hernandez St ☎0910 933 4760. Right by the bus terminal, this local hangout built in native materials, including bamboo and coconut, hosts live bands on Fri and Sat at 8pm. Expect dancing, drinking (beer P45) and belting out at the karaoke; basic meals are served, too (P150). Daily 8am–11pm.

DIRECTORY

Banks and exchange There are two ATMs, one at the Rural Bank of Donsol on Clemente St (Mon–Fri 8am–5pm, Sat 8am–noon), that only accepts Visa cards, and another at the Municipality Building. Some of the accommodation options, including *Giddy's Place* (see opposite), will take credit cards, but the only resort offering currency exchange (US dollars and euros) at the time of research was the *Elysia* (see opposite).

Sorsogon City

4

There are few attractions in **SORSOGON CITY**, although it serves as a base to explore the area's natural sights and has a range of good accommodation. Along the pier, vendors crack open large clams and display them in buckets. The **boardwalk** on the pier is a good place to watch the sun set, with views of Mount Pulag and Mount Bulusan. Every year, the **Kasanggayahan festival** (roughly Oct 17–23) celebrates the town's history with street parades, traditional dances and beauty pageants.

Museum and Heritage Center
Capitol Compound • Mon–Sat 9am–5pm • Free

The small **Museum and Heritage Center** displays a number of ancient artefacts, including burial jar covers dating back as far as 1000 BC that were found in caves in Bacon. Among the other exhibits are beautiful Chinese porcelain bowls from the Ming dynasty, chairs with Chinese-inspired designs and anchors believed to have been used during the Spanish colonial era. Highlights include the skull of a sperm whale, the skeletal system of a dolphin and a 10m long vertebra of a whale shark that was washed ashore at nearby Donsol in 2010.

ARRIVAL AND INFORMATION

SORSOGON CITY

By bus Buses use the Grand Terminal 2km south of the city centre, a P40 tricycle ride away. Local buses make the trip to Legazpi (every 15min; 1hr 30min). Philtranco runs a daily service to and from Manila (10–12hr), as do a number of local companies (13 daily).

By jeepney Jeepneys travel to Gubat (every 10min; 30min; P25), Bacon (every 10min; 30min; P17) and Bulan (every 30min; 2hr; P75).

By van Regular vans connect the city to Legazpi (every 15min; 1hr 15min; P85).

Tourist information The provincial tourist office is in the Capitol Compound (Mon–Fri 8am–noon & 1–5pm; ☎056 421 5632, ⓔsorsogonprovincial_tourism@yahoo.com).

ACCOMMODATION AND EATING

Fernando's Hotel N. Pareja St ☎056 211 1357, ⓦfernandoshotel.com. At the time of writing, this hotel was undergoing major renovations, including construction of a swimming pool. As well as their simple budget rooms, they have cosy coconut-and-bamboo-clad rooms (P1600), and new deluxe ones with private balconies (P2000).

There's wi-fi at the restaurant only. 🛜 **P1000**

Fritz Homestay Block 21, Executive Village, Tugos ☎0939 915 2327, ⓦfritzhomestay.com. This welcoming homestay 1km north of town is more of a B&B – the twenty-odd rooms are nicely decorated with wrought-iron bed frames, wooden wardrobes and lampshades made with shells. The most expensive (P1800) are particularly spacious, with knick-knacks dotted about. There are also two little swimming pools in the backyard, and a restaurant (with wi-fi) serving Filipino dishes. 🛜 **P1300**

★**Siama Hotel** Sitio San Lorenzo, Bibincahan ☎02 514 2653, ⓦwww.siamahotel.com. This chic designer hotel offers stylish rooms with creative furniture made from wood. The welcoming rooms are set around an inviting 25m pool with a giant over-water hammock – a pleasant spot to sip a cocktail at sunset. The hotel organizes pick-up from Legazpi airport. Wi-fi available in the lobby only. 🛜 **P8500**

Una Pizzeria 3257 Pareja St ☎056 255 0942. Probably the best restaurant in town, this welcoming place offers pizzas (P140) and pasta dishes (P122), served in a couple of airy rooms with scattered wooden tables and a few paintings adding colour to the walls; the mellow background music and the two retro sofas add to the inviting atmosphere. Also open for breakfast. Daily 8am–9pm.

DIRECTORY

Banks There are a number of banks (including BPI, PNB and Allied Bank) on Rizal St and Magsaysay St.

Shopping Kasanggayahan Village at the Capital Compound (daily 8am–9pm) has a dozen or so shops selling souvenirs and local products including pili nuts.

Rizal Beach

A short tricycle ride beyond the barangay of **Gubat**, which lies about 12km east of Sorsogon City on the eastern tip of the province, **Rizal Beach** stretches for 2km in a perfect crescent. It's a pleasant spot that can be suitable for **surfing** between October and January; for further information contact Gubat Inc (☎0905 242 1693), who rent boards (P150/hr) and organize lessons (P150/hr).

ARRIVAL AND DEPARTURE   RIZAL BEACH

By bus Several companies connect Manila to Gubat (5 daily; 12hr).

By jeepney Jeepneys from Gubat travel to Bulusan (every 15min; 45min; P38) and Sorsogon City (every 10min; 30min; P25).

By tricycle A tricycle from Gubat to Rizal Beach is P50 (10min).

ACCOMMODATION

Lola Sayong Eco-Surfcamp Rizal Beach, ☎0999 406 1497, ⓦlolasayong.org. An excellent budget choice, offering beachfront bamboo cottages and tents, both with shared bathrooms. There are plenty of shady palm trees and hammocks for relaxing, as well as a communal kitchen and restaurant serving local dishes (P80–100). Surfboard rental (P800/day) and surf lessons (P350/hr) are also available. An extra environmental fee (P25/day) is added to your bill. Camping (1–2-man tent) **P150**, cottages **P800**

Bacon and around

The small town of **BACON** (pronounced "backon"), 9km north of Sorsogon City by jeepney, has a grey-sand beach with a handful of resorts. Just a ten-minute tricycle ride west is the black-sand **Libanon Beach**, where surf hammers dramatically against immense, black rocks that were spewed out centuries ago by Mayon. The volcano is visible in the distance.

Paguriran

Bacon is a good base for exploring some of the **islands** in the eastern half of Albay Gulf. The best of these is **Paguriran**, a circle of jagged rock, much like the rim of a volcano, inside which is a seawater lagoon that's wonderful for swimming. The access point from the mainland is **Paguriran Beach**, 20km east of Bacon, from where you can walk across

to the island at low tide; make sure to check your timings. Otherwise, you'll have to hire a boatman to paddle you across (P150). Paguriran Beach is a wonderful spot to while away a few hours – the water is crystal clear, and there are lovely views over the neighbouring islands.

ARRIVAL AND DEPARTURE

BACON AND AROUND

By jeepney Regular jeepneys connect Sorsogon City to Bacon (every 10min; 30min; P17) and Paguriran Beach (every 20min; 1hr 30min; P44).

By tricycle A tricycle from Bacon to Paguriran Beach is P500 (45min).

ACCOMMODATION

Unless otherwise stated, the accommodation listed below has limited **wi-fi**, usually only available in public areas.

Fisherman's Hut Brgy Caricaran ☎0909 515 8758. Small, welcoming resort 1km east of Bacon, offering a series of comfortable rooms in cute A-frame nipa huts with private bath; four are duplexes that can sleep up to four, while one has a kitchenette with microwave. ☎ **P2000**
Paguriran Beach Resort Paguriran Beach ☎0918 650 3941. This simple resort on beautiful Paguriran Beach is a nice little place to while away a day or two; there's one cosy a/c A-framed hut with private bath, sleeping five (P3500),

as well as two smaller a/c rooms with thatched roof and shared bath. **P1800**
Sirangan Beach Resort Brgy Caricaran ☎0919 582 2732. This boutique hotel 1km east of Bacon features spacious, tasteful rooms with natural materials such as granite and rattan throughout. Each has its own character; some have fabulous sea views from their four-poster beds. There's a dive shop and snorkelling out in front of the resort. ☎ **P4500**

Bulusan Volcano National Park

Mount Bulusan, in the heart of **Bulusan Volcano National Park**, is one of three active volcanoes in the Bicol region. Trekking has resumed following a series of ash explosions and earthquakes in November 2010 and another small eruption in October 2016, but it remains essential to check the situation before considering an ascent. From **Lake Bulusan** a 6.3km trail (3hr) leads to Aguingay Lake at 940m above sea level. This is where trekkers camp before setting off early to ascend the volcano in time for sunset. At the peak is the Blackbird Crater Lake (1565m), from where there are wonderful 360° views over Mount Mayon to the north, the Philippine Sea and Masbate to the west, the Pacific to the east, and as far afield as the Visayas to the south. Although it is possible to climb the volcano year-round, the **best months** are April and May. If you're feeling really energetic, you can join the **Sky Run**, a yearly race to the volcano's peak that starts in **Bulusan town**, 8km from Lake Bulusan – the record holder is a Kenyan who raced to the peak and back in 3hr 47min in June 2013.

ARRIVAL AND INFORMATION

BULUSAN VOLCANO NATIONAL PARK

By jeepney You can take a jeepney to the town of Irosin from Sorsogon City (every 15min; 45min; P45) or Bulan (15min; 30min; P25) and then another towards Bulusan town (hourly; 30min; P20) – you'll need to jump off at the junction to the volcano, so ask the driver where to get off.
Guides and information Hikers will be refused access by rangers if an eruption warning is up; for guides and

up-to-date details about the state of the volcano, contact the environmental organization AGAP, who can also provide accredited guides (P350 registration fee; guides P1000/group of five; ☎0919 223 1536, ☎agapbulusan @yahoo.com). You should also consult the Philippine Institute of Volcanology and Seismology website (☻phivolcs.dost.gov.ph).

ACCOMMODATION

Balay Buhay Bee Farm ☎0912 790 7046, ☻balaybuhaybeefarm@gmail.com. A lovely bee farm, 5km south of Lake Bulusan, offering accommodation in pleasant grounds with one thousand bee colonies, a tilapia

pond and a freshwater shrimp hatchery. There's also a pretty stone swimming pool with fresh water flowing directly from a spring. As well as simple cottages, there are twin rooms (P1400) and rooms with two sets of bunks (P1500). **P1000**

4

Masbate province

The province of **Masbate** ("maz-bah-tee") lies in the centre of the Philippine archipelago. It comprises the **island of Masbate**, site of the small capital of **Masbate City**, plus two secondary islands – **Burias** and **Ticao** – and numerous smaller islands. There are a number of attractions here – exceptional beaches on Masbate island, such as **Bituon**, for example, along with immense caves in thick jungle such as **Kalanay** and **Batongan** – but it's the infrastructure that's lacking. This is slowly changing, however, with an increased emphasis on tourism and a new ferry route to Manila via Caticlan (and Boracay).

The position of Masbate at the heart of the Philippines leads to some complicated **cultural blending**, with a mix of **languages** including Cebuano, Bicolano, Waray, Ilonggo, Tagalog and Masbateño. The province has long had something of a reputation for violence, with an image throughout the Philippines as a lawless "Wild East" frontier. Like many isolated areas of the archipelago, Masbate does seem a law unto itself and political killings are certainly not unheard of, but its reputation for unfettered goonish violence is mostly unfair. It is highly unlikely that tourists will feel any less **safe** here than in most other parts of the country.

The Wild East moniker is, however, apt for reasons other than lawlessness: Masbate ranks second only to the landlocked province of Bukidnon, Mindanao, in raising **cattle**. There's even an annual **rodeo** in Masbate City in the first or second week in April, where cowboys do battle for big prize money. If you're on the island on a Thursday, take the time to visit the **Uson Livestock Auction Market**, 42km southwest of Masbate City. It is one of the country's largest, with traders from various islands selling carabao, pigs, horses, chickens and goats.

4

Masbate City

The provincial capital of **MASBATE CITY** is attractively situated, nestling between the sea and the hills, but spoilt slightly by unstructured development. The best time to come is during the **Rodeo Masbateño**, a four-day orgy of bull-riding and steer-dogging held every April (around April 3–16).

A number of activities and sights around Masbate City together make a good day-trip by **bangka**. The tourist office (see p.226) should be able to help with arrangements for bangka rental, or you could bargain directly with a fisherman at the pier close to the main transport terminal. Expect to pay around P1000 for a small boat, or P2500 for a medium-sized one.

Pawa boardwalk

4km southwest of Masbate City centre • Jeepney P15; tricycle P75 (15min)

The **Pawa boardwalk** was built primarily to shorten the distance to school for students in the barangay of Pawa. The 1.3km path extends into protected **mangroves** at each side, where migratory birds can be seen, particularly at low tide. The **Pawa Women Mangrove Guardians Association** (☏0910 811 5215), housed in a hut along the boardwalk, organize boat paddling, fishing, shell collecting and mangrove planting. They can also rustle up meals, although make sure to give them at least one day's notice.

Buntod Sandbar

P50 conservation fee • From Masbate City, take a tricycle to the barangay of Nursery (P50), where there are bangkas for private hire (for a round trip including waiting you'll pay P500 for up to three people, P800 for larger groups; 10min)

Out in the pass between Masbate and Ticao islands, in a marine protected area, the **Buntod Sandbar** is a popular spot at the weekend but empty during the week. After paying your conservation fee at the large open-fronted hut, you can relax at a picnic table – be sure to bring some supplies – or on one of the four floating platforms. There's decent snorkelling, too – and equipment for rent at the hut (P50/day).

ARRIVAL AND DEPARTURE

By plane The airport is on the southern edge of town; a tricycle to the centre is P50 (5min). Cebu Pacific and PAL fly to Masbate from Manila (1 daily; 1hr 15min).

By boat Masbate City's ferry pier is west of the centre. There are also boats to Cawayan, on the southern side of Masbate island, from Bogo on Cebu (daily noon; 5hr; P350) and to Mandaon, on the west side, from Roxas (2 weekly; 4hr 30min; P450) and Cajidiocan on Sibuyan (1 weekly; 4hr; P450). Bangkas connect Masbate with Lagundi on Ticao Island (every 30min 8am–4pm; 45min; P80).

Destinations (ferries) Batangas (Super Shuttle: roll-on-roll-off; 1 weekly; 12hr; P555); Bulan, Bicol (Kulafo: 1 daily Mon–Sat; 4hr; P200); Cebu (Cataingan: Super Shuttle: roll-on-roll-off: 1 weekly; 10hr; P555; Trans-Asia: 2 weekly; 12hr; P625); Manila (Montenegro Lines: 1 daily; 11–12hr; P850); Pilar, 15km south of Donsol, Sorsogon province (3 fast crafts daily; 2hr; P394; Denica Lines: 1 roll-on-roll-off daily; 4hr; P230); Pio Duran, Albay (Medallion Transport: 1 daily; 3hr 30min; P200; Isarog: 1 daily; 3hr 30min; P200).

By bus and jeepney Buses, jeepneys and vans use a terminal on Diversion Rd on the southern edge of town, a little beyond the fishing port.

INFORMATION

Tourist information The provincial tourist office (Mon–Fri 8am–5pm; ☎ 056 333 2220, ✉ gerardopresado@yahoo .com) is in the Capitol Building, while the city tourist office is in the City Hall (Mon–Fri 8am–noon & 1–5pm; ☎ 056 588 2402, ⊛ masbatecity.gov.ph). Both can advise on itineraries, although they have little in terms of printed materials.

ACCOMMODATION AND EATING

7-AR Golden Beach Resort Nursery Blvd ☎ 056 582 0175. This pleasant resort is one of the best options in town – the a/c rooms with flatscreen TVs are clean and comfortable. Doubles have a small lounge area, but the singles are very poky. There's a lovely garden with an inviting pool with loungers, a breezy jacuzzi, a thatched restaurant and a nice café with a few books and magazines. Wi-fi at reception only. ☏ **P2500**

Baywalk Garden Blvd Extension, Ibingay St ☎ 056 333 6648, ✉ baywalkghotel@yahoo.com.ph. Pleasant hotel with spacious, well-kept rooms with polished wooden furniture. There's a garden with a couple of shaded areas for breakfast. Wi-fi at reception only. ☏ **P1350**

Doux Seduction Quezon St ☎ 0928 328 8123. This cute café, with bright-yellow walls and wooden crates for chairs, has a bit of a French theme going on, with postcards of Paris and a giant Eiffel Tower. It serves an excellent array of coffees as well as cakes, breads and pastries. They also have wi-fi. Daily 10am–10pm.

★ **Ham's Cup** Ibañez St ☎ 056 582 0205. Located on the ground floor of the *Balay Valencia Hotel*, this chic yet cosy café is good for lunch or dinner, serving international dishes such as burgers (P80), salads (P89) and potatoes with spicy dip (P100), as well as teas and coffees (P50). Daily 1pm–midnight.

★ **Legacy Suites** Purok 8, Masbate Circumferential Rd ☎ 056 582 0210, ⊛ legacysuites.net. This place may look big and impersonal from the outside, but inside you'll find spotless, colourful rooms with a/c and flatscreen TVs, and cosy communal areas with beautiful wooden furniture. There's also a restaurant and an outdoor patio with mini-waterfalls. ☏ **P1350**

MG Hotel Punta Nursery ☎ 056 333 5614, ✉ MG_ hotel2013@yahoo.com. One of the city's best hotels offers spacious a/c rooms with very decent-sized beds (by Filipino standards). Pricier rooms also have a fridge, with the most expensive options (P1650) set around the small pool area. Wi-fi at the restaurant only. Rates include breakfast. ☏ **P1200**

Tio Jose Steak Grills Ibingay St ☎ 056 582 0193. This popular restaurant is a stab at a US-style bar, with sizzlers, steaks and grills (P200) on the menu, as well as Spanish-style tapas. Dishes include *calamares fritos* (P180), onion rings (P95) and buttered chicken (P155), plus plenty of Filipino dishes. It gets pretty lively in the evenings, when locals belt out karaoke. There's wi-fi, too. Daily 11am–11pm.

DIRECTORY

Banks There are plenty of banks along Quezon St, including DBP and Land Bank.

Internet access Loyola on Ibanez St (daily 8.30am–9.30pm; P13/hr; ☎ 0907 111 1054).

Police The police station is in the City Hall (☎ 056 582 0875).

Bituon Beach

The sand at **Bituon Beach** (aka Bagacay Beach), 14km south of Masbate City and 2km down a dirt road from the barangay of **Bagacay**, is not as blindingly white as some, but that's a minor quibble. Some 2km long, the beach, with palm trees at the edge and beautifully clear shallow water, is nonetheless a pretty crescent bay.

ARRIVAL AND DEPARTURE	BITUON BEACH

By jeepney From Masbate City it's a short jeepney ride to Bagacay (hourly; 20min; P20); they stop on the main road from where you can either walk to Bituon Beach (20min) or take a tricycle down the track (P40; 5min).
By tricycle A tricycle all the way from Masbate City (1hr 30min) should cost P300.

ACCOMMODATION

Cocoview Lagoon About 5km north of Bituon, this pleasant stretch of land has freshwater pools and picnic huts that attract scores of *masbateños* over the weekends. They also have a few simple a/c rooms for overnight stays. **P1000**

Batongan Cave

20km inland from Mandaon • Local guide P500; ask around where the jeepney drops you off, or organize in advance at the Masbate City tourist office (see opposite) • Jeepneys (hourly; 45min; P80) and buses (hourly; 1hr) run from Masbate City towards Mandaon; ask the driver to let you off at the caves; there are also boats to Mandaon from Roxas, in Panay (2 weekly; 4hr 30min; P450) and Cajidiocan on Sibuyan (1 weekly; 4hr; P450)

The town of **MANDAON** is 64km west of Masbate City on the opposite coast. The trip by jeepney takes you along a scenic road that passes through pastureland, paddy fields and a number of isolated settlements inhabited by subsistence farmers. There's not much in Mandaon itself, but it's a good base for exploring two of the island's most noted natural wonders: **Kalanay Cave** on the northwest coast 40km from Mandaon, and, 20km nearer town, **Batongan Cave**. Both make excellent day-trips, but Batongan is the better of the two, with immense caverns and a large population of bats whose guano is collected and used as fertilizer. About 100m away is an **underground river**, which you can swim in. It's easy to get lost in these parts and if you fall and get injured you might not be found for days, so don't explore the caves or the river without a **local guide**.

4

Palani Beach

About 5km north of **BALUD** on Masbate's western coast is **Palani Beach**, a wonderful, 5km-long virgin stretch of sand fringed with palm trees and lapped by crystal-clear waters. There are only a handful of simple resorts here, but if you're happy to stay in basic accommodation then it's a wonderful place to unwind for a few days. During the week you'll have the entire beach to yourself, while on weekends it gets busy with *masbateños* from all over the island. You can also camp here.

ARRIVAL AND DEPARTURE	PALANI BEACH

By jeepney Regular jeepneys make the journey from Masbate City to Balud (hourly; 3hr; P100), from where you can take a tricycle to Palani Beach (15min; P100).

ACCOMMODATION

Bataga Resort Palani Beach ☎ 0920 735 9395. One of the very few resorts along this beautiful stretch of coast, this simple place consists of a handful of basic fan and a/c rooms with cold showers; all are very simple, but it's a great place to get away from it all. **P500**

Placer

On Masbate island's southwest coast, the small town of **PLACER** doesn't offer much to visitors, but it does have a pleasant stretch of beach with a few newish resorts. The waters around here are rich in giant squid, scallops and, in particular, **crabs** – the provincial tourist office in Masbate City (see opposite) can help organize a visit to a crab production plant.

ARRIVAL AND DEPARTURE

PLACER

By jeepney Regular jeepneys make the journey from Masbate City to Placer (hourly; 2hr; P140). There are also boats from Bogo on Cebu (daily noon; 5hr; P350) to Cawayan, which is 60km north of Placer.

ACCOMMODATION

Virginia Beach Resort Pasiagon ☎ 0939 627 3269. One of the best places to stay on the whole of Masbate island, this pretty resort is a 5min tricycle ride from Placer. As well as one *kubo* beach hut (P1500), there are three tastefully furnished rooms facing a leafy pool area with wooden four-poster beds, kitchenette with fridge and kettle, and patios with cushioned rattan seating. The resort organizes bangka hire (P2500 return trip) to nearby islands. 🛜 **P1800**

Ticao Island

Beautiful and laidback **Ticao Island**, across the Masbate Passage from Masbate City, is well worth the one-hour bangka trip. The infrastructure is mostly basic and the roads can be very difficult in the rainy season, but Ticao is home to beautiful scenery and lovely **beaches** with crystal-clear waters, and it's deliciously unvisited. A convenient way to get around is to hire a bangka for around P3000 and explore the coast. Ask the boatman to take you to **Talisay**, the island's finest beach, and then on to **Catandayagan Falls**, the only waterfall in the country – and one of the very few in the world – where fresh water cascades directly into the sea. It's an impressive sight, plunging 60m into the emerald-green waters below. It's a perfect spot to have a swim, too.

ARRIVAL AND DEPARTURE

TICAO ISLAND

By boat Bangkas connect Masbate pier to Lagundi, on Ticao's southwest coast (every 30min 8am–4pm; 45min; P80); there are also bangkas from Bulan in Sorsogon province to San Jacinto on the northeast of Ticao Island (5 daily; 1hr; P100) and from Pilar to Monreal in the north (2 daily; 1hr 30min; P145).

ACCOMMODATION

Altamar Boutique Resort ☎ 02 817 7463, 🌐 ticao altamar.com. Set in large, lush grounds, this lovely resort consists of a hilltop villa, Yellow House, with a welcoming lounge and four cosy private rooms decorated with vases, rugs, books and wicker and wood furniture. There are also attractive cottages set around the grounds, with neat and tidy rooms, although they are smaller than in the main building, and not quite as homely. Activities include kayaking, horse-riding along the beach and island-hopping trips. Full board only; rates are per person. 🛜 Rooms and cottages **P3500**

★**Ticao Island Resort** ☎ 02 893 8173, 🌐 donsolecotour .com. This friendly place has four welcoming budget rooms and, on a pretty stretch of beach, nine comfortable a/c cabañas (P2600) with parquet flooring and spacious bathrooms. The resort grows its own vegetables, and the restaurant menu includes delicious home-made bread, pizza and pasta. Staff can organize fishing trips, kayaking, firefly river tours, horseriding and cooking lessons. There's limited wi-fi available in the restaurant only. Full board only; rates are per person. 🛜 **P1700**

SNORKELLING AND DIVING FROM TICAO ISLAND

Ticao Island is surrounded by spectacular **dive sites**, one of the best known being the huge Manta Bowl, the cleaning and feeding station for local manta rays. There are five different dive sites within the bowl, with depths ranging from 14 to 29 metres. Most of these are for advanced divers, so if you're after something less intense, head north of Ticao to the island of **San Miguel**, which has another twelve dive sites, better suited to less experienced divers. Night dive options are available at the **Pasil Ree**, found in front of *Ticao Island Resort* (see above). The waters in the **Ticao Pass**, to the east of Ticao island, are rich in plankton and attract many types of sharks including black-tip reef sharks, tiger sharks, hammerheads and even the mighty whale shark; many of these sharks can be spotted while diving and snorkelling here.

The best way to organize **dive or snorkel trips** to these sites is to contact the excellent dive shop at *Ticao Island Resort* (☎ 02 893 8173, 🌐 donsolecotour.com), which also offers PADI and SSI dive courses. Manta Bowl (see p.228) also lies within easy reach of Donsol and trips can be arranged from here too.

Catanduanes Island

Once known as the "Land of the Howling Winds" thanks to its reputation for typhoons, the eastern island province of **Catanduanes** has rebranded itself as "The Happy Island" in honour of the affability and resilience of its people. Ripe for exploration, it's a large, rugged, rural island with endless stretches of majestic coastline. While **surfers** have known about Catanduanes for some time, attracted to the big waves off **Puraran Beach** on the wild east coast, the island has barely felt the impact of tourism, although with four flights a week from Manila and improvements to the main road around the island, this is slowly changing. There are several good beaches within easy reach of the capital **Virac**, along with the immense caves in **Lictin**, while the undeveloped west coast offers the opportunity to blaze a trail into areas few travellers see. Above all Catanduanes is a friendly, down-to-earth place to hang out for a few days, adjusting to a slower pace of life and travel.

When Filipinos think about Catanduanes they think mostly of **bad weather** – the island lies on the exposed eastern edge of the archipelago, smack in the middle of the "typhoon highway". Unless you are a surfer (surf season is roughly July–Oct), the best time to visit is from March to June, when the chances of rainfall are slight and the wind is less wicked. During the wet season (July–Nov), the island can be hit half a dozen times by **typhoons**, causing extensive damage to crops and homes and sometimes loss of life.

Virac

VIRAC is an anonymous provincial town, busy with mercantile activity and the noise of jeepneys. There is a small central plaza with a cathedral and a lively market, and an interesting local **museum**, but for most visitors Virac will simply be a base for exploring the rest of the island.

Museo de Catanduanes

Old Capitol Building, Santa Elena St • Mon–Fri 8am–4pm • P50

The **Museo de Catanduanes**, within the same building as Virac's tourist office, is worth a look. Artefacts include fishing implements and trumpet shells used to send out signals to local communities. Objects from the Spanish colonial era include the intricately decorated walking cane of a Spanish congressman, which he allegedly used to accessorize his sharkskin coat and felt hat.

Around Virac

You will find some good **beaches** west of Virac in the villages of **Magnesia** and **Palawig**, particularly good for sunbathing and swimming, and east at **Buenavista**, although Puraran (see p.230) is the best for surfing. Inland from Palawig there are enormous limestone **caves** near the village of **Lictin**. To get there you'll need to find a guide in Lictin (there are no established rates, but P500 is a reasonable amount to pay); contact the tourist office in

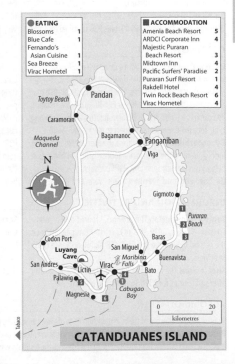

● EATING		■ ACCOMMODATION	
Blossoms	1	Amenia Beach Resort	5
Blue Cafe	1	ARDCI Corporate Inn	4
Fernando's		Majestic Puraran	
Asian Cuisine	1	Beach Resort	3
Sea Breeze	1	Midtown Inn	4
Virac Hometel	1	Pacific Surfers' Paradise	2
		Puraran Surf Resort	1
		Rakdell Hotel	4
		Twin Rock Beach Resort	6
		Virac Hometel	4

CATANDUANES ISLAND

Virac (see below) before setting out, or ask at the barangay hall in Lictin or in any of the village stores. The best known is **Luyang Cave**, whose waters are said to have healing properties. Another good short trip from Virac is to the **Maribina Falls**, between the barangays of Marinawa and Binanwahan – thus the name – fifteen minutes inland by jeepney. The waterfall plunges more than 10m into a crystal-clear pool that's good for swimming.

Puraran Beach

30km northeast of Virac • Surfboard rental and lessons P350/hr • One morning jeepney from Virac passes Puraran (1hr; P50) on its way to Gigmoto at 10.30–11am; there are also jeepneys from Virac to Baras (hourly; 40min; P40), from where it's a P150 tricycle trip (20min) to the beach; beach resorts can arrange a tricycle back to Baras

The break at beautiful **Puraran Beach** is referred to as **Majestic** by surfers. Majestic is fickle but it's generally thought that the best bet is to come here between **July and October**, when low-pressure areas lurking out in the Pacific help kick up a swell (though if these areas turn into tropical storms or typhoons, surfing is not advisable).

Luckily, you don't have to be a surfer to enjoy a few days on a beach as lovely as this. Extensive **coral gardens** just offshore make for wonderful snorkelling, and swimming is safe inside the line of the reef and away from the rocks – ask for advice at your resort before heading out, though, as it is not unknown for swimmers to get into trouble. Puraran is still mercifully undeveloped, with just three basic resorts.

ARRIVAL AND DEPARTURE   CATANDUANES ISLAND

By plane Virac's airport is 4km west of the town. A tricycle into Virac will cost around P50, or less if you walk away from the airport waiting area. Cebu Pacific has flights from Manila (4 weekly; 1hr 10min).

By boat From Tabaco, there are ferries to Virac (2 daily; 8am and 2pm; 3hr 30min; P240, plus P30 terminal fee) and a new fast craft to San Andres (2 daily, 7am and 12pm; 1hr 30min; P320, plus P30 terminal fee). From Guijalo port in the Caramoan Peninsula you can hire a private bangka to Codon port on the western coast of Catanduanes island (45min; P1500), from where you can catch a tricycle to Virac (1hr; P500).

GETTING AROUND

By rental car Hiring a car with a driver is a good if expensive way to see the island; try the drivers at the airport, visit the provincial tourist office in Virac (see below) or simply ask your accommodation to arrange it. For P2000–3000, for instance, you can get a return trip to Puraran Beach including waiting time; for a full day exploring expect to pay P4000–5000.

By motorbike Motorbikes are a cheaper way of exploring independently; the provincial tourist office in Virac (see below) can help arrange rental (P500/day).

By bus, van and jeepney Buses, vans and jeepneys to destinations on the west side of Catanduanes leave from the barangay of Gogon in Virac. From Gogon, buses and vans to Pandan (buses every 2hr; 4hr; vans hourly 1–5pm; 3hr; P150) pass through Caramoran (bus 3hr 30min; vans 2hr 30min; P150); there are also jeepneys to San Andres, with the first departure at 6am, and sporadic departures thereafter (20min; P30). From Virac pier, vans run to Bagamanoc (every 2hr until 1pm and then hourly thereafter; 1hr 30min; P80) and Viga (hourly; 1hr 15min; P80); there are also local buses to Bagamanoc (noon & 2pm; 2hr).

INFORMATION AND ACTIVITIES

Tourist information The provincial tourist office (Mon–Fri 8am–5pm; ☏ 0929 399 8437, ⊛ tourism.gov.ph) is on the second floor of the Old Capitol Building on Santa Elena St in Virac.

Surf lessons The resorts at Puraran Beach (see opposite) offer surf lessons for P350/hr including board rental.

Services All the services are in Virac. There are a few banks, including PNB and BDO, on the main plaza and a branch of DBP on the ground floor of the Old Capitol Building, just below the tourist office. The post office is at the back of the municipal building.

ACCOMMODATION

If you're keen to stay out of town, but within reach of Virac's amenities, try the *Twin Rock* or *Amenia Beach* resorts. The resorts at **Puraran Beach** are very laidback and it is not unusual to end up staying for longer than you had planned. Note that electricity is often limited to a few hours a day, and that **wi-fi** at all the resorts is very unreliable, and often only available at their restaurants.

VIRAC

ARDCI Corporate Inn 4th Floor, ARDCI Corporate Building, San Roque ☏0998 988 2476, ⓦardci innvirac.com. On two floors of an office block with floor-to ceiling windows, this is a good option; rooms are comfortable and the bathrooms have rain showers. There's a café with views over the rice paddies and Virac. Breakfast included. Limited wi-fi. ☏ **P1300**

Midtown Inn San José St ☏0947 563 8165, ⓦcatmidinn.com. One of the best options in town, just off the main roundabout, with a little communal lounge on the first floor. Most rooms have a/c, cable TV and private bathrooms with hot showers. Limited wi-fi. ☏ **P1344**

Rakdell Hotel San Pedro St ☏052 811 0881, ⓔjoshpampanga@yahoo.com. Budget option with acceptable a/c rooms with private bath and hot shower – but its location opposite a popular nightspot means that it can be noisy. On the plus side, there's a roof-deck restaurant where guests can enjoy their meals. Limited wi-fi. ☏ **P1000**

Virac Hometel Virac Diverson Rd, San Roque ☏0919 994 5079. This cosy guesthouse is set in a large garden, filled with bamboo huts for dining. Inside there's lots of polished wood, and clean and simple a/c rooms. Traditional Filipino breakfast is included. Limited wi-fi. ☏ **P1200**

AROUND VIRAC

Amenia Beach Resort Palawig Beach, San Andres ☏0915 353 0020. Some 12km west of Virac, the real draw here is the lovely beach outside, which is popular with day-trippers but is also a pleasant spot to stay. The nine rooms here, named after local trees, are appealing enough, with

decent-sized beds, and there are a couple of swimming pools. **P2000**

Twin Rock Beach Resort Brgy Igang ☏047 252 9978, ⓦtwinrockcatanduanes.com. About 10km south of Virac, this is one of the island's most developed resorts, with leafy grounds on a lovely stretch of beach in front of two jagged rock formations. It offers a range of room options, from claustrophobic rock cottages without pool access to larger deluxe a/c rooms (P1650) with pool access included. There's a zipline over the sea, a climbing wall, kayaks and a pool with two slides. The noisy karaoke is a drawback. Limited wi-fi. ☏ **P600**

PURARAN BEACH

Pacific Surfers' Paradise ☏0917 738 2941. Lovely thatched wooden cottages (a/c P1500) towards the middle of the beach, decorated with native materials and patterns of tree rings on the floors. There's also a nipa restaurant serving Filipino dishes. **P800**

Puraran Surf Resort ☏0915 764 9133, ⓦpuraransurf .com. First resort on the beach, with rooms in a concrete block at the back, as well as seven simple, welcoming bamboo and palm-leaf cottages (P600) with wooden beds. There are also a couple of cottages with a/c (P1800), and a restaurant. **P400**

Majestic Puraran Beach Resort ☏0929 424 3818, ⓦmajesticpuraran.com.ph. Six rustic fan-cooled thatched cottages set around a wide garden at the far end of the beach, with wooden balconies with swinging hammocks. There are also a couple of a/c rooms in a concrete block, which are not nearly as nice (P1000). Surf lessons (P350 p/hr) and massages are also available. **P650**

4

EATING

Unless you're staying in one of the two upmarket resorts, the best **restaurants** can be found in the city of Virac. The only places to eat at Puraran Beach are within the three simple resorts.

VIRAC

Blossoms Salvacion St ☏0932 710 0576. The most atmospheric restaurant in town, with wooden chairs set around a breezy dining area. They serve pasta (P65–80) and pizza (P125), as well as seafood (P195), noodles (P45) and cakes (P55) such as mango and walnut. Mon–Sat 7am–10pm.

Blue Café Gogon ☏0915 420 8434. This cosy café, located on the second floor of Virac Town Centre shopping mall, offers a good selection of savoury dishes such as pastas (P110–140) and panini (P55), as well as waffles (P65) and cakes (P35). Daily 10am–9am.

Fernando's Asian Cuisine Gogon ☏0908 977 1162. On the third floor of Virac Town Centre mall, this large and friendly restaurant filled with cosy booths and long tables

serves all kinds of Asian cuisine, from Japanese and Thai to Korean and Chinese, as well as Filipino. Dishes include aubergine and beef hot pot (P180), Korean *bibimbap* (P200) and California maki sushi (P120). It also offers fabulous city views. Daily 11am–2pm and 4–9pm.

Sea Breeze Pier Side, PPA Building, Brgy Salvacion ☏0906 494 6597. Located by the pier, with shaded wooden huts by the beach, this is a pleasant spot for a beer (P50) and a sea breeze; the food, however, is less than average. Free wi-fi. Daily 7am–1am.

Virac Hometel Virac Diverson Rd, San Roque ☏0919 994 5079. Set in the garden of a cosy B&B, with tables in individual thatched bamboo huts. Typical Filipino plates include sizzling chicken (P190) and *bistek* (P235), as well as pasta dishes (P170). Daily 7am–9pm.

Mindoro

BANGKA, SABANG

5

Mindoro

Within a few hours of Manila, yet worlds away, Mindoro remains undeveloped even by Philippine provincial standards. Much of the island is wild and rugged, with some near-impenetrable hinterlands and an often desolate coastline of wide bays and isolated fishing villages. The island, seventh largest in the archipelago, is divided lengthways into two provinces, Mindoro Occidental and Mindoro Oriental; the latter is the more developed and visited. Most travellers head this way only for the beaches, scuba diving and nightlife around picturesque Poblacion (Puerto Galera town) on Mindoro Oriental's northern coast, a short ferry trip across the Isla Verde Passage from Batangas, but there is much more to Mindoro than this. Few people, Filipinos included, realize that the island is home to several areas of outstanding natural beauty, all protected to some degree by local or international decree.

ARRIVAL AND DEPARTURE   MINDORO

BY PLANE

San José airport In the south of Mindoro Occidental, the airport is served by one daily flight (1hr) from Manila with Cebu Pacific. There is no airport serving Puerto Galera.

BY BOAT

Manila to Puerto Galera A good way to reach Puerto Galera and Sabang from Manila is to buy a combined bus-boat ticket with Si-Kat (☎02 708 9628, ☜sikatferrybus. com; daily 8.30am; arrive Sabang 12.15pm and Muelle pier 1pm; P800); the bus departs from their office at City State Tower, 1315 Mabini St, Ermita.

Batangas City to Puerto Galera and northern Mindoro The main ferry port for departures to Muelle pier in Poblacion (Puerto Galera town) is Batangas City (see p.116). There are frequent departures (daily 6.30am–5pm) from Batangas to Muelle pier (P230), Sabang (P230) and White Beach (P270) on large outriggers, easy to find on arrival at Batangas Port Terminal 3; companies running them include Father and Son Shipping Line (FSL; ☎043 287 3047, ☜puertogaleraferry.net).

A chartered outrigger will cost at least P4000 one-way. All passengers must also pay the terminal fee (P30), and an environmental fee (P50) upon arrival. In addition, Montenegro Lines (☎043 740 3201) operate a car ferry from Batangas City to Balatero, 3km west of Poblacion (daily 7am & noon; 2hr; passengers P170).

Batangas City to Calapan and Abra de Ilog Port Montenegro Lines (☎043 740 3201) run ferries every other hour to Calapan (P240), 44km southeast of Galera, and Abra de Ilog Port (6 daily; P260), 30km west. Fast Cat (☎632 816 1183) also runs between Batangas and Calapan (midnight, 1.30am, 6am, 9am, 11am, 2.30pm, 6pm and 8pm; P190) in just 1hr 30min.

Batangas City to San José Montenegro Lines (☎043 740 3201) operate ferries to San José (Mon, Wed & Fri 6pm; P726).

Roxas to Caticlan (for Boracay) Roxas (163km southeast of Puerto Galera) is a key link on the Strong Nautical Highway route to Boracay, and there are regular ferries departing for Caticlan (4hr). Starlite Ferries (☎02 724 3034) runs three times daily (1am, 9pm & 11pm, returning noon & 4pm; P420; ☎043 723 9965), while Montenegro Lines (☎043 740 3201) has five daily boats (usually 4am, 10am, 4pm, 8pm & midnight; P460).

Bulalacao to Caticlan (for Boracay) Bulalacao, 44km south of Roxas, has two daily departures to Caticlan with

WHITE FAN CORAL, MINDORO

Highlights

❶ Puerto Galera The area around this picturesque coastal resort has fine beaches, challenging treks and scuba diving for every level. **See p.237**

❷ Tribal visits Get an intriguing insight into a marginalized culture by meeting the island's original inhabitants, the Mangyan. **See p.243**

❸ Mount Halcon Mindoro's highest peak is a serious hiking challenge through mist-shrouded jungle with jaw-dropping vistas of the whole island. **See p.247**

❹ Mounts Iglit-Baco National Park See the rare tamaraw, a type of water buffalo, as you trek through some of the most enchanting countryside on Mindoro. **See p.252**

❺ North Pandan Island Idyllic island hideaway just off the west coast, a tranquil resort offering scuba diving, snorkelling or the chance to just laze on the bone-white sands. **See p.253**

❻ Apo Reef Superlative diving in one of the most pristine marine environments in the world, where sharks, rays and other pelagics are common sightings; you can spend the night on a remote islet, too. **See p.254**

HIGHLIGHTS ARE MARKED ON THE MAP ON P.236

5

Fast Cat (📞 632 816 1183; 10am & 10pm, returning 3am & 3pm; 3hr; P375).

San José to Cuyo Island and Taytay Montenegro Lines operates ferries to Cuyo Island and Taytay in Palawan, but there are no set schedules and services operate on demand.

BY BUS

Manila to San José Dimple Star Transport (📞 02 517 9677) runs two direct bus routes to Mindoro from Manila (3 daily) from Ali Mall in Cubao and Pasay to San José, both via Batangas port (10hr). From here some buses take the ferry between Batangas and Abra de Ilog Port before continuing on to San José via Sablayan, while other buses take the ferry between Batangas and Calapan and then continue on to San José via Roxas. Tickets will be at least P1100 one-way.

HIGHLIGHTS

1. Puerto Galera
2. Tribal visits
3. Mount Halcon
4. Mounts Iglit-Baco National Park
5. North Pandan Island
6. Apo Reef

5

Mindoro Oriental

Most visitors head to **Mindoro Oriental**, which is more accessible and developed than its poorer neighbour across the mountains, to dive in the marine reserve at **Puerto Galera**, in the north of the province. Nearby **Mount Malasimbo** is also protected because of the biodiversity of its thickly jungled slopes. To the east of Puerto Galera, near the port of **Calapan**, is **Mount Halcon** – at 2587m, Mindoro's tallest peak and a difficult climb even for experienced mountaineers. The south of the island is less populated than the north, with few tourists making it as far as **Roxas** on the southeast coast unless they're taking a ferry to Caticlan (for Boracay) from **Bulalacao**, around 44km south of Roxas.

Puerto Galera

One of the country's most popular resorts, **PUERTO GALERA** (meaning "Port of the Galleons") boasts some of the most diverse coral reef diving in Asia and gorgeous, sugar-sand beaches, as a result of which the whole area is often mobbed during national holidays. Arriving by ferry is a memorable experience, the boat slipping gently through aquamarine waters past a series of headlands fringed with haloes of sand and coconut trees. Brilliant white yachts lie at anchor in the innermost bay and in the background looms the brooding hulk of Mount Malasimbo, invariably crowned with a ring of cumulus cloud.

Founded by the Spanish in 1574, the town was once an important port and served as Mindoro's capital until 1837, when Calapan assumed the role. Today it's a natural choice for escaping Manileños, so book ahead if you're planning to visit during Easter and summer weekends. There's also plenty on offer in addition to diving, including excellent snorkelling, trekking into the mountains and beach- and island-hopping by bangka.

Poblacion (Puerto Galera town)

Poblacion, Puerto Galera town itself, occupies a marvellous location, overlooking Muelle Bay on one side, with green hills behind it. Despite its picturesque location, the town is a little chaotic – filled with tricycle traffic, and offering few good restaurants and places to stay. Other than watching the bangkas phut-phut back and forth from one of the waterfront cafés and bars near Muelle pier, there's not much to see or do. Most tourists move straight on to the beaches and dive resorts, but with some time to kill you might visit the small **Excavation Museum** or take a glance at the canon-flanked marble **Cross at Muelle**, near the pier; it was erected by the Spanish to commemorate the sinking of the battleship *Canonero Mariveles* in 1879 during a storm.

■ ACCOMMODATION			
Blue Crystal Beach Resort	7	Marco Vincent Dive Resort	3
Coco Beach Island Resort	1	Mountain Beach Resort	9
El Cañonero	10	Summer Connection	2
Kalaw Place	4	Sunset at Aninuan Beach Resort	6
Luca's	8	Tamaraw Beach Resort	5

● EATING	
Ciao Italia	1
Luca's Cucina Italiana	2

PUERTO GALERA AREA

Python Cave, Tamaraw Falls, Calapan, Roxas & San José ▼

5

PUERTO GALERA ORIENTATION

Though Puerto Galera does have a commercial centre (aka **Poblacion** or **Puerto Galera town**), the name is generally used to refer to the whole area between **Sabang**, 5km to the east, and **White Beach**, 8km to the west. Most visitors head straight for Sabang and the nearby beaches of **Small La Laguna** and **Big La Laguna**, home to a diverse range of accommodation, diving, restaurants and nightlife. There are a couple of resorts near the village of **Palangán**, about halfway along the road from Puerto Galera to Sabang. Northeast of Palangán there's a small isolated cove at **Sinandigan** with a handful of very peaceful options. In the other direction, picturesque White Beach has plenty of accommodation and is popular with partying Manileños at the weekends. For the best beaches and more of a remote experience, walk – or take a tricycle – further west to beautiful **Aninuan Beach** with its range of plush resorts; or **Talipanan Beach**, which has a couple of comfortable and affordable places to stay.

Excavation Museum

Nautical Hwy at P. Concepcion St • Daily 8–11.30am & 1.30–5pm • Free (donation suggested)

Located near the town hall and within the grounds of the Immaculate Conception Church, the **Excavation Museum** contains a small but intriguing collection of items excavated from gravesites and underwater wrecks in the region – some items date back to 200 BC. Highlights include fragments of ancient Chinese porcelain and Siamese pottery, as well as Ming dynasty burial jars.

Sabang and around

Set in a pretty cove, **Sabang** is jam-packed with hotels, restaurants and dive schools, and appeals to primarily foreign tourists. Despite its popularity, there's not much of a beach here, so it's not great for swimming; and there's a very visible girlie-bar scene that comes as a shock to many visitors. At night the small rabbit warren of streets behind the beach can feel a little seedy. If you arrive here by bangka from Batangas City, you'll be dropped right on the beachfront.

Small La Laguna

Just a few minutes' walk northwest along the coast from Sabang beach, **Small La Laguna** is the ideal choice if you're looking for a range of friendly accommodation in a quiet location – most of it right on the water – with good dive operators and a handful of informal bars and restaurants. The beach here is still not great, however, so if you're looking for something more tropical, head around the headland to Big La Laguna (see below).

Big La Laguna

The sheltered cove of **Big La Laguna** has dive shops and a few good accommodation options, some with convivial beach-style bars and restaurants attached. With largely clean sands, this is the best spot in the Sabang area for swimming, and there's safe snorkelling over the offshore coral reef (boats are prohibited). Further west lies pretty **Coco Beach**, dominated by the plush *Coco Beach Island Resort* (see p.243) and pretty much the preserve of the resort's guests.

Palangán and Sinandigan Cove

To the southeast of Sabang lies quiet **Sinandigan Cove**, also known as Coral Cove, dominated by the Escarceo Point lighthouse. Other than a few abandoned resorts, there's not much here, but it makes for a lovely walk from Sabang and offers spectacular coastal views. Six kilometres to the southwest you'll find the barangay of **Palangán**, home to a few quiet and comfortable places to stay. Some are on the ridge above the road, with marvellous views across Puerto's bays and islets, and are just a short walk from the beach. Not all of these resorts have dive centres, but they can all help arrange diving through operators in Sabang.

White Beach

A once quiet crescent of sand, spectacular **White Beach** has in recent years been populated by small resort hotels and cottage rooms popular with Filipino families. Unlike Sabang, there are not many girlie bars and fewer scuba divers too, but it does have a number of lively discos and bars that can get a bit noisy. White Beach gets especially busy at peak times, notably New Year and Easter, when backpackers and students from Manila hold all-night rave parties on the sand. There are still some quieter spots on the beach, but those looking for an isolated and quiet beach experience should head on to Aninuan and Talipanan (see below).

Aninuan and Talipanan

By far the two best beaches in the Puerto Galera area, **Aninuan** and **Talipanan** both have vast swathes of empty golden sand and good range of accommodation options, from upmarket resorts to laidback guesthouses. While slightly more difficult to reach via public transport, they can both be accessed by walking along the shoreline (20–30mins from White Beach) and, when the tide is in, via a pathway that leads up over the headland. Aninuan is more popular, while Talipanan is for those seeking real solitude. There's no nightlife and no karaoke – just you, the fishermen and the fireflies.

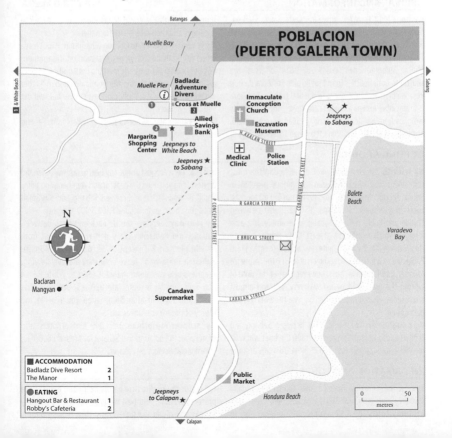

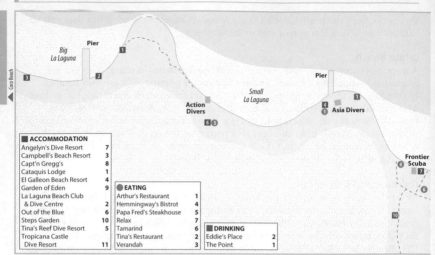

ACCOMMODATION

Angelyn's Dive Resort	7
Campbell's Beach Resort	3
Capt'n Gregg's	8
Cataquis Lodge	1
El Galleon Beach Resort	4
Garden of Eden	9
La Laguna Beach Club & Dive Centre	2
Out of the Blue	6
Steps Garden	10
Tina's Reef Dive Resort	5
Tropicana Castle Dive Resort	11

EATING

Arthur's Restaurant	1
Hemmingway's Bistrot	4
Papa Fred's Steakhouse	5
Relax	7
Tamarind	6
Tina's Restaurant	2
Verandah	3

DRINKING

Eddie's Place	2
The Point	1

ARRIVAL AND INFORMATION

PUERTO GALERA

By boat Most travellers arrive at Puerto Galera via boat from Batangas (see p.116) at Muelle pier in Poblacion, or direct to Sabang (see p.238) and White Beach (see p.239). Though no boats travel direct to Aninuan or Talipanan, Minolo Shipping Lines (❶043 287 3614) offers a free shuttle to both beaches from Muelle pier. For Abra de Ilog Port, further west in Mindoro Occidental (the road to Abra is impassable except on foot or trail bike), there are daily bangkas from Balatero at around 10.30am (around P250; 1hr), providing the seas aren't too rough (check with your hotel), although a safer way to get there is to head back to Batangas and then take a ferry from there.

By jeepney Jeepneys to Calapan (1hr 30min; P100) leave when full from the Petron petrol station on the southern edge of Poblacion from early morning until mid-afternoon; a/c minivans also make the trip from a depot 2km further out of town; they're slightly more expensive, but will get you there quicker.

By bus One Calapan-bound jeepney leaves from Sabang each morning.

GETTING AROUND

By tricycle Tricycles are always available and the most convenient way to zip between the various beaches in Galera, though drivers are notorious for ripping off tourists. Locals pay around P30/person (P50 at night) between Muelle pier/Poblacion and Sabang for example, but as a foreigner you'll be asked for at least P200/tricycle (getting them down to P100 is quite an achievement). From Poblacion to White Beach reckon on at least P160, more for Aninuan and Talipanan. Note, however, that at the time of writing the road to Talipanan was very bad and almost impassable when it rains, so walking via the beach is the best option.

By bangka Bangkas regularly ply between Sabang and White Beach (40min); for around P1500 the boat will wait for you (one-way will cost P1000-plus). You can arrange bangkas between just about any beach; rates will depend on how long you need the boat for and your haggling skills. Small pumpboats travel between Sabang and Big/Small La Laguna beaches for around P200 (P400 at night).

By jeepney Jeepneys shuttle back and forth between Sabang and Poblacion (they depart up the hill from Muelle pier, on P. Concepcion St; 6am–6pm; 15min), although these won't leave until they are overflowing. Jeepneys also run along the west coast to White Beach and Aninuan. Most routes are P20–25, but note that most stop running after 5pm, when you'll be at the mercy of the tricycle drivers.

By scooter/motorbike You can rent scooters and motorbikes in Poblacion and Sabang for around P800/day; try asking at *Badladz Dive Resort*.

INFORMATION AND TOURS

Tourist information There's a small tourist office (daily 7.30am–5pm; ❶043 287 3051) at Muelle pier.

Jeepney tours There are a couple of tour operators in town, but their offices are hardly ever open and they're pretty unreliable. Your best bet is to hire a local jeepney to take you round the sights; most drivers have photos

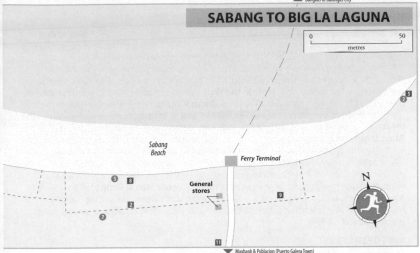

▲ Bangkas to Batangas City

SABANG TO BIG LA LAGUNA

5

Sabang Beach

Ferry Terminal

General stores

N

▼ Maxbank & Poblacion (Puerto Galera Town)

and descriptions of local attractions plastered up inside their jeepneys to give you an idea of where to go. A day's private hire costs around P1700, and as the price is for the whole jeepney, it's cost-effective to join up with other travellers.

ACCOMMODATION

With direct boats from Batangas to Sabang and White Beach, there's really little need to stay in **Poblacion (Puerto Galera town)**; that said, if you want to escape the beach scene, there are a couple of decent hotels here. Accommodation choices in **Sabang** range from small resorts to more expensive dive resort options. Generally speaking, the accommodation to the west of the main road, which is closer to the nightlife, is pricier than that to the quieter east. **White Beach** is now very popular, and room prices have rocketed. It can be hard to find a decent budget room, particularly at weekends and holidays; it's definitely worth booking in advance. **Aninuan Beach** has the best range of both upmarket and mid-range resorts, while **Talipanan** has some good budget options. Note that though **wi-fi** is available in most resorts listed here, it's often unreliable and limited to public areas such as the lobby or poolside.

POBLACION (PUERTO GALERA TOWN)
Badladz Dive Resort Muelle pier ☎ 043 287 3693, ⓦ badladz.com; map p.239. Geared to divers rather than beach-lovers, with great bay views and spacious rooms with hot water, a/c and cable TV. There's also a dive shop (see box, p.242). Wi-fi in public areas. ☞ P1490

★**The Manor** Yacht Club Rd, Brgy Santo Nino ☎ 0926 937 7908, ⓦ themanorpuertogalera.com; map p.239. The only luxury offering in the town is this modern mansion, on a ridge above the Yacht Club (500m west of the Immaculate Conception Church) with spectacular views in all directions. Each room is individually decorated and features high-quality furnishings and modern art – the "Presidential Suite" and "Indonesian Room" are particularly impressive. There are also a couple of houses for rent, which are great for families. In the grounds you'll find tennis courts and an infinity pool, and there's a free boat shuttle from the Yacht Club. ☞ P3880

SABANG BEACH
Angelyn's Dive Resort ☎ 0915 266 1564, ⓦ angelynsdiveresort.com; map pp.240–241. Good location right on the beach, at the far western end, and only a short walk from dive operators, bars and restaurants. All rooms have a/c, cable TV and mini-fridges and some have private balconies. There's also a small open-air restaurant. Wi-fi in the restaurant. ☞ P2350

Capt'n Gregg's ☎ 0917 540 4570, ⓦ captngreggs.com; map pp.240–241. Turn left at the end of the road in Sabang, and it's a 2min walk along the beach to get to this popular, well-established resort catering mainly to divers, with acceptable rooms (the cheapest come with fans only, but all have flatscreen TVs), decent food and useful advice from the resident divers in the dive shop, many of whom have lived in Sabang for years. ☞ P1400

★**Garden of Eden** ☎ 043 287 3096, ⓦ cocktaildivers .com; map pp.240–241. Just east of Sabang Pier, this is one of the area's most attractive and relaxed resorts, with

5

DIVING IN PUERTO GALERA

The beauty of scuba diving around Puerto Galera is the number and variety of **dive sites** that can be reached by boat in a matter of minutes. These offer something for everyone, from exhilarating dives in raging currents to gentle drifts along sheltered coral reefs.

A good option for novices is West Escarceo, a drift dive sloping down gently from 5m to 30m. Look out for electric clams in the small caves here and big schools of snapper, trevally and sweetlips. Just west of here, **Hole in the Wall** is another popular spot to see large schools, particularly of drummer fish and batfish. The **Sabang Wrecks**, two wooden wrecks and a steel yacht, are home to surgeonfish, moray eels, lionfish, and even quirky frogfish and stargazers. In the shallow areas around the sea grass you can also see green sea turtles. Finally, don't miss the **Alma Jane Wreck**, where advanced divers can safely swim below deck to explore the cargo holds. The ship is now a refuge for lionfish and rabbitfish, among others.

A more challenging dive is the **Canyons**, a healthy reef split into three slab-like sections with deep troughs (hence the name) and some fierce currents. It's the best place in the area to encounter large pelagics such as sharks and barracuda. **Verde Island Dropoff** is another for advanced divers only: a rocky pinnacle 400m off Verde Island, where sloping reefs and coral-carpeted walls are home to banded sea snakes, scorpionfish, nudibranchs and a variety of colourful reef fish.

DIVE OPERATORS

There are dozens of dive operators in Sabang, Small La Laguna and Big La Laguna, and a smattering in White Beach and the beaches nearby. Rates are P1700–1800 for a dive with full equipment, or P1250 if you bring your own wetsuit and buoyancy control device; the more dives you do, the cheaper it gets. Reckon on around P14,000 for a one/two day PADI course. Established firms include:

Action Divers Next to Out of the Blue villas, Small La Laguna ☎ 043 287 3320, ⓦ actiondivers.com.

Asia Divers Next door to El Galleon resort, Small La Laguna ☎ 043 287 3205, ⓦ asiadivers.com.

Badladz Adventure Divers Badladz Dive Resort,

Muelle pier, Poblacion (Puerto Galera town) ☎ 0927 268 9095, ⓦ badladz.com/diving.

Frontier Scuba Near Angelyn Beach Resort, Sabang ☎ 043 287 3077, ⓦ frontierscuba.com.

---

thatched fan-cooled bungalows (ones with a/c are P3500) set in a tropical garden with a lagoon-shaped pool. There's also a good beachfront restaurant. ☞ **P2500**

★**Steps Garden** ☎ 043 287 3046, ⓦ stepsgarden .com; map pp.240–241. Discreetly tucked into the western end of the cove, some 60m inland, Swedish-owned *Steps* has a wide variety of comfortable a/c huts spread through the lovely hillside gardens (inspired by the Greek island of Santorini). There's also an attractive pool, a good restaurant and friendly staff. ☞ **P1600**

Tina's Reef Dive Resort ☎ 043 287 3046, ⓦ tinasreef .com; map pp.240–241. Offering some of the cheapest accommodation in Sabang, as well as a decent restaurant (see p.245), this is a good budget choice, set right at the eastern end of the beach. Clean, simple fan rooms are scattered up the hillside. Deluxe rooms (P2500) are larger and have a/c. Wi-fi in public areas. ☞ **P1500**

Tropicana Castle Dive Resort Sabang Rd ☎ 043 287 3075, ⓦ tropicanacastleresort.com; map pp.240–241. Set on the main road coming into Sabang from Poblacion, this extraordinary faux-German *schloss*, owned and operated by the Maierhofer family, has medieval-themed rooms with four-poster beds and all mod cons, although it's seen better

days. There's a swimming pool, a small spa and a restaurant, which are also rather tired-looking. Many guests are on all-in packages from Europe that include diving. Wi-fi in the restaurant. ☞ **P1990**

SMALL LA LAGUNA

El Galleon Beach Resort ☎ 043 287 3205, ⓦ asiadivers.com; map pp.240–241. Professionally run, tropical-style hotel with airy bamboo a/c rooms, many with balconies, ranging from no-frills budget to spacious sea-view cottages (US$170); there's also a pleasant seaside restaurant (see p.245). ☞ **US$59**

★**Out of the Blue** ☎ 043 287 3357, ⓦ outoftheblue .com.ph; map pp.240–241. Sophisticated villas and apartments on the hillside above the beach, 30m back from the sand, most of which feature huge sea-view windows and balconies. There are also two pools, and a great restaurant, *Verandah* (see p.245). Spotty wi-fi. ☞ **US$125**

BIG LA LAGUNA

Campbell's Beach Resort ☎ 043 287 3466, ⓦ campbellsbeachresort.com; map pp.240–241. Set at the far end of the beach, and offering cosy, well-furnished rooms with a/c, hot water and cable TV. Backpacker rooms with bunks are also available at their sister resort, *Scandi Divers*, located next door. Limited wi-fi. 📶 Dorms US$14, doubles US$44

Cataquis Lodge 📞 0916 316 9877; map pp.240–241. Brightly coloured, no-frills concrete huts with a/c, cable TV and hot water, in an exceptional location just paces from the sea. There are cheaper wooden cottages with fans at the back (P700). P1500

La Laguna Beach Club & Dive Centre 📞 043 287 3181, 🌐 llbc.com.ph; map pp.240–241. Substantial resort with palm-roofed rooms and cottages surrounding a beautiful swimming pool. All rooms have a/c, hot water, cable TV and DVD player. On site are a reputable diving school, a first-class restaurant and *Gecko Bar* with a large balcony for sunset-watching. Patchy wi-fi. 📶 US$65

COCO BEACH

Coco Beach Island Resort 📞 0917 883 9334, 🌐 cocobeach.com; map p.237. Situated in a remote cove and reachable only by private bangka (they'll collect you in Batangas or at Muelle pier), this secluded resort has airy rooms built of indigenous materials. There's a large outdoor swimming pool in the grounds, and a full range of activities on offer, including day-trips, diving and tennis. You'll have to depend on the resort's bangkas to take you anywhere, even out for dinner, though there are several in-house restaurants. Limited wi-fi. 📶 P3500

PALANGÁN

Blue Crystal Beach Resort 📞 043 287 3144, 🌐 bluecrystalbeachresort.com; map p.237. For those seeking a remote escape without foregoing everyday luxuries, this imposing colonnaded building right on the seashore may be the answer. Rooms have a/c, cable TV and are grandly decorated with heavy furnishings, and some have kitchenettes. There's also a decent pool and beautiful coastal vistas. In fact the only downside is that the beach here isn't that great. Wi-fi in reception. 📶 US$70

DAY-TRIPS AROUND PUERTO GALERA

MANGYAN VILLAGES AND MUSEUM

Two Mangyan tribal villages (see box, p.246) are easily accessible from Puerto Galera, while others require a bit more effort in the form of some stiff uphill hiking, but are rewarded with a more genuine experience. To get the most out of your visit it's worth calling the **Mangyan Heritage Center** in Calapan (see p.246), who can provide an interpreter and cultural etiquette tips. The **Baclaran Mangyan** village is just a thirty-minute walk from Poblacion, while the barangay of **Dulangan** is a short jeepney ride from Baco, 34km southeast of Puerto Galera. Some 12km beyond the town of Baco itself (and not far from the Mangyan village), the small **Mindoro Heritage Museum** (daily 9am–5pm; P50; 📞 043 743 0038) at the *Dolce Vita Di Jo Resort* contains a rare collection of artefacts from each of Mindoro's Mangyan tribes.

TAMARAW FALLS

Off the main road to Calapan lie a number of caves and thundering waterfalls, and thirty minutes from Puerto Galera, in the barangay of Villaflor, the **Tamaraw Falls** (P25) is the mother of all cascades. Here cool mountain water plummets over a 132-metre precipice and into a natural pool and man-made swimming pool. The falls have become a popular sight (hence the entrance fee), so avoid going at the weekend, when they are overrun. Lots of travellers hire scooters or motorbikes (P800/day) in town to save the cost of a guided tour (and to spend more time at the falls). The cheapest option is to take the Calapan-bound jeepney at Poblacion and ask to get off at the falls, which are right beside the road (30min; around P40).

MOUNT MALASIMBO

One of the best day-treks is from White Beach into the foothills of **Mount Malasimbo** (1168m), where there are a number of tribal communities, as well as waterfalls with cold, clear pools big enough for swimming. To tackle the summit itself, pick up the trail at Talipanan Beach (take a tricycle) and through the Iraya Mangyan village just inland. Total trek time is around 5hrs for a reasonably experienced hiker (no permits necessary).

PYTHON CAVE AND HOT SPRINGS

This popular day-trek takes you 3km out of town along the Calapan road, from where a narrow, unsigned 2km trail leads up to the immense **Python Cave** through thick vegetation and piping-hot springs deep enough for a swim. Tricycles will ask for at least P400 for the return trip (including the wait).

5

★**Kalaw Place** ☎0917 532 2617, ⊛kalawplace.com .ph; map p.237. This is something special, a gracious and relaxed family-run resort on a promontory to the north of the road just before you reach Palangán. Options range from rooms in the main house to a whole wooden cottage (P3800), good for up to six people. All rooms are beautifully furnished in native style and many boast expansive bamboo balconies with fabulous views. The owners prepare the food served in the restaurant, including vegetarian dishes. ⊜ P1900

WHITE BEACH

Marco Vincent Dive Resort ☎043 287 3590, ⊛marcovincent.com; map p.237. Set a few hundred metres back from the beach, with plush a/c rooms set around a central courtyard with pool, this hacienda-style development is as grand as it gets in White Beach. There's a dive centre on site. ⊜ P5575

Summer Connection ☎043 287 3688, ⊛www .summerconnection.net; map p.237. At the attractive western end of the beach, *Summer Connection* has managed to retain much of its original charm despite having added a modern concrete block. The simple nipa huts at the back are the least expensive option, but there are also clean and functional standard rooms (P2500) with a/c, cable TV, fridge and shower; deluxe rooms (P2800) have hot water. Spotty wi-fi in public areas. ⊜ P800

ANINUAN

Sunset at Aninuan Beach Resort ☎0917 495 7945, ⊛aninuanbeach.com; map p.237. Right on the sand halfway along the beach, this marble-floor complex has tastefully styled a/c rooms which look out over the sea. The reef right in front of the resort is perfect for snorkelling, and there's a relaxing pool, open-air bar and a good restaurant. Wi-fi in public areas. ⊜ P5500

Tamaraw Beach Resort ☎0921 279 5161, ⊛bit.ly/ tamarawresort; map p.237. *Tamaraw* has an unbeatable location on the sand at the White Beach end of Aninuan, and pleasant rooms with balconies overlooking the sea, perfect for watching the sunset. The main building is an ugly motel-style box with simple, sparsely furnished rooms; the separate cottages are more appealing (P2000). They also do good, reasonably priced food, mostly salads and grills with rice. Wi-fi in the lobby. ⊜ P800

TALIPANAN

El Cañonero ☎0905 611 8154, ⊛elcanoneroresort .com; map p.237. At the Aninuan beginning of Talipanan Beach, this small resort on a silky stretch of sand offers simple a/c doubles with mini fridges, or thatched family rooms with bamboo bunks (P3100). It also has as an attached restaurant and pizzeria. P2400

Luca's ☎0916 417 5125, ⊛lucaphilippines.com; map p.237. At the far end of the beach, *Luca's* has well-designed rooms with a/c, cable TV, fridge and hot water, plus genuine Italian food at the beautifully situated restaurant (see opposite). ⊜ P1500

Mountain Beach Resort ☎0906 362 5406, ⊛mountainbeachresort.com; map p.237. In the middle of the beach, offering a good choice of rooms, from basic doubles to nipa huts with kitchens and cable TV (P1800), and a/c bungalows on the sand (P3000). ⊜ P1300

EATING

Restaurants are quite overpriced in the whole of the Puerto Galera area, so be prepared to pay more than you might be used to in other parts of the Philippines. Most of the area's resorts have their own simple restaurants, and in-hotel places are the only option at **Aninuan** and **Talipanan**. Outside of these, there are good restaurant scenes at **Sabang**, though the places here are generally more expensive, and at **White Beach**, which has some small-scale cafés and restaurants serving simple, relatively inexpensive food.

POBLACION (PUERTO GALERA TOWN)

Hangout Bar & Restaurant Muelle pier ☎0920 461 0570; map p.239. Popular spot for a drink or light meal as you watch the boats come and go in the beautiful natural harbour. The menu includes tasty pizzas, pancakes and toasted sandwiches (from P150). Daily 7am–7pm.

Robby's Cafeteria Calapan North Rd ☎0927 632 8244; map p.239. Popular with tourists and locals, *Robby's* is one of Poblacion's many Italian restaurants. The menu features delicious pizzas (P180) and classic steaks (P600). Daily 8am–9pm.

SABANG BEACH

Hemingway's Bistrot ☎043 287 3560, ⊛hemingways-bistrot.com; map pp.240–241. On the front towards the western end of the beach, German-owned *Hemingway's* is renowned for offering the finest Western cuisine on the strip, with a top-class chef, imported ingredients (including Angus beef from the US and German Paulaner beer), and the highest prices in Puerto Galera: traditional *Nürnberger Rostbratwürste* sausage starts at P475, with the finest "Cowboy" rib-eye steak (21oz or 600g) running to P2695. Daily 10.30am–10.30pm.

Papa Fred's Steakhouse ☎043 287 3361, ⊛steakhouse-sabang.com; map pp.240–241. Just east of Sabang Pier, this popular place specializes in meat dishes (Fred is a German expat), serving hefty, perfectly grilled steaks (from P695) alongside a decent selection of Filipino favourites and superb seafood (P365–595). The lunch menu is a bit cheaper (P345). Also has a great wine list. Daily 8am–10.30pm.

Relax ☎0920 708 4471; map pp.240–241. A friendly little restaurant off the main alley through town serving mainly excellent Thai and Filipino fusion dishes like chicken curry and adobo, plus a few Western offerings (P200–250). Daily 6am–11pm.

Tamarind ☎043 287 3085; map pp.240–241. On the front at the western end of the beach, *Tamarind* is one of Sabang's most popular restaurants, offering tropical charm, wonderful ocean vistas and tasty international and Filipino dishes. The menu includes burgers (P350) and steaks (P890). Daily 8am–11pm.

★**Tina's Restaurant** ☎043 287 3046, ⬙tinasreef .com; map pp.240–241. At the far eastern end of the beach, this is a pleasant little restaurant with chequered tablecloths, bamboo chairs and nice sea views, serving a range of Filipino, German and Asian dishes at reasonable prices (P150–300), as well as breakfasts. The mango pancakes are exceptionally good. Daily 7.30am–10.30pm.

SMALL LA LAGUNA

Arthur's Restaurant El Galleon Beach Resort ☎043 287 3205, ⬙asiadivers.com; map pp.240–241. Great views and good European and Filipino cuisine (mains P350–500) cooked up by a French chef continue to make this a popular Small La Laguna choice. They also offer themed buffet nights (P350–500), such as Mongolian on Wednesdays and Sundays, and Indian on Fridays. Daily 7am–10pm.

★**Verandah** Out of the Blue ☎043 287 3357, ⬙outoftheblue.com.ph; map pp.240–241. Perched high above the beach, this is the best restaurant in Small La Laguna and serves salads, excellent Australian Wagyu beef steaks (P650) and pizzas (from P220), either in the tasteful wood-furnished interior or out on a breezy terrace overlooking the ocean. There's also a decent wine list (from P750). Daily noon–3pm & 6–10pm.

WHITE BEACH

★**Ciao Italia** ☎0906 352 7633; map p.237. Perched on the cliffside at the western end of the beach, this cute restaurant offers wonderful views, as well as tasty Italian dishes – think home-made pasta and thin-crust pizzas with authentic ingredients such as olives and artichokes (P280–P380). Daily 8am–11pm.

TALIPANAN BEACH

★**Luca's Cucina Italiana** Luca's ☎0916 417 5125, ⬙lucaphilippines.com; map p.237. Italian seems to be the order of the day in Puerto Galera, and few places are as good and as relaxed as *Luca's*. At the far western end of the beach at the resort of the same name, it's a tranquil spot with beachside views and authentic Italian food such as thin-crust pizzas and hearty pasta dishes with tangy tomato sauce (mains P200–480). Daily 6am–10pm.

DRINKING

Most of the dive resorts in **Sabang** have their own bars where visitors tend to congregate at the end of the day for a beer. Outside of the places listed below, Sabang's night scene is dominated by girlie bars, and gets seedier as the night progresses. **White Beach** is lined with small-scale cafés and restaurants which serve Puerto Galera's trademark cocktail, the "**Mindoro Sling**" (basically a combo of rum, Sprite and various fruit juices). For something a bit more romantic and low-key, head to the resorts in **Aninuan**, most of which have good beach bars.

SABANG BEACH

Eddie's Place ☎043 287 3126; map pp.240–241. Right on the seashore near the pier, *Eddie's* is a breezy spot for a sunset beer or mango shake, and a good place to wait for the ferry. Two pool tables in the back. Daily 24hr.

SMALL LA LAGUNA

The Point El Galleon Beach Resort ☎043 287 3205, ⬙asiadivers.com; map pp.240–241. Though it's located on the headland between Sabang and Small La Laguna, this popular sunset drinks spot with amazing views is part of the *El Galleon* resort, with a huge cocktail list (drinks from P120) and food available from the hotel menu. Daily 10am–midnight.

DIRECTORY

Banks and exchange In Poblacion (Puerto Galera town), Allied Savings Bank (Mon–Fri 9am–3pm; ☎042 442 0203), near the turn-off for Muelle pier, exchanges foreign currencies and has an ATM, but is not always online, so bring enough pesos, or dollars, for your time here. The well-stocked Candava Supermarket at 62 P. Concepcion St also changes dollars. In Sabang, Maxbank (on the road heading back to Poblacion) has an ATM that usually accepts international cards. Otherwise the nearest banks with international Cirrus/Maestro links are in Calapan or Batangas (there are also ATMs at Batangas port).

Clinics and pharmacies The Puerto Galera Medical Clinic is in Axalan St in Poblacion, a short walk up the hill from Muelle pier, opposite the church. There are a number of other rudimentary clinics in the town; if in doubt you can always ask the dive operators, who know where the best doctors are. There are also a few small pharmacies in town.

Police station The police station (☎043 281 4043) is inside the municipal compound.

5

Calapan

About 45km east of Puerto Galera, the busy port city of **CALAPAN** is the capital of Mindoro Oriental. It's not a tourist destination, depending for most of its livelihood on trade, but it has good transport connections and is the base for a trek up **Mount Halcon** (see opposite), the fourth-highest mountain in the country and supposedly the toughest to climb. Calapan's main road is **J.P. Rizal Street**, which is only 500m long and runs past Calapan Cathedral south to Juan Luna Street.

Mangyan Heritage Center

Santo Niño St, Ibaba East • Mon–Fri 8.30am–noon & 1.30–4.30pm • Free • ☎ 043 441 3132, ⊚ mangyan.org • Tricycles from the city centre are around P20

West of Calapan Pier along Quezon Drive, the **Mangyan Heritage Center** is a library, archive and research and education centre, and is the place to go for an in-depth introduction to the culture of Mindoro's oft-misunderstood Mangyan peoples (see box below). There's usually a small exhibition of photos, books and handicrafts on display, and you can learn how to write your name in Mangyan script.

ARRIVAL AND INFORMATION   CALAPAN

By boat Arriving in Calapan by ferry from Batangas City (see p.116), the city centre is a 15min ride away by tricycle (P35).

By bus and jeepney If you're heading for Puerto Galera, many resorts will send transport to meet you if you book and pay in advance. Otherwise you can take a jeepney (every 45min 6am–5pm; 1hr 30min; P100) from the petrol station out beyond the Provincial Capitol building on J.P. Rizal St (tricycles charge P10 to the depot). Many of these jeepneys don't go as far as Sabang or White Beach, so you'll need to change to

tricycle or taxi at Poblacion (Puerto Galera town). For Roxas (3–4hr), jeepneys head out from the market, small buses leave from a terminal on the corner of Roxas and Magsaysay streets, and there are also minivans from the Angel Star terminal on Mabini St (every 15min daily 5am–5pm; P200; ☎ 02 783 0886), while larger Dimple Star buses leave from the ferry pier (2 daily; P950), destined for San José via Roxas.

Tourist information The main tourist office for Mindoro Oriental is in the Provincial Capitol building on J.P. Rizal St (daily 9am–4pm; ☎ 043 288 5622).

ACCOMMODATION AND EATING

Accommodation options in Calapan don't set the pulse racing and most are located outside the centre. Note that **wi-fi** at the places listed below is usually only available in public areas, such as the lobby or the restaurant, and is pretty unreliable. In terms of **eating**, a walk along the traffic-clogged length of J.P. Rizal St in town will take you past the usual Filipino fast-food outlets, including *Jollibee*, *Chowking* and *Mister Donut*.

Anahaw Island View Resort Brgy Balite ☎ 0920 477 6169, ⊚ anahawislandviewresort.blogspot.ae. Located

just west of the city, this resort offers simple native cottages with fan (or a/c for P850), as well as cottages with

---

THE MANGYAN

It's estimated that there are around one hundred thousand of Mindoro's original inhabitants, the **Mangyan**, left on the island, who have a way of life not much changed since they fought against the invading Spanish in the sixteenth century. With little role in the mainstream Philippine economy, the tribespeople, who divide into eight tribal groups, subsist through slash-and-burn farming of taro and yams, a practice the elders insist on retaining as part of their culture despite the destruction it causes to forests.

You may well see Mangyan as you travel around the island, often wearing only a loincloth and machete and carrying produce for market, but if you want to actually visit them in their villages, it's best to go with a guide who can act as an interpreter. You can break the ice with a few treats such as cigarettes, sweets and matches, but if you want to take photographs make sure you have permission. Treks to Mangyan villages are possible in several parts of the island (see box, p.243). Visit the Mangyan Heritage Center in Calapan (see above) for a more in-depth introduction to the culture.

CLIMBING MOUNT HALCON

Rugged **Mount Halcon** rears up dramatically from the coastal plain of Mindoro Oriental, 28km southwest of Calapan. At an altitude of 2586m, it's Mindoro's highest peak, and surrounded by some of the most extensive tracts of rainforest on the island. Conquering the summit is a major target of mountaineers from all over the globe, though since 2006 the trails have been officially closed. In 2013 hikes unofficially resumed, with the blessing of the local Mangyan community, though the situation remains confusing. Don't even think about climbing Mount Halcon on your own – hire a Mangyan guide at **Bayanan**, just south of Calapan city.

Unusually for the Philippines, Halcon is not of volcanic origin, created instead by a massive geological uplifting millions of years ago. The total climb – the barangay of Dulangan and Halcon combined – is longer than that to the summit of Mount Everest from Base Camp; allow four to five days for the ascent and descent. There are many obstacles, not the least of which is the sheer volume of **rain** that falls on the mountain. There is no distinct dry season here and heavy rain is virtually a daily occurrence, resulting in an enormous fecundity of life – massive trees, dense layers of dripping moss, orchids, ferns and pitcher plants – but also making the environment treacherous and potentially miserable for climbers. Another irritation is the *limatik*, a kind of small leech that quietly clings to your boots and skin. You'll be sleeping on the mountain for at least three nights, so will need to bring a tent and other equipment. Make sure you have good waterproof clothing and a waterproof cover for your backpack.

PRACTICALITIES

The lower slopes of Mount Halcon are about an hour from Calapan; to **get there**, take a jeepney to Baco (around P30), where you should register at the town hall. From Baco take a tricycle (P35/person) up an unsealed track to the barangay of Bayanan, where you pay P50 to the barangay head and can organize guides. You can also approach the mountain from Puerto Galera, taking a jeepney for Calapan and getting off at the Baco turn-off. Chartering a van at Baco market to Bayanan will cost at least P1000. Expect to pay P2000 per person (in a group) for the climb, including **permit** and **guide fees** but excluding food and water, plus P50 for entry to the trail. Check ⦿pinoymountaineer.com for up-to-date **information** on the ascent.

---

or without hot tubs (P1500–2000) and deluxe rooms in the main building (P1500). There's a covered pool area and waterside restaurant, but there's not much of a beach and the water is quite dirty. Wi-fi in the restaurant. ☞ P600
Calapan Bay Hotel Nautical Hwy (Quezon Drive), Salong ⦿0920 477 6169. Bright and clean a/c rooms with

cable TV and hot water. There's also an atmospheric restaurant with a patio overlooking the ocean. ☞ P1200
Parang Beach Resort Brgy Parang ⦿043 288 6120. Some 15min southeast of town, with a number of plain but comfortable and well-kept rooms in tin-roofed cottages right on the shore, plus a beachside restaurant. P1350

DIRECTORY

Banks There are numerous banks with ATMs along J.P. Rizal St, including Metrobank (Mon–Fri 9am–5pm; ⦿043 288 1985).
Immigration The immigration office (Mon–Fri 8–5pm;

⦿043 288 2245), where you can extend visas, is at J. Luna St.
Internet access There are plenty of internet cafés on J.P. Rizal St, near the junction with Bonifacio St.

Roxas

Unless you just have a penchant for rough-road driving and are planning to head across the mountains to San José and beyond, the main reason for heading down the east coast to **ROXAS** is to take the ferry to Caticlan (for Boracay) or Romblon. Roxas is a busy town, with a lively **market** (Wed & Sun) and a few hotels and beach resorts with long, hot stretches of grey sand at **Dalahican Beach**, 5km along the coast from Dangay pier.

As ferries leave around the clock, there's really little reason to stay in Roxas unless you're too late to get onward transport to San José or Calapan. If you find yourself with a few hours to kill while waiting for a ferry, the best thing to do is to head for the Dalahican Beach resorts, which have day rates for non-guests (although most get very busy on weekends).

5

By bus Buses and jeepneys run north and south from Roxas, leaving from near the market on Administration St, and from Dangay pier on the eastern edge of town. Heading north to Calapan is simple enough and there are a series of minivan depots on Magsaysay St which operate cramped but speedy trips (3–4hr). A couple of jeepneys journey west over the mountains to San José (2hr) every morning, while comfy a/c Dimple Star (see p.236) buses run to San José and north to

Calapan (for Manila) twice a day.

By ferry Roxas is a key link on the Strong Nautical Highway route to Boracay, and there are regular ferries departing for Caticlan (4hr) from Dangay pier (P20 by tricycle from the market). Starlite Ferries runs twice daily (☎ 043 723 9965; 9pm & 11pm, returning noon & 4pm; P420) and Montenegro Lines has five daily boats (usually 4am, 10am, 4pm, 8pm & midnight; P460).

INFORMATION

Tourist information There's a tourist office (Mon–Fri 8am–5pm; ☎ 043 289 2824) at the entrance to Dangay pier.
Banks and exchange The Allied Savings Bank on

Administration St has an ATM (Mon–Fri 9am–3pm; ☎ 043 289 2749). There's a Mercury Drug pharmacy next to Roxas Villas, and a doctor's surgery at the *RL Ganan Hotel*.

ACCOMMODATION AND EATING

Cruzsmart Beach Resort Dalahican Beach ☎ 043 289 2421. Simple resort with a pool (P75 for non-residents) and a/c rooms which are rentable in 4-, 12- and 24hr segments. It also has pergolas for rent (P250/half-day), but the bad news is that there is also karaoke. Limited wi-fi available. 📶 **P900**

LYF Hotel Roxas market, Bagumbayan ☎ 043 289 2819. Painted brilliant orange, this place has small, lean fan and a/c rooms with cable TV, although some have no windows, and the walls are very thin. The canteen serves up some good food. Wi-fi in public areas. 📶 **P350**

South of Roxas

The coastal road south from Roxas trundles through **Mansalay** and on to the small town of **Bulalacao**, the jumping-off point for a bangka ride to some beautiful and remote islets, including Target, Aslom, Buyayao and **Tambaron Island**.

By bus The road between Bulalacao and San José is surfaced all the way, making the journey to the airport just 45min. Vans and jeepneys ply the coast north to Roxas (1hr) and Calapan (4–5hr), and across to San José, but you

can also catch the twice daily service north and south on Dimple Star buses (p.236).
By bangka From Bulalacao you can hire bangkas to the islands for P1000–1500.

ACCOMMODATION

Tambaron Green Beach Resort Tambaron Island ☎ 0929 893 7871, 🌐 tambaron.com. This charmingly isolated resort has dorms and simple cabañas set amid trees on a beach frequented by green sea turtles; there are also "executive" rooms facing the sea (P1500). There's

night-time electricity and a communal kitchen. Meals are P175–250 /person, and the bangka to the island is P600 one-way. Wi-fi is available in common areas. Closed June–Oct. 📶 Dorms **P200**, cabañas **P500**

Mindoro Occidental

Aside from a few intrepid wildlife enthusiasts and divers around Sablayan, **Mindoro Occidental** remains wonderfully undiscovered, and travellers with flexible travel plans and a penchant for bumpy jeepney rides will have their efforts rewarded with wild jungle-covered mountains, remote beaches, and maybe meetings with a few local Mangyan people along the way.

San José on the southwest coast has the only functioning airport on Mindoro and makes a logical gateway for trips north to the fishing town of **Sablayan**, itself the jumping-off point for a sight no scuba diver should miss, the **Apo Reef Marine Natural Park**, a vast reef complex offering some of the best diving in the world. As well as organizing a trip from

5

Sablayan, you can do so in advance at a dive shop in Manila (see p.84) or Busuanga (see box, p.398). Sablayan is also a base for a visit to the **Mounts Iglit-Baco National Park**, home to the tamaraw – a dwarf buffalo endemic to Mindoro and in acute danger of extinction – and to **Sablayan Watershed Forest Reserve**, a lowland forest with beautiful **Lake Libuao** at its centre. The northwest of the island is little-visited, though there are some unspoilt beaches around the town of **Mamburao**, the low-key capital of Mindoro Occidental.

San José

On Mindoro's southwest coast, the intensely sun-bleached and noisy port town of **SAN JOSÉ** is a quintessential Philippine provincial metropolis, with traffic-dense streets lined with pharmacies, cheap canteens and fast-food outlets. Travellers usually only see San José as they pass through on their way from the airport to Sablayan or the Mounts Iglit-Baco National Park (see p.252), for which permits can be obtained here. Though Apo Reef is close by, there are no major dive operators in town and it's best to organize a trip through the *Pandan Island Resort* (see p.254) or in Sablayan (see p.252).

San José is bounded on its northern edge by the **Pandururan River**, beyond which are the pier and the airport. Arriving by jeepney from Roxas, or bus from Sablayan, you'll find yourself on **Cipriano Liboro Street** in the west of town. From here it's a short walk (or tricycle ride; P10) to the main thoroughfare, **Rizal Street**, which runs across town and turns into the National Highway in the east, where it runs inland to Magsaysay.

ARRIVAL AND DEPARTURE

SAN JOSÉ

By plane Northwest of town, San José Airport is a 20min (P20) tricycle ride from the centre; you could also take one of the private cars that act as airport taxis, for which you'll pay at least P100 (fix the price before you get in). The airport is served by one daily flight from Manila (45min) with Cebu Pacific, whose office is at the airport.

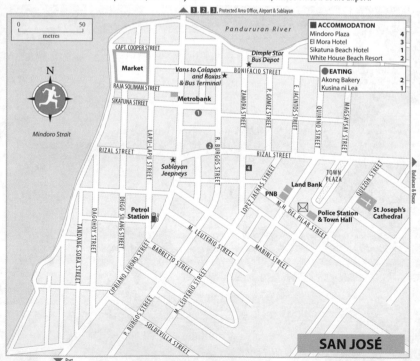

By boat Cheap flights have superseded boats to San José, and there's little benefit from taking a ferry here. Nonetheless, Montenegro Lines operates ferries to Batangas (Sun, Tues & Thurs 6pm; P726), and less regular services to Cuyo Island and Taytay in Palawan (check in advance). One route worth checking out is the "Bunso boat" to Coron (see p.394), an informal bangka service that usually departs Tues & Fri 9am (P1200; buy tickets from any agent in town). The boat returns from Coron Mon, Wed & Fri. The trip is supposed to take 6hr but can take much longer. You must embark via a smaller boat from the beach in front of central San José (another P20).

By bus Buses leave from the Dimple Star depot (☎ 0921 568 6449) on Bonifacio St at 6am, 11am, 3pm, 5pm, 7pm, 8pm and 11pm for Sablayan (3hr), Mamburao (5–7hr) and Abra de Ilog (7hr), while vans for Calapan via Roxas leave from just outside the bus terminal on Bonifacio St at 3.30am and 2pm (check the latest times in advance). All of these services continue on to Batangas by ferry, and then Manila by bus, but if you're not planning to stop anywhere along the way, it's almost as cheap (and much quicker) to fly. If you want to reach Puerto Galera, you'll need to take a bus to Abra de Ilog, then a jeepney to the Abra de Ilog pier at Wawa on the north coast, and finally take (or charter) a bangka the rest of the way.

By jeepney Two or three jeepneys depart every morning (check in advance) from just south of Rizal St on C. Liboro for Sablayan (3–4hr) and Roxas (2hr).

INFORMATION

Permits and guides You can apply for a permit (free) and organize a local guide for Mounts Iglit-Baco National Park (you'll meet the guide at the park entry station) at the Protected Area Office (Mon–Fri 8am–4pm; ☎ 043 491 4200) in the LIUCP Building on Airport Rd.

Banks and exchange There are a number of banks, including PNB on M.H. Del Pilar St, and Metrobank on Sikatuna St (at Liboro St), both of which have ATMs. There are a handful of small internet cafés along Rizal and Liboro streets, though places frequently open and close.

ACCOMMODATION

Unless you arrive too late to move on, there's little reason to **stay** in San José, but if you find yourself with a night here, the choices are between one of the budget options in town, or spending a little more out at the beach on the edge of town in the barangay of San Roque.

Mindoro Plaza Zamora St ☎ 043 491 4661. Friendly, central option with shabby but clean double rooms with fans and old TVs, plus some rooms with a/c (P1100). There's also an on-site canteen. Wi-fi in the lobby. ☞ P750

El Mora Hotel Brgy San Roque 1 ☎ 043 491 4869, ⓦ elmorahotel.com. Hip boutique hotel with a choice of five themed rooms (Japanese, Filipino, etc) all with a/c and cable TV; there's also a swish pool and a restaurant serving a range of sandwiches, soups, noodle dishes and sizzling seafood or pork dishes. Free shuttle to the airport. ☞ P2500

Sikatuna Beach Hotel Airport Rd, Brgy San Roque ☎ 043 491 4108, ⓦ sikatunabeachhotel.com. Pleasant beachside spot with friendly staff and simple, ageing rooms with cable TV (some with a/c look out to the ocean; P1500). It could do with renovation, and it's worth haggling for a lower rate and checking your room before paying. There's also a decent open-sided restaurant with wi-fi. ☞ P1500

White House Beach Resort Airport Rd, Brgy San Roque ☎ 0999 138 5854, ⓦ whitehousephilippines .com. One of the best options in the city, this marble-floored house boasts five spacious and comfortable a/c rooms with cable TV and ocean-view balconies. Free wi-fi in the dining room. ☞ P2500

EATING

Sit-down **dining options** in San José principally revolve around the hotels, and of these the best options are the restaurants at *Sikatuna Beach Hotel*, *El Mora Hotel* and the canteen at the *Mindoro Plaza*.

Akong Bakery Rizal St. The best bakery in town is a 24hr haven of tempting aromas – fresh-from-the-oven *pandesal* (a soft, sweet and slightly salty bread roll) and other pastries are knocked out throughout the day for a handful of pesos. Daily 24hr.

Kusina ni Lea Sikatuna St ☎ 043 457 0442. Inexpensive soups, sandwiches and local dishes in a traditional Filipino-style wooden dining hall (mains P130–200), cooled by a/c. Daily 6.30am–11pm.

Sablayan

A very bumpy 40km north of San José, the unhurried fishing town of **SABLAYAN** is the perfect jumping-off point for several nearby attractions, including Mounts Iglit-Baco

5

National Park, the Sablayan Watershed Forest Reserve and Apo Reef. The town, small enough to cover on foot, has a central plaza (with free wi-fi) with a town hall, and a stretch of scrappy black-sand beach lined by bangkas.

ARRIVAL AND INFORMATION   SABLAYAN

By bus There are buses and jeepneys north to Mamburao (3hr) and Abra de Ilog (4hr), and south to San José (3–4hr) from the bus station, which is at the southern edge of town on the National Highway. The slightly faster Dimple Star services (with onwards boat-bus connections for Batangas and Manila; 4 daily; 8–10hr) leave from their terminal, also on the National Highway. The pier is a 5min walk south of the bus station.

Tours, permits and guides To arrange permits for Mount Iglit-Baco National Park (free), guides and boats to North Pandan Island and the Apo Reef Marine Natural Park, head to the friendly Sablayan Eco-Tourism Office (Mon–Sat 8am–noon & 1–5pm; ☎ 0998 546 5917, ⓦ sablayan.net) in the town plaza.

ACCOMMODATION AND EATING

Camalig Restaurant National Hwy ☎ 0912 961 1465. A wide range of dishes (P50–280) from local seafood and sweet-and-sour pork (P160) to noodles (P60–85), burgers and pastas, as well as vegetable options such as steamed okra with fish sauce (P95) and mixed veg in oyster sauce (P85). The restaurant is a 5min tricycle ride (P10) from the main plaza. Daily 11am–9pm.

Gustav's Place Santo Niño ☎ 0939 432 6131, ⓦ gustavs-place.com. This simple Austrian-owned resort, a little out of town, has a number of cosy thatched bungalows in a palm-shaded garden by the seafront. There are two nipa huts with fan, as well as one standard fan bungalow (P1400) and one deluxe air-con bungalow (P2200). There is also a simple restaurant. Limited wi-fi. 🛜 P800

GVD Restaurant Viguilla St ☎ 0919 566 3410. Conveniently located in the centre of town, and specializing in seafood, with various sushi and sashimi, as well as Filipino favourites such as adobo and *bulalo*. Kids get to amuse themselves on toy bikes in the playground. Mains P140–200, and merienda P25–40/person. Daily 6am–10pm.

Sablayan Adventure Camp Punta, Poblacion ☎ 0917 850 0410, ⓦ sablayanadventurecamp.com. Out by the pier, this cheery establishment has spacious a/c rooms set in cottages looking out to the beach, although the walls dividing the rooms don't stretch to the ceiling, meaning you'll hear everything that your neighbours do. They also have a fairly basic restaurant and can arrange boats to Pandan. P800

La Sofia Apartelle 483 P. Urieta St, Brgy Buenavista ☎ 043 743 0209. The simple but clean and modern rooms (P750) in the new wing of *La Sofia Apartelle* have a/c and cable TV. Fan-cooled rooms with shared bathroom in the older main building are basic but clean. Limited wi-fi available. 🛜 P450

Mounts Iglit-Baco National Park

The isolated and wonderfully raw jungles of **Mounts Iglit-Baco National Park** are dominated by the twin peaks of **Mount Baco** (2488m) and **Mount Iglit** (2364m). It can take up to two days of tough hiking to reach the peak of Mount Iglit, while the vegetation is so dense that there have been no officially recorded ascents of Mount Baco.

There are also a number of more leisurely treks through the foothills to areas in which you are most likely to see the endangered **tamaraw** (*Bubalus mindorensis*), a dwarf buffalo endemic to the island; numbers are now rising every year, and the 2016 annual headcount identified some 430 individual animals in the wild. The tamaraw, whose horns grow straight upwards in a distinctive "V" formation, has fallen victim to hunting, disease and deforestation in the past, and to create more awareness of its plight there is talk of designating it the country's national animal. The Sablayan Eco-Tourism Office (see above) can advise on visits to the **Tamaraw Conservation Program**, known as the "Gene Pool Farm", a small laboratory where scientists are trying to breed the tamaraw in captivity.

Apart from tamaraw, the park is also prime habitat for the Philippine deer, wild pigs and other endemic species such as the Mindoro scops owl and the Mindoro imperial pigeon. It's also home to two **Mangyan** groups – the Tau-Buid and Buhid – some of whom you are likely to meet on guided hikes.

ARRIVAL AND INFORMATION

By bus/jeepney Reaching the park by public transport from Sablayan means taking one of the regular buses or jeepneys south along the coastal road to the barangay of Popoy, then a jeepney up the bumpy and rutted track to the park itself.

Guided hikes To visit the park, you'll first have to secure a permit (free) and arrange a guide (P1500–2000 for up to three days), either in San José at the Protected Area Office

MOUNTS IGLIT-BACO NATIONAL PARK

(see p.251) or the Sablayan Eco-Tourism Office (see opposite). Both of these offices can help put together all of the logistics for your trip, including camping options. Guided hikes usually include a 3hr stroll to the park bunkhouse (aka station 2) where you can stay the night, before the steep hike up to Mt Magawang (just above station 3; 2hr) where you should see the famed tamaraw (and can also spend the night).

Sablayan Watershed Forest Reserve

Entry permits cost P50 and must be secured from the Sablayan Eco-tourism Office in advance • Hire a vehicle and driver in Sablayan (P2500 for a day-trip), or take a bus along the coastal road and ask to be dropped at the turn-off for the penal colony, near the town of Pianag; buses and jeepneys run from Pianag for the return trip

The **Sablayan Watershed Forest Reserve** is unusual among protected wilderness areas because it surrounds the **Sablayan Prison and Penal Farm**, a huge open "prison without bars" established in the 1950s and surrounded by agricultural lands worked by the prisoners. The inmates also produce handicrafts, and are distinguishable from the guards by their orange T-shirts, saying "minimum" or "medium", depending on their crime (maximum-security inmates are kept away from visitors).

Nearby are a number of villages where staff and prisoners' families live; beyond the last of these villages is a motorable track that ends at the edge of the dense **Siburan Rain Forest**, close to Lake Libuao and the largest lowland forest on Mindoro.

Both the forest and the whole reserve are superb **birdwatching** spots; you might see species such as the endangered bleeding-heat pigeon, serpent eagle and black-hood coucal; prisoners can act as guides (P150), taking you to the best birding areas and pointing out individual species.

Lake Libuao

The entry permit for the Sablayan Watershed Forest Reserve (see above) includes access to the lake

Within the grounds of Sablayan Prison Farm, shallow and roughly circular **Lake Libuao** is covered in lotuses and alive with birds, including kingfishers, bitterns, egrets and purple herons. An undulating footpath around the shore makes for some wonderful walking, taking you through the edge of the forest and through glades from where there are views across the water; you'll see locals balanced precariously on small wooden bangkas fishing for tilapia. If you're reasonably fit you can walk round the lake in three hours, starting and finishing at the penal colony, though allow an hour to get between the colony and the main road.

North Pandan Island

Idyllic **North Pandan Island**, ringed by a halo of fine white sand, coral reefs and coconut palms, lies 2km off the west coast of Mindoro. In 1994 a sanctuary was established around the eastern half of the island so the **marine life** is exceptional; with a mask and snorkel you can see big grouper, all sorts of coral fishes, even the occasional turtle (sharks are very rare, however).

The island is the site of the well-run *Pandan Island Resort* (see p.254), but is open to day guests from 8am to 6pm. On most days the resort's scuba-diving centre organizes day-trips to **Apo Reef** (see p.254), and longer overnight safaris both to Apo and to Busuanga, off northern Palawan (see p.394), if there are enough passengers. Even if you don't dive, there's plenty to keep you occupied on and around the island itself, including kayaking, jungle treks, windsurfing and sailing.

5

ARRIVAL AND DEPARTURE

By boat If you want to visit the island for the day, contact the Sablayan Eco-Tourism Office (see p.252) who can arrange transport on the *Pandan Island Resort* bangka (P200 for one person and P50 for each additional person, plus a P100 fee to set foot on the island); to get to the departure point, you need to take a tricycle to "Punta". Once

NORTH PANDAN ISLAND

there, the *Pandan Island Resort's* dive shop will kit you out for snorkelling (P200/person) or a "fun dive" (P1650). There's also an additional "environmental fee" of P275 for divers and P55 for non-divers; guests at the resort also pay these fees.

ACCOMMODATION AND EATING

★ **Pandan Island Resort** ☏ 0919 305 7821, ⊛ pandan .com. This well-run, back-to-nature private hideaway was developed by the French adventurer who "discovered" the island in 1986. As well as the budget rooms, there are standard double bungalows (P1800), larger bungalows for four (P2800) and family houses for up to six (P3750). During the diving season (Nov–May) the island is so popular that all

rooms are often taken, so it's important to book in advance. Guests are required to take at least one buffet meal (P470) at the resort restaurant every day, and this is no bad thing: the chef dishes up excellent European and Filipino cuisine (try the tangy fish salad in vinegar) and the beach bar serves some unforgettable tropical cocktails. Limited wi-fi available. 📶 **P900**

Apo Reef Marine Natural Park

Lying about 30km off the west coast of Mindoro, magnificent **Apo Reef Marine Natural Park** stretches 26km from north to south and 20km east to west, making it a significant marine environment and one of the world's great dive destinations. There are two main atolls, separated by deep channels, and a number of shallow lagoons with beautiful white sandy bottoms. Only in three places does the coral rise above the sea's surface, creating the islands of Cayos de Bajo, Binangaan and **Apo**, the largest.

Apo Island is home to a ranger station and a lighthouse, and you can spend a magical night here in tents (turtles often lay eggs on the beach), though the experience comes at a price. The diving is really something special, with sightings of manta rays, sharks (even hammerheads), barracuda, tuna and turtles fairly common. Most of the Philippines' 450 species of coral are here, from tiny bubble corals to huge gorgonian sea fans and brain corals, along with hundreds of species of smaller reef fishes such as angelfish, batfish, surgeonfish and jacks.

ARRIVAL AND INFORMATION

Fees Experiencing Apo Reef isn't cheap. For starters, everyone who visits needs to pay an "environmental fee": P2450 to dive and P650 for everyone else (including snorkellers). Transport by boat (1hr 30min from *Pandan Resort*) is extra, and you'll pay additional fees if you want to dive (as opposed to just snorkel).

Tours from Pandan Island Resort *Pandan Resort* rates for scuba-diving trips to Apo Reef depend on the boat and the number of people on it, with per-person prices ranging from P14,170 (two people) to P9290 (eight people) for three dives plus equipment. Overnights cost considerably more: per-person rates range from P24,050 for two people

APO REEF MARINE NATURAL PARK

to P16,700 for eight people for six dives plus equipment. If you just want to snorkel, a day-trip to the reef (including environmental fees and food) costs P7620 per person for two people; groups of eight pay P2740 per person.

Tours from Sablayan You can visit the reef on one of the liveaboard trips offered by many dive operators in Coron Town in Busuanga (see box, p.398) or Manila, or organize a trip with the Sablayan Eco-Tourism Office in Sablayan (see p.252); a ten-person boat out to the reef is P8000 for a day-trip and P8500 for overnight (snorkelling only). There is also a P1000 guide fee and the P650 environmental fee, and you must bring your own food and drink.

The northwest

It's hard to believe that the quiet, relatively isolated west-coast town of **MAMBURAO**, 80km north along the coastal road from Sablayan, is the capital of Mindoro Occidental. With a population of around forty thousand, Mamburao is significant only as a trading and fishing town, although the coastal road is undeniably scenic, with blue ocean on one side and jungled mountains on the other. North of town there are some alluring stretches of white-sand **beach**, which are slowly being developed for tourism. The best of these is **Tayamaan Bay**, 4km north of Mamburao, where day-trippers can use the beach at the Tayamaan Beach Resort for P30.

North of Mamburao the road forks. From here, jeepneys and some buses head northwest along the coast to Palauan or northeast to **ABRA DE ILOG**, near the north coast; the journey to Abra de Ilog takes you past dazzling green paddy fields and farmland planted with corn. The easily motorable road ends at the Abra de Ilog pier at **Wawa**, 1km past Abra de Ilog, although the coastal track to Puerto Galera is a popular route with bike riders, and hikers have also made the trip.

ARRIVAL AND DEPARTURE   THE NORTHWEST

By bus The most comfortable way to traverse the west coast is via the 4–5 daily services on Dimple Transport, which shuttle between Mamburao and San José (5–7hr), Sablayan (2–3hr) and Abra de Ilog (2hr), with connections to Batangas and Manila.

By boat From the Abra de Ilog pier at Wawa, the easiest way to get to Puerto Galera is to take a bangka. There are sometimes morning passenger bangka services, but don't be surprised if you end up having to charter your own (about 2hr; P1500–2000).

ACCOMMODATION

MAMBURAO
La Gensol Plaza Hotel National Hwy ☎043 711 1072. No-frills hotel where the cheapest rooms are fan singles with tiny cold showers, though they also have larger, more comfortable doubles with a/c and cable TV (P1400). Wi-fi at reception. 📶 P900

ABRA DE ILOG
★**Tuko Beach Resort** Munting Buhangin Beach

☎0918 528 2173, 🌐tukobeachresort.com. Though a 20min bangka ride from Abra pier (P800), this tranquil, plush German-owned beach hotel is by far the most enticing and comfortable option in the region, with monkeys in the trees and dolphins frolicking offshore. Accommodation is in spacious fan cottages (a/c ones cost P1900 per person), and breakfast and dinner is included (add P350 per person for full board). Rates are per person. P1650

Boracay and the Western Visayas

CAMBUGHAY FALLS, SIQUIJOR

Boracay and the Western Visayas

The Visayas, a collection of large and small islands in the central Philippines, are considered to be the cradle of the country. The western half of this sprawling group contains an absorbing array of islands of all sizes, which offer everything from powdery beaches and dazzling coral reefs to thickly forested mountains. This spectrum of natural assets provides superb opportunities for diving, snorkelling and other watersports, as well as great hiking. There are also a few surprisingly pleasant towns where you can enjoy small-scale urban life.

The jewel in the crown of **the Western Visayas** is undoubtedly **Boracay**, which though diminutive in size utterly dwarfs the larger islands surrounding it in terms of its touristic profile. By contrast, the **Romblon** group to the north and sizeable **Panay** to the south are far less visited, although the latter is home to the country's liveliest festival, **Ati-Atihan**. Yet further south, the largest island of **Negros**, famed for sugar-cane production, has a varied assortment of attractions and is conveniently located between the smallish but enticing islands of **Guimaras** and **Siquijor**, both favourites of the discerning traveller. Wherever you go in this region, the locals are invariably welcoming and more than happy to assist you in having a great time.

As with the whole of the Visayas, those who live in the western half are quite a diverse bunch. Visayan is the umbrella **language** group in the Visayas, the most widely spoken form of which is Cebuano (see box, p.315), the native language of Cebu. Cebuano has an audible presence in eastern Negros and Siquijor, due to their proximity to Cebu. The language with most speakers in the westernmost regions is Ilongo, although Panay has tongues as diverse as Aklan, Karayan and Kuyan; all contain elements of Malayo-Polynesian. Even the modest-sized islands of Romblon are home to several linguistic varieties. This diversity of languages is a symptom of the region's fractured topography; many of these islands are culturally and economically isolated from those around them.

Boracay

Some 350km south of Manila, and just off the northeastern tip of Panay, the island of **BORACAY** is famed for the picture-perfect **White Beach**, a quality dining and wild nightlife scene, plus activities from scuba diving to kitesurfing. It may be only 7km long and 1km wide at its narrowest point, but Boracay has over thirty beaches and coves, and enough accommodation options to suit all budgets. Watching the graceful *paraws* (sailing boats) setting sail at sunset is worth the journey on its own.

Though Boracay is popular with domestic tourists, they are outnumbered by foreigners, both on package and independent holidays; this gives the island a strong

ATI-ATIHAN FESTIVAL

Highlights

❶ Boracay Though overdeveloped, Boracay's White Beach is still one of the best anywhere, with great dining and nightlife; and there's so much to do, you'll never be bored. **See p.261**

❷ Romblon This little-visited island group includes relaxed Romblon Town and challenging Mount Guiting Guiting on neighbouring Sibuyan. **See p.269**

❸ Ati-Atihan Festival, Kalibo The biggest bash in the Philippines: wild costumes, outdoor partying and copious food and drink. **See p.284**

❹ Silay Stay in the converted mansions of sugar barons and visit a sugar-cane factory in Silay, blessed with some fine architecture. **See p.293**

❺ Mount Kanlaon National Park Active volcano at the centre of dense forest offering some extreme trekking and climbing. **See p.295**

❻ Sugar Beach Negros' most delightful strip of sand is a superb place to unwind and a good jumping-off point for magnificent Danjugan Island. **See p.296**

❼ Apo Island Robinson Crusoe-esque hideaway off Negros, with excellent diving. **See p.303**

❽ Siquijor Very laidback island with a reputation for sorcery and a fine balance between gentle commercialization and unspoilt natural beauty. **See p.303**

HIGHLIGHTS ARE MARKED ON THE MAP ON P.260

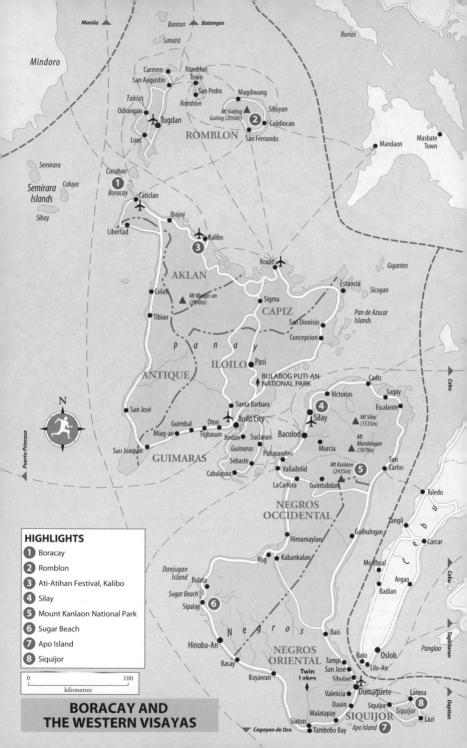

BORACAY AND THE WESTERN VISAYAS

HIGHLIGHTS

1. Boracay
2. Romblon
3. Ati-Atihan Festival, Kalibo
4. Silay
5. Mount Kanlaon National Park
6. Sugar Beach
7. Apo Island
8. Siquijor

0 _____ 100
kilometres

N

international feel. For all its beauty, Boracay is far and away the most developed island resort in the Philippines, a situation which has its downsides – it can be hard to relax with the constant blare of music on the beach and the hum of tricycles on the island's main road. Many resort owners are aware of how fragile the island is and organize beach clean-ups and recycling seminars. The authorities have finally woken up to some of the island's problems, and threats to demolish resorts that have been built without permission have actually come into effect, plus a beach **smoking ban** has been in force for several years. For all the hordes of visitors hell bent on partying, locals are keen to keep the island a family destination; overt public displays of affection are discouraged and **topless sunbathing** is only tolerated in quiet parts of the less frequented beaches.

6

White Beach

To many visitors, the 4km talcum-powdery sand strip of **White Beach** *is* Boracay, and while the carnival of activities, touts and tourists is hardly an accurate representation of Philippines beach life, it is certainly fun. A short walk along the beach takes you past restaurants serving a veritable United Nations of cuisines, including Greek, Indian, Caribbean, French, Thai and more. The beach is also dotted with interesting little bars and bistros, some of them no more than a few chairs and tables on the beach, others where you can sit in air-conditioned luxury eating Chateaubriand and smoking Cuban cigars.

Not so long ago, bangkas from Caticlan would pull up directly to White Beach, at one of three **boat stations**. Though the stations themselves have disappeared, their names continue to be used to describe the three respective segments of the beach. The smartest places to stay are mostly towards the quieter far north section of the beach, beyond Boat Station 1. To the south in Boat Station 2 the lively heart of the beach focuses on **D'Mall**, a warren of outdoor lanes and one main street, which is packed with cafés and shops. Things gradually quieten down as you move south towards Boat Station 3, where there's a clutch of budget accommodation set back from the beach.

Around the island

Most visitors fall in love with White Beach, but you shouldn't leave out **Puka Beach** on the north coast, so named for its famous shiny white seashells (*puka*). A pleasant way to get there is to hire a bangka on White Beach (P800 one-way), and then take a tricycle back (P200). Immediately north of White Beach sits the little village of **Diniwid** with its 200m beach, accessible from White Beach on a path carved out of the cliffs. At the end of a steep path over the next hill is the tiny **Balinghai Beach**, enclosed by walls of rock. On the other side of the island, **Bulabog Beach** has developed from a small fishing village into a popular kitesurfing destination.

Around 500m north of Bulabog Beach, Mount Luho (P60 entry) is an easy ascent. The tallest point on the island (though only about 100m high), it affords terrific

---

WET SEASON ON BORACAY

The two distinct **climatic seasons** in the Philippines have a marked effect on Boracay. Because of the island's north–south orientation, White Beach takes the brunt of onshore winds during the wet season (June–Oct), so don't expect it to look at its well-barbered best at that time. The waves can be big, washing up old coconuts, seaweed and dead branches. Many beachfront resorts and restaurants are forced to erect unsightly tarpaulins to keep out the wind and sand, and some even close during July and August, the wettest months. The onshore wind makes for some thrilling windsurfing and kitesurfing, but other ocean activities move to calmer waters on the island's east side.

360-degree views of the island and neighbouring Romblon. On the northeast side of Boracay, **Ilig-Iligan Beach** has coves and caves, as well as thick jungle, which is full of flying fox fruit bats.

ARRIVAL AND DEPARTURE

Travelling to and from Boracay has never been easier, and long-distance **ferries** have largely been superseded by countless **flights**. Unless you're coming from Carabao Island in the Romblon group, all visitors must pass through the hectic little town of **Caticlan**, from where frequent bangkas shuttle visitors across to **Cagban pier** in the south of Boracay (15min). Boats cost P25 during the day and P30 at night, plus P75 environmental fee and a P100 boat terminal fee. From Cagban it's just a short tricycle journey to White Beach (P150) or you can jump in a shared van (P20). If you're flying in and have booked to stay at one of the pricier resorts, you might be met at the airstrip by a hotel representative.

By plane Cebu Pacific and PAL flights connect Caticlan with Manila and Cebu. The same destinations are served from Kalibo as well, which also has a handful of flights to other Asian countries (see pp.283–284). Caticlan airstrip is a 3min tricycle ride (P50/person) from the ferry terminal, or you can walk it in less than 10min. As well as at the airport ticket offices, flights can be booked through Filipino Travel Center inside the Boracay Tourist Center (see p.264).
Destinations from both airports Cebu (5–7 daily; 55min); Manila (21–27 daily; 1hr 10min).

By boat From Mindoro there are regular Montenegro Shipping Lines (☎036 288 7373) and Starlite (☎036 288 7495, ⊛starliteferries.com) ferries from Roxas to Caticlan (8 daily; around 4hr; from P460). For Romblon there are slow bangkas from Caticlan to Looc on Tablas, plus a car ferry to Odiongan. Alternatively you can negotiate with a boat captain on White Beach to take you to Carabao, and then travel onwards to the main island group.
Destinations Looc (on Tablas; 2 daily; 4hr); Odiongan (5 weekly; 3hr); Roxas (on Mindoro; 6 daily; 4hr).

By bus and van Buses drop you on the main road through Caticlan, about 1km from the pier and airport, from where there are tricycles to take you the rest of the way. Many vans from Kalibo (particularly from the airport) will take you all the way to the ferry pier.
Destinations Iloilo (hourly until 4pm; 6hr); Kalibo (every 10–15min; 1 hr 30min); San José (6 daily; 3hr 30min).

GETTING AROUND

By tricycle Fares should be no more than P200 for a trip along the length of the island's main road – make sure you agree a fare before you climb on board as some drivers have a habit of adding "extras" at the end of the journey. Electronic tricycles ("e-trikes"), supposedly introduced to eventually replace petrol-fuelled ones, charge similar rates.

BORACAY

● EATING
Indigo	2
Seb'varia	3
Tesebel's	1

■ **ACCOMMODATION**
Amihan Backpackers	6
Balinghai Beach Resort	2
Discovery Shores	5
Fridays	4
Nami	3
Shangri-La's Boracay Resort & Spa	1

■ **DRINKING & NIGHTLIFE**
Red Pirates Pub	1

Banyugan Beach
Puka Beach
Bat Cave
Punta-Bunga Beach
Punta Bunga MAIN ROAD
Yapak
Hagdan
Punta-Ina
Balinghai Beach
Ilig-Iligan
Shell Museum
Ilig-Iligan Beach
Diniwid Beach
Diniwid
► Fairways & Bluewater
Lapuz-Lapuz Beach
Horse Riding Stables
Mount Luho
Lapuz-Lapuz
SEE 'WHITE BEACH' MAP FOR DETAILS
Balabag
Bulabog
Hangin Kite Center
White Beach
Bulabog Beach
Boracay Rock
SULU SEA
Ambulon
Tulubhan
SIBUYAN SEA
N
Malabunot
Tambisaan
Manoc-Manoc
Crocodile Island
Cagban Beach
Cagban Ferry Pier
Manoc-Manoc Beach
Laurel Islands
Tabon Strait
Boats to Boracay
Panay
Caticlan Airport
0 1 kilometre

BORACAY'S ACTIVITY BONANZA

Boracay has the biggest range of **activities** to be found anywhere in the Philippines. In addition to the sports below, there are numerous dive sites and operators (see box, p.265)

KITESURFING AND WINDSURFING

Windsurfing has been popular in Boracay since the 1990s, and more recently the **kitesurfing** boom has seen the island emerge as one of the world's premier locations for this sport. Boarders gather on Bulabog Beach to take advantage of the constant wind during the peak season, while in the off-season the focus shifts to White Beach. There are a number of schools offering both windsurfing and kitesurfing equipment rental and lessons (see below) covering everything from basic introductory classes (P2900) to full-blown courses (P19,000).

OTHER WATERSPORTS

Other watersports on offer include **jet-skiing** (P2000/30min), **waterskiing** (P1500/15min), **banana boat rides** (P300/person), **boat hire** (sailing boats P2750/hr; speedboats P4000/hr), **glass-bottom boat rides** (P800/person), **fly-fishing** (P800 for 15min), **ocean kayaking** (P600/hr or P1000 for 30min in a completely translucent "Crystal" kayak – immediately north of *Red Pirates Pub*; call ☎036 288 2818), **parasailing** (P2500) and even **mermaid swimming** (yes, you read that correctly – stick on a mermaid tail and take to the ocean; P2000 for 3hr; call ☎0917 324 3947).

For a true adrenaline experience, you can try **flyboarding** (P8500/30min; price includes return transport to Carabao Island, lunch and drinks; call ☎0910 230 0000), which involves a jet propulsion tube sending riders several metres above the water. More natural highs can be achieved by **cliff diving** at Ariel's Point, a thirty-minute boat ride away from White Beach; trips can be arranged through *Boracay Beach Club* at Boat Station 1 (☎036 288 6770; P2500 for a full day out including transport, lunch and unlimited beers).

LAND SPORTS

On land, the choices are equally extensive. Take your pick from: **quad biking** (P2500/hr); **golf** at Fairways & Bluewater, Newcoast (from P2000; ☎036 288 5587, ⓦfairwaysandbluewater.com.ph); **horseriding** in Balabag (P750/hr; ☎036 288 3311); **ziplining** at Mount Luho (P1200); **zorbing** (P600); and **mountain biking** (P150/hr; ☎00920 384 3430). One of the nicest rides is to cycle from Punta Bunga to Tambisaan Beach, where the shoreline is dotted with installation art, including the famous Boracay Sandcastle. Up in the air you can get great views from even a ten-minute **helicopter ride** (P3750/person).

TIBIAO ACTIVITIES

Several hours away at **Tibiao** (see p.281), on the Panay mainland, are a host of adrenaline-inducing options including **whitewater kayaking**, **canyoning**, **trekking** and more **ziplining**: excursions here from Boracay can be arranged through Tribal Adventures (see below).

OPERATORS

You'll find **touts** offering almost all of the activities above along the beach, but for specialist activities it's best to head direct to the operators.

Allan B. Fun Tours Near Boat Station 2, White Beach ☎036 288 5577, ⓔallan_b68@yahoo.com. The go-to guy for many of the touts on White Beach, Allan B.'s is one of the most reliable places to arrange activities.

Filipino Travel Center Boracay Tourist Center (see p.264) ☎036 288 6499, ⓦfilipinotravel.com.ph. Offers the usual activities, plus flights and tours in other parts of the Philippines. There's also a useful notice board here advertising new boat services, adventure tours, activities, nightlife and accommodation.

Funboard Center Northern end of Bulabog Beach ☎0927 343 4071, ⓦwindsurfasia.com. Windsurfing (rental from P800/hr; lessons P3200/2hr) and kitesurfing (full kit rental P2500/3hr; lessons P3000/1hr 30min)

specialists who offer lessons from beginner to pro.

Hangin Kite Center Bulabog Beach ☎0998 995 3289, ⓦhanginkite.com. One of the best established kitesurfing schools offering rental, storage, lessons and more. Beginner lessons cost P2900 (90min) and there are various courses up to the full one with IKO Certification (9hr/P19,000). The scene shifts to White Beach from May–Oct.

Tribal Adventures Boracay Sandcastles, Boat Station 1 ☎036 288 3207, ⓦtribaladventures.com. Professional operator running a host of adventurous trips around the Philippines. Their all-inclusive three-day Tibiao trip takes in hiking and whitewater kayaking (from P15,000/person, minimum of four).

6

6

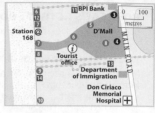

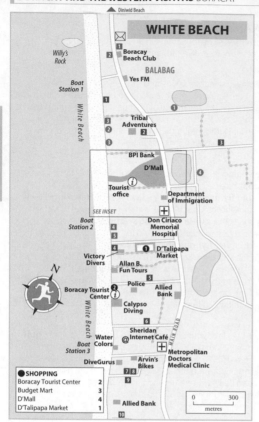

■ **ACCOMMODATION**

Bamboo Bungalows	12
Dave's Straw Hat Inn	9
Fat Jimmy's	13
Frendz Resort	2
Lishui Beach Resort	14
Moreno's Cottages	7
The Muse Hotel	1
Nigi Nigi Nu Noos 'e' Nu Nu Noos	4
Ocean Breeze Inn	6
Orchids Resort	8
Pinjalo Resort Villas	5
Seabird International Resort	11
Tree House Beach Resort	10
W Hostel	3

● **EATING**

Aria	7
Cyma	8
English Bakery and Tea Rooms	1
Hobbit Tavern	5
Lemon i Café	6
Manana	2
Papa's BBQ House	4
Real Coffee and Tea Café	10
Steakhouse Boracay	3
True Food Restaurant	9

■ **DRINKING & NIGHTLIFE**

Bombom Bar	7
Club Paraw	2
Coco Bar	6
Cocomangas Shooters Bar	1
Epic	8
Plagia Sand Bar	3
Summer Place	5
Wave Bar & Lounge	4

● **SHOPPING**

Boracay Tourist Center	2
Budget Mart	3
D'Mall	4
D'Talipapa Market	1

By bangka You can hire four- to six-person bangkas or *paraw* for around P800/hr.

By scooter Many resorts and a number of outlets on the main road rent scooters for P400–500 per day.

INFORMATION

Tourist information The Department of Tourism has a small, ineffectual tourist office (☏ 036 288 3689) in D'Mall, on the right-hand side as you enter from the beach. A few minutes' walk to the south, the Boracay Tourist Center (daily 9am–10pm, shop open until 11.30pm; ☏ 036 288 3704, ⊛ touristcenter.com.ph) is far more useful; as well as sending mail, exchanging cash and selling maps, it also holds a branch of Filipino Travel Center (daily 9am–6pm; see box, p.263).

Listings The *Boracay Sun* (⊛ boracaysun.com) and expat newspapers, plus *My Boracay* mini-guide are all distributed free and have the latest details of what's new and happening in Boracay.

ACCOMMODATION

There are over three hundred **places to stay** on Boracay, which means that except at peak times (Christmas, Easter and Chinese New Year, when prices can rise by as much as fifty percent) you should be able to find a room simply by taking a stroll down White Beach. Rates have increased sharply in recent years, with the best rooms in high-end places going upwards of US$500 a night, but there are still cheapies out there, especially away from the beach. Broadly speaking, the beach is divided into three sections: **Boat Station 1 and north** is high end, **Boat Station 2 and around** is generally mid-range, while the lanes behind the beach **south of Boat Station 3** hold a selection of budget backpacker options, plus a smattering of mid-range and high-end places. At the mid-to-upper end, there are usually great advance online deals, and budget places will often give decent discounts for longer stays or at slack times.

WHITE BEACH
BOAT STATION 1 AND POINTS NORTH

★**Discovery Shores** At the northern end of White Beach, beyond Boat Station 1 ☎036 288 4500, ⍟discoveryshoresboracay.com; map p.262. At the upper end of Boracay's price spectrum, *Discovery Shores* features bright, spacious and ultramodern rooms and suites stretching back up the hill behind the beach. All rooms are luxurious and contain an impressive array of amenities, which include iPod dock and flatscreen TV. The premier rooms have an expansive outdoor living area with a large jacuzzi and views down to the sea. There's also a pool, bar, two superb restaurants (see p.267) and a spa. ☞ **P19,000**

Frendz Resort 100m towards the beach from Main Rd ☎036 288 3803, ⍟frendzresortboracay.com; map p.264. Tucked halfway between the beach and main road, the simple cottages at *Frendz* present no-frills laidback living. The native huts have double beds, hot and cold showers and nice verandas. There are also separate male and female dorms (a/c and fan) and a café with wi-fi. Bring a padlock for your locker. Two-night minimum stay for online bookings. ☞ Dorms **P450**, doubles **P2000**

Fridays Right at the northern end beyond Boat Station 1 ☎036 288 6200, ⍟fridaysboracay.com; map p.262. One of Boracay's first resorts, and still one of the best, *Fridays* occupies a prime spot at the northern end of the beach and offers comfortable deluxe and premier rooms, and top-notch premier suites which enjoy great ocean views. All rooms are decked out in traditional Filipino style but with modern facilities, and there's a decent pool. Although it's only a three-star property, the service and amenities run close to five star. ☞ **P18,810**

The Muse Hotel On the beachfront, Boat Station 1 ☎036 288 2288, ⍟themuseboracay.com; map p.264. Dazzling white marble luxury hotel, with a snazzy lobby and spacious, comfortable rooms arranged around a rectangular pool. The rooms themselves feature toothpaste-white linens and light pine furniture, plus mini-bars and cable TVs. There is also a café, roofdeck and spa. ☞ **P12,800**

BOAT STATION 2 AND AROUND

★**Bamboo Bungalows** Just north of D'Mall ☎036 288 6324, ⍟bbboracay.com; map p.264. Great choice in the heart of the action, a stone's throw from D'Mall. There's a range of cottages and apartments set around the lush garden, and some rooms at the front of the main building with beach views. Discounts off the rack rate are always available. ☞ **P4000**

Fat Jimmy's 200m inland, south of D'Mall ☎0922 875 3088, ⍟fatjimmysresort.com; map p.264. One of a

DIVING AROUND BORACAY

Boracay's diving isn't as varied or extreme as diving in Palawan or Puerto Galera, but there's still enough to keep everyone happy. The dive sites around the island, all easily accessible by bangka, include gentle drift dives, coral gardens and some deeper dives with a good chance of encounters with sharks. At **Crocodile Island**, fifteen minutes southeast of Boracay, there's a shallow reef that drops off to 25m and a number of small canyons where sea snakes gather. **Big and Small Laurel** are neighbouring islets with some of the best soft coral in the Visayas and shoals of snappers, sweetlips, eels, sea snakes, morays, puffers and boxfish. Probably the star attraction for divers here is **Yapak**, where you freefall into the big blue, eventually finding at 30m the top of a marine wall where there are batfish, wahoo, tuna, barracuda and cruising grey reef sharks. **Lapu Wall** is a day-trip from Boracay to the northern coast of Panay, but the diving is some of the most challenging in the area, with overhangs and caverns. Another good day-trip is north to Carabao Island (see p.272), in the province of Romblon, where there are splendid reefs, some peaceful, powdery beaches and a resort if you want to stay overnight.

DIVE OPERATORS

There are dozens of licensed dive operators along White Beach. A **Discover Scuba** introductory session with a dive master costs around P3000, while a full PADI **Open Water Course** (3–4 days) costs P22,000. For certified divers, one dive goes for P1500 (P2000 for nitrox), less for multiple packages. Of the countless dive operators on the island, the following are well established and PADI five-star rated:

Calypso Diving Boat Station 2 ☎036 288 3206, ⍟calypso-boracay.com.

DiveGurus Boat Station 3 ☎036 288 5486, ⍟divegurus.com.

Fisheye Divers Boat Station 1 ☎036 288 6090, ⍟fisheyedivers.com.

Victory Divers Boat Station 2 ☎036 288 6056, ⍟victorydivers.com.

Water Colors Boat Station 3 ☎036 288 6745, ⍟watercolors.ph.

6

number of budget resorts along a path next to D'Mall. Relaxed, quiet and friendly, *Fat Jimmy's* has sixteen simple but charming fan or a/c rooms, five of which have their own small patio garden (P3000). Family rooms sleep four with a bunk bed for the kids and rates include a choice of Filipino or American breakfast. 📶 **P1800**

Lishui Beach Resort On the beach, 100m south of D'Mall ☎036 288 3301, ✉lishui@outlook.ph; map p.264. Nine tastefully furnished a/c rooms with fridge, cable TV, telephone and spacious porch, plus one suite at the front of the property looking out over the ocean. Floors are tiled, the whitewashed walls are decorated with tasteful Filipino art and the surrounding gardens are lush and peaceful. Breakfast and welcome drink included. 📶 **P5500**

Nigi Nigi Nu Noos 'e' Nu Nu Noos 5min walk north of the Boracay Tourist Center ☎036 288 3101, 🌐niginigi.com; map p.264. Long-standing and enduringly popular White Beach guesthouse featuring Indonesian-style cottages set in tranquil tropical gardens. All of the spacious cottages have thatched pagoda roofs and shady verandas. Also has a decent, very popular bar-restaurant. Breakfast and mineral water included. 📶 **P6195**

Pinjalo Resort Villas Down the footpath beside the Tourist Center, on the left ☎036 288 2038, 🌐pinjalo.com; map p.264. Good-value, comfortable accommodation close to the beach but away from the noise of the bars and clubs. Standard rooms are on the small side, making it worth the extra for the deluxe options (P5400). All rooms are tastefully furnished and look onto peaceful gardens or the pool. 📶 **P4100**

Seabird International Resort Set back from the beach a short walk north of D'Mall ☎036 288 3047, 🌐seabirdboracay.com; map p.264. An oldie but a goodie, *Seabird* continues to renovate to keep up with the new crowd and offers a range of rooms set in pleasant and quiet gardens just a minute's walk back from the beach. Good coffee, pancakes, breakfasts and fish in the restaurant. 📶 **P3300**

BOAT STATION 3 AND POINTS SOUTH

Dave's Straw Hat Inn Down the path next to Angol Point Beach Resort ☎036 288 5465, 🌐davesstrawhatinn.com; map p.264. *Dave's* is a charming, homely little resort with comfortable a/c and fan rooms, plus good food. Fan rooms are one of the best deals on the island, while even deluxe doubles (P2490) have extra roll-out beds so a family of four can fit in at no extra charge. Wi-fi in reception only. 📶 **P1820**

Moreno's Cottages At the southern end of the beach opposite Dave's Straw Hat Inn ☎036 288 2031, ✉boracayjojo29@yahoo.com; map p.264. This friendly, locally run option has small and simple fan and a/c huts set around a pleasant garden, just a 2min walk from a lovely section of White Beach. 📶 **P1500**

Ocean Breeze Inn Just inland, a few mins' walk south of Boracay Tourist Center ☎036 288 1680, 🌐oceanbreezeinn.info; map p.264. You can choose between a/c rooms (P2000) in the pleasant sky-blue painted house or the more humble but airy nipa huts (fan) in the adjacent plot. Wi-fi in the house only. 📶 **P1200**

★**Orchids Resort** A short walk inland from Moreno's Cottages ☎036 288 3313, 🌐orchidsboracay.com; map p.264. Owned by an affable American, *Orchids* offers great-value rooms and nipa huts a few minutes' walk from White Beach. Standard fan rooms are clean and have hot showers while the fan cottages offer more space and have cosy verandas with hammocks. A/c rooms also have cable TV, and there's wi-fi throughout, for a fee of P50/day. A few minutes' walk up the hillside, *Orchids* also has newer, thatch-roofed concrete villas with two beds in the a/c downstairs and a living room with cable TV, kitchen and balcony upstairs (P2500). 📶 **P915**

Tree House Beach Resort At the southern end of the beach ☎036 288 4386, ✉damariotreehouse@yahoo.com.ph; map p.264. Rooms may be slightly dated, but they're comfortable, quiet and nicely furnished. A/c rooms cost double, while the dorm rooms are cheap, but cramped and very simple. Owner Mario also cooks a mean pizza. 📶 Dorms **P350**, doubles **P1000**

ELSEWHERE ON BORACAY

Amihan Backpackers East of Main Road, inland from and south of Boat Station 3 ☎036 286 3203, 🌐amihanbackpackersboracay.com; map p.262. Dorm-only hostel offering unbeatable prices on slightly higher ground, around 10min walk inland. Clean but simple with no frills – don't expect towels or cooking facilities. Good views from the rooftop area. Dorms **P350**

Balinghai Beach Resort Balinghai Beach ☎036 288 3646, 🌐balinghai.com; map p.262. If you're looking for desert-island solitude and don't mind being a tricycle ride from the buzz of White Beach, *Balinghai* fits the bill. On a small, secluded cove surrounded by cliffs on the northern part of Boracay, it's set into a steep slope with lots of steps, and boasts a handful of private bungalows and houses built from local materials, with consideration for the environment. Each house is different and prices vary accordingly. One has a tree in the kitchen and another is carved from the rock face, with a balcony facing the sunset. There is also a small restaurant with separate bar. 📶 **P4800**

Nami On the cliffside 20m above Diniwid Beach ☎036 288 6753, 🌐namiresorts.com; map p.262. Reached by steep steps or a rickety lift, the spacious and stylish villas at this upmarket place, on the next cove along from White Beach, offer 180-degree ocean views, jacuzzi, butler service and DVD players. Service, however, doesn't quite hit the mark. 📶 **P11,500**

Shangri-La's Boracay Resort & Spa Brgy Vapak ☎ 036 288 4988, ⊛ shangri-la.com; map p.262. Perched above its own private beach, the *Shangri-La* presents a range of attractively styled rooms and villas which blend comfortably into the lush hills. Service is top-notch, and all of the usual *Shangri-La* chain facilities are on offer, along with nature trails and a dive centre. The palatial Presidential Villa costs a staggering P144,500 a night. 🛜 **P19,000**

★**W Hostel** Balabag ☎ 036 288 9059, ⊜ whostel boracay@gmail.com; map p.264. Excellent new hostel within easy walking distance of the beaches on both sides of the island, decked out in bright colours with murals and ethnic hangings on lacquered walls. A simple free breakfast is included, and there's a large well-equipped kitchen for self-catering, making this a top choice. Friendly, knowledgeable staff complete the picture. 🛜 Dorms **P750**, doubles **P2500**

6

EATING

Boracay has a more diverse dining scene than most cities in the Philippines, and even in a two-week stay you can only sample a fraction of the options. Many restaurants are listed in the local info booklet *My Boracay*, which has meal discount vouchers. As well as the listings below there are also plenty of **local vendors** who set up barbecues on the beach at sundown to cook everything from fresh lapu-lapu and squid to tasty local bananas sprinkled with muscovado sugar. Conversely, the big international chains also have a noticeable presence. A **cautionary note**: to be wary of the big seafood buffet places on the seafront, as sometimes the fish isn't quite as fresh as it appears and can cause stomach problems.

CAFÉS

English Bakery and Tea Rooms Short way east of Main Road, Balabag ☎ 036 288 3158; map p.264. The only remaining branch of the *English Bakery* in Boracay serves up great breakfasts (P135–195), yoghurts, cakes and shakes, as well as lunch deals like fish and chips (P230). Shaded tables looking out over a small lagoon make a great spot to escape the heat and enjoy a cup of Lyons English tea and some banana bread. Daily 6am–6pm.

★**Lemon i Café** D'Mall ☎ 036 288 6781, ⊛ lemoni cafeboracay.com; map p.264. Terrific bright and airy little café. Breakfast items include eggs Benedict and delicious coconut pancakes (both P260). For lunch or dinner there's outstanding pan-fried mahi-mahi with warm potato salad and lemon butter garlic sauce (P420), lemon and thyme roast chicken with sautéed potatoes (P480) and a range of lemon desserts. Drinks (P75–250) range from refreshing calamansi juice to "lemonijito" and other cocktails. Free wi-fi. Daily 8am–11pm.

Real Coffee and Tea Café Boat Station 2 ☎ 036 288 5340, ⊛ facebook.com/RealCoffeeAndTeaCafe; map p.264. The upstairs location overlooking the beach is pleasantly removed from the hubbub. The bamboo interior harks back to a simpler time when this was the first "real" coffee (P90–160) on the beach. Good breakfasts (P180–350), as well as a great selection of teas (try the punchy ginger tea, P90) and cookies. Free wi-fi. Daily 7am–7pm.

RESTAURANTS

Aria Beach entrance to D'Mall ☎ 036 288 5573, ⊛ aria .com.ph; map p.264. This popular Italian place offers attractive alfresco dining under the palms. Pizzas (P410–650) and pastas (P360–470) are reliably good, and coffee and desserts are available from neighbouring *Café del Sol*. Daily 11am–11pm.

Cyma D'Mall ☎ 036 288 4283, ⊛ cymarestaurants.com; map p.264. The owners may not be Greek, but *Cyma* serves

the best tzatziki (P175) in Boracay in a tiny but boldly decorated restaurant. Delicious *horiatiki* (Greek salad; P370), chicken souvlaki (P390) and baklava (P220) are also on the menu, and it's worth checking the specials board. Daily 10am–11pm.

Hobbit Tavern D-Mall ☎ 036 288 6687, ⊛ facebook .com/HobbitTavernBoracay; map p.264. Western-themed restaurant serving large portions of roulade and burgers (both around P400), as well as juicy steaks (around P1500). Live country and folk music at lunchtime and in the evening. Free wi-fi. Daily 8am–1am.

★**Indigo** Discovery Shores, north of Boat Station 1 ☎ 036 288 4500, ⊛ discoveryshoresboracay.com; map p.262. The place to come for a splurge, with tables on the sand and in the suave interior. Classy dishes such as blackened grouper or mussel Madras curry cost P795, while a US Angus steak will set you back P2695. Creative set menus are also available. The hotel's *Sands* restaurant is also good, but less costly. Daily noon–10pm.

Manana Between boat stations 1 and 2 ☎ 036 288 5405; map p.264. This lively Mexican restaurant serves tasty fajitas (P363), enchiladas and chimichangas (P352–550), which can be enjoyed in the brightly decorated interior or on tables out on the beach to the backbeat of Latino tunes. A giant frozen mango daiquiri (P148) rounds the meal off perfectly. Daily 10am–10pm.

Papa's BBQ House Opposite side of pond from D'Mall ☎ 036 288 1101; map p.264. Brightly lit, reliable local joint serving whole roast chicken for P210, as well as meals such as pork adobo and chicken curry (both P150). Daily 24hr.

Seb'varia Bulabog Beach ☎ 036 288 2527, ⊛ bit.ly/ Sebvaria; map p.262. Attached to the Hangin Kite Center (see box, p.263), this breezy shack with a sand floor serves a range of international cuisine such as Thai green curry, scampi tagliatelle and currywurst (mains P290–450). Daily 8am–11pm.

Steakhouse Boracay Boat Station 1 ☎036 288 6102, ⓦfacebook.com/SteakhouseBoracay; map p.264. Excellent steak and salad restaurant, which enjoys a great upstairs location overlooking the beach. Imported steaks (P730–795) are the mainstay, but the local ones (around P500) are also worth a try. Free wi-fi. Daily 10am–11pm.

Tesebel's On the main road, just off Puka Beach, ☎036 288 6705; map p.262. This long-standing restaurant is nothing fancy but people go back for the delicious fresh seafood, which includes garlic prawns with buttered honey (P200) and tangy *sinigang* soup with the catch of the day.

Head here for a lazy lunch if you're in the Puka Beach area. Daily 6am–11pm.

★**True Food Restaurant** Next door to Mango-Ray Resort, a short walk south of D'Mall ☎036 288 3142, ⓦfacebook.com/TruefoodBoracay; map p.264. Tastefully decorated restaurant where delicious Indian meals can be enjoyed while sitting on cushions around a low table. There are dishes from all over the Subcontinent including *aloo jeera*, biriani, pakora and *masala dosa*, and the menu also extends to North Africa, with some couscous offerings. Most dishes in the P400–600 range. Daily noon–10.30pm.

DRINKING AND NIGHTLIFE

Nightlife in Boracay starts with drinks at sunset and continues all night. Hard-core partiers don't warm up until around midnight, with many dancing and drinking until sunrise. As well as the listings below, there are countless other options which range from upscale resort bars to beach shacks.

BARS

BomBom Bar Right on the beach, 100m north of D'Mall; map p.264. An atmospheric little chilled-out beach hut, with seats on the sand where you can listen to local musicians come together for jam sessions on native instruments. Daily 8am–1am.

Coco Bar Red Coconut Resort, Boat Station 2 ☎036 288 3507, ⓦfacebook.com/CocoBarInBoracay; map p.264. This loud and lively bar serves cocktails (P150–200) and offers itself as a "husband daycare centre". Free wi-fi. Daily 6am–11.30pm.

Plagia Sand Bar Boat Station 1 ☎036 288 3161; map p.264. Trendy bar where you can sip cocktails (P125–330) on sofas under a huge canopy on the sand. The nightly fire poi dancers are the best on the island (from 9pm), and there are flavoured hookahs available while you watch the show. Daily 5pm–midnight.

Red Pirates Pub South end of White Beach, beyond Boat Station 3 ☎036 288 5767, ⓦfacebook.com/RedPiratesPub; map p.262. Bare feet and sarongs are the order of the evening at this relaxed little beach club far from the madding crowd. The music ranges from reggae to chill-out, and tribal to ethnic and acoustic sounds. The owner, Captain Joey, has a sailing boat and offers sunset cruises, adventure tours and snorkelling trips around the island. Free wi-fi. Daily 10am–4am.

Summer Place 200m south of D'Mall ☎036 288 3144, ⓦboracaysummerpalace.com; map p.264. U-shaped bar facing the beach, with a dancefloor and music until the sun comes up, or until the last customer leaves. Daily 10am–4am.

CLUBS

Club Paraw Boat Station 1 ☎036 288 6151; map p.264. Spilling out onto the sand, this popular club plays everything from techno to r'n'b. There's a P150 cover in peak season, but it includes a drink. Daily 10am–3am.

Cocomangas Shooters Bar On the main road inland from Boat Station 1 ☎036 288 6384, ⓦcocomangas.com; map p.264. (In)famous for drinking games involving potent cocktails, this place stays raucous until the wee hours. Cover charge (P100) on Sat. Daily 10am–3am.

Epic On the edge of D'Mall ☎036 288 1417, ⓦepicboracay.com; map p.264. In the daytime, *Epic's* kitchen turns out tasty dishes from its international menu, and in the evening it transforms into one of the most popular clubs on the strip. Resident DJs serve up dance music from 10pm and guest DJs for party nights. Free wi-fi. Daily 11am–2am.

Wave Bar & Lounge Hennan Regency, near Boat Station 2 ☎036 288 6111, ⓦfacebook.com/WaveBarAndLounge; map p.264. Part of an upmarket resort, this trendy, modern beach lounge bar-club hosts DJs whose tunes are piped out to the dancefloor via state-of-the-art Swiss "plane wave" speakers. Happy hour till 10pm. Free wi-fi. Daily 5pm–3am.

SHOPPING

Boracay Tourist Center Halfway between Boat Stations 2 and 3 ☎036 288 3704, ⓦtouristcenter.com.ph; map p.264. Sells everything from beachwear to foodstuffs, and contains a travel agency, internet café and postal service, plus they can deliver groceries. Daily 8am–11.30pm.

Budget Mart Where D'Mall meets the main road ⓦbudgetmart.com.ph; map p.264. Boracay's most accessible decent-sized supermarket. Daily 7am–11.30pm.

D'Mall Behind the beachfront restaurants; map p.264. D'Mall has a warren of alleys packed with stalls and boutiques where you can pick up everything from clothes to dive gear and imported foods. Most shops 9/10am–9/10pm.

D'Talipapa Market map p.264. Sprawling market with the best and cheapest selection of beachwear in Boracay, plus a fruit, veg and wet market, with simple restaurants that will cook your freshly bought produce. Daily 8am–11pm.

DIRECTORY

Banks and exchange There are numerous banks with ATMs on Boracay, but during peak season they sometimes run out of cash by the afternoon or at weekends, so it's best to go on weekday mornings. All banks offer exchange. There's an Allied Bank on the beach path at Boat Station 3, and another on the main road inland from the Boracay Tourist Center, which also changes cash. A number of private exchange agents and resorts will also change cash.

Hospitals and clinics The main hospital is the 24hr Don Ciriaco Senares Tirol Senior Memorial Hospital (☎ 036 288 3041) on the main road a little south of D'Mall. The Metropolitan Doctors Medical Clinic, towards the southern end of the main road (☎ 116 or ☎ 0918 926 3112, ⓦ facebook.com/MDMCBoracay), can also provide first aid or deal with emergencies and will send a doctor to your hotel.

Immigration Visa extensions (see p.48) are available at the small Department of Immigration office next to *Nirvana Beach Resort*, just off Main Rd south of D'Mall (Mon–Fri 7.30am–5.30pm; ☎ 036 288 5267).

Internet access Most resorts and many restaurants and cafés in Boracay have free wi-fi. Getting online otherwise is a little more expensive than in many parts of the country; reckon on anything between P25 and P50/hr. The internet café at the Boracay Tourist Center is convenient and has fast connection for P50/hour. Other options are the business centre at *Nigi Nigi Nu's* (P40/hr), and the *Sheridan Internet Café* (P50/hr) at Boat Station 3.

Laundry The place you're staying will probably arrange laundry for you, but for a cheaper service there are several launderettes on the island which charge around P40/kg: Laundry Wascherei Is a little south of Boat Station 3, Lavandera Ko is next to *Cocomangas*, and Speedwash is on the main road inland from Boat Station 3.

Pharmacies There are pharmacies selling most necessities in D'Mall, Boracay Tourist Center and D'Talipapa.

Police The police station (☎ 036 288 3066) is a short walk inland between Boat Stations 2 and 3, immediately behind the Boracay Tourist Center. If you have lost something, you can ask the friendly staff at the local radio station, YES FM 91.1 (☎ 036 288 6107, ⓦ yesfm911boracay.blogspot .co.uk), to broadcast an appeal for help. They claim to have a good record of finding lost property, from wallets and passports to Labrador puppies. The station office is on Main Rd close to Boat Station 1.

Post The post office in Balabag, inland from northern White Beach, is open Mon–Fri 9am–5pm.

Romblon

Off the northern coast of Panay, between Mindoro and Bicol, the province of **ROMBLON** consists of three main islands – **Tablas**, **Romblon** and **Sibuyan**, plus a dozen or so more smaller islands. The province is largely overlooked by visitors because of limited transport connections, and once you're here, to put it simply, there's not that much to do. However, as Boracay becomes increasingly crowded, Romblon makes an ever-more appealing option, and little by little it is making its way onto travellers' radars, aided by the opening of new resorts and activities, particularly on the southernmost island of **Carabao**. For now, though, most of Romblon remains wild and untouched and is home to some beautiful and rarely visited **beaches** and coral reefs, making it an excellent off-the-beaten-track destination for **scuba diving. Mount Guiting Guiting**, on Sibuyan, also offers one of the country's most challenging hikes.

ARRIVAL AND DEPARTURE   ROMBLON

BY PLANE

Tugdan Airport There's a small airport at Tugdan on Tablas Island, which is served by four weekly flights from Manila with Cebu Pacific subsidiary Cebgo (1hr 10min). Jeepneys meet flights and run to Looc (40min; P60) and San Agustin (P90; 1hr). If you don't have too much luggage, you can take a habal-habal (P75) to Looc or to destinations further afield. Many resorts across the island group can arrange airport pick-up, although it will cost far less to make your own way.

BY BOAT

From Batangas 2GO operate ferry services from Batangas to Odiongan, on Tablas Island (Tues & Fri 9pm; 6hr; P1000) and Romblon Town (Wed & Sat 11pm; 7hr; P1100), which carries on to Roxas on Panay (see p.282). Montenegro Shipping Lines (☎ 043 740 3201) has a slower service (Mon, Thurs & Sat 5pm) for Odiongan (10hr; P762) and on to Romblon (13hr; P954). Finally, Navios Shipping Lines (☎ 0908 146 2243) has sailings (Sun & Wed 4pm) to San Agustin (9hr; P850) then Cajidiocan on Sibuyan's east coast (12hr; P950).

From Mindoro There are three weekly bangkas from Roxas on Mindoro to Odiongan (3–4hr; P150).

From Panay and Boracay 2GO run five weekly services from Caticlan to Odiongan (2hr) and two weekly from Roxas (5hr; P670). Alternatively, there are also bangkas (2 daily; 3– 4hr; P100) from Caticlan to Looc, or you can charter bangkas in

Boracay itself for Carabao Island. From Tabon Baybay port there are also small boats to Carabao (2 daily; 45min; P100). If the sea is calm and the weather OK, there are also daily bangkas every morning from Roxas to Sibuyan Island (4–5hr; P180).

From Masbate Cajidiocan is linked by occasional bangkas with Mandaon on Masbate.

GETTING AROUND

BY BOAT

From Tablas Island There are bangkas from San Agustin on Tablas to Romblon Town (2 daily; 1hr; P100–150), and San Fernando on Sibuyan (1 daily; 2hr; P250). There are also bangkas from Santa Fe to Carabao (2–3 daily; 40min; P80). Direct Odiongan–Romblon ferries run three times per week.

From Romblon Island There are bangkas from Romblon Town to San Agustin (2 daily; 1hr; P100–150) on Tablas, and Magdiwang (1 daily; 2hr; P250) and San Fernando on Sibuyan (1 daily; 2hr 30min; P300). Twice a week, Navios ferries (⊙0908 146 2243) go from Romblon to Cajidiocan (2hr) on Sibuyan.

From Sibuyan Island Daily bangkas run from San Fernando to San Agustin on Tablas and Romblon Town (both 2hr 30min; P300). There are also daily bangkas from

Magdawing to Romblon Town (2hr; P250), and twice weekly ferries from Cajidiocan to Romblon (2hr).

BY ROAD

Once you've made it to the islands, the main modes of transport are jeepneys, tricycles and motorbikes, with the odd bus.

By jeepney Jeepneys run set routes and tend to be most frequent in the mornings. Odiongan to San Agustin (1hr 40min), by way of example, costs P50.

By tricycle and motorbike taxi Motorbike taxis are one of the speediest if not always most comfortable ways to get around. Short journeys cost as little as P50–100 and a full day-trip around P1000–1200, excluding petrol.

By van and motorbike Resorts can also help to arrange transport, including van and motorbike hire (P500/day).

Tablas Island

Tablas, the largest and best connected of the Romblon group, is a narrow island with a sealed coastal road. Chartering a jeepney for a tour around the island is worth considering. The road that cuts across the island from Concepcion to Odiongan is a real thrill, winding along a ridge with views as far as Sibuyan in the east and Boracay in the south on clear days.

Odiongan and San Andres

If you arrive by air, it's typical to head first to **ODIONGAN**, the island's main town, which has a few simple places to stay. From Odiongan it's easy to explore the beautiful northwest coast up to **SAN ANDRES**, a neat and tidy little place with paved roads and low-rise wooden houses. The town has a beautiful sweeping bay of fine sand on one side, and on the other dazzling paddy fields that stretch to the foothills of **Mount Kang-Ayong** (Table Mountain), which can be climbed with a guide – ask at the town hall in the plaza.

6

Calatrava and San Agustin

The next town north of San Andres is **Calatrava**, from where you can charter a bangka for the short hop to the **Enchanted Hidden Sea**, an incredibly beautiful 40m-wide pool of water barely 10m from the sea through a gap in the rocks. To most local folks the pool is an enchanted place, home to supernatural beings, though you're more likely to see white-breasted eagles, monkeys, butterflies, sharks and turtles.

For bangkas to Romblon or Sibuyan, go by bus or jeepney to dull **San Agustin** on the northeast coast; the only reason to stay over here is if you miss the last one.

Looc and Santa Fe

The sleepy town of **LOOC**, a scenic place huddled among palm trees against a curtain of jungled hills and facing a wide natural harbour, is not really worth going out of your way but is a useful entry point from Caticlan. Further south, the district of **Santa Fe** is home to some good beaches, although the town itself is little more than the jumping-off point for boats to Carabao.

Looc Bay Marine Refuge and Sanctuary

Arrange snorkelling through the KOICA office beside the pier (daily 8am–4pm; P100, snorkel & mask rental P50; ☎0935 590 2204)

Looc's main attraction is the **Looc Bay Marine Refuge and Sanctuary**, an area of the bay guarded 24 hours a day to allow corals damaged by dynamite fishing to regenerate. The guards, all volunteers, are stationed on a bamboo platform; you can organize a visit to snorkel from it through the KOICA office.

INFORMATION

Tourist information The tourist office is in the Capitol Building on Looc's town plaza (daily 8am–noon & 1–5pm; ☎0995 393 0805) but is often left unmanned and not much help anyway.

TABLAS ISLAND

Services In Odiongan, there's a small internet café and BPI bank with ATM on the plaza, plus a PNB bank with ATM on Formilleza St.

ACCOMMODATION AND EATING

ODIONGAN

Islands Gourmet Deli Quezon St ☎0919 483 8531. The best food in Tablas is served up in this cosy little restaurant decked out in native materials. Organic ingredients are sourced locally to make tasty dishes ranging from stone-baked pizzas to BBQ chicken and pork (all P80–200), plus delicious smoothies. Daily 7am–9pm.

Lyn's Snack Bar Rizal St ☎042 567 5812. Directly below the *Odiongan Plaza Lodge*, this place has outdoor seating

where you can fill up on cheap local dishes (from P80). Daily 6am–8pm.

Odiongan Plaza Lodge Rizal St ☎042 567 5760. Convenient for a short stay due to its central location opposite the town hall on the plaza, this place has well-kept a/c rooms with tiled floors and hot showers. P1000

Sato Dizon Arcade Just off MA Roxas St, 200m north of the Plaza ☎042 567 6070. Painted bright yellow, this modern business/accommodation complex has fan and a/c

(P800) doubles, a large suite and a dorm. Wi-fi in lobby and upstairs lounge. 🛜 Dorms **P200**, doubles **P300**

SAN AGUSTIN

August Inn Town plaza ☎ 0919 592 2495. An adequate little lodging house with a/c rooms. Most rooms share communal bathrooms, although some of the doubles are en suite (P800). **P400**

Kamella Lodge Town plaza ☎ 0919 610 7104. Next door to *August Inn*, this place has small, ordinary a/c rooms that are acceptable for a short stay. **P400**

LOOC

Angelique Inn Gonzales St, southeast cnr of Plaza de la Paz ☎ 0916 344 6946. *Angelique* offers basic rooms, a bit dusty but with clean linen, all with shared bathrooms. The simple restaurant, which has wi-fi, is one of the few places to eat in town, though the food at *Bantigue Resort* is better. 🛜 **P800**

Bantigue Resort Brgy Punta, 2km southeast ☎ 0927 627 2614. The large bonsai trees and sizeable bamboo replica of the Eiffel Tower make this seaside resort a unique choice. There's not much competition, but the large well-furnished rooms and decent restaurant are the best in the Looc area. 🛜 **P2000**

SANTA FE

By the Sea Resort Campong Beach ☎ 0999 664 3917, 🌐 bythesearesort-tablas.com. Lovely little Italian-owned dive resort, with huts nestled into the hillside above a pretty stretch of white sand, where there's also a pool. Rates sound expensive, but include three top-notch meals a day, plus snacks, drinks and even Italian wine with dinner. Wi-fi in restaurant only. 🛜 Full board **P7600**

Morel's Private Island Resort Guinbiyaran Bay ☎ 0936 976 5630, 🌐 morelisland.com. Sitting on its own tiny island, this charming resort has a budget beach cottage with kitchen sleeping six (P1800), and small, attractive rooms, mostly with shared bathrooms. The resort can arrange pick-up from Santa Fe, a 20–30min drive from the pier at Guinbiyaran and then a short bangka ride. Alternatively they can arrange a boat direct from Boracay (P5000). 🛜 **P1200**

Carabao Island

Only 6km wide from the capital of **San José** on the east coast to **Lanas** on the west, beautiful little **Carabao Island** is an idyllic place where fishing is the main industry and tourism has only just begun to have an impact. **Divers** arrive on day-trips to explore the dozen well-known dive sites in the reefs around the island, although, if you want to stay longer, there are a few decent resorts at **Inobahan Beach**, the island's best – a 1km stretch of powdery white sand a couple of minutes' walk from **Port Said**, where bangkas arrive. It's easy to hire a motorbike in San José to get around; an enjoyable ride takes you to **Tagaytay Point**, the highest point on the island from where there are magnificent views across to Boracay and beyond. Note that Carabao's electricity supply is only switched on for part of the day.

ACCOMMODATION AND EATING   CARABAO ISLAND

INOBAHAN BEACH

Republic of Inobahan Beach Resort ☎ 0918 330 3718. This once-tiny place has now expanded to fifteen rooms (some a/c), including four thatched cottages, each spacious enough for three. There's also a small restaurant – intriguingly named the *Sir Polyon Lounge* – serving breakfast, soup, hamburgers and grilled meat and fish. **P750**

White Beach Dive & Kite Resort ☎ 0939 774 7410, 🌐 carabao.whitebeachdivers.com. Formerly the friendly and popular *Ivy's Vine*, this place is under new management as of early 2014 and has improved the rooms and facilities.

There's a selection of simple beach fan and smarter a/c rooms (P2600), plus a dive and kitesurfing centre. 🛜 **P1500**

LANAS BEACH

Lanas Beach Resort ☎ 0915 214 1002, 🌐 lanasbeachresort.com. British-run resort on a beautiful and quiet stretch of beach. The seven a/c apartments and suites are well designed and set in lush landscaped grounds. The restaurant is highly recommended too, serving a range of dishes, including burgers and Thai green curry. 🛜 **P1800**

Romblon Island

Romblon Island has been extensively quarried for decades to get at the beautiful Romblon marble, a favourite with the rich and famous in Manila. It's a picturesque island, with a pretty harbourside capital, an interior buzzing with wildlife and a coastal road, partly cemented, that you can whip around in half a day past some enticing beaches. **Romblon Town** itself is a pretty place, with Spanish forts, a venerable cathedral and breathtaking views across the Romblon Strait.

Romblon Town

One of the most attractive towns in the Philippines, low-rise **ROMBLON TOWN**, the provincial capital, sits at the back of a deep, twisting bay, with red-roofed houses lining the water's edge and thickly jungled hills behind. Happily dozing in the balm of a more sedentary age, the town feels decades behind the rest of the Philippines. In the mornings, the only sound is that of crowing cockerels, and most activity stops for a siesta in the afternoons. The town has developed a small but discerning and somewhat quirky expat community. The only time the place gets busy is around the second Saturday of January for the **Fiesta of Santo Niño**, celebrating the failure of the Spanish to steal the holy image of baby Jesus from the local cathedral.

6

The town has a few sights, all reachable on foot. Slap in the middle, overlooking the quaint little Spanish plaza, is **St Joseph's Cathedral**, a richly atmospheric church built in 1726. Overlooking the seafront are the remains of renovated **Fort San Andres** (dawn–dusk; P10) and less well preserved **Fort San Pedro**, reminders of the risk Romblon Town once faced from pirates.

Beaches and resorts

Romblon island has some good beaches with very simple hut accommodation on the coast near **Lonos**, 3km south of Romblon. Around 500m long, **Bonbon Beach** is accessed from the road between Romblon and Lonos, and has a gently sloping ocean floor that makes it safe for swimming. A little south of here, **Tiamban Beach** (P40) is a short stretch of white sand backed by palm trees and wooden refreshment shacks. Further still, a number of resorts have sprung up along the stretch of coast from Tiamban south to **Ginablan** and the nearby barangay of **San Pedro**.

| ACCOMMODATION | ROMBLON ISLAND |

ROMBLON TOWN

D'Maestro Inn West corner of the harbour ☎ 0975 942 6014, ✉ mingranemaestro@yahoo.com.ph. The simple but clean fan and a/c (P800) rooms in this family guesthouse are all en suite – it's the cheapest deal in town. **P500**

Romblon Plaza Roxas St ☎ 042 507 2269, ✉ puntacorazonresort@yahoo.com. Two blocks back from the pier, this four-storey building has en-suite doubles with fans, a/c rooms (P1200) and superior suites. The hotel has its own very pleasant rooftop restaurant with daily P99 specials and good views of the cathedral. 🛜 **P700**

★**Stone Creek House** Gov. Fetalvero Ave ☎ 0906 212 8143, ✉ stonecreekhouseromblon@gmail.com. Just beyond the covered market, this three-storey boutique hotel boasts three splendid units, crowned by the spacious self-catering penthouse suite (P3500), complete with classy decorations and top-notch appliances. 🛜 **P2500**

ELSEWHERE ON THE ISLAND

Dream Paradise Mountain Resort Brgy Mapula, 9km southwest of Romblon Town ☎ 0908 748 2272. This lushly landscaped complex of ochre buildings blend well into the hillside setting overlooking tranquil rice paddies. Most rooms are a/c (P1200) but there are a couple with fans. There's a refreshing pool and cute "marble zoo". 🛜 **P400**

Lamao Beach Resort Brgy Lamao, 14km east of Romblon Town ☎ 0948 413 8079, 🌐 facebook.com/ LamaoBeachR. Four spacious and neatly tiled nipa huts (P800), smaller huts with shared bathrooms and two a/c rooms (P1800), all set in a peaceful beachfront compound with a large pool and simple restaurant. **P400**

San Pedro Beach Resort Brgy San Pedro, 12km southwest of Romblon Town ☎ 0928 273 0515, ✉ yolamingoa@yahoo.com. A few minutes' drive south of Ginablan, this charming, relaxing hideaway has cottages nestled along a hillside overlooking sandy Talipasak Beach. There's home cooking in the restaurant and staff can arrange island-hopping and trekking. **P800**

EATING

ROMBLON TOWN

Café Old Sailor Just inland from the harbourfront ☎ 0999 519 1766. Small German-owned *bierkeller* serving schnitzel, wursts and goulash for P290–450, as well as a range of imported beers. Stays open later when there's a crowd. Free wi-fi. Daily 7am–9pm.

J, D & G Just inland from the harbourfront ☎ 0917 876 0072. The Italian owner makes sure that the pizzas and pasta dishes here (P200–350) pass muster. There's also tasty fresh fish and some fine desserts. Free wi-fi. Daily 6am–9pm.

★ **Romblon Deli** Near the ferry pier. This welcoming place has great food and the most reliable travel information in town. Owner Dave, from Cheshire in the UK, and his Filipina wife Tess, offer a taste of Blighty for homesick Brits in the form of bangers and mash (P275), fish and chips (P245) and some good old-fashioned northern hospitality. Free wi-fi. Daily 7am–9pm.

ACTIVITIES

Anchor Bay Water Sports 3km west of Romblon Town ☎ 0918 247 9942, ⊛ anchorbaywatersports.com. The island's best watersports outfit offers windsurfing rental (P700/half-day), paddling in their custom-built kayaks (P160/hr), fishing and snorkelling. There's also a great restaurant – try the P350 marlin special – and some simple concrete huts for overnighting.

Ducks Diving San Pedro ☎ 0929 440 7135, ⊛ the-three-p.com. Professional Swiss diving centre, which specializes in macro diving for avid underwater photographers but also offers fun dives from P1500 when not booked up.

Sibuyan Island

The easternmost of the Romblon group, verdant **Sibuyan Island** has everything the adventurous traveller could dream of: a sparkling coastline; a thickly forested interior; and a couple of daunting mountain peaks, most notably the ragged, saw-like bulk of **Mount Guiting Guiting**. Dubbed "The Galapagos of Asia", the island boasts an extraordinarily rich range of **wildlife**, including 700 plant species and 131 species of bird. Five mammal species (one fruit bat and four rodents) are unique to the island.

Much of Sibuyan was declared a nature reserve in 1996. However, this has not prevented the island from being targeted as a potential mineral-mining site, and although resistance has so far succeeded, corporations continue to conduct research. Sibuyan's 47,000 residents, mostly subsistence farmers and fishermen who rely on the forest and the ocean to supplement their meagre incomes, see relatively few tourists, but some who know every cove, trail and cave on the island are happy to act as guides. Most Sibuyan residents live in three towns, **San Fernando**, **Cajidiocan** and **Magdiwang**; most boats dock at the latter.

Mount Guiting Guiting

Permits (P300), guides and porters (both P1000/day) can be organized at Mount Guiting Guiting Natural Park headquarters (☎ 0928 490 1038) • The park is accessed by an 8km tricycle ride from Magdiwang (P100)

Rising directly from the coastal plain to a height of 2050m, the extinct volcano **Mount Guiting Guiting** is an unforgettable sight. This is not a climb to be undertaken lightly, and if you plan on doing any serious trekking or climbing, you'll have to bring all your equipment with you. The trail to the top of the mountain (affectionately known as G2 by climbers) starts from the **Mount Guiting Guiting Natural Park** headquarters. It begins gently enough, winding through pleasant lowlands, but soon becomes very steep and culminates in a precarious traverse across "the knife edge" to the summit. Even experienced mountaineers regularly fail to summit, and you'll need to allow three days for the round trip (guide compulsory) including ten hours for the ascent.

Next to Guiting Guiting is **Mayo's Peak** (1530m), a secondary summit that, like its neighbour, is cloaked in mossy forests, ferns and rare orchids. The trek to the top is more straightforward, requiring only 24 hours. Check at the park headquarters for more information and advice.

ACCOMMODATION   SIBUYAN ISLAND

Sanctuary Garden Resort By the start of the trail up Mt Guiting Guiting ☎ 0920 217 4127. This well-located place provides a great alternative to a beach stay, and offers everything from camping and dorm beds to a/c rooms with fridges, TVs and DVD players (P1800). They also rent out bicycles for P200/day . ☞ Dorms P250, doubles P1200

Vicky's Place M.H. Del Pilar St, Magdiwang ☎ 0920 530 8533. Next to the elementary school, this family home features bright, airy guest rooms with a shared bathroom. There's also a good restaurant in the garden. P600

Panay

The substantial, vaguely triangular-shaped island of **PANAY** has been largely bypassed by tourism, perhaps because everyone seems to get sucked towards **Boracay** off its northern tip instead. There's room enough on Panay, though, for plenty of discovery and adventure: the island has a huge coastline and a mountainous, jungle-filled interior that has yet to be fully mapped.

Panay comprises four provinces: **Antique** ("ant-ee-kay") on the west coast; **Aklan** in the north; **Capiz** in the northeast; and **Iloilo** ("ee-lo-ee-lo") running along the east coast to the capital of the province, **Iloilo City**, in the south. The province that most interests tourists is Aklan, whose capital, **Kalibo**, is the site of the big and brash **Ati-Atihan festival**, held in the second week of January (see box, p.284). This doesn't mean that you should give the rest of Panay the brush-off. The northeast coast was badly affected by Typhoon Yolanda, but it still offers bangka access to a number of unspoilt islands, while on the west side, Antique is a raw, bucolic province of picturesque beaches and scrubby mountains.

6

ARRIVAL AND DEPARTURE PANAY

By plane There are four major airports on Panay, all served by daily flights from Manila. Panay's principal airport is in Iloilo and has flights from Manila, Cebu, Davao and Puerto Princesa. On the north coast there are airports at Roxas, Kalibo and Caticlan. Roxas only has a few flights per day, while busier Kalibo and particularly Caticlan are mainly used by visitors on their way to Boracay. Kalibo is also served by international flights from around Asia, so is an alternative port of entry into the Philippines. See individual town accounts for flight schedules.

By boat Frequent passenger ferries link Iloilo with Bacolod on nearby Negros; a few also sail to Manila and Cebu. Large bangkas ply the route to Guimaras. In the north, Caticlan is served by boats from Roxas on Mindoro Oriental (see p.248) and a couple of destinations on Tablas Island in the Romblon group (see p.271). Roxas receives ferries from Batangas (see p.116) via Romblon Town and bangkas from Sibuyan, as well as ferries from Mandaon on Masbate.

Iloilo City and around

ILOILO CITY is a useful transit point for Guimaras (see p.285) and has good ferry connections to many other Visayan islands, but there's nothing to keep you here for more than a day or two. The **city centre** occupies a thin strip of land on the southern bank of the Iloilo River, with views across to Guimaras. **General Luna Street** runs for nearly 3km along the northern boundary of the centre, and is one of the city's major arteries, lined with banks, hotels and restaurants. It's worth heading across the river to the **Smallville Commercial Complex** for dining and nightlife, made all the more attractive by the proximity to the splendidly landscaped new riverside **Esplanade**. For more of a sense of history, the old areas of **Molo**, 3km west of town, and **Jaro**, 3km north, both make pleasant distractions. There are also more adventurous pursuits to be enjoyed around Iloilo, including trekking and caving in **Bulabog Puti-An National Park**, and trips to local Ati villages.

Over the fourth weekend of January, the **Dinagyang** festival (🐦facebook.com/ DinagyangSailoiloFestival), loosely based on Kalibo's Ati-Atihan, adds some extra frenzy to the city. The **Paraw Regatta** falls in the third week of February and includes a race across to Guimaras.

Plaza Libertad and J.M. Basa Street

In the southeastern quadrant of the city is **Plaza Libertad**, where the first flag of the Philippine Republic was raised in triumph after Spain surrendered the city on December 25, 1898. There's little to remind you of the history, though – the square today is a concrete affair with fast-food restaurants and busy roads on all sides. The few old residential and commercial buildings that survive date back to Spanish and American colonial periods, and are mostly in **J.M. Basa Street**, which runs past the square linking Ledesma Street to the port area.

6

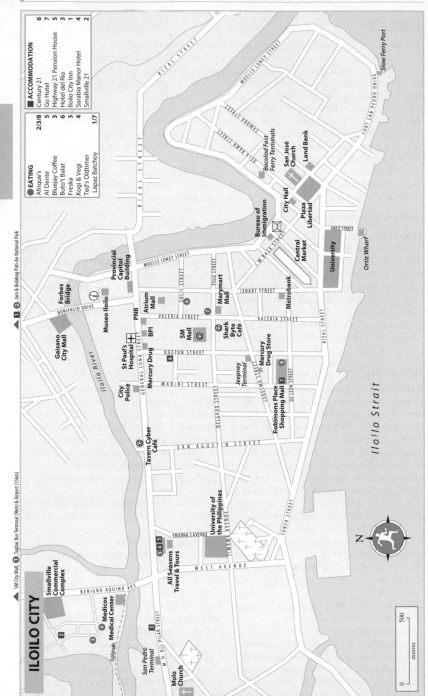

ILOILO CITY

● EATING		■ ACCOMMODATION	
Afrique's	2/3/8	Century 21	6
Al Dente	5	Go Hotel	7
Bluejay Coffee	3	Highway 21 Pension House	5
Buto't Balat	6	Hotel del Rio	3
Freska	3	Iloilo City Inn	1
Kogi & Vegi	3	Sarabia Manor Hotel	4
Ted's Oldtimer	4	Smallville 21	2
Lapaz Batchoy	1/7		

Museo Iloilo

Bonifacio Drive, just south of the river • Mon–Fri 9.30am–5pm • P50 • A short walk north of General Luna St, or hop on a Jaro-bound jeepney

An engaging and clearly presented repository of Iloilo's cultural heritage, the **Museo Iloilo** has a diverse range of exhibits including fossils, shells and rocks indicating the age of Panay Island. There are also ornamental teeth, jewellery excavated from pre-Spanish burial sites, pottery from China and Siam, coffins, war relics and some modern art, including large wooden sculptures.

Molo

Molo can be reached by taxi (P7), or on foot from the city centre in 30min by heading west down M. H. Del Pilar St, or by tricycle or jeepney (10min; P7)

On the western edge of the city, the district of **Molo** makes for an interesting wander. In the sixteenth and seventeenth centuries, Molo was a Chinese quarter, much like Parian in Manila. The main sight is **Molo Church** (St Anne's), a splendid nineteenth-century Gothic Renaissance edifice made of coral, with rows of female saints lining both sides of the aisle.

Asilo de Molo

Open to visitors daily 10am–noon & 1–4pm • Donation expected • ☎ 033 338 0252, ⓦ asilodemolo.com

About 1km west along the road from Molo Church is the **Asilo de Molo**, formerly an orphanage where vestments were hand-embroidered by orphan girls under the tutelage of nuns. The orphans have since been transferred to Manila, and the Asilo, still run by the Sisters of the Daughters of Charity, is now home to Iloilo's elderly poor, who also turn out local handicrafts.

Jaro

Taxi (P60–70), or jeepneys marked Jaro or Tiko (10min; P7), or about a 45min walk

Three kilometres north of the centre across the Forbes Bridge, the historical enclave of **Jaro** is worth exploring. You can also wander among the old colonial homes of sugar barons and mooch through a number of dusty old antique shops, where prices are lower than in Manila. Jaro's **plaza** is an inspiring little piece of old Asia, dominated by Jaro Cathedral, and lined with *bibingka* stalls and colourful flower shops.

Jaro Metropolitan Cathedral

Jaro Plaza

The Spanish-era **Jaro Metropolitan Cathedral**, with its ivory-white stone facade and dignified but crumbling old belfry that was partially destroyed by an earthquake in 1984, is the seat of the Catholic diocese in the Western Visayas. Steps either side of the main doors lead up to a platform and the Shrine to the Divine Infant and Nuestra Señora de la Candelaria (Our Lady of Candles).

Nelly Garden mansion

Set back from Luna St, south of Jaro Plaza • P100; tours P1000 per group (min five) – for tours, reserve at least three days in advance with the Iloilo tourist office (see p.278)

The grandiose **Nelly Garden mansion** stands down a picturesque driveway lined with eucalyptus. The mansion, which has murals on the walls and a U-shaped dining room with a fountain in the middle, can only be visited by arrangement.

Bulabog Puti-An National Park

Foreigners P100, Filipinos P10; guide P150 • Ranger's office cabins P250/person, Dingle homestay P500/person • To reach the park independently from Iloilo City, charter a taxi (P2000–3000, depending on vehicle size and how long you stay) or take a jeepney to Dingle (1hr), then tricycle (P20/person) to the park entrance; or book a trip through the tourist office (see p.278)

Some 40km north of Iloilo, **Bulabog Puti-An National Park**, established in 1961, sits along a ridgeline of intact primary forest. The region's caverns were used as a hideout by

6

6

revolutionary forces during the Spanish period, and inscriptions penned on the cave walls still bear testament to this time. Today the park offers a healthy choice of adventurous outdoor pursuits such as trekking and cave exploration, plus the chance to spot monkeys, pythons and a host of creepy-crawlies.

You can easily visit as a day-trip from Iloilo, but for those who want a closer look, an **overnight stay** can be arranged at the simple cabins in the ranger's office, or at a homestay in Dingle. You can get to Bulabog Puti-An independently – in which case hiring a **guide** on arrival is recommended – but for fuller exploration it's worth arranging a trip in advance through the tourist office.

ARRIVAL AND DEPARTURE ILOILO CITY

By plane Iloilo's airport is at Cabutuan, 15km from the city. A taxi to the city centre costs about P400, or you can take a share-van for P60/person. Cebu Pacific (☎ 033 333 0015) and PAL (☎ 033 333 0040) have ticket offices at the airport. Air tickets can also be obtained at travel agents or any of the city's Western Union offices.
Destinations Cebu (4–6 daily; 45min); Davao (1–2 daily; 1hr 10min); Manila (9–13 daily; 1hr 10min); Puerto Princesa (3 weekly; 1hr).
By boat Slow ferries from Cebu and Manila arrive at the wharf on the eastern edge of the city, a 15min walk or short jeepney/tricycle ride from General Luna St. Fast ferries for Bacolod leave a few hundred metres beyond the post office on Muelle Loney St. Ortiz wharf, used by bangkas (P15) from Hoskyn on Guimaras, is at the southern end of Ortiz St near the market.
Destinations Bacolod (frequent; 1hr); Cagayan de Oro (1 weekly; 14hr); Cebu City (8 weekly; 12–13hr); Hoskyn (on

Guimaras; every 30min; 15min); Manila (2 weekly; 24hr); Puerto Princesa (3 weekly; 25–27hrs).
By bus and minivan Most buses now arrive at the Tagbac bus terminal, 9km northeast on the outskirts of town, from where it's a 20min ride into town by taxi (P120) or jeepney (P15). The most comfortable and reliable bus company is Ceres Liner (☎ 033 329 1223), which has frequent a/c and ordinary services. Non-stop minivans from here are slightly quicker, but more expensive. Both services are most frequent until 1pm. For San José, capital of Antique in the west, and Libertad to the north, you'll need to head to the old San Pedro terminal on M.H. Del Pilar St in the west of town.
Destinations Caticlan (every 45min–1hr; 6hr); Estancia (every 20min; 3hr 30min); Kalibo (every 30min; 4–5hr); Roxas (every 30min; 3hr); San José (every 30min–1hr; 2hr 30min).

GETTING AROUND, INFORMATION AND TOURS

By taxi and jeepney There are plenty of taxis in Iloilo, but the city centre is compact enough to cover on foot. There's a jeepney terminal on Ledesma St.
Tourist information The helpful tourist office (Mon–Fri 8am–5pm; ☎ 033 337 5411) is in the grounds of the Capitol Building on Bonifacio Drive, one block north of J.M. Basa St and next to the Museo Iloilo.

Tours The tourist office has a list of accredited travel agencies, guides and drivers and can help you arrange trips in the surrounding region including to Guimaras, Bulabog Puti-An National Park and the churches of the south coast. All Seasons Travel & Tours (daily 8am–5pm; ☎ 033 336 7182), at the *Sarabia Manor Hotel* (see opposite), offer tours of the city and further afield, as well as flight tickets and vehicle rental.

ACCOMMODATION

Century 21 Quezon St ☎ 033 335 8821, ✉ centuryhotel@yahoo.com. Mid-sized, glass-fronted building offering basic, affordable rooms with a/c and cable TV. Singles are among the cheapest in town for this sort of quality, and family rooms for four are good value at P1800. Wi-fi in the lobby only. 🛜 **P1200**
Go Hotel Robinsons Mall, Ledesma St at Mabini St ☎ 033 335 3376. Increasingly popular franchise, always attached to a Robinsons Mall. Rooms are bright, modern and comfortable. The earlier you book online, the better the price. 🛜 **P1000**
Highway 21 Pension House General Luna St ☎ 033 335 1220, ✉ highway21_hotel@yahoo.com. Excellent budget choice close to the *Sarabia Manor Hotel* with

modern rooms and staff who are on the ball. All rooms have a/c, cable TV and hot water, but some are windowless. Good location not far from the Esplanade and Smallville. 🛜 **P800**
★**Hotel del Rio** M.H. Del Pilar St, Molo ☎ 033 335 1171, 🌐 hoteldelrio.com.ph. Stylish and very professional hotel in a pleasant location on the river. Standard rooms have a/c, fridge, cable TV, king-size bed and river views. Superior (P3552) and deluxe rooms (P4388) are newer and more tastefully styled, but don't overlook the river. There's also a popular coffee shop and a good pool. 🛜 **P2925**
★**Iloilo City Inn** 113 Seminario St, Jaro ☎ 033 320 2186. This friendly place enjoys a quiet location close to the

sights in Jaro and has clean, comfortable a/c rooms at affordable prices. Downstairs, *Bavaria* serves good German food and beer and has wi-fi. The roof deck has views of the nearby cathedral. 📶 P850

Sarabia Manor Hotel General Luna St ☎033 335 1021, 🖰sarabiamanorhotel.com. Iloilo's biggest hotel has been given a new lease of life by a change of ownership. The cheapest "Budget" rooms are very small but the "Economy" and "Travellers" rooms are good value while the "Corporate" rooms are fancier and include breakfast. All

dozen room types come with a/c and have cable TV. Promo rates usually available. 📶 P825

Smallville 21 Smallville Commercial Complex, Diversion Rd ☎033 501 6821, 🖰smallville21hotel .com. This new addition to the home-grown *21* chain is perfect for those who want to have some of the city's best nightlife and restaurants on their doorstep. Rooms are well kept, modern and fitted with dark wood furnishings. Breakfast included. 📶 P1800

EATING

Across the river from the city centre, **Smallville Commercial Complex** has everything from coffee shops and restaurants to bars featuring live bands, and full-blown clubs like *Aura*, *Ice* and *MO2*. **Coffeebreak** is a citywide chain which does good coffee and cakes.

Afrique's 107 Castilla St, Jaro ☎033 320 0554, 🖰facebook.com/AfriquesPizza; Red Square Building, Smallville ☎033 509 4900. Atmospheric restaurant in a lovely old colonial house right behind Jaro cathedral. The menu is largely Italian and includes a huge range of pizzas along with specialities such as *osso bucco* pasta, all around P300. They also have a more modern branch at Smallville. Daily 10am–10pm.

Al Dente Sarabia Manor Hotel, General Luna St ☎033 336 7183, 🖰sarabiamanorhotel.com. Stylish, reasonably priced Italian restaurant serving seafood and chicken paella for two (P275) and a range of delicious pasta dishes (P145–295). Also does fish and chips. Free wi-fi. Daily 11am–10pm.

Bluejay Coffee Smallville Commercial Complex, Diversion Rd ☎033 333 3961, 🖰bluejaycoffee.com. Relaxed blend of comfy chairs and tasty food, serving all-day American, Filipino, German or Spanish breakfasts for P245. The chunky apple and tuna salad sandwich (P195) is also excellent, as is the coffee (P80–160). Free wi-fi. Mon–Sat 6am–midnight, Sun 8am–midnight.

★**Buto't Balat** Solis St ☎033 509 6770. A haven of tropical tranquillity and greenery in the midst of the downtown mayhem, this popular restaurant offers

candlelit dining under thatched cabanas surrounding a small pond. Dishes to try include chilli shrimps (P295), pork Bicol Express (P185), beef *kare kare* (P325), and there's fish by weight. Daily 10.30am–10pm.

★**Freska** Smallville Boardwalk, Diversion Rd ☎033 855 3271. *Freska* continues to make Illonggo dining easy with its mouthwateringly good-value daily lunch and dinner buffets for P299. Over forty dishes are on offer, including green mango salad, chicken *Inasal* (marinated and grilled – an Iloilo speciality), BBQ pork and a delicious dessert line-up. Your thirst can be quenched by the huge selection of imported beers. Daily 11.30am–2.30pm & 5.30–10.30pm.

Kogi & Vegi Boardwalk, right off Esplanade ☎033 331 9589. Pleasantly decorated modern Korean restaurant, where you can enjoy well-prepared, authentic dishes such as beef *bulgogi* (P350), *tukbokki* stir-fried rice (P280), soups and, of course, *kimchi* (P280). Daily 10am–10pm.

Ted's Oldtimer Lapaz Batchoy Valeria St & SM City Mall ☎033 337 0804, 🖰facebook.com/TedsLapazBatchoy. Though the precise origins of *batchoy*, the famed Illonggo dish (see box below), are something of a mystery, *Ted's*, open since 1945, is without question *the* place to get an authentic helping of it (P90). Daily 8am–8pm.

DIRECTORY

Hospital St Paul's Hospital is at the eastern end of General Luna St (☎033 337 2741), towards the junction with Bonifacio. The new Medicus Medical Center is just off the Esplanade (☎033 328 7777).

Immigration The Bureau of Immigration (☎033 509 9651) is at the Old Customs House on Aduana St.

Internet access All of the big malls have internet cafés, including Netopia on the second floor of SM City, or you

---

ILOILO SPECIALITIES

Iloilo City is one of the best places in the country to try **seafood**, and it's also known for a number of unique regional Illonggo delicacies, including **pancit Molo soup**, a garlicky noodle soup containing pork dumplings, which is named after the Molo area of the city and is sold at numerous street stalls. **Batchoy**, an artery-hardening combination of liver, pork and beef with thin noodles, is also widely available.

could try *Tavern Cyber Café* at the *Riverside Inn* on General Luna St, or *Shark Byte Café* on Yulo St (both daily 9am–7pm; P15/hr).

Pharmacies There are pharmacies in every mall. There's also a large branch of Mercury Drug opposite St Paul's Hospital on

General Luna St (daily 7am–11pm; ☎ 033 338 3181).

Police The main city police department is in General Luna St (☎ 033 337 5511).

Post Iloilo's main post office is below the Bureau of Immigration on Aduana St.

The south coast

Heading southwest from Iloilo City along the coastal road – the only road – takes you through the atmospheric Spanish-era towns of **Oton**, **Tigbauan**, **Guimbal**, **Miag-ao** and **San Joaquin**. Each has a historic **church**, notably Tigbauan's Baroque church (22km from Iloilo City) and Guimbal's Catholic (35km from Iloilo) church, which stands close to a number of ruined seventeenth-century watchtowers.

Miag-ao Church
Miag-ao, 40km west of Iloilo

Pride of place along the southwest coast goes to **Miag-ao Church** (also known as the Church of Santo Tomas de Villanueva), built by the Augustinians between 1786 and 1797 as a fortress against Moro invasions. Declared a national landmark and a UNESCO World Heritage Site, the church is built of a local yellow-orange sandstone in Baroque-Romanesque style, a unique example of Filipino Rococo.

ARRIVAL AND DEPARTURE   THE SOUTH COAST

By car The easiest way to visit the church towns of the southwest is to hire a vehicle and driver in Iloilo for a day-trip, which should cost P2500–3000.

By bus and jeepney If you have time, it's simple enough to travel between the towns by public transport. All buses

from Iloilo City bound for San Joaquin (1hr) pass through Oton (10min), Tigbauan (15min), Guimbal (25min) and Miag-ao (50min), and plenty of jeepneys also ply the west-coast route.

ACCOMMODATION

Anhawan Beach Resort Oton ☎ 0917 597 3214, ⓦ anhawanbeach.com. Not too far from Oton town, this overpriced resort offers several different room types, all of which have a/c. There's also a decent pool and spa, plus an extensive activity line-up including jet-skiing, kayaking and horseriding. ☎ P3360

Bantayan Beach Resort Guimbal ☎ 033 315 5009. Named after the squat, Spanish-era watchtower on the property, this place has a/c cottages, now all fully renovated (P1900). There's a pool table and free wi-fi in the restaurant. ☎ P1500

The west coast

Most of the west coast of Panay, made up largely of the province of **Antique**, is untouched by tourism. This is one of the poorest areas of the Philippines, with a solitary coastal road connecting a series of isolated villages and towns. It's an attractive coastline with a savage backdrop of jungled mountains that are only just beginning to be explored and climbed. The journey along the province's coast, from **San José** in the south to **Libertad** in the north, provides an excellent opportunity to experience a simple provincial life, shielded from the rest of the Philippines by mountains on one side and sea on the other.

San José

SAN JOSÉ is a busy little port town whose major claim to fame – apart from being capital of Antique – seems to be that its cathedral has the tallest bell tower in Panay. There are no tourist sights here, just a chaotic wharf, a cracked plaza and a main street, the National Highway, lined with pawnshops, canteens and rice dealers. The town's annual **Binirayan festival**, held from April 30 to May 2, commemorates the thirteenth-century landing of ten Malay chieftains who established the first Malayan settlement in the Philippines.

Tibiao

About halfway along Panay's west coast, **TIBIAO** is best used as a base for **whitewater kayaking**, **rafting** and **trekking** on the Tibiao River, at the head of which the town stands. Tibiao also stands in the shadow of Panay's highest peak, **Mount Madja-as** (2090m) – it's possible to climb this daunting peak, but a permit and guide are essential. The town itself is a relaxed spot, with a lively central plaza – complete with basketball court – less than 200m inland from the long stony beach full of fishing boats.

Tibiao Eco Adventure Park

Daily 8am–5pm • Entry P50, zipline P300, guided kayaking tours P900 • From Tibiao take a shared tricycle (P8) 3km north to the junction at Importante, then a habal-habal ride (P70), or a 40min walk; you can also visit as part of a tour with Katahum Tours (see below)

A few kilometres inland is the **Tibiao Eco Adventure Park** (aka TEA Park), which opened in 2012 and offers a host of outdoors activities from gentle introductory kayaking lessons through to whitewater rides, canyoning and rapelling. For many visitors, the highlight is the 1km long zipline through the lush jungle.

ARRIVAL AND DEPARTURE   THE WEST COAST

By bus San José's bus station is in Isabel St, 1km west of the centre, and the pier is on the western edge of the town.

Buses running between San José and Caticlan pass through Tibiao.

ACTIVITIES

Katahum Tours Tibiao ☎ 0947 531 6518, ⊛ katahum .com. Tour operator (as well as a fish spa and hotel) where you can arrange everything from gentle day-tours to rafting and trekking.

Tribal Adventures Professional adventure operator running whitewater kayaking trips from their base in Boracay (see box, p.263).

ACCOMMODATION AND EATING

SAN JOSÉ

Centillion House 2000 Brgy Bantayan ☎ 036 540 9403, ⊛ centillionhouse.com. Set above a small shopping mall, this place has clean, well-maintained rooms with a/c and cable TV, and also serves the best meals in town. P1500

TIBIAO

Homtel University of Antique Campus, Main Rd ⊛ bit. ly/HomtelAntique. Twelve simple fan rooms mostly with shared bathrooms, set in the peaceful university campus. The singles are extremely small but great value (P300), the doubles rather overpriced. P1000

Kasa Raya Travelers Inn Near the crossroads at Importante ☎ 0917 524 7875, ⊛ facebook.com/

KasaRayaInn. Comfortable modern rooms, some fan, some a/c, all including breakfast. The knowledgeable owner Alex runs eco-trips to inland and islet destinations. ☏ P700

Kayak Inn Beyond TEA Park, in the foothills outside Tibiao ☎ 0905 906 2380. Simple lodge by the river with basic bamboo nipa huts each with a *kawa*, a large wok-like bath heated by fire (originally used for cooking muscovado sugar; P200). P500

La Westview 200m east of the plaza ☎ 0936 830 6437, ⊛ bit.ly/LaWestview. Smooth bar/restaurant that was being refurbished at the time of writing. They offer a small selection of chicken, pork or beef dishes in original or spicy sauces for P80–130. There's a good internet outlet at the front. Daily 8am–10pm.

The east coast

Panay's **east coast** – from Iloilo City north to **Estancia** – is an undeveloped area of wilderness and sun-drenched barangays rarely seen by tourists. There are some wonderfully pristine islands off the coast, many of them unfamiliar even to locals, but to explore them you'll need time on your hands, patience and a willingness to spend nights camped on beaches. This region was badly hit by Typhoon Yolanda, with heavy loss of life. It has largely got back on its feet, but developing tourism is still not a priority.

Roxas

ROXAS, the capital of Capiz province, is renowned for its seafood, and also has a reputation among Filipinos as being a hotbed of witches and shamans. The city is well connected by air, sea and land. However, aside from taking a trip out to the pleasant if unremarkable stretch of golden sand and row of seafood restaurants at **Baybay Beach**, 3km north of town en route to the port, there is little to keep visitors in Roxas for long. You may want to have a quick look at the local historical artefacts in the **Ang Panublion Museum** (Mon–Sat 9am–5pm; free; ☎033 621 2070, ⓦangpanublionmuseum.weebly. com) on the elongated traffic-choked plaza in the town centre.

In late 2013, Roxas became the headquarters for the Yolanda relief operation in devastated northern Panay. While Roxas proper escaped without too much serious damage, many of the famous seafood shacks (and resorts) at Baybay were damaged or destroyed, though these are now all fully operational again.

ARRIVAL AND INFORMATION   ROXAS

By plane The airport, 10min north of the city by jeepney or tricycle (P20) in Arnaldo Blvd, is served daily from Manila by PAL and Cebu Pacific flights, both of which have offices there.

By boat Ferries dock at the Calusi pier, 3km west of Baybay Beach. Tricycles run out to the pier for P20, plus there are P10 jeepneys. Providing the weather is agreeable, bangkas leave every morning for Sibuyan Island in the Romblon group (4–5hr). There are also ferries to Batangas (2 weekly;

13hr) via Romblon Town (5hr) and to Mandaon on Masbate (4 weekly; 5hr).

By bus Services for Iloilo, Kalibo and Estancia use the new bus terminus 4km south of the Panay River, reachable by tricycle. Direct services stop early, so another alternative is to catch one of the frequent buses to Sigma (till 6.45pm), and then change there for Kalibo or Caticlan.

Destinations Caticlan (every 30min–1hr; 3hr); Iloilo (every 20–30min; 3–4hr); Kalibo (every 30min; 2hr).

ACCOMMODATION

ROXAS

Halaran Plaza Hotel Opposite City Hall, Rizal St ☎036 621 0649. In a central location, *Halaran* has a choice of spacious and comfortable fan and a/c rooms (P750) with solid wooden floors and high ceilings, although they can be a bit noisy. 📶 **P550**

Roxas President's Inn Rizal Ave at Lopez Jaena St ☎036 621 0208, ⓦroxaspresidentsinn.com. This hotel is strewn with antiques. Rooms are cosy and clean, with a/c, cable TV and hot showers attached. There's also a convivial café, and wi-fi in the lobby. 📶 **P1904**

BAYBAY BEACH

Grand Gazebo ☎036 650 0522, ⓦbit.ly/GrandGazebo. Attractive, locally owned place just over the road from the beach, with bright, spacious a/c rooms with flatscreen TVs, set around a pleasant lawn. Breakfast included. 📶 **P1800**

San Antonio Resort ☎036 621 6638, ⓦthe sanantonioresort.com. A range of rooms from tiny budget rooms to luxurious suites overlooking an attractive lagoon just back from the beach. There's also a pleasant pool (with poolside wi-fi), and kayaking on the lagoon. 📶 **P1300**

EATING

ROXAS

Café 1927 P. Gomez St ☎036 621 6185, ⓦbit.ly/Cafe1927Roxas. Just down the road from Halaran Plaza, this laidback place with old vinyl discs and licence plates on the walls serves good combo meals and breakfast such as beef tapa for under P100. Salmon steak, sandwiches and pasta cost P120–230. Mon–Sat 7.30am–10pm.

BAYBAY BEACH

Alma's Grill ☎0930 168 3006. In a bright-yellow building on the seashore, *Alma's* serves standout *gambas* (P300 for six people), grilled fish and smaller snacks like squid or catfish on a skewer (both P150). Daily 7am–10pm.

Coco Veranda ☎036 621 6185, ⓦfacebook.com/CocoCerandaCapiz. Pretty beachside restaurant with

---

TINDOG CAPIZ!

Visitors to Roxas can help with the ongoing Yolanda recovery effort by taking one of the provincial tourist office's **"Tindog Capiz!"** ("Arise Capiz!") tours (☎033 337 5411, ⓔcapiz .tourism@yahoo.com). **Voluntourism** trips were already in place prior to Yolanda, but have more focus and purpose than ever in the years since. Projects include house and school building, mangrove replanting, food production and livelihood training programmes.

friendly service and a huge seafood menu. As well as excellent crab, scallops, oysters, mussels and prawns, there's also pink salmon sashimi (P185/100g), plus meat dishes, cocktails and desserts. Free wi-fi. **Daily 10am–10pm.**

Kalibo

KALIBO, the capital of Aklan province, is the biggest – in fact the only – attraction of Panay's **north coast**, which from Roxas in the east to Caticlan in the west (see p.262) is mostly industrial and has no notable beaches. Served by flights from around Asia, Kalibo lies on the well-trodden path to Boracay; for most visitors, this is simply the place to transfer from plane to bus.

The town's major thoroughfare is **Roxas Avenue**, which runs into town from the airport in the southeast, with most streets leading off it on a southwest–northeast axis. It's really just another small town, full of tricycles and fast-food outlets, but it does have an interesting **museum**, and every second week of January it hosts what is probably the biggest street party in the country, the **Ati-Atihan**, an exuberant festival that celebrates the original inhabitants of the area and the later arrival of Catholicism (see box, p.284).

Museo It Akean

San Martelino St at Archbishop Reyes St • Mon–Sat 8am–noon & 1–5pm • P15 • ☏ 036 268 9260

Kalibo is home to one of Panay's best museums, the **Museo It Akean**. Though modest, it's the only museum to document the cultural heritage of the Aklañons (Aklan people), and contains exhibits of the area's old *piña* textiles, pottery, religious relics, literature and Spanish-era artefacts, many on loan from affluent local families. Among the most interesting exhibits are rare costumes that were worn by Aklan tribespeople during festivals. Despite serious earthquake damage in the 1980s, the museum building retains some of the original features; since its construction by the Spanish in 1882, it has also been used as a school, a courtroom and a garrison.

Bakhawan Eco-tourism Centre and Mangrove Park

Bakhawan, around 3km east of town • Daily 8am–5pm • P20

A short tricycle ride from town, the **Bakhawan Eco-tourism Centre and Mangrove Park** is the site of a mangrove replanting project. The project was principally initiated to prevent flood and storm surges, but also benefits local wildlife and affords visitors the chance to experience this little-seen habitat up close. Once here, you can walk along a pretty 1km-long boardwalk through the tangled mangrove thickets to the beach.

ARRIVAL AND DEPARTURE
KALIBO

By plane The 10min tricycle ride into town from the airport, a distance of about 6km, costs P40. Air Asia, PAL (☏ 036 262 3260) and Cebu Pacific (☏ 036 262 5407) all have ticket offices at the airport; Cebu Pacific also has an office on Toting Reyes St, near the junction with Quezon Ave.

Domestic destinations Cebu (3–6 daily; 50min); Manila (10–12 daily; 1hr 10min).

KALIBO

● **EATING**
Goto	2
Latte Coffee Café	3/5
Mary's	1
Peking House	4
Roz & Angelique's	6

■ **ACCOMMODATION**
Ati-Atihan County Inn	5
Kalibo Inn	3
Marzon	4
RB Lodge	1/2

6

ATI-ATIHAN: KEEP ON GOING, NO TIRING

Ati-Atihan is a quasi-religious mardi gras held every January in Kalibo. The culmination of the two-week event is a procession through the streets on the third Sunday of the month, a sustained three-day, three-night frenzy of carousing and dancing. Transvestites bring out their best frocks, and schoolgirls with hats made of coconuts join aborigines, celebrities and priests in fancy dress. Throw in the unending beat of massed drums and the average Filipino's predisposition for a good party, and the result is a flamboyant alfresco rave that claims to be the biggest and most prolonged in the country. The Ati-Atihan mantra *Hala Bira, Puera Pasma* translates as "Keep on going, no tiring."

The festival's **origins** can be traced to 1210, when refugees from Borneo fled north to Panay. Panay's Negrito natives, known as Atis, sold them land; both parties celebrated the deal with a feast, which was then repeated year on year. The fancy-dress element derives from the lighter-skinned Borneans blacking up their faces in affectionate imitation of the Atis. Later, Spanish friars co-opted the festival in honour of the **Santo Niño**, spreading the word among islanders that the baby Jesus had appeared to help drive off a pirate attack. It was a move calculated to hasten the propagation of Catholicism throughout the Philippines, and it worked. Ati-Atihan has since become so popular that similar festivals have cropped up all over the Visayas. Historians generally agree, however, that the Kalibo Ati-Atihan is the real thing.

International destinations Busan, South Korea (8 weekly; 4hr 55min); Kuala Lumpur, Malaysia (4 weekly: 3hr 45min); Seoul, South Korea (5 daily; 5hr 15min); Singapore (4 weekly; 3hr 40min); Taipei, Taiwan (2 weekly; 3hr).

By boat Ferries arrive in Dumaguit Port, a 15min jeepney ride (around 12km) outside Kalibo. There is a service every five days to Manila with Moreta Shipping Lines (☎ 036 262 3003), who have a ticket office on Regalado St, near the junction with Acavedo St. Shuttle buses take passengers from Kalibo's Ceres Liner terminal to Caticlan

port, from where ferries run to several other destinations (see p.275).

By bus and van Regular buses and vans serving Caticlan (the jumping-off point for Boracay) arrive and depart directly from the airport (1hr 30min; P200). Cheaper buses and vans (P111) to Caticlan leave from the Ceres Liner terminal on Osmeña Ave, from where there are also regular buses and vans to all other destinations listed.

Destinations Caticlan (every 20min; 1hr); Iloilo (every 20–30min; 4–5hr); Roxas (every 30min; 2hr); San José (hourly; 4–5hr).

ACCOMMODATION

Good accommodation can be hard to find during the Ati-Atihan, when rates double or triple, so if you're visiting during the festival, make sure you've booked a room (and, if you want to fly in, your plane ticket) in advance.

Ati-Atihan County Inn D. Maagma St ☎ 036 268 6116, ⊛ bit.ly/AntiAtihanCountyInn. Government-owned place offering good-value rooms with fans or a/c, cable TV and hot showers, set around a communal living area that has wi-fi. 🛜 Dorms ‾P150‾, doubles ‾P840‾

Kalibo Hotel 467 N. Roldan St ☎036 268 4765, ⊛ kalibo-hotel.com. Well-furnished, airy, a/c rooms in a good location on the eastern edge of Kalibo, within walking distance of Gaisano Mall and other shops. Staff are efficient and helpful, and can arrange plane and ferry tickets. 🛜 ‾P1232‾

★**Marzon** Santa Monica, 2km southeast of town ☎036 268 2188, ⊛marzonhotelkalibo.com. Surprisingly upscale hotel for this part of the world

– perhaps a sign of things to come. Owned by the same company as *Marzon* in Boracay, this modern hotel on the road out to the airport has comfortable, stylish rooms and a huge swimming pool. *Latte Coffee Café* (see opposite) and *Roz & Angelique's* (see opposite) are also right next door. 🛜 ‾P1800‾

★**RB Lodge** Original branch: N. Roldan St; new branch: G. Pastrana St ☎036 268 5200, ⊛facebook .com/RBLodgeKalibo. Good-value hotel with a surprisingly chic modern branch just around the corner from the original. The cheapest fan rooms are small and dark but the better a/c rooms (P1150) are quiet and tastefully furnished. There's also an internet café and a coffee shop. 🛜 ‾P450‾

EATING

Kalibo's dining options have improved in recent years, particularly out in Santa Monica on the way to the airport. In town there are a few independent places, but otherwise it's a choice of hole-in-the-wall carinderias or fast-food chains which include *Chowking*, *Jollibee* and *Andok's*.

★**Goto** N. Roldan St at Veteran St ☎0919 643 5955. Chilled-out rooftop restaurant serving burgers, buffalo wings, onion rings and the like for P100–220, plus a range of beers and cocktails. Simple and inexpensive Filipino cuisine is served in the downstairs dining room. Daily 10.45am–1am.

Latte Coffee Café Archbishop Reyes St & Santa Monica ☎036 268 9026. There are two branches of this pleasant coffee shop in Kalibo, both of which sell great coffee, sandwiches and light meals (P150–175), alongside Havaiana flip-flops. Free wi-fi. Both daily 7am–9pm.

Mary's G. Pastrana St ☎036 268 8204, ⓦbit.ly/ MarysKalibo. Clean, bustling canteen-style place serving huge bowls of noodles (from P55), sandwiches, desserts and coffee. Daily 8am–6pm.

Peking House Martyrs St ☎036 268 4752. Kalibo's most popular Chinese restaurant is often full of folk enjoying delicious but inexpensive food such as seafood fried rice and noodle dishes. Mains P100–200. Daily 11am–9pm.

Roz & Angelique's Santa Monica ☎036 268 3512. A popular dining spot for Kalibo's well-to-do, this formal restaurant has an extensive menu featuring everything from crispy pata (P400, good for three) to crêpes (P140), burgers, sandwiches, crème brûlée and shakes. No MSG is used in the cooking; free wi-fi. Daily 10.30am–9pm.

6

DIRECTORY

Hospital The Dr Rafael S. Tumbokon Memorial Hospital (☎036 268 4917), an immense, modern, rose-pink building, is on Mabini St.

Internet access There are many small internet cafés, including *Ed's Video Place* on G. Pastrana St (daily 8am–9pm; P15/hr), and *Rovic's* on Luis Barrios St.

Post The post office is in the Provincial Capitol Building, off Osmena Ave in the south of town.

Guimaras

Separated from the Panay mainland by the narrowest slither of ocean, the small island of **GUIMARAS** is best known for producing the tastiest mangoes in the Philippines. The bounteous fruit is celebrated on the third weekend of April at the **Manggahan Guimaras festival** in San Miguel, the island's capital, which includes an eating contest that sees competitors consuming as many of the super-sweet mangoes as they can in thirty minutes.

The island has some good, affordable **resorts**, exceptional **beaches** – especially around **Nueva Valencia** on the southwest coast – and a few enticing **islands** offshore. Its undulating **interior** makes it a beautiful place to explore by mountain bike – main roads are reasonably signed, though there are a bewildering array of secondary roads, trails and tracks. There's also a smattering of history, with defiant old Spanish churches and the country's only **Trappist monastery**. During the Filipino–American War, General Douglas MacArthur, then a first lieutenant, built the wharf near Buenavista, which is still being used by ferries today.

Guimaras has been affected by a couple of oil spills during the last decade or so, and although the beaches look to the casual observer as if they are back to their pristine best, it will take decades for the island's mangrove ecosystems – and fish stocks – to fully recover.

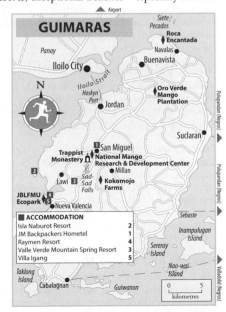

GUIMARAS

Airport

Panay

Iloilo City

Siete Pecados
Roca Encantada
Navalas
Buenavista

N

Iloilo Strait

Hoskyn Port

Jordan

Oro Verde Mango Plantation

Pulupandan (Negros)

Suclaran

Trappist Monastery

San Miguel
National Mango Research & Development Center

Millan

Lawi

Sad-Sad Falls

Kokomojo Farms

Pulupandan (Negros)

JBLFMU Ecopark

Nueva Valencia

Sebaste

Inampulugan Island

Sereray Island

Nao-wai Island

Valladolid (Negros)

Taklong Island

Cabalagnan

Guiwanon

■ ACCOMMODATION	
Isla Naburot Resort	2
JM Backpackers Hometel	1
Raymen Resort	4
Valle Verde Mountain Spring Resort	3
Villa Igang	5

0   5
kilometres

Jordan and San Miguel

Tourists only visit **JORDAN**, in the north of the island, because most bangkas from Iloilo arrive at Hoskyn port 2km to the west. Nearby **SAN MIGUEL**, the capital, is on the island's major crossroads and, although few people choose to stay here, it has most of the facilities, including a couple of ATMs, as well as several simple local restaurants.

6

Kokomojo Farms

Around 4km from San Miguel • Free • ☎ 033 337 7620

You could hardly leave Guimaras without a visit to one of the **mango plantations**. All have just the right soil, elevation and exposure to the elements to produce succulent fruit ready for the main harvest season in April and May. The most visitor-friendly plantation on the island is **Kokomojo Farms**, near Millan, roughly in the centre of Guimaras, where the owners will show you around personally if you call ahead.

Our Lady of the Philippines Trappist Monastery

2km south of San Miguel

Founded in 1972 by Americans, **Our Lady of the Philippines Trappist Monastery** lies on the main road southwest from San Miguel. Orchards grow assorted tropical fruit, and there's an interesting souvenir shop where monks sell banana fries, cashews, guava jelly, mango jam and even holy water under the Trappist Monastic Products brand name. Unfortunately, you cannot enter the monastery itself, although you can attend one of the seven daily church services.

Sad-Sad Falls

1.5km west of the San Miguel to Nueva Valencia road, down an unmarked track about 500m south of Guimaras Memorial Gardens Park; about a 10min walk from the car park (P10).

Guimaras has some pretty waterfalls in its hinterland, the best of which is **Sad-Sad Falls**, south of San Miguel. You can swim in the chilly mountain pool formed by the gushing water, or just have a picnic.

Nueva Valencia and the south

NUEVA VALENCIA in the southwest is nothing more than a ramshackle crossroads town. However, it's close to a couple of the island's better resorts and the **JBLFMU Ecopark** (dawn to dusk; P50), a convoluted promontory featuring a marine sanctuary, a sea cave with coral, sea grass monitoring station and a butterfly garden.

Taklong and Sereray islands

Bangkas can be hired from P350/hr through resorts or direct from boat owners

Exploring the beautiful islands and islets in the south of Guimaras by bangka makes a good day-trip. Off the southwest coast is **Taklong Island**, a marine reserve whose mangroves and beds of sea grass are breeding grounds for hundreds of marine species. Off the southeast coast there's **Sereray Island** and **Nao-wai Island**, both with tiny sandy coves where you can picnic and swim.

Navalas and the north

The seventeenth-century **Navalas Church**, an atmospherically decrepit relic of the Spanish regime, is a good starting point for exploring the barangay of **NAVALAS** on Guimaras' northern coast. A short walk away on a promontory overlooking Iloilo Strait stands a villa known as **Roca Encantada** (Enchanted Rock) or, more sneeringly, Lopezville, vacation house of the wealthy Lopez clan who hail from Iloilo.

Siete Pecados

30min by bangka from Navalas • Small boats (fitting four to six people) charge P400 for the first hour, then P150 for succeeding hours • Bring your own snorkel; many accommodations rent them out

Opposite the Roca Encantada's promontory is a picturesque group of coral islets called **Siete Pecados** (Isles of the Seven Sins). The largest of these has an impressive house perched on top, but the others are bare. There are no beaches, but it's worth the trip for the snorkelling.

6

ARRIVAL AND INFORMATION

GUIMARAS

To/from Panay Frequent bangkas (20min; P14) leave Ortiz wharf in Iloilo City for Hoskyn port on the west coast of Guimaras. Some resorts can send a bangka to collect you at Iloilo for P1500.

To/from Negros There are two ferries daily from Sebaste on the southeast coast to Pulupandan (P80–100), which also receives two daily bangkas from Suclaran (P80) further

up the east coast. There is also a daily bangka (P80) from Cabalagnan on Guimaras' south coast to Valladolid, south of Bacolod.

Tourist Information On arrival at Hoskyn port, look for the Guimaras Tourism Assistance kiosk (daily 7.30am–4.30pm; ☎ 0999 332 1727).

GETTING AROUND

By jeepney Open-sided minivans and jeepneys make regular circuits of the island's major towns and ports and can be useful for touring the island if you're not laden down with luggage. Jeepneys charge P13 per section (eg Jordan to San Miguel or SM to Nueva Valencia); the journey from Jordan to Nueva Valencia (45min–1hr) costs P25.

By tricycle and habal-habal Since many of the resorts lie off the main jeepney and minivan routes, hiring a tricycle or habal-habal is the most convenient option for

getting to your accommodation. Most journeys should cost P100–200; a full day's sightseeing by tricycle goes for P1200. The east and south coast ports will set you back around P350–500 from most resorts.

By motorbike and bicycle To get the most out of exploring the island on two wheels, it's worth enquiring about a guide at the tourism assistance kiosk in Hoskyn. Many resorts rent out mountain bikes (P300/day) and motorbikes (P500–600/day).

ACCOMMODATION AND EATING

Guimaras is small enough that it doesn't matter too much where you **stay**. Even if you choose the solitude of a resort on one of the smaller islands nearby, it's easy to hop on a bangka back to Guimaras itself. **Eating** is almost exclusively in the resorts, apart from some humble local joints, mainly in San Miguel, serving *lechon* and the like.

Isla Naburot Resort Naburot Island, off the west coast of Guimaras ☎ 0918 909 8500. Beautiful and romantic, *Isla Naburot* has six private cottages built partly from flotsam and jetsam, with driftwood for window frames and shells for walls. There's no electricity; after dark you'll have to read by paraffin lamp and eat by candlelight. Top-class meals from local produce are included in the room rate. Activities include fishing, swimming, island-hopping, snorkelling and scuba diving. Full board P6000

JM Backpackers Hometel San Miguel ☎ 033 581 2164, ⓦ bit.ly/JMBackpackersHomotel. The only choice if you want a central location in the capital, this fine modern hostel has compact rooms, some with a/c (P1200) and all featuring cable TV and separate shower and toilet cubicles. 🛜 P700

Raymen Resort Alubihod, 1.5km west of Nueva Valencia ☎ 033 396 0252, ⓦ raymenresort.com. Located on the island's southwest coast, *Raymen Resort* has clean a/c rooms with TV (from P1450) and hot showers in a

building set back from the beach, as well as cheaper fan rooms. There's a simple restaurant – avoid weekends if you don't like karaoke. 🛜 P700

★ **Valle Verde Mountain Spring Resort** Off the San Miguel–Nueva Valencia road ☎ 0918 730 3446. A great alternative to the beach, friendly *Valle Verde* offers simple rooms set in a lush valley looking down towards pretty Lawi Bay. The seven rooms range from rustic fan huts to more comfortable a/c cottages (P1500). As well as a natural spring at the bottom of the hill, there's a large and inviting spring-water pool (P65 for non-residents). Wi-fi in the restaurant only. 🛜 P800

Villa Igang 2km west of Nueva Valencia ☎ 033 394 0024, ✉ matr.corp@gmail.com. Enjoying a stunning location within the JBLFMU Ecopark (one-off entry fee required), this resort has four cute cottage-style fan rooms and a variety of a/c rooms (from P1700). Wi-fi in the restaurant only. 🛜 P1000

DIRECTORY

Banks San Miguel has the island's only two ATMs.
Internet access The most relaible outlet is *Café Manila* (daily 7.30am–6pm; P15/hr) in San Miguel.
Hospitals Medical care is better than you might expect,

with a provincial hospital in San Miguel and others at Buenavista and Nueva Valencia.
Police The Philippine National Police station is in the barangay of Alaguisoc in Jordan.

6 Negros

The island of **NEGROS**, fourth largest in the country and home to 3.5 million people, lies at the heart of the Visayas, between Panay to the west and Cebu to the east. Shaped like a boot, it's split diagonally into the northwestern province of Negros Occidental and the southeastern province of Negros Oriental. The demarcation came when early missionaries decided that the thickly jungled central mountain range was too formidable to cross, and this is still felt today with each side of the island speaking different main languages – Cebuano to the east and Ilonggo to the west.

THE BITTER HISTORY OF SUGAR IN NEGROS

Land reform – or the lack of it – has been at the root of simmering discontent on Negros that began in the 1970s under Ferdinand Marcos and continues to this day. All of Negros's sugar-producing land is held by two percent of the people, and half the arable land by five percent. Negros's gentry see the land as a way of life, while the Church, the New People's Army (NPA; see p.441) and various peasant organizations see it as a source of food. The NPA has been screaming about land reform for years, intimidating *hacienderos* and seizing land. The *hacienderos* have responded with private armies and acts of repression, turning Negros into a battleground for the struggle between rich and poor, in which the rich have all the guns.

In the 1970s and 1980s this struggle was played out against the background of Ferdinand Marcos's thieving dictatorship. Marcos monopolized sugar trading, placing it in the hands of crony **Roberto Benedicto**, who ended up controlling 106 sugar farms, 85 corporations, 17 radio stations, 16 television stations, a Manila casino, a *Holiday Inn* and a major piece of the national oil company. Known as the Sugar Czar, he effectively controlled the supply chain, allowing him to steal tens of millions of dollars from his neighbours on Negros by paying them a quarter of the price he received when he resold their sugar. For good measure Marcos gave him control of the bank that was the planters' principal lending agency.

In 1974, as prices of sugar on the world market rose steadily, Benedicto began hoarding, speculating that the price would continue to rise. When sugar prices plummeted in 1984, Benedicto responded by paying planters less for their sugar than it cost to grow. The planters took their land out of cultivation and, as a result, production in 1985 was half that of ten years earlier. Thousands were thrown out of work and hunger and malnutrition set in on a massive scale. Benedicto got out of the sugar business and was promptly appointed Philippine ambassador to Japan.

In 1981, the **Pope** visited Negros and thrust the island into the international limelight with his words of condemnation ("injustice reigns"), in stark contrast to Imelda Marcos's message that "Negros is not an island of fear, but an island of love". Five years later Marcos was overthrown, and **Cory Aquino** gave the impression during her election campaign that she was willing to give up her family's hacienda north of Manila in the name of nationwide land reform. But once elected she produced a watered-down land bill which she dumped in the lap of a newly elected Congress dominated by landed oligarchs. "She might as well have appointed a crack addict to run her drug treatment programme," said an opposition senator.

As for Benedicto, he was allowed to keep US$15 million of the fortune he amassed, and he lived quietly in Negros until his death in 2000. Although no longer ruled by a single overlord, since the millennium the Negros sugar-cane industry has been in gradual decline, trying to compete with globalized market forces. Meanwhile, even when they do have work, the 300,000 labourers who toil in the fields continue to survive on barely subsistence wages of P100–150 per day.

Today, Negros is known as "Sugarlandia"; its rich lowlands grow two-thirds of the nation's sugar cane, and you'll see evidence of this in the vast silver-green expanse of sugar-cane plantations stretching from the Gulf of Panay across to the gentle foothills off the volcanic mountains of the interior and beyond. The mountains rise to a giddy 2465m at the peak of **Mount Kanlaon**, the highest mountain in the Visayas. For the intrepid, this means there's some extreme trekking and climbing on Negros, from Mount Kanlaon itself to **Mount Silay** in the north.

From **Bacolod**, the capital of Negros Occidental, you can follow the coastal road clockwise to **Silay**, a beautifully preserved sugar town with grand antique homes and old sugar locomotives. Much of the north coast is given over to the port towns through which sugar is shipped to Manila, but at the southern end of the island around **Dumaguete** there are good beaches and scuba diving, with a range of excellent budget accommodation. The **southwest coast** – the heel of the boot – is home to the island's best beaches, and remains charmingly rural and undeveloped, with carabao in the fields and chocolate-coloured roads winding lazily into the farming barangays of the foothills.

Brief history

Among Negros's earliest inhabitants were dark-skinned natives belonging to the **Negrito** ethnic group – hence the name Negros, imposed by the Spanish when they set foot here in April 1565. After appointing bureaucrats to run the island, Miguel López de Legazpi placed it under the jurisdiction of its first Spanish governor. Religious orders wasted no time in moving in to evangelize the natives, who were deemed ripe for conversion to the true faith. The latter half of the eighteenth century was a period of rapid economic expansion for Negros, with its **sugar industry** flourishing and Visayan ports such as Cebu and Iloilo open for the first time to foreign ships. In the last century, the rapacious growth of the sugar industry and its increasing politicization were to have disastrous consequences that are still being felt today (see box opposite).

ARRIVAL AND DEPARTURE   NEGROS

By plane The main airports on Negros are Bacolod and Dumaguete, both with flights from Manila and Cebu City.
By boat The biggest and busiest ports on the island are Bacolod and Dumaguete, which are connected by regular ferries with Manila and Mindanao. Bacolod also has ferry connections with Iloilo on Panay, while Dumaguete and its satellite ports have various services to Cebu, Tagbilaran (Bohol) and Siquijor. Many other coastal towns have smaller ferries and bangkas going to neighbouring islands as well as to other destinations on Negros itself. Boats from San Carlos, on the east coast, head to Toledo (7 daily; 2hr) on Cebu, while Cadiz has connections to Bantayan Island.

Bacolod

On the northern coast of Negros, **BACOLOD** is a half-million-strong provincial metropolis, known as the "City of Smiles" and famed for its flamboyant **Masskara Festival** (third week of Oct). Its tourist attractions aren't significant enough to make you linger for more than a day or two, but it's a major transit point and a good base from which to visit nearby historic towns such as Silay and Victorias, or to arrange more adventurous excursions to Mount Kanlaon.

The old **city centre**, chaotic and choked with traffic, is best defined as the area around the **City Plaza** at the northern end of Araneta Street. North of here, Bacolod's main thoroughfare, and the city's social hub, is **Lacson Street**, which runs past the Provincial Capitol Building and has good restaurants, shops and bars. There are more places to stay, eat and party 3km south of the town centre at the **Goldenfields Commercial Complex**.

Negros Museum

Gatuslao St • Mon–Sat 9am–6pm • P100 • ☎ 034 433 4764

Housed in an elegant Neoclassical building dating from the 1930s (though badly damaged by a storm in 2012), the **Negros Museum** details five thousand years of island

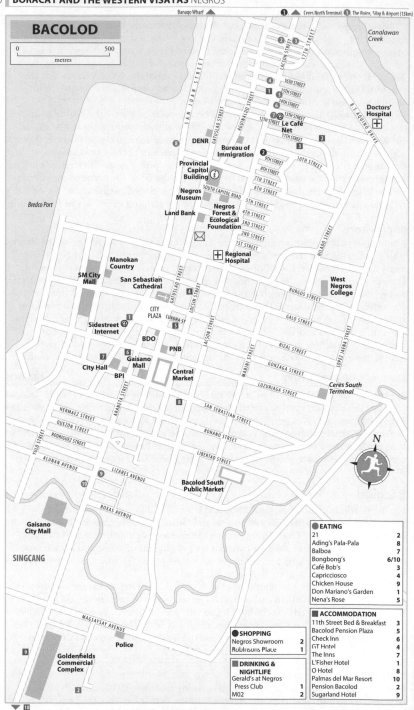

BACOLOD

0 _____ 500
metres

Banago Wharf

Ceres North Terminal   The Ruins, Silay & Airport (15km)

Canalawan Creek

B.S. AQUINO DRIVE

Doctors' Hospital

Le Café Net

DENR

Bureau of Immigration

Provincial Capitol Building

Negros Museum

Land Bank

Negros Forest & Ecological Foundation

Regional Hospital

Manokan Country

SM City Mall

San Sebastian Cathedral

CITY PLAZA

Sidestreet @ Internet

BDO   PNB

Gaisano Mall

City Hall

BPI

Central Market

West Negros College

Ceres South Terminal

HERMAEZ STREET
QUEZON STREET
RODRIGUEZ STREET
ALUNAN AVENUE
LIZARES AVENUE
ROXAS AVENUE

Bacolod South Public Market

Gaisano City Mall

SINGCANG

MAGSAYSAY AVENUE

Police

Goldenfields Commercial Complex

Bredco Port

SHOPPING

| Negros Showroom | 2 |
| Robinsons Place | 1 |

DRINKING & NIGHTLIFE

| Gerald's at Negros Press Club | 1 |
| M02 | 2 |

EATING

21	2
Ading's Pala-Pala	8
Balboa	7
Bongbong's	6/10
Café Bob's	3
Capricciosco	4
Chicken House	9
Don Mariano's Garden	1
Nena's Rose	5

ACCOMMODATION

11th Street Bed & Breakfast	3
Bacolod Pension Plaza	5
Check Inn	6
GT Hotel	4
The Inns	7
L'Fisher Hotel	1
O Hotel	8
Palmas del Mar Resort	10
Pension Bacolod	2
Sugarland Hotel	9

history and has artefacts from other parts of Asia. Its star exhibit is the "iron dinosaur" steam engine on the upper floor, once used to haul sugar cane. The 1930s Provincial Capitol Building next door is another of the city's few architectural highlights.

Negros Forest and Ecological Foundation

South Capitol Rd, opposite the Provincial Capitol • Mon–Sat 9am–noon & 1.30–4pm • P25 • ☎ 034 433 9234, Ⓦ negrosforests.org

The rescue centre at the **Negros Forest and Ecological Foundation** is an unexpected reprieve from the streets. It's not a huge site, but conservationists do what they can to care for endangered animals endemic to Negros, including leopard cats, the Visayan spotted deer, the writhed hornbill and the Negros bleeding-heart pigeon.

The Ruins

Talisay • Daily 10am–8pm • P100 • ☎ 034 476 4334, Ⓦ theruins.com.ph • Round-trip taxis cost around P300, depending on how long you stay, or take a P50 tricycle ride from the crossroads immediately south of the North bus terminal

Seven kilometres north of the Provincial Capitol Building, on the edge of town, **The Ruins** make a great short excursion from the city. Officially the Don Mariano Ledesma Lacson Mansion, it is billed as the "Taj Mahal of Negros", more for its sad story of love lost than its architectural splendour, although it does have a haunting beauty. The Lacsons were one of the island's pre-eminent sugar families in the nineteenth century. When Maria Lacson died during pregnancy with the couple's eleventh child, Don Mariano was inconsolable and set about building a memorial mansion. During the outbreak of World War II, the building was razed to prevent it being used as a headquarters by the Japanese. The fire left behind the building's complete superstructure, including the double-M motif used throughout. Mariano died in 1948, and the building was forgotten about until his great-grandson decided to open it to the public. There is also an atmospheric restaurant, *Don Mariano's* (see p.293).

ARRIVAL AND DEPARTURE   **BACOLOD**

By plane Bacolod-Silay Airport is located 15km northeast of town and is linked to Bacolod by taxi (P500), shuttle buses from SM City Mall (P150) or, cheapest but least convenient, by jeepney from the North bus terminal to Silay (P14), from where it's a short tricycle ride (P15/person or P60 for private hire). Philippine Airlines has offices at the airport (☎ 034 435 2011), as do Cebu Pacific (☎ 034 435 2156), who also have an office in Victoria Arcade in Rizal St (☎ 034 434 2052).
Destinations Cebu City (5–7 daily; 45min); Davao (3 weekly; 1hr 10min); Manila (10–14 daily; 1hr 15min).
By boat Most ferries come from Iloilo and dock at Bredco port, a short walk or tricycle ride (P20) west of City Plaza. Oceanjet (☎ 034 708 8201), 2GO (☎ 034 435 4965) and Weesam Express (☎ 034 709 0830) have ticket offices here. Long-distance ferries to Manila and Mindanao leave less often and use the old Banago wharf, 8km north of Bacolod. Jeepneys from Banago into town cost P25/person. Smaller vessels for Guimaras leave from either Pulupandan or Valladolid, 20km and 25km southwest respectively.
Destinations Cagayan de Oro (1 weekly; 21–22hr); Iligan (1 weekly; 14hr); Iloilo (every 20–40min; 1hr); Manila (4 weekly; 20–24hr); Ozamiz (1 weekly; 18–19hr).
By bus Ceres Liner buses (☎ 034 434 2387) drop passengers at one of two main terminals. The South

terminal, for destinations south, is on Lopez Jaena St, just east of the old city, while the North terminal is around 4km north of town on the National Highway (continuation of Lacson St). Buses from the North terminal head along the coastal road to Cadiz, from where there are boats to Bantayan Island; some continue on to San Carlos and round the long way (313km) to Dumaguete, while others board ferries at San Carlos for Toledo on the western coast of Cebu and continue on to Cebu City. The quickest way to Dumaguete is from the South terminal down the west coast and then via the inland road that runs from Kabankalan across the mountains. A few services cover this route directly, but most of the time you'll need to change in Kabankalan. Buses heading south along the coast road for Sipalay also leave from the South terminal.
Destinations Cadiz (every 15–30min; 1hr 30min); Cebu City (7 daily; 8–10hr); Dumaguete (every 30min; 6–7hr); Sagay (every 30min–1hr; 2hr); San Carlos (every 30min–1hr; 3hr); Silay (every 10–15min; 20min); Sipalay (hourly; 4–5hr).
By jeepney Jeepneys, FX vans and tricycles cost P7 for journeys within 5km. For Silay (P14) you'll need to change at the North bus terminal. Jeepneys to Pulupandan (40min; P25) and Valladolid (50min; P30) leave from outside the South terminal.

6

INFORMATION AND ACTIVITIES

Tourist information The Negros Occidental Tourism Center (Mon–Fri 8am–5pm; ☎ 034 432 3240) is in the Provincial Capitol Building.

Hiking and cycling To arrange hiking or biking trips in

the foothills of Mt Kanlaon, contact the tourist office, the DENR on Gatuslao St (☎ 034 434 7411, ⓦ denr.gov.ph), or local guide, Angelo Bibar (☎ 0917 301 1410, ⓔ angelobibar@gmail.com).

ACCOMMODATION

Hotels are spread throughout the city but there are three main areas to choose from: foodies will relish the uptown choices around the northern section of **Lacson St**; bargain-hunters are best off in the shabbier **town centre**; and nightlife fiends will find surprisingly quiet accommodation around **Goldenfields**, a modern complex 3km south of town and also the city's red-light district.

CITY CENTRE

Bacolod Pension Plaza Cuadra St, opposite City Plaza ☎ 034 433 4547, ⓔ bacpensionplaza@yahoo .com. Not to be confused with *Pension Bacolod*, this place is bigger and more central, with 66 old but well-maintained a/c rooms.

Check Inn Luzuriaga St ☎ 034 432 3755, ⓦ checkinn .com.ph. Decent-value option near the old town centre with modern, clean and comfortable rooms, the best of which are on the business floor (from P1000), set around the roof garden. 🛜 **P900**

GT Hotel Locsin St at Galo St ☎ 034 432 1888, ⓦ gthotels.com.ph. One of the city's newer hotels, with friendly staff and attractive, modern rooms styled in muted tones. Mod cons include central a/c, low lighting, flatscreen TV and fridge. 🛜 **P1410**

★**The Inns** San Juan St ☎ 034 704 2746, ⓦ iconhotelph .com. The former Sylvia Manor has been fully refurbished under new ownership in boutique style with bold colours and no small measure of artistic flair. The great-value rooms exude a warm atmosphere, and the ground floor *Hot N' Juicy* restaurant does excellent seafood. 🛜 **P1200**

O Hotel 52 San Sebastian St ☎ 034 433 7401, ⓦ ohotel .com.ph. Large, modern motel-style hotel with brightly coloured lobby and rooms, all with cable TV, fridge and mini-bar, although those facing the front are noisy. There's also an ATM in the lobby. 🛜 **P1400**

LACSON STREET

★**11th Street Bed & Breakfast** 14 11th St ☎ 034 433 9191, ⓦ bit.ly/11StreetBB. A great-value pension set around a leafy courtyard with a fountain, just a few

minutes' walk from the Lacson St restaurants. Rooms are clean and simple with cable TV and bathrooms, and a/c rooms (P850) have hot water. Breakfast included. 🛜 **P550**

★**L'Fisher Hotel** Lacson St ☎ 034 433 3731, ⓦ lfisherhotelbacolod.com. One of Bacolod's best top-end hotels, this glass-fronted establishment is in a great location right on Lacson St. The deluxe rooms are extremely comfortable, with a/c, cable TV, fridge and safe. There's also a 24hr poolside café that offers buffet lunches and dinners. Within the same complex are two more modest sister hotels, of which *L'Fisher Chalet* (P1600) is better value than *L'Fisher Ecotel*. 🛜 **P4000**

Pension Bacolod 11th St ☎ 034 433 3377. Not as welcoming as the *11th Street B&B* along the road, this popular cheapie is still great value, though both the walls and mattresses are thin. The cheapest rooms have shared bathrooms. Wi-fi only in the lobby. 🛜 **P290**

ELSEWHERE IN THE CITY

Palmas del Mar Resort J.R. Torres Ave, 2km southwest of Goldenfields ☎ 034 434 3587, ⓦ palmasdelmarresort .net. Family resort in a residential area close to the sea, with a good range of accommodation, including regular a/c rooms, family rooms and cottages. There's a decent-sized pool and the restaurant serves local specialities and European dishes. You might have the pool to yourself on weekdays, but weekends can get busy. 🛜 **P1500**

Sugarland Hotel Araneta St ☎ 034 435 2691, ⓦ sugarlandhotel.com. Good-value modern hotel with stylish and well-kept a/c rooms. There's also a small pool and a couple of good restaurants in the hotel, plus a massage service. 🛜 **P2200**

EATING

Bacolod's dining scene has moved uptown and upscale in recent years, with a cosmopolitan range of trendy cafés and restaurants along northern **Lacson St**, while time-tested favourites still hold their own in the **old city**. As well as the listings below, it's worth checking out the row of identikit chicken restaurants at **Manokan Country**.

★**21** 21st St at Lacson St ☎ 034 435 3852, ⓦ 21restaurant.com. Popular with Bacolod's elite and middle classes, this institution dishes out amazing *batchoy* (noodle soup with crispy pork; P110) and excellent seafood,

from blue marlin with herb butter (P285) to good old-fashioned fish and chips (P265). White tablecloths and attentive service complete the picture. Daily 10am–11pm.

Ading's Pala-Pala San Juan St, opposite the fish market

☎ 034 458 1594. Massive fish restaurant with indoor and outdoor seating, where you can get the catch of the day at market rates, plus delights like crab-meat soup (P170) or shrimp tempura (P200). Daily 11am–3pm & 5–11pm.

Balboa 13th St at Lacson St ☎ 034 435 8642. *Balboa* is a clean, bright diner with a Negrense twist. Along with diner staples including pizza (P259–299) and spare ribs (P149), local offerings include *kare kare* (P249) and *lechon kawali* (P159). Daily 11am–10pm.

Bongbong's Araneta St ☎ 034 704 2530, ⊛ facebook .com/bastapasalubong. For a real taste of Sugarlandia, *Bongbong's* sells everything from banana-honey chips to *piyaya* (a hardened pancake with sugar melted inside) and delicious *bay ibayi* (sugar and coconut bar). They also have outlets at the ferry terminal, on the plaza and at the corner of 13th St at Lacson St. Daily 9am–11pm.

Café Bob's 21st St at Lacson St ☎ 034 709 1091. Super-popular diner that efficiently turns out pizzas (P200–325), sandwiches and burgers (P90–200), plus coffees (P60–140). It also a huge range of imported goods for sale in the deli (closes at 9pm). Free wi-fi. Daily 8am–midnight.

Capriccioso 15th St at Lacson St ☎ 034 432 9558, ⊛ facebook.com/capricciosodeli. Trendy little deli-restaurant serving soups, pasta dishes (P240–315), paninis (P200–230) and specials such as the "Capriccioso Platter" of cold meats and cheeses for P850, good for four. Free wi-fi. Daily 10.30am–9.30pm.

★ **Chicken House** Araneta St ☎ 034 842 3096. An oldie but a goodie, *Chicken House* has been serving up sumptuous roast chicken (P80) and other grilled meat for three decades and continues to draw in the local crowds with its distinctive flavours and low prices. Other branches at the north end of Lacson St. Daily 10am–10.30pm.

Don Mariano's Garden Talisay ☎ 0942 082 0375. Tucked discreetly at the back of the lawn facing The Ruins, with an a/c interior and patio seating, this classy restaurant serves an international menu featuring burger mushroom quesadilla (P190), *pollo con funghi* (P250 and pork *sisig* (P160). Daily 8am–8pm.

Nena's Rose 14th St at Lacson St ☎ 034 458 1771. Simple canteen-style favourite with colourful paintings on the wall, great for delicious Inasal chicken, pork, liver and *bangus* (milkfish), all between P35–150, making it superb value. Daily 11am–2pm & 5pm–midnight (Sat till 2am).

DRINKING AND NIGHTLIFE

The city's nightlife district is cited as **Goldenfields Commercial Complex** in Singcang, but while there are a few regular bars and clubs, in truth many of the places here are girlie bars catering to an exclusively male crowd, so the atmosphere is rather seedy.

Gerald's at Negros Press Club San Juan St ☎ 034 704 3655. This small, friendly venue in the press building is pleasantly located overlooking City Plaza. Drinks are cheap (San Miguel P48), there's live music from 8.30pm and snacks to stave off hunger. Daily 5pm–midnight.

MO2 Goldenfields ☎ 034 433 6026. Chain bar-club serving reasonably priced drinks (San Miguel P55) and featuring nightly live music from 9pm. Also has a quieter punkah-cooled outdoors sitting area. Daily 8pm–2am.

SHOPPING

Negros Showroom Lacson St at 9th St ☎ 034 433 8833. This extensive showroom has top-quality handicrafts from all over the island. Daily 9.30am–7pm.

Robinsons Place Lacson St, 1km north of B.S. Aquino Drive ⊛ robinsonsmalls.com. Located on the northern section of Lacson St, this popular countrywide mall has dozens of shops to supply your everyday needs, as well as clothes stores and fast-food outlets. Daily 10am–9pm.

DIRECTORY

Cinema There's a Cineplex cinema at Robinsons Place on the northern section of Lacson St (☎ 034 441 0453, ⊛ robinsonsmovieworld.com).

Hospitals Bacolod Doctors' Hospital (☎ 034 433 2741, ⊛ thedoctorshospital.com) is on B.S. Aquino Drive, northeast of the centre.

Immigration The Bureau of Immigration is at the back of the National Bureau of Investigation office on Aguinaldo St (☎ 034 433 8581).

Internet access The malls have internet outlets, or you can try Sidestreet Internet (daily 8am–1am; P20/hr) on San Juan St.

Police Police headquarters is at Magsaysay Ave, south of the centre, in Singcang (☎ 034 434 1152).

Post The post office is on Gatuslao St, near the junction with Burgos St (Mon–Fri 9am–5pm).

Silay

The elegant town of **SILAY**, about 15km north of Bacolod, is an atmospheric relic of a grander age, when Negros was rich from its cultivation of sugar cane. In the late eighteenth century it was talked about as the "Paris of Negros", with music performers from Europe arriving by steamship to take part in operettas and *zarzuelas*. This passion for music and the arts gave Silay – and the Philippines – its first international star, **Conchita Gaston**, a mezzo-soprano who performed in major opera houses in Europe in the postwar years. Japanese forces occupied the city in World War II, after which the sugar industry declined and Silay lost its lustre – many of its European residents departed for home. Today, Silay's major tourist draw is its **ancestral homes**, most of them built between 1880 and 1940. Some of the best are open to the public or have been converted into hotels, offering a glimpse of what life was like for the sugar barons.

The main road runs through Silay as **Rizal Street**, passing the central public plaza halfway along its kilometre strip of shops, hotels and restaurants. The major annual festival in town, the **Kansilay**, lasts one week and ends every November 13 with a re-enactment of a folk tale showing the bravery of a beautiful princess who offered her life for justice and freedom.

The Balay Negrense Museum

Cinco de Noviembre St, a 5min walk west of the central plaza • Tues–Sun 10am–5pm • P60 • ☎ 034 714 7676, ⓦ balaynegrense.com

The **Balay Negrense Museum** was once the home of Don Victor Gaston, eldest son of Yves Leopold Germaine Gaston, a Frenchman who settled in Silay in the mid-nineteenth century. After World War II, the house was left deserted; by 1980, it was a sad ruin, known only by locals for the ghosts that were said to roam its corridors. Now restored by the Negros Foundation, the house is a glorious monument to Silay's golden age, with rooms of polished mahogany furnished with antiques donated by locals.

Don Bernardino-Ysabel Jalandoni House Museum

Rizal St • Tues–Sun 9am–5pm • P60 • ☎ 034 495 5093

Hard to miss at the northernmost end of Rizal Street is the pink **Don Bernardino-Ysabel Jalandoni House Museum**, known throughout town as the Pink House. Built in 1908, it gives some idea of the luxury of the time and features displays of antique law books and Japanese occupation currency. The price includes a guided tour – ask them to show you the huge metal vat in the garden, which was used to make muscovado sugar.

Manuel and Hilda Hofileña ancestral house

Cinco de Noviembre St • Tues–Sun 10am–5pm • P60 • ☎ 034 495 4561

The first ancestral home in Silay to open its doors to the public, the **Manuel and Hilda Hofileña ancestral house** is one of the last vestiges of the city's artistic history. The house holds a gallery of works collected by Manuel and Hilda's son, Ramon, which includes contemporary Filipino painters and masters such as Juan Luna and Amorsolo, as well as two nude sketches of Ramon in a state of arousal. Also on display are countless fascinating antiques and curiosities which include part of a meteorite fragment, one of Negros's oldest pieces of pottery and (allegedly) the world's smallest dolls, visible through a magnifying glass. An incongruously modern DVD collection caps it off.

Church of San Diego

Zamora St, on the north side of the public plaza

Built in 1925, the **Church of San Diego** is a dramatic sight, with a great illuminated crucifix on top of the dome that is so bright at night that it was once used by ships as a navigational aid. Behind the church are the ruins of the original sixteenth-century Spanish church, now converted into a grotto and prayer garden.

Guinhalaran

About 2.5km from town; 10min by tricycle or jeepney (P20)

Silay is known for **pottery** made from the red clay endemic to the area. In the barangay of **Guinhalaran** on the National Highway, you can visit the potters and watch them making high-quality jars and vases, which are for sale at bargain prices.

Hawaiian Philippines Sugar Company

About 7km from town; 15min by tricycle (P25) • Hours vary • ☎ 034 495 2085 • Visits can be arranged through the tourist office (see below)

Just a short drive from Silay, this historic **Hawaiian Philippines Sugar Company** mill offers the chance to take a ride on one of the famed "iron dinosaurs" and see the workings of a genuine sugar mill. North from here along the rugged coast is Victorias Milling Company (ⓦvictoriasmilling.com), the largest integrated mill and sugar refinery in Asia.

ARRIVAL AND INFORMATION   SILAY

By bus and jeepney Buses and jeepneys from Bacolod either terminate at the southern end of Rizal St, from where it's a short walk to the centre, or pass right through the plaza. Tricycles to the airport cost P15/person, or P60 for the whole vehicle; vans cost P50.

Tourist information The Silay tourist office (Mon–Fri 8am–noon & 1–5pm; ☎034 495 5553) is in the central plaza. The helpful staff can arrange informal guided tours of some ancestral houses that aren't usually open to the public, and will open the small historical museum (same hours) opposite the office for you.

Internet *JForce Internet café* is two blocks north of the plaza on Burgos St.

ACCOMMODATION AND EATING

Café 1925 4 J. Ledesma St ☎034 714 7414. This pretty little place dishes up Italian classics, sandwiches (P110–200), pasta (P135–195), squid balls (P55) and excellent coffee. Free wi-fi. Tues–Sat 9.30am–9.30pm, Sun 10.30am–9.30pm.

El Ideal 118 Rizal St ☎034 495 4430, ⓦbit.ly/2mK8BYR. Established in 1920, this bright and airy café-deli does a range of sweet and savoury items, including noodles (P89), sandwiches and rice meals (P100–200), cassava cake (P180), and *halo-halo* (P85). Daily 6.30am–6pm.

★**German Unson Heritage House** Zamora St, 150m east of the plaza ☎034 432 2943, ⓦfacebook.com/

German.Unson. This superbly renovated property, full of original furniture and artwork, exudes period charm while offering modern comforts. The biggest of the four ample-sized rooms (P2300) has a huge shower and oval stone bath. There are balconies, gardens and complimentary breakfast. ☞ P1800

Winbelle Pension Hauz In arcade off Rizal St, behind the cathedral ☎034 495 5898, ⓔwinbellehomes @yahoo.com. The best budget choice in town, this place offers functional, average-sized rooms with bright-yellow walls. Wi-fi in the lobby area only. ☞ P1800

Mount Kanlaon

Thirty kilometres southeast of Bacolod, **Mount Kanlaon** (2435m) is the tallest peak in the central Philippines and one of the thirteen most active volcanoes in the country. Climbing it offers a potentially dangerous challenge, with the real possibility of violent eruptions – climbers have died scaling it – and the crater's rim is a forbidding knife-edge overhanging an apparently bottomless chasm. The dense surrounding **forest** contains all manner of wonderful fauna, including pythons and tube-nosed bats, and locals believe the mountain is home to many spirits. It also features in Philippine history – it's where President Manuel Quezon hid from invading Japanese forces during World War II.

There are three main routes up the volcano itself. The **Guintubdan trail** is the easiest and most common ascent, but even this should not be underestimated. From here, although it's only 8km to the top, the trail is best broken with an overnight stop (see p.296). The 14km-long **Mananawin trail** works best over three days and offers the chance to really get to know the region, while the short, steep **Wesey trail** is very exposed and only for experienced tropical mountaineers. It goes without saying that for whichever route you choose, you'll need a guide.

ARRIVAL AND INFORMATION   MOUNT KANLAON

By jeepney Guintubdan is 2hr by jeepney from Bacolod, with a change at La Carlota.

Guides Whichever way you choose to ascend, a permit (P500) and guide (P700/day) are mandatory, and a porter (P500) might come in handy. The easiest way to make all of these arrangements is through the DENR (☎034 434

7411, ⓦdenr.gov.ph), or directly with Angelo Bibar (☎0917 301 1410; ⓔangelobibar@gmail.com). Contact Angelo as far in advance as possible (ideally a month) and he can arrange everything from permits, guides and porters to tents and meals. Various other agents and hotels throughout Negros also run trips.

ACCOMMODATION

Neither of the options below provide eating options, so come prepared with enough food to last your stay.

The Pavilion Guintubdan ☏034 460 2582. Clean and simple accommodation, with cold showers, in an attractive lodge nestled in the forest. Dorms P150, twin P1000
Rafael Salas Nature Camp Guintubdan ☏034 461 0540. Just up the road from *The Pavilion*, this nature camp is the headquarters of the 300-hectare Rafael Salas Nature Park, named after the late statesman who was a native of Bago City. It's not quite as pretty as *The Pavilion* but still feels like the ultimate in luxury after a night on the mountain. Dorms P10, doubles P500

Sagay and around

SAGAY is a hectic industrial and fishing city 15km east along the coast from the sugar port of **Cadiz**, at the mouth of the Bulanon River. Head for the city plaza and take a look at the **Legendary Siete**, or Train Number Seven, an "iron dinosaur" that once hauled lumber for the Insular Lumber Company and now stands in the middle of the plaza, restored and sparkling in all her 75-tonne liveried glory.

Sagay Marine Reserve

Free • Bangkas leave from Sagay wharf (30min; P70/person)

Sagay is the jumping-off point for one of the Philippines' least-visited natural wonders, the beautiful **Sagay Marine Reserve**. The sanctuary boasts some marvellous beaches, and with its maximum of seventy visitors per day, its reef remains a picture of health; with a mask and snorkel you can see giant clams, puffer fish, immense brain corals and the occasional inquisitive batfish.

ARRIVAL AND DEPARTURE   SAGAY AND AROUND

By bus Regular buses from Bacolod stop in Cadiz (1hr 30min) and Sagay (2hr) on their way along the coastal road.

By boat There are three services each week from Cadiz (usually early morning) for Bantayan Island, off the north coast of Cebu (3–4hr).

Sipalay and around

Nearly 200km south of Bacolod, on the heel of Negros, **SIPALAY** is the access point for the lovely resorts of **Sugar Beach** and **Punto Ballo**, a few kilometres north and south of town respectively. There are a couple of hotels in town, but given the proximity of the beaches there's no need to stay unless you arrive late. Sipalay's historical focal point is the plaza and the church, but these days most activity centres around its pier and the main drag, **Alvarez Street**, where there are numerous canteens, bakeries and convenience stores.

Punta Ballo and Campomanes Bay

Punto Ballo can be reached by tricycle from Sipalay (P150 direct with a driver, or P300 through a resort); it's a 25–30min walk from Punta Ballo to Campomanes Bay

Just 6km south of Sipalay, **Punto Ballo** has a pretty stretch of beach and offers great snorkelling and diving from the shoreline. A couple of kilometres south, **Campomanes Bay**, also known as Maricalum Bay, is a natural harbour that's said to be deep enough to hide a submarine. Shaped like a horseshoe and 2km wide and backed by steep cliffs, it's a fantastic day-trip with some good snorkelling and scuba diving, though there's no accommodation here.

Sugar Beach

Resorts can arrange boat transfer, picking you up from Poblacion Beach in Sipalay (P350/boat for 4–6); a cheaper, less direct alternative is to take a tricycle to Nauhang (P150), then a small paddle boat across the creek (P20), and walk around the headland – better still, ask to be let off the bus in Montilla, 5km northeast of Sipalay, only a P50 tricycle ride from Nauhang

Although it's just 5km as the crow flies from Sipalay, the absence of road access to beautiful **Sugar Beach**, cut off by knobbly green hills, makes it feel more like an island. While it may not have the white sand and azure waters of Boracay, it offers a relaxed vibe, plus a good selection of small resorts ranging from ultra-budget to mid-range.

ARRIVAL AND INFORMATION

SIPALAY AND AROUND

By bus If you're coming from Dumaguete, the quickest bus route follows the coast south around the toe of the island and then north through Hinoba-an, but an equally scenic option is to head north and then across the mountains to Kabanklan before travelling south for Sipalay. Buses from Bacolod or Dumaguete stop at Poblacion Beach in Sipalay Town. For moving on, there are hourly buses from Sipalay for Bacolod (5–6hr), but only one direct service for Dumaguete (5am; 5hr), so you're best hopping on the first southbound bus and then changing in Hinoba-an. You may even require a further change at Bayawan.

Tourist information There's a small tourist office at the beach end of Alvarez St in Sipalay (Mon–Fri 8am–noon & 1–5pm; ☎ 034 473 2101).

ACCOMMODATION AND EATING

SIPALAY

Driftwood City On the town beach ☎ 0920 900 3663. Simple beach café (under the same ownership as *Driftwood Village* on Sugar Beach) serving pizza and pasta dishes (P100–150). They can also arrange bangkas to Sugar Beach (P350). Daily 7am–7pm.

Jamont Hotel Mercedes Blvd ☎ 034 473 0350. The most comfortable place to stay in town has clean but characterless rooms right behind the beach. They also have a nice pool, and their *La Verandah* beach restaurant is fairly decent. 📶 P1200

PUNTA BALLO

★**Artistic Diving Beach Resort** ☎ 0905 220 5594, ⊕ artisticdiving.com. Beachfront accommodation in simple fan or a/c (P990) rooms, fan or a/c bungalows (P1590). and larger villas with cable TV (P2290). There's also a decent bar and restaurant with wi-fi, plus a pool and dive centre. 📶 P500

Sipalay Easy Diving & Beach Resort ☎ 0917 300 0381, ⊕ sipalay.com. Pleasant fan bungalows and even smarter a/c stone cottages (from P2750), with spacious verandas and attractive rattan and wooden furnishings, set in hillside gardens looking down to the white-sand beach. Wi-fi in the restaurant. 📶 P1600

SUGAR BEACH

Bermuda Next to Takatuka Lodge ☎ 0920 529 2582, ⊕ bermuda-beach-resort.com. *Bermuda* offers spacious and tastefully decorated fan-cooled beachfront bungalows (P1650) and smaller a/c rooms (P1450) at the rear of the property. The restaurant serves Italian and Thai cuisine, but the Filipino dishes are recommended. Charge for wi-fi. 📶 P1050

Big Bamboo Beach Resort Just north of the centre of the beach ☎ 0999 671 6666, ⊕ bigbamboobeachresort .com. Accommodations range from tiny overpriced nipa huts just bigger than the mattress, to larger bamboo cottages (P1400) and through to concrete a/c rooms (P1700); there's also a dorm and simple restaurant. 📶 Dorms P300, doubles P600

★**Driftwood Village** Halfway along the beach ☎ 0920 900 3663, ⊕ driftwood-village.com. A backpacker favourite with a superb vibe, Swiss-owned *Driftwood* has a wide range of budget huts, some with private bathrooms, set in palms behind the beach. There's also a basic dorm, an excellent restaurant that does great Thai and fish, and a lively bar. Wi-fi in restaurant. 📶 Dorms P250, doubles P450

Sugar Rocks Music Bar Northern end of the beach ☎ 0908 429 8413. It's worth the clamber up the hill to get to this cosy nook of a bar overlooking the beach. Drinks are reasonably priced, and some rooms are also available, though you're better off staying down on the beach. Mon–Sat 9am–2am.

Sulu Sunset Beach Resort Towards the northern end of the beach ☎ 0919 716 7182, ⊕ sulusunset .com. German-owned *Sulu* has simple but attractive fan cottages – which look straight out onto the beach – and a larger bungalow (P1350). The restaurant serves Filipino food, a few European dishes including schnitzel, and cold beer. Free transfer from Sipalay if you stay three nights or more. Wi-fi in restaurant. 📶 P650

★**Takatuka Lodge** The furthest south of the resorts ☎ 0920 230 9174, ⊕ takatuka-lodge.com. Wonderfully wacky *Takatuka* displays the unhinged creativity of its Swiss-German owners. Each room features one-of-a-kind furnishings, from the pink Cadillac bed in the Superstar room, to the microphone light fittings in Rockadelic. All rooms have verandas and cost around P400 more for a/c and hot showers. The restaurant serves Filipino and international dishes – some of the best food on the beach , with menu items such as *tuktoro-ok* (crispy fried chicken with creamy, green coconut-pandan rice and a Malay peanut sauce). There is also a reputable dive centre here. Wi-fi costs P50 per day. 📶 P1275

6

6

Danjugan Island and Bulata

Lying 3km off the southwest coast of Negros and accessible through the small town of **Bulata**, about 10km north of Sipalay, **Danjugan** (pronounced "Danhoogan") **Island** is a little gem. Managed as a nature reserve by the Philippine Reef and Rainforest Foundation (PRRCFI; ⊚ prrcf.org) NGO, it's entirely fringed by vibrant coral reefs. Danjugan is so well forested that it's home to rarities such as the white-bellied sea eagle and barebacked fruit bat. Around five thousand **bats** of various species reside in a **cave** on the island; resident pythons feed on them from the rocky ledges by the entrance.

There are also a number of small **islets**, including Manta Island and Manta Rock, and three protected offshore **reefs**, home to about 570 species of fish. An overnight stay (see below) is a truly magical experience, as you're lulled to sleep by the sound of lapping waves on the beach.

ARRIVAL AND DEPARTURE	DANJUGAN ISLAND AND BULATA
By bus and tricycle Buses driving the coastal road pass through Bulata. For Danjugan, ask to be let off at Crossing Remollos, a short walk from the pick-up point for the island's bangka service, which should be arranged in advance.	**Tours** Day-trips to Danjugan from the *Punta Bulata Resort & Spa* (see below) and some of the Sugar Beach resorts cost P1950, including transfers, lunch, snacks, a trekking guide and kayaking. A shorter ecotour costs P950.

ACCOMMODATION

★ **Danjugan Sanctuary** ☏ 034 441 6010, ⊚ danjugan island.ph. The atmosphere at *Danjugan Sanctuary* is extremely sociable and blissfully relaxed. Accommodation is in beautifully designed rooms at Typhoon Beach (P3950 per person) or more basic huts at Moray Lagoon. Rates include return transfers, all meals, a boat tour, trekking guide, plus snorkel and kayak use. Wi-fi at certain spots. 🛜 Full board **P5900**

Punta Bulata Resort & Spa Accessed along a 2km dirt road from Cartagena ☏ 034 713 4888, ⊚ puntabulata .com. The resort has a good range of comfortable huts, rooms and family cabins (for six), all a/c. There's also a spa, a pleasant bar and a hillside native-style restaurant with ocean views. Wi-fi in common areas. To get here, take the coastal road bus and ask to be let off at Cartagena, from where you can take a tricycle or arrange with the resort to send one. 🛜 **P2700**

Dumaguete

DUMAGUETE ("dum-a-get-eh"), known in the Philippines as the City of Gentle People, is capital of Negros Oriental and lies on the southeast coast of Negros, within sight of the southernmost tip of Cebu Island and Siquijor. With its attractive architecture, laidback university town ambience and lovely **seafront promenade**, shaded by acacia trees and coconut palms and lined with lively bars and restaurants, it's easy to see why the town is increasingly becoming a mainstream tourist destination.

While Dumaguete doesn't possess major sights, it is a great base from which to explore the region. **Day-trips** include the Twin Lakes of Balinsasayao and Danao (see p.305) and dolphin- and whale-watching at Bais (see box, p.305), while scuba diving can be arranged from the affordable resort accommodation around Dauin (see p.304).

St Catherine of Alexandria Cathedral

Governor Perdices St, Quezon Park

Dumaguete is centred on the grand **St Catherine of Alexandria Cathedral**, which dominates Quezon Park. The cathedral was originally built in 1754, although the current version dates from 1957. Standing next to the cathedral is the **belfry**, which was completed in 1867, and its statue of the Lady of Lourdes is a popular site of worship in its own right.

Silliman University

Anthropological Museum: SE corner of main campus, near the church • Daily 8am–noon & 2–5pm • Mon–Sat P50, Sun & hols P100

The oldest Protestant university in the Philippines, **Silliman University**'s strong reputation has largely been built on the work of its marine laboratory, which has spearheaded efforts to protect the island's mangroves and stop illegal fishing. The university also has an interesting **Anthropological Museum** housing some Song and Ming dynasty porcelain, as well as relics from minority tribes in the Philippines.

ARRIVAL AND DEPARTURE DUMAGUETE

By plane Dumaguete's small airport is in Sibulan, 4km north of the centre. PAL (☏ 035 532 9888) has offices at the airport, as does Cebu Pacific, also with an office on Governor Perdices St (☏ 035 225 6850). Tricycles make the trip to the city for P100 or less; there are also jeepneys (P7) from outside the airport perimeter fence, or you can haggle with one of the private car and van drivers who greet incoming flights: P250–300 is reasonable into town, or P550–700 to Dauin.

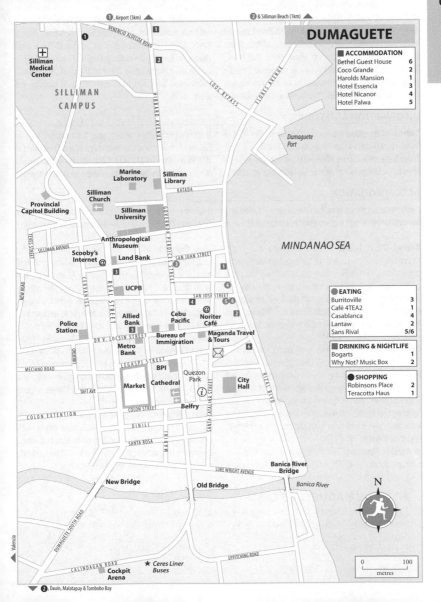

DUMAGUETE

■ ACCOMMODATION
Bethel Guest House	6
Coco Grande	2
Harolds Mansion	1
Hotel Essencia	3
Hotel Nicanor	4
Hotel Palwa	5

MINDANAO SEA

● EATING
Burritoville	3
Café 4TEA2	1
Casablanca	4
Lantaw	2
Sans Rival	5/6

■ DRINKING & NIGHTLIFE
Bogarts	1
Why Not? Music Box	2

● SHOPPING
Robinsons Place	2
Teracotta Haus	1

6

Destinations Cebu (4 weekly; 40min); Manila (4–6 daily; 1hr 25min).

By boat The ferry pier is near the northern end of Rizal Blvd, within easy walking distance of the centre. A tricycle costs P20. 2GO (☎ 035 225 4435) have a weekly ferry to Manila on Wed, while Cokaliong (☎ 035 255 3599) and George & Peter Lines (☎ 035 422 8431) between them have ferries most nights direct to Cebu. Oceanjet (☎ 0923 725 3734) run daily services to Tagbilaran on Bohol. For Dapitan on Mindanao, FastCat (☎ 0918 908 6995) run a fast daily service (3hr), while Aleson Shipping (☎ 035 422 8762), George & Peter Lines and Montenegro Shipping Lines (☎ 035 422 3632) all have slower boats. For Siquijor, GL Shipping Lines (☎ 035 480 5534), Aleson, Montenegro and Oceanjet all operate services, mostly to Siquijor Town or, less frequently, Larena. Alternatively, you can take *Coco Grove Beach Resort*'s private yacht to Tambisan at

3.30pm for P450. For southern Cebu, it's quicker to cross from one of the ports near Dumaguete (see box below).

Destinations Cebu City (8 weekly; 6–7hr); Dapitan (6–7 daily; 3–4hr); Manila (1 weekly; 19hr); Siquijor (9–11 daily; 45min); Tagbilaran (1–2 daily; 2hr).

By bus and jeepney The Ceres Liner terminal (☎ 035 225 9030) is on Governor Perdices St, 1km south of Quezon Park. A tricycle costs P20, but if you haven't got much luggage you can walk it almost as fast. For departures to the north of the island, it's worth making sure that you get on an express bus, which will shave hours from journey times. There are hourly buses to Sipalay (4–5hr), with changes in Kabankalan or Hinoba-an, and Bacolod (6–7hr). For the short hop to Dauin, there are plenty of jeepneys and buses going back and forth most hours of the day and night.

INFORMATION AND TOURS

Tourist information In town, there's a tourist office kiosk in Quezon Park (Mon–Fri 8am–5pm; ☎ 035 225 0549).

Tours There are a number of decent travel agencies and tour operators in town who can arrange trips to nearby attractions.

Harold's Mansion (see below) runs good budget trips to Casororo Falls, Bais and dive trips to Apo Island. Orientwind at 201 Flores Ave (☎ 035 422 5298, ⓦ orientwind.com.ph) offers an extensive line-up of tours in the region and beyond.

ACCOMMODATION

Dumaguete has plenty of inexpensive accommodation in the city centre or within walking distance of it, but rooms can get booked up fast in high season. Another option is to base yourself in Dauin (see p.302) and see Dumaguete on a day-trip.

Bethel Guest House Rizal Blvd ☎ 035 225 2000, ⓦ bethelguesthouse.com. In an excellent location on the seafront, this modern four-storey building has clean studio rooms and doubles, some with a sea view (for which you'll pay extra). Rooms at the front are big and bright, with picture windows. Staff are efficient and friendly, and there's a reasonable restaurant. Strictly no alcohol or smoking. 🛜 **P1300**

Coco Grande Hibbard Ave, just north of Silliman University ☎ 035 422 0746, ⓦ cocograndehotel.com. Under the same ownership as *Coco Grove* on Siquijor and *Apo Island Resort* on Apo, this remains one of the best places in town. The lobby and lounge are quaintly old-fashioned, while the spacious rooms and suites (P4200) are attractively styled and come with a/c, cable TV and fridge. Breakfast included. 🛜 **P1400**

★**Harolds Mansion** 205 Hibbard Ave, just north of Silliman University ☎ 035 422 3477, ⓦ haroldsmansion

.com. Owned by affable adventurer Harold Biglete, this hostel offers great-value rooms plus a sociable roof-deck restaurant where you can get on the wi-fi. A/c rooms (P1000) have cable TV and hot-water showers; fan rooms are actually preferable, as the a/c units can be noisy. Harold is a great source of travel information and can arrange all sorts of tours. They also have a basic ecolodge up in Valencia (see p.302). Simple breakfast included. 🛜 Dorms **P300**, doubles **P600**

Hotel Essencia 39 Real St ☎ 035 422 1137, ⓦ hotel-essencia.com. This nine-storey hotel has become rightfully popular for its clean, comfortable and stylish rooms in a central location. Staff are friendly, and there's a good restaurant, as well as a spa. 🛜 **P1600**

Hotel Nicanor San José St ☎ 035 226 3330, ⓦ hotelnicanor.com. Modern, comfortable rooms with a/c, cable TV, hot showers and free wi-fi. Standard rooms are windowless, making it worth the extra P400 to upgrade to a larger superior room. 🛜 **P1350**

FROM DUMAGUETE TO CEBU

To get to **Cebu island** from Dumaguete, take a van, jeepney (P12) or tricycle (P120) north to Sibulan from where there are boats to Lilo-An (every 30min; 30min; P45–70); from Lilo-An, buses run up the east coast to Cebu City. Alternatively, continue beyond Sibulan to Tampi, from which boats go to Bato on Cebu (every 1hr 30min; 30min; P70). From Bato, buses go north to Moalboal, and then on to Cebu City. You can get a chit (a numbered scrap of paper which guarantees you a place; you'll still pay on the bus) for the connecting Cebu bus at the Sibulan pier ticket office.

Hotel Palwa Locsin St ☎035 422 8995, bit.ly/ HotelPalwa. One of the town's cheaper options, offering small but nicely styled a/c rooms with flatscreen TV, and there's also a pleasant café. Wi-fi in the lobby. �internet **P1198**

EATING

Dumaguete has an expanding food scene which features everything from fresh seafood stalls to quality international cuisine.

Burritoville San Juan St, two blocks inland ☎035 522 4554, ⓦfacebook.com/BurritovilleDumaguete. Colourful new Tex-Mex joint run by a chef from Arizona, who concocts tasty nachos (P150), tacos (P170–190) and burritos (P210–330). Daily 8.30am–9pm

★**Café 4TEA2** 145 Hibbard Ave, 1km north of Harold's Mansion, ⓦfacebook.com/4tea2 ☎0924 377 7003. Unique Russian restaurant with a whimsical flying-teapot mural in the front patio. Feast on truly gigantic portions of pasta (P130), pepper beefsteak or cheesy giant meatballs (both P185). There's a Russian buffet for P295 on Sat. Daily 7am–11pm.

Casablanca Rizal Blvd ☎035 422 4080, ⓦdumaguete-restaurants.com. Movie-themed, Austrian-owned restaurant which offers fine European cuisine to a mainly expat clientele. Most dishes such as pasta and Indian chicken curry cost under P300, though the signature Brazilian beef tenderloin at P665 is undeniably excellent. *Casablanca* also has its own bakery and deli, a decent wine list and a changing daily menu. Daily 7am–11pm.

★**Lantaw** 201 Flores Ave, around 1km north of the ferry port ☎035 421 1296, ⓦbit.ly/LantawDumaguete. Deservedly Dumaguete's most popular seafood restaurant, with a spacious interior, large courtyard and sea-facing wooden deck. Excellent-value dishes include *sinigang* shrimp soup (P160), served in more of a vat than a bowl, and sizzling marlin (P185). Daily 11am–10pm.

Sans Rival Bakery: San Jose St; restaurant: Rizal Blvd ☎035 421 0338, ⓦbit.ly/SansRival. The original little cake shop on San Jose St still turns out delicious cakes and coffee, while its larger sister round the corner on Rizal serves a host of tasty but inexpensive meals including tapas (P155–220) and sizzling shrimp *sisig* (P280). Daily: bakery 9am–9pm; restaurant 10am–11pm.

DRINKING AND NIGHTLIFE

Nightlife is mostly focused on **Rizal Blvd**, although, like many Philippine port towns, the scene gets a little sleazy here as the night wears on.

Bogarts North end of Rizal Blvd ☎0906 865 9485. Small, popular Swiss-owned bar-restaurant playing fairly eclectic and varied music, and with wheat beer and other international brands on the drinks menu. Meals such as schnitzel and pasta are P200–300. Daily 8am–1am.

Why Not? Music Box 70 Rizal Blvd ☎035 225 7725, ⓦwhynotdumaguete.com. The most popular nightlife venue in town, *Why Not?* has a selection of bars plus a disco that's very popular with ladyboys. There's also a games room, internet café and even a deli. Daily 10am–2am.

SHOPPING

Robinsons Place On the southern edge of town ⓦrobinsonsmalls.com. Decent-sized mall with supermarket, National Book Store, plenty of clothes and electronics stores, cafés and restaurants, plus a bouncy castle for kids. Daily 10am–8pm.

Terracotta Haus Silliman University Co-operative, ⓦfacebook.com/TerracottaHausSouvenirShop. For Negros souvenirs including basketware and bags, seek out the tiny souvenir kiosk in the Silliman University Co-operative. Daily 9am–5.30pm.

DIRECTORY

Hospitals Dumaguete's best hospital is the Silliman Medical Center (☎035 420 2000) on Venencio Aldecoa Rd. **Immigration** Dumaguete's bustling immigration office is at Lu Pega Building, 38 Dr V. Locsin St, at the end of a narrow shopping arcade signed off Dr V. Locsin St (Mon–Fri 8am–5pm; ☎035 225 4401). **Internet access** As you'd expect of a university town,

there's no shortage of internet cafés, especially around the campus. One of the best places to get online is Klassik Cyber Zone on Silliman Ave (P15/hr). **Police** The main police station is at the west end of Dr V. Locsin St, near the Central Bank. **Post** The post office is on Santa Catalina St.

Valencia and around

An 8km drive inland and uphill from the coast, the town of **VALENCIA** offers fresh air, thundering waterfalls and adventurous trekking nearby, and a quirky museum. While there are a few places to stay here, Valencia can easily be visited as a day-trip (or half-day-trip) from Dumaguete or Dauin. The town itself has an attractive main square and a few cafés, but the reason to come out here is to experience the beauty of the mountain scenery.

Casororo Falls

Apolong • P10 • Habal-habal from Valencia to drop-off point of Casaroro Falls, P150 round-trip or you can take one of the day-trips from Harold's Mansion in Dumaguete (see p.300; P300/person).

It's a steep 5km drive up from Valencia to the starting point of the steps down to **Casororo Falls**. Once you've descended the steps, it's a 400m scramble up the valley, with a couple of quite tricky river crossings before you round a bend to view the towering 30m falls, surrounded by lush tropical greenery. Locals (or your habal-habal driver) might offer to show you the way, in which case it's a good idea to tip them a small amount.

Mount Talinis

You can either hire local guides (P700/day) and porters (P500/day) or take an organized trip from Harold's Mansion in Dumaguete (see p.300) – they can arrange day-hikes (P2750–3500), overnight treks (P4750–5500) and full mountain assaults

The challenging trail up **Mount Talinis** (1903m) begins at Apolong near the entrance to Casororo Falls and *Harold's Eco Lodge*. There are several different routes up the mountain, all of which require two to three days of steep jungle-trekking through dense foliage, but are rewarded by steaming fumeroles, tranquil lakes and spectacular views. You're definitely best with a guide for this trek, and you will need to bring tents, sleeping bags and food with you.

Cata-al WWII Museum

Jose Romero Rd at Legarda St • Daily 8am–5pm • Free, but donations welcome

The slopes of Mount Talinis were a hotbed of activity during World War II and were bombarded by US ships trying to force out the entrenched Japanese forces. Local resident Felix Constantina V. Cata-al (aka "Tantin") has been hunting out war memorabilia from the surrounding forests since he was a boy, and his huge and captivating collection is now on display at the **Cata-al WWII Museum**. Samurai swords, dog tags, old uniforms and radios are just a few of the bewildering array of items on show. Indeed, Cata-al's collection now has so many missile shells that he's ingeniously constructed a stair balustrade from them.

ARRIVAL AND DEPARTURE — VALENCIA AND AROUND

By bus, van and jeepney Regular jeepneys leave Dumaguete for Valencia (P12); you can also take a tricycle (P30/person). Vans and jeepneys can be chartered for around P1500, tricycles for P250–300. Alternatively, you could hire a tricycle at Bacong, halfway between Dumaguete and Dauin, for the steep ride up to Valencia (P100).

ACCOMMODATION

The Forest Camp On the road up to Casororo ⓣ0917 312 0853. This family-run camp has grown over the years and now has a few attractive cabins where you can overnight, as well as day-use cottages (P300–500). There's also a network of trails, some lovely pools and a simple restaurant. P80 entrance fee if you're not staying. **P1000**

Harolds Eco Lodge Casororo Trailhead, Apolong ⓣ0915 290 9931, ⓦharoldsmansion.com. Ultra-simple huts and a dorm without toilets at the start of the trail to Casororo Falls. There's a pool table and 24hr electricity, though. Dorms **P250**, doubles **P500**

Dauin and around

South of Dumaguete is beach-and-dive-resort country, with a decent range of accommodation. However, beaches are brown sand and the sea can be choppy from November to May, which makes the nearby island of Siquijor (see p.305) a more appealing prospect for pure beach enthusiasts. This said, divers will find the quality of nearby dive sites more than adequate compensation.

DAUIN is a popular port of call 15km south of Dumaguete. The beach has a dramatic backdrop of palm trees and ruined watchtowers, which were built in the nineteenth century as protection against raiding Moro pirates.

Malatapay market

Malatapay, Zamboanguita, 20km southwest of Dumaguete and 10km southwest of Dauin • Wed dawn–noon • Most of the resorts in Dauin arrange trips to the market (20min drive); alternatively, flag down a jeepney or charter a tricycle (P250–300 round-trip from Dauin including waiting time)

One of the most unusual markets in the Philippines is held every Wednesday in the seaside barangay of **Malatapay**. Buyers and sellers at **Malatapay market**, also known as **Zamboanguita market**, still use the traditional native barter system, with farmers from the surrounding villages and Bukidnon tribespeople from the interior meeting with fishermen and housewives to swap everything for anything – livestock, fish, exotic fruit, strange vegetables and household items. You'll have to be up bright and early to visit

---

APO ISLAND AND OTHER DIVE SITES

Tiny, volcanic **Apo Island**, 7km off the south coast of Negros, has become a prime destination for divers, most of whom head out for the day from Dumaguete, Dauin or Siquijor. Site of one of the Philippines' first and most successful marine reserves, Apo has a series of reefs teeming with marine life, from the smallest nudibranch to the largest deepwater fish. The sanctuary area is on the island's southeast coast, while much of the flat land to the north is occupied by the only village, home to four hundred fisherfolk and farmers. Non-divers needn't be bored; Apo has some fantastic snorkelling and it's a great little island to explore on foot.

Organized trips from Dumaguete or Dauin cost P1000–3000 per person depending on the level of comfort and number of people in your group, or you can travel independently on one of the regular bangkas from Malatapay. The trip takes about 45 minutes and the price is fixed at P2000 for a small bangka (good for four), P3000 for a large bangka (up to ten people), or alternatively you can arrange a place on one of the four daily *Liberty Lodge* shuttles (P300/person; see below). General **admission** to the marine sanctuary, where you can snorkel with turtles in guided groups of four, is P300, though it can get rather like a watery zoo.

Among other dive sites, **Calong-Calong Point** off the southern tip of Negros is known for its dazzling number of smaller reef fish. Nearby is **Tacot**, a tricky deep dive where sharks are common. From the coastal towns to the south of Dumaguete, you can take a bangka to Siquijor (see p.305), where sites such as **Sandugan Point** and **San Juan** go as deep as 65m, and where you can expect to see tuna, barracuda and sharks – plus, from March to August, manta rays.

Sightseeing trips to Apo can be arranged through most hotels in Dumaguete, but for dive trips you're best to book through dive resorts in Dauin or Siquijor – *Atmosphere* (see p.304), *Liquid* (see p.304) and *Coco Grove Beach Resort* (see p.309) are all recommended. In Dumaguete, *Harold's Mansion* (see p.300) runs day-trips (1–3 dives P2000–3300), or you can just snorkel (P1200).

APO ISLAND ACCOMMODATION

Apo Island Beach Resort ☎ 0939 915 5122, ⓦ apoislandresort.com. A few minutes' walk over a path from the village, under the same ownership as *Coco Grove* in Siquijor and *Coco Grande* in Dauin, this lovely little place sits at the back of a tiny isolated sandy cove, hemmed in by rocks. It's expensive, and the beach and restaurant can get overrun with day visitors, but once they've left, the true magic of this location reveals itself. Breakfast included. Dorms P800, doubles P2700

Liberty's Lodge ☎ 0920 238 5704, ⓦ apoisland

.com. Set above the main beach, *Liberty's* offers good views and reasonable rates for the sweet little rooms, which are inclusive of all meals. Wi-fi for P50/day (if there is electricity) in the restaurant. Shuttle boats run to Malatapay four times a day. 🛜 P2150

Mario Scuba Diving & Homestay ☎ 0906 361 7254, ⓦ mariosscubadivinghomestay.com. In the thick of the village, this humble place offers the cheapest rates on the island, either in the eight-bed dorm or simple private en-suite rooms. Dorms P250, doubles P600

the market: the bartering begins at first light and is usually more or less finished by noon. Malatapay is also the departure point for boats to Apo Island (see box, p.303), so a visit to the market and island can easily be combined.

Tambobo Bay

Most resorts can arrange trips, or you can hop on any bus or jeepney (P70) from Dumaguete or Dauin heading south along the coast – get off at Siaton and then take a tricycle for the last few kilometres (P50/person) to the beach; if you have your own vehicle it's far simpler to leave the main road at Mayabong Crossing (Km39) from which it's a beautiful but very bumpy 10km to Tambobo

Forty kilometres south of Dumaguete, at the very southern tip of Negros near the small town of Siaton, **Tambobo Bay** is a beautiful, serpentine bay, popular with foreign yachties for the protection it affords from storms, but also for its laidback lifestyle and pretty mangrove- and palm-fringed beaches. It's a great place to spend a lazy afternoon swimming and snorkelling, and there are also a few decent places to stay.

ARRIVAL AND DEPARTURE

By bus and jeepney Buses and jeepneys leave Dumaguete for Dauin (20–30min), Malatapay (40min), Zamboanguita (45min) and Siaton (1hr) from either the Ceres Liner terminal or the area around the market. An alternate route to Valencia leaves the main highway at Bacong, halfway between Dumaguete and Dauin; tricycles can be chartered from here for the steep ride up to Valencia for P100.

DAUIN AND AROUND

ACCOMMODATION

DAUIN

Atlantis Brgy Lipayo, 800m north of Dauin ☎035 425 2327, ⍇atlantishotel.com. A/c cottages with TV, mini-bar and private bathrooms, set amid lovely gardens, and for a little more, you can get sea views. *Atlantis* is primarily a dive resort, though it offers non-divers a large pool, loungers on the sand and day-trips to Dumaguete, Bais (for dolphin- and whale-watching) and Apo Island. ☞ **P4000**

★**Atmosphere** Maayong Tubig, 5km south of Dauin ☎035 400 6940, ⍇atmosphereresorts.com. British-owned *Atmosphere* is easily the most upmarket place in this part of the world. Beautiful suites, apartments and penthouses, with state-of-the-art facilities and wonderful outdoor bathrooms, are spread through well-manicured gardens. There's also a quality dive shop, the excellent Sanctuary spa, a top-class restaurant and a lovely infinity pool. The Kids Cove day-care centre also makes *Atmosphere* a good choice for families. ☞ **P11,500**

★**Liquid** Brgy Bulak, 2km north of Dauin ☎0917 314 1778, ⍇liquiddumaguete.com. Run by a friendly British-Canadian couple, this low-key dive resort has eight attractively decked-out beach huts (P1600), all with sea views, and six a/c cottages (P3300). There are also some cheaper concrete rooms at the back, discounted if you dive. There's wi-fi at the sociable pool bar and at the upstairs restaurant, which serves tasty meals and has a small bakery. ☞ **P1000**

Mike's Dauin Beach Resort Poblacion, Dauin ☎0916 754 8823, ⍇mikes-beachresort.com. Attractive, small-scale and homely resort on a pretty stretch of beach. Rooms are spread over two floors in one large block, and there's a lovely pool down by the beach. Also has a popular dive centre. ☞ **P3300**

Pura Vida Brgy Lipayon, Dauin ☎035 425 2274, ⍇pura-vida.ph. Stylish option with a range of tastefully designed native fan and a/c huts, and a lovely beachside pool. Wi-fi in reception and at the restaurant. ☞ **P3900**

TAMBOBO BAY

Kookoo's Nest ☎0919 695 8085, ⍇kookoosnest.com .ph. Wonderfully remote little British-run place with simple cottages on stilts overlooking a pretty cove at the entrance to Tambobo Bay. There are kayaks for rent and the restaurant turns out tasty meals and snacks. **P1150**

EATING

DAUIN

Cat's Acacia Café Opposite the public market ☎0936 651 6729. Simple restaurant with a shady courtyard, serving the likes of burgers (P175), pizza and other continental cuisine (P300–400). Daily 7am–10pm.

MALATAPAY

Dream Resort Just along from the Apo Island bangka station ☎0915 629 9606. Opened in 2013 by a British-Filipino couple, this lovely little café right on the seashore makes a great stop after a visit to to Malatapay market or Apo Island. They serve decent omelettes (P80), pancakes (P60), coffee and juices, plus home-made mango ice cream. There were also rooms under construction at the time of writing. Daily 7am–late.

6

> **WHALE-WATCHING AROUND BAIS**
>
> The city government operates the cruise vessels *Dolphin I & II*, *Vania I & II* and *Horizon* out to view the **whales and dolphins** in Bais Bay, each of which accommodates 15–20 people (P3000–4000). Tours operate all the way through to October, and bookings are recommended at least a month in advance, especially during the peak whale-watching season (March–Sept) – to arrange, call the tourist office (see below) or ☎035 402 8174. It is also possible to just turn up at Bais pier and negotiate with local boatmen or, more easily, to take a day-trip from Dumaguete.

Bais and around

The town of **BAIS**, about 40km north of Dumaguete, is a good place to see **dolphins and whales** in Bais Bay as they migrate through the Tanon Strait separating Negros from Cebu. Tours run between March and October (see box above).

Twin Lakes

Daily 8am–5pm • Foreigners P100, Filipinos P10; kayak rental P100/hr • From Bais either take a jeepney to Amlan (P15) and then a motorcycle taxi up to the lakes (P350 round-trip) or hire a van from Bais or Dumaguete (around P3000); day-trips and hikes from Dumaguete can be booked through *Harold's Mansion* in Dumaguete (see p.300) from P500/person including lunch

Nestled in a jungled crater 15km west from the main coastal road, the **Twin Lakes** of Balinsasayao and Danao make for an excellent day out. Getting there is part of the adventure and is best done by motorbike, as the last part of the track is often inaccessible to larger vehicles. Alternatively, you can make the strenuous 15km **hike** in from the little town of **San José**, nearly midway between Dumaguete and Bais. The hike takes you past a couple of waterfalls, where you can swim, and through settlements of the indigenous Bukidnon people who inhabit the area. Once at the lakes, it's possible to rent a kayak and head out onto the water, and to hire a pair of binoculars to check out the wildlife, which includes tarictic hornbills, monkeys and eagles; there's also a café.

ARRIVAL AND INFORMATION   BAIS AND AROUND

By bus and jeepney Bais lies on the main coastal road and is well served by buses and jeepneys from Dumaguete (1hr).

Tourist information The tourist office (Mon–Fri 8am–5pm; ☎035 402 8338) is in the public plaza in the centre of town.

ACCOMMODATION AND EATING

Campuyo Aroma Beach Resort Manjuyod ☎0928 407 2999. A few kilometres north of Bais and right on the beach, *Aroma* has clean, a/c rooms with cable TV. They also have a restaurant with free wi-fi and can arrange dolphin-watching trips. 🛜 P900

La Planta Hotel Mabini St ☎035 402 8321, 🌐 laplanta.com.ph. Clean and comfortable twin rooms in a quaint and cosy place that used to be the city's power plant. Also has a pool and a decent restaurant. P1450

Siquijor

Small, laidback **SIQUIJOR** lies between the islands of Cebu, Negros and Bohol and makes a worthwhile stop on a southern itinerary. Very little is known about the island and its inhabitants before the arrival of the Spanish in the sixteenth century, who named it the Isla del Fuego ("Island of Fire") because of the eerie luminescence generated by swarms of fireflies. This sense of mystery still persists today, with many Filipinos believing Siquijor to be a centre of **witchcraft** (see box, p.305). Shamans aside, the island is peaceful, picturesque and a pleasure to tour, whether by bike, tricycle, motorbike or jeepney – the entire 72km coastal road is paved (a rare delight in the Philippines) and traffic is light. The **beaches** alone make it worth a visit, but there are also **mountain trails**, waterfalls and old churches to explore as well as decent scuba diving. The island is gradually becoming more popular, a process that will only be

SORCERORS ON SIQUIJOR

Every Good Friday, herbalists from around Siquijor and from the rest of the Visayas and Mindanao gather in **San Antonio**, in Siquijor's pea-green hinterlands, to prepare potions made from tree bark, roots, herbs and insects. The culmination of this annual Conference of Sorcerers and Healers – now rebranded the **Folk Healing Festival** because it sounds less menacing – is the mixing of a mother-of-all potions in a large cauldron. As the mixture is stirred, participants gather in a circle and mumble incantations said to imbue it with extraordinary healing powers. The ceremony takes place on Good Friday in the belief that on Christ's day of death, supernatural forces are free to wander the earth. The brew is evidently strong, with wide-ranging powers that include provoking a good harvest, securing a spouse or getting rid of that troublesome zit. The festival attracts spiritualists and tourists from across the Philippines and beyond – be sure to book your accommodation well in advance if you plan to visit at that time.

accelerated if the private airport, whose runway has already been extended, is opened to commercial flights as planned.

Most places to stay are within half an hour of the port towns of **Siquijor** and **Larena**, notably around **San Juan**, south of Siquijor, and at **Sandugan**, north of Larena. A number of resorts have certified **dive operators** who will take you on trips to places such as Sandugan Point and Tambisan Point, both known for their coral and abundant marine life. At Paliton Beach there are three submarine caves where you can see sleeping reef sharks, and at Salag-Doong Beach, on the eastern side of the island, divers have occasionally reported seeing manta rays and shoals of barracuda. Further afield but still within easy reach, Apo Island (see box, p.303) is another dive favourite, and is worth a visit even if you stay above water.

Siquijor Town

SIQUIJOR TOWN is a likeable enough place though without anything to keep you there for long. There is an atmospheric eighteenth-century church on the seafront, the **Church of St Francis of Assisi**, which was built in 1783 partly from coral. You can climb its bell tower for views across the town and out to sea.

The north coast

Some slow ferries arrive at the port of **LARENA**, from where the beaches of Sandugan are only a brief jeepney or tricycle ride to the north. From the pier it's just a short walk to Larena's centre, which has a town hall, plaza and church, but not much else. There are a couple of basic lodges, but with plentiful jeepneys and tricycles to nearby Sandugan, there's really no need to stay.

Six kilometres northeast of Larena is the village of **SANDUGAN**, where there's a beach and a number of resorts, one with professional **scuba-diving** facilities. To reach the beach, take a tricycle or jeepney from Larena to Sandugan and then negotiate the rutted path that leads to the shore. All the tricycle drivers know it, so you won't get lost.

The west coast

Twenty minutes west of Siquijor you come to beautiful and undeveloped **Paliton Beach**, 1km down a bumpy track from the main road (take the turn-off at the church in Paliton Town), but well worth the journey. A west-facing cove of sugary-white sand, Paliton is sheltered from big waves by the promontory of **Tambisan Point**, and has views of tropical sunsets you'll never forget.

A few kilometres further south, the small town of **SAN JUAN** has an unusual focal point: the sulphurous **San Juan de Capilay Lake**, where locals gather (especially at

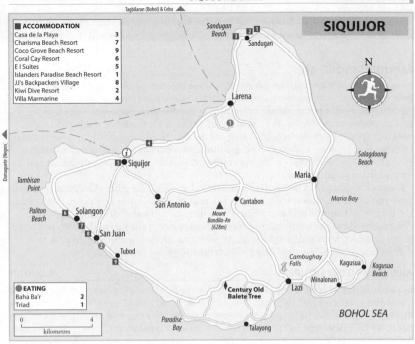

weekends) to wallow in the eggy water, said to have miraculous healing qualities. For more energetic activity, try the scenic but strenuous trek from San Juan along a jungled trail to San Antonio.

The east coast

Siquijor's picturesque east coast is a rural littoral of sun-bleached barangays and hidden coves, some of the most secluded around **Kagusua Beach**, reached through **Minalonan** and then the sleepy little fishing village of **Kagusua**. There's a sealed road from the village to the edge of a low cliff, where steps take you down to the sand and a series of immaculate little sandy inlets. To proceed north from Kagusua you'll have to backtrack to the coastal road at Minalonan, where you can catch a jeepney through sleepy **Maria** and on to **Salagdoong**, which has a resort popular with locals at weekends. For Salagdoong Beach, look out for the signposted turning about 6km north of Maria. You can walk it in about twenty minutes from the main road.

Southern Siquijor

The main east-coast road meets the island's north–south dissecting road at **Lazi**, with its delightful nineteenth-century church built of coral and stone. Right opposite it is the oldest convent in the Philippines, a low-rise wooden building now sagging with age, but still beautiful. A couple of kilometres inland from Lazi, **Cambughay Falls** are the island's most accessible and popular waterfalls. Steep steps lead down to the pretty falls, which are a pleasant spot for a picnic or a swim.

Continuing clockwise, the main road cuts a fair distance inland, passing the **Century Old Balete Tree**; sheltered under its massive branches are a few stalls and a popular pond with a fish spa (P20). If you have a motorbike, you can explore the partly paved tracks that lead down to the coves around **Talayong** and **Paradise Bay**. You may also pass the island's main **dairy farm** – Siquiyor is famed for its fresh milk, which is quite a rarity in the Philippines.

Mount Bandila-an

You can enquire about guides at the tourism assistance centre in Siquijor Town, although many resorts can also offer advice and arrange for a local to show you the way • Access is via either the village of Cantabon (take a tricycle or jeepney from Larena), or Cangmonag in the south

At 628m and right at the island's heart, **Mount Bandila-an** is Siquijor's highest point and accessible to anyone who's reasonably fit. It lies at the centre of the island in an area that suffered serious damage during World War II, when acres of forest were razed by retreating Japanese troops. Now the entire area is part of the Siquijor Reforestation Project; while rehabilitation is not yet complete, wildlife such as the leopard cat and long-tailed macaque survive.

Mount Bandila-an can be climbed in a day, and you'll need a guide. On the way to the peak you'll pass the **Stations of the Cross**, where a solemn religious procession re-enacting the Passion of Christ is held every Easter, and there are a number of springs and caves. Ask your guide to point out another huge old balete tree at the side of the trail, said to be home to spirits, imps and guardians of the forest. To ask their permission to pass, the polite thing to say is "*tabi tabi lang-po*" ("excuse me, please step aside").

ARRIVAL AND DEPARTURE   SIQUIJOR

By plane Until plans for the public airport are completed, Siquijor is not accessible by plane.

By boat GL Shipping Lines (☎035 480 5534), Aleson (☎035 422 8762), Montenegro (☎035 422 3632) and Oceanjet (☎0923 725 3734) operate eleven daily services from Dunaguete, mostly to Siquiyor Town but some to Larena (45min–1hr 30min). Oceanjet also has a combined service from Cebu to Tagbilaran, then Dumaguete and finally on to Larena (3 weekly; 4hr 50min). *Coco Grove Beach Resort* (see opposite) runs a private yacht from Tambisan to Dumaguete at 12.30pm, returning at 3.30pm. Onwards boat tickets can be arranged through most resorts or directly at Siquijor Town and Larena piers.

INFORMATION

SIQUIJOR TOWN
Tourist information There's a tourism assistance centre (Mon–Fri 8am–noon & 1–5pm; ☎035 344 2088) at the pier in Siquijor Town, which has a few maps and brochures and can also help arrange transport and guides.
Services There are a few banks with ATMs in town, plus some small internet cafés, including the intriguingly named Melbon Rub (☎035 480 9026).

THE NORTH COAST
Tourist information There's a friendly private tourist office (daily 8am–9pm) in a building by the pier in Larena, which also has a pleasant café and a well-stocked souvenir shop.
Services Larena has a post office and an Allied Bank with an ATM. You can get online at Mykel's Internet, next to the pension of the same name.

GETTING AROUND

If you've booked accommodation in advance, you may get a free pick-up from your port of arrival; otherwise there are tricycles from the main port of Siquijor, and jeepneys from Larena. You could also arrange a tour through your resort.

By bike and motorbike Renting a bicycle or motorbike is the cheapest and best way to get around the island. Bicycles can be rented from certain resorts, including *Kiwi Dive* (see opposite). Motorbikes can be rented from around P300/day from many resorts, or at Scandinavian Rent-A-Motorbike (☎0939 640 5132) on the National Highway in Siquijor Town.

By bangka To travel the coast by sea, charter a bangka in Larena, Siquijor Town or Lazi.

ACCOMMODATION   SIQUIJOR

SIQUIJOR TOWN
E I Suites Behind the church ☎035 480 9069, ⓦfacebook.com/BellviewOfficial. Clean, modern en-suite rooms in a smart new building above a decent restaurant.

Close to the port and all amenities. 📶 P1200
★**Villa Marmarine** Candanay, 2.5km east of Siquijor Town ☎0919 465 9370, ⓦwww.marmarine.jp/en. Wonderful place on a peaceful stretch of beach, with

spacious, well-constructed huts and rooms (a/c P2500), as well as a fine restaurant serving authentic Japanese and Filipino food. The tennis-mad owner conducts lessons on the resort's court. 🛜 P1200

THE NORTH COAST

Casa de la Playa Sandugan ☎035 377 2291, ☜siquijorcasa.com. German Terry and local Emely have established a New Age tropical spa that offers yoga sessions, food made with organic vegetables from the resort's own garden and even massages from a local shaman. Accommodation is in a range of lovingly built fan and a/c huts, and houses with kitchenettes (P1700), either in a pretty garden bursting with frangipani and white *sampaguita* blossom or right on the beach. 🛜 P1100

Islanders Paradise Beach Resort Sandugan ☎035 377 2412, ☜islanders-paradise-beach.com. Seven simple cottages with porches where you can relax and watch the waves lap and sun set. Guests are welcome to join in the weekly Sunday school. 🛜 P950

Kiwi Dive Resort At the eastern end of Sandugan Beach (turn right at the end of the path) ☎035 424 0534, ☜kiwidiveresort.com. Pleasant, small-scale resort with attractive stone cottages on a low hill overlooking a private cove, all with bathrooms and the better ones with solar hot water. Omelettes, nourishing stews, curry, fish, spaghetti and vegetarian dishes are some of the tasty options available at the restaurant. One of the owners is a dive instructor and can organize trips to nearby sites. They also rent out mountain bikes (P250/day) and motorbikes (P500/day). 🛜 P500

THE WEST COAST

Charisma Beach Resort Solangon, 2km northwest of San Juan ☎0908 861 9689, ☜charismabeachresort.com. British-owned place with dorm beds, simple bamboo cottages right on the beach and spick-and-span, white, motel-style rooms arranged around a swimming pool (P1400–2650). Wi-fi in the restaurant. 🛜 Dorms P450, doubles P1000

★**Coco Grove Beach Resort** Tubod, 2km southeast of San Juan ☎035 481 5008, ☜cocogroveresort.com. By far the island's most luxurious resort, Australian-owned *Coco Grove* occupies a prime stretch of palm-fringed beach. Rooms range from modest but tasteful standards to newer executive suites and luxury villas, all of which have a/c. There are three restaurants, two pools, a swim-up bar, a reputable dive centre, kayaks, spa, and wi-fi in the common areas. The resort has regular entertainment programmes and also runs dive trips most days to Apo Island (including lunch at sister *Apo Island Beach Resort*; see box, p.303). They even run their own daily yacht to Dumaguete. 🛜 P3500

Coral Cay Resort Solangon Beach, 3km west of San Juan ☎0919 269 1269, ☜coralcayresort.com. This resort is owned by an expat and his Filipina wife. Accommodation ranges from clean, simple rooms with fan and cold shower to spacious a/c cottages with a small living area and separate bedroom (P3930). The restaurant menu is surprisingly urbane for such an isolated place, featuring coq au vin and Australian Chardonnay. Jeepney tours, trekking, scuba diving, mountain bikes and anything else you care to ask for can all be arranged. Wi-fi in restaurant. 🛜 P1140

JJ's Backpackers Village 1.5km northwest of San Juan ☎0918 700 0467, ✉jiesa26@yahoo.com. Good budget choice owned by a friendly Aussie and his Filipina wife, where the simple rooms have fans and shared bathrooms. There are also tents for rent and a dorm. Wi-fi in common areas. 🛜 Tent P300, dorms P300, doubles P500

EATING

SIQUIJOR TOWN

The main drag in Siquijor Town, Rizal St, is chock-a-block with cheap canteens and bakeries selling fresh *pan de sal*.

THE NORTH COAST

Triad Restaurant Larena ☎035 377 2236. Perched atop a hill a short ride from Larena, *Triad* offers tasty food and expansive views over the coast from its massive circular dining area. Dishes on offer include nachos and dip (P130), *lechon kawali* (P100), baked New Zealand mussels (P250), plus cakes and shakes. Daily 7am–9pm.

THE WEST COAST

Baha Ba'r 500m south of San Juan ☎0998 548 8784, ☜baha-bar.com. Hip place with a shady courtyard and smart upstairs wooden deck, where you can enjoy breaded calamari, chicken tacos (both P150) and fresh fish (P200–300) while listening to live acoustic music (except Sun). Come for the fine Fri evening fish and *lechon* buffet, then head across the road to see the live bands at *Czar's*. Daily 10am–9pm.

6

Cebu and the Eastern Visayas

CHOCOLATE HILLS, BOHOL

Cebu and the Eastern Visayas

The Eastern Visayas, a collection of jigsaw-shaped islands in the heart of the Philippines, are considered the cradle of the country. It was here that Ferdinand Magellan laid a sovereign hand on the archipelago for Spain and began the process of colonization and Catholicization that has since shaped so much of the nation's history. The islands were also the scene of some of the bloodiest battles fought against the Japanese during World War II, and where General Douglas MacArthur waded ashore to liberate the country after his famous promise, "I shall return".

7

Comprising thousands of islands and atolls, this relaxing region is a bounty of tropical sands and coral reefs; everywhere you turn, there seems to be another beach or dive site. There are four major island groups – **Cebu**, **Bohol**, **Samar** and **Leyte** – but it's the hundreds of tropical enigmas in between that make this part of the Philippines so irresistible.

Of the smaller islands, some are world-famous for their scuba diving, such as **Malapascua**, off the northern tip of Cebu; some for their extraordinary better-than-Boracay beach life, such as **Panglao**; and some for the ability to take you back in time to the Philippines as it once was, such as **Biliran** and **the Camotes**. Travelling here is a slow, easy-going, and ultimately rewarding experience.

The Eastern Visayas suffered a great deal of damage back in 2013, with a substantial quake in Bohol in October, and then in November **Typhoon Yolanda** tore through the region, leaving a band of destruction along its path (see box, p.360). Numerous destinations were affected, including southeastern Samar, Tacloban, Ormoc, the Camotes, Bantayan and Malapascua. While most areas have returned to normal, some parts, in particular eastern Leyte and southeast Samar, remain a shadow of what they once were, and the legacy of both disasters continues to be felt. Although we have provided the most up-to-date information possible, note that some places are still under renovation, while others, left out of this edition, will reopen in the future.

Cebu

Right in the heart of the Visayas, nearly 600km south of Manila, the island of **CEBU** is the most densely populated in the Philippines and home of the second-largest metropolis, **Cebu City**, an important transport hub with ferry and air connections to the rest of the country. Cebu is a long, narrow island – 300km from top to bottom and only 40km wide at its thickest point – with a mountainous and rugged spine. Most tourists spend little time in the towns, heading off on island-hopping adventures to the north or venturing west for world-renowned scuba diving. The closest beaches to Cebu

TARSIERS

Highlights

❶ **Cebu City** It's not Manila, but the Philippines' second-biggest metropolis is still a hectic introduction to modern Filipino life. Beyond the packed malls and thronging markets, there's plenty to savour in its museums, churches and happening restaurant and bar scene. **See p.315**

❷ **Malapascua** A little nugget of paradise north of Cebu, boasting the dazzling Bounty Beach, plenty of islets to explore and scuba diving with thresher sharks. **See p.334**

❸ **Pescador Island Marine Reserve** Off the coast of Moalboal, tiny Pescador is only 100m long, but has a glorious reef attracting whale sharks and divers from around the world. **See p.338**

❹ **Bohol** Everything good about the Philippines in one compact island package: superb diving, fine beaches, Gothic churches, the postcard-perfect Chocolate Hills and, uniquely, tarsiers – the world's smallest primates. **See p.342**

❺ **Beaches** Beaches, beaches and more beaches. From Alona Beach's restaurant- and bar-lined strip to the pinch-yourself-you're-dreaming blue of Bantayan and White Beach, the Eastern Visayas has them by the bucket-load. **See p.345, p.339 & p.332**

❻ **Tacloban and beyond** Help support the post-Yolanda relief effort in Leyte by spending your tourist pesos where the natural disaster hit hardest. **See p.361**

HIGHLIGHTS ARE MARKED ON THE MAP ON P.314

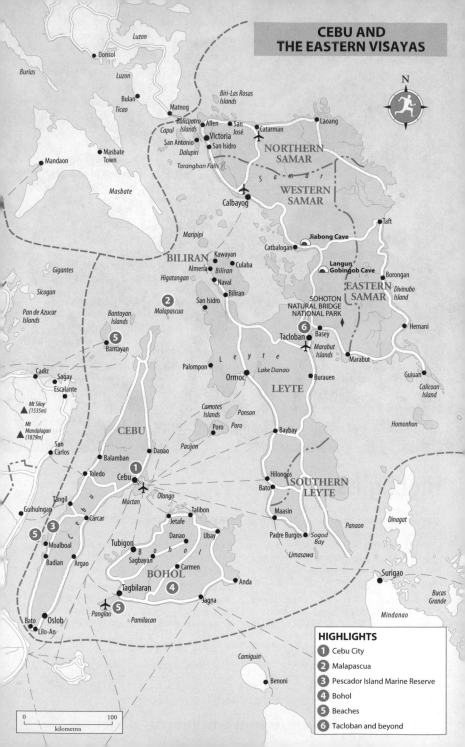

CEBU AND
THE EASTERN VISAYAS

N

Luzon

Donsol

Burias

Luzon

Ticao

Bulan

Matnog

Biri-Las Rosas Islands

Balicuatro Islands

Capul   Allen   San José   Catarman   Laoang

San Antonio   Victoria

Dalupiri   San Isidro

Tarangban Falls

NORTHERN SAMAR

Masbate

Mandaon

Masbate Town

Masbate

Calbayog

WESTERN SAMAR

Taft

Maripipi

Jiabong Cave

Gigantes

BILIRAN   Kawayan

Almeria   *Biliran*   Culaba

Catbalogan

Langun Gobingob Cave

Borongan

Sicogan

Higatangan   Naval

San Isidro   Biliran

EASTERN SAMAR

Divinubo Island

Pan de Azucar Islands

(2) *Malapascua*

San Isidro

SOHOTON NATURAL BRIDGE NATIONAL PARK

Hernani

Bantayan Islands

(5)

Tacloban   Basey

Marabut Islands

Guiuan

Bantayan

Palompon

Leyte   Lake Danao

Marabut

Calicoan Island

Cadiz

Sagay

Escalante

Ormoc   Burauen

LEYTE

Homonhon

Mt Silay (1535m)

Camotes Islands   *Ponson*

Baybay

Mt Mandalagan (1879m)

San Carlos

CEBU   Danao

Poro   *Poro*

Balamban

Cebu

Pacijan

Hilongos

SOUTHERN LEYTE

Toledo

Olango

Bato

Dinagat

Tangil

Mactan

Talibon

Maasin

Guihulngan

Carcar   Jetafe

Panaon

(5)

(3)   *Cebu*

Tubigon   Danao   Ubay

Padre Burgos   *Sogod Bay*

Moalboal

Sagbayan   *Bohol*

Limasawa

Badian   Argao

Carmen

Surigao

Tagbilaran   **BOHOL**   Anda

Bucas Grande

(4)

Panglao   Jagna

Mindanao

Bato   Oslob

(5)

Lilo-An

Pamilacan

Camiguin

Benoni

HIGHLIGHTS	
(1)	Cebu City
(2)	Malapascua
(3)	Pescador Island Marine Reserve
(4)	Bohol
(5)	Beaches
(6)	Tacloban and beyond

0   100
kilometres

City are the resort-fringed sands on **Mactan Island** to the southeast, although they are by no means the best. Head north instead to the marvellous island of **Malapascua**, where the toothpaste-white beach is as fine as Boracay's; to tranquil **Bantayan** off the northwest coast; or to really get away from it all, to the isolated **Camotes Islands**. Alternatively, to the south of Cebu City, you can cross to the west coast diving haven of **Moalboal** to explore its offshore caves and canyons. Finally, down in the south, **Oslob** has become famous for nose-to-nose encounters with whale sharks.

ARRIVAL AND DEPARTURE   CEBU

By plane Getting to Cebu is simple. There are dozens of flights daily from Manila to Cebu City and less frequent flights from a number of other key destinations within the Visayas (Kalibo and Tacloban), the rest of the Philippines (Camiguin, Siargao, Coron, Davao and Puerto Princesa) and the rest of Asia (Hong Kong, Seoul, Singapore and Taipei).

By ferry Cebu's position in the middle of the country makes it an excellent place to journey onwards by ferry, with frequent sailings to Luzon, Mindanao and elsewhere in the Visayas.

Cebu City

7

Gateway to the Visayas, **CEBU CITY** is the Philippines' second-largest city, home to nearly a million people. Nicknamed the "Queen City of the South", it's peppered with historic attractions and is worthy of a day or two's exploration before moving on to the beaches and islands beyond. While a far easier introduction to urban life in the Philippines than Manila, Cebu is not without its problems: streets are often clogged with smoke-belching jeepneys, and "rugby boys" (see box, p.43) are common. The October 2013 Bohol earthquake (see box, p.343) also shook Cebu, not that the happy-go-lucky Cebuanos would let you know it. Buildings have been restored and it's very much a modern, happening metropolis: the current trend is for colossal shopping malls, praiseworthy restaurants and buzzing coffee shops.

A QUICK GUIDE TO CEBUANO

Filipino (Tagalog) might be the official language and English the medium of instruction, but **Cebuano**, the native language of Cebu, is the most widely spoken vernacular in the archipelago, not used only in Cebu but also throughout most of the central and southern Philippines. Cebuano and Tagalog have elements in common, but also have significant differences of construction and phraseology – it's quite possible for a native Manileño to bump into a native Cebuano and not be able to understand much of what he or she says.

Cebuano is evolving as it assimilates slang and colloquialisms from other Visayan dialects, as well as from Tagalog and English. Confused? You will be. Most Cebuano conversations veer apparently at random between all three languages, leaving even Filipino visitors unable to grasp the meaning.

Bold vowels below indicate where to lay emphasis.

SOME CEBUANO BASICS

Good morning	Ma**a**yong b**u**ntag	**Yes**	O-**o**
Good afternoon	Ma**a**yong h**a**pon	**No**	Dili
Good evening	Ma**a**yong gab**i**	**OK**	Sigi
How are you?	Kumus**ta**?	**How much is this?**	Tag-pila ni?
I'm fine	Ma**a**yo man	**Expensive**	Mahal
Very well	Ma**a**yo ka'**a**yo	**Cheap**	Bar**a**t
What's your name?	Umsay pangalan ni mu?	**Idiot!**	Amaw!
Where are you from?	Tag**a** din ka?	**Go away!**	Layas!
		Who?	Kins**a**?
Thank you	Sal**a**mat	**What?**	Unsa?
You're welcome	Wal**a**y sapay**a**n	**Why?**	Ngan**o**?
Goodbye	Ari na ko	**Near/Far**	D**u**ol/Lay**o**

Many of Cebu's attractions are associated with Magellan's arrival in 1521 and are to be found near the **port** in the old part of the city. West of here, a seething cobweb of sunless streets spreads out between **Carbon Market** and **Colon Street**, the latter anchoring the oldest mercantile quarter in the country. You can explore the area on foot, picking your way carefully past barrow boys selling pungent fruits, hawkers peddling fake mobile-phone accessories and, at night, pimps whispering proposals from dark doorways. A vibrant, humming, occasionally malodorous area of poorly maintained pavements and thick diesel fumes, it's not a mainstream tourist sight, but it's worth some of your time in order to experience the daily realities and pulsating energy of downtown Cebu.

Further inland, the excellent **Casa Gorordo Museum** and **Museo Sugbo** are rich with colonial splendour and offer more historical insights, while for a break from the serious stuff, **Tops Lookout** is true to its name; it offers a sigh-triggering view across the city, along with a much-needed breath of fresh air.

Cebu City's main tourist event is the Mardi Gras-style **Sinulog festival** in January (see box opposite).

Magellan's Cross
Magallanes St • Daylight hours • Free

Cebu City's spiritual heart is an unassuming stone rotunda in the middle of busy Plaza Sugbo that houses the **Magellan's Cross**. The first of the conquering Spaniards to set foot in the Philippines, Magellan began a colonial and religious rule that would last four hundred turbulent years. The rotunda's ceiling is exquisitely painted with a scene depicting his landing in Cebu in 1521 and the planting of the original cross on the shore. It was with this crucifix that Magellan is said to have baptised the Cebuana Queen Juana and her followers. The cross that stands here today, however, is only a modern reproduction, apparently containing fragments of the conquistador's original.

Basilica del Santo Niño
President Osmeña Blvd, next to the Cross of Magellan • Daily 9am–7pm • Free

Heralded by vendors selling religious icons and amulets offering cures for everything from poverty to infertility, the **Basilica del Santo Niño** was first founded in 1565 – making it the oldest church in the country – and is home to probably the most famous religious icon in the Philippines: the statue of the **Santo Niño**. The figure, which looks like an extravagantly dressed children's doll, is said to have been presented to Queen Juana of Cebu by Magellan after her baptism, considered the first in Asia, in 1521. Another tale has it that 44 years later, after laying siege to a pagan village, one of conquistador Miguel López de Legazpi's foot soldiers found a wooden chest that had survived the bombardment inside a burning hut. Inside this box was the Santo Niño. If you want to see the statue, let alone touch it, you'll have to join the queue of devotees that often squirms through the doors and outside.

CEBU CITY ORIENTATION

Cebu City's main north–south artery is **President Osmeña Boulevard**, running from the Provincial Capitol Building down to **Plaza Independencia**. Beyond this is a jumble of streets that in true Philippine urban tradition appears to have no particular centre. Return visitors may cite the earthy, careworn charms of Colon Street and the **port** as the beating heart of Cebu, while others focus on the hotel and bar hub of **Fuente Osmeña**, 1km north, but these days the best dining and shopping are to be found in the malls at the **Ayala Center** and the trendy residential northern suburbs of **Lahug** and **Banilad**. Thirty minutes' drive north of the city proper, **Mandaue** is an industrial suburb that functions as one of the city's economic and transport hubs.

SINULOG

Almost as popular as Kalibo's Ati-Atihan (see box, p.284), the big, boisterous **Sinulog festival**, which culminates on the third Sunday of January with a wild street parade and an outdoor concert at Fuente Osmeña, is held in honour of Cebu's patron saint, the Santo Niño. The Santo Niño statue itself (see opposite) is brought on a boat from Mandaue to the city proper, festooned with candles and garlands, and then paraded through the streets. Sinulog is actually the name given to a swaying **dance** said to resemble the current (*sulog*) of a river and supposedly evolved from tribal elders' rhythmic movements. Today, it's a memorable, deafening spectacle, with hundreds of intricately dressed Cebuanos dancing through the streets to the beat of noisy drums. Most of the action happens on President Osmeña Boulevard, but to escape the crowds, grab a spot on one of the nearby roads where security is less zealous and you can slip underneath the velvet ropes and join the dancers. For information about Sinulog and details of the exact route, which varies every year as the festival grows, visit ⓦ sinulog.ph. If you plan to visit Cebu City during Sinulog, make sure you book accommodation well ahead of time.

7

Carbon Market
MC Briones St • Daily 6am–6pm • Free

No longer the coal unloading depot from which its name is derived, **Carbon Market** is now an area of covered stalls where the range of goods on offer, edible and otherwise, will leave you reeling – shining fat tuna, crabs, lobsters, coconuts, guavas, avocados, mangoes and more. The market is alive from well before dawn and doesn't slow down until after dark.

Fort San Pedro
Near the port area at the end of Sergio Osmeña Blvd • Mon–Sat 8am–8pm • P30

When he arrived in 1565, conquistador Miguel López de Legazpi set about building **Fort San Pedro** to guard against marauding Moros from the south. It was here, on December 24, 1898, that three centuries of Spanish rule in Cebu came to an end when their flag was lowered and they withdrew in a convoy of boats bound for Zamboanga, on Mindanao – their way station for the voyage to Spain. The fort has been used down the centuries as a garrison, prison and zoo, but today is little more than a series of walls and ramparts. On Sundays, the park opposite, **Plaza Independencia**, gets packed out with locals playing ball games and enjoying picnics.

Cebu Metropolitan Cathedral
Legazpi St • Daily 9am–7pm • Free

An imposing sixteenth-century Baroque structure, **Cebu Metropolitan Cathedral** has felt the force of nature and conflict several times in its four hundred-year history. An early version was completely destroyed by a typhoon before construction was finished, and the cathedral was almost razed to the ground during World War II. It was quickly rebuilt, and then renovated in 2009, but damaged (only superficially, thankfully) once again by the October 2013 earthquake.

Yap-Sandiego Heritage House
Mabini St • Daily 9am–12am • P50 • ☎ 032 514 3002

Distilling the essence of Cebu before the mall and mobile era is the **Yap-Sandiego Heritage House**, which was built between 1675 and 1700 and is one of the oldest homes in the Philippines, evidenced by the dusty antiques and warp and weft of the floorboards. It's owned by a descendant of the original residents; current landlord Val Sandiego, a choreographer and antique collector, still – somewhat bizarrely – stays over at weekends with his extended brood. The house is located across the road from the overtly patriotic, flag-waving **Heritage of Cebu Monument**.

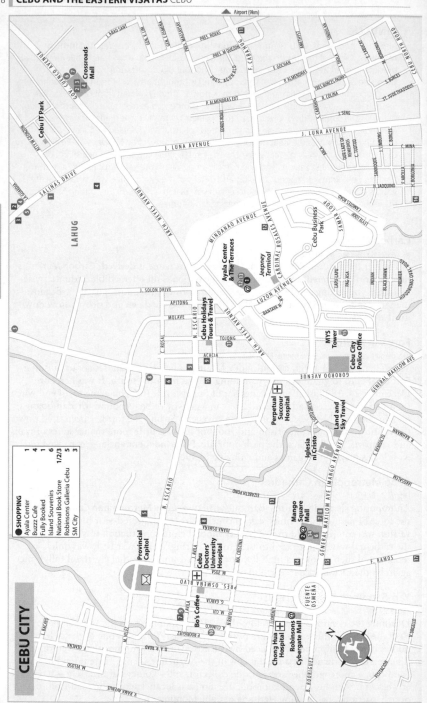

CEBU CITY

Airport (9km)

Crossroads Mall

Cebu IT Park

LAHUG

SALINAS DRIVE

J. LUNA AVENUE

GOV. CUENCO AVENUE

ARCH. REYES AVENUE

Ayala Center
& The Terraces

Cebu Business
Park

Jeepney
Terminal

MINDANAO AVENUE

CARDINAL ROSALES AVENUE

LUZON AVENUE

J. SOLON DRIVE

APITONG

MOLAVE

ACACIA

N. ESCARIO

C. ROSAL

TOJONG

Cebu Holidays
Tours & Travel

MYS
Tower

Cebu City
Police Office

GORDORO AVENUE

GENERAL MAXILOM AVE

Perpetual
Succour
Hospital

Land and
Sky Travel

Iglesia
ni Cristo

Elizabeth Pond

Mango
Square
Mall

Provincial
Capitol

Cebu
Doctors'
University
Hospital

JUANA OSMEÑA

PRES. OSMEÑA BLVD

N. ESCARIO

GENERAL MAXILOM AVE (MANGO AVENUE)

Chong Hua
Hospital

Robinsons
Cybergate Mall

Bo's Coffee

FUENTE
OSMEÑA

F. RAMOS

M. VELOSO

V. RAMA AVENUE

SHOPPING

Ayala Center	1
Buzzz Cafe	4
Fully Booked	1
Island Souvenirs	6
National Book Store	1/2/3
Robinsons Galleria Cebu	5
SM City	3

N

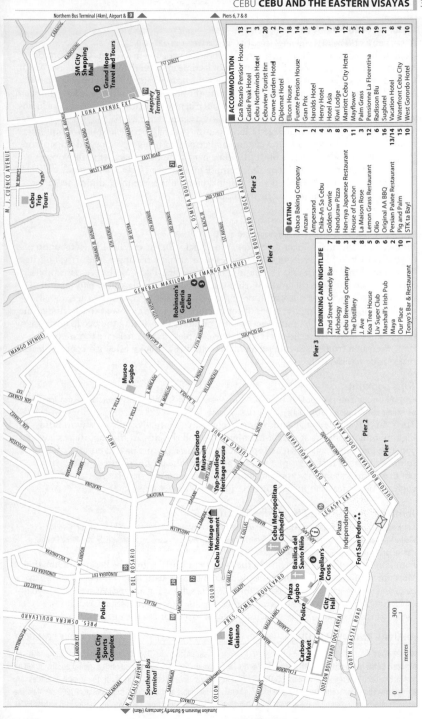

Northern Bus Terminal (4km), Airport & **9** ▲   ▲ Piers 6, 7 & 8

■ ACCOMMODATION	
Casa Rosario Pension House	13
Castle Peak Hotel	11
Cebu Northwinds Hotel	3
Cebuview Tourist Inn	20
Crowne Garden Hotel	2
Diplomat Hotel	17
Elicon House	18
Fuente Pension House	14
Gran Prix	15
Harolds Hotel	6
Henry Hotel	1
Hotel Asia	7
Kiwi Lodge	16
Marriott Cebu City Hotel	12
Mayflower	5
Palm Grass	22
Pensione La Florentina	9
Radisson Blu	19
Sugbutel	21
Vacation Hotel	4
Waterfront Cebu City	8
West Gorordo Hotel	10

● EATING	
Abaca Baking Company	7
Anzani	1
Ampersand	2
Chika-An Sa Cebu	4
Golden Cowrie	5
Handuraw Pizza	8
Han-nya Japanese Restaurant	9
House of Lechon	11
La Maison Rose	3
Lemon Grass Restaurant	12
Olio	6
Original AA BBQ	16
Persian Palate Restaurant	13/14
Pig and Palm	15
STK ta Bay!	10

■ DRINKING AND NIGHTLIFE	
22nd Street Comedy Bar	7
Alchology	8
Cebu Brewing Company	3
The Distillery	4
J. Ave	8
Koa Tree House	5
Liv Super Club	9
Marshall's Irish Pub	6
Maya	2
Our Place	10
Tonyo's Bar & Restaurant	1

7

Casa Gorordo Museum

35 Lopez Jaena St, off Mabini, off the eastern end of Colon St • Tues–Sun 10am–6pm • P80 • ☎ 032 255 5630

Built in the 1850s by wealthy merchant Alejandro Reynes, the marvellous **Casa Gorordo Musum** building is one of the few structures of its time in Cebu that survived World War II. Owned by a succession of luminaries, including the first Filipino Bishop of Cebu, Juan Isidro de Gorordo, it was acquired in 1980 from the bishop's heirs and opened as a museum three years later. In 2014, the museum closed for extensive structural renovations, including the addition of a new shop and café, and reopened again in late 2016.

The house is a striking marriage of late Spanish-era architecture and native building techniques, with lower walls of Mactan coral cemented using tree sap, and upper-storey living quarters built entirely from Philippine hardwood held together with wooden pegs. The interior offers an intriguing glimpse into the way Cebu's aristocracy once lived, and is elegantly furnished with original pieces like a Viennese dining set, a German piano and Catholic icons from Spain.

Museo Sugbo

MJ Cuenco Ave • Mon–Sat 9am–6pm • P75 (including guided tour) ☎ 032 239 5626

Housed in the former Carcer del Cebu (provincial jail), the excellent **Museo Sugbo** traces the island's history from early Chinese and Siamese trading to the arrival of the Spanish and the modern era. The highlights are the first-floor World War II exhibits, including banned "guerrilla money" that was issued after the Japanese had instituted their own currency, and possession of which was punishable by death. There are also wartime notices detailing the types of foods Filipinos weren't allowed to eat: one of the few staples not on the list was sweet potato, meaning that during the occupation, many people survived on these alone. Towards the complex's rear, a separate room houses finds excavated from Plaza Independencia, including a spooky fifteenth-century death mask made of gold leaf.

Tops Lookout

Busay • P100 • Return taxi P1500 including waiting time; Busay jeepneys (P8) from SM City and Ayala Center stop 1km from Tops, from where there are habal-habals (P300 round trip), or you can brave the steep walk up

The road that winds northwards out of Cebu City eventually finds its way to **Busay**, the high mountain ridge that rises immediately behind the city. At the top, there's a wide concrete lookout area known as **Tops Lookout**, where visitors pay an entrance fee, buy some barbecued chicken from a vendor and watch the plum-coloured sunset. It's popular at dusk, so don't expect romantic solitude, but the view is great and the air cooler and cleaner than in the concrete jungle 600m below.

Jumalon Museum and Butterfly Sanctuary

Jumalon St, Basak • Mon–Sat 9am–5pm • P50 • ☎ 032 261 6884, ⓦ jumalonbutterflysanctuary.com • Taxis cost P200 (20min); alternatively, take any jeepney heading along Cebu South Rd to Friendship Village or Basak, get off at the Holy Cross Parish Church and look out for Jumalon St near Basak Elementary School

Four kilometres west of the centre in the largely residential suburb of Basak, the **Jumalon Museum and Butterfly Sanctuary** is lepidopteran heaven, with rooms full of glass display cases and a large garden at the back with butterflies fluttering around. As well as everyday species, such as monarchs and viceroys, there are also rare examples such as albinos, melanics, dwarfs and conjoined twins. It's home to a fascinating art gallery, too.

ARRIVAL AND DEPARTURE   **CEBU CITY**

BY PLANE

Mactan Cebu International Airport Cebu flights land at Mactan Cebu International Airport (☎ 032 340 2486, ⓦ mactan-cebuairport.com.ph) on Mactan Island. There is a tourist information counter in the arrivals hall where you can pick up the Department of Tourism's city and island map. The arrivals hall also has car rental booths including Avis, Friends and Thrifty; all the rental agencies are reputable and offer cars from around P3000 per day. The departure tax from Cebu for international flights is P750, while domestic departure tax is P200; this is now included in almost all airfares.

Getting into town White taxis are generally cheaper than yellow taxis, but there isn't much difference between them. Getting into town, 8km across the suspension bridge, should cost P250–350 on average, though it varies depending on your destination and the time of day; in heavy traffic, fares can hit P450 or more. MyBus, a welcome new airport transfer running to and from Mactan from SM City Cebu, is also now in service (every 20–30mins, 6am–10pm; P25; ⓦ facebook.com/MyBusPH).

Airlines Air Asia (☎ 032 341 0226), Cebu Pacific (☎ 032 341 2550) and Tiger Airways (☎ 032 340 9813) all have representatives at the airport, as well as offices in town; other airlines include Asiana Airlines (☎ 032 342 8062); Cathay Pacific (☎ 032 340 3254); Korean Air (☎ 032 340 5431); Philippine Airlines (☎ 032 340 9780); PAL Express (☎ 032 415 9901); and Silk Air (☎ 032 340 0042).

Routes Both Cebu Pacific and PAL operate flights to dozens of regional cities, including Manila, Davao, General Santos, Iloilo, Kalibo and Tacloban. To get to Camiguin and Siargao, Cebu Pacific currently operates daily flights. Air Asia runs flights to Manila, as well as international routes to Kuala Lumpur, Seoul, Singapore and Taipei.

Domestic destinations Bacolod (8 daily; 45min); Cagayan de Oro (5 daily; 45min); Camiguin (1 daily; 45min); Caticlan (3 daily; 1hr); Clark (6 weekly; 1hr 25min); Davao (6–9 daily; 1hr); Iloilo City (4–6 daily; 50min); Kalibo (3–7 daily; 50min); Manila (at least 30 daily; 1hr 10min); Puerto Princesa (1 daily; 1hr 15min); Siargao (1–2 daily; 1hr); Tacloban (3–4 daily; 45min); Zamboanga (1 daily; 1hr 5min).

BY BOAT
ESSENTIALS

Piers The arrival point for ferries is one of eight large piers stretching along the harbour area beyond Fort San Pedro. Pier 1 is closest to Fort San Pedro, just a few minutes on foot, while Pier 8 lies several kilometres to the northeast. Jeepneys and buses line up along nearby Sergio Osmeña Blvd for the short journey into the city. Taxis wait to meet arriving ferries.

Tickets and information As well as ticket offices at the piers, travel agents and hotels throughout the city can book ferry tickets (see p.323). Generally speaking, tickets for fast ferries on the main inter-island routes are very reasonably priced, at P200–500 per single (add an extra 25–50 percent to that for a/c or business class). Slower services are, as you'd expect, cheaper, and should cost no more than P100–200 one-way, depending on the popularity of the route. The shipping pages of local newspapers are a good place to get up-to-date ferry information. There's also a shipping schedules channel on the local Sky Cable TV network, available in some hotels. For a helpful introduction to inter-island ferry schedules, visit ⓦ schedule.ph.

SHIPPING LINES AND FERRIES
The three main fast boat companies are Oceanjet, Weesam and 2GO. 2GO is a conglomerate of companies (Cebu Ferries, Negros Navigation, SuperCat and SuperFerry) acquired by the Chinese government, which operates both fast and slow ferries and generally – alongside rival operator OceanJet – offers the most comfortable and professional service. Confusingly, routes operated by SuperCat still go under this name, and you may also see reference to the other old company names in outdated print material and signage. For a full list of ferry companies and their contact details, see Basics (see p.25).

DESTINATIONS
Cebu is connected by boat to almost every major port in the Philippines and a number of minor ones (see box, pp.322–323). Fast boat and catamaran services link Cebu with Bohol and Leyte all within 3hr, but these services are more expensive than regular ferries (for example, Cebu–Tagbilaran costs from P400 for a ticket compared with P210 for the slower Cokaliong service). As well as ferries to Dumaguete, another way to Negros is to ride the bus to Bato, Lilo-An or Toledo, and take a ferry or big bangka (see p.300).

BY BUS
Bus terminals Ceres Liner (☎ 032 345 8650) is the main bus company in Cebu and operates out of two terminals. The Northern bus terminal, served by jeepneys marked "Mandaue" (P8), is on the coastal road, 4km east of the city centre, and is used by buses and jeepneys for destinations north of the city (all every 20–30min). The Southern bus terminal, for buses south, is on Bacalso Ave, west of President Osmeña Blvd and is accessible by jeepneys marked "Basak" (P8).

Destinations from Northern terminal Danao (for Camotes; frequent; 1hr); Hagnaya (for Bantayan; every 30min; 3hr 30min); Maya (for Malapascua; every 30min; 4hr).

Destinations from Southern terminal Badian (4hr); Bato (4hr); Lilo-An (3hr); Moalboal (3hr); Oslob (4hr); Toledo (for San Carlos; 2hr 30min).

BY CAR
Car and driver You may prefer to charter a car with driver to get around the island; many tourists simply flag down a taxi and negotiate a flat rate with the driver, usually P2500–3000 for the day for a one-way trip to Moalboal or Maya, for example. Many of the bigger hotels have their own cars with drivers, but charge significantly more.

Rental companies Many firms, including Alamo and Avis, have kiosks at the airport. In town, Alamo is at the *Waterfront Cebu City*, Salinas Drive (☎ 032 232 6888) and Hertz is at the *Marriott*, Cardinal Rosales Ave (☎ 032 411 5800).

7

7

CEBU FERRY SCHEDULES

Note that **ferry schedules constantly change**, especially those for slower boats. The best resource is the local English-language newspapers, which print updated timetables on a daily basis.

DESTINATION	TYPE	COMPANY	FREQUENCY	DURATION
BILIRAN				
Naval	Slow	Roble Shipping	4 weekly	9hr 30min
BOHOL				
Tagbilaran	Slow	2GO	5 weekly	5hr
	Slow	Cokaliong	1 weekly	5hr
	Slow	F.J. Palacio Lines	3 weekly	5hr
	Slow	Lite Shipping	2–3 daily	5hr
	Slow	Trans-Asia Shipping Lines	1 weekly	5hr
	Fast	Oceanjet	10 daily	2hr
	Fast	SuperCat	3 daily	2hr
	Fast	Weesam	5 daily	2hr
Tubigon	Passenger	Aleson Shipping	4 daily	1hr 20min
	Passenger	Island Shipping	4 daily	3hr
	Passenger	Kinswell	3 daily	3hr
	Passenger	Lite Shipping	2 daily	3hr
	Passenger	MV Star Crafts	15 daily	1hr 20min
CAMOTES				
Poro	Slow	E. B. Aznar Shipping	3 weekly	4hr 30min
	Fast	Oceanjet	3 daily	1hr 30min
LEYTE				
Hilongos	Passenger	Roble Shipping	3 daily	4hr 30min
Maasin	Slow	Cokaliong	4 weekly	6hr
	Fast	WeeSam	2 daily	3hr
Ormoc	Slow	Lite Shipping	1 daily	6hr
	Slow	Roble Shipping	1 daily	6hr
	Fast	Oceanjet	5 daily	2hr 30min–3hr
	Fast	SuperCat	5 daily	2hr 30min–3hr
	Fast	Weesam	1 daily	2hr 30min–3hr
LUZON				
Manila	Passenger	2GO	5 weekly	23hr
	Passenger	Gothong Lines	4 weekly	23hr

GETTING AROUND

By bus Cebu City's Bus Rapid Transit System is still a pipe dream, meaning jeepney and vans are the principal public transport.

By taxi Taxis are plentiful and it's not hard to find a driver who's willing to use the meter. The tariff is P3.50 per 500m plus a flagfall of P30; a typical cross-city trip costs P200–250 outside rush hour.

By jeepney and van Jeepneys and open-sided Isuzu vans painted in outrageous colours ply dozens of cross-city routes. From Colon St, they run almost everywhere: east to the piers and the SM City Mall, north to Fuente Osmeña, northeast to Ayala Center and south to Carbon Market. There are also jeepneys along N. Escario St, north of Ayala Center, heading east to Mandaue and west and southwest to the Provincial Capitol Building, Fuente Osmeña and the Colon St area. The standard fare for each leg, or part thereof, is P8.

INFORMATION

Tourist Information The main tourist office is the Department of Tourism's Cebu regional office (Mon–Fri 8am–5pm; ☎ 032 254 2811) in the LDM Building on Legazpi St, near the junction with Lapu-Lapu (close to Fort San Pedro). There's also a branch at the airport (opening hours vary). As well as information about the festival, the Sinulog Foundation website (🌐 sinulog.ph) has a wealth of information about the city.

Maps Of the city maps available, the best is *EZ Map* (P249), which is available at bookshops and some hotels, but there

MASBATE				
Masbate City	Passenger	Cokaliong	1 weekly	13hr 30min
	Passenger	Super Shuttle	1 weekly	13hr 30min
	Passenger	Trans-Asia Shipping Lines	2 weekly	13hr 30min
MINDANAO				
Cagayan de Oro	Passenger	2GO	3 weekly	8–10hr
	Passenger	Gothong Lines	1 weekly	8–10hr
	Passenger	Lite Shipping	3 weekly	8–10hr
	Passenger	Super Shuttle	1 weekly	8–10hr
	Passenger	Trans-Asia Shipping Lines	1 daily	8–10hr
Dapitan	Passenger	Cokaliong (via Dumaguete)	4 weekly	9hr
	Passenger	George & Peter Lines (via Dumaguete)	5 weekly	9hr
Iligan	Passenger	2GO	1 weekly	13hr
	Passenger	Cokaliong (via Ozamiz)	5 weekly	13hr
	Passenger	Trans-Asia Shipping Lines	2 weekly	13hr
Nasipit	Passenger	2GO	1 weekly	10hr 30min
	Passenger	Cokaliong	4 weekly	10hr 30min
	Passenger	Gothong Lines	1 weekly	10hr 30min
Ozamiz	Passenger	2GO	1 weekly	8hr
	Passenger	Gothong Lines	1 weekly	8hr
	Passenger	Cokaliong	5 weekly	8hr
Surigao	Passenger	Cokaliong	6 weekly	7hr
Zamboanga	Passenger	George & Peter Lines	2 weekly	16hr
NEGROS				
Dumaguete	Passenger	Cokaliong	5 weekly	4–6hr
	Passenger	George & Peter Lines	5 weekly	4–6hr
	Passenger	Oceanjet (via Tagbilaran)	2 daily	4–6hr
PANAY				
Iloilo City	Passenger	Cokaliong	4 weekly	12hr
	Passenger	Trans-Asia Shipping Lines	3 weekly	12hr
SAMAR				
Calbayog	Passenger	Cokaliong	3 weekly	11hr
	Passenger	F.J. Palacio Lines	3 weekly	11hr
Catbalogan	Passenger	Roble Shipping	2 weekly	12hr
SIQUIJOR				
Siquijor Town	Passenger	Oceanjet (via Tagbilaran and Dumaguete)	1 daily	4hr 50min

are plenty of free maps to pick up from hotel receptions, tourist kiosks and at Mactan airport.

Newspapers There are a number of English-language local newspapers, including the *Cebu Daily News* (w cdn.ph), and the *Sun Star Cebu* (w sunstar.com.ph), both of which have ferry timetables, events listings and restaurant reviews.

TOURS

Travel agents These can be found in most malls and hotels and can arrange tours of the city, ferry tickets, flights and vehicle hire (with driver). A few to try include: Cebu Trip Tours (M.J. Cuenco Ave ☏032 268 5470, w cebutriptours.com); Grand Hope Travel and Tours (Lower Ground Level, SM City Mall, Juan Luna Ave ☏032 233 8263, w grandhopetravel.com); and Land and Sky Travel (Rivergate Complex, General Maxilom Ave ☏032 254 0101, w landskytravel.com).

ACCOMMODATION

Some of the cheapest accommodation in Cebu City is in the old **Colon Street** area, though the streets in this neighbourhood can be a little daunting at night, with roaming pimps and a number of shabby massage parlours and girlie bars. Hotels around **Fuente Osmeña** are better, and, further out, glitzier options near the **Ayala Center** and in **Lahug** and **Banilad** are close to the city's hyper-real malls and many of the more fashionable restaurants.

COLON STREET AND AROUND

Cebuview Tourist Inn 200 Sanciangko St ☎032 254 8333, ⓦcebuviewtouristinn.com. Reasonably comfortable and secure, offering a/c rooms with cable TV and Filipino breakfasts (P75). Long-term deals are available and it's right in the mix of the shopping and fast-food outlets outside. ☞ **P800**

Elicon House P. del Rosario at Junquera St ☎032 255 0300, ⓦelicon-house.com. This eco-hostel is rooted in permaculture philosophy, with more than a whiff of hippy bohemia about it. For those who value sociable common spaces, delicious vegetarian food and safe, secure accommodation (with CCTV), it's great value. No-frills a/c rooms are clean if uninspiring, and there's cable TV and – obviously – an on-site bike museum. ☞ **P1045**

Palm Grass 68 Junquera St ☎032 412 2462, ⓦpalmgrasshotel.com.ph. Pitched as Cebu's first heritage hotel, *Palm Grass* is a new addition off Colon St, decorated in faux-vintage maps, teak furniture and gold curtains. Deluxe rooms are well lit and modern, while staff are super-helpful. Breakfast is included, and there is a mini rooftop bar – great for sunset beers. ☞ **P1300**

FUENTE OSMEÑA AND AROUND

Casa Rosario Pension House 101 E. Ramon Aboitiz St ☎032 253 5134, ⓦcasarosario.net. This long-running all-rounder is on a quiet side street just minutes from Fuente Osmeña. All of the boldly painted a/c rooms have cable TV and attractive furnishings. There's a welcoming breakfast bar in the lobby. ☞ **P1200**

Diplomat Hotel 90 F. Ramos St ☎032 253 0099. Popular hotel in a good location set back from F. Ramos St. Standard rooms are perfectly adequate, while superior rooms are bigger, brighter and some have decent views. All rooms are a/c and have hot water, cable TV and fridge. ☞ **P1300**

Fuente Pension House 0175 Don Julio Llorente St ☎032 412 4988, ⓦfuentepensionhouse.com. The spotlessly clean lobby makes the *Fuente* seem like a boutique hotel at first glance, but the rooms are simple and good value. All have hot water and cable TV, and the rooftop restaurant has free wi-fi. They offer 24hr rates, regardless of when you check in, and reliable airport and pier pick-up and drop-offs. ☞ **P1189**

Gran Prix F. Ramos St at General Maxilom Ave ☎032 254 1295, ⓦgranprixhotels.com/cebu. Economy hotel in a great location near chaotic Fuente Osmeña with small, modern a/c rooms (many without windows, though), and *Jollibee* vouchers for breakfast. Wi-fi in lobby only. ☞ **P1399**

Hotel Asia 11 Don Jose Avila St ☎032 255 8534, ⓦhotelasiacebu.com. In a good location north of Fuente Osmeña, this neat, well-run Japanese-themed hotel has an airy white-tiled lobby, plenty of Mt Fuji motifs and well-appointed, box-sized rooms, each with a high-tech toilet. Larger, deluxe rooms (some laid-out tatami-mat-style) have stone bathtubs. Restaurant *Han-Nya* is open 24hr and transports you straight to downtown Tokyo. ☞ **P1950**

★The Mayflower Villalon Drive ☎032 255 2700, ⓦmayflower-inn.com. "Shop local, eat local, sleep local" is this hotel's motto, and it's easy to see why: its eco-credentials are plastered over the walls. There's a friendly organic café, a mini forest garden (with resident turtles), a games room and an adjoining folk art museum stuffed with all sorts of oddities. Erratic wi-fi. ☞ **P1375**

Vacation Hotel 35 Juana Osmeña St ☎032 253 2766. The best a/c rooms at this charming mid-range choice, north of Fuente Osmeña, are on the second floor, with balconies overlooking the small pool. Downstairs, some rooms at the front have little verandas centred around a garden, but others are darker and less enticing – ask to see a few. ☞ **P1888**

AYALA CENTER AND AROUND

Harolds Hotel 146 Gorordo Ave ☎032 505 7777 ⓦharoldshotel.com.ph. With a bustling all-day café and 360-degree rooftop live music bar (Mon–Thurs & Sun 5pm–midnight, Sat & Sun till 1am), this business hotel is an exciting proposition. Daily rates are on the high side, but over-the-counter promos are great value. Rooms come fitted with mini-bars, rainfall showers and comfy memory foam beds. Weak wi-fi. ☞ **P3800**

Kiwi Lodge 1060 G. Tudtud St, Mabolo ☎032 232 9550, ⓦkiwilodge.centralcebu.com. Small hotel in a residential area south of Ayala Center, with a range of comfortable a/c rooms at reasonable prices. Superior rooms in the new wing (P2100) have flatscreen TVs and safes. ☞ **P1400**

Marriott Cebu City Hotel Cardinal Rosales Ave ☎032 411 5800, ⓦmarriott.com. The *Marriott* is housed in a twelve-storey building near the Ayala Center. There are over three hundred rooms, all remodelled in sleek, modern style, plus three restaurants, a poolside café and a health club. ☞ **P5050**

Pensionne La Florentina 18 Acacia St ☎032 231 3118. Family-friendly cheapie in a rambling old building set back from Gorordo Ave. The best rooms on the upper floors have a/c and cable TV, while the pokey street-level veranda is the ideal place to plan your next move. No café, but the Ayala Center is just a short walk away. Wi-fi in reception area only. ☞ **P950**

West Gorordo Hotel 110 Gorordo Ave ☎032 231 4347, ⓦwestgorordo.com. Another permaculture hub from the team behind the *Mayflower* and *Elicon House*. Bright, clean and comfy rooms with a/c and cable TV in an ideal location close to the mall madness of Ayala. Downstairs, *Journeys*

Café is stacked with guidebooks and maps, making it a great spot to meet other travellers. 🛜 **P1595**

LAHUG AND BANILAD

Cebu Northwinds Hotel Salinas Drive ☎032 233 0311, ⓦcebunorthwinds.com. Close to Lahug's bars and restaurants, as well as the workday action of Cebu IT Park, this business hotel has a/c, cable TV and a coffee shop and restaurant. More expensive superior rooms on the hotel's front side are bigger, but overlook the traffic rush. Wi-fi in public areas. 🛜 **P1500**

Crowne Garden Hotel Salinas Drive ☎032 412 7517, ⓦcrownegardenhotel.com. In a price war with *Cebu Northwinds* across the road, this hotel just edges it for service. Its entrance is hidden around the back of a car park, but don't let that put you off: rooms are bright, clean and comfortable and have a/c, hot water, cable TV and fridge. Free wi-fi in the lobby only; breakfast costs extra (P300). 🛜 **P1350**

★**The Henry Hotel** Banilad ☎032 520 8877, ⓦthehenryhotel.com. The owners have clearly raided every second-hand store in the country to create this spectacular hipster pad. The lobby features cartoon statues, vintage movie props and traffic lights, plus there's an impressive pool and pop-art-themed restaurant and cocktail bar. Great dining and nightlife options are on the doorstep, but for downtown sightseeing you'll need to arrange a cab with one of the bow-tie-wearing bellhops. 🛜 **P7500**

Waterfront Cebu City Salinas Drive ☎032 232 6888, ⓦwaterfronthotels.com.ph. A mid-city landmark, the *Waterfront* is a brash slice of Las Vegas, Cebu-style. Despite the name, it's nowhere near the coast. A world unto itself, with a 24hr casino, several upscale restaurants and bars, and a gym and large pool, this is as showy as the city gets. 🛜 **P4100**

ELSEWHERE IN THE CITY

Castle Peak Hotel F. Cabahug St at President Quezon St, Mabolo ☎032 233 1811, ⓦcastlepeakhotel.net. Affordable hotel in a quiet area east of Ayala. Although showing signs of age, the rooms are spacious and the bathrooms well maintained. There are two decent on-site restaurants, *The Pizza Pub* and *The Dining Room* – the latter does a recommended *lechon*. Popular with Chinese salarymen. 🛜 **P1888**

★**Radisson Blu** S. Osmeña Blvd ☎032 402 9900, ⓦradissonblu.com. Cebu's City's premier international hotel is a gigantic palace with a monstrous lobby, hundreds of spacious, tastefully decorated rooms and the most overwhelming breakfast spread (included) in the city at *Feria* – cooking stations offer everything from Korean BBQ to French crêpes. Better still, the service is so good that you'll rarely have to lift a finger. 🛜 **P6800**

Sugbutel S. Osmeña Blvd ☎032 232 8888, ⓦsugbutel.com. The economy version of Japan's capsule hotels, this bizarre green-and-white budget stopover has the cheapest comfy beds in the city. Large rooms have been subdivided into train-like compartments which house two–six bunk beds, each of which has an overhead light, small safety box and plug socket. The lobby feels like a train station waiting room, but it's functional and – most importantly – dirt cheap. Patchy wi-fi. 🛜 Dorms **P265**, doubles **P1450**

EATING

Cebu's cosmopolitan dining scene is seriously on the up, offering everything from excellent snack joints to Michelin-star restaurants. Though there are places to eat all over downtown, many of the best options are to be found in the city's malls, notably **The Terraces** at the Ayala Center, a tastefully designed food court overlooking atmospheric gardens. North of the centre, the malls **Crossroads** and **Banilad Town Center** (BTC) are also home to the city's best international restaurants. Fast-food chains and coffee shops are so commonplace that it can feel as if there's one on every corner.

COLON STREET AND AROUND FUENTE OSMEÑA

Han-nya Japanese Restaurant Hotel Asia, 11 J. Avila St ☎032 255 8536, ⓦhotelasiacebu.com. Japanese cuisine served around the clock in a lattice-screened restaurant with raised seating areas, on the ground floor of *Hotel Asia*. Udon and *yaki soba* noodles start at P210; if you're in the mood for a blow-out, try the jumbo-sized beef tenderloin *teppanyaki* (P460). Daily 24hr.

Persian Palate Restaurant Mango Square Mall, General Maxilom Ave ☎032 236 0448; Ayala Center ☎032 232 6898 ⓦpersianpalaterestaurant.com. Well-spiced Indian and Middle Eastern dishes, including biryanis (P295), samosas (P110) and baba ganoush (P165). There are four other outlets, including one at Ayala. Daily 10am–8pm.

The Original AA BBQ M.J. Cuenco Ave at Legaspi Ext. Opposite Plaza Indepencia, this branch of the low-key, self-service, Cebu-wide chain offers a butcher's shop's worth of authentic Filipino skewered meats and fish. Dishes like sweet and sour pork (P100) and baked scallops (130) bring in locals by the busload. Daily 10am–9pm.

STK ta Bay! Paolito's Seafood House 6 Orchid St ☎032 253 4732, ⓦstktabay.com. *STK* stands for Cebu's three most famous cooking methods – *sugba* (grill), *tuwa* (soup) and *kilaw* (ceviche) – while the wall of fame showing a who's who of Filipino diners underlines the restaurant's credentials. Set up in Paolo Alcover's home, diners are seated among family heirlooms and instruments, including locally made guitars and an enormous goatskin drum. Despite the distractions, the food remains the star: try the adobo eel (P150) or black pepper-crabs (P295). Daily 9am–2pm & 5–11pm.

AYALA CENTER AND AROUND

Handuraw Pizza Gorordo Ave ☏ 032 231 3398, ⓦ handurawpizza.com. Serving thin-crust concept pizzas with a hearty Cebuano twist, this beloved citywide franchise has come a long way since opening in 2004. Go local with a Tinapa Delight, topped with smoked milkfish (small P208, large P398). Live music most nights. Mon–Thurs & Sun 10am–midnight, Fri & Sat 10am–2am.

★House of Lechon Acacia St ☏ 032 231 0958. To go the full hog in the company of smiling, grease-chinned locals, there really is nowhere better in Cebu. With cherry-red, succulent barbecued pig that's been voted the best in the city (no small feat with so much competition), the restaurant prices its secret-recipe *lechon* by weight (250g, P200; or P230 for the spicy version). Daily 10am–10pm.

Lemon Grass Restaurant Garden Level, The Terraces, Ayala Center ☏ 032 233 8601. Staff at this bright, garden-view restaurant really know how to lure customers through the door. Thai and Vietnamese dishes are as close to authentic as you can expect round here, with lots of well-seasoned and spicy coconut curries. The *banh xeo* (sizzling Vietnamese crêpes; P255) are also delicious. Daily 11am–11pm.

The Pig and Palm MYS Tower, Pescadores Rd ☏ 032 255 8249, ⓦ thepigandpalm.ph. Located on the ground floor of the MYS Tower, this Spanish tapas restaurant is run by Michelin-starred British chef Jason Atherton and his Filipino wife, Irha. The creative sharing plates are highly recommended, with dishes like beef-and-foie-gras burgers (P690) and tipples made with bacon butter bourbon (P275). Tues–Sun 8am–12am.

LAHUG AND BANILAD

Abaca Baking Company Crossroads Mall, Banilad ☏ 032 262 0969, ⓦ theabacagroup.com. Tucked away at the back of the Crossroads Mall, this small but sophisticated café has a wide-ranging menu offering everything from gourmet sandwiches (P150) to cupcakes and Danishes (P80), all served up by sleek staff clad in black. Hands down, it's the hippest breakfast spot in the city. Daily 7am–10pm.

Ampersand Banilad Town Center (BTC) ☏ 032 348 0575. Trendy, popular terrace restaurant and bar with gastro-pub dishes such as burgers, sliders and creative sharers such as crab and artichoke *arancini* (P300) and mango *sriracha* chicken pizza (P350). Daily 10am–2pm & 6pm–1am.

Anzani Panorama Heights, Nivel Hills ☏ 032 232 7375, ⓦ anzani.com.ph. Run by Italian chef Marco Anzani and his Filipino wife Kate, this classy hilltop restaurant is an award-winner for Mediterranean fusion cuisine. Dishes are pricey (mains P900), but for something totally different, try the ostrich carpaccio (P470) or pan-seared crocodile tail (P755). The couple also own restaurants all over the city. Daily 11.30am–2pm & 5.30pm–midnight.

Chika-An Sa Cebu Salinas Drive ☏ 032 233 0350. A Cebu institution that serves popular rustic food such as chicken or pork BBQ sticks (P72), *lechon kawali* (crispy pork; P179), sizzling *bangus* (milkfish; P169) and various soups. There's another branch in SM City Mall. Daily 10.30am–2pm & 6–9.45pm.

★La Maison Rose 371 Gorordo Ave ☏ 032 268 5411, ⓦ facebook.com/LaMaisonRoseCebu. Affectionately known as "the Pink Restaurant", this converted villa looks like the French embassy from the street, but is made up of a smart restaurant, outdoor patio and *La Vie Parisienne*, a patisserie and fine-food emporium. In the restaurant, dishes such as duck confit (P650) and escargots (P180) make it a culinary utopia for Francophiles, but with fresh-baked pastries (P25) and macarons (P50), the patisserie is worth a pit stop too. Daily 12–11pm.

Olio Crossroads Mall, Banilad ☏ 032 238 2391, ⓦ oliocebu.com. Highly rated, high-end fusion restaurant specializing in seafood and steaks, with a tempting but wallet-emptying wine list (P1100–4700). The 400g New York steak (P1600) is a carnivorous treat. Other crackers include herb-crusted rack of lamb with crispy potatoes (P1550), or for a lighter bite there's spinach and rocket salad (P750). Daily 11am–2pm & 6–11pm.

7

DRINKING AND NIGHTLIFE

Cebu, like its big sister Manila, is a city that never – or rarely – sleeps. You don't have to walk far in the centre to pass a pub, karaoke lounge or a music bar, although you'll want to choose your venue carefully. Many of the biggest clubs are to be found in **Mango Square** on General Maxilom Ave, though some are distinctively seedy; others change their name so often it can be hard to keep up with what's going on. While many of the most appealing places are at the **malls**, a more cosmopolitan drinking scene is emerging, with the epicentre around the trendy **Cebu IT Park** and **Crossroads Mall** in Banilad.

BARS

★Cebu Brewing Company Crossroads Mall, Banilad ☏ 063 998 845 2508, ⓦ cebubrewing.com. Craft beer lovers are in for a treat. With four draught brews on taps, dozens of bottles from around the world to sample and rotating ale specials, including drops flavoured with mango and coconut (P125), this pokey pub is hop heaven. Upstairs, you'll find *Qube Gallery* (Tues–Sat 10am–7pm), a dinky hub for southern Filipino art. Tues–Sat 4pm–midnight.

The Distillery Crossroads Mall ☎ 032 266 9064, ⓦ thedistillery.com.ph. One for real night owls, this connoisseur's drinking hole is set up like a liquor store, yet turns into a lively party spot with DJs and fresh-faced young waifs supping on single malts. Mon–Thurs & Sun 6pm–3am, Fri & Sat 6pm–4am.

Koa Tree House 55 Gorordo Ave ☎ 032 318 4853. Little more than a cluster of wooden tables, this open-fronted saloon offers cheap beers, regular live music and a weekend flea market. *Kukuk's Nest*, which is across the road, is a 24hr art-inspired bar-restaurant where you'll find more of the same. Mon & Sun 6pm–1am, Tues–Sat 6pm–2am.

Marshall's Irish Pub General Maxilom Ave ☎ 032 412 6418, ⓦ marshallsirishpub.com. A long-running favourite along the street from Mango Square, *Marshall's* has great happy hour deals (P50 beers 4–7pm) and live acoustic music every night. Daily 10am–3am.

Maya Crossroads Mall, Banilad ☎ 032 238 9522, ⓦ theabacagroup.com/maya. The place to whet your sombrero with an exhaustive tequila list (from P210), as well as blue agave tasting tours (P1100). There are also authentic Mexican dishes including burritos and fajitas (from P295) and energetic salsa classes (Wed at 8.30pm). Mon–Thurs & Sun 5pm–midnight, Fri & Sat 5pm–2am.

Our Place Pelaez St at Sanciangko St ☎ 032 416 8243, ⓦ ourplacecebu.com. *Our Place* remains a Cebu stalwart, straight from the pages of Graham Greene. A small upstairs bar is cooled by clunky ceiling fans, where expats swill San Miguel (P50) into the early hours and complain about the hardships of life in the tropics. Daily 7am–11pm.

Tonyo's Bar & Restaurant The Hangar, Salinas Drive. Big, boisterous, open-sided drinking hall with cheap beers such as San Miguel and Tanduay for P50, and *pulutan* (bar snacks, such as grilled pork belly) for P85. There's a big TV for sports, and live music from 9pm. Popular with young Filipinos and the Cebu IT Park crowd. Daily 24hr.

CLUBS

22nd Street Comedy Bar Mango Square ☎ 032 263 1728, ⓦ 22ndst.tripod.com. Styled on a New York basement club, this off-street showcase for stand-ups has live comics nightly. The weekly schedule also includes live bands and karaoke. Daily 8pm–3am.

Alchology Mango Square ☎ 0943 548 3923, ⓦ bit.ly/Alchology. Next to the huge *J.Ave* club, *Alchology* is the long-running heart of the slightly seedy Mango Square party district, with the best light show in the city and group VIP tables for a minimum of P3000. Fri & Sat 10pm–6am.

Liv Super Club City Time Square, Mandaue ☎ 032 406 8080, ⓦ livsuperclub.com. International DJs and *Coyote Ugly*-inspired bar dancers draw thousands from downtown to this warehouse club located out by Park Mall, about 4km northeast of SM City Shopping Mall. A strict dress code is enforced. Fri P200, Sat P300, free otherwise. Wed–Sat 8.30pm–6am.

SHOPPING

BOOKSHOPS

Fully Booked Level 2, The Terraces, Ayala Center ☎ 032 417 1400 ⓦ fullybookedonline.com. This branch of the country's best bookstore has a broad range of titles and also sells magazines and stationery. Mon–Thurs & Sun 10am–9pm, Fri & Sat, 10am–10pm.

National Book Store SM City Mall ☎ 032 231 5496; Ayala Center ☎ 032 231 4006; Mango Plaza ☎ 032 268 3055; ⓦ www.nationalbookstore.com. A great YA and kids' selection as well as plenty of bestsellers, staff picks and classics, plus stationery and writing supplies galore. Mon–Sat 9am–8pm, Sun 9am–7pm.

MALLS

Life revolves around the mall in Cebu, and aside from the big four below, Crossroads Mall and Banilad Town Center (BTC), both in Banilad, are worth checking out for their happening bar and dining scenes.

Ayala Center Cebu Business Park ☎ 032 516 3025, ⓦ ayalamallcebu.com. Opened in 1994, the Ayala Center still welcomes around 135,000 shoppers every weekend. It plays host to a huge selection of local and international stores, along with coffee shops, cinemas, dentists and internet cafés – and the excellent The Terraces dining complex. Daily 10am–9pm (later for The Terraces).

Robinson's Galleria Gen. Maxilom Ave at Sergio Osmena Blvd ☎ 032 231 5030, ⓦ robinsonsmalls.com. More than two hundred shops, a 3D cinema, open-air American-style food court and the largest flower-power guitar you're ever likely to see. Daily 10am–9pm.

SM City Juan Luna Ave ☎ 032 231 0557, ⓦ smsupermalls.com. Another megamall, this retail labyrinth has all the usual shops, movie theatres and services – plus a bowling alley – spread between the old Southern Wing and the newer Northern Wing. Another location at SM Seaside City, southwest of the city. Daily 10am–9pm.

SOUVENIRS

Besides the malls, there are also a half-dozen souvenir stalls inside the airport departure lounge. As well as Alegre on Mactan (see p.331), for handmade guitars and ukuleles, you could also try Borromeo St, a 10min walk south of Colon St.

Island Souvenirs P. Burgos St ☏ 032 236 5062, ⓦ theislandsgroup.com. A peso's throw from The Cross of Magellan, this downtown emporium sells Cebu-branded T-shirts, hats, bags and all sorts of fun-in-the-sun, Visayan-inspired goodies. Look for the bright-green "I Heart Cebu"

monogram outside. Daily 9am–6pm.

The Buzzz Cafe Robinson's Galleria ☏ 977 813 4396, ⓦ boholbeefarm.com. A first for Cebu, this fine food shop and café from the wildly popular Bohol farm-to-fork outfit showcases a variety of gourmet honeys, tropical fruit-flavoured jams, organic teas and honey wine. Daily 8.15am–5.15pm.

DIRECTORY

Banks and exchange There is no shortage of places to change currency, particularly along the main drag of President Osmeña Blvd, on Fuente Osmeña and in all shopping malls. The main banks are BDO, PNB and Allied. Beware the 24hr exchanges in the bar districts unless you really want to – rates are often substantially lower than elsewhere. Also try to use guarded indoor ATMs if you need to withdraw cash late at night – ATM muggings are not unheard of.

Cinemas Ayala Malls 360 in the Ayala Center (see opposite) has the most comfortable movie theatre in Cebu, and shows the latest movies in English daily.

Consulates A number of countries have consular offices in Cebu, among them the UK, at Villa Terrace, Greenhills Rd, Mandaue City (☏ 032 238 9055) and the US, *Waterfront Cebu City*, Salinas Drive, Lahug (☏ 032 231 1261), though these are open only part-time and don't offer a full consular service.

Emergencies ☏ 161.

Hospitals Among the best equipped are Cebu Doctors' University Hospital, President Osmeña Blvd (☏ 032 253 7511, ⓦ cduh.com.ph); Chong Hua Hospital, Don Mariano Cui St, just north of Fuente Osmeña (☏ 032 255 8000, ⓦ chonghua.com.ph); and Perpetual Succour Hospital on Gorordo Ave (☏ 032 233 8620, ⓦ perpetualsuccorhospital. com).

Immigration The Cebu Immigration District Office is on the Level 2 of J. Centre Mall on A.S. Fortuna St, Mandaue

(usually daily 8am–6.30pm; ☏ 032 345 6441). You can extend your 30-day visa to 59 days here in a few hours. There's also a sub-office on the ground floor of the Gaisano Mactan Island Mall Annex Building on Quezon Ave in Lapu-Lapu, Mactan Island (usually daily 8am–6.30pm; ☏ 032 495 2852).

Internet access Most malls have internet cafés, often on higher floors; Netopia is on level 4 of the Ayala Center. There are also net cafés in Mango Square on General Maxilom Ave. Most hotels, restaurants and coffee shops have free wi-fi.

Pharmacies There are large pharmacies in all malls, and you'll also find 24hr pharmacies that are often little more than holes in the wall, but carry a good stock of essentials. There's a big branch of Mercury drugstore at Fuente Osmeña, and a Watson's just round the corner on President Osmeña Blvd.

Police The main Cebu City Police Office is on Gorordo Ave (☏ 032 231 5802), while there is another handy branch south of Fuente Osmeña close to Cebu State College (☏ 032 253 5636). There's a branch of the tourist police unit opposite Cebu City Hall near Fort San Pedro (☏ 032 412 1838).

Post The main post office (Mon–Fri 8am–noon & 1–5pm; ☏ 032 416 3989, ⓦ phlpost.gov.ph) on Quezon Blvd, close to the port area at the back of Fort San Pedro, has a packing service. There's also another branch in the Capitol complex.

7

Mactan Island

The closest beaches to Cebu City are on **MACTAN ISLAND**, which is linked to the main island of Cebu by the Mandaue–Mactan Bridge and the Marcelo Fernan Bridge. Off the southern coast of Mactan and linked by two short bridges is **Cordova Island**, a relatively undeveloped slab of land with a couple of secluded, upmarket resorts on the beach. While the sands and scuba diving on these islands don't compare with Malapascua, for instance, they are easier to reach, and the many package-style resorts here (see p.380) offer plenty of watersports and day-trips to nearby islands.

Lapu-Lapu

On the island's northern shore, close to the Mandaue–Mactan Bridge, the small capital of **LAPU-LAPU** has a heaving central market, a mall, a post office and some small hotels, but not much for tourists. For many, an obligatory souvenir purchase is a handmade **guitar** from one of Mactan's world-famous Cebuano guitar factories (see p.331).

THE BATTLE OF MACTAN AND THE DEATH OF MAGELLAN

Everything seemed to be going well for Portuguese explorer **Ferdinand Magellan** when he made landfall in Samar early in 1521 and claimed the pagan Philippines for his adopted country, Spain, and the true religion, Catholicism. He stocked up on spices and sailed on, landing in Cebu. It was here that he befriended a native king, Raja Humabon and, flush with his conquest of the isles, promised to help him subdue an unruly vassal named **Lapu-Lapu**. Early on the morning of April 27, 1521, Magellan landed at Mactan and tried to coerce Lapu-Lapu into accepting Christianity. Lapu-Lapu declined and when Magellan continued to hector he angrily ordered an attack. As his men fled quickly to their ships, Magellan, resplendent in polished body armour, backed away towards safety, but was felled by a spear aimed at his unprotected foot. Lapu-Lapu's men quickly moved in for the kill. In the north of Mactan, at the Mactan Shrine, are two memorials to the battle: **Magellan's Marker** and **Lapu-Lapu's Monument** (an odd cross between King Neptune and Rambo, sculpted in bronze). Seventeen months later, on September 8, 1522, the last remaining ship in Magellan's original fleet sailed into Seville with eighteen survivors on board. After three years, and the loss of four ships and 219 lives, the first circumnavigation of the globe was complete.

7

The east coast

The beach on Mactan's **east coast** is not especially attractive and in some cases has been expensively dredged, groomed and landscaped to try to make it look like a tropical beach should, with the predictable result that it looks fake. Most of the clientele at the resorts are rich Filipinos, and package tourists from Hong Kong, Japan and South Korea.

ARRIVAL AND DEPARTURE   MACTAN ISLAND

By jeepney Mactan is a P15 ride from the terminal by Cebu City's SM City Mall on J. Luna Ave Extension, close to the *Radisson Blu Cebu*. In Lapu-Lapu, jeepneys stop near the small market square, where you can catch another onwards towards the beaches dotted along Mactan's east coast.

By taxi From the airport to anywhere on Mactan is a short journey that costs no more than P200 by taxi. Getting to Cordova takes a little longer and will cost up to P250.

INFORMATION AND ACTIVITIES

Scuba diving Simon Timmins (☎ 032 345 0071, ⌨ sidive. com) is an experienced instructor who offers very competitive rates for dives and PADI packages – Open Water costs from P13,500. He can also help to organize trips to swim with the whale sharks in Oslob (see box, p.341). Scotty's Dive Center, inside the plush *Shangri-La's Mactan*

Resort & Spa on Punta Engaño Rd (☎ 032 231 0288, ⌨ divescotty.com) is also highly recommended for dive courses and trips from Mactan.

Tours An island-hopping day-trip, bookable through most resorts, costs between P2000–3600.

ACCOMMODATION AND EATING

Lapu-Lapu has a handful of functional, affordable hotels with a/c and restaurants. On Mactan's **eastern shore** there are about twenty beachfront resorts, mostly overpriced mid-range resorts or top-of-the-line international affairs set up for the package crowd, but there are a couple of cheaper options in **Maribago**. While there's some good dining here, it's also expensive.

LAPU-LAPU

Bellavista Hotel Quezon Hwy, Lapu-Lapu City ☎ 032 340 7821, ⌨ thebellavista-hotel.com. The bright blue box of the *Bellavista* has sleek, modern rooms, with good amenities. There's a pool and travel desk, and room rates include breakfast and round-trip airport transfers. ⌨ **P2500**

Hotel Cesario Quezon Hwy, Lapu-Lapu City ☎ 032 340 0214. Mid-range hotel with a/c rooms, use of the rooftop pool at the *Bellavista* next door, and a buffet breakfast included in the rate. Free airport transfers are a bonus. ⌨ **P1400**

Manna STK Food House Mactan Shrine, Lapu-Lapu ☎ 032 340 6448. One of three waterfront point-and-cook seafood grills hidden behind the souvenir market at the Mactan Shrine, this stands out for its vast selection of shellfish and friendly service. Get the likes of meaty prawns (P650/kg) or grouper (P850/kg) grilled, sautéed in garlic, or fried. Daily 8am–10pm.

EAST COAST

Abaca Boutique Resort & Restaurant Punta Engaño Rd ☎ 032 495 3461, ⓦ abacaresort.com. It's hard not to fall In love with this jaw-dropping honeymooners' getaway on the northeast tip of Mactan. Villas are graced with an infinity pool and butler service, while the spa and Californian-inspired kitchen ensure that most guests rarely leave the compound. 🛜 **P15,900**

Plantation Bay Resort & Spa Marigondon ☎ 032 505 9800, ⓦ plantationbay.com. Home to one of the world's largest man-made saltwater lagoons, this colossal resort offers all manner of water's edge activities, including a comprehensive scuba programme. Rooms range from poolside villas to riverboat suites. It's usually packed with Chinese and Korean families. 🛜 **P11,800**

★ **Shangri-La's Mactan Island Resort** Punta Engaño Rd ☎ 032 231 0288, ⓦ shangri-la.com. The ultimate in Cebuano luxury, the Mactan *Shangri-La* is super-comfortable and has every amenity imaginable. There are five hundred rooms, eight restaurants and bars, and it has a speedboat, yacht, luxury sedan or helicopter to meet you at the airport. There are plenty of activities on offer, including scuba diving, windsurfing, banana-boat rides and, for relaxation, the renowned Chi Spa. 🛜 **P12,500**

WEST COAST

Lantaw Floating Native Restaurant Cordova ☎ 032 514 2959, ⓦ facebook.com/LantawFloating NativeRestaurant. Fresh fish and fantastic sunsets are the order of the day at this native Cebuano over-water restaurant anchored off the western coast. The breezy terrace attracts large parties and families, while its beer promos and piled seafood plates make it a messy affair. Dishes from P220. Daily 11am–11pm.

SHOPPING

Alegre Guitar Factory Pajac–Maribago Rd, Lapu-Lapu ☎ 032 340 4492. A visit to this famous guitar factory offers the chance to see instruments being made, as well as doing a little souvenir shopping. The cheapest steel-stringed acoustics (from P2800) are not that well constructed, but for serious enthusiasts there are top-quality models made with Indian rosewood or mango wood (P80,000). The factory is a P250–300 taxi ride from central Cebu. Daily 8am–6pm.

DIRECTORY

Banks There are multiple ATM branches across the island. **Hospital** The best hospital is the Mactan Doctor's Hospital (☎ 032 236 0000, ⓦ mactan.cduh.com.ph), near the airport in Basak.

Police In Lapu-Lapu, the police station (☎ 032 341 1311) is on Basak Maringondon Rd at the intersection with the Quezon National Highway.

Olango Island

Five kilometres east of Mactan Island, **Olango Island** supports the largest concentration of **migratory birds** in the country. Of the 97 species found here, about 48 – including egrets, sandpipers, terns and black-bellied plovers – use the island as a layover on their annual migration from breeding grounds in Siberia, northern China and Japan to Australia and New Zealand. The island is also home to about sixteen thousand resident native birds, which live mostly in the northern half; the southern half is made up of expanses of mudflats and mangroves – this is where you can find the rudimentary **Olango Island Wildlife Sanctuary** (daily 9am–5pm; P100; ☎ 0915 386 2314, ⓦ olangowildlifesanctuary .org). The reserve is at its best during peak migration months: September to November for the southbound migration and February to April northbound.

ARRIVAL AND TOURS   **OLANGO ISLAND**

Day-trips Most resorts on Mactan can organize an island-hopping day-trip to Olango (around P2500 including snorkelling equipment), though you could visit independently.

By boat There are regular bangkas (every 40min; P50) to Santa Rosa on Olango Island from the wharf near the *Mövenpick* at the far north of Mactan Island, or you can hire your own bangka from Maribago Wharf to the island and back for around P2000. From the small Santa Rosa wharf, it's a short 15min tricycle ride (P150) to the wildlife sanctuary.

ACCOMMODATION

Nalusuan Island Resort & Marine Sanctuary ☎ 032 516 6432, ⓦ nalusuanislandresort.com. One of the few places to stay close to the island, *Nalusuan* is set on an islet rising out of Olango's western coastal reef and has a choice

7

of fan rooms or stilted a/c cottages on the water. The open-air restaurant specializes in seafood caught on the doorstep and there are nightly campfire cookouts. There are kayaks and paddleboards available to explore the area, but better yet, the house reef is fabulous for snorkelling. Note that there's no electricity in the daytime, and wi-fi is limited to the restaurant. 🛜 **P3500**

Toledo and Balamban

On the west coast of Cebu, less than two hours from Cebu City by road, **TOLEDO** has several daily ferries to **San Carlos** in Negros (see below) – make sure that you get there before mid-afternoon, as Toledo isn't a place you'd choose to stay. You're better off heading twenty minutes north to the town of **BALAMBAN**, which has slightly more to offer with its clutch of deserted black-sand **beaches**.

ARRIVAL AND DEPARTURE   TOLEDO AND BALAMBAN

By bus Buses leave Cebu City's Southern bus terminal for Toledo from 5am daily (2hr 30min; P70). If you're heading from Cebu City to Negros, catch an early bus to Toledo to make sure you don't miss the last ferry.

By ferry Several ferries and ROROs, including fast E. B. Aznar Shipping (1hr; P225; ☎ 032 467 9447) and slow Lite Shipping (2hr; P180; ☎ 032 255 1721) run daily to San Carlos in Negros.

ACCOMMODATION AND EATING

The Ranch Resort Laguna Rd, Toledo ☎ 933 619 6690, 🌐 ranchresort.com.ph. Given the very few options in town, this powder-blue saloon-style Texan farmhouse is by far the best choice, even if it is about 8km south on the main westcoast highway. The highlights are its five pools and horse-riding opportunities. Wi-fi in lobby only. 🛜 **P1800**

Sailor's Cabin Abucayan, Balamban (look out for the big white and blue entrance) ☎ 032 465 2816, 🌐 sailors-cabin.com. Accommodation in this German-owned place comprises three types of apartments, with cable TV and private bathrooms. The menu at the restaurant (daily 6am–9pm) includes Wiener schnitzel (P139) and Hungarian goulash (P159), while the owner can organize trips to undiscovered areas of the rural west coast. 🛜 **P1000**

Bantayan Island

Just off the northwest coast of Cebu, quiet, bucolic and pancake-flat **BANTAYAN ISLAND** is the place to go for pleasant, low-key resorts, a smattering of sparkling sandy beaches and friendly open–armed welcomes. While Malapascua takes the lion's share of visitors this far north, that makes Bantayan all the quieter: visitors here are occupied by little more than sand, sunshine and seafood. The island was badly hit by Typhoon Yolanda in November 2013; many residents still live in temporary housing, but the island is on its way to making a full recovery. Most of the resorts and beaches are around the little town of **SANTA FE** on the southeast coast, which is where ferries from mainland Cebu arrive at the boat terminal.

● EATING	
Balikbayan	4
Blue Ice	3
Caffe del Mare	2
MJ Square	1

■ ACCOMMODATION	
Amihana Beach Cabanas	2
Bantayan Cottages	1
Budyong Beach Resort	4
Kota Beach Resort	5
Yooneek Beach Resort	3

Madridejos

0   2 kilometres

N

Atop Atop
Virgiv Island
Hilantagaan Island

Bantayan
NATIONAL ROAD

Santa Fe Pier

Sugar Beach

Hagnaya (Cebu)

Cadiz (Negros)

Hilotongan Island

Doong Island

BANTAYAN ISLAND

Bantayan Town

Along the west coast, the port town of **BANTAYAN** has no decent accommodation, but it's worth a quick visit. There's an elegant Spanish-style plaza on the south side of which stands the **Saints Peter and Paul Church**. The original structure was torched by marauding Moros in 1640, with eight hundred local folk taken captive and sold as slaves to Muslim chieftains in Mindanao. Every Easter during Holy Week, Bantayan holds solemn processions of decorated religious *carozzas* (carriages), each containing a life-sized statue representing the Passion and death of Jesus Christ. Thousands turn out to join in the processions, many setting up camp on the beaches because the resorts are full.

ARRIVAL AND DEPARTURE   BANTAYAN

By bus To reach Bantayan from Cebu City you can take a bus (7 daily; 3hr 30min) from the Northern bus terminal to the port town of Hagnaya, where you pay a P10 pier fee and P170 for the ferry crossing to Santa Fe (6–7 daily; 1hr).
By taxi Taxis from Cebu to Hagnaya can be negotiated for around P2000, and as little as P700 on the way back.

By bangka There are big bangkas to Bantayan from Cadiz on Negros. Coming from Malapascua, bangkas can be chartered for around P3000–3500, but only take this route in good weather. If you intend to stay in Santa Fe, you can get a tricycle from the pier to your accommodation, though some resorts can send a representative to collect you at the pier.

GETTING AROUND

By habal-habal The only local transport is a habal-habal, known on Bantayan as a *tricikad*.
By motorbike It's fun to hire a motorbike or moped

(P200/day) and tour the island yourself by the coastal road, though inspect the rental thoroughly beforehand.

INFORMATION

Money There's a PNB with ATM on Rizal Ave in Bantayan Town, but it's best to bring enough cash to last your stay. Currency can be changed at many resorts and at the

MoneyGram exchange office across from the Santo Niño Parish Church in Santa Fe.

ACCOMMODATION

Amihan Beach Cabanas East side of Santa Fe ☎032 438 9285, ⓦamihan-beach.com. Six lovely bamboo-and-nipa cabins spread around a sandy courtyard, a coconut shell's throw from hammock-hung palms and the clear sea. Rooms come with mosquito nets, cable TV, hot and cold showers, and there is a breezy restaurant. The only downside is the storm-damaged beachfront. 🛜 P2700
Bantayan Cottages Santa Fe ☎032 438 9358, ⓦbantayancottages.com. On the main road into town, not far from the centre, this cheap-and-cheerful option has cut-price backpacker rooms in the main house and a selection of veranda-fitted deluxe rooms with king-size beds, a/c and TVs around an orchid-scented garden (P1600). 🛜 P700
Budyong Beach Resort A short ride west of Santa Fe ☎032 438 9285, ⓦbudyong.byethost7.com. A good selection of simple beachfront fan and a/c nipa-thatched cottages (P800–2200) set around a well-groomed coconut

grove on Santa Fe's loveliest stretch of beach. There's a simple restaurant here, and the resort is within easy walking distance of the town centre. Wi-fi at reception only. 🛜 P800
Kota Beach Resort On the main Santa Fe beachfront ☎032 438 9042, ⓦkotabeachresort.com. Next door to *Budyong*, *Kota* has a range of tightly packed cottages set in regimented lines on a lovely stretch of beach. The superior cottages (P3400) are right on the sand, and for those on a budget, the economy and fan rooms at the back offer decent value. Wi-fi in the restaurant only. 🛜 P900
Yooneek Beach Resort A short ride west of Santa Fe ☎032 438 9124, ⓦyooneekbeachresort.com. Plonked on a quiet part of Sugar Beach, this laidback, nine-room complex has a variety of a/c and fan rooms, some with balconies, fridges and TVs. It's also home to one of the best backpacker bars on the beach. 🛜 P1590

EATING AND DRINKING

Bantayan has a way to go before it becomes a culinary destination, but there are a few places to try after a hard day at the beach. A great cheap breakfast option is to buy banana bread from the bakery by the main junction in Santa Fe and some fresh mangoes from the market across the road.

Balikbayan Santa Fe ☎0921 438 9216. Friendly restaurant in the backstreets of Santa Fe, with cosy pergolas dotted around a pretty garden. There's decent pizza and set menus of grilled seafood and rice (P148); the

house *halo-halo* is as tasty as you'll find anywhere in Cebu. Daily 7am–11pm.
Blue Ice On the main strip in Santa Fe. This popular Swedish-owned, bamboo-built tiki bar has MTV videos,

7

weekend live music and dancing in the evenings. There's an extensive selection of mains including chicken dishes, steaks, seafood and pizza. Mains around P295. Daily 8am–late.

Caffe del Mare On the main strip in Santa Fe ☎0942 572 2749. *Caffe del Mare* is straight from the just-like-Mama-made-it Italian cooking school, offering antipasti, home-made pastas, authentic pizzas and Milanese-flavoured pork. Locals love the generous happy hour too

(1–5pm; San Miguel P40). Daily 7am–midnight.

★**MJ Square** Off the main strip in Santa Fe ☎032 438 9013. This community collective of lively, pop-up style restaurants has a dozen or so choices with everything from Tex-Mex burritos and burgers to cupcakes, coffee and cheap Filipino eats. Two to try are the *Bantayan Burrito Company* and *Cupcake Island Bakery*. Daily 10am–11pm.

Malapascua Island

Eight kilometres off the northern tip of Cebu, the tiny island of **MALAPASCUA** is often erroneously touted as the next Boracay, largely due to **Bounty Beach**, a blindingly white stretch of sand on the island's south coast. Yet Malapascua is a world apart from its Western Visayan counterpart, and the islanders have no interest in seeing their paradise lost.

The island's trump card is its world-class **diving**, and it is also renowned for the chance to see thresher sharks congregate in shallow waters (see box below). The sting in the tail is that Malapascua was just emerging onto the main tourist stage when **Typhoon Yolanda** struck. Almost every roof on the island was destroyed, and most of the local population was left without shelter. Substantial private reparations and contributions have helped the island get its groove back and, in spite of recent challenges, the inhabitants of Malapascua remain some of the warmest people you'll meet. They're also renowned for their love of a party, especially during the annual fiesta from May 11–12 when the whole island gets into carnival mode.

Around the island

It's worth taking a stroll in the cool of the late afternoon to explore the island's glorious main beachfront. You'll also find, radiating from the jetty, a web of traffic-free sandy lanes home to beach bars, low-key seafood grills, and divers relaxing after the drama of the sea. For more of an adventure, you can **walk** the entire circumference of the island in a few hours, a journey which will take you through sleepy fishing villages lined with mangroves to remote white-sand beaches.

DIVING AT MALAPASCUA

Although some shallower dive sites around Malapascua were damaged by Yolanda, the major attraction – the distinctively tailed **thresher sharks** – remain in residence, and anyone staying more than a few days is almost guaranteed a sighting. The vortex of this activity is **Monad Shoal**, the only place in the world where the trident-tailed swimmers can be seen like clockwork before sunrise and just before sunset. At shallow depths of around 20m, they congregate on the sea plateau in huge numbers, using the seamount as a symbiotic cleaning station where fish remove (and eat) parasites from the sharks' skin. There are also plenty of wrecks in the vicinity, including the passenger ferry **Doña Marilyn**, which went down in a 1988 typhoon and is now home to scorpionfish, flamefish and stingrays. Dive companies collect a P150 marine conservation tax per day, and there is an additional charge of P50 to visit Monad Shoal.

DIVE OPERATORS

Divelink ☎032 541 6711, ⓦ divelinkcebu.com.
Evolution Diving Resort (see opposite).
Malapascua Exotic Island Dive and Beach Resort (see opposite).

Sea Explorers Philippines ☎0917 320 4158, ⓦ sea-explorers.com.
Thresher Shark Divers ☎0917 795 9433, ⓦ malapascua-diving.com.

Kalanggaman and Carnasa islands

Day-trip bangka hire costs from P4000 to either islet; group tours from P800/person

Whether you're diving or not, don't miss the opportunity for a day-trip to unwind on **Kalanggaman**, a beautiful, tiny islet that consists of no more than a spectacular narrow, arcing sandbar, a handful of windswept trees and some shaded picnic benches. Another full-frontal stunner in the area – two hours northeast of Malapascua by bangka – is **Carnasa Island**, a tropical paradise where you land at a picturesque bay fringed by palm trees.

ARRIVAL AND DEPARTURE
MALAPASCUA ISLAND

From Cebu Most visitors head from Cebu City's Northern bus terminal to Maya by Ceres Liner bus (3–4hr; P180, P200 a/c) or private taxi (P3500), and then take a bangka (hourly; P100) across to the island. The last boat to Maya is usually at 4pm, although boatmen may try to tell you it's earlier to get you to charter a bangka (P1500 depending on the boatman and your bargaining skills). When its low tide, you'll likely need to transfer to a smaller boat to get you to the shoreline (an additional P20 at each end).

From Bantayan You'll need to charter a bangka from Malapascua (2–3hr; P3000–3500); only undertake this trip if the weather is fair and set to stay that way.

From Leyte There is a daily boat at 7am from San Isidro to Maya (2hr; P300), returning at 10am. From the city of Bogo, one hour south, operator Super Shuttle Ferry runs a daily service to Palompon at 12pm (returning at 7.30am).

INFORMATION AND ACTIVITIES

Money There are no banks on Malapascua, so it's best to bring enough pesos with you. The closest ATM is in Bogo on the mainland.

Internet Most resorts have free wi-fi; note that there's a tiny internet café at the bangka terminal on Logon village beach.

Sunset cruises Sunset cruises involving swimming, snorkelling, and cliff jumping can be great fun (P1000/person); to arrange one, ask at your resort.

ACCOMMODATION

There are about a dozen **dive resorts** on Bounty Beach and a number of others dotted around the island. Budget rooms at the most popular book up fast in peak season. Bear in mind that **swimming pools** are illegal on the island, and even though many have been built, they are a major drain on the island's water resources; the best accommodation providers don't have them.

BOUNTY BEACH

★ **Evolution Diving Resort** Far eastern end of the beach ☎ 0917 631 2179, ⓦ evolution.com.ph. If only all dive resorts were like this. Run by two of the island's most experienced and passionate technical divers – David (Irish) and Matt (English) – this welcoming, sixteen-room hideaway is tucked away on the loveliest stretch of real estate on the island. Rooms are split between fabulous bungalows and newly constructed deluxe rooms further back from the beach, while the personable staff make sure that your A–Z of diving needs is taken care of. Wi-fi in bar area only. 📶 **P1900**

Malapascua Exotic Island Dive and Beach Resort Far eastern end of the beach ☎ 032 516 2990, ⓦ malapascua.net. One of the best-established resorts on the island, the motel-style *Exotic* escaped lightly from Yolanda, with only two rooms suffering damage. There's a huge range to choose from, including standard a/c to pricey beachfront deluxe rooms (P4600). Full board is available (P1350 extra) and it's Dutch-owned, which explains the in-house European bakery and Heineken on draft. Wi-fi in the restaurant only. 📶 **P2800**

Mike & Diose's Aabana Beach Resort Far eastern extreme end of the beach ☎ 0917 875 4736, ⓦ aabana .de. A collection of simple fan beach huts, plus tricked-out deluxe cottages with a/c, cable TV, DVD player, and fridge (P2150). It's tucked away in a garden, by some fishing boats and next door to *Evolution*. Management are as friendly as can be. Wi-fi doesn't reach the back rooms. 📶 **P650**

Ocean Vida Beach and Dive Resort Middle of Bounty Beach ☎ 0917 570 7249, ⓦ ocean-vida.com. Plush rooms right on the beach make Swiss-German-owned *Ocean Vida* a popular choice for both divers and sun-seekers. Prices are high (P4700–5200 for a sea view, including breakfast and beach towels), but then so is the quality of service and rooms, and the restaurant-bar is one of the liveliest on the strip. 📶 **P3400**

AROUND THE ISLAND

Buena Vida Resort & Spa On the lane behind Bounty Beach ☎ 915 283 0258 ⓦ buenavida-malapascua.com. For those seeking a respite from early-morning dives and late-night beach bars, this perfumed oasis, hidden in the

7

7

riddle of lanes off the beach, is a rare blissed-out sanctuary. There are twelve fabulous en-suite garden rooms, all with private wooden terraces, hammocks and chill-out beanbags. For a tranquil treat, checkout the on-site Vida Spa, the only one on the island (massages from P850). Run by the same team behind *Ocean Vida*. ☎ P3900

Hiltey's Hideout Homes On the lane behind Bounty Beach ☎ 0918 287 0999, ⓦ hilteyshideout.com. Cheap, centrally located accommodation run by affable German Volker Hiltebrandt. Block-built around a garden, the fan and a/c rooms are simple affairs with bamboo furniture, but what keeps it packed is the fact that its in striking distance of the beach. Long-term discounts are available (from P800 a night), making it popular with backpackers completing dive courses. ☎ P1300

Tepanee Beach Resort Logon Beach ☎ 0917 302 2495, ⓦ tepanee.com. On a lovely headland just west of Bounty Beach, *Tepanee's* Italian owners have glamorized Logon Beach, causing locals to nickname the area the "Italian Quarter". A/c ocean-view cottages and rooms are decorated with bamboo furniture and have queen-size beds. This is the place to come for a zoned-out beach holiday. ☎ P2300

★**Villa Sandra** 200m east of the bangka pier ☎ 926 993 8262, ⓦ facebook/VillaSandraMalapascua. A rambling place atop the only hill in town, this backpacker hideaway is owned by Jonjon, a reggae-loving Filipino who knows a thing or two about distilling the perfect chill-out vibe for travellers. Rooms vary from six-bed dorms with personal fans (P350) to thatched bungalows (P800); if you want to go really cheap, sling up a hammock (P200). Also worth a visit for its bargain vegetarian food. ☎ P350

White Sand Bungalows Logon Beach ☎ 032 318 8666, ⓦ whitesand.dk. Overlooking the boat landing, this low-key collection of six fan nipa huts is as simple as Malapascua gets. The balconies come draped with hammocks and out front, on a raised wooden platform, is a Thai restaurant, *Aroi Mak* (seafood from P300). ☎ P1200

EATING AND DRINKING

Amihan Logon Beach ☎ 0977 817 8390, ⓦ amihanrestaurant.com. Next door to island favourite *Angelina's*, this Italian-run joint is part of *Tepanee Beach Resort* (see above) and comes with a fabulous crow's-nest view above the beach line of foaming surf. Lunch is a steal (P300 for pizza or pasta with a beer or soft drink) while dinner is a more refined affair. Daily 7am–10pm.

★**Angelina** Logon Beach ☎ 0915 340 4906. Easily the best (and most expensive) place to eat on the island, *Angelina's* serves top-quality Italian dishes on gingham tablecloths looking out over pretty Logon Beach. Top dishes include beef or fish carpaccio (P355) and *tartar di tonno* (P365), but the wood-fire pizza (from P320) and pasta dishes are also excellent. Daily 8am–10pm.

Ging Ging's In the maze of lanes behind Bounty Beach. Long-running backpacker favourite *Ging Ging's* serves Filipino food in a hard-to-find dining room that is often packed with diners on a shoestring. The menu cuts a fine balance between mains for less than P100 (soup P20, noodles from P35), plus pricier seafood gems like shrimp and crab-fried rice (P150–350). Daily 7am–10pm.

Kokoy's Maldito Logon Beach. The island's prime sunset beach bar, barn-like *Maldito's* has pool tables, table football, happy hours, an outdoor screen for live sports, and plenty of other reasons to keep you socializing later than planned. Drinks are a bargain at P50 for beers, or P40 for rum. Daily 7am–midnight.

The Camotes Islands

About 30km northeast of Cebu City, the friendly, peaceful **CAMOTES ISLANDS** are named after camotes, the sweet potatoes which thrive on the islands' rocky topsoil cover. Known as the "lost horizon of the south", the island group once sheltered Magellan's fleet; it now serves as a refuge for travellers, thanks to a reliable ferry route from Cebu and Danao. The two principal islands, **Pacijan** and **Poro**, are linked by a mangrove-shaded causeway. While those two islands are seeing increasing visitors, the third, **Ponson**, is as off-the-track as this part of the country gets. Villages have little in the way of modern services, and residents experience daily power outages.

Pacijan

The main town on Pacijan is **SAN FRANCISCO**, on the eastern edge of the island, where the causeway runs across to Poro. "San Fran" has a pretty 150-year-old church, but little else to detain you; most of the resorts are scattered around the powdery sands of the northwest and along Santiago Bay to the south.

Beaches

A ten-minute habal-habal ride from **Consuelo**, on Pacijan's west coast (where boats arrive), **Himensulan Beach** is a short, attractive stretch of oceanfront with a handful of resorts. Pacijan's widest stretch of sand is **Santiago Beach**, another ten minutes around the toe of the island, which also has a selection of hotels to choose from. In the northwest of the island, low-key **Bakhaw Beach** (also referred to as Borromeo Beach) is the closest the Camotes gets to the sugar-white-sand of Boracay.

Lake Danao and around

Greenlake Park P20; boat rides P100/person; kayak rental P50/hour

To get the lay of the land, make for the **Arquis Viewing Deck** in the heart of the island. From here you can see guitar-shaped **Lake Danao**, an extensive body of murky water, and the site of the privately owned **Greenlake Park** where you can take *sakanaw* (local boat) trips or a kayak out to the mangroves, then have lunch in one of the simple shorefront restaurants.

Tulang

P20/person, or P300–500 for private boat

North of Lake Danao lies **Tulang**, a picturesque islet lapped by turquoise waters, which has good snorkelling and diving and is accessible by a short bangka ride from Tulang Daka Beach.

Poro

Across the causeway on the more rugged Poro, **Buho Rock Resort** (P20) is stretching the use of the word resort (there are no rooms or places to eat), but it does have a lovely swimming spot, slides and six-metre-high rock platforms where you can dive into the sea. At the eastern edge of the island near MacArthur, you can swim in a series of subterranean sea caves at **Bukilat** (P10), while easier swimming awaits at **Busay Falls** just a short walk from Tudela on the south coast.

Ponson

Take a ferry from Tudela on Poro's south coast (2hr), or a bangka from Puerto Bello on Poro's northeast coast to Kawit (20min; P50)

To really get away from it all, make for the easternmost and smallest of the Camotes, **Ponson**, where there are several quiet, attractive white-sand beaches. Bangkas arrive at the main settlement of Kawit. You're likely to attract attention on Ponson, as few travellers make it this far; the interest is genuine – the locals will simply want to find out where you're from.

ARRIVAL AND DEPARTURE · THE CAMOTES ISLANDS

By boat The Camotes are accessible by fast ferry from Cebu City with OceanJet (daily at 6am & 3pm; 1hr 30min; P500). The reliable Jomalia Shipping (☎ 032 346 0421) connects Danao to Consuelo on Pacijan (6–7 daily; 2hr; P200), while Super Shuttle Ferry has a service from Poro to Danao daily at 1pm (returning at 5pm; 3hr; P300). Danao is 1hr from Cebu City's northern terminal by bus; a taxi costs P800–1000. There's a P20 terminal fee to leave Danao. Jomalia Shipping also connects Tudela (on Poro) and Pilar (on Ponson) with Ormoc on Leyte (daily 5.30am & 7.30am, returning at 3pm & 5pm; 1–2hr 30min). This route is subject to change, so check ahead of any planned travel.

Money There's a post office at the town hall in Poro and a DBP Bank with an ATM, but this doesn't accept foreign cards or exchange, so bring enough cash to last.

GETTING AROUND

By motorbike Hiring a motorbike is the easiest way to get around; most resorts can rent one for around P400–500 per day.

By habal-habal Short trips cost P50. From the Consuelo pier on Pacijan to San Francisco costs P100, and a full-day island tour is P1000.

ACCOMMODATION

The Camotes' resorts are rustic and low-key affairs, so there is little in the way of **wi-fi**; those that do have it – or, at least, say they do – are prone to power blackouts and patchy connections.

DANAO

Danao Coco Palms Resort 2km south of the port ☎ 02 406 2921, ⓦ facebook.com/DanaococoPalmsResort. If you're stuck in Danao for the night, the cottages at this popular pool resort aren't a bad place to spend the night. Prices are higher at the weekends (P500). **P350**

PACIJAN

Bellavistamare B&B Santiago Beach ☎ 032 318 0804, ⓦ facebook.com/BvmareCamotes. This clean, budget option enjoys a good location looking out over the broad expanse of Santiago Beach. There's a choice of fan or a/c doubles (P1450) and family rooms, plus you can hire snorkelling gear (P300/day). **P950**

Keshe Beach Resort Bakhaw Beach ☎ 0929 892 5792. Ideal for those seeking real isolation, *Keshe* has just three simple nipa huts on one of the island's most alluring beaches. There's a half-hearted café which can turn out basic dishes, or guests are free to cook for themselves. If you stay here, it's a good idea to hire a motorbike to get around. **P1500**

Mangodlong Rock Resort Heminsulan Beach ☎ 032 328 0500, ⓦ camotesislandph.com. The most upmarket choice on the Camotes, *Mangodlong Rock* has a range of clean, comfortable beachfront units with cable TV set around a large oceanfront garden and pool. **P2200**

Santiago Bay Garden and Beach Resort Santiago Beach ☎ 032 345 8599 ⓦ camotesislandph.com. Owned by the same team behind the *Mangodlong Rock Resort*, this hotel has a huge choice of room types, all set on a prime slice of hillside overlooking pretty Santiago Beach. The villas (P2500) and bungalows (P3000) are the best value, but the fan rooms offer a budget alternative and full use of the resort's facilities, which include two pools. Free wi-fi in the restaurant only. 🛜 **P1000**

PORO

Flying Fish Resort 5km east of Esperanza ☎ 0908 876 5427 ⓦ camotesflyingfishresort.com. Snorkelling – and the off-beach coral shelf – is the chief draw at this very isolated resort on the north of the island. The reef was badly damaged by Yolanda, but it's still a great place to hang out for a few days. Seafront a/c cottages include breakfast (P2200), but there is no wi-fi and power can be hit and miss. **P1000**

My Little Island Hotel Esperanza ☎ 032 267 6539 ⓦ mylittleislandhotel.com. If you don't mind being away from the beach, you'll find some of the best-value rooms on the island at this quiet, clean, business hotel. There's a restaurant and swimming pool, and the reception staff are as helpful as they come. If you're feeling particularly

---

DIVING AT MOALBOAL

Pescador Island, thirty minutes by bangka from Panagsama, is one of the best dive sites in the country; it's surrounded by a terrific reef that teems with marine life, and is renowned for its swirling **sardine shoals**. Barely 100m long, the island is the pinnacle of a submarine mountain reaching just 6m above sea level and ending in a flat surface, making it look from a distance like a floating disc. The most impressive of the underwater formations is the **Cathedral**, a funnel of rock that is open at the top end and can be penetrated by divers. Pelagic fish are sometimes seen in the area, including reef sharks and hammerheads, while at lesser depths on the reef there are Moorish idols, sweetlips, fire gobies and batfish. There are at least ten other dive sites around Panagsama, including the gentle Balay Reef, Ronda Bay Marine Park, Airplane Wreck (which was sunk by Savedra Dive Center) and Sunken Island (an advanced site).

Arranging diving trips is easy, with a **dozen operators** at Panagsama Beach. Dives typically cost P1200/1900 for a boat dive, with or without equipment.

DIVE OPERATORS

Blue Abyss Dive Shop South end of Panagsama Beach ☎ 032 474 3036, ⓦ blueabyssdiving.com.

Freediving Philippines North end of Panagsama Beach ☎ 0928 263 4646, ⓦ freediving-philippines.com. For something a little different, try a free-diving course at this outfit. The aim is to train guests how to hold their breath longer and dive deeper unassisted.

Prices start at US$125/day.

Quo Vadis Dive Resort (see p.340).

Savedra Dive Center North end of Panagsama Beach ☎ 032 474 3132, ⓦ savedra.com.

Seaquest Dive Center Beside Panagsama Beach northern junction ☎ 032 232 6010, ⓦ seaquestdivecenter.com.

exravagant, splurge on the penthouse suite with custom bed, kitchen, living room, and rose-petal-filled jacuzzi (P6300). 📶 **P1800**

EATING

Pito's Sutokil Santiago Beach, Pacijan. Laidback and popular little beach café serving breakfasts (P65–95), simple meals (P90–110) and seafood (P300) right on the sand. *Nena's Bar & Grill* next door serves similar dishes. Daily 5am–10pm.

Moalboal and around

Three hours by road and 89km from Cebu City, on the southwestern frontier of Cebu Island, lies the sleepy inland town of **MOALBOAL**, jumping-off point for the nearby resorts of **Panagsama Beach**, the boozy hangout for travellers and scuba divers chasing the **sardine run** (see box opposite). Sun-worshippers looking for a Boracay-style sandy beach will be disappointed – there isn't one: the shoreline is rocky in places and not generally suitable for recreational swimming. Nonetheless, Panagsama's village makes up for this in other ways, with a great range of accommodation, marvellous sunset views over distant Negros and good discounts on diving and rooms. Sunbathing by resort pools, diving and drinking take centre stage, and there's little else to do in town. If baking on the sand is top of your list, head 8km north to **White Beach**, an attractive strip with several far quieter mid-range resorts. Note that – confusingly – the whole area around Panagsama is often referred to as Moalboal.

Away from the coast, the jagged limestone peaks and lush river valleys of Cebu's central mountains offer white-knuckle canyoning, hiking, kayaking, mountain biking and horseriding all within easy reach of Panagsama.

White Beach (8km)

SeaQuest Dive Center Ven'z Kitchen @

ATM

Freediving Philippines

Cyan Adventures

Savedra Dive Center

ACCOMMODATION
Chief Mau	1
Love's Beach & Dive Resort	6
Maya's Native Garden	3
Moalboal Backpacker Lodge	2
Quo Vadis Beach Resort	5
Tipolo Beach Resort	4

DRINKING AND NIGHTLIFE
Chili Bar	1
Pacitas Disco Bar	2

EATING
The French Coffee Shop	1
Lantaw	3
The Last Filling Station	4
The Pleasure Principal	2

Planet Action Adventure

Blue Abyss Dive Shop

0   100
metres

PANAGSAMA BEACH

N

Kawasan Falls

Badian • P10 • P30 by southbound bus, P400 return trip by tricycle; it's a 20min walk from the main road to the falls

With such a spellbinding oceanfront in Panagsama Beach, it may come as a surprise to learn that **Kawasan Falls** is the most popular place to swim in Moalboal, even if it is 17km to the south. Made up of a series of cascades – some as high as 20m – this jungle-fringed waterfall is a great place for a taster of Cebu's interior.

ARRIVAL AND DEPARTURE

MOALBOAL AND AROUND

By bus A number of bus companies, including Ceres Liner (⊙ 032 345 8650), run regular services to Moalboal town from Cebu City's Southern bus terminal (3hr; P160), but make sure that the driver knows where you want to get off,

as most buses continue beyond Moalboal. Moalboal proper is on the road that follows the coast; however, Panagsama Beach and White Beach are a P100/P150 tricycle ride (respectively) from the main road where buses drop

SECURITY IN SOUTHERN CEBU

At the time of writing, several governments advised against all but essential travel to southern Cebu, including the municipalities of Dalaguete, Badian, Santander and Sumilon Island, due to the threat of terrorism. Anticipating kidnapping threats to foreign visitors and attacks by terrorist groups, the US Embassy issued a warning in November 2016. Soon after, the UK and Canadian Embassies followed suit. This may be a short-term warning, and it has so far not significantly affected tourist numbers. However, if planning to travel here, check the latest government advice ahead of time, and use your common sense.

passengers. Heading south for Lilo-An and Bato, for onward ferries to Negros and Dumaguete, there are regular Ceres Liner buses (1hr 30min; P80), or you can arrange a van through one of the resorts (P1500–2000).

By taxi A quicker option from Cebu City than the public bus is to negotiate a rate with a taxi driver – P2000 is a reasonable price.

INFORMATION AND ACTIVITIES

Money Moalboal has a number of ATMs which accept foreign cards.

Cooking classes Ven'z Kitchen in Panagsama (P1300/person, P2000/two people; ☏ 032 474 3981, ⓦ facebook. com/VenzKitchen) is a dinky cooking school offering a great hands-on introduction to the hybrid Spanish-Asian cuisine of the Philippines. Tutors are super-friendly Ven and Venz; they'll guide you around the local market to select ingredients before returning to the kitchen to show you how to make dishes such as pork adobo and *biko*, a gooey desert made with sticky rice, brown sugar and coconut milk. Great fun.

Outdoor activities To get away from the dive scene and explore the wild hinterlands of western Cebu, head for Planet Action Adventure (☏ 0917 583 0062, ⓦ action-philippines.com) at the *Tipolo Beach Resort* (see p.340). Jochen and Jinky can organize caving, trekking, canyoning and mountain-biking tours, with most day-trips starting at P3000. Also highly recommended for jungle tours is Cyan Adventures (☏ 032 474 3400, ⓦ cyan.ph), which has an office beside *The French Coffee Shop* (see opposite).

ACCOMMODATION

PANAGSAMA BEACH

Chief Mau 50m inland from the beach path's north end ☏ 0942 742 4535, ⓦ facebook.com/ChiefMau Moalboal. This newcomer knows how to keep budget backpackers' happy. Set around a sociable bar terrace with a driftwood shack vibe, you'll find both fan and a/c six- and eight-bed dorms, a handful of privates (P800 fan, P1500 a/c), plus board games and weekly Sat beer pong. You can't beat the banana pancakes, either. ⓦ **P350**

Love's Beach & Dive Resort A 5min walk from Quo Vadis ☏ 032 474 3086, ⓦ lovesbeachresort.com. Attractive and well-cared-for resort on a quiet section of coast. There's a wide variety of fan and a/c (P2800) rooms to choose from, a decent pool, free wi-fi in the public areas, and a lovely restaurant looking out to Pescador Island. Breakfast included. ⓦ **P1700**

Maya's Native Garden Opposite Tipolo Beach Resort ☏ 032 474 3053, ⓦ mayasnativegarden.com. You won't find a more exotic setting in Moalboal. With five thatched, stilted native huts, centred around a rough-and-ready garden (look out for hummingbirds), *Maya's* excels, with clean, affordable rooms and friendly service. For local craft beers (P150) and Mexican food, prop up on a stool at the restaurant-bar out the front. ⓦ **P800**

Moalboal Backpacker Lodge North end of the beach path ☏ 0917 751 8902, ⓦ moalboal-backpackerlodge .com. One of the cheapest places to stay, this buzzy backpacker hangout has three very simple mixed dorms (P300) and four private rooms and cottages, some of which have their own bathroom (P950). Pride of place in the lobby is an upcycled truck-turned-breakfast-bar. ⓦ **P300**

Quo Vadis Dive Resort At the beach path's southern end ☏ 032 474 3068, ⓦ quovadisresort.com. Attractive place, set in coastal gardens, with a relaxed poolside atmosphere. Economy rooms are in a block at the back, while stylishly decorated a/c nipa huts and cottages are closer to the front (P2950). There's also a bar-restaurant looking straight out to sea, and a great dive shop on-site. ⓦ **P1780**

Tipolo Beach Resort South of the centre ☏ 0917 583 0062, ⓦ tipoloresort.com. Lovely little seaside resort owned by the friendly folk behind Planet Action Adventure and *The Last Filling Station*. A/c rooms look out onto an attractive garden, with the sea beyond, and are tastefully furnished in bamboo, with tiled floors, hot showers and mini-bars. ⓦ **P1500**

WHITE BEACH

Blue Orchid At the beach's northern end ☏ 0929 273 1128, ⓦ blueorchidresort.com. Beautifully isolated

SWIMMING WITH WHALE SHARKS AT OSLOB

Once a sleepy little town, **Oslob**, at the southern tip of Cebu, has become famous for the near-guaranteed chance to swim with **whale sharks** off the coast of Tan-awan, a barangay of Oslob. Marine biologists raise **ethical questions** about the adverse effects of human–whale shark interaction and doubt whether the Oslob population can even be considered wild anymore, but while the opportunity to swim with the animals remains, tourists flock here on a daily basis. Visitors are given a mandatory orientation, and those who plan to swim with the gentle giants are required not to wear sunscreen, not to use flash photography, and not to get closer than 5m to the whale sharks. Unfortunately, these rules are often flaunted the moment a shark is sighted from the boat.

The most painless way to arrange a visit is to book through **Oslob Whale Sharks** (☎ 0925 548 8687 ⓦ oslobwhalesharks.com; from P2650/person for a group of four), or a dive shop in Cebu, Moalboal, Panglao (in Bohol) or Dauin (on Negros). Tours from Cebu leave early morning and head first for the whale sharks, then stop for lunch before heading back to the city. It's far cheaper to arrive independently by Ceres Liner bus from Cebu (3–4hr) and then organize the trip in Tan-awan. A thirty-minute boat ride (the maximum duration) costs P600 per person, or P1200 for snorkelling. Given the large number of visitors, a morning visit is recommended.

ACCOMMODATION

Casa Bonita Tan-awan ☎ 032 515 4010, ⓦ oslobwhalesharks.com. Good all-rounder with simple a/c rooms with shared or en-suite bathrooms (P700–1500) and conveniently located within walking distance of Tan-awan pier. Book via Oslob Whale Sharks. Dorms <u>350</u>
Sharky Hostel Oslob Tan-awan ☎ 0923 151 4909.

With a choice of dirt-cheap eight- or ten-bed mixed dorms, this spartan guesthouse has little more than an outdoor terrace and travel desk to recommend it. But what it lacks in character, it makes up for with a stellar location. Stay here and you'll be one of the first out on the boat in the morning – the dock is 50m away. <u>P350</u>

---

property at the end of the road with a landscaped garden, pool, dive school, well-designed rooms, massage pavilions and nose-to-nose views of Negros across the Tañon Strait. The resort is showing signs of age, but remains a good choice for peace and quiet. Wi-fi in the restaurant and pool areas only. 🛜 <u>P3000</u>
Dolphin House Southern end of the beach ☎ 032 358 5419, ⓦ moalboal.net. Long considered the most sophisticated place to stay on White Beach, this dive and spa resort is pricey (deluxe bungalows and suites start at P6000), but has a lovely pool and a very professional on-site diving school. Note that the shoreline is rocky

here. 🛜 <u>P3400</u>
★ **Hale Manna** Next to Blue Orchid ☎ 032 316 2603, ⓦ halemanna.com. If there's a more relaxing place in Cebu, we've yet to find it. Overlooking a landscaped tropical garden with yucca huts, pool and an unbeatable strip of white beach out front, this former family home has been turned into a beautifully decorated Cebuano-meets-Hawaiian lodge that celebrates the best of both heritages. The owner founded Cebu's *Handuraw Pizza* chain, so it's little surprise that the restaurant serves fantastic thin-crust pizzas (P348). <u>P3300</u>

EATING

PANAGSAMA BEACH

The French Coffee Shop North end of the beach path ☎ 0906 353 4315. This friendly place offers freshly brewed, bottomless coffee (P80–120), croissants and crêpes (P220) and great breakfasts (try the Parisienne, P250), as well as daily specials. Free wi-fi. Daily 6am–10pm.
Lantaw Opposite Chili Bar ☎ 0915 278 5388. Hidden from the beach path, above the Neptune Diving Shop, this bamboo hut kitchen has mastered the tricky art of Indian, Indonesian and Thai cuisines. Come for deliciously zingy curries, stay for the epic sea views. Mains from P200. Daily 7am–10pm.

The Last Filling Station Tipolo Beach Resort ☎ 0917 583 0062, ⓦ tipoloresort.com. Right at the heart of the Moalboal scene, this laidback place rustles up tasty international dishes and top-notch wood-fired pizzas (P275), as well as freshly baked bread and heaped breakfasts (P195). Free wi-fi. Daily 6.30am–10pm.
★ **The Pleasure Principal** North end of the beach path ☎ 032 474 3988. Basque-style fish, Arabic-spiced pizzas, Indian curries and Godzilla-sized shellfish (P200–600) are the speciality at this deservedly popular jack-of-all-trades fusion restaurant on the main strip. Daily 7am–10pm.

7

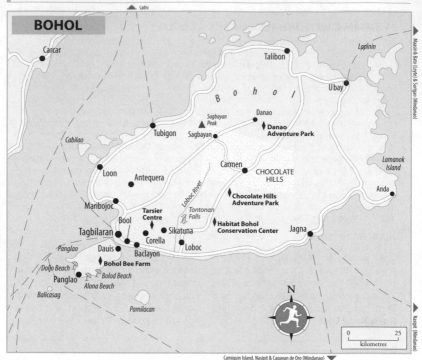

DRINKING AND NIGHTLIFE

PANAGSAMA BEACH

Chili Bar Midway along the beach path ☎ 0928 503 3413. In spite of legendary Swedish owner Lars's passing, this waterfront bar remains resolutely popular with divers ("get out of that wet suit and into a dry martini"). Great sea views, two pool tables and cut-price beers to the last man or woman standing. Daily 9am–late.

Pacitas Disco Bar Just north of Tipolo Beach Resort. An empty waterfront garage six days a week, *Pacitas* comes alive on Sat nights, when it functions as the biggest disco in the area, attracting a healthy crowd of locals and boozed-up travellers. Cover charge P50, including one drink. Sat 9pm–3am.

Bohol

BOHOL, a two-hour boat ride south of Cebu, is an attractive little island where life today is pastoral and quiet. The only sign of heavy tourist activity is on the beautiful beaches of **Panglao**, a magnet for scuba divers and sun-worshippers, which is close to the utilitarian port capital of **Tagbilaran**. Most visitors only leave the beach for a day-tour taking in Bohol's most famous attractions: the postcard-perfect **Chocolate Hills**, a glimpse of the world's smallest primate, the endangered **tarsier**, lunch on the **Loboc River** and a visit to the **Blood Compact** site, memorial to Bohol's violent past. Those with more time can be rewarded by trips to other parts of the province, including the adventure centre at **Danao**, the attractive island of **Pamilacan** and the forgotten-by-time beaches of **Anda**.

Bohol is also renowned for its wonderfully creaky Spanish churches – many of them built with coral, which can be found all over the island – though several were damaged during the October 2013 quake (see box opposite). May is **fiesta** month on Bohol, with island-wide celebrations including barangay festivals, beauty pageants, street dancing and solemn religious processions. Another highlight is the annual Bohol Day on July 22.

OCTOBER 15, 2013 QUAKE

On October 15, 2013, Bohol was shaken up by a magnitude 7.2 earthquake, which struck the whole island. The quake did damage as far away as Cebu City. On Bohol, more than two hundred people died and thousands of homes and buildings were destroyed (including the Chocolate Hills Complex and some of the island's beloved Spanish-era churches). While houses and modern buildings have been reconstructed, and tourist sights have returned to normal, many of the Spanish churches remain covered by scaffolding, and for now their future remains unknown.

ARRIVAL AND DEPARTURE   BOHOL

By plane There's an airport in Tagbilaran (see below), but Panglao Island International Airport, scheduled to open late 2017, also known as New Bohol International Airport, is intended to be the new gateway to Bohol.

By boat Tagbilaran is Bohol's principal port (see below),

though there are services from Jagna (see p.351), Tubigon and Ubay (see p.350). Starcraft also operates fast ferries to Cebu from Jetafe (3 daily; 1hr), in the northwest, and VG Shipping Lines operates a slow ferry from Talibon (2 daily; 4hr), in the north.

Tagbilaran

There are plenty of hotels and lodges in **TAGBILARAN**, the hectic port capital of Bohol, but with so many beaches and sights nearby, there's no real reason to stay here. From Tagbilaran, you can be on Panglao Island in less than twenty minutes; even the Chocolate Hills, hidden in the hinterlands, are less than an hour away by road.

Aside from the **museum**, the only sight in Tagbilaran itself is the **Cathedral**, opposite the plaza in Sarmiento Street, a nineteenth-century hulk standing on the site of an original that was destroyed by fire in 1789. Located on the edge of town is **Island City Mall**, which is packed full of shops, cafés and restaurants. The **Tagbilaran City Fiesta** takes place on May 1.

National Museum

Plaza Rizal • Daily 8am–5pm • Free

Set in the former home of Carlos Garcia (the fourth President of the Philippine Republic), the **National Museum** isn't worth a special trip, but if you have some time to kill before catching a ferry or bus, the presidential memorabilia and anthropological collection of shells will help pass half an hour.

ARRIVAL AND DEPARTURE
TAGBILARAN

By plane Air Asia, Cebu Pacific and PAL have flights to Tagbilaran from Manila (1hr 15min). The airport lies less than 2km outside Tagbilaran; tricycles into town cost P70, and taxis are only a little more on the meter.

By boat The ferry pier in Tagbilaran is off Gallares St, a 1km tricycle ride from the city centre. Taxis and vans for hire wait like hawks to meet passengers arriving on ferries. The Cebu–Tagbilaran route is operated by several fast ferry companies (2hr; P400–1000) including Oceanjet (12 daily; P400 normal, P500 a/c, P1000 business) and SuperCat (3 daily). Other operators such as Cokaliong (1 weekly), F.J. Palacio Lines (3 weekly), Lite Shipping (2–3 daily) and Trans-Asia Shipping Lines (1 weekly) also have cheaper

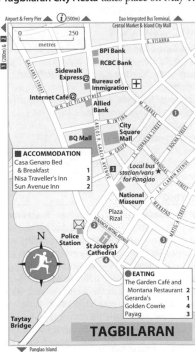

TAGBILARAN

slower services (4–5hr; P195) on this route. Bear in mind that the Cebu Passenger Terminal has airport-style security and charges a P25 terminal fee, so plan to arrive at least 30min in advance.

Destinations Argao (2 daily; 2hr), Cagayan de Oro (3 weekly; 10hr), Cebu City (hourly; 2–5hr); Larena, Siquijor (2 daily; 3hr 30min), via Dumaguete (2 daily; 2hr).

By bus All bus journeys around the island start at Dao Integrated Terminal, near Island City Mall and the Central Market, 10min outside Tagbilaran by jeepney or tricycle. Buses leave here (every 30min–1hr) for all destinations both clockwise and anticlockwise around the main coastal road, as well as along the cross-island road via Carmen and the Chocolate Hills. For Alona Beach, the most convenient buses leave from a scrap of waste-ground at the corner of Hontanosas and F. Rocha streets.

Destinations Anda (2hr 30min); Baclayon (20min); Bool (10min); Carmen (1hr 30min); Jagna (1hr 30min); Tubigon (1hr 30min); Ubay (4hr).

By taxi, van and tricycle Travel agents and most hotels in Tagbilaran and Panglao can arrange car or van hire, but the cheapest way is to negotiate directly with a taxi, which should cost P2000–3000/day, depending on your destination. If you're heading for Panglao, it's not hard to find a taxi, van or tricycle at the airport or pier to whisk you across the bridge and out to the beaches. If you negotiate a little, you won't pay more than P500 for a taxi to Alona, or P250 for a tricycle.

By jeepney Jeepneys leave from Dao, making trips clockwise and anticlockwise around the coast, but they stop often and become uncomfortably overloaded, so are best used only for short trips (P10 to Baclayon, for example).

By motorbike The whole island is accessible by motorbike – a cheap, fun and flexible way to see Bohol. Rentals are easily available in Tagbilaran and Panglao (around P500/day).

INFORMATION AND ACTIVITIES

Tourist information You can find small information kiosks at the airport and ferry pier. The Bohol department of tourism is one of the country's most proactive provincial tourist boards and can provide plenty of up-to-date information, maps, ideas and itineraries. Visit the friendly staff at Governor's Mansion on CPG Ave (☎ 038 412 3666, ⓦ boholtourismph.com).

Tours and activities For a highly recommended

backwater paddle through island mangroves at night, book a trip with Kayakasia, an outfitter based out of Maribojoc (☎ 0932 855 2928, ⓦ facebook.com/Kayakasia Philippines). Under cover of darkness, Rey Donaire and his informative guides lead small group tours on a 2hr paddle along the palm-lined Abatan River, finishing up beside hundreds of fireflies that glow in the moonlight (P1950). It just may well be the highlight of your trip to Bohol.

ACCOMMODATION

Casa Genaro Bed & Breakfast Franklin St, off Graham Ave ☎ 038 501 8910, ⓦ casagenaro.com. Situated just north of the ferry terminal, this 1950s-era house has delightful touches, with wooden interiors and quirky furnishings. The seven deluxe suites all have private bathroom, balcony or veranda, and cable TV. This is a real rustic find. P2500

Nisa Traveller's Hotel 14 CPG Ave ☎ 038 411 3731, ⓦ nisatravellershotel.com. The best budget option in town, featuring good a/c doubles (P700), hot water and clean bathrooms, as well as more expensive rooms with

king-size beds (P1300). Note that rooms at the front contend with constant traffic noise. P500

Sun Avenue Gallares St ☎ 038 412 5601. A great location midway between the pier and downtown makes up for the pokey standard rooms here, some of which have no windows. Deluxe rooms have a/c and cable TV (P1350). Request one at the back for a better night's sleep, or else prepare for a barrage of tricycle honks from 5am. Free wi-fi in the lobby. The well-run café serves oddities such as durian-flavoured coffee. P800

EATING

★**The Garden Café and Montana Restaurant** Plaza Rizal ☎ 038 411 3701. Established by the Bohol Deaf Academy and providing training for up to forty deaf students, *The Garden Café* has a menu mixing Mexican and Filipino dishes (P150–300). You can communicate with the staff in writing or with sign language (a few basic signs are listed in the menu). Upstairs, it's a completely different story at *Montana Restaurant* (though part of the same business), a fun-filled Wild West-themed pub-restaurant with moose heads on the wall, wooden booths and cowboy-booted staff. The

finger-lickin' American BBQ is a sure-fire winner (P150–350). Daily: café 6.30am–10pm; restaurant 11am–10pm.

Gerarda's J.S. Torralba St ☎ 038 412 3044. A short walk from Plaza Rizal, *Gerarda's* is easily Tagbilaran's most sophisticated restaurant. Popular with local Filipino celebrities, it's a riot of wooden furniture and parquet floors with diners tucking into heaped seafood plates of *gambas* and succulent pork. A sign of its enduring popularity, a second outlet, *Gerarda's Dos*, has opened on CPG Ave. Daily 8am–2pm & 5–10pm.

Golden Cowrie Venancio P. Inting Ave ☎ 038 411 1323. Sister to the long-popular Cebu institution, serving thoroughly Filipino food. Affordable set menus from P139, or you can opt for individual dishes such as sizzling prawns (P149). Daily 10am–2pm, 5–9pm.

Payag S. Matig-a St ☎ 038 412 2527. Hidden on the second floor of an antiquated Spanish-era home, this terrace-style restaurant's sizzling pork *sisig* (P160) and BBQ *lechon* (P175) is as authentic as any you'll find anywhere in Bohol. Daily 10am–10pm.

DIRECTORY

Banks There are plenty of banks with ATMs on CPG Ave. You can also change money in Tagbilaran City Square Mall.
Hospitals The Governor Celestino Gallares Memorial Hospital (☎ 038 411 4831 ⊛ gcgmh.doh.gov.ph) is on M. Parras St.
Immigration The Bureau of Immigration (☎ 038 235 6084) is on CPG Ave, a 10min walk north of the downtown core.

Internet access To get online, try the internet café on M.H. Del Pilar St, or Sidewalk Express around the corner on CPG Ave. Many coffee shops have free wi-fi, including *Bo's Coffee* and *Buzzz Café* in Island City Mall.
Police The police station is near City Hall, behind St Joseph's Cathedral.
Post The post office is west of St Joseph's Cathedral.

Panglao Island

Across one of two bridges from Tagbilaran, **PANGLAO** boasts beautiful beaches, first-rate diving and historic Spanish churches. The whole island is enjoying increasing popularity, nowhere more so than **Alona Beach**, and while there is now a great choice of hotels and restaurants, this also means higher room and food prices. With a controversial international airport planned for 2019 and a colossal *Hennan* luxury hotel already on the beachfront, things are changing at pace. Despite rapid development, quieter stretches of white sand can still be found, particularly at **Bolod Beach**, **San Isidro Beach** and **Bikini Beach**, all on the south coast, and **Doljo Beach**, near the westernmost tip of the island.

Away from the reefs and beaches, Panglao has two main towns, **Dauis** and **Panglao**, on the east and west sides of the island respectively, both of which centre around pretty Spanish churches. The rest of the interior feels like a giant replica of a batik, filled with nipa huts and flowering palms – perfect for short walks, cycle rides, or motorbike tours.

Bohol Bee Farm
Dao, Dauis • Daily 8am–5pm • ☎ 038 510 1822, ⊛ boholbeefarm.com

Near Dao on the island's southern coast, **Bohol Bee Farm** is one of the island's star attractions and offers the chance to tour an organic bee and vegetable farm. Afterwards, you can sample the delicious produce at the restaurant or buy some of the goodies to

DIVING AT PANGLAO

The **reef** at the western end of Panglao, a few minutes by bangka from Alona Beach, has healthy soft corals, a multitude of reef fish and perpendicular underwater cliffs that drop to a depth of 50m. This is where most of the island's dive sites are, though you can go further afield to **Doljo Point** and **Cervira Shoal**, or use Alona Beach as a base for diving at Cabilao (see p.351). Dives typically cost around P1500, plus equipment, but as always, the more dives you do the cheaper it gets. Day-trips also run to **Balicasag**, a beautiful halo of coral with steep drop-offs to the southwest.

DIVE OPERATORS

Genesis Divers Peter's House (see p.347) ⊛ genesisdivers.com. The longest-running operator on Alona is still going strong, despite increasing competition from new kids on the block, with very professional instructors. P1250 per dive; cheaper multi-

dive deals are available.
Sea Explorers Alona Vida Beach Resort (see p.347) ⊛ sea-explorers.com. Offering dive safaris and island-hopping, Sea Explorers are one of the best outfits in Alona. P1350 per dive, excluding equipment.

take home. They have accommodation on the farm too (see opposite), and you can try their produce elsewhere at the *Buzzz Café* chain (see p.348).

Pamilacan Island

Boat tour P3500–4000/person; every Wed there are large group boat tours for P1500/person – alternatively, take a bus to Bacalayon and arrange a trip with Pamilacan Island Dolphin & Whale Watching Tours (P2500–3000; ☎ 038 540 9279, ⓦ whales.bohol.ph)

Off the south coast of Panglao Island is whale territory, and the tiny **Pamilacan Island** is a prime jumping-off point for **whale-watching and dolphin-spotting**. Once home to generations of whalers, the island now excels at community-focused tourism; boat crews make the daily ocean run in converted whaling ships, armed with eco credentials rather than harpoons and nets. The best time of year to visit is from February to June.

ARRIVAL AND DEPARTURE   PANGLAO ISLAND

From Tagbilaran Almost everyone arrives at Alona by van (P500–600) or tricycle (P250) from Tagbilaran port or airport, in which case you'll be dropped as close to your accommodation as possible (you'll need to walk to get to some of the beach cottages).

From elsewhere in Bohol You might arrive via Dao Integrated Terminal (see p.344), from where there are jeepneys and buses to Panglao. These services will drop you on the main road, from where it's a 5min walk down to the beach.

INFORMATION AND TOURS

Banks There's a BPI ATM on the Alona Beach access road. There are also plenty of places to change money in Alona, but it's best to hunt around to find the most competitive rates.

Tourist information There is no official tourist information centre in Alona, just a number of glorified confectionary shops that dispense tours. In case of any trouble, there is a tourist police assistance centre at Rona's Corner (☎ 038 502 8365).

Tours Seashine Tours (☎ 038 502 9038, ⓦ seashine travelandtours.com), a stone's throw from the beach, can book all ferry tickets, as well as arrange day-trips around Bohol, van hire and boat trips (P1800–2500 for the day). Alternatively, try German-owned Valeroso Travel and Tours (☎ 038 502 9126, ⓦ ralleontour.com). Standard rates in Alona Beach are P500 for an evening fireflies tour, or P700 for a day-trip to Oslob to see the whale sharks.

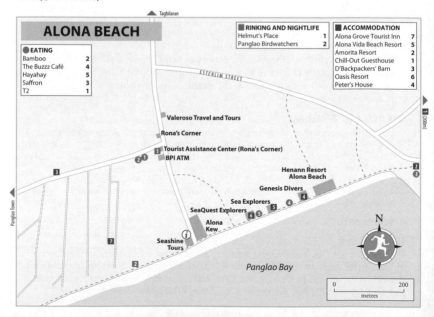

ALONA BEACH

Tagbilaran

EATING
Bamboo — 2
The Buzzz Café — 4
Hayahay — 5
Saffron — 3
T2 — 1

DRINKING AND NIGHTLIFE
Helmut's Place — 1
Panglao Birdwatchers — 2

ACCOMMODATION
Alona Grove Tourist Inn — 7
Alona Vida Beach Resort — 5
Amorita Resort — 2
Chill-Out Guesthouse — 1
D'Backpackers' Barn — 3
Oasis Resort — 6
Peter's House — 4

ESTERLIM STREET

Valeroso Travel and Tours
Rona's Corner
Tourist Assistance Center (Rona's Corner)
BPI ATM

Henann Resort
Alona Beach
Genesis Divers
Sea Explorers
SeaQuest Explorers
Alona Kew
Seashine Tours

Panglao Town

Panglao Bay

N

0   200
metres

ACCOMMODATION

Hotel prices have gone skywards in **Alona**, and there are hardly any budget options on the beach, but if you don't mind a short walk or tricycle ride to the sea, there are still a few cheapies to be found.

ALONA BEACH

Alona Grove Tourist Inn Set back from the western end of the beach ☎038 502 4200, ⓦfacebook.com/AlonaGroveGouristInn. One of a number of off-beach budget resorts with a row of simple thatched huts, some with a/c, fridge and cable TV. Popular with money-conscious backpackers. ☎ P700

Alona Vida Beach Resort Halfway between the main access road and the east end of the beach ☎038 502 9180, ⓦalonavida.com. Excellent rooms decorated in earthy tones just a few metres back from the beach. Deluxe and superior rooms (P4200–5200) come with fridges, mini-bars, kettles, safety deposit boxes and room service, plus there's one budget room, though it's a little too close for comfort to the lively Coco Vida bar. Sea Explorers dive centre (see box, p.345) is also on-site. ☎ P2400

★**Amorita Resort** Along the clifftop at the beach's eastern end ☎038 502 9002, ⓦamoritaresort.com. The infinity pool overlooking the sea at this fabulous clifftop retreat is one of the many highlights at this luxury resort, which includes polished service, stunning food, free bikes, day-beds and a very good cocktail bar. Rooms are huge, with balconies, flatscreen TVs and rainfall showers. Superb, if pricey. ☎ P8000

Chill-Out Guesthouse A 10min walk from the eastern end of the beach ☎038 502 4480 ⓦchilloutpanglao.com. Tricky to find, this delightful guesthouse is all the more rewarding for being away from the beach action. Spotless rooms with private balconies and fan or a/c (P1600) are dotted around a tropical garden, and there's a social restaurant to sink a beer away from the crowds. It's justifiably popular, so book in advance. ☎ P1350

D'Backpackers Barn Hontanosas Rd, towards Panglao ☎038 502 4968, ⓦbackpackersbarn.com. Right by the main road, this cowboy-themed newcomer is already a firm favourite, despite the obvious lack of beachfront. D'Backpackers offers clean four-bed dorms, fan and a/c rooms (P1200–1400), and a common area with hammocks, dartboard and board games. Wi-fi in common areas only. ☎ P400

Oasis Resort Eastern end of the beach ☎038 502 9056, ⓦseaquestdivecenter.com. In the thick of things in the middle of Alona Beach, this sprawling dive resort has a lovely pool, bucolic garden and great people-watching opportunities; there's a garden lounge, as well as a beachfront cocktail bar and restaurant. Standard rooms have bamboo-frame beds, whirring fans and a veranda, while the deluxe options (P3300) come with pool or garden views and enough room to loll around like a whale. ☎ P2400

Peter's House Eastern end of the beach ☎038 502 9056, ⓦgenesisdivers.com. One of the last genuine budget options on the beach, Peter's has four simple and cosy nipa rooms above the bar. Owned by Genesis Divers (see box, p.345), the hotel has an in-house divers-only policy during peak season; deals are available. ☎ P1200

BOLOD BEACH

Amarela Resort Brgy Libaong, western part of Bolod Beach ☎038 502 9497, ⓦamarelaresort.com. Perched on top of a hill looking out to the sea, Amarela is an intimate, sophisticated hideaway with stylish rooms, good amenities and its own art gallery. Heavy wood furnishings define the rooms, all of which have a/c, balconies, hot showers, cable TV and DVD players. There's a well-stocked DVD library, and the popular restaurant enjoys wonderful views. From the main house, steps lead down to a pretty stretch of white beach, plus there's a cracking pool. ☎ P6000

Bohol Beach Club Bolod Beach ☎038 502 9222, ⓦboholbeachclub.com.ph. Large VIP resort split into two wings named after the Philippines' two monsoons: "Habagat", with recently renovated native-style cottage blocks, and the plusher "Amihan", which boasts more elegant rooms surrounding two swimming pools. Watersports are on offer, along with a range of other highlights including a gym, pizzeria and herb garden for the restaurant. Day visitors can use the beach and pool for P600, of which P450 goes towards food and drinks. ☎ P11000

Bohol Bee Farm Dao, Dauis ☎038 510 1822, ⓦboholbeefarm.com. As the name suggests, this ranch-style place offers the unique opportunity to get busy with the bees. As well as getting to enjoy the farm's organic produce from the vegetable and herb garden in the excellent restaurant, overnight guests are given a complimentary tour. Comfortable cottages with a/c, cable TV and hot water are dotted throughout the property, and there's a pool and ocean swimming platform. Free wi-fi in the lobby, and the store selling organic goodies is the pride of Bohol. ☎ P3000

ELSEWHERE ON THE ISLAND

★**Bohol Coco Farm** Southern Coastal Rd ☎0906 807 1869, ⓦfacebook.com/BoholCFarm. Ideal for those seeking peace, quiet, organic produce and fellow-minded travellers, this Filipino-run eco-farm 5km east of Alona Beach's bright lights feels like a world apart. The farm features stripped-back nipa huts and mixed dorms. Motorbikes are a bargain P250/3hr. Walk-ins often have to

7

look elsewhere, so book ahead. Wi-fi doesn't reach the rooms. 🛜 Dorms P350, huts P800

Momo Beach House Doljo Beach 📞 02 553 9549, 🌐 momobeachhouse.com. It's hard not to fall in love with this sensuous, eco-beach-house on the north coast.

Furnished with shabby-chic wicker armchairs and chaise lounges, the gazebo-like communal area and restaurant overlook a stunning arc of coconut palm beach and an oceanfront pool. 🛜 P7200

EATING

ALONA BEACH

Bamboo On the main road by Rona's Corner 📞 038 503 8328. Formerly the Gallic-flavoured *L'Elephant Bleu*, this restaurant has been rebooted as an international all-rounder with vegan burgers, pastas and curries on the menu (P220–690). Confusingly, next door, but in the same complex, is *The French House*, a sophisticated bar with live music and movie nights. Daily 11am–2pm & 5–10pm.

Buzzz Café Centre of the beach 📞 0917 304 0661, 🌐 boholbeefarm.com. Owned by *Bohol Bee Farm* (see p.347), this dependable breakfast and lunch spot serves excellent waffles with bacon and eggs (P200), ice cream (P60), and regulars from the farm's restaurant menu. The second-floor dining area looks out over the beach; packaged local delicacies are on sale downstairs. Free wi-fi. Daily 7am–11pm.

Hayahay Eastern part of the beach 📞 038 502 9288, 🌐 hayahay.net. Promising the best pizza in town, *Hayahay* lives up to the billing, serving mean thin-crusts. Try the Balicasag with salmon and tuna (P270). Daily 7am–midnight.

Saffron Amarito Resort, at the east end of the beach 📞 038 502 9002, 🌐 amoritaresort.com. One of a new breed of trendy places to eat in Alona, *Saffron*'s team of chefs present Filipino salads, chicken and inventive seafood. Among its mouthwatering signatures are sea-bass ceviche, tuna *kinilaw* and line-caught white marlin (P355–475). Perfect for a date night. Daily 11am–10pm.

T2 Bar, Café & Restaurant At Rona's Corner 📞 0908 593 5155, 🌐 facebook.com/T2Restaurant. This popular 24hr joint caters for bleary-eyed new arrivals, as well as those who haven't left from the night before. The kitchen dishes up burgers, pizzas and pastas for a mix of expats and divers (mains P250–400). Quiz nights every Mon. Daily 24hr.

DRINKING AND NIGHTLIFE

Nightlife mainly revolves around resort and dive-shop bars, but there are a few independent party places by the beach turn-off.

ALONA BEACH

Helmut's Place Rona's Corner. Owned by a German biker, this enduringly macho biker bar has friendly service, live sports, a pool table, plus decent European food. Beers P45. Daily 10am–2am.

Panglao Birdwatchers Towards the beach's western end 📞 0912 710 8328 🌐 panglaobirdwatchers.com. Aussie-run beachfront bar (hence the super-cold beers) that's big on sunset happy hours, booming tunes and good times. If the quirky staff, cocktails, live sports and zingy tacos (from *Woody's BBQ Shack* next door) don't convince you, little else will. Early till late.

The interior

In addition to the ubiquitous Chocolate Hills, which appear on every tourist brochure and postcard from Manila to Mindanao, Bohol's **interior** hosts a range of sights worth exploring. Take your pick from historic churches, markets, river cruises, waterfalls, a tarsiers sanctuary, and a jungle adventure camp.

Antequera Market

Sun 7am–noon • 🌐 www.antequera-bohol.lgu.ph • Bus or jeepney from Tagbilaran (P40), or visit as part of a day-trip (from P2000 for a vehicle)

A number of resorts offer half-day trips to the town of **ANTEQUERA**, 20km north of Tagbilaran, to see the lively Sunday **market**. Craftsmen and traders from around the island congregate to sell handicrafts such as baskets, hats and various home decor items like linen tablecloths, mirrors and attractive bowls made from stone or coconut shells.

Philippine Tarsier Sanctuary

Daily 9am–4pm • P50 • Hiking guides P500 per group of two for 4hr • 📞 0908 937 8094, 🌐 tarsierfoundation.org • No flash photography • Bus or jeepney (P30) from Tagbilaran to Corella and then a tricycle for the last 4km; or stay on the bus towards Sikatuna and ask to be dropped at the entrance, from where it's a 500m walk to the sanctuary

Ten kilometres northeast of Tagbilaran outside the village of Corella, the **Philippine Tarsier Sanctuary** is dedicated to protecting what is left of the native population of tarsiers, saucer-eyed creatures you will see on posters throughout the country. Often mistakenly referred to as the world's smallest monkey, the cuddly **tarsier** – all 10–15cm of it – is more closely related to the lemur, loris and bushbaby and has been around for a staggering 45 million years.

After a brief induction at the base camp, knowledgeable **guides** lead visitors into the jungle, but spotting the sanctuary's hundred-or-so free-to-roam residents among the foliage can be challenging, especially as the creatures are nocturnal and rarely move. Upon being found, the tarsier study visitors with wide-eyed curiosity, sometimes swivelling their heads a disconcerting 180 degrees to get a better look.

Group tours tend to visit the unaffiliated and for-profit **Loboc Tarsier Sanctuary** as part of a cruise on the Loboc River; however, this is best avoided. Here, rehabilitated creatures are often kept in enclosures and caretakers have been known to let visitors manhandle the endangered critters.

Loboc River

Private boats cost P800 for the return trip (1hr); all-you-can-eat floating barge buffet P450 per person (daily 11am–3pm)

Eleven kilometres east of Corella, the town of **Loboc** is the starting point for enormously popular **jungle boat trips** along the **Loboc River** to **Tontonan Falls**. Whichever way you choose to cruise, it's a very touristy, if lovely, journey past idyllic villages, green paddies, twisted roots and towering palms. The majority of visitors are whisked away on a floating restaurant barge, stopping off at riverside shacks to see local women sing and dance, before arriving at the somewhat underwhelming waterfall.

Habitat Bohol Conservation Center

Bilar • Daily 7.30am–5pm; night safaris 5–6.30pm • P45 (including guided tour); night safaris P900 • ☎ 038 535 9400, ⓦ facebook.com/HabitatBoholWildlifeAdventure

THRILL-SEEKING IN BOHOL

Bohol's interior is packed with **activities** that'll encourage you to step out of your comfort zone. From stand-up paddleboarding down a jade river to ziplining on a bicycle or surfboard (yes, really) above the forest canopy, the Eden-like combination of the island's jungle, rivers and mountains provides the perfect backdrop to let loose and get wild. Here are some places to embrace your inner Tarzan or Jane.

Chocolate Hills Adventure Park ☎ 0932 667 7098, ⓦ bit.ly/ChocHillsAdventurePark. Based at the Chocolate Hills, activities include an eco-trail canopy walkway (P200), Tarzan high-rope challenges (from P300) and a bike or surf zipline (P450).

Danao Adventure Park ☎ 038 510 0050, ⓦ danaoadventurepark.com. A few kilometres from the small town of Danao, north of the Chocolate Hills, Danao Adventure Park occupies an area of rugged jungle-covered massif cut by deep valleys. Established in 2006, the park has become the centre for outdoors pursuits in Bohol, offering everything from river trekking (P300), white-knuckle-inducing "plunge" canyon swinging (P700), climbing (P100–400), extreme caving (P550) and kayaking (P300). The easiest and quickest way to get here is to arrange a car and driver through your resort (around P3000 return); alternatively, take a bus from Tagbilaran to Danao via Sagbayan (3hr; P85), where you can charter a tricycle (P100).

SUP Tours Philippines ☎ 038 537 9011, ⓦ suptoursphilippines.com. Running fantastic stand-up paddleboarding and biking trips along the Loboc and Abatan Rivers (as well as further afield in Negros, Palawan and Siargao), this Belgian-Filipino paddle centre is based on a bend of the river at *Fox and Firefly Cottages* (see p.350). The real star is the outfit's full-day journey into the island interior along a jade-like river, but for those who want something less strenuous, shorter three-hour waterfall and estuary excursions are available. Various paddleboarding trips, including waterfall and river tours start at P1650. They also do guided mountain biking (from P950).

Halfway between Loboc and Carmen, the **Habitat Bohol Conservation Center** is a bird and butterfly park – and a popular tour-group stopover – with over 150 different types of lepidopterans and plenty of bats, insects and fireflies. Night safaris can be organized, in order to see nocturnal wildlife, including – of course – tarsiers. Proceeds from the tours go towards better habitat protection.

The Chocolate Hills

Viewpoint Daily dawn to dusk • P50 • **Adventure Park** Daily 8.30am–5.30pm • P60; buggy tours P900/1hr • **Sagbayan Peak** Daily dawn to dusk • P50 • To get to the Adventure Park or Viewpoint independently, take a bus to Carmen (hourly; 2hr; P60) from the Dao terminal in Tagbilaran, and then hop on a habal-habal (around P50); a round trip by taxi costs P2500; for Sagbayan Peak, take a bus from Tagbilaran to Sagbayan town, then rent a habal-habal

Renowned throughout the Philippines, the surreal **Chocolate Hills** are one of the country's biggest tourist attractions. Some geologists believe that these unique 40m mounds – there are said to be 1776 of them if you care to count – were formed from deposits of coral and limestone sculpted by centuries of erosion. Most locals, however, will tell you that the hills are the calcified tears of a broken-hearted giant; others prefer the idea that they were left by a giant carabao with distressed bowels.

What you think of the hills will depend largely on the time you visit. During the glare of the day, the light casts harsh shadows and the hills lose their definition. But at **dawn or dusk** they look splendid, especially during the dry season (Feb–June) when the scrub vegetation covering the hills is roasted brown. At such times, they really do live up to their billing.

Most visitors head for the 360-degree viewpoint at the government-run **Chocolate Hills Viewpoint**. Built atop one of the unearthly formations, it's reached by a winding road and a steep climb up two hundred or so rough-hewn steps. The site was badly damaged by the October 2013 quake (see box, p.343) and renovations were still ongoing at the time of research.

Different views are on offer at the privately run **Chocolate Hills Adventure Park**, where the main draw is a host of thrilling activities (see box, p.340). The centre also offers ATV and buggy tours around the bases of the hills.

Prior to the earthquake, visitors wanting solitude to escape the crowds would continue further north to **Sagbayan Peak**, northwest of Carmen. The area, however, was the epicentre of the Bohol quake and has since been reborn as a Disneyfied funfair.

ACCOMMODATION AND EATING — THE INTERIOR

★**Fox and the Firefly Cottages** By the Petron Gas Station, Baranggay Valladolid ☎0947 8933 022, ⊛ suptoursphilippines.com/foxandthefireflycottages. Five hundred metres off the main Loboc Rd, this chilled-out collection of riverside cabanas is a great place to soak-up the sights and sounds of the Bohol jungle for a day or two. With great home-made food, lovely staff and a choice of six-bed dorms or comfy privates, the only decision is whether to read a book by the riverside or hop on a paddleboard. 🛜 Dorms P450, doubles P1800

Nuts Huts 2km north of Loboc ☎0920 846 1559, ⊛ nutshuts.org. Started by two friendly Belgians, this riverside resort has reached its twenty-year milestone. There are simple dorms with mosquito nets and far bigger rooms with private bathroom and balcony, and the perched-up outdoor restaurant has attractive views across the dense green canopy of rainforest. Activities on offer include rafting, trekking or mountain biking. Dorms P400, doubles P1200

The west and north coasts

Bohol's pretty northwest coast is lined with mangroves and dotted with Spanish-era ruins, and is also the access point for the dive sites of **Cabilao Island**. Further north, **Tubigon** has fast craft to Cebu, while on the opposite side of Bohol to Tagbilaran, the agricultural town of **Ubay** has handy transport connections to Leyte.

Maribojoc
Take a bus or jeepney from Tagbilaran (30min)

The pretty coastal town of **MARIBOJOC** lies just 14km from Tagbilaran and is worth a quick stop. The town is the site of the old Spanish **Punta Cruz watchtower**, one of a number of old watchtowers of note on Bohol. Once a lookout for marauding pirates, Punta Cruz is now a viewing deck from where you can gaze across to Cebu and Siquijor.

Cabilao Island
Bus to Loon from Tagbilaran (1hr; P30) and then change to a jeepney (P10) or habal-habal (P70) for Mocpoc pier on Sandingan Island; bangkas from Mocpoc to Cabilao cost P20 (20min)

Off the radar for most divers, the pretty little island of **Cabilao** has a handful of modest, but very comfortable resorts, making it an appealing option. With limited beachfront, these chilled-out resorts can also arrange trips to local dive sites such as the **Wall at Cambaquiz**, where there are turtles and baby sharks, and **Shark View Point**, where one of the attractions – apart from sharks, as you'd expect – is the easy-to-miss pygmy sea horse.

Lapinig

Just offshore from Ubay, the undeveloped island of **Lapinig** offers good diving, some of it for experts only in extreme subterranean caves. To explore, you can rent a bangka for the day (P1500–2000) at the small pier in Ubay, but the easiest way to dive is to arrange a trip through one of the operators in Panglao (see box, p.345).

ARRIVAL AND DEPARTURE
THE WEST AND NORTH COASTS

By boat Kinswell Shipping Lines and Starcraft operates fast ferries between Cebu City and Tubigon (11 daily; 1hr 20min), while Lite Shipping runs a slower ferry (2 daily; 2hr 30min). Super Shuttle Ferries depart from Ubay to Bato on Leyte (daily; 3hr 30min).

ACCOMMODATION

CABILAO ISLAND
Polaris Dive Centre On the main beach on the northwest coast ☏ 0918 903 7187, ⓦ polaris-dive.com. Family-style resort with a choice of cottages ranging from simple wooden treehouses to more substantial a/c doubles and bungalows (P3250). At low tide, the nearby sandbar is ideal for snorkelling; kayaks are also available. **P1860**
Pura Vida On the northeast coast ☏ 0917 321 8557, ⓦ cabilao.com. From the same team as *Pura Vida* in Dauin, Dumaguete (see p.304), this sibling offers the same standard lodgings at a range of budgets all the way up to a honeymoon suite. There are five economy rooms on the beachfront, while deluxe a/c rooms (P5200) sit atop a small cliff looking out over the ocean. There's also a popular beach bar and the Sea Explorers dive centre. **P3900**

The south coast

Most travellers only make it this far in order to catch the boat from the busy little port town of **Jagna** to Camiguin Island and Mindanao. But those that have the time to stop for a few days are spoilt with beautiful beaches and diving at **Anda**, as well as a few Spanish-era ruins along the way.

Bool

Some 5km east of Tagbilaran, the coastal fishing town of **BOOL** is said to be the oldest settlement on the island. It's also the location of the **Blood Compact Site**, marked by a bronze sculpture on the seafront, as well as dozens of tour buses stopping off for photo opportunities. This is the spot where local chieftain Rajah Sikatuna and Miguel López de Legazpi concluded an early round of Philippine–Spanish hostilities in 1565 by signing a compact in blood. Every year for one week in July, Boholanos gather in Bool for the **Sandugo Festival**, which, apart from the usual beauty pageants and lashings of roast pig, includes an eyebrow-raising re-enactment of the blood ceremony. Plans are afoot to develop the area into the much bigger **Bohol Friendship Park**.

Baclayon Church

Museum daily 8am–5pm • P50

About 2km east of Bool, **BACLAYON** is the site of **Baclayon Church**, the oldest stone church in the Philippines, which was badly damaged by the 2013 quake. Much of the newer Augustinian facade collapsed, along with the upper half of the bell tower. The rest dates back to 1595 and was declared a national historical landmark in 1995. While the renovations continue apace, notably on the newly restored belfry, the church's convent functions as an intriguing **ecclesiastical museum** housing a number of priceless religious icons and oddities.

Anda and around

Buses run from Tagbilaran (3hr)

Around 100km east of Tagbilaran, the countless white-sand coves of beautiful Guindulman Bay have made the once forgotten town of **ANDA** an emerging choice for those looking to escape Panglao's commercialized beach scene. Most of the resorts which have popped up in recent years are high-end, although there are also a few budget options. Offshore, **Lamanok Island**'s haematite cave paintings add credence to Anda's claim as the "cradle of Boholano culture", while on land there are several caves offering clear-water swimming – **Kabagno Cave** has a 6m-deep pool.

ARRIVAL AND DEPARTURE

By boat Super Shuttle Ferry runs three times a week from Jagna to Balbagon on Camiguin Island (Mon, Wed & Fri; 2hr).

Cokaliong Shipping Lines also operates a daily service from Jagna to Nasipit on Mindanao (daily 11.55pm; 5hr 30min).

ACCOMMODATION

THE SOUTH COAST

ANDA

Amun Ini Beach Resort and Spa 10km east of town ☎ 038 510 6230, ⌂ amunini.com. Meaning "this is ours" in the local Ilonggo dialect, this remote hideaway, reached after a long drive, has a private beach, infinity pool and the kind of exemplary service that means you'll be handed a cold-pressed towel as soon as you start sweating. ☎ **P12,200**

Anda Cove Northern end of the beach ☎ 0995 432 5179, ⌂ facebook.com/AndaCoveRetreatResort. Sometimes it's possible to do everything right. Set up as a socially conscious enterprise, as well as a yoga and meditation retreat, this beachfront resort shelters eight lovely rooms that are perfect for unwinding. You can snorkel, sunbathe on the private beach, or give something back by helping at the community centre or in the organic

garden. ☎ **P3500**

Anda White Beach Resort Northern end of the beach ☎ 0917 700 0507, ⌂ andabeachresort.com. For pure beach-lovers, this place can't be beaten, with attractive rooms, the best of which front onto a bright white strip of sand. There's also a palm-fringed pool, kayaks, an on-site dive shop and a buzzy bar. Wi-fi in public areas. ☎ **P5000**

Blue Star Dive and Resort 1km north of the market ☎ 0949 946 5386, ⌂ bluestardive.com. One of the first to venture this far east, British-owned *Blue Star* still stands out for scuba-lovers and has a good dive centre, pool, a tiny beach at low tide, and good snorkelling on the house reef. There is a choice of ten standard bungalows, or ocean- and pool-view a/c rooms (P4990), all of which are spacious and tastefully designed. Wi-fi reaches some rooms. ☎ **P3600**

Samar

The island of **SAMAR**, between Bicol and Leyte and 320km from top to toe, has yet to take off as a major tourist destination, which is both a shame and a blessing. Administratively divided into three parts, **Northern**, **Western and Eastern Samar**, large parts of each remain unspoilt, wild and beautiful. Homonhon Island in Eastern Samar is where **Ferdinand Magellan** is reputed to have set foot for the first time on Philippine soil in 1521, but these days the island is better known as the arrival point for many of the Philippines' worst storms. **Typhoon Yolanda** rocked southeastern Samar in November 2013, devastating numerous cities, towns and villages in its path. As well as the terrible human costs, the typhoon's aftermath continues to have serious economic implications.

The typhoon's ongoing impact is evident in the east-coast surfing mecca of Guiuan, which has so far failed to live up to its pre-Yolanda promise, or to **Sohoton Natural Bridge National Park**, a prehistoric wilderness in Western Samar, which continues to be overlooked. Further north, however, the towns of **Calbayog** and **Catbalogan** offer plenty of adrenaline-rush activities in their hinterlands, including the chance to explore some of Southeast Asia's biggest cave systems.

ARRIVAL AND DEPARTURE
SAMAR

By plane There are airports at Calbayog and Catarman, both served by PAL to Manila. Cebu Pacific also flies to Calbayog.

By boat Coming from Cebu there are numerous slow ferry connections to various ports along Samar's west coast, including Calbayog and Catbalogan. Ferries from Matnog on Bicol in Luzon arrive in Allen, in the northwest of the island.

By bus and minivan Tacloban on neighbouring Leyte is linked to Samar by regular buses and minivans, crossing the 2km San Juanico Bridge. From Manila, several operators including Philtranco (philtranco.net) cross on the Matnog–Allen ferry and run down the coastal road to Catbalogan (17–23hrs).

7

Northern Samar

Served by flights from Manila and boat from Luzon, **Northern Samar** is primarily used as an entry and departure point to and from the island, but there are also some beautiful islands offshore. The **Balicuatro** and **Biri Island** groups are slowly being developed for tourism, but most remain wonderfully pristine and untouched.

Allen

Arriving from Luzon by bus or ferry, your first taste of Samar is the small port town of **ALLEN**, in northwestern Samar, which has basic services and amenities but little else of interest to travellers. Most people head straight from the boat onto a bus or van, or out to the nearby Balicuatro or Biri Islands.

ARRIVAL AND DEPARTURE
ALLEN

By boat Roll-on, roll-off ferries from Matnog on the southernmost tip of Bicol (Luzon) make the return trip to the Balwharteco terminal in Allen, several times each morning (1–1hr 30min). As in other ports, there is a terminal fee of P20.

By bus and jeepney Dozens of buses and jeepneys run

east every day from Allen to Catarman (1hr; from P60) and beyond, as well as south to Calbayog (2hr) and Catbalogan (4hr), where you can catch an onward bus to the southern half of the island. Buses heading south and east from Allen also pick up passengers at the port itself.

ACCOMMODATION

Birmingham Allen Beach Resort Rizal St, Allen 07731 911 8103 birminghamallen.com. There's no real beach here, but this four-room resort is a great option for a stopover, with tasty food, clean rooms, and helpful

staff. As a welcome bonus, it's in a great location in which to see the to-die-for sunsets as the sun dips behind Dalupiri Island. **P2000**

The Balicuatro Islands

The remote, marine-protected **Balicuatro Islands**, off Samar's northwest coast, afford the chance to find your own slice of paradise for the day, although currently only a couple of them have anywhere to stay. The capital of **Dalupiri Island**, where most bangkas arrive, is **San Antonio**, a sleepy barangay with dozens of little bangkas that can take you on day-trips to tranquil islands nearby.

The rest of the islands, also largely unexplored by tourists, are mostly home to farmers and fishermen. **Capul**, for example, is a picturesque little atoll about one hour from the San Isidro Sea Port on Samar, with the empty shell of a seventeenth-century fortified stone church built by the Spanish, and an almost derelict coastal road that takes you past some incredible coves and beaches.

ARRIVAL AND DEPARTURE   THE BALICUATRO ISLANDS

By boat Scheduled morning bangkas leave from Victoria, 8km south of Allen, to San Antonio on Dalupiri (30min). Private bangka trips can also be arranged direct to resorts on Dalupiri from San Isidro (P500), 7km south of Victoria. There is one morning bangka from Looc ferry terminal in

Allen to Capul (1hr), or you can arrange a private trip for around P600.
Money and services There are no ATMs on the islands. San Antonio in Dalupiri has a pharmacy and a small medical clinic.

ACCOMMODATION

Crystal Sand Beach Resort 1km south of San Antonio, Dalupiri ☎0917 336 9740, ☜crystalsand beachresort.weebly.com. Run by Swedish-Filipino couple Karl and Cora (who cooks up a storm in the kitchen), this popular lobster-pink hotel is blessed with a fantastic beach and super-helpful management. A/c rooms come with king-size beds, cable TV, and fridges. Beds in the backpackers' station are a steal. Dorm P500,

doubles P1400
Octopussy Bungalow Resort Dalupiri, 500m south of Flying Dog beach ☎0906 515 7376, ☜octopussy .ch. Concrete-and-thatch cottages in pretty, if very remote, gardens. There are few places to eat in the area, but this Swiss-Filipino-run resort also offers half (P700pp) and full board (P1000pp). P1350

Catarman

The ramshackle north coast port city of **CATARMAN** is served by flights from Manila and – though it has never been a tourist destination – makes a good point of entry to Northern Samar if you want to save yourself a long bus or ferry journey. It's also only a short hop from the Biri group of islands.

ARRIVAL AND INFORMATION   CATARMAN

By plane PAL operates a daily flight from Manila and has offices at the airport, and also on J.P. Rizal St in town.
By bus and van Buses from the terminal behind the market. A quicker way for destinations south, rather than a public bus, is to take a Grand Tours or D'Turbanada van, which both leave hourly.

Destinations Allen (hourly; 1hr); Calbayog (hourly; 2hr); Catbalogan (hourly; 3hr); Tacloban (hourly; 7hr)
Money There are a few banks with ATMs in Catarman, including a BDO Bank on Anunciation St and a Security Bank on Del Pilar St.

ACCOMMODATION

Café Eusebio Bed and Breakfast 1071 Anunciation St ☎055 500 9245. This is the closest thing that Catarman has to a boutique hotel. Located next to shops, banks and restaurants, *Café Eusebio* has modern rooms, designer fixtures and fittings, and great Filipino breakfasts. It also does great coffee and cakes in the café, where there's wi-fi. ☞ P1500
Pink City Pension House Roxas St ☎055 500 9183. True to its name, this place has bright-pink rooms set

around a central water feature. Standard rooms have a/c and cable TV, but for hot water you'll need to fork out for an executive or family room (P1500–1800). There's free wi-fi in the lobby. ☞ P1000
Sasa Pension House Jacinto St ☎055 251 8031, ☜sasapensionhouse.webs.com. The clean, comfortable fan and a/c rooms at this four-storey, family-run pension offer great value, and it's often fully booked as a result. The cheapest rooms have shared bathrooms. ☞ P900

EATING

Beehive Resto-Bar 211 Bonifacio St ☜facebook .com/BeehiveGelera. A new, family-run place, the *Beehive* offers hearty mains such as steak and rice or salmon and veg, as well as a great selection of freshly

baked cakes. Before paying up, the only decision is whether to take a slice of blueberry cheesecake (P158), mango cake (P128), or chocolate brownie (P108) to go. Daily 8am–midnight.

Michz Café Western end of Jacinta St ☎ 055 500 9519, ⓦ bit.ly/MichzCafe. Popular café serving pastas, salads and the best pizza in town, including a devilishly spicy tuna and pepperoni half-and-half (mains P75–300). Cool down afterwards with a Willy Wonka-esque *halo-halo* (P75). Daily 8am–10pm.

Our Nest 2nd floor Ortiz Bldg, Marcos St ☎ 0916 476 4702. Filipino café specializing in an eclectic list of highly calorific goodies such as fried chicken and garlic, seafood with rice, steak, sizzling *sisig*, nachos and sinful iced chocolate. If you're in town for a while, you'll be back more than once. Mon–Sat 10am–midnight.

Biri-Las Rosas Islands
P50 marine protection fee

Somewhere among the tantalizingly undeveloped cluster of idyllic outcrops known as the **Biri-Las Rosas Islands**, you'll be able to find one to call your own for the day. Most of the islands are only inhabited by poor fisherfolk, and the infrastructure is non-existent, but there are a few places to stay. Beyond the white sand, there are a number of more beguiling attractions, including weird rock formations, majestic cliffs, tidal pools and – at the right time of year, after the annual monsoons – sea waterfalls.

7

ARRIVAL AND DEPARTURE THE BIRI-LAS ROSAS ISLANDS

By boat Bangkas from Lavezares, 8km east of Allen, go to Biri (P60; 1hr) until an hour before sunset. Alternatively, you can charter a boat from San José (where all buses stop)

for around P1500 for a day-trip; bear in mind that restaurant options on the islands are slim, so it's likely that you'll have to provide food for you and the boatman.

ACCOMMODATION

Biri Resort & Dive Centre Just south of Biri town, Biri Island ☎ 0915 174 1386 ⓦ biri-resort.com. Rebuilt following Yolanda in a bid to drive tourism and support the local recovery effort, this dive centre is a worthy place to stay, particularly as it continues to

support the island's damaged coral gardens through the Biri Initiative (ⓦ biri-initiative.org). Boat dives start from P1400, and there's a decent café on site, *The Reef Bar & Grill*. P3500

Western Samar

Western Samar is dominated by its limestone topography, and has **caves**, gorges and waterfalls galore. Aside from the famous **Sohoton Natural Bridge National Park**, most natural attractions are still relatively undiscovered, and there is little tourist footfall and infrastructure. The provincial towns of **Calbayog** and **Catbalogan** are the best bases for exploring the region.

Calbayog and around

Sitting pretty, wedged between the Calbayog River on one side and the Samar Sea on the other, **CALBAYOG** makes a pleasant enough place for a stop on the west coast on your way through Samar. **Bangon and Tarangban Falls** are within easy reach of the city on the way to Catbalogan. To get to the falls, take a jeepney to Tinaplacan, and then walk (45min), or take a habal-habal direct (20min). Once there, you can swim in the plunge pool at Bangon Falls, or hike up to Tarangban Falls.

Guinogo-an Cave
Free • Take a jeepney from Calbayog to Lungsod, from where you can hire a boat (P300–350 return), then walk the last 15min to the cave – bring a torch

After entering **Guinogo-an Cave**, you'll quickly find yourself wading through chest-deep water, before you emerge into a series of vaulted caverns, home to *kabyaw* (fruit bats), snakes, spiders and crabs. It's far safer to take a guide with you, which can be organized through the tourist office (see p.356). The vast Calbiga cave system is also accessible from Calbayog, but it's best to organize trips here through Trexplore (see box, p.356).

ARRIVAL AND DEPARTURE

By plane The airport is 8km out of town; a tricycle into the centre costs P120.

Destination Manila (6 weekly; 1hr 10min).

By boat Calbayog has three weekly ferries for Cebu departing at 7pm (Mon, Wed & Fri; 11hr), operated by Cokaliong (☎ 055 533 8959). The return ferry comes back at the same time (Tues, Thurs & Sat). The ticket office is at the port, which lies on reclaimed land 2km from town. Tricycles into town charge P30.

By bus and jeepney Buses and jeepneys arrive at the Capoocan transport terminal north of the river, 10min by tricycle from the town centre.

CALBAYOG AND AROUND

Destinations Allen (jeepneys; 2hr); Catarman (4 daily; 2hr 30min); Catbalogan (every 30min; 2hr); Tacloban (every 30min; 4hr).

By van A quicker alternative to the bus is to take a Grand Tours or Van-Vans shuttle van, which leave from their private terminals. Grand Tours is on the corner of Burgos St and the National Highway, while Van-Vans can be found at the bus station and on Bugallon St.

Destinations Allen (hourly; 1hr 45min); Catarman (hourly; 2hr); Catbalogan (every 30min; 1hr 30min); Tacloban (via Catbalogan; 3hr–3hr 30min).

INFORMATION

Tourist information Next to City Hall, Calbayog's friendly tourist office (Mon–Fri 8am–5pm; ☎ 055 2091 4041, ⊕ facebook.com/Calbayog.Tourism) has a few brochures about local attractions and can offer transport advice as well as helping to arrange guides.

Services Opposite the Legislative Hall there's a post office, plus a daily produce market in Orquin St, on the northern edge of town near the river. There are several banks with ATMs.

ACCOMMODATION AND EATING

Carlos n' Carmelos Nijaga St ☎ 055 209 4055. Simply the best ribs in the Eastern Visayas. This fast-food favourite wows locals and newcomers alike with sizzling grilled-rib platters as well as burgers, pastas, tacos, cheese sticks and fancy fries. Mains around P200. Mon–Sat 8am–9pm, Sun 8am–8pm.

Ciriaco Hotel South of town on the National Hwy ☎ 055 209 6521, ⊕ ciriacohotel.com. By far Calbayog's best hotel, with excellent rooms, the more expensive of which look straight out to sea. There's a lobby café and a pool. Staff bend over backwards to help. 📶 **P2400**

S&R Bed & Breakfast Northwest of town on the National Hwy ☎ 055 533 9026 ⊕ srbedbreakfast .blogspot.com. This hotel is comfy, clean and cosy. The single-storey red-and-yellow block overlooks a clean garden, while the five rooms have mini balconies, cool tiled floors, queen beds and TVs. Deluxe rooms, with deep-soaking tubs, cost extra (P1650). 📶 **P1300**

S.O. Coffee Nijaga St ☎ 055 209 6038. Next door to *Carlos n' Carmelos*, this smart little coffee shop (S.O. stands for Special Occasions) has cakes, smoothies, a line-up of dishes (nachos, garlic rice and baby back ribs), party supplies and toys. Brewed coffee P30. Free wi-fi. Mon–Sat 8am–10pm.

SAMAR UNDERGROUND

Catbalogan is not known as the capital of **caving** in the Philippines for nothing. Below the surface, a whole new world exists; it's a must-see on any visit. Of the many caves in Samar, **Jiabong**, just 12km from Catbalogan, is the easiest to explore, and has plenty of weird and wonderful features, including a ceiling carpeted with miniature stalactites. Further away, some 50km south of the city, **Langun-Gobingob** in Calbiga stretches 7km through twelve different chambers, and is one of the largest cave systems in Southeast Asia. This utterly dark environment is home to blind crabs, fish and thousands of fluttering bats. Both caves offer extreme caving – plenty of wading, swimming and squeezing through narrow spaces, with only your guide's lantern (or your torch) to guide you. **Permits** are required.

CAVING TRIPS

Trexplore Allen Ave, Catbalogan ☎ 055 251 2301, ⊕ trexplore.weebly.com. The best way to get underground is to arrange a guided trip through local cave guru Joni Bonifacio at the Trexplore outdoor shop. If there's anything Joni doesn't know about the subterranean passages below the Catbalogan jungle, then it's not worth knowing about. He can arrange day- or overnight trips to the caves including meals, permits, equipment and transport (P3000–7000/person; minimum two people).

Catbalogan and around

Seventy kilometres south of Calbayog, the bustling port town of **CATBALOGAN** is the capital of Western Samar. For travellers, the city is mostly of interest as a base from which to head out climbing, canyoning and caving in the labyrinthine **cave systems** found within a couple of hours drive of the city (see box opposite); it's also a popular birdwatching area.

Ulot Torpedo Boat Extreme Ride

P1850 (for up to five people) • ☎ 0917 314 9885 ⓥ facebook.com/TorpedoBoat • Take a bus or shuttle van bound for Borongan from Tacloban or Catbalogan and jump off at Samar Island National Park in Brgy Tenani; book in advance

Ulot Torpedo Boat Extreme Ride is a community-run initiative located on the cross-island Taft-Paranas Road that heads to Borongan on the east coast, 16km from the Catbalogan junction. The organization is successfully bringing visitors to a once-remote part of Samar. The idea is simple: a torpedo-shaped pumpboat whisks you up through the rapids into the island's last virgin forest, where you embark on a jungle adventure involving trekking, swimming and wildlife-watching. The longest river in Samar, the 90km Ulot was named for the local term for monkey, but it's unlikely you'll see any. Instead, keep your eyes peeled for soaring hawks and eagles.

ARRIVAL AND INFORMATION

CATBALOGAN AND AROUND

By ferry Roble Shipping has a twice-weekly ferry service to Cebu (Tues & Fri 7pm; 12hr), which leaves from the Catbalogan pier at the end of Allen Ave.

By bus and van Buses leave from the Catbalogan Bus Terminal, between Pier 1 and Pier 2, departing every 30min–1hr.

Destinations Borongan (5hr); Calbayog (2hr); Catarman (4hr); Tacloban (3hr).

By van A quicker alternative to the buses is to take a Duptours, Grand Tours or Van-Vans vehicle. All three companies have regular services for Calbayog and Tacloban, which leave from their private terminals – Grand Tours and Van-Vans on San Bartolome St, and Duptours just around the corner on Allen Ave. For Catarman, you need to transfer in Calbayog.

Destinations Calbayog (every 30min; 1hr 30min). Tacloban (every 30min; 2hr).

Money and services Catbalogan has most things a traveller should need, and ATMs aren't hard to come by.

ACCOMMODATION AND EATING

Café Maria Rosario Rizal Ave ☎ 055 543 8679. This is the place for home-made cakes, shakes and frappes, which the sweet-toothed locals can't get enough off. Savoury delights like baked macaroni and spaghetti bolognese are also on the menu. Set meals from P130. Daily 9am–10pm.

Casa Cristina 152 San Roque St ☎ 055 251 2840, ⓦ casacristinahotel.com. A cheap-and-cheerful option with brightly painted rooms. Budget options share communal bathrooms, while deluxe a/c rooms (P1250) come with cable TV, hot and cold water and en-suite bathrooms. However, none of the rooms have windows. 📶 **P900**

City Grill Del Rosario St. Modern café-restaurant which churns out home-fried specialities like sizzling pork ribs, chicken wings and beef steaks, making it one of the most popular joints in town. Live music and acoustic performances at weekends are another draw. Mains P150–300. Daily 9am–10pm.

Hotel San Francisco 2 San Francisco St ☎ 055 543 8384. In hardly a close competition, this 28-room hotel is the most modern in the city. With the odd design flourish, IKEA-style furniture and token contemporary art on the walls, it certainly looks the part. It's quiet, comfortable and clean. A small breakfast is included, too. Wi-fi in the lobby only. 📶 **P1450**

Rolet Hotel Mabini Ave ☎ 055 251 5512. Starting to show signs of age, this was once the best option in town, with a/c rooms, slightly worn furniture, cable TV and good bathrooms. The friendly proprietors, Odie and Lolit Letaba, can answer most travel-related questions on the area. 📶 **P950**

Sohoton Natural Bridge National Park

Best known for a rock that has formed a natural bridge across a gorge, the **Sohoton Natural Bridge National Park** includes some remarkable limestone caves and chasms, and lowland rainforest where you can see, even around the park's picnic areas, monitor lizards, macaques and wild boar. Heavy rains cause flash floods, and the park is often closed during the monsoon from late November to early March.

Much of the area can be toured by boat and kayak, although to reach the **natural bridge** itself you'll have to get out and walk; and as there are few marked trails, you'll need to hire a **guide** to find your way around. The boat trip into the park is spectacular, heading up the **Cadacan River**'s estuary, which is lined by mangroves and nipa palms. As you approach, the river begins to twist and is then funnelled into a gorge of limestone cliffs and caves.

The most accessible of the park's many impressive caves is **Panhuughan I**, which has extensive stalactite and stalagmite formations in every passage and chamber. If you're lucky you might come across a number of specialized spiders and millipedes that eke out lives here in total darkness, and there have been many significant archeological finds in the caves, including burial jars, decorated human teeth and Chinese ceramics. During World War II, Filipino guerrillas used the caves as hideouts in their campaign against the occupying Japanese forces.

ARRIVAL AND INFORMATION   SOHOTON NATURAL BRIDGE NATIONAL PARK

Access The park is in the southern part of Samar, with the only approach being through Basey, on Samar's southwest coast, where you can arrange a bangka for the 10km-long, 2hr river trip to Sohoton. The quickest way to get to Basey is via Tacloban on Leyte, from where you can catch an early minivan or jeepney from the New Bus Terminal (40min; P30); a tricycle will then take you to the Basey Municipal Tourist Office, near Basey's plaza.

Fees, guides and information It's both complicated and expensive to get into the heart of the park. At the regional tourist office (☎ 055 276 1471) you pay the P200 entrance fee, and can arrange a guide (P400), head torch (P400) and a bangka to take you to and from the park; prices fluctuate wildly between P1200–1700/person for a six-seater, so be prepared to haggle.

Marabut Islands

A hundred kilometres southeast of Catbalogan lies the small settlement of Marabut. This is the jumping-off point for exploring the **Marabut Islands**, a striking collection of toothy limestone karsts rising out of the sea only a few hundred metres offshore, and reminiscent of Krabi's outcrops on Thailand's Andaman Coast and the rock formations in Halong Bay, Vietnam. There's no **accommodation** on any of the islands, but there are some options on the mainland.

ACCOMMODATION   MARABUT ISLANDS

Caluwayan Palm Island Resort Brgy Caluwayan, 17km northwest along the coast from Marabut ☎ 0977 3545 692, ⊛ caluwayanresort.com. *Caluwayan* offers luxurious accommodation with a/c and TV, in lovely native-style cottages on a stretch of beach. There is a choice of rooms, villas and cottages, and plenty of distractions, including kayak hire (P200/hr), rock climbing and a stellar infinity pool. ☎ __P2500__

Eastern Samar

Eastern Samar is surf country, particularly around **Borongan**, and further south on beautiful Calicoan Island, which is accessed from the small and sleepy town of **Guiuan**. **Calicoan** island has plenty of beaches, caves and lagoons and was only just starting to see tourism development when Yolanda devastated the island, and almost entirely demolished Guiuan. Slowly, the area is beginning to recover.

The bus trip from Catbalogan across to the east coast is one of the great little road journeys in the Philippines, taking you up through the rugged, jungle-clad interior past isolated barangays and along terrifying cliff roads. After four hours, the bus emerges from the wilderness onto the typhoon-battered east coast at Taft and turns south towards Borongan.

Borongan and around

BORONGAN has good surf at most times of year, and the entire coastline remains largely untouched by developers and hotels. Confident surfers can slip off the country's main surfing circuit to discover reef and beach breaks all to themselves here. If the surf's not up, you could always hire a bangka and take a trip along the coast, or out to the pretty island of **Divinubo**, dubbed the hidden paradise of Eastern Samar. It's an idyllic day-trip destination for exploring and snorkelling, but as there are no facilities on the island, make sure that you take something to eat and drink.

ARRIVAL AND INFORMATION

By bus and jeepney There are a few buses that ply the mountain route between Borongan and Catbalogan (5hr), as well as jeepneys and vans for Guiuan. The Duptours terminal is on Real St, and Van-Vans is on E. Cinco St.

Tourist information The small tourist office (Mon–Sat

BORONGAN AND AROUND

8am–4pm; ☎ 0917 426 9167) is in the Provincial Capitol Building facing Borongan plaza.

Money There's a Metrobank on Abogado St, and a PNB across from the Uptown Mall next to *Hotel Dona Vicenta*, both of which have ATMs.

ACCOMMODATION AND EATING

Boro Bay Hotel North of town on Baybay Blvd ☎ 0917 533 5618, ⓦ facebook.com/BoroBayHotel. Situated away from the bustle of downtown, this quiet property has an impressive pavilion-style lobby and entrance, and welcoming and friendly staff. The clean rooms have all the mod cons, including a/c, cable TV and en-suite showers with hot water. Basic breakfast included of beef or milkfish, with egg over rice. 🛜 **P1500**

Hotel Dona Vicenta Real St ☎ 0908 256 9747. The most luxurious accommodation in the town is to be found at this grand-looking business hotel on the main highway. Comfortable, box-like rooms and junior suites (P1680) have cable TV, although many suffer from being too close to the noisy bar, which often stays open until 2am. The higher you go – towards the presidential suite, no less – the better the mountain and ocean views. There's a refreshing pool, too. 🛜 **P980**

Pirate's Cove Beach & Surf Resort Brgy Bato, on a peninsula 1km east of town ☎ 0999 158 3710, ⓦ piratescovesurf.weebly.com. Looking like a cross between a crashed cruise ship and an Antoni Gaudí masterpiece, this long-running, eclectic resort has interesting rooms that range from a treehouse to family cottages, all of which have kitchens. The resort also has a pool, jacuzzi, and one of the most impressive, if downright weird, Scalextric set-ups you're ever likely to encounter. 🛜 **P1500**

Rawis Resort & Restaurant Real St ☎ 0906 287 4719. Aside from at the hotels, Borongan's dining options are limited, which makes this international all-rounder overlooking the estuary and Baybay beach a solid option. It has live music almost every night, cold beers and meals such as chop suey and fried chicken (mains P100–295). Daily 10am–1am.

7

Guiuan and around

At the far end of the road in southeast Samar, protruding out into the Leyte Gulf like a skeletal finger, is **GUIUAN** and the forgotten-by-time surf outpost of **CALICOAN ISLAND**. Such exposed topography meant that when Typhoon Yolanda hit in 2013, with vicious 400km/h winds, the area stood no chance. The casualties were lower than they could have been – fewer than two hundred people were killed – but the storm caused untold damage to the area's hotels and restaurants, and the emerging surf scene was literally wiped off the map. Nonetheless, the resilient community is starting to recapture its pre-Yolanda spirit. This is paving the way for the re-emergence of remote surf camps along Calicoan's **ABCD Beach**, and fishermen eager to show you **Kantican** and **Tubabao** – Eastern Samar's best white-sand islands – by bangka.

Calicoan Island

Catch a jeepney to Sulangan via ABCD Beach from Guiuan Terminal (P30), or charter a habal-habal for a round trip (P300–350)

Accessible across the Guiuan bridge, **Calicoan Island** ticks a lot of boxes – quiet towns, empty beaches, frothing surf and grand sunsets. Prior to Yolanda, it was rapidly developing, but most surf camps were completely destroyed in the almighty storm. The island was thrown back to far simpler times, and there are still few resorts to choose from.

Most surfers base themselves in Guiuan, content with day-trips to ABCD Beach, for the Pacific reef breaks. The best surfing season is from June to October.

By bus and jeepney The quickest way to get to Guiuan is with a Van-Vans or Duptours shuttle bus from Tacloban, which leave when full (3hr 30min). Regular buses will take nearly double that time. If coming from Borongan, a jeepney is by far your best bet (3hr).

Tourist information The Guiuan Tourism Council, based

at the Town Plaza (Mon–Sat 9am–6pm; ☎0917 426 9167), can help with information on the region.

Money There's a PNB ATM near the Guiuan Integrated Transport Terminal, as well as a Metrobank and Landbank in town.

ACCOMMODATION AND EATING

La Luna Beach Resort North of Sulangan Bridge, Calicoan ☎0905 288 7516 ⓦresortlaluna.com. Owned by long-time Italian ex-pat Giovanni, this little four-room resort – two look out to sea (P200 extra), two are out the back – is a great place to detox for a few days, with its saltwater pool and well-stocked bar. Remote, but worth the effort of getting here. ☎ P2500

Misty Blue Boathouse 50m from Tanghay View Lodge, Brgy Luboc ☎0906 251 9663. With a great oceanfront setting and a laidback vibe, this Aussie-run resort and beach bar is a real treat. Expect wood-fired

pizzas, BBQ chicken, pastas, burgers and cold beers in the restaurant. Owner Greg is a mine of information. Mains P200–350. Daily 10am–9pm.

Tanghay View Lodge 2km north of Guiuan town, Brgy Luboc ☎0915 416 8067. This very clean, three-storey oceanfront property overlooks Tubabao Island and the Leyte Gulf. It's run by the gregarious Susan Tan, and not only does she keep the place spick and span, she's also responsible for efficient, friendly staff. The lodge is home to the best restaurant in town, with a Filipino menu that changes daily (mains P50–150). ☎ P1500

Leyte

The east Visayan island of **LEYTE** ("LAY-tay"), separated from Samar to the north by a mere slither of ocean, the San Juanico Strait, is another sizeable chunk of the Philippines that has a great deal to offer visitors but is regularly overlooked. You could spend months here and still only scratch the surface: the coastline is immense, the interior rugged and there are lakes and mountains that are well off the tourist map, known only to farmers who have tilled their shores and foothills for generations.

TYPHOON YOLANDA

On November 8, 2013, **Typhoon Yolanda** (known internationally as Haiyan) hit the southeastern tip of Samar with wind speeds of up to 315kph. The superstorm left a broad band of destruction through northern Leyte, northern Cebu, northeastern Panay and finally Busuanga, in Palawan, before leaving the archipelago. Yolanda made landfall near Guiuan, which was almost completely obliterated, and 2m-plus storm surges wreaked havoc in Tacloban. In spite of a huge **international relief effort**, many of the worst affected areas remained without power, clean water and supplies for weeks. Looting became a major problem, while in unaffected regions businesses and individuals rallied to raise funds and support.

Economically, the recovery period will be counted in years, but for the families of the six thousand dead the losses are clearly irreparable: many remain missing, and allegations surrounding the mismanagement of rehabilitation funds still plague government agencies. Aid groups remain in Tacloban and their presence can still be felt, particularly because sustained support is needed to help rebuild homes and repatriate families who continue to live in temporary housing. **Tourism** can have a vital role here; in Cebu and Bohol, where other seismic natural disasters have recently hit, much-needed cash injections have made a life-changing difference to the speed and scale of recovery.

However, the worst hit areas in Leyte haven't been so lucky. While the principal tourist sights, including Sohoton National Park, are open, the islands continue to receive only a trickle of tourists compared to elsewhere in the Eastern Visayas. For the most part, tourist infrastructure remains minimal, and beyond the main cities of Tacloban and Ormoc there are few hotels and travel operators. But the good news is that local agencies are working tirelessly to change this, and tomorrow is beginning to look brighter.

In the sixteenth century, Magellan passed through Leyte on his way to Cebu, making a blood compact with the local chieftain as he did so. But to many Filipinos and war historians, the island will always be associated with **World War II**, when its jungled hinterlands became the base for a formidable force of guerrillas who fought a number of bloody encounters with the Japanese. It was because of this loyalty among the inhabitants that General Douglas MacArthur landed at Leyte on October 20, 1944, fulfilling the famous promise he had made to Filipinos, "I shall return".

Around the provincial capital of **Tacloban**, the usual arrival point, there are a number of sights associated with the war, notably the **Leyte Landing Memorial**, marking the spot where MacArthur waded ashore to liberate the archipelago. Tacloban is also now remembered as the site of the worst of Typhoon Yolanda's devastation – as well as the powerful winds and rain, a huge storm surge decimated large chunks of the city (see box opposite). To the north of Tacloban is the beautiful island of **Biliran** and, a short bangka ride away from Biliran, the islands of **Maripipi** and **Higatangan**, which both have terrific beaches, rock formations and caves. To the south of the bayside town of **Ormoc**, the coastal road takes you through the ferry ports of **Baybay** and **Maasin** before reaching **Padre Burgos**, which is gaining a reputation for its scuba diving and whale shark encounters.

ARRIVAL AND DEPARTURE   LEYTE

By plane Leyte's only major airport is at Tacloban, served by daily flights to Manila and Cebu.

By boat Fast ferry connections link the port of Ormoc with Cebu, and there are also boats from Cebu and Bohol to Bato, Baybay, Hilongos, and Maasin on Leyte's west coast.

By bus Buses to Leyte operate from Manila, and there are also regular daily services from Biliran to Tacloban and Ormoc, and from Samar via the San Juanico Bridge.

Tacloban and around

On the northeast coast, **TACLOBAN** is associated by most Filipinos with that tireless collector of shoes, Imelda Marcos, who was born a little south of here in the small coastal town of Tolosa to the prominent Romualdez family. In her youth, Imelda was a local beauty queen, and referred to herself in later life as "the rose of Tacloban". The famed **San Juanico Bridge**, presented by Ferdinand to Imelda as testimony to his love, is another legacy of the Marcos connection. You'll probably see it when flying in or out of the airport, which still bears the Romualdez name.

Typhoon Yolanda will live long in the memory for the survivors in Tacloban, which became the epicentre of recovery efforts (see box opposite). Although most hotels and restaurants are now back on their feet, at the time of writing thousands of residents were still living in temporary shelters (which were designed to house them for a few months, not years), and low-cost housing units on the city outskirts remained unfinished. As an indication of just how important the relief work is, President Duterte has taken a personal stake in the new resettlement sites, ordering government agencies to urgently address bottlenecks in the worst hit areas.

In many ways, though, it's business as usual in the city itself, and Tacloban remains a typically frenetic Filipino city, with most activity centred around the port and the market. There are few tourist attractions, though if you are here for a day or two you'll find that the city has everything you need: good accommodation, numerous travel agencies, and banks and restaurants crammed into the grid-like centre between **Avenida Veteranos** and **J. Romualdez Street**.

The city's major fiestas are the Mardi Gras spectacles of **Pintados-Kasadyaan**, a celebration of the body-painting traditions of the island's ancient tattooed warriors, and **Sangyaw**, a carnival with parades and floats. Both are held in the last week of June.

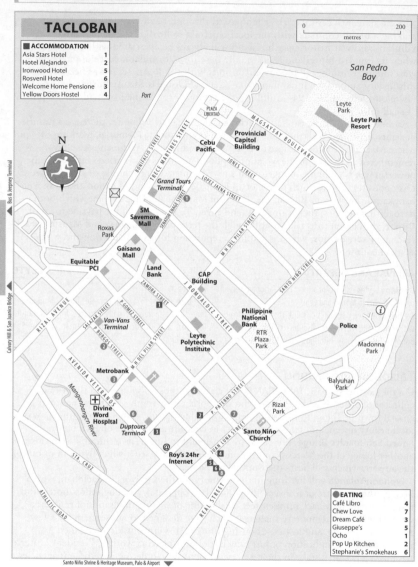

TACLOBAN

ACCOMMODATION	
Asia Stars Hotel	1
Hotel Alejandro	2
Ironwood Hotel	5
Rosvenil Hotel	6
Welcome Home Pensione	3
Yellow Doors Hostel	4

EATING	
Café Libro	4
Chew Love	7
Dream Café	3
Giuseppe's	5
Ocho	1
Pop Up Kitchen	2
Stephanie's Smokehaus	6

Santo Niño Shrine & Heritage Museum, Palo & Airport

Santo Niño Shrine and Heritage Museum

Real St, 2km south of town • Mon–Fri 8am–5pm • P230 for up to three people, including guide

The first stop on any tour of Tacloban should be to gawp at the **Santo Niño Shrine and Heritage Museum**. A grand folly of a house that Imelda Marcos ordered built but, in fact, never slept in, it was sequestered by the government after the Marcos regime was overthrown. Inside, there is evidence aplenty that nothing was too opulent or tasteless for the Iron Butterfly. Her personal chapel has sparkling diamond chandeliers, gold-framed mirrors and an expensive replica of the miraculous Santo Niño de Leyte (the original resides in the **Santo Niño Church** opposite Rizal Park in Real Street).

San Juanico Bridge

Free · Take a bus from the New Bus Terminal to anywhere on Samar (Marabut, Basey, Borongan, Guiuan) and jump off beforehand (20min, P30)

Completed in 1973, the monumental, humpbacked landmark of **San Juanico Bridge** stretches from Leyte to Samar, and at 2.16km is the longest bridge in the Philippines. Though such a statistic may not be all that impressive, its arch-shaped truss design is still an engineering marvel. On a good day, the bridge offers fabulous views across the San Juanico Strait to Tacloban and beyond.

Calvary Hill

Ave Veteranos, on the western edge of the city, 1km from the centre

It's worth the sweat of a walk up to the top of **Calvary Hill**. This is a place of pilgrimage during Holy Week before Easter and the ascent is marked by the fourteen **Stations of the Cross**, with a five-metre statue of the Sacred Heart of Jesus at the summit. A good time to start the climb is late afternoon, so you reach the top in time to watch the sunset.

Palo and around

A taxi to Palo costs P220–320, tricycle P120 and jeepney P20

About 5km south of Tacloban is the small town of **PALO**, known for its associations with MacArthur and the liberation. It was at Palo's **Red Beach**, about 1km from the town centre, that MacArthur waded ashore on October 20, 1944, fulfilling his famous vow to return. The spot is marked by the dramatic **Leyte Landing Memorial**, an oversized sculpture of the general and his associates, among them Sergio Osmeña walking purposefully through the shallows to the beach.

ARRIVAL AND INFORMATION

TACLOBAN AND AROUND

By plane Daniel Z. Romualdez Airport is located on a spit of land southeast of Tacloban, 10km by road from downtown. A jeepney into town costs P13, a tricycle around P120. Air Asia, Cebu Pacific (☎053 325 8486) and PAL (☎053 325 7832) currently have ticket offices at the airport, and Cebu Pacific (☎053 321 9410) has an office on Senator Enage St. There is a P150 airport terminal fee to pay before clearing security.

Destinations Cebu (3 daily; 50min); Manila (10 daily; 1hr 10min).

By bus and jeepney Buses and jeepneys from all points arrive at the New Bus Terminal in Abucay, 2km west of the city. Services to destinations within Leyte and Samar run regularly, but are most frequent in the mornings.

Destinations Borongan (4hr 30min); Calbayog (hourly; 4hr); Catbalogan (hourly; 3hr); Catarman (hourly; 6hr); Maasin (hourly; 5hr); Manila (3 daily; 24hr); Naval (every 30min; 3hr); Ormoc (hourly; 3hr).

By van Many of the bus routes are also covered by the far quicker Duptours Shuttle Services, Grand Tours and Van-Vans minivans, each of which leaves from their designated terminal: Duptours opposite the *Welcome Home Pensione* on Santo Niño St; Grand Tours from Trece Martires St, near the post office; and Van-Vans terminal on P. Burgos St.

Destinations Catbalogan (every 30min; 2hr); Maasin (every 30min; 4hr); Naval (every 30min; 2hr 45min); Ormoc (every 30min; 2hr 30min).

Tourist information The regional tourist office on Magsaysay Boulevard on Kanhuraw Hill can provide information, maps and travel tips (☎053 832 0901).

ACCOMMODATION

Accommodation ranges from quirky budget rooms to affordable mid-range places. As tourists start to drip-feed back to Leyte, Tacloban will see the lion's share of the windfall, so by the time you read this, there will probably be more boutique-style hotels to rival the ones listed here.

Asia Stars Hotel Zamora St ☎053 321 5388, ⓦasiastarshotel.com. Unattractive from the outside, but the rooms are fine, the staff friendly and the central location unbeatable. Quiet doubles with fan or a/c, all with private shower, plus some rooms which have cable TV and a fridge. Deluxe rooms have bigger beds (P1800). 🛜 P1200

Hotel Alejandro P. Paterno St ☎053 321 7033. From the outset more museum than hotel, this bragging old-timer in an attractive 1930s colonial villa was used as a refuge for evacuees in World War II. Rooms are tastefully styled and have a/c, cable TV, and fridges, although not all have external windows. There's a fascinating display of historic photographs, and downstairs the restaurant and coffee shop have wi-fi. Worth a look round, even if you're not staying. 📶 **P1800**

Ironwood Hotel P. Burgos St at Juan Luna St ☎053 321 9999, ⓦ ironwoodhotel.com. Sleek, modern, and a world apart from the competition. A great new addition to Tacloban, the *Ironwood* is a business hotel with a fine selection of premium doubles, kings and deluxe executive suites (P5000). Rooms come with flatscreen TVs, MP3-compatible radios, and fragrant bathroom amenities, but you'd expect as much for the price. 📶 **P3250**

Rosvenil Hotel 302 P. Paterno St ☎053 321 2676. Part Spanish farmhouse ranch, part Swiss mountain lodge, this homely mid-range option has clean if bare-boned rooms with comfy beds and a choice of a/c or fan. Out front is a sociable garden, and the hotel is in walking distance to all the downtown restaurants. 📶 **P1480**

Welcome Home Pensione South end of Santo Niño St, opposite the Caltex petrol station ☎0917 7027166, ⓦ welcomehomepensione.com. Across the road from the Duptours terminal, this place offers good-value fan or a/c rooms (shared bathroom or en suite), and bargain family rooms (P1400). Gets booked up frequently, so reserve ahead. For free wi-fi, head to the coffee shop next door. **P800**

★**Yellow Doors Hostel** P. Burgos St at Juan Luna St ☎0921 600 0165, ⓦ facebook.com/HelloYellowDH. The most stylishly designed backpackers' in the Eastern Visayas, this surprising find is the first hostel of its kind in Tacloban, and will be hard to beat. A three-storey building abandoned after Typhoon Yolanda, it's standout features include upcycled furniture recovered from the debris, a book swap library and a lovely chill-out area on the roof. Rooms are minimalist but funky. 📶 Dorms **P800**, doubles **P1250**

EATING

These days Tacloban has a pretty sophisticated **restaurant** scene, including weekend pop-ups and American-style smokehouses. In between meals, there are plenty of local specialities to **snack** on – *binagul*, a hot sticky concoction made of coconut and nuts, and chocolate *meron* can be bought freshly made every morning from hawkers along Rizal Ave.

Café Libro P. Gomez St at Santo Niño St ☎053 523 2738. Quirky little café obsessing over the three C's – coffee, cakes and cookies (all from P30). There is a well-thumbed secondhand book exchange, so lingering over a cup of freshly brewed coffee and a peanut butter or red velvet cupcake (both P100) is the norm here. Mon–Sat noon–9pm.

Chew Love P. Gomez St ☎0917 310 8286. If any restaurant can create a social media buzz in Tacloban, it's *Chew Love*. Don't be put off by the twee, candy-cane look of this emoji-influenced café-restaurant. Past the eye-popping wall-art mural and toy-town design, it's a fun place to eat. There are plenty of fish, steak, pork and chicken soul-food dishes to choose from, served with heart-shaped rice (P170–200). Understandably, it's popular with families and teenagers. Mon–Sat 11am–8.30pm.

Dream Café 222 M.H. Del Pilar St ☎053 325 8222, ⓦ dreamcafe.ph. Australian-Filipino-owned, this jack-of-all-trades diner serves all-day breakfasts (P95–190), burgers (P145–285), paninis (P195–265), Aussie rib-eye steaks (P895), freshly baked breads, packed lunches and imported wines. The terrace is one of the few places in the city to grab a cold beer, while on Fri and Sat nights, it hosts live acoustic shows. Daily 8am–11pm.

★**Giuseppe's** 173 Ave Veteranos ☎053 321 4910. It seems like every town in the Philippines has an Italian place like this, but *Giuseppe's* is a genuine cut above the rest. The stone-baked pizzas (P350–600) are as good as you'll find in this part of the world, and there's also ravioli ragu, baked lasagne, spaghetti marinara (P300–350) and top-notch coffee. It's as sophisticated as the Tacloban dining scene gets. Daily 11am–10pm.

Ocho Senator Enage St ☎053 325 4171, ⓦ ocho.ph. Stylish restaurant where you choose from super-fresh salads, fish, fruit and desserts laid out at the back of the restaurant, or opt for market-fresh fish or shellfish cooked to your taste. For something different, try one of the *amapalaya* specials (bitter tropical melon with fish). Two can dine for around P500. Daily 10am–10pm.

Pop Up Kitchen 194 P. Burgos St ☎0917 623 1889. Also known as *POUKI*, this burger bar is doing great things with the humble meat patty and French fry. Take your pick from mango salsa, avocado or a wasabi burger (P200–250) – the latter comes served on a scale of one to ten, depending on how hot you can handle it. Daily 11am–11pm.

Stephanie's Smokehaus Ave Veteranos ☎0917 323 3747. Ludicrously popular buffet restaurant, where P250 buys a great-value, all-you-can-eat spread. It's hugely popular with locals, and queues out the door aren't unheard of at weekends. Daily 10am–2pm & 5–9pm.

DIRECTORY

Hospital There are a number of private hospitals and medical clinics in the city, including Divine Word Hospital on M. H. Del Pilar St, and R.T. Romualdez Hospital and Mother of Mercy Hospital south of the city centre.

Internet Roy's 24hr Internet on P. Paterno St is just one of the many small internet places dotted around downtown.
Police Local police headquarters are located on the P. Paterno Extension near the RTR Plaza Park.
Post office There's a post office near the harbour on Trece Martirez St.

Biliran

The beautiful and largely undiscovered Eden of **Biliran** lies off the north coast of Leyte, connected by a bridge. An autonomous island province governed from **NAVAL**, the sleepy capital on the west coast, Biliran is the Philippines in microcosm: there's a lengthy coastline of deep coves and palm-fringed white beaches; a mountainous interior; and the **Sampao rice terraces**, the island's own small version of Banaue's agricultural steps at Iyusan.

Among the many natural wonders are nearly a dozen thundering **waterfalls**, most with deep, clear pools that are perfect for swimming: Kasabangan Falls is in the barangay of Balaquid on the south coast; Casiawan Falls, a little further along the coast near Casiawan village; and Tinago Falls, near Gabibihan, is in the island's east. For something different, and to see where the future of tourism in Biliran may lie, stop at the **Canaan Hills Farm & Honey Garden** outside Caibiran. A tropical fruit farm, landscaped garden and organic café, it paints a romanticized picture of rural Leyte life.

Two of the best **beaches** on Biliran are on opposite sides of the island, but even on a day-trip you'll have time to see them both. On the east coast, near Culaba, is the deserted Looc White Beach, while the Shifting Sand Bar, 45 minutes by bangka towards **Higatangan** from Naval, is a 200m-long curving spit of sand surrounded by shallow water.

Maripipi and Higatangan islands

For Maripipi there are two boats daily from Naval (10am & 10.30am; 1hr; P60), which both return at 5am the following day; two boats run daily to Higantangan (noon & 1pm; 40min; P40) and return the following morning – unless you charter a bangka (P2000–4000), overnighting is necessary on both islands

If you get to Biliran, make sure that you allow enough time to take a bangka to some of the surrounding islands. **Maripipi** is a picturesque place for a backwoods adventure, dominated by a stunning 924m volcano, while Higatangan Rocks on **Higatangan Island** is well worth a visit. The beach here is beautiful, and the rocks have been carved into extraordinary formations by time and tide. Both islands have simple, often power-free (or power-limited) places to stay.

ARRIVAL AND DEPARTURE   BILIRAN

By bus and minivan There are buses and Duptours minivans to Naval from Tacloban and Ormoc (both every 30min; 2–3hr).
By boat Roble Shipping (☏053 500 7898) have four ferries a week from Cebu City to Naval (Mon, Wed, Fri & Sat; 9hr), but if you want to save time, it's far quicker to take a fast ferry to Ormoc then a minivan from there.

GETTING AROUND

By bus and jeepney From Naval there are sporadic buses and jeepneys north to Almeria (20min; P25), Kawayan (40min; P30) and east to Caibiran and Culaba (1hr; P60), but no further in either direction.
By habal-habal To explore the island at leisure, it's most convenient to hire a habal-habal to take you around for the day (P900–1200). Alternatively, try Biliran Island Rent-A-Car (from P4000; ⓦ tourism.biliranisland.com).

INFORMATION

Tourist information The small tourist office (Mon–Fri 8am–5pm; ☏053 500 9571) and museum is on the second floor of the Provincial Capitol Building in Naval. To explore the more remote areas of the islands and to find the waterfalls, it's best to employ the services of a local guide (P300–400/day) – staff at the tourist office can help arrange one. It's also worth checking out ⓦ biliranisland. com, ⓦ tourism.biliranisland.com and ⓦ biliran.ph.
Services There are Metrobank and PNB banks, both with ATMs, on P. Inocentes St near the WAD Mall in Naval.

7

ACCOMMODATION AND EATING

As tourism has yet to really take off on Biliran, hotels and guesthouses are accustomed to **power blackouts**, and **electricity** often only runs at certain times of the day. In conditions such as this reliable **wi-fi**, particularly on the remoter islands, is still a few years away.

NAVAL

Chamorita 5km south of town ☎091 8608 3499, ⓦchamoritarp.com. Owned by American expat Leo, and located just off the island ring road, this homely waterfront resort has a mixture of a/c rooms, including budget options for backpackers (P500), standard doubles and deluxe rooms (P1500) with French-louvre windows and power-showers. There's a restaurant and bar on site, and a whole host of activities on offer. 🛜 **P950**

D'Mei Residence Inn 213 P. Inocentes St ☎053 500 9796, ✉dmei.residence.inn@gmail.com. Hands down the best overnight option in Naval, with attractive, clean and brightly painted a/c rooms with flatscreen TVs. Considering the noise outside, the rooms are surprisingly quiet. There's a handy mini-mart on the ground floor. Wi-fi in communal areas only. 🛜 **P1100**

Marvin's Seaside Inn 2km north of town, Brgy Atipolo ☎0921 424 1002, ✉ marvinsseasideinn @yahoo.com. A far better bet than staying in town, *Marvin's* is a quiet, safe and clean choice with seaside rooms (without views or any kind of beach) in the main banana-yellow block, and larger, nicer rooms (P1800) set around the pool in a building across the road. All rooms come with cable TV and hot showers, and the restaurant has a decent range of Western and Filipino dishes. Wi-fi in reception. 🛜 **P1200**

MayLaka 7km south of town ☎0920 919 6844 ⓦmaylaka.com. The closest thing Biliran has to a

boutique lodge, this new (if pricey) addition to the island's resort line-up has a restaurant, bar and spa. A/c rooms go the extra mile with flatscreen TVs, rainforest showers, mini-bars and folded towel animals. A new budget option is set to open in late 2017. 🛜 **P3920**

ELSEWHERE ON BILIRAN

Agta Beach Resort Almeria, 12km north of Naval ☎0906 225 6265 ⓦagtabeachresort.com. Something of a scuba pioneer, *Agta* was the first dive resort on Biliran, and continues to prioritize what's under the sea rather than what's on land. This means that its rooms could do with an update, but staff make up for it by being amiable and eager to help. 🛜 **P1200**

MARIPIPI AND HIGANTANGAN ISLANDS

Higantangan Island Beach Resort Higatangan ☎0910 573 5963, ⓦhigatanganislandresort.com. A good range of slightly dated, simple rooms and cottages spread through manicured gardens on the shore. During the day, the resort can arrange local hikes, bike and kayak rental, and provide a free shuttle to a nearby sandbar. At night, the resort runs on a generator. **P800**

Napo Beach Resort 20min habal-habal from pier, Maripipi ☎0921 212 5164 ⓦnapobeachresort.com. For those who won't mind if the power generator cuts out at night or not, Maripipi's only place to stay is an attractive shoestringers' resort with budget rooms and brightly painted fan (P1600) and a/c (P2500) huts set at the base of mountains. Breakfast included. **P700**

Ormoc and around

For such a small, quiet town, **ORMOC**, on Leyte's west coast, has endured a surprising amount of turmoil in its recent history. Scene of some of the bloodiest battles during World War II, Ormoc Bay, at the mouth of the Isla Verde River, hides dozens of shipwrecks. In 1992, floods caused untold damage and resulted in the loss of eight thousand lives. Then, in 2013, Yolanda tore through the city, demolishing countless homes and damaging almost every roof. The city has recovered well, though, and its bay-side park is a lovely place to watch the sunset.

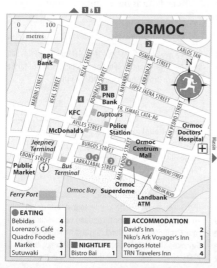

ORMOC

● EATING		
Bebidas	4	
Lorenzo's Café	2	
Quadro Foodie		
Market	3	
Sutuwaki	1	

■ NIGHTLIFE	
Bistro Bai	1

■ ACCOMMODATION	
David's Inn	2
Niko's Ark Voyager's Inn	1
Pongos Hotel	3
TRN Travelers Inn	4

Lake Danao National Park

Lake raft rental P150/hr • Jeepney from Ormoc (P60) or hire a van for the day (P3000)

Lake Danao National Park, 19km away from Ormoc and at a far cooler 650m above sea level, makes for a pleasant half-day trip. Once there, you can hike to a number of different waterfalls, including Inawasan Falls (30min), Tigbawan Falls (2hr) and Mag-aso Falls (3–4hr). For something more relaxing, you can explore the park's lake by renting a raft.

ARRIVAL AND DEPARTURE
ORMOC

By ferry Oceanjet (5 daily; ☎032 255 7560 in Cebu), SuperCat (5 daily; ☎032 233 7000) and Weesam (1 daily; ☎053 561 0080) all have fast ferry sailings between Cebu and Ormoc (2hr 30min). 2GO (☎053 561 9818), Lite Shipping (☎053 561 6036) and Roble Shipping (☎053 255 7631) run slower services for Cebu (5–6hr).

By bus, jeepney and van The main bus terminal and jeepney terminal are next to each other on Ebony St, near the

pier. Jeepneys also operate some of the routes below but are far slower. The quickest way to move on is with a Duptours Shuttle Services van, which costs slightly more than the buses, and leaves from the terminal on Bonifacio St (P120 for Tacloban).

Destinations Baybay (hourly; 1hr); Maasin (hourly; 3hr); Naval (every 30min; 3hr); Tacloban (hourly; 3hr).

ACCOMMODATION

★**David's Inn** Carlos Tan St ☎053 255 7618. Set a few blocks back from the main action, this well-run, friendly guesthouse is the kind every traveller likes to stumble into after a long day. The rooms (all en suite) are decent, with a/c, hot water and cable TV, and some have a terrace (P1050). Snacks and beers are on offer too. ☏ **P800**

Niko's Ark Voyager's Inn Real St ☎053 561 0258 ⓦnikosarkboutiquehotel.com. Niko's is a unique concept. Decked out to look like the inside of Captain Nemo's submarine, this boutique hotel has ship's cabins for rooms, with nautical memorabilia, lifebuoys, and frigate ropes hung from the walls. Bunk-bed dorms for shipmates are a bargain, and there are capsule-like single rooms (P550) and doubles with power-showers and flatscreen

TVs. Lovely, if a little odd. ☏ Dorms **P300**, doubles **P900**

Pongos Hotel Bonifacio St ☎053 561 9722. During Yolanda, Pongos flung open its doors to help as many people as possible in the aftermath – and people in Ormoc continue to have a soft spot for it. It has a vast array of rooms, ranging from tatty doubles in the main building to better a/c rooms (P1300) in the new building. ☏ **P800**

TRN Travelers Inn 32 Rizal St ☎053 255 7700, ⓦtrntravelersinn.com. This long-running budget hotel has small but clean rooms, and is a dependable choice. All rooms are a/c and have cable TV. Tiny singles start from P700, but the majority of rooms are more spacious doubles. There's also a snack bar, coffee shop, gym and music lounge. Wi-fi reaches some rooms. ☏ **P1300**

EATING

Bebidas Malacadios St ☎053 560 8098. Bebidas welcomes you with a billboard proclaiming "Coffee – do stupid things faster with more energy". Inside, there's lively artwork, free wi-fi, and the menu includes favourite staples such as spaghetti and sandwiches (P15–60), coffees, brownies and desserts. It's also a popular night-time drinking spot. Daily 9am–2am.

Lorenzo's Café Larrazabal St ☎053 561 6216. Pleasant Starbucks clone with indoor seating and people-watching tables outside, which look across to the sea. The menu

includes sandwiches, salads and pastas (P130–160). Daily 7.30am–11pm.

Quadro Foodie Market Larrazabal St. Across from the seafront park by the harbour, a vast array of stalls at this lively night market sell an A to Z of cheap meals, street snacks and cold beers. Fri–Sun 5pm–2am.

Sutuwaki Larrazabal St ☎0928 406 2603. Popular open-sided restaurant by the harbour where you choose from the meat and fish at the counter and get it cooked to order. Daily 10am–midnight.

DRINKING

Bistro Bai Real St ☎053 561 2259 ⓦbistrobai.wixsite .com/mysite. To see where Ormoc locals let their hair down, there's really only one joint in town. A bar, grill,

restaurant, coffee shop and live-music venue rolled into one, Bistro chalks up everything from cold-brew coffee and kare kare to breakfasts and funk nights. Daily 8am till late.

DIRECTORY

Hospital The city's most convenient hospital is Ormoc Doctors' Hospital (☎053 560 8222), on the corner of Aviles St and San Pablo St.

Internet access There are a number of interent cafés dotted around town between Osmeña and Aviles streets.

Police Ormoc's police station is on J. Navarro St at Aviles St.

7

The southwest coast

If you're heading south along the coast, you'll find several towns which offer transport connections with Cebu and thus an alternative gateway to the diving to be found further south at Padre Burgos (see below). Fifty kilometres south of Ormoc, the frenetic port of **BAYBAY** is a functional town with a very busy wharf area and a main street lined with *carinderias*, convenience stores, pawnshops and a few banks. About halfway between Baybay and Maasin, clean, easy-going **HILONGOS** has a number of canteens huddled around a simple pier, but nowhere to stay. A little south of Hilongos, the port town of **BATO** is a useful jumping-off point for Padre Burgos. At the mouth of the Maasin River, the otherwise dull, industrial port of **MAASIN** makes a good starting point if you're heading for the far south of Leyte, an area that's opening up for scuba diving and whale-shark-watching, particularly around Sogod Bay.

ARRIVAL AND INFORMATION   THE SOUTHWEST COAST

By boat Both Baybay (Cokaliong: 3 weekly; Roble Shipping: daily; 6hr) and Hilongos (Gabisan Shipping *Gloria G1*: daily; Roble Shipping: daily; 3hr 30min) are connected by regular ferries to Cebu and have onwards transport connections by bus, jeepney and van further south. From Maasin, Cokaliong runs slow ferries to Cebu City (4 weekly; 6hr), while Weesam Express runs two fast services (daily; 3hr; check ahead of travel). From Ubay on Bohol, Super Shuttle Ferry runs trips to Bato (daily; 3hr 30min).

By bus If you're arriving by air in Tacloban you can catch an a/c minivan direct to Maasin (4hr; P220). Otherwise, buses from Tacloban take up to 6hr. A trip from Ormoc should take around 3hr (P170).

Tourist information You can get up-to-date information on diving and whale-shark-watching from any of the resorts, particularly *Peter's Dive Resort* and *Sogod Bay Scuba Resort* (see opposite).

ACCOMMODATION

Caimito Beach Hotel R. Kangleon St, 7km south of Maasin ☎ 053 570 1139 ⓦ caimitobeachhotel.com. This nine-room pool resort is a short drive along the coast, but worth it for the waterfront location, pools and patios. Tiled floor rooms are no-frills, but come with extra perks including mini-bar, tea-and-coffee-making facilities and bathroom amenities. Single rooms are available (P1300). 📶 P2300

Villa Romana Hotel R. Kangleon St, Maasin ☎ 053 381 2228. A mix of Spanish bodega-style and downtown Filipino, this central hotel is a reliable option to break up a journey. It's on the waterfront, overlooking the Port of Maasin, and within walking distance of the city's best shops, bars and restaurants. 📶 P1350

Padre Burgos and around

The area around **PADRE BURGOS** on Leyte's southern tip has developed as an under-the-radar **scuba-diving** destination, with dozens of sites, including the impressive **Napantao Marine Sanctuary**. The region has a frontier atmosphere, and remains firmly off the main tourist path. Those who come this far are rewarded with eerily quiet deep-wall and cave dives in **Sogod Bay** and unpredictable **whale shark** sightings that – on a good day – can beat anywhere in the country.

Limasawa Island

Bangkas leave Padre Burgos 3–4 times early in the morning for Magallanes Brgy on Limasawa (45min; P60)

It was atop a prominent hill on tiny **Limasawa Island** that Magellan is said to have conducted the first Catholic Mass in the Philippines on March 31, 1521. After an often choppy boat ride from Padre Burgos, visitors can walk up 450 concrete steps to a monument at the top of the hill, from where there are commanding views over the whole island.

Coral Cay Conservation

In the village of Napantao on Panaon Island • ☎ 0044 207 620 1411 ⓦ coralcay.org

Established more than thirty years ago in the UK, **Coral Cay Conservation** is an international group with an ongoing project in Southern Leyte, focused on protecting the coral reefs in and around Padre Burgos and **Panaon Island**, further east across Sogod Bay. Volunteers are welcomed to the headquarters in the village of **Napantao**, where a variety of programmes are available, including everything from two-week stints to more immersive four-month marine conservation surveys.

ARRIVAL AND DEPARTURE

By ferry The closest major port to Padre Burgos is Maasin, which is served by ferries from Cebu City (see p.322).
By jeepney Jeepneys head up the coast to Maasin (1hr;

PADRE BURGOS AND AROUND

P40) from where there are transport connections to the rest of Leyte.

ACCOMMODATION

★**Peter's Dive Resort** Padre Burgos ☎0917 791 0993, ⓦwhaleofadive.com. For those who want excellent service and plenty of time in the water beyond the pebble beach, this is a superb option. There's affordable accommodation in dorms, better standard rooms or duplex cottages (P1740). The views of Sogod Bay are breathtaking. The main building's lower terrace has a games room, and there's a pool and an excellent little restaurant where the owners serve home-cooked food. Cheaper rates for divers. 🛜 Dorms P400, doubles P1560

Sogod Bay Scuba Resort Lungsodaan, 1km north of town ☎0915 520 7274, ⓦsogodbayscubaresort.com. Don't be put off by the concrete rooms: the real draw is the professional diving outfit and the location, a flipper's throw from the best scuba sites. Even if you're not here to dive, the owners can help arrange everything from trekking to motorbike hire and caving trips. Wi-fi in public areas. 🛜 P1100

Southern Leyte Divers San Roque, Macrohon ☎0921 663 1592, ⓦleyte-divers.com. This small, German-owned lodge, run by Gunther and Alona, is some 15min northwest of Padre Burgos by jeepney, with charming native-style cottages and hammocks in a lazy beachside location. The terrace restaurant serves Bavarian sausages, fish dishes and curry; the owners can, of course, arrange all sorts of diving trips. Limited wi-fi. P1600

7

Palawan

BACUIT ARCHIPELAGO

Palawan

Tourism is on the up in Palawan, and for good reason. Surrounded by the 1,780-odd islets that make up Palawan province, the main island is the fifth largest in the Philippines, with a lush jungle-swathed interior surrounded by floury white beaches lapped by gin-clear waters and overlooked by towering limestone outcrops. Its location southwest of Luzon on the very edge of the archipelago, as close to Borneo as it is to Manila, has seen Palawan influenced by many external cultures and religions, and it instantly has a different feel to the rest of the Philippines. While the centres of Coron, El Nido, Sabang and Puerto Princesa have become popular tourist hubs, the southern part of the 450km-long, sword-shaped main island remains largely unexplored. But whichever parts of the province you choose to visit, you'll be treated to a Jurassic landscape of coves, beaches, lagoons and forests. Offshore, meanwhile, despite some damage from dynamite fishing and coral bleaching, there's always an untouched reef to discover.

8

The capital of Palawan, **Puerto Princesa**, is the main entry point and is close to the mangrove islands of **Honda Bay** and the immense flooded cave systems that make up the mind-boggling **Underground River**. Further north you'll find the pretty beach resort town of **Port Barton**, the old fortress town of **Taytay** and the incredibly beautiful islands and lagoons of **El Nido** and the **Bacuit archipelago**. Some areas are still relatively unaffected by tourism, such as the friendly little fishing village of **San Vicente** and nearby **Long Beach**, one of the finest stretches of sand anywhere. Undeveloped **southern Palawan** contains some of the least-visited areas in the whole country, from the remains of a Neolithic community in the **Tabon Caves** and the turtle and cockatoo sanctuaries at **Narra** to **Brooke's Point**, the access point for **Mount Mantalingajan**.

The **Calamian group** of islands, scattered off the northern tip of the main island of Palawan, has a deserved reputation for some of the best **scuba diving** in Asia, mostly on sunken World War II wrecks. Even if you're not a diver, there's plenty to do here. The little town of **Coron** on Busuanga is the jumping-off point for trips to mesmerizing **Coron Island**, with its hidden lagoons and volcanic lake and, to the south, the former leper colony of **Culion**.

Note that while most tourist hubs now have ATMs, smaller places such as Sabang and Port Barton do not, so it's wise to bring enough cash for your stay.

ARRIVAL AND DEPARTURE

By plane There are currently two main airports in Palawan: at Puerto Princesa on the main island and Busuanga Island in the Calamian chain. At the time of writing, finishing touches were being made to an expansion project to create a new Puerto Princesa International Airport (in the same location as the old

PORT BARTON

Highlights

❶ Dining out in Puerto Princesa With its top-notch seafood restaurants, this is the best place in Palawan to indulge in the local cuisine. **See p.377**

❷ Underground River Pass under limestone cliffs and through sepulchral chambers on a boat trip along the world's longest navigable subterranean river – a true wonder of nature. **See p.383**

❸ Port Barton A laidback and convivial beach town with simple accommodation, rustic nightlife and a pristine bay of reefs and untouched islands. **See p.384**

❹ Long Beach Enjoy one of the nation's most alluring stretches of bone-white sand – and get there before the developers arrive. **See p.384**

❺ Bacuit archipelago Explore the majestic limestone islands, beaches and lagoons that stud the bays around El Nido. **See p.390**

❻ Scuba diving around Coron Some of the wildest diving in Asia, around sunken Japanese World War II wrecks. **See box, p.398**

❼ Lake Kayangan Hop on a bangka to a hidden blue lagoon off Coron Island, from where you scramble uphill to this dazzling volcanic lake. **See p.397**

HIGHLIGHTS ARE MARKED ON THE MAP ON P.374

airport), which opened in May 2017; note that international destinations may increase by the time you read this. Those wanting to fly directly to El Nido can do so via the town's privately run Lio Airport, served by AirSwift (☎ 02 318 5941, ✇ air-swift.com) only.

Destinations (from Puerto Princesa) Angeles (Philippine Airlines: 3 weekly; 1hr 30min); Cebu (Cebu Pacific: 2 daily; 1hr 15min); Iloilo City (Cebu Pacific: 1 daily; 1hr 5min); Manila (Air Asia, Cebu Pacific & Philippine Airlines: 11 daily; 1hr 20min); Taipei, Taiwan (Philippine Airlines: 1 weekly; 3hrs).

Destinations (from Busuanga) Cebu (Philippine Airlines; 1 daily; 1hr 30min); Manila (Cebu Pacific, Philippine Airlines, Skyjet: 2 daily; 1hr 15min).

Destinations (from El Nido) Cebu (1 daily; 1hr 40min); Manila (4 daily; 1hr 15min).

By boat 2GO (☎ 02 528 7000) operate a ferry between Puerto Princesa, Coron and Manila, departing Puerto Princesa on Saturdays at midnight (14hr to Coron, 30hr to Manila). There's also a RoRo ferry with Montenegro (☎ 043 740 3201) to Puerto Princesa from Iloilo via Cuyo (4 weekly; 36hr) to Iloilo, including a stopover in Cuyo.

GETTING AROUND

By bus, jeepney and van Services run throughout the main Palawan island. From Puerto Princesa you can travel south to Brooke's Point and Quezon or north to Sabang, Roxas, San Vicente, Taytay and El Nido. While jeepneys are

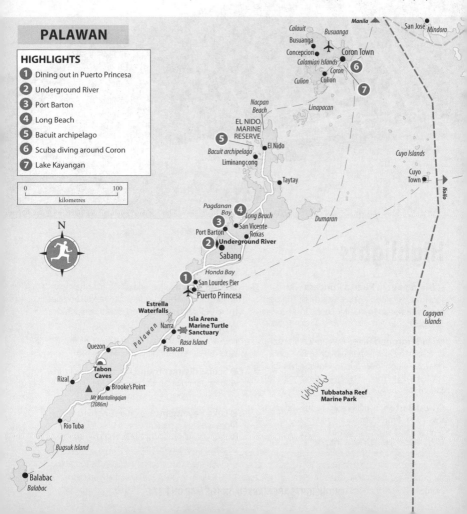

the cheapest way to travel, they're slow and you have to change often; vans run between all the main tourist hubs and are the most convenient transport for travellers. Lexxus Shuttle (☎ 0915 347 9593) and Recaro Vans (☎ 0909 351 3037) are two reliable van services.

Puerto Princesa

PUERTO PRINCESA is the only major urban sprawl in Palawan, and its population of just over 250,000 makes up a third of the island's total. Even so, it manages to live up to its name as the "City in the Forest" – a few minutes' wander up any side street will soon find you amid greenery. Southeast Asia's first carbon-neutral city, it's an eco-friendly capital where the mall is entirely run on solar power and littering can earn you a prison sentence. There are a few sights around Puerto Princesa, as well as a couple of worthwhile ones in the city itself, although most visitors treat it as a one-night stop on the way to or from Palawan's beaches and islands. **Rizal Avenue**, the main drag, runs west from the airport 3km through the centre of the city to the ferry port. Just east of the port along the seafront, the lively **Bay Walk** promenade is a popular spot for an evening stroll, with a string of alfresco seafood shacks along the water's edge.

Immaculate Conception Cathedral

Plaza Cuartel, Rizal Ave • Daily 6am–7pm • Free

At the west end of Rizal Avenue, on **Plaza Cuartel** is the **Immaculate Conception Cathedral**, a pretty white- and blue-painted Neo-Romanesque structure with twin towers. The plaza has a memorial dedicated to the 143 American soldiers who were burnt alive near the city by the retreating Japanese Army during the "Palawan Massacre" of 1944.

Palawan Museum

Mendoza Park, Rizal Ave • Mon, Tues, Thurs & Fri 8.30am–noon & 2–5pm • P20

The small **Palawan Museum** offers an overview of the history, art and culture of the region. Most of the exhibits are fossils and old tools but there are, at least, informative English captions. Look out for shells in the biology section and, in the archeological displays, the Neolithic-era Manunggul burial jar.

ARRIVAL AND DEPARTURE   **PUERTO PRINCESA**

By plane Puerto Princesa airport (see p.372) is located at the eastern edge of the city on Rizal Ave. A small tourist office (☎ 048 434 4211) opens to meet flights. Most local hotels will arrange to pick you up for free; tricycles to the centre cost around P50. Of the airline offices at the airport, Philippine Airlines is open daily (8am–4.30pm; ☎ 048 433 4565), while Cebu Pacific (☎ 048 433 554) and the other airlines open for flights only.

By boat Services to and from Puerto Princesa (see opposite) arrive and depart from the port at the western end of Malvar St, a short walk north of Rizal Ave.

By bus, jeepney and van Most services depart from the San José terminal (also known as "New Market" after the market next door), 7km north of the centre. Tricycles charge P100–120 from the city centre to San José; you can also catch multicabs (a minivan version of a jeepney; P15) and jeepneys from the corner of Rizal Ave and the National Highway (junction 1). Departures to all points north are most frequent in the early mornings; the times quoted here are guidelines only. Vans are typically 25 percent faster than buses and slightly more comfortable, but are also correspondingly more expensive. Daytripper Palawan (☎ 0917 848 8755, ✆ daytripperpalawan.com) is a good option, with services from Puerto Princesa to El Nido leaving in the mornings or the afternoons (P850–950).

Destinations Brooke's Point (4 daily; 5hr); El Nido (10 daily; 6–8hr); Port Barton (5 daily, 7.30am–4.30pm; 3hr); Quezon (hourly, mornings; 4hr); Roxas (10 daily, mornings; 3hr); Sabang (8 daily, 6.30am–3pm; 2hr 30min); San Vicente (2 daily; 5hr); Taytay (10 daily, mornings; 5hr).

8

8

PUERTO PRINCESA

Puerto Princesa Airport

City Coliseum, ◄

San José Bus Terminal (7km), Palawan Adventist Medical Center, Iwahig Penal Colony, Butterfly Eco-Garden and Tribal Village, Crocodile Farm & Baker's Hill

Topstar

ABREA ROAD

F. VILLAROSA ROAD

Rent-a-Bike

Bureau of Immigration

Air Philippines Express

MANALO EXTENSION

N

0 — 100 metres

Soapy Laundry

Trip Buddies

Island Paradise Tours

A. RENGEL ROAD

RIZAL AVENUE

TRINIDAD RD.

ABAD SANTOS EXTENSION

ABUEG STREET

Corazon Travel & Tours

NATIONAL HIGHWAY

LAGAN STREET

Provincial Capitol Building

Tubbataha Reef Natural Park Office

Multicabs and Jeepneys to San José

BALTAN STREET

FERNANDEZ STREET

Provincial Hospital ◄

MALVAR ST.

LACAO STREET

BDO

CARANDANG STREET

Allied Bank

BPI   Metrobank

MANALO STREET

ABAD SANTOS STREET

ABUEG STREET

H. MENDOZA ST.

Mercury Drug

Palawan Museum

Fish Port

Unitop Mall

Mendoza Park

VALENCIA ST

MANALO ST

MABINI STREET

BONIFACIO STREET

Bay Walk Park

Market

BUNGAN STREET

RIZAL AVENUE

MANGA ST

BURGOS STREET

ROXAS STREET

ROXAS STREET

GOMEZ STREET

DEL PILAR ST

QUEZON STREET

QUEZON STREET

LS. DOROHOY

R. MENDOZA STREET

REYNOSO STREET

Coast Guard

MALVAR STREET

CONCEPCION

Immaculate Concepcion Cathedral

Plaza Cuartel

TAFT STREET

SANDOVAL STREET

Port

Coron, Manila, Cuyo & Iloilo ◄

● EATING	
Badjao Seafront Restaurant	8
Haim Chicken Inató	7
KaLui	3
Kinabuchs Grill & Bar	5
Painted Table	2
La Terrasse	4
Viet Ville	1
White Fence Café	6

■ ACCOMMODATION	
Blue Lagoon	5
Canvas Boutique Hotel	3
Casa Linda Inn	6
Dolce Vita Hotel	1
Hibiscus Garden Inn	8
Palo Alto B&B	2
Puerto Pension	4
Purple Fountain Inn	7

■ DRINKING	
Itoy's Coffee Haus	2
Palaweño Brewery	3
Tiki Restobar	1

GETTING AROUND

Tricycles The standard fare per person within the city – including the airport and port – is P10 (more after 9pm), while hiring a tricycle privately will cost P50 for a short hop (more in the evenings).
Motorbike rental There are numerous motorbike rental

shops near the airport on Rizal Ave, all charging around P600/day for a scooter or P1000/day for the bigger motorbikes. Rent-a-Bike (☎048 433 0598, ⊛rent-a-bike .ph) on Rizal Avenue is a reputable operator and will also deliver to your hotel.

INFORMATION

Tourist office Provincial Capitol Building, Rizal Ave, 1km west of the airport at the junction with the National Highway (Mon–Sat 9am–5pm; ☎048 433 2968).
Underground River permits If you're planning to visit the Underground River independently (see p.383), you can

arrange a permit on the spot if you take your passport along to the park office in the City Coliseum, north of the centre via the National Highway at San Pedro (daily 8am–5pm; ☎048 723 0904).

ACCOMMODATION

Puerto Princesa's many places to **stay** are concentrated on and around Rizal Ave; the most pleasant are towards the eastern end of the strip. Those in the leafy northern suburbs are a tricycle ride from the centre. **Wi-fi** is more reliable here than in other parts of Palawan, but it's often only available in public areas.

Blue Lagoon Purok Malaya ☎048 433 0118, ⊛bluelagoon.com.ph. Close to Rizal Ave, offering clean, comfortable cottages with cable TV and fridge. Staff are friendly and welcoming and there's a decent restaurant. ☞ **P2500**
★**Canvas Boutique Hotel** National Hwy ☎0917 807 1360, ⊛canvasboutiquehotel.com. One of the best and most innovative accommodation options in the city, this modern industrial-style boutique hotel is covered in murals by local artists and offers chic rooms with polished concrete floors and creative touches such as bamboo speakers and colourful lamps. There's also a pool area with plants and sunken seating, and an excellent restaurant (see p.378). **P3000**
Casa Linda Inn Trinidad Rd ☎048 433 2606. Simple, friendly and convenient place off Rizal Ave, with the bonus of good European and Asian food in the breezy café. The large rooms are arranged around a spacious courtyard garden. All are native style, with wooden floors and walls made of dried grass. **P1000**
Dolce Vita Hotel 4 Victoria Romasanta St, San Pedro ☎048 434 5357, ⊛hotels-palawan.com. This German-owned hotel, northeast of the centre, has romantic canopy beds and fancy bathrooms set in two-storey pavilions (cable TV, breakfast and a/c included). There's a decent pool and bar, as well as family rooms (P4000) and suites (P3400). ☞ **P2500**
Hibiscus Garden Inn Manalo Extension ☎048 434 1273, ⊛puertoprincesahotel.com. Just south of the airport, with great staff and friendly service, and huge rooms with spotless

tiled floors, a/c, cable TV and hot showers. There's also a peaceful garden with hammocks and outdoor tables where breakfast is served. The attached restaurant serves some of the best pizzas in town. Free airport pick-up. ☞ **P1800**
Palo Alto B&B Kawayanan St, Libis San Pedro ☎048 434 2159, ⊛paloalto.ph. Some 4km north of town (a 15min tricycle ride), this large, family-run B&B with a pool and a restaurant is housed in several impressive buildings constructed with wood sourced from sustainable Palawan forests, and set around a central lawn and forested area. Cheaper rooms are on the small side but have a/c, flatscreen TVs and good bathrooms. The whole place could do with a little bit of sprucing up, but overall it's a comfortable option. **P2700**
★**Puerto Pension** 35 Malvar St ☎048 433 4148, ⊛puertopension.com. Located at the back of the lively Bay Walk promenade, this three-floored nipa-hut-style building is set in a lush tropical garden. The cosy a/c rooms all have mini-fridges and cable TV, and are decorated with local Palaweño artwork. There's also a lovely rooftop restaurant with spectacular bay views, and free use of an outdoor hot tub in the evenings. ☞ **P1946**
★**Purple Fountain Inn** 269 Manalo Extension ☎048 434 2430, ⊛purplefountaininn.com.ph. Set around a leafy courtyard with the eponymous purple fountain, this quirky inn offers bright, kitsch rooms with stained-glass windows and fun artwork. All have a/c, quality wooden furniture, TVs and hot water. It also has an excellent restaurant, the *White Fence Café* (see p.378). ☞ **P1800**

8

EATING

★**Badjao Seafront Restaurant** Abueg St, Bagong Sikat ☎048 433 9912. Open-air, native-style restaurant with terrific views of the sea. It's reached on foot from Abueg Rd, at

the end of Bonifacio St across a dainty bamboo bridge. Expect to pay about P500 a head for a meal of fresh, tasty grilled seafood such as sizzling squid. There are also a couple of

8

veggie dishes including stuffed aubergine and breaded okra (P245). If you're here in the evening, getting transport back to the centre can be tricky, so you might want to pay a tricycle driver P200 to wait for the return trip. Daily 10am–10pm.

★**Haim Chicken Inatô** 294 Manalo Extension ☎048 433 2261. Despite sounding like a fast-food chicken chain, this family-run restaurant serves quality Filipino dishes. You can dine on mains such as grilled tuna belly (P175), *ginataang ubod ng rattan* (young rattan vine with coconut milk and small fish; P117) and vegetable curry (P160) while seated in bamboo huts decorated with vibrant artwork. Daily 10am–10pm.

KaLui 369 Rizal Ave ☎048 433 2580, ⊛kaluirestaurant .com. Everyone who comes to Princesa seems to end up at this pretty bamboo restaurant, where waiters in tribal garb greet you at the door. It's a bit overrated, but the beautifully crafted daily set meals (good for two; P625) are built around either seafood or meat, and most come with a salad and a small portion of fresh, raw seaweed. À la carte items include shrimps in garlic butter (P285) and tuna steak (P245). Reservations are essential for dinner (call or ask at your hotel). Mon–Sat 11am–2pm & 6–11pm.

Kinabuchs Grill & Bar Rizal Ave ☎048 434 5194. The huge and enticing bar and garden at this Filipino restaurant is usually packed. The main attraction is the *tamilok* or "mangrove worms" (P135), believed to be an aphrodisiac rich in protein (actually a mollusc that tastes a bit like squid). Equally adventurous and more palatable dishes include Croc à la Bicol Express, with crocodile meat (P345), while the classic Filipino food is also excellent; try the sizzling seafood *sisig* (P230) or *singang na baboy* (P190). Daily 4pm–1am.

Painted Table Canvas Boutique Hotel, National Hwy ☎0917 807 1360. This hotel café and restaurant is a stylish, modern place to eat, serving Filipino cuisine alongside popular Western dishes. Try the soy-fried chicken with Palawan honey glaze (P365) or local mussels in a ginger and lemongrass broth (P260). If you're here with a large group, ask to sit at the eponymous brightly coloured painted table. Daily 7am–10pm.

La Terrasse Rizal Ave ☎048 434 1787, ⊛laterrasse palawan.com. Upscale but reasonably priced Filipino/ European fusion restaurant – the airy interior is elegant and the food a delight. The menu focuses on wholesome, "slow" foods and organic, free-range ingredients. Highlights include Tuscan pork roulade (P290) and sizzling chicken teriyaki (P235). They also have a few vegetarian dishes such as spicy aubergine with tofu (P180). Daily 11am–11pm.

Viet Ville 13 Santa Lourdes ☎0977 456 7599. Located on the way up to Honda Bay, this traditional Vietnamese restaurant is one of the few that remain in the city, situated in the former refugee village that was created when many fled to the city in the 1970s and 1980s. The menu includes classic beef *pho* (P105), *chao long* (Vietnamese porridge; P105) and shrimp in tamarind sauce (P215). A few veggie dishes are also available. Daily 9am–9pm.

White Fence Café Purple Fountain Inn, 269 Manalo Extension ☎048 434 2430. This colourful, country-style hotel café is filled with odd knick-knacks and shows old black-and-white films on the TVs around the walls. They serve classic international fare, such as pasta (P230), pizza (P320), soups and salads (P125) and barbecue ribs (P285). Daily 8am–9pm.

DRINKING

Itoy's Coffee Haus Rizal Ave ☎048 434 9918. Convivial local café chain with a huge range of coffee-based drinks (P60–185). They also have decent desserts, including cassava pudding (P60), and free wi-fi. Daily 6am–11pm.

Palaweño Brewery 28 Manalo St ☎048 725 6950, ⊛palawenobrewery.com. The first and only craft brewery in Palawan, this small bar was set up by two Filipina women, and also offers microbrewery tours.

Beers (P170) use indigenous flavours from Palawan and P400 buys you a tray of four to sample. Mon–Sat 1–9pm.

Tiki Restobar Jct 1, Rizal Ave ☎048 434 1797. This big, busy open-sided bar on the city's main junction is getting to be a major venue for live bands (nightly from 9.30pm). They also serve set meals and seafood dishes (P140). Daily 6pm–2am.

TUBBATAHA REEF NATURAL PARK
Located in the middle of the Sulu Sea, 181km southeast of Puerto Princesa, **Tubbataha Reef Natural Park** has been inscribed on the UNESCO World Heritage List thanks to its huge number of marine species. Unsurprisingly, it has become a magnet for scuba divers, who reach it on liveaboard boats – most departing from Puerto Princesa between March and June. The reef is one of the finest in the world, with sightings of sharks, manta rays and turtles a daily occurrence. Dive operators in Manila, Puerto Princesa and Coron Town can arrange **packages** from around US$1600 for a one-week trip, including onboard accommodation and meals, the conservation fee of P3000, and up to four dives a day. For details see ⊛expeditionfleet.com or ⊛moonshadow.ch or visit the park office on Manalo Extension in Puerto Princesa (☎048 434 5759, ⊛tubbatahareef.org).

TOURS FROM PUERTO PRINCESA

There are several attractions around Puerto Princesa that you can easily visit in a day or less, including **Honda Bay** (see below) and the **Underground River** (see p.383), though note that for the latter you need to sort out a permit at least a day in advance (see p.384). Many hotels and agents in the area sell essentially the same tours, taking in the nearest sights for around P600 per person in a minivan, or P500–700 by tricycle.

Most "city" tours take in the **Palawan Butterfly Eco-Garden and Tribal Village** (daily 8.30am–5pm; P50), where you can see butterflies, tandikan (small native peacocks), bearcats (a member of the civet family) and leopard geckos, as well as meet some of Palawan's native tribespeople; and **Baker's Hill** (daily 7am–8pm; free), a beautiful sculpture-filled garden with an excellent bakery selling *hopia ube*, mooncake-like pastries filled with bright purple *ube* (purple yam). Some tours also visit the **Iwahig Prison and Penal Farm** (daily 8am–7pm; free), an interesting "Prison Without Bars" established in 1904, and the **Crocodile Farm and Nature Park** (Mon–Sat 9am–noon & 1–4pm, Sun 2–4pm; P50), though the welfare of the animals at the latter is a bit suspect and it's probably best avoided.

RECOMMENDED TOUR OPERATORS
Corazon Travel and Tours Junction 1, Rizal Ave ☎ 048 433 0508.

Island Paradise Tours Rizal Ave ☎ 048 433 2245.
Topstar Rizal Ave ☎ 048 433 8247.
Trip Buddies Rizal Ave ☎ 048 723 0160.

DIRECTORY

Banks and exchange Banks in the centre include Allied Bank, Metrobank, BDO and BPI on the same stretch of Rizal Ave (all with ATMs), between Mendoza Park and the National Highway.

Hospitals and clinics There are two good hospitals, the Palawan Adventist Medical Center (☎ 048 433 4666) on the National Highway, 4km north of the city centre; and the Provincial Hospital, 1km north of the city centre on Malvar St.

Immigration The office on Rizal Ave, near *La Terrasse* restaurant (Mon–Fri 8am–4.30pm; ☎ 048 433 2248) can easily extend visas on the spot.

Laundry Soapy Laundry, Rizal Ave (Mon–Sat 8am–noon & 1–8pm, Sun 1.30–8.30pm).

Pharmacies Mercury Drug (daily 6am–midnight; ☎ 048 433 3875) on Rizal Ave, opposite Mendoza Park. The branch at the Alicon Building, Malvar St (☎ 048 434 8618) is open 24hr.

Post The main post office is on Burgos St at Rizal Ave.

8

Honda Bay

Picturesque **Honda Bay**, 10km north of Puerto Princesa, is a shallow, lagoon-like expanse of water, backed by the spectacular range of mountains on the main island. The bay contains seven low-lying **islands**, most of them little more than sandbars fringed by mangrove swamp and small beds of coral – perfect for a day of island-hopping, lounging and snorkelling. Note that Snake Island, formerly one of the most popular visitor destinations, has been sold to a private owner and is now off limits.

To snorkel at the lush **Pambato Reef**, the best place in Honda Bay for coral and giant clams, you can join a tour from Puerto Princesa (see box above); boats moor up at a floating pier with a giant turtle-shaped roof. Some trips take in the swanky **Dos Palmas resort on Arreceffi Island**, where the day-guest rate will usually be included in the price of your tour.

Luli Island

A laidback stop in Honda Bay, **Luli Island** sinks and rises with the tide and is sometimes almost completely covered by water. At low tide it has a beautiful beach, where locals create imaginative sand sculptures. There is also a large area where operators often encourage the rather dubious practice of fish feeding. Although you may see visitors taking part, it's not advisable, and is in fact banned on the reef itself.

Cowrie Island

As the main lunch stop for tours of Honda Bay, **Cowrie Island** has a number of thatched cabanas, as well as a fine sandy beach – great for swimming and sunbathing, but not so much for snorkelling, as it's not close to the reef. This island provides a welcome rest during a tiring day of swimming.

Starfish Island

Starfish Island is a sandbar backed by mangroves named after the abundant **horned sea star** (starfish) that carpet much of the inner shallows here. The island has some fine snorkelling towards the northern end, but it's not advisable as the water is so shallow that it's difficult to avoid touching the coral, causing damage to it and yourself. As a result, lots of tour operators no longer stop here.

Isla Pandan

Isla Pandan, managed by the *Legend Hotel* in Puerto Princesa, offers expensive beach huts (P600), umbrellas, table and chair sets (P400) and massages – along with everything from paddleboards to buckets and spades. Simple seafood meals are also available from local vendors.

ARRIVAL AND INFORMATION   **HONDA BAY**

Organized tours Corazon Travel and Tours at Junction 1, Rizal Ave in Puerto Princesa (☎048 433 0508) offer Honda Bay tours for P1450/person, including pick-up and drop-off at local hotels, transport to the San Lourdes pier, stops at three islands (usually Luli, Cowrie and Pandan) and a buffet lunch. While this is convenient, you can save money if you're in a large group by arranging tours independently (see below).

By boat Outrigger bangkas tour Honda Bay from the San Lourdes pier, 11km north of Princesa. At the pier, the Honda Bay Boat Owners Association (daily 7am–5pm; ☎0929 864 9255 or ☎0908 635 3326) rents bangkas for P1300–1500 depending on the size of the vessel – there's also a P21/person terminal fee. Boats are rented by the day, and it's usual to make just three stops, plus Pambato Reef, but

you can specify which islands you want to visit. You can rent masks, fins and booties (reef shoes) for P100 each. It's good to tip your boatmen if they've looked after you well. To get to the pier, the departure point for which is signposted around 1km off the National Highway, hotels can arrange minivans (P1500) or tricycles (P400–500), which comes with the convenience of return transport guaranteed. It's cheaper to grab a tricycle on the street (P100–150 one-way), though you might have to wait a while to get one heading back.

Island fees There are fees payable to visit Luli Island (P50), Cowrie Island (P75), Pambato Reef (P50), *Dos Palmas* resort (P500), Starfish Island (P50) and Isla Pandan (P150).

Southern Palawan

A journey through southern Palawan represents one of the last great travel challenges in the Philippines. Much of the area is sparsely populated, with limited accommodation and nothing in the way of dependable transport, communications or electricity. The major attractions, south of **Quezon** village, are **Tabon Caves** – among the country's most significant archeological sites. On the east coast, around **Brooke's Point**, there are hardly any buses and few jeepneys, but if you do make it here you'll find unspoilt countryside, quiet barangays and deserted, palm-fringed beaches backed by craggy mountains.

Narra and around

The small town of **NARRA**, about two hours by bus and 92km south of Puerto Princesa, makes a good introduction to southern Palawan: there are several empty beaches in the area as well as **Rasa Island**, 3km offshore, the only place in the wild where you can see the endangered **Philippine cockatoo**. Around 250 of the estimated wild population of only one thousand reside here, although their habitat is threatened by plans for a 15MW coal-fired power plant less than 1km from the island; fierce opposition seems to have stalled the plans for now, but whether it will eventually be built remains to be seen. The island is a thirty-minute boat trip from the village of Panacan, a short tricycle ride from Narra. Further offshore, the **Isla Arena Marine Turtle Sanctuary** is a major nesting site for green turtles, where the tiny hatchlings are protected before being released into the wild. The main hatching season is between February and April.

Inland, the most rewarding excursion is to the **Estrella Waterfalls**, around 15km from Narra on the road back to Puerto Princesa. The water is wonderfully fresh and pure (you can swim here), and the falls are surrounded by lush jungle inhabited by monkeys.

ACCOMMODATION	NARRA AND AROUND
Crystal Paradise Resort Sea Rd, Antipuluan ☎0917 809 9600, ⊛crystalparadiseresort.com. On the edge of Narra, this resort has good rooms and luxurious villas with	their own pools (from P10,000). There's also a spa and staff can arrange trips to the nearby attractions. Wi-fi is available, but it's unreliable. ☎ P3500

Tabon Caves and around

It was inside the **Tabon Caves** in 1962 that archeologists discovered a fragment of the skull dubbed "**Tabon Man**", dating back 22,000 years, which made it the oldest-known human relic from the archipelago at the time. Crude tools and evidence of cooking fires going back some fifty thousand years have been unearthed in the caves, along with fossils and a large quantity of Chinese pottery dating back to the fifth century BC. Most of these artefacts have been transferred to the National Museum in Manila for preservation, though some are on display in the caves. It's still intriguing to wander through the damp caverns and tunnels, which may have been a kind of Neolithic workshop for making stone tools; researchers are still working here and are happy to show visitors the latest finds.

Quezon

The Tabon Caves are accessible from **QUEZON**, a fishing village consisting mainly of wooden houses on stilts, around 150km southwest of Puerto Princesa. Before visiting the caves, stop first at the **National Museum** (Mon–Fri 9am–4pm; free) near Quezon wharf for orientation and information. There are actually more than two hundred **caves** in the area, but only 38 have been established to be of archeological and anthropological significance. Of these, only seven are **open** to the public; Tabon is the most interesting. You can visit Tabon independently but it's much better to set up a tour via one of the operators in Puerto Princesa (see box, p.379).

ARRIVAL AND DEPARTURE	TABON CAVES AND AROUND
Tours Hotels and travel agents in Puerto Princesa (see p.375) organize day-trips to the Tabon Caves for around P1200/person.	**By bus and bangka** You can catch a bus from Puerto Princesa to Quezon (4hr). At Quezon wharf, bangkas can be chartered for P800 for the 30min ride to the caves and back.

ACCOMMODATION	
Tabon Village Resort Tabon ☎0910 239 8381. A good place to stay near the caves, with very rustic native cottage-style accommodation with fans and private bathrooms right on the water, plus a floating restaurant. P550	**Villa Esperanza Resort** Tabon ☎0935 103 2820. One of the best resorts in the area with simple fan rooms set around a beachside garden; rooms with a/c (P650) are also available. There's also a decent restaurant. ☎ P300

Brooke's Point and Mount Mantalingajan

Deep in the southern half of Palawan, a four- to five-hour drive south of Puerto Princesa, the town of **BROOKE'S POINT** is flanked by the sea on one side and formidable mountains on the other. It was named after eccentric nineteenth-century British adventurer James Brooke, who became the Rajah of Sarawak (now Malaysia) after helping a local chieftain suppress a revolt. From Borneo he travelled north to Palawan, landing at what is now Brooke's Point and building an imposing **watchtower**, the remains of which stand next to a newer **lighthouse**. Today, the main attraction here is the ascent of nearby **Mount Mantalingajan** (2086m), Palawan's highest peak. It's a seriously tough climb, which can take up to a week, so make sure you come well prepared; there's no equipment for rent locally. The usual route actually starts on the west coast from the barangay of Ransang near **RIZAL** (6hr from Princesa by Charing Bus Lines). Enquire at Rizal town hall or call Fidel (☎0909 911 1600), who can help to arrange a guide and porter.

ACCOMMODATION   BROOKE'S POINT AND MOUNT MANTALINGAJAN

Silayan Lodge Brooke's Point plaza ☎0928 347 0075. Functional rooms in the centre of town, opposite the town hall; the cheapest have fan and shared bathrooms, but you can pay a little extra for a/c and en-suite facilities. **P200**

Sunset Lodge Brooke's Point ☎0927 519 2579. A range

of basic a/c (P500) and fan rooms with or without bathrooms, as well as a restaurant and disco (which can sometimes get quite noisy). There's also a good seafood restaurant next door. Limited wi-fi. ≈ **P250**

Northern Palawan

Most visitors to Palawan focus their time in **northern Palawan**, a wild mountainous land that crumbles into the mesmerizing islands of the Calamian chain (see p.393). Two hours north of Puerto Princesa, the UNESCO World Heritage-listed **Underground River** meanders past a bewildering array of stalactites, stalagmites, caverns, chambers and pools. From here, **Port Barton** makes for a soothing stopover on the journey north to **El Nido**, with a wide range of accommodation options and enticing snorkelling spots in the bay. El Nido town itself is a little chaotic, but occupies a very scenic spot and is the gateway to the clear waters and jungle-smothered limestone islands of the **Bacuit archipelago**.

Sabang

The jumping-off point for the Underground River is **SABANG**, a small village and laidback beach resort some 78km and two hours north of Puerto Princesa by road. The Underground River aside, Sabang's main appeal is its lovely white, palm-fringed **beach** facing St Paul's Bay. Many people just come here for the day to see the Underground River, but it's well worth staying for a couple of nights. As well as sunbathing and swimming (pay attention to the flags, though, as currents can be strong), there's an 800m **zipline** (daily 7am–5pm; P350) at the far eastern end of the beach, and the promise of **jungle trekking** (see opposite). You could also simply settle down in one of the numerous **massage shacks** (P500/hr) dotted along the beach.

ARRIVAL AND INFORMATION   SABANG

By bus, jeepney and van There are daily morning buses (2–3hr) from the San José terminal in Puerto Princesa to Sabang. Lexxus Shuttle (☎0915 347 9593) also have regular services to Sabang, departing from Puerto Princesa's wharf between 8am and 6pm. For El Nido, Lexxus Shuttle vans leave Sabang at 7.30am, 8.30am, 1pm, 2pm and 4.30pm (5.5hr). You can also catch a jeepney to the junction at Salvacion (7am, 10am, noon & 2pm) and change there. For Port Barton, vans leave Sabang at

7.30am, 8.30am, 1pm and 2pm (3.5hr). You can buy a van seat in advance at the Lexxus stand near the wharf.

By boat Unscheduled bangkas sometimes do the Sabang–Port Barton route (2hr 30min; P1200/person, P7200/boat), and might even continue on to El Nido (9hr) if there's demand – ask at the travel centre in *Green Verde* hotel (see opposite).

Information and tours There are a number of tour companies along the beachfront, including the one at

Green Verde hotel (📞 0910 978 4539). All can assist with everything from banqkas and buses to motorbike rental, as well as Underground River permits and Port Barton boats. They can also help arrange a host of local activities from ATV rides (P800/hr) and jungle trekking (P200/person) to mangrove boat rides (P250 for 45min); prices are guidelines only and vary between companies.

ACCOMMODATION

Most places to **stay** on Sabang are aimed at backpackers, with cold showers and electricity from 6pm to 11pm only; only the resorts have **wi-fi**.

Blue Bamboo 📞 0910 797 0038. Owned by a friendly local woman, this place has cottages set on a hillside and is located on the other side of the village from the beach (a 15min walk west from the wharf); it's perfect for anyone looking to escape it all and live like a local. The budget backpacker rooms are very simple, but great value, while the family rooms (P1200) are large, with lovely bamboo furniture and great views over the bay. P600

★ **Daluyon Beach and Mountain Resort** 📞 048 433 6379, 🌐 daluyonbeachandmountainresort.com. Tucked away at the eastern end of the beach, these attractive two-storey cottages have thatched roofs and luxurious rooms that open out to the sea. There's an attractive pool, 24hr power and a restaurant and bar (see below). 📶 P7600

Green Verde 📞 0910 978 4539. Towards the middle of the beach, offering small, clean and simple fan rooms with 24hr electricity and cold showers. There's also a helpful travel service (see above) and a restaurant (see below). P600

Hilmyna Beach Resort 📞 0916 245 0456. Just east of *Green Verde*, this is a popular choice with private nipa huts right on the beachfront. All have a fan, mosquito nets and charming wooden balcony. There's also an attached restaurant serving grilled fish, sandwiches, pastas and meat dishes. P800

Sheridan Beach Resort & Spa 📞 048 434 1448, 🌐 sheridanbeachresort.com. Ultra-posh (and expensive) hotel, right in the middle of the beach, with well-designed, modern rooms, a huge pool and a host of extras, plus a good restaurant (see below). Pick-ups from Princesa P3000. 📶 P6557.60

★ **Thalets Beach Cottages** 📞 0916 237 9599. Located east of *Green Verde*, and offering basic beach-facing nipa huts with private balconies, bamboo floors and mosquito nets. They also have a busy restaurant. P500

EATING AND DRINKING

Green Verde Green Verde hotel 📞 0910 978 4539. This wooden beach-house restaurant is a good budget choice, with a garden of individual cabañas facing the beach; expect spiced ginger pork (P175), lemongrass tuna (P175) and vegetable curry (P145). Daily 7am–9pm.

Pawikan Restaurant and Coco Beach Bar Daluyon Beach Resort 📞 048 723 0889, 🌐 daluyonresort.com. This refined resort restaurant makes for a quiet evening, with frozen margaritas, pizza and pasta and excellent Filipino dishes on offer; mains P300–600. Daily 6–10pm.

South Seas at the Sheridan Sheridan Beach Resort & Spa 📞 048 434 1448, 🌐 sheridanbeachresort.com. A decent range of local and international dishes served at tables looking over the beach. The native chicken *tinola* (with green papaya, chilli and pepper; P330) is good. This is also the best place in Sabang for a coffee (P130). Daily 6am–11pm.

★ **Tangay Tarabidan** Right on the beach, this simple yet excellent restaurant serves some of the best food in Sabang. They specialize in vegetarian and halal meals, although they have lots of fish dishes too. Plates include tofu steak with teriyaki ginger (P130), aloo gobi masala (P185) and pad Thai (P195). Mon–Thurs & Sun 7am–10pm, Fri 7am–5pm, Sat 6–10pm.

The Underground River

🌐 ppur.com.ph

Recognized by UNESCO as a World Heritage Site and voted as one of the "new Seven Wonders of Nature" in 2012, the **Underground River**, officially **Puerto Princesa Subterranean River National Park**, is a unique underwater river system that cuts through the limestone hills for 8.2km before emptying out into the South China Sea. The **caves** are completely natural and unlit, ranging from low-lying passages to vast, cathedral-like caverns. Because of the site's popularity and fragile ecosystem, visitor numbers are restricted to a daily quota of nine hundred visitors, which is reached every day during peak season (Nov–May); make sure you book your visit ahead of time.

8

Visiting the Underground River

After sorting out your permit (see below), you take a twenty-minute bangka from Sabang to the next bay along. Languid **monitor lizards** often congregate near the rangers' hut here, while macaque monkeys hang out in the trees, looking to grab any loose snacks – don't feed them (or the lizards). After showing your pass and getting your audioguide at the rangers' hut, you take a 150m hike through the forest to the river mouth, where boats depart. The audioguide commentary gives the low-down on the history and ecology of the caves, as well as singling out interesting rock formations inside, including the 62m high "**Cathedral**", a vast chamber that soars into the darkness and contains stalactites that resemble Mary, Jesus and friends; there's also one named "Sharon Stone" for the actress's infamous pose in the movie *Basic Instinct*. There are also more than four thousand bats living in the caves and numerous swallows.

Visitors get to see just 1.5km of the caves on the regular 45-minute tours; you can travel up to 4.3km into the system, but you'll need to arrange a special permit at least three days in advance. Afterwards, if you're feeling energetic, you can hike back from the mouth of the river to Sabang, a 5km trip through lush scenery, though this is steep and sometimes slippery, especially after rain.

ARRIVAL AND INFORMATION   **THE UNDERGROUND RIVER**

Permits Permits (P250) can be arranged at the park office in the City Coliseum in San Pedro, Puerto Princesa (☎ 048 723 0904; see p.377), at least one day in advance. It's best to secure a permit for 8am–9am (before the day-trippers arrive), but even if you're issued a different time you can just turn up at the wharf, show your permit and pay the P40 terminal fee – they'll probably put you on the next boat that has space. If you haven't pre-organized a permit in Puerto Princesa, local agents in Sabang (try *Green Verde*'s travel centre; see p.383) can make the necessary arrangements up until 8pm the day before you want to go. If you join an organized tour (see p.379), permits will be arranged for you.

By boat Your permit will specify the time you need to report to Sabang wharf for the 20min bangka ride (P700 for up to six) to the cave. Boat trips start daily at 8am and the last boat leaves at 3.30pm.

By van Renting a whole van for a day-trip to the Underground River will cost at least P3500.

Tours Day-tours (see p.379) from Puerto Princesa to the Underground River cost around P1500/person and include all fees and a basic lunch buffet. If you want to stay on in Sabang they'll drop you off after the tour.

Port Barton and around

On the northwest coast of Palawan, roughly halfway between Puerto Princesa and El Nido, **PORT BARTON** is far less developed than its busier neighbours and more peaceful, too. The streets are all dirt tracks, there are no day-trippers and the rhythms of Filipino life continue alongside the groups of backpackers lounging around in the increasing number of budget beach hotels. The hotels face crescent-shaped **Pagdanan Bay**, with its magical sunset views – **Port Barton Beach** itself, a gorgeous strip of sugary sand, is great for swimming.

Minutes away are fourteen pristine white-sand islands, and a number of top-notch dive and snorkelling sites in **Port Barton Marine Park**. Note that **electricity** is usually available between 6pm and midnight only, and that there are no banks. All minivans will drop you at the village's tourism office, where you are required to register and pay a P50 environmental fee. Remember to take proof of this with you when you go on a tour of the Port Barton Marine Park islands, otherwise you won't be able to go.

Pagdanan Bay

You can rent a bangka from Port Barton for a day of island-hopping in **Pagdanan Bay**, aka Port Barton Marine Park. Popular targets include the spectacular coral at **Twin Reef** and **Aquarium Reef** (both a few minutes' ride from Port Barton); the former in particular offers vast banks of hard coral, including plenty of spiny staghorn, and hordes of tropical fish. There are also certain places where you can spot sea turtles. The bay islands themselves are

traditional desert island types where you can swim or just chill out. Most trips take in the beach at **Exotic Island**, which has the odd monkey and a number of thatched beach huts for relaxing. You can wade across the narrow sandbar to **Albaguen Island**, which also has accommodation. Most tours stop for lunch at lush **Paradise Island**.

ARRIVAL AND DEPARTURE

PORT BARTON AND AROUND

By bus, jeepney and van From Puerto Princesa you can take a minivan to Port Barton (3hr; P350) with either Recaro Vans (7.30am, 9am, 11am, 2pm & 4pm; ☎0909 351 3037) or Lexxus Shuttle (4 daily, 7.30am–4.30pm; ☎0917 686 1118). Alternatively, take the daily bus (9am; 3hr 30min) from the San José terminal (see p.375). The bus arrives in Port Barton on Rizal St, close to the beach and the town centre. The last option is to catch a bus, van or jeepney to Roxas, from where a daily jeepney runs to Port Barton (1hr) at around 9am, or to San José (at the Port Barton road junction), from where you can charter a motorbike or tricycle (P400–500) for the bumpy last 22km – this is not recommended during or after heavy rain, though. Some resorts can also arrange pick-ups from the San José

turn-off. In the other direction jeepneys leave Port Barton for Roxas at around 9am; from Roxas you can pick up services to El Nido, but be prepared to wait. At the time of writing, the road to Port Barton was undergoing major renovations and was partly unpaved, making for a very bumpy ride whichever method of transport you take.

By boat By far the most appealing way to reach Port Barton is by boat. Unscheduled bangkas sometimes do the Sabang–Port Barton route (2hr 30min; P1200/person, P7200/boat), and there might also be services to El Nido (P1500/person, P9000/boat; 4hr 30min) if there's demand. Enquire at *Greenviews Resort* (see below). Local bangkas run to and from San Vicente in the mornings (45min–1hr; P100/person), or you can charter one for P1000.

TOURS AND ACTIVITIES

Boat tours Friendly and professional Jensen (☎0921 626 9191) can organize both private and group tours to the islands in Pagdanan Bay, as can many of the larger resorts such as *Greenviews* (see below) and *Deep Moon* (see below).

Scuba diving Aquaholics Dive Centre (☎0998 193 6585, ⓦportbartondiving.com), in the middle of Port Barton beach, charge around P4000 for three dives.

ACCOMMODATION

Buses and boats arriving in Port Barton are met by staff from any number of **hotels**; take a look before making a choice. High season runs from mid-November to May – you'll get much cheaper deals outside this period. Few places have **wi-fi**; when available it's usually in public areas only.

PORT BARTON

★Ausan Beach Front Cottages ☎0926 707 4154, ⓦausanbeachfront.com. This place has cottages and basic nipa huts, some with colourful murals on the walls and balconies. They are also one of the few places here with a/c rooms (P1950). The treehouse room (P1550) is particularly popular. Limited wi-fi. ☞ **P1250**

★Deep Moon Resort ☎0917 449 9212, ⓦdeepgold resorts.com. On the beach a short walk from Rizal St, with big A-frame cottages right on the sand (P1200), resembling Swiss chalets, all with balconies and private bathrooms. Those on a budget should ask for the cheaper ones at the back. They also have seating in their lovely wooden reception area. Patchy wi-fi in the restaurant. ☞ **P900**

Elsa's Beach Resort ☎0906 308 0733, ⓔelsas beachresort@gmail.com. Near the southern end of the strip, *Elsa's* enjoys a great location on a pleasant stretch of beach, with an excellent restaurant and comfy cottages (some facing the garden). Limited wi-fi. ☞ **P1000**

Greenviews Resort ☎0929 268 5333. At the far northern end of the beach, offering spotless nipa huts with fans and bathrooms (cold showers only) within a lush

garden that attracts giant birdwing butterflies, sunbirds and the odd monitor lizard. Owners Dave and Tina Gooding are extremely helpful and give great advice for onward travel. They also have a separate outdoor bar area (away from the cottages) with nightly live bands. **P1700**

Summer Homes ☎0946 995 7608, ⓦsummerhomes-palawan.com. One of the few places with 24-hour electricity (solar-powered), this place offers a range of colourful beachfront cottages (P2000) set around a lawn, as well as simple, clean and comfortable brick rooms at the back. They take credit cards and have a restaurant. Kayaks (P400/day) and motorbikes (P700/day) are also available to rent. Limited wi-fi. ☞ **P950**

PAGDANAN BAY ISLANDS

Blue Cove Island Resort Albaguen Island ☎0908 562 0879, ⓦbluecoveresort.com. An extremely tranquil collection of nipa huts (some with hot showers) overlooking the bay. The resort can arrange bangka pick up from Port Barton for P800/couple. Limited wi-fi. ☞ **P1200**

Coconut Garden Island Resort Cacnipa Island ☎0918 370 2395, ⓦcoconutgarden.palawan.net. Wonderfully remote spot with attractive A-frame huts (P1700–1850) and cheaper rooms in a block at the back. It's a lovely place to while away the days, but there are also a host of activities on offer from volleyball to kayaking. The resort can arrange bangka pick-up from Port Barton or San Vicente for P250–300/person. Limited wi-fi. 📶 **P860**

EATING AND DRINKING

Most of the **restaurants** in Port Barton are at the resorts; head for *Elsa's* or *Greenviews*. **Nightlife** is not part of Port Barton's appeal – there are a couple of local karaoke bars, but everything tends to shut down by 10pm.

Jambalaya Cajun Café 📞0915 315 3842. This welcoming Cajun-style café on the beach next to the main pier is one of the few restaurants not located at a resort. Its curries (P400) and fish (P400) are overpriced, but its jambalaya (P270), a Louisiana-style mix of spicy rice, fresh fish and veg, is a bestseller. There's also free internet when it decides to work. Daily 8am–9pm.

San Vicente

About 15km north of Port Barton is the sleepy fishing village of **SAN VICENTE**, accessible by bangka or a bone-shaking jeepney ride from Princesa. It has a small market, a petrol station and a couple of snack stalls but little else; it does offer an alternative to taking longer bangka rides between Port Barton and El Nido however, as it has road links to the north coast and Taytay.

The only reason to linger around here is **Long Beach**, a so-far undeveloped 14km stretch of sand south of town that ranks as one of the most extraordinary beaches in the country – you can see both ends only on a brilliantly clear day. Enjoy its unspoilt feel while you can, as a planned new airport has already prompted the development of large resorts, and it is only a matter of time before the beach is "discovered" by package tours.

ARRIVAL AND DEPARTURE   SAN VICENTE

By plane There are plans to open an airport, though no one knows quite when that will be.

By bus, van and jeepney From Princesa there are buses (4–5hr) and vans (4 daily). For moving on, you can either wait for a bus or van, or locals should be able to rustle up a driver; count on P2000 for the rough, bumpy 2hr 30min ride to Taytay (only the main highway between Roxas and Taytay is surfaced).

By boat A bangka leaves for Port Barton at 8am (P100), otherwise you can charter a boat for the 45min journey (P1000).

By motorcycle To get to Long Beach, you will need to catch a lift on a motorcycle from San Vicente's market, near the pier, for around P50.

ACCOMMODATION

Picardal Lodge 📞0919 239 2224. A short walk from the pier, this simple, friendly place has half-decent rooms and cottages set amid greenery. They can assist with island-hopping. Wi-fi is limited to common areas. 📶 **P800**

Taytay

On the northeast coast of Palawan, about 140km north of Port Barton by road and 50km south of El Nido, the quaint and friendly town of **TAYTAY** ("tie-tie") was capital of Palawan from the earliest days of Spanish conquest in the seventeenth century until Princesa assumed the role in 1903. Today there's little to show of this history save the impressive **Fuerza de Santa Isabel** (daily 9am–5pm; P30), the squat stone fortress built by the Spanish between 1667 and 1738. As with many places in Palawan, the main attractions lie **offshore** – you can tour the wonderfully untouched islands in the bay by chartering a bangka for the day from the harbour (P2000–3000). **Elephant Island** is best known for its hidden lagoon: it's a wonderful place to swim, with a natural skylight in the rock which acts like a roof.

ARRIVAL AND INFORMATION   TAYTAY

By bus, van and jeepney All transport from Puerto Princesa and El Nido will drop you at the bus terminal on the edge of town; tricycles should shuttle you to the harbour (for tours of the bay) for P100.

Services There are a couple of banks in Taytay but neither have ATMs – you may be able to get a cash advance with your credit card at Palawan Bank In an emergency. Electricity is available from 5pm until 5am.

ACCOMMODATION AND EATING

TAYTAY TOWN

Casa Rosa ☎0920 895 0092. Pleasant little resort on a hill behind the town hall, with clean, good-value rooms plus cottages (P1190) set in attractive gardens. The excellent café (mains P150–275) offers spectacular fort and ocean views and serves delicious home-cooked pizzas, fish and grilled chicken, as well as sandwiches, and has wi-fi. They can also offer tours including kayaking, dolphin-watching, birdwatching and waterfall trips (P1500–3500). 🛜 **P700**

Pem's Pension House and Restaurant Rizal St ☎0917 300 7660 or ☎048 723 0463. Located near the fort, and offering single rooms with a shared bathroom, plus charming wooden cottages with private bathrooms, either with fan (P700) or a/c (P1300). Wi-fi in the lobby only. 🛜 **P600**

TAYTAY BAY ISLANDS

Apulit Island Resort Apulit Island ☎02 894 5644, ⓦelnidoresorts.com. Run by *El Nido Resorts*, this swish hideaway is close to Taytay town and offers accommodation in luxury cottages built on stilts over the water; you can spot baby sharks from your balcony. The resort has various bars and restaurants, including a lovely little bar high on a rocky cliff at the back of the beach, reached by 109 steps. Price is for full board for two people. 🛜 **P25,500**

★**Flower Island Resort** Flower Island ☎0917 504 5567, ⓦflowerisland-resort.com. This idyllic, eco-friendly, all-inclusive resort features 24 romantic and attractively furnished nipa huts scattered along the shore, equipped with bathrooms, fans (some have a/c) and verandas with hammocks. The restaurant serves buffet meals. Rates are per person. 🛜 **P5717**

El Nido and the Bacuit archipelago

8

With its scruffy beach, narrow, tricycle-choked streets and unplanned rows of concrete hotels, the small but booming resort town of **EL NIDO**, in the far northwest of Palawan, comes as quite a surprise for somewhere that's marketed as paradise. But though the town makes a poor first impression, El Nido's **surroundings** are jaw-dropping, hemmed in between spectacular jagged cliffs and an iridescent bay littered with jungle-smothered limestone outcrops. One of the most popular tourist hubs in Palawan, El Nido is becoming increasingly crowded and expensive. You can still find good-value options compared to some other places in the Philippines, but many visitors are now looking to the nearby beaches of **Corong-Corong** and **Caalan** to escape the noise and crowds of El Nido.

The town is the departure point for trips to the mesmerizing **Bacuit archipelago**, where the **El Nido marine sanctuary** is the largest such reserve in the Philippines. The archipelago's striking beauty has not gone unnoticed by developers, who have established a number of **exclusive resorts** on some of the islands. If a rate of more than US$250 a night (per person) for a taste of paradise is too much for you, stay on the mainland and island-hop by day. Note that El Nido now has 24hr electricity, although blackouts (or brown-outs as locals call them) are still common.

DIVING AND SNORKELLING AROUND EL NIDO

The waters off El Nido are popular with **divers**, especially those looking to do a PADI course. **Snorkelling** is good, too, though much of the reef system has been killed off over the years due to crown-of-thorns starfish, bleaching and dynamite fishing. There are a few reliable **dive operators** in El Nido, who can also advise about trips to the Tubbataha Reef (p.378) and Apo Reef (p.254).

DIVE OPERATORS

El Nido Marine Club El Nido Beach ☎0917 774 3210. Dives from P2800; PADI from P19,000.

Palawan Divers Calle Hama ☎0939 958 1076, ⓦpalawan-divers.org. Three dives from P4200; PADI from P23,500.

Sea Dog Diving Serena St ☎0916 777 6917. Dives P1500 per person.

EL NIDO AND THE BACUIT ARCHIPELAGO

■ ACCOMMODATION	
Dolarog Beach Resort	7
Golden Monkey	2
Kalinga	3
Lagen Island Resort	8
Miniloc Island Resort	6
Morning Walsh Resort	5
The Nest El Nido Beach Resort	1
Overlooking Resort	4

El Nido Taraw Via Ferrata

Brgy Maligaya Zone 1 • Daily 9am–5pm • 45min tour P400/person; tickets are sold from the office at the start of the climb • ☎ 0977 171 4960

Don't miss the climb to the top of the marble cliffs of **Mount Taraw**, the ridge that backs the town, via the **El Nido Taraw Via Ferrata** canopy walk. It's a strenuous haul, via a series of rope bridges and metal staircases (a harness keeps you hooked to the metal guide ropes), but the views are magnificent. Rates include mandatory guide.

El Nido beaches

The El Nido bayfront has ravishing views, but the **beach** itself is average and not especially attractive for swimming thanks to the heavy bangka traffic. **Caalan** or **Corong-Corong**, just a short walk north and south of town respectively, are much quieter, although still not great for swimming – Caalan is full of rocks and coral. A better option is **Nacpan Beach**, a vast swathe of white sand, reachable via a 40-minute tricycle ride north of El Nido; take insect repellent as the sandflies can be voracious.

The Bacuit archipelago

The main reason that most people visit El Nido is to go **island-hopping** (see box below) around the enchanting **Bacuit archipelago**, 45 limestone outcrops riddled with karst cliffs, sinkholes and idyllic lagoons.

Cadlao Island and Helicopter Island

The dramatic tower of rock just off El Nido is **Cadlao Island**. The star here is **Ubugon Cove** at the back of the island, hemmed in by jagged rock, where you can snorkel, but this is also one of the few islands that you can explore on land, too. One-hour trekking tours (P2300 for three people) take in the unusual saltwater Makaamo Lagoon. Near Cadlao Island, **Dilumacad Island** (aka **Helicopter Island**) has a gorgeous 300m-long beach covered in shards of rare blue coral and lots of multicoloured shells.

Miniloc Island

Miniloc Island, 45 minutes by boat from El Nido, boasts one of the area's greatest treasures, the **Big Lagoon**, with glass-clear aquamarine water surrounded by towering limestone cliffs that look like a cathedral rising up from below. Tours aboard small bangkas take a spin around the lagoon, but usually don't stop, while those on larger bangkas will have to wade through. Nearby, the similarly awe-inspiring **Small Lagoon** is only accessible by kayaking (P300 extra; see box below) through a small gap in the rocks.

Matinloc Island

One of the largest islands in the group, **Matinloc Island** takes a bit longer to reach (around an hour from El Nido), but is well worth the journey, and has several intriguing targets tucked away along its jagged shore. **Hidden Beach** lies around a tight bend in the rocks, a gorgeous cove hidden from view. On the other side of the island is the **Matinloc Shrine**, completed in 1993 – this Catholic shrine is usually quiet and windswept other than on May 31, when it's mobbed by believers for the Feast of the Lady of Matinloc.

Matinloc's main draw is **Secret Beach**, reached by a tiny gap you can swim through; on the other side is a spellbinding cove facing a white-sand beach surrounded by steep rock walls. Tours also usually stop in the Tapiutan Strait off Matinloc for the chance to see **turtles**, but it depends on weather conditions.

ISLAND-HOPPING IN THE BACUIT ARCHIPELAGO

Bacuit archipelago **tours** (generally 9am–4pm) have been standardized into packages, and prices are set by the local government. They cost P1200–1400 per person (including lunch) depending on the islands visited, plus a P200 ecotourism development fee valid for ten days. Numerous places offer trips; one of the best options is the *El Nido Boutique and Artcafé* on Serena St in El Nido (☎0920 902 6317, ⊛elnidoboutiqueandartcafe.com). **Tour A** takes in the attractions of Miniloc and Shimizu islands; **Tour B** goes to Snake Island, Cudugnon Cave and points south; **Tour C** goes to Matinloc's Secret and Hidden beaches; and **Tour D** takes in Cadlao Island and Ipil Beach, among others. The highlights are scattered throughout each itinerary, to encourage several days of touring, but you can also choose a combo tour, taking in the highlights of A and B or A and C, for example. At the time of writing, the Tourism Office were in the process of rebranding each tour, so the destinations may change.

If time is short you can **charter your own boat**, taking in all the best locations; reckon on P4000–5000 per bangka. Another option is a **kayak tour**, bookable via *El Nido Boutique and Artcafé* or Northern Hope Tours on Calle Real (☎0939 902 2216, ⊛northernhopetours.com): trips to Cadlao and Miniloc both cost around P1900. If you simply want to stay put on a **beach** for a few hours and do some snorkelling, you can charter a boat for P1200 to Seven Commandos Beach on the mainland, which has a small bar behind a lovely strip of sand; P1300 to Helicopter Island or P1600 to Shimizu Island (prices are for two people).

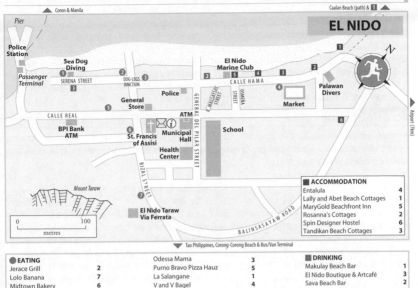

ACCOMMODATION	
Entalula	4
Lally and Abet Beach Cottages	1
MaryGold Beachfront Inn	5
Rosanna's Cottages	2
Spin Designer Hostel	6
Tandikan Beach Cottages	3

● EATING					■ DRINKING	
Jerace Grill	2	Odessa Mama	3		Makulay Beach Bar	1
Lolo Banana	7	Purno Bravo Pizza Hauz	5		El Nido Boutique & Artcafé	3
Midtown Bakery	6	La Salangane	1		Sava Beach Bar	2
		V and V Bagel	4			

8

Southern islands

The main attractions in the southern archipelago include **Snake Island**, a serpentine sandbar lapped by crystal-clear waters, making it a great spot for sunbathing and a dip at low tide; and **Pangalusian Island** with its long, palm-fringed, white-sand beach, perfect for swimming and snorkelling at any time.

ARRIVAL AND DEPARTURE

EL NIDO AND THE BACUIT ARCHIPELAGO

By plane El Nido is a 6km tricycle ride (P200) from the El Nido airport, also called Lio Airport. Privately owned, it has flights with AirSWIFT (☎02 318 5941, ⊚air-swift .com) to and from Manila (1hr 15min); tickets can be booked in advance through Manila booking agents or the *El Nido Boutique and Artcafé* (see p.392). There's a 10kg luggage allowance, although you can buy extra up to 20kg. **By boat** Daily fast ferries (4hr), operated by Montenegro Lines, leave for Coron at 6am and cost P1760; there are onward ferries to Manila from Coron. Arrange your ticket at least one day in advance from one of the many tour operators in town or *El Nido Boutique and Artcafé*, which can also arrange tickets for all other boats. There are also daily bangkas to Coron leaving at 8am (P1500 including lunch; 8–9hr), but as they are slower, less comfortable and more vulnerable to weather-related delays, the ferry is a

much better choice. For other destinations you generally have to charter your own bangka: it's P9000 to Port Barton (4hr 30min) and P12,500 to Sabang (7hr).

By bus and van The bus and van "terminal" is in Corong-Corong, a 10–15min walk or P20 tricycle ride from El Nido town. Regular and a/c buses run till 6pm to Puerto Princesa (via Taytay and Roxas) with Roro and the more comfortable Cherry; they take around 8hr. More expensive, but faster and more convenient (and offering hotel pick-ups), vans to Puerto Princesa (6hr; P700) also leave throughout the day; try Alpha Sierra Transport Services (☎0998 433 9714). Daytripper Palawan (☎0917 848 8755, ⊚daytripper palawan.com) is also a good option, running to Taytay (P400; 1hr 30min) and Roxas (P700; 3hr 30min). For Port Barton change in Roxas (or the San José turn-off), and for Sabang jump off at the Salvacion turn-off.

TAO PHILIPPINES

Tao Philippines (⊚taophilippines.com) offer a unique way to travel between El Nido and the Calamian islands. Five-day (and four-night) tours aboard a traditional Paraw sailing boat explore the remote string of jewel-like islands between El Nido and Coron Town on Busuanga. Guests live like locals, camping and sleeping in native villages along the way. Trips run from October to early June and cost P28,500 per person (more during peak seasons), including food.

INFORMATION

Tourist office Inside the DENR building near the town hall on Calle Real in El Nido, one block inland from the beach (daily 8am–8pm; ☎ 0917 841 7771).

El Nido Boutique and Artcafé The travel centre (daily 7am–8pm; ☎ 0920 906 6317, ⊚ elnido boutiqueandartcafe.com) of this café on Serena St (see opposite) is a good source of up-to-date local information. You can book tours, boats and ferries, and change money. Credit cards accepted.

Banks and exchange There are two ATMs in El Nido: one outside the Municipal Hall and the other at the BPI Bank on Calle Real.

ACCOMMODATION

You should book ahead (especially at Christmas and Chinese New Year) for El Nido town's **budget accommodation**; rates are a bit higher at quieter and prettier **Corong-Corong** or **Caalan** beaches. **Wi-fi** can be unreliable, and is usually only available in public areas of places listed.

EL NIDO

Entalula Calle Hama ☎ 0920 906 6550, ⊚ entalula .com; map p.391. Elegant beachfront option with standard a/c rooms beautifully crafted from wood and nipa; there are also four fan-cooled cabañas (P3000); all have hot water and sea-view verandas. ☞ **P2800**

Lally and Abet Beach Cottages Off Calle Hama ☎ 0917 850 2948, ⊚ lallyandabet.com; map p.391. Long-established, well-run resort at the northern end of town on the shore, with 35 a/c rooms and lovely wooden cottages (P2400–4500). Patchy wi-fi. ☞ **P1800**

MaryGold Beachfront Inn Calle Hama ☎ 0917 642 7722, ⊚ mgelnido.com; map p.391. Charming beachfront accommodation with spotless country-cottage and seaside-themed rooms. The more expensive (P2950) are at the front, with sea views and balconies. Limited wi-fi. ☞ **P2350**

Rosanna's Cottages Calle Hama ☎ 0920 605 4631; map p.391. Formerly a top budget choice, *Rosanna's* has moved a little upmarket, but still offers friendly service and beachfront rooms, these days with a/c and solar-powered hot water. Limited wi-fi. ☞ **P1800**

★**Spin Designer Hostel** Balinsasayaw Rd at Calle Real ☎ 0917 566 7746, ⊚ spinhostel.com; map p.391. Trendy backpacker hostel with mixed dorms, female dorms and single or twin private doubles. There's also a lounge area with cable TV, basic kitchen equipment for use, self-service laundry and free breakfast. Wi-fi in the lobby. ☞ Dorms **P1000**, doubles **P3000**

Tandikan Beach Cottages Calle Hama ☎ 0919 944 6312; map p.391. In a fine location with sea and mountain views, and offering nine simple fan cottages (and some with a/c; P1500). You'll wake in the morning to find a flask of hot water on your balcony for coffee. Wi-fi at reception. ☞ **P1200**

CAALAN BEACH

Golden Monkey ☎ 0929 206 4352, ⊚ golden monkeyelnido.com; map p.389. Peaceful little British-Filipino owned resort with well-constructed garden and smart rooms with views in the main block, as well as beachfront huts (P4500). They also have kayaks for rent (P500). Wi-fi works sometimes. ☞ **P4180**

Kalinga ☎ 0921 570 0021; map p.389. One of the cheaper options on peaceful Caalan Beach. There are a variety of attractive rooms and huts set in a garden just back from the sand, all of which have TV and hot water. If you want a/c, add P500 to the room price. Unreliable wi-fi. ☞ **P3200**

The Nest El Nido Beach Resort ☎ 0917 714 5779; map p.389. Swish and friendly family-owned new resort on the quiet Caalan beachfront, with luxury cottages built around a lush garden. There are spectacular views from the restaurant, which serves up huge and delicious Filipino-style breakfasts. Weak wi-fi. ☞ **P5800**

CORONG-CORONG

Dolarog Beach Resort Dolarog Beach ☎ 0927 420 7083, ⊚ dolarog.com; map p.389. Peaceful beachside accommodation with thatched cottages and rooms in a grassy coconut grove on a quiet and rather isolated stretch of private beach, 4km south of Corong-Corong. The resort is well run, serves excellent meals and is easy enough to reach from town by tricycle (P20/person) or bangka (about P200/boat). You can also arrange for staff to meet you at the airport. Limited wi-fi. ☞ **P4800**

★**Morning Walsh Resort** ☎ 0946 037 5394, ⊚ morningwalsh@yahoo.com; map p.389. A private home, owned by the lovely Nelma, in the middle of laidback Corong-Corong Beach, with ten spacious rooms, individually decorated and with beautifully carved wooden furniture, private bathrooms and a/c. There's also a large garden filled with quirky sculptures, beachside massage huts and kayaks for rent. **P2000**

Overlooking Resort Just off Taytay-El Nido National Hwy ☎ 0916 631 7078, ⊚ el-nido-overlooking.com; map p.389. Stunning resort, perched on a cliff high up in the tree canopy, overlooking Bacuit Bay. The plush cottages blend modern and traditional designs, and there are also private villas (P7900), one with its own infinity pool (P15,250). Wi-fi in public areas. ☞ **P5250**

BACUIT ARCHIPELAGO

★**Lagen Island Resort** Lagen Island ☎ 02 894 5644,

Welnidoresorts.com; map p.389. Operated by *El Nido Resorts*, this private island paradise has superb beaches and diving, with stylish tropical accommodation in fan-cooled or a/c cottages. Package rates include meals and watersports. Rates are for two people in a double room and cover full board. Limited wi-fi. � **P27,800**

★**Miniloc Island Resort** Miniloc Island ☎02 894

5644, Welnidoresorts.com; map p.389. An *El Nido* resort, *Miniloc* offers a coastal village vibe, with beautifully stylish native-style cottages. At the reef, just offshore, guests get the chance to swim with huge 1.5m jackfish. Rates are for two people in a double room and cover full board. Spotty wi-fi. � **P27,300**

EATING

Jerace Grill Rizal St ☎0917 678 8002; map p.391. Right on the beachfront, this loud and lively restaurant is popular with both locals and travellers, and serves up classic Filipino dishes, as well as excellent fresh seafood. Choose your "catch of the day", and it'll be grilled right in front of you on the shore, and served with rice and vegetables (P200 depending on size). Daily 2–11pm.

★**Lolo Banana** The Bazaar, Rizal St ☎0916 213 3860; map p.391. Set in a sandy courtyard lined with stalls, tropical plants and bunting, this funky alfresco bar and restaurant serves everything from panini (P200) to tapas plates (P70) and fajitas (P180). Daily 2–11pm.

Midtown Bakery Rizal St; map p.391. The best bakery in town, with the usual buttery buns, white bread and *pandesal* (bread rolls), plus a tempting array of cakes such as the delicious egg-custard tart, all for a few pesos – plenty of budget travellers load up here. Mon–Sat 7am–7pm.

Odessa Mama Calle Hama ☎0927 655 0360; map p.391. This Ukrainian restaurant is an unexpected find in El Nido, offering delicious home cooking that's popular with travellers, as evidenced by the notes scrawled across the

walls. Try the *varenyky* (dumplings stuffed with cottage cheese and honey; P200) and classic borsch (beetroot soup; P150). Daily 7am–11pm.

Purno Bravo Pizza Hauz Calle Real ☎0929 220 4366; map p.391. With chairs and tables set around a large wood-fired oven, this place offers good pasta (P230) and Italian-style pizza – try their signature El Nido (P390) topped with mushrooms, ham, peppers, olives, onions, pineapple and mozzarella. Daily 11am–11pm.

La Salangane 33 Serena St ☎0916 648 6994, Wlasalangane.com; map p.391. Stylish place overlooking the beach, with a cool bar and great Filipino/French cuisine. Try the beef in black pepper sauce (P370) and a classic French tarte tatin (P245) for dessert. Daily 7am–10.30pm.

★**V and V Bagel** Calle Hama ☎0977 456 6241; map p.391. Freshly baked New York-style bagels with a host of appetizing fillings, from classic Italian (P240) to the "Delicatessen" (cream cheese, smoked salmon, red onions and capers; P280). They also do huge burgers (P265), delicious home-made cakes and refreshing coffee frappés. Great for vegetarians. Daily 7.30am–8.30pm.

DRINKING

El Nido Boutique and Artcafé Serena St, Calan Beach ☎0920 902 6317, Welnidoboutiqueandartcafe.com; map p.391. The heart of El Nido's visitor scene, thanks to its excellent travel centre. The food at the café isn't great, so it's better to just go for a drink at the bar and enjoy the live music. Daily 6.30am–11pm.

★**Makulay Beach Bar** Makulay Lodge ☎0916 401 9590; map p.391. The perfect place for sunset cocktails

(P250), set on a small stretch of sand at the beginning of Caalan Beach. Lie back on sunken deck chairs and enjoy the views. Happy hour 4–7pm. Daily 9am–11pm.

Sava Beach Bar Calle Hama ☎0946 350 9188; map p.391. This stylish bar, with chairs and loungers out on the sand, is one of liveliest on El Nido beachfront. The tunes are just as good as the colourful cocktails (P200) and usually have everyone up and dancing. Daily 4pm–2am.

The Calamian Islands

The island-hopping, kayaking, diving and trekking in the **Calamian Islands**, north of mainland Palawan, in many ways trumps that in the parent island, especially when it comes to its world-famous **wreck-diving**. From the main settlement of **Coron Town** on the largest island, **Busuanga**, you can explore the awe-inspiring islands and reefs of Coron Bay, beginning with the lagoons and coves hidden among the staggering limestone cliffs of **Coron Island**. Southwest is **Culion Island**, an intriguing former leper colony. The waters around the Calamians are also feeding grounds for the endangered **dugong** – the best tours to see them are arranged by *Club Paradise* on Dimakya Island (see p.396).

Busuanga Island

Busuanga is the largest island in the Calamian group, but is mostly wild and undeveloped, with little to see beyond the lively fishing community of **Coron Town** on the south coast and its hinterlands. Coron Town is the main base for exploring the **shipwrecks** in adjacent **Coron Bay**, but non-divers will find the pristine snorkelling, swimming and hiking trails nearby just as enticing.

Coron Town and around

With its narrow streets and ramshackle wharf, **CORON TOWN** retains an old-fashioned provincial charm, although like most Filipino towns its roads are congested with an ever-growing number of tricycles. Refreshingly, you won't see any fast-food chains here, and there are a good number of restaurants and accommodation options. Coron Town is a major resort-in-the-making, with regular flights from Manila helping to ramp up development and ambitous land-reclamation projects in the pipeline. The phenomenal views across the bay to Coron Island never get old; these are best appreciated from the top of **Mount Tapyas**, a steep 30 to 45-minute hike along a trail which starts at the end of San Augustin Street.

Maquinit Hot Springs

7km east of Coron Town • Daily 8am–8pm • P150 • Tricycles charge about P300 return from Coron Town (they usually wait for 2hr); private minivan rental is P1200–1500, and some boat tours of Coron Bay include the springs

Facing Coron Bay, the **Maquinit Hot Springs** comprise a series of enticing open pools of spring water that feed into each other before cascading into the sea; the springs are 36°C, making it best to visit during rain or the cool of the evening.

CORON TOWN AND THE CALAMIAN ISLANDS

ACCOMMODATION

Club Paradise	1
Coral Bay Resort	3
El Rio y Mar	2
Sangat Island Dive Resort	4

ARRIVAL AND DEPARTURE

By plane Flights arrive at Busuanga (Coron) Airport, with its small terminal building and handful of sari-sari stores (30min by van/jeepney from Coron Town; P150). There's a tourist information counter next to the baggage claim (📞 0918 725 4665), but no ATM. All the airlines have offices in town, and tickets can also be booked through Calamian Islands Travel and Tours (📞 0917 532 2719, 🌐 coron-travel .com) on Rosario St.

Destinations Cebu (Cebu Pacific: 1 daily; 1hr 40min); Manila (Cebu Pacific & PAL Express: regular daily flights; 1hr).

By boat The 2GO Manila–Coron ferry service leaves Manila at 4pm on Fri, arriving in Coron Town at 6am on Sat

INFORMATION

Tourist information The helpful tourist centre in Coron Town faces the market (Mon–Fri 9am–noon & 1–5pm; 📞 0920 662 0057).

Banks and exchange There are several banks in Coron Town, most of which have ATMs that accept foreign cards.

ACCOMMODATION

There are plenty of **places to stay** in Coron Town, and some of the best resorts in the Calamians lie off the **north coast of Busuanga**, a bus and boat ride from the airport and a 1hr drive from town.

CORON TOWN

Coron Village Lodge 134 National Hwy 📞 0928 202 0819, 🌐 coronvillagelodge.com; map p.396. A bamboo-fronted lodge, surrounded by lush tropical plants, this former family home has 25 clean and simple rooms with a/c and private bathrooms. There's also a rooftop bar and restaurant. Wi-fi in public areas. 📶 **P950**

Darayanon Lodge 132 National Hwy 📞 0917 894 4593, 🌐 darayanon-coron.weebly.com; map p.396. Rambling hotel with decent deluxe rooms in the newer wing (P2300); the older rooms at the front are a bit shabby and damp. The pool is a nice extra, as is the leafy garden. The alfresco restaurant serves good breakfast, lunch and dinner. Unreliable wi-fi. 📶 **P1400**

BUSUANGA ISLAND

morning; it departs 1hr later for Puerto Princesa, arriving at 9pm on Sat. On the way back, it leaves Puerto at midnight on Sat night/Sun morning, stopping off in Coron Town at 2pm on Sun, leaving at 3.30pm, and arriving in Manila at 5.30am on Mon morning. For El Nido, Montenegro Lines operate a daily fast ferry leaving at noon (4hr; P1760). There are also daily morning bangkas to Coron leaving at 8am (P1500 including lunch; 8–9 hr), but as they are slower, less comfortable and more vulnerable to weather-related delays, you're much better off taking the ferry. Both are bookable through any resort or guesthouse. Both ferries and bangkas arrive and depart from the public pier next to *Sea Dive Resort*.

BPI is the best, up on the National Highway (Cirrus, Plus, Visa, Electron and MasterCard accepted; P200 fee); Allied Savings Bank on Don Pedro St takes Visa. Western Union (Mon–Sat 8am–6pm, Sun 8am–5pm), on Real St, also sells air tickets.

8

The Funny Lion Sitio Jolo, Poblacion V 📞 632 856 1443, 🌐 thefunnylion.com; map p.396. This contemporary boutique resort is located just north of the town and offers spectacular views of the bay. Rooms are sleek and well appointed, and there's a beautiful infinity pool and a good restaurant. **P6400**

★ **KokosNuss Resort** National Hwy 📞 0919 776 9544, 🌐 kokosnuss.info; map p.396. The first resort as you approach Coron Town from the airport, 1km north of town. Accommodation is set around a lovely garden area with hammocks and a small pool. Rooms range from quaint thatched bungalows with a/c (P1980) to eco-rooms with solar-heated showers (P1900) and cave-style rooms with fans. A range of luxury rooms were under construction at

---

CORON TOWN TOUR OPERATORS

Most hotels can arrange various **tours** of the islands and attractions near Coron Town, but it's worth shopping around as itineraries and prices vary. The following **operators** are recommended.

Calamian Tourist Boat Association At the town pier behind the market, this basic outfit has its own fixed prices for island-hopping.

Calamianes Expeditions 11 San Augustin St 📞 0919 305 4363, 🌐 corongaleri.com.ph. An excellent, eco-friendly budget choice. They need a minimum of five people to run tours, but will pair you with other groups to make up the numbers. Coron

Island trips, for example, start at just P650/person including lunch, but excluding snorkel gear (P150) and entrance to Kayangan Lake (P300).

Sea Dive Resort 3 Don Pedro St 📞 0918 400 0448, 🌐 seadiveresort.com. In addition to their recommended dive trips (see box, p.398) this in-hotel operator is a good possibility for tours.

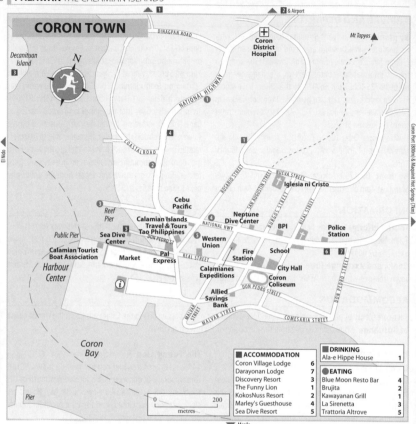

8

the time of writing. Weak wi-fi. 🛜 **P1740**

Marley's Guesthouse National Hwy ☎0929 772 5559, 🌐marleyguesthouse.wixsite.com/marleysguesthouse; map p.396. A real backpacker hangout, inspired by the owner's love of reggae and Bob Marley, this place has simple fan double rooms with shared bathrooms; those with a window cost P100 more. There's also a communal kitchen, lounge and funky alfresco bar. Poor wi-fi. 🛜 **P400**

Sea Dive Resort 3 Don Pedro St ☎0918 400 0448, 🌐seadiveresort.com; map p.396. Popular divers' resort offering simple, comfortable options, from budget doubles with shared bathroom to en-suite fan (P900) and a/c rooms (P1600). The walls are quite thin, however, so noise can be an issue. There's a decent restaurant, bar and limited wi-fi, and the dive facilities are first-rate. Visa and MasterCard accepted (three percent surcharge). It is also a well-equipped dive operation (see box, p.398). 🛜 **P450**

EATING

CORON TOWN

Blue Moon Resto Bar National Hwy ☎0929 538 7181;

THE NORTH COAST

Club Paradise Dimakya Island ☎02 719 6971, 🌐clubparadisepalawan.com; map p.394. Slick, German-owned place with cosy, modern a/c cottages a stone's throw from the beach and a fabulous reef just offshore, where turtles and dugongs have been sighted. Rates are per person and cover full board. Wi-fi in reception. 🛜 **P11,600**

El Rio y Mar Port Caltom, San José ☎02 838 4964 or ☎02 668 3929, 🌐elrioymar.com; map p.394. Set on a 500m-stretch of beach facing a lagoon (it's on a promontory, not an island), with an infinity pool. The 24 spotless, beautifully maintained native or cedar cabañas all have hot water, TV and video, and there's basic wi-fi at the restaurant. The many activities, including kayaking, sailing, fishing and snorkelling, cost extra, as do diving and tours. Wi-fi in the restaurant. 🛜 **P7600**

map p.396. A British/Filipino-owned bar and restaurant with international, Filipino and Thai dishes. The burgers

(P300) are exceptionally good and the tiger prawns in coconut milk (P450) aren't bad either. There aren't any veggie dishes on the menu, but ask and they'll make them for you. They show live sports on TV here too, and it's a good spot for a drink. Daily 9am–2am.

★**Brujita** National Hwy ☎0916 660 7430; map p.396. Specializing in vegetarian dishes, this is one of the best and most popular restaurants in town – arrive early to get a table. The menu includes vegetable curry with coconut milk and chickpea curry with mung beans (both P160). It's a hit for meat and seafood too, with plenty of chicken dishes (P190) and fresh fish. Daily 9am–10pm.

Kawayanan Grill National Hwy ☎0917 574 4586; map p.396. Atmospheric Filipino restaurant with thatched candlelit cabañas and a lush garden. Great place for drinks, with good cheap cocktails (P70), and decent food, too; the seafood platter (P395) is ideal for sharing, and the crocodile

sisig (P285) is also a novel option: a sizzling plate of crocodile meat flavoured with calamansi (local lime), garlic and chilli. Daily 11am–11pm.

La Sirenetta Reef pier ☎0998 474 2517; map p.396. Reached via the alleyway beside Coron Divers and Coron Reef Pension House, La Sirenetta has one of the best locations in town, out on a pier opposite Sea Dive Resort, with views across the bay. Tasty margaritas and great seafood: dishes include mahi-mahi with mango (P380) and coconut and basil curry with fish and fresh veg. Best to come in the evenings as many of the dishes are not available for lunch. Daily 11am–10pm.

★**Trattoria Altrove** Rosario St ☎0918 464 4671; map p.396. This breezy top-floor restaurant has a romantic air and some of the best Italian food you'll find anywhere in the Philippines. The giant thin-crust pizzas (P380–645) are particularly popular, and are topped with authentic ingredients. Daily 5–10pm.

DRINKING

Ala-e Hippie House 5 Nueva St ☎0975 580 6812; map p.396. This reggae-loving hippy bar is hidden high on a hill above Coron Town and offers spectacular sunset views from its balcony, as well as live reggae music. Covered in posters, artwork and tie-dye wall hangings, seats are on cushions on the floor. You'll be treated like a good friend, but may have to put up with warm beers. Daily 9am–11pm.

8

Coron Bay Islands

The primary reason to stay in Coron Town is to explore the spellbinding islands and coves scattered around **Coron Bay** – also a fantastic destination for **wreck-diving** (see box, p.398). Bangka trips are easy to arrange, but it's worth comparing the various packages on offer (see box, p.395). **Coron Island** is the most popular destination, but you should also try to spend some time on the smaller, less-visited islands.

Coron Island

Sea Dive Resort (see opposite) offers day-trips (usually 8am–4pm) for around P1500 for a bangka of up to four people; the Calamian Tourist Boat Association (see box, p.395) charges P2000 – these prices do not include the various admission fees, and lunch is usually an extra P250/person

Most hotels and tour operators in Coron Town offer day-trips to **Coron Island**, an enchanting cluster of jagged limestone cliffs and peaks just fifteen minutes across the bay. The island offers truly spectacular landscapes and some rich snorkelling sites, though visitors are confined to the northern coast; Coron is the traditional home of the **Tagbanua** people and the rest of the island is strictly off limits to outsiders. The Tagbanua in the two main east-coast communities of **Banuangdaan** (Old Coron Town) and **Acabugaonow** make most of their income from charging admission fees to the island's various attractions; this supplements their traditional sources of livelihood, fishing and bird's-nest collecting.

Tours involve plenty of snorkelling and swimming. In between Coron Island and Coron Town you'll typically stop at **Lake Kayangan** (see below) and **Siete Picados Marine Park** (P100), which offers a relatively rich spread of coral and marine life (sea snakes, sea fans, clownfish and whale sharks are sometimes spotted on the deeper side of the reef).

Lake Kayangan

Daily 8am–4pm • P300

To visit volcanic **Lake Kayangan**, boats dock at a gorgeous lagoon rimmed with coral and turquoise waters – here the Tagbanua have a small hut with basic information

---

WRECK-DIVING IN CORON BAY

Most divers come to the Coron area for the World War II **Japanese shipwrecks**. There are 24 wrecks in all, all sunk in one massive attack by US aircraft on September 24, 1944. Among the most interesting are:

Akitsushima A big ship lying on her side with a crane once used for hoisting a seaplane. Between Culion and Busuanga islands, near Manglet Island, the wreck attracts huge schools of giant batfish and barracuda.

Irako The best of the wrecks and still almost intact; it's home to turtles and enormous groupers, who hang in the water and eyeball you as you float past. A swim through the engine room reveals a network of pipes and valves inhabited by moray eels and lionfish, which have spines that deliver a hefty dose of poison.

Morazan Maru Japanese freighter sitting upright at 28m. Large shoals of banana fish, giant batfish and pufferfish the size of footballs can be seen, especially around the mast, bow and stern. It's easy to get into the cargo holds, making this a good wreck-dive for beginners.

Taiei Maru Japanese tanker covered with beautiful corals and a large variety of marine life. The deck is relatively shallow at between 10m and 16m deep, and is well suited to wreck-dive beginners.

DIVE OPERATORS

There are a dozen or so dive operators in Coron Town. The following are reliable.

Neptune Dive Center National Hwy ☎0912 760 7492, ⓦneptunedivecenter.com.

Sea Dive Resort 3 Don Pedro St ☎0918 400 0448, ⓦseadiveresort.com.

8

about the island and the tribe, with staff on hand to answer any questions. The lake itself is reached by climbing up a steep flight of steps – at the top, turn left along a narrow path to tiny **Kayangan Cave** for awe-inspiring views of the lagoon below. The main path continues down to the lake, where you can snorkel in the warm waters and spy schools of odd-looking needlefish and plunging cathedral-like rock formations.

The rest of the island

Lake Barracuda (P200) is encircled by jagged limestone outcrops that give way to lush jungle, but is only really worth the additional entrance fee if you are on a **dive trip**; on the surface the water is the usual temperature, but 18m down it heats up so much that you can drift along on hot thermals. To the west are the **Twin Lagoons** (P200), hemmed in by jagged pillars of limestone towering over the water like abstract sculptures. Boats dock at the end of the first lagoon, where you can swim through a low-lying water tunnel into the second one, a tranquil and very deep inlet. Odd coral formations cling to the sides of the lagoon, looking like a sunken city under the surface. A little further along the coast is **Skeleton Wreck** (P100 fee), a sunken Japanese fishing vessel easily viewed by snorkellers, and a series of narrow **beaches** backed by sheer cliffs. Tours usually stop for lunch on one of these (Banol Beach is the most popular), but each one charges a P200 fee.

The southern islands

The Calamian Tourist Boat Association (see box, p.395) runs tours for P3500/boat; Calamianes Expeditions (see box, p.395) charges P950/person

One hour south of Coron Town lies the enticing trio of **Malcapuya Island** (P150), **Banana Island** (P200) and **Bolog Island** (P100), classic desert islands where the main activity is lounging on the beach. Malcapuya has monkeys inland, while Bolog features alluring **Malaroyroy Beach**, a curving bar of silky white sand.

Sangat Island

Sea Dive (see p.396) charges P3500/boat, while the Calamian Tourist Boat Association (see box, p.395) rate is P2500 and Calamianes Expeditions (see box, p.395) charges P950/person

Sangat Island, west of Coron Town (1hr 30min by boat), is yet another craggy, picture-perfect tropical island. As well as plenty of coral gardens laced with tropical fish, the island is close to eleven World War II shipwrecks, some of which can be explored by snorkellers at low tide.

ACCOMMODATION   CORON BAY ISLANDS

★**Coral Bay Resort** Potototan Island ☎0916 544 1843, ⓦcoralbay.ph; map p.394. Comfy, rustic, chilled-out accommodation in fan-cooled wooden huts on a 900m white-sand beach about 1hr 30min from Coron Town by bangka (free transfer from the Coron Town office if you stay two nights or more). You can trek around the island or snorkel just offshore on a beautiful reef teeming with tropical fish. Slow, patchy wi-fi. 🛜 P3400

Discovery Resort Decanituan Island ☎0918 398 7125, ⓦdiscoverydiversresort.com; map p.394. Popular, laidback resort, a 10min bangka ride from Coron Town, with a 24hr shuttle service back and forth. The seventeen bungalows all have private bathrooms and terraces with

fine views of the bay. Staff are friendly and there's a good restaurant with sporadic wi-fi. The beach here is nothing special, but there are kayaks available, with which you can get to nicer ones nearby. 🛜 P1800

★**Sangat Island Dive Resort** Sangat Island ☎0919 617 5187, ⓦsangat.com.ph; map p.394. Established by a British expat in 1994 on a gorgeous island – 30min from Coron Town – with a giddy interior of cliffs and jungle and a shore of coves and coral reefs. Accommodation is in thirteen native-style beachfront and hillside cottages (with fans), and they specialize in diving courses. Free (limited) wi-fi or P100/hr for internet. Rates are per person and cover full board. 🛜 US$105

Culion Island

Few travellers make it to the curious island of **Culion**, around two hours south of Coron Town by boat. In 1904 the Americans decided to create an isolated but self-sufficient leper colony here – it became the world's largest **leprosarium**, a place that inspired fear and often revulsion. Today the leper colony has all but been erased, but haunting monuments of the island's past remain, as well as some untouched, empty beaches. Like Busuanga, Culion is quite large and undeveloped, but the main attractions lie in the pretty little capital, **Culion Town**. The approach to town is dominated by the striking coral-walled **La Inmaculada Concepción Church**, which was rebuilt in 1933 on the site of an older fortified Spanish chapel, completed in 1740. Beside it is the old lighthouse, with tremendous views north to Coron Town.

Culion Museum

Culion Sanatorium and General Hospital compound • Mon–Fri 9am–noon & 1–4pm • P200

The intriguing **Culion Museum**, housed in the island's former leprosy research lab (built in 1930), details the history of the colony. Featuring medical relics and photographs from the early twentieth century, with a vast archive of patient records that you can browse, it also maintains the rooms where doctors worked, complete with original, rather frightening-looking equipment.

ARRIVAL AND INFORMATION   CULION ISLAND

By boat Culion can only be reached by bangka from Coron Town; a large outrigger (P180 plus P20 terminal fee) leaves daily at 1/1.30pm from Coron Town (1hr 30min). Boats return at around 7.30am/8.30am – so you'll have to stay overnight unless you rent a private bangka from the Calamian Tourist Boat Association (see box, p.395) for a return trip (2hr

one-way; P2500–3500), or join the tour (P1150/person) with Calamianes Expeditions (see box, p.395).

Tourist information Inside the town hall (Mon–Fri 9am–5pm; ☎0917 552 2277).

Services There are no banks or ATMs, and credit cards are rarely accepted, so bring enough cash for your stay.

ACCOMMODATION AND EATING

Hotel Maya Culion Town ☎0939 254 2744. Next to La Inmaculada Concepción Church, Culion's best hotel is actually a teaching hotel operated by the Jesuit-run Loyola College of Culion. Rooms are spacious and comfortable and service is friendly. Single rooms are available (P550). Wi-fi in public areas only. 🛜 P1100

Tabing Dagat Lodging House Culion Town ☎0921 653 1470. A 5min walk from the port, opposite the local government offices, this is a comfy option offering doubles with shared bathrooms or larger a/c en-suites with balconies (P750). There's also a decent Filipino restaurant. Credit cards accepted. Unreliable wi-fi. 🛜 P900

8

Mindanao

KADAYAWAN FESTIVAL, DAVAO

9

Mindanao

Mindanao, the massive island at the foot of the Philippine archipelago, is in many ways the cultural heart of the country, a place where indigenous tribes still farm their ancient homelands and Christians live alongside Muslims who first settled here in the fourteenth century. Spanish rule came late to much of Mindanao, and was tenuous at best throughout the nineteenth century; when the Americans occupied the islands, it was here they met their most bitter resistance. Today, the island remains a conflict zone: in spite of a peace pact between the Moro Islamic Liberation Front (MILF) rebels and the government early in 2014, the island has become mired in anti-government insurgencies, terrorist attacks and tourist kidnappings. With the exception of the islands of Camiguin and Siargao, caution is advised against travel anywhere on the island, and certain parts should be avoided altogether. Note that at the time this book went to print, in June 2017, Mindanao was under martial law following the Islamist-militant attack on the city of Marawi in the ARMM (see box, p.405).

North Mindanao, which sees the most tourist activity, is comparatively safe and accessible, although the lively gateway city of **Cagayan de Oro** (CDO) was the site of a number of roadside explosions and grenade blasts in 2016. From the north coast, most visitors make a beeline for the pint-sized island of **Camiguin**, one of the country's most appealing tourist spots and an island with more volcanoes per square mile than anywhere else in the world. Elsewhere, northeast Mindanao is rich in ecotourism potential and offshore islands. Highlights include the ancient wooden boat discovered at **Butuan**, the spellbinding **Enchanted River** and the surfing and backpacker hotspot of **Siargao**.

The **southeast** is home to Mindanao's largest city, **Davao**, a diverse and friendly place best known for its fresh fruit. Davao itself is not a city of legendary sights, but the nearby countryside and coast offer plenty of attractions, from **Samal Island** to the **Philippine Eagle Center**. Davao is also the gateway to **Mount Apo**, the nation's highest peak and – when it's open for business again following a temporary closure at the time of research – a magnet for trekkers and climbers.

Much of western Mindanao is part of the **Autonomous Region in Muslim Mindanao** (ARMM), an area of huge tourism potential, but where the security situation is in a state of flux (see box, p.433). We have removed most of our coverage of the region; check the current **security** situation before considering a visit.

Cagayan de Oro and around

Sprawled along the north coast of Mindanao, the city of **CAGAYAN DE ORO** (CDO) makes an ideal introduction to the island, with its smattering of sights and fine restaurants, and a handful of enticing attractions in the mountains beyond, including

Highlights

❶ **Whitewater rafting on the Cagayan de Oro River** Shoot the rapids near the city of Cagayan de Oro; the full 15km course offers four hours of thrills in a beautiful setting. **See box, p.407**

❷ **Lanzones festival, Camiguin** Visit this dazzling little island in October, when the colourful four-day Lanzones festival is held. **See p.410**

❸ **Enchanted River** This magical, remote lagoon is a deep cove of crystalline water crammed with colourful tropical fish – a visual delight. **See p.416**

❹ **Siargao Island** With tranquil resorts, powdery beaches, top-notch surfing and laidback nightlife, Siargao is a backpacker's dream. **See p.417**

HIGHLIGHTS ARE MARKED ON THE MAP ON P.404

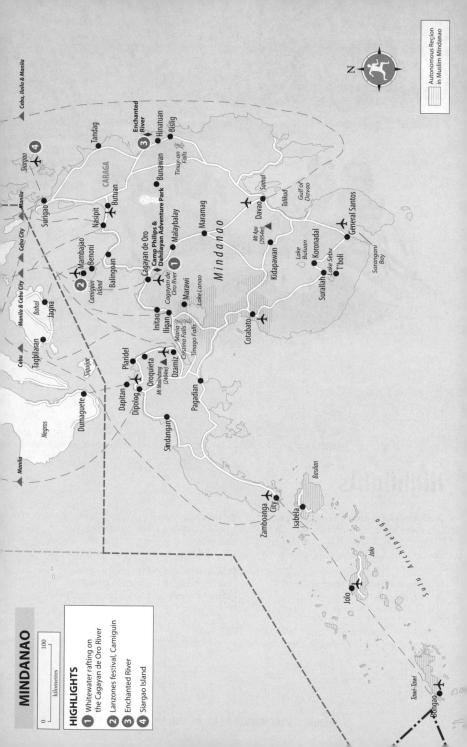

MINDANAO

0	kilometres	100

HIGHLIGHTS

1. Whitewater rafting on the Cagayan de Oro River
2. Lanzones festival, Camiguin
3. Enchanted River
4. Siargao Island

Autonomous Region in Muslim Mindanao

N

Mindanao

CARAGA

Cebu, Iloilo & Manila
Tandag
Enchanted River
Hinatuan
Bislig
Siargao
Surigao
Manila
Nasipit
Buttuan
Bunawan
Tinuy-an Falls
Mambajao
Benoni
Cagayan de Oro
Camp Philips & Dahilayan Adventure Park
Malaybalay
Maramag
Davao
Samal
Talikud
Gulf of Davao
Balingoan
Camiguin Island
Initao
Iligan
Marawi
Lake Lanao
Mt Apo (2954m)
Kidapawan
Koronadal
Surallah
Lake Sebu
T'boli
General Santos
Sarangani Bay
Maria Cristina Falls
Tinago Falls
Cagayan de Oro River
Cotabato
Ozamiz
Oroquieta
Mt Malindang (2404m)
Plaridel
Dapitan
Dipolog
Sindangan
Pagadian
Zamboanga City
Isabela
Basilan
Jolo
Jolo
Sulu Archipelago
Bongao
Tawi-Tawi
Cebu, Iloilo & Manila
Cebu City
Manila & Cebu City
Jagna
Bohol
Tagbilaran
Cebu
Manila
Dumaguete
Negros
Siquijor

whitewater rafting on the Cagayan de Oro River (see box, p.407). Sitting on the eastern bank of the river, the city stretches from **Vicente de Lara Park** in the north, with its age-old mahogany trees, to circular **Gaston Park** in the south, once the site of city executions, bullfights and parades.

Southwest of the park, you'll find the **San Augustine Cathedral**, a dour off-white stone edifice, with immense stained-glass windows, rebuilt in the 1950s. A couple of kilometres northeast of **Xavier University**, the hip, modern heart of the city revolves around the **Limketkai Center**, an upscale mall, and the adjacent **Rosario Strip**. At weekends, locals can also be found flooding into outposts of the city's two largest shopping mall chains, **Centrio Ayala Mall** and **SM City Mall**.

Museum of Three Cultures

Capitol University, Corrales Ave, 2km north of Plaza Divisoria • Mon–Fri 9am–noon & 1.30–5.30pm, Sat 9am–noon • P50 • ☎ 088 856 2832, ⓦ cu.edu.ph

The **Museum of Three Cultures** is devoted to the Christians, Muslims and seven indigenous traditions (or "Lumad") of northern Mindanao. The first gallery is dedicated to history, with exhibits on the Huluga Caves, early trade with China and the Butuan boats (see p.415). The most interesting section is dedicated to the M'ranao

---

THE MINDANAO PROBLEM

Because of its volatile political situation and advice from Western governments to avoid visiting mainland Mindanao altogether, you should always check the **current situation** before travelling. Politically, things are fluid and confusing; a number of factions and splinter groups are calling for varying degrees of autonomy from Manila.

The thorniest issue involves Mindanao's Muslims (known as Moros), who are seeking self-determination. The **Moro National Liberation Front** (MNLF) started a war for independence in the 1970s that lasted until 1987, when it signed an agreement accepting the government's offer of autonomy. As a result, the **Autonomous Region in Muslim Mindanao**, or ARMM, was created in 1990, covering the western provinces of Basilan, Lanao del Sur, Maguindanao, Sulu and Tawi-Tawi, plus Marawi City. The **Moro Islamic Liberation Front** (MILF) splintered from the MNLF in 1981 and refused to accept the accord. At the height of the fighting, more than 750,000 people were displaced and about four hundred people killed. The fighting continues today, and the group is in the habit of making uneasy truces.

Unfortunately, Mindanao's problems don't end with MILF. In the early 1990s another disaffected group of fighters founded **Abu Sayyaf**, whose name means "Bearer of the Sword". Based on **Basilan Island**, off Mindanao's south coast, Abu Sayyaf is said to have ties to a number of Islamic fundamentalist organizations, including al-Qaeda and Islamic State.

In November 2009, 57 people (including 34 journalists) were tortured and murdered in what was dubbed the **Maguindanao Massacre**, apparently for attempting to register a rival candidate for the upcoming elections; the perpetrators were a private militia controlled by the powerful Ampatuan clan, who were arrested and tried in 2010. Since the massacre, which led to the president declaring a state of emergency, numerous ceasefires between the government, military and various rebel groups have come and gone.

At least four Muslim rebel groups continue to operate on the island, and since 2015 there has been an increase in **bomb threats** and the **kidnapping** of foreign nationals and tourists. Abu Sayyaf beheaded a Canadian hostage in April 2016, for example, and there were multiple attacks in November 2016, including some specifically targeting foreigners. In May 2017, the **Maute** rebel group, with the backing of Islamic State, attacked Marawi city in the ARMM and took several hostages. President Duterte declared martial law on Mindanao, and at the time of writing at least twenty civilians had been killed in the fighting.

The current UK government advice is to avoid all but essential travel to north and eastern Mindanao – excluding Camiguin and Siargao – and avoid the rest of the island completely.

9

CAGAYAN DE ORO

Macabalan Wharf (4km)

Eastbound Bus Terminal

& Limketai Mall

Capitol University Medical Center, Centrio Ayala Mall & Museum of Three Cultures

Airport, Great White Water Tours, CDO Bugnay River Rafting & SM City Mall

EATING	
Bigby's Café & Restaurant	1
Cucina Higala	3
Restaurant Damaso	5
Thai Me Up	2
Vjandep Bakeshop	4

NIGHTLIFE	
Somewhere Else	1

N

MARCOS BRIDGE

MAGSAYSAY STREET

C.M. RECTO AVENUE

Cagayan De Oro
Medical Center II

M. H. DEL PILAR STREET

NACALABAN ST.

Vicente de
Lara Park

Provincial
Capitol

GENERAL CAPISTRANO STREET

MACAHAMBUS STREET

KALAMBAGOHAN STREET

AKUT STREET

LUNA STREET

Land
Bank

Iglesia ni
Cristo

Cagayan de Oro
River

MONTALBAN STREET

TIANO BROTHERS STREET

Kagay
Whitewater
Rafting

MABINI STREET

DON APOLINAR VELEZ STREET

Library

YACAPIN STREET

P. PACANA STREET

BORJA STREET

BURGOS STREET

RIZAL STREET

GOMEZ STREET

PABAYO STREET

CRUZ TAAL STREET

CORRALES AVENUE

T. NERI STREET

Plaza
Divisoria

ABEJUELA STREET

Tourism
Showcase

Mercury
pharmacy

DBP

Cyberium @

Domain
@

T. CHAVEZ STREET

Police

City
Hall

PCMC
Hospital

Xavier
University
Building

XAVIER UNIVERSITY
CAMPUS

HAYES STREET

GAERLAN STREET

Museo de Oro

Gaston
Park

SAN AGUSTIN STREET

Viajero
Outdoor
Centre

San Augustine
Cathedral

DOLORES STREET

0	50

metres

ACCOMMODATION	
Budgetel	2
CDO Hotel Xentro	4
GC Suites	6
Miami Inn	5
Red Planet	1
Seda Centrio	3

of Marawi, an area at the heart of the Moro dispute. Exhibits cover Islamic brass work, giant ceremonial swords and traditional *torogan*-style houses.

Museo de Oro

Xavier University, Corrales Ave • Tues–Sat 9am–noon & 1–5pm • P70 • ☎ 088 853 9800, ⓦ www.xu.edu.ph

Part of Xavier University's campus, **Museo de Oro** (Museum of Gold) is one of the country's most important collections of folkloric artefacts. The museum is split into three exhibits: the ethnic history of Northern Mindanao, the ethnology of Mindanao, and the Francisco Demetrio SJ Gallery, which contains art and historical artefacts. The museum is an informative and useful introduction to Mindanao's complicated make-up – just don't come expecting any gold; despite the name, there's no haul of booty.

Dahilayan Adventure Park

40km southeast on the highway to Davao • Daily 8am–5pm • Ziplines package P600; ziplines and rafting combo package from P2199 • ☎ 0922 880 1319, ⓦ dahilayanadventurepark.com • A van and driver from CDO should cost P2500–3000/day

Billed as Mindanao's most extreme playground, the **Dahilayan Adventure Park** makes for an entertaining day out, primarily for its long **zipline** and refreshingly cool alpine location, in the hills some 1370m above sea level. The **Dahilayan Zip Zone** comprises three ziplines: an exhilarating 320m section, a tamer 150m segment, and the 840m finale, where you are chained into a full-body harness before hurtling down the mountain at 90km/hour. There's also whitewater rafting – either come with a group or call in advance and they should be able to place you in a boat (minimum six).

ARRIVAL AND DEPARTURE   CAGAYAN DE ORO AND AROUND

By plane Laguindingan International Airport is 33km northwest of the city – about an hour's drive. The airport is accessible by jeepney (P40 to Laguindingan turn-off, then P20 shuttle to the airport), but the most convenient transfers are with LAX Shuttle (P249), which picks up at the Centrio Ayala Mall, or with Magnum Express, which leaves from Magnum Radio in CM Recto (P249). Philippine Airlines has ticket offices at the airport (daily 4am–7pm; ☎ 088 555 0752) and on the ground floor of the East Annex Building at Limketkai Mall (Mon–Sat 8.30am–5pm, Sun 8.30am–noon; ☎ 088 857 2294). Cebu Pacific (Mon–Sat 8am–5pm; ☎ 088 586 3936) has a ticketing office at 89

Hayes St, Cagayan De Oro.
Destinations Bacolod (1 weekly; 1hr 10min); Cebu City (6–7 daily; 50min); Davao (1–2 daily; 55min); Iloilo (3 weekly; 55min); Manila (12–13 daily; 1hr 30min); Tagbilaran (1 weekly; 45min).
By bus The Eastbound bus terminal is near the Limketkai Center, 3km east of the centre (off Recto Ave), while the Westbound Bus and Jeepney Station lies 6km west of the centre on the Iligan road. From either, you can take a jeepney (P10–12) or a taxi (around P50) into town.
Destinations from Eastbound terminal Balingoan (for Camiguin; every 45min till 5pm; 1hr 45min); Butuan (every

RAFTING THE CAGAYAN DE ORO RIVER

Whitewater rafting along the fourteen major rapids of the Cagayan de Oro River gained popularity after former president Gloria Macapagal-Arroyo took a ride here in 2002. The jumping-off point is at the barangay of **Mambuaya**, a thirty- to forty-minute ride from the city proper. The wet months (Sept and Oct) are best for intermediate and professional levels (when the rapids range from class 3 to 4), while the rest of the year is more suitable for beginners.

RAFTING OPERATORS

CDO Bugsay River Rafting ☎ 088 85015 808, ⓦ cdorafting.com. Reliable operator offering a variety of packages for beginner through to advanced paddlers (P1200–3500).
Great White Water Tours ☎ 088 310 5415, ⓦ riverraftingcdo.com. This decent company offers

half-day (P1400) or full-day tours (P2000). Rates include transfers, guides, equipment, snacks and meals.
Kagay Whitewater Rafting ☎ 088 852 1021, ⓦ kagaycagayandeororafting.com. The most popular outfit in the city offers 2–4hr trips on the upper, mid and lower levels of the river (P1200/P1800/P2000).

9

45min till 5pm; 4hr); Davao (every 30min; 6–8hr); Surigao (2 daily; 6hr).

Destinations from Westbound terminal Dipolog (2 daily; 6–7hr); Iligan (hourly; 1hr 30min); Marawi (hourly; 3hr); Ozamiz (hourly; 4hr); Zamboanga (hourly; 12hr).

By boat Macabalan Wharf is 4km north of the centre; regular jeepneys make the journey back and forth. 2GO runs three services to Cebu from CDO, while Trans-Asia has

a daily service to Cebu. Super Shuttle Ferry also operates to Cebu every Sat, while Lite Shipping has services to Cebu, Dumaguete and Jagna on Bohol.

Destinations Bacolod (weekly; 21hr); Cebu City (daily; 10hr); Dumaguete (3 weekly; 7hr); Iloilo (3 weekly; 14hr); Jagna (4 weekly; 6–7hr); Manila (daily; 35hr); and Tagbilaran (3 weekly; 10hr).

INFORMATION AND ACTIVTIES

Tourist office The Cagayan De Oro Tourism Showcase is on Don Apolinar Velez St (Mon–Fri 8am–noon & 1–5pm). The website ⓦ cdoguide.com is also helpful.

Viajero Outdoor Centre This is a one-stop hub for those seeking camping, caving and mountaineering excursions

across northern Mindanao. The owners rent out ropes, tents, safety gear and more. They're also an excellent source of local information, and can arrange all kinds of trips into the jungle (137 Archbishop Hayes St; Mon–Sat 10am–7pm; ☏ 088 857 1799, ⓦ facebook.com/ViajeroOutdoorCentre).

GETTING AROUND

By tricycle Most locals use tricycles to get around the city (6am–10pm; P6–10 for city trips)

By jeepney Jeepneys start at P6.50.

ACCOMMODATION

Budgetel Corrales Ave, north of C.M. Recto ☏ 088 856 4200, ⓦ budgetel.com.ph. Handy for the Eastbound bus terminal, this hotel is the city's cheapest deal. It offers 34 en-suite a/c singles, twins and doubles, as well as enormous sixteen- and eighteen-bed dorms with shared bathrooms. There's a laundry, too. Wi-fi in the lobby area. 🛜 Dorms P250, doubles P990

CDO Hotel Xentro Corrales Ave, behind Pelaez Sports Center ☏ 088 850 1922, ⓦ hotelxentro.com. The newest hotel in Cagayan De Oro, with great-value deals for single travellers (P800). The pros are that it's bright, clean and modern, and there's a range of rooms from seven-bed dorms to deluxe suites; the downside is that its popular with groups, so can get noisy. If you fancy a massage, try the spa on the ground floor. Patchy wi-fi. 🛜 P1300

★**GC Suites** 4th Floor, Grand Central Building, Hayes St ☏ 088 858 1234, ⓦ gcsuitescdo.com. The closest this city has to a boutique hotel, GC Suites offers a variety of a/c single and double rooms decorated in homage to musical icons such as The Beatles and Bob Marley, and with TVs and clean en-suite bathrooms. Guests are given a voucher for a

free meal, redeemable at one of six restaurants in the same complex. 🛜 P988

Miami Inn Vamenta Blvd ☏ 088 858 1901. One of many identikit downtown hotels, this budget cheapie stands out for its quiet location on the Cayagan De Oro River and rainbow-coloured a/c rooms. Also has a coffee shop, 24hr reception and laundry service. Wi-fi in public areas. 🛜 P900

Red Planet C.M. Recto Ave ☏ 063 2519 0888, ⓦ redplanethotels.com. Between Centrio Ayala Mall and the Limketkai Center, this candy-cane-coloured hotel is as switched-on to traveller needs as Cagayan De Oro gets. All rooms have a/c, a power shower, and a flat-screen TV. 🛜 P1400

Seda Centrio C.M. Recto Ave ☏ 088 323 8888, ⓦ sedahotels.com. Sharing a roof with the Centrio Ayala Mall (where it seems half of the city lives), this business hotel, spread over six floors, is a functional stopover. Rooms are clean and comfy, and fitted with all mod cons including fast wi-fi, iPhone docks and widescreen TVs. It's popular with out-of-town shoppers, hence the inflated prices. 🛜 P3700

EATING

Cagayan de Oro is the best place to eat in northern Mindanao, with a range of affordable **restaurants**. The centre of the action is where A. Velez crosses Hayes and Chavez streets, while a couple of kilometres east, the **Limketkai mall** also has a good mix of restaurants.

Bigby's Café & Restaurant Centrio Ayala Mall ☏ 088 880 0822, ⓦ bigbyscafe.net. Local chain offering a fusion of Western and Filipino dishes, from "Rack a Bye Baby" (P399) and pork chops (P285) to burgers (P249). Don't miss the Midnight Dream Cake (P99/slice). Also one at SM City CDO. Daily 9am–10pm.

★**Cucina Higala** 222 Capistrano St ☏ 088 881 1570, ⓦ facebook.com/pg/CucinaHigala. This Filipino restaurant combines traditional Mindanaoan recipes with modern techniques. Try its *sinuglaw* (seafood ceviche with grilled pork) or *humba* (braised pork belly stew) prepared sous-vide-style. Mains P200–400. Daily 11am–2pm & 5–10pm.

Restaurant Damaso Chavez St ☎0935 591 8479, ⓦfacebook.com/RestaurantDamaso. A great bet for breakfast, this place serves up smoked chorizo, beef *tapa*, eggs, vegetable rice and salads. They also make tasty Sriracha chicken wings (P190), grilled swordfish (P225) and ribs (P330). Daily 7am–10pm.

Thai Me Up Centrio Ayala Mall ☎0916 124 6266. Not a fetish club, but a superb Thai restaurant, with an open-air dining room perfect for warm evenings. Expect the usual dishes – tom yung, pad thai and *som tam* (papaya salad) from P150 – but also the odd Filipino dish that's sneaked its way onto the menu. Daily 10am–11pm.

Vjandep Bakeshop 78 Tiano Brothers St ☎088 858 4027, ⓦvjandep.com. Locals say you haven't been to Cagayan De Oro if you haven't eaten at *Vjandep Bakeshop*, the city's most popular bakery. Its especially popular for its *pastels*, bread buns filled with custard (P140 for a dozen); other fillings include pineapple, jackfruit and mango. Daily 7am–5pm.

NIGHTLIFE

Somewhere Else Corrales Ave ☎0997 536 8175, ⓦfacebook.com/pg/SomewhereElseCDO. DJs are flown in from Manila and Cebu to play here, the city's see-to-be-seen party place. The menu features around thirty imported beers – Mindanao's biggest selection. They do bar snacks, too. Mon–Thurs & Sun 5pm–1am, Fri & Sat 5pm–3am.

DIRECTORY

Hospitals and clinics The Capitol University Medical Center is on Iligan Rd east of the city centre (☎082 856 4730, ⓦcumccdo.com). The Cagayan De Oro Medical Center II is on Nacalaban St (☎088 2271 1874).

Internet access There are numerous places for internet access near Xavier University: Cyberium and Domain on Plaza Divisoria both charge P20/hr. There is free wi-fi at the SM City Mall, south of the city.

Iligan and around

Some 90km west of Cagayan de Oro, the port city of **ILIGAN** is served by regular ferries from Manila and Cebu, making it an alternative gateway to Mindanao if you're travelling on a budget. Little more than a village in the early 1900s, it boomed as an industrial centre after the creation of a hydroelectric power scheme in the 1950s, but was almost completely rebuilt after a devastating fire in 1957. Famed for its **waterfalls**, it's a friendly, laidback place with a population of around 300,000. The best cluster of cascades lies on the west side, on the highway towards Ozamiz and Zamboanga.

Maria Cristina Falls

8.5km southwest of Iligan on the highway to Ozamiz and Zamboanga • Daily 9am–4pm • P35; zipline P200 • ☎063 221 3988 • It's 150m to the park entrance from the main road jeepney stop; walking to the falls from the entrance takes 20min (800m), or you can take the park shuttle (P10)

The most impressive cascade in the region, and located within the **NPC Nature Park**, the **Maria Cristina Falls** serves as the main source of power for much of Mindanao. The twin falls (named after two heartbroken girls who are supposed to have jumped from the top), plunge 100m into the torrential Agus River, and are at their best on Saturday and Sunday at 11am, when the Agus VI Hydroelectric Plant upstream releases the most water. There is a zipline here, too.

Timoga Springs and Macaraeg-Macapagal House

9.5km west of Iligan on the highway to Ozamiz and Zamboanga • **Timoga Springs** Daily 9am–6pm • P100 • **Macaraeg-Macapagal House** Mon–Fri 8am–5pm, Sat–Sun 9am–4pm • Free • ☎063 223 6992

Just 1km beyond the Maria Cristina Falls, the ice-cold, crystal-clear **Timoga Springs** flow freely to a collection of privately owned swimming pools and resorts that can all get very crowded in summer.

Next door to the springs, right on the highway, is the **Macaraeg-Macapagal House**, sometime home to both Diosdado Macapagal, the ninth president of the Philippines, and Gloria Macapagal-Arroyo, the fourteenth president. As a child, Gloria spent many happy

9

days in this house, which was built in 1950 by her maternal grandfather, and the handsome property has been well maintained, preserved as it would have looked in the 1950s. There's not much inside other than family portraits, including a sultry study of the ex-president from 1983, and a statue of Gloria as a child outside, playing on a swing.

Tinago Falls

15km southwest of Iligan, off the Zamboanga road • P10 • Jeepneys will drop you off on the highway, from where you can hike or take a habal-habal to the falls (P40/bike; arrange a return pick-up)

The **Tinago Falls**, a beautiful ribbon of water cascading 73m into a deep-blue pool, get their name from their location, nestled in a dramatic ravine (*tinago* means hidden). They became locally famous when they featured in the 2011 Pinoy movie *Forever and a Day*. From the top it's a tough walk down four hundred or more steps into the ravine; take plenty of care if it's raining.

ARRIVAL AND INFORMATION

By bus The northbound bus terminal, off Bonifacio Ave, 3km north of the centre, serves Cagayan de Oro. The southbound terminal off Roxas Ave, just south of the centre, serves western and southern destinations. Jeepneys and taxis are usually easy to find near both terminals.
Destinations from northbound terminal Cagayan de Oro (hourly; 1hr 30min).
Destinations from southbound terminal Dapitan (several daily; 4hr) Marawi (hourly; 2hr); Ozamiz (hourly; 2hr); Zamboanga (8 hourly; 10hr).

ILIGAN AND AROUND

By boat Ferries from Cebu and Manila dock on the edge of the downtown area. If you walk towards the first traffic circle, you'll find plenty of taxis and jeepneys.
Destinations Cebu (7 weekly; 13hr); Manila (3 weekly; 34hr).
Tourist information The tourist office (Mon–Fri 8am–5pm; ☎063 221 3426, ⓦiligancitytourism.yolasite .com) is at Bahay Salakot on leafy Buhanginan Hill, next to City Hall at the far eastern end of Quezon Ave; take a taxi or jeepney here from downtown.

GETTING AROUND

By jeepney Most jeepney rides around town cost P6.50.
By taxi A/C taxis charge P30 then P2.50/300m, while

non-a/c "PU" taxis run fixed routes for a set rate of P30. Taxis should charge around P100/hr for tours of the waterfalls.

ACCOMMODATION AND EATING

Cheradel Suites Bro. Raymond Jeffrey Rd ☎063 221 4926. Kitschy collection of rooms and suites in a six-building complex around a small pool. Rooms are modern and comfortable and have a/c and cable TV; the biggest Presidential Suite (P9500) has three bedrooms plus a kitchen. 🛜 **P1850**
Mariano's Home Cooked Specialities Meadow Lark St ☎0917 717 5071, ⓦfacebook.com/MarianosHCS. The Mariano family know how to cook up a storm. They offer an exiting range of Filipino-European creations in

their fine-dining restaurant, where dishes range from pan-seared snapper with clams to herb-roasted chicken with pumpkin mash and beef short rib. Mains P200–400. Mon–Sat 4–9.30pm.
Red-C Residences Tambo Highway ☎063 221 4926. The "C" may as well stand for convenient – this new-ish, no-frills inn is a stone's throw from the bus station and a P7 jeepney ride to downtown. The medium-sized rooms have decent hot and cold showers and cable TV. There's also a café beside the hotel. 🛜 **P779**

Camiguin Island

Around 20km off the north coast of mainland Mindanao, little **Camiguin Island** ("cam-ee-*gin*") is one of the country's most appealing tourist spots, offering ivory beaches, iridescent lagoons and jagged mountain scenery. There's no shortage of adventure here, with reasonable scuba diving and tremendous trekking and climbing in the rugged interior, especially on volcanic **Mount Hibok-Hibok**. Another major tourist draw is the annual **Lanzones festival**, held in the fourth week of October. Revellers dressed only in lanzones leaves stomp and dance in the streets as a tribute to the humble fruit, one of the island's major sources of income.

The beauty of Camiguin is that it doesn't really matter where you stay, as you can visit all the sights easily from anywhere. The **coastal road** is only 64 km long, making it entirely feasible to circle the island in a day. If you don't want to depend on public transport, consider renting a motorbike for day-trips.

Mambajao and around

There's no reason to hang around in **MAMBAJAO** ("mah-bow-ha"), the island's capital, other than to sort out the practicalities of your stay. Of the nearby beaches, **Cabua-an Beach**, to the east, near the barangay of Balbagon, is marginally the closest, with some nice coral close to the shore and half a dozen decent resorts. **Agoho Beach**, 7km west of Mambajao, is wider and sandier, with many resorts – an ideal place to base yourself for all sorts of activities, including scuba diving and volcano climbing.

Katibawasan Falls

P30 • Tricycle or minivan to the falls from Mambajao P300–400

Easily accessible by road – or you can trek along a marked trail from Balbagon (2hr) – the impressive **Katibawasan Falls** is a narrow, 70m-high cascade with a crystal-clear plunge pool at the bottom, perfect for a chilly swim. A number of souvenir stalls also congregate at the base of the falls.

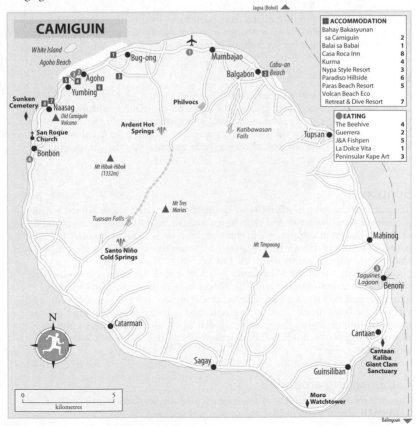

CAMIGUIN

Jagna (Bohol)

White Island
Agoho Beach
Bug-ong
Mambajao
Cabu-an Beach
Balgabon
Agoho
Yumbing
Sunken Cemetery
Naasag
Old Camiguin Volcano
Philvocs
San Roque Church
Ardent Hot Springs
Katibawasan Falls
Tupsan
Bonbon
Mt Hibok-Hibok (1332m)
Mt Tres Marias
Tuasan Falls
Santo Niño Cold Springs
Mt Timpoong
Mahinog
Taguines Lagoon
Benoni
N
Catarman
Cantaan
Cantaan Kaliba Giant Clam Sanctuary
Sagay
Guinsiliban
Moro Watchtower
Balingoan

0   5
kilometres

■ **ACCOMMODATION**
Bahay Bakasyunan sa Camiguin	2
Balai sa Babai	1
Casa Roca Inn	8
Kurma	4
Nypa Style Resort	3
Paradiso Hillside	6
Paras Beach Resort	5
Volcan Beach Eco Retreat & Dive Resort	7

● **EATING**
The Beehive	4
Guerrera	2
J&A Fishpen	5
La Dolce Vita	1
Peninsular Kape Art	3

9

Ardent Hot Springs
Daily 6am–10pm • P30

Some 3km inland from the barangay of Tagdo, **Ardent Hot Springs** can be reached in about an hour on foot from either Mambajao or Agoho Beach. The water in these pools, which lie in a developed park in a jungle valley, is warmed by the volcanic interior of Mount Hibok-Hibok and can reach 40°C. The best time to visit is from late afternoon or after dark, when you can sit in a pool with a cold drink and gaze at the stars. There's a little restaurant, a coffee shop and accommodation in a number of simple cottages.

Mount Hibok-Hibok
Permit to climb the volcano P200 • Most resorts can recommend a local guide (day-trip P2000–2400); a highly recommended expert is Barry Gorres (☎ 0975 211 9546)

In the northwest of the island, Camiguin's only active volcano, **Mount Hibok-Hibok**, had its last major eruption in 1951, with tremors and landslides that killed five hundred people. At a relatively modest 1332m, it can be climbed in four to five hours, but the strenuous trail crosses some steep slopes and treacherous rocks, and the hike shouldn't be attempted alone. Along the way, you'll see steam vents and hot pools, and at the top there's a crater lake. Views from the summit are unforgettable.

Philvocs
Mon–Fri 8am–5pm

At **Philvocs**, an easy 3km trip inland from Mambajao by tricycle, volcanologists who monitor Mount Hibok-Hibok are happy to talk to visitors about their work, and have a number of spectacular photographs of past eruptions.

White Island
P20 • Return pump-boat trips from the pier next to Paras Beach Resort in Yumbing cost P450

About halfway between Mambajao and Bonbon, off the island's northwest coast, lies one of Camiguin's most popular attractions, **White Island**, a dazzling serpentine ribbon of sand only visible at low tide and easily reached by bangka from Yumbing. The views and the water are gorgeous, but there's no shade, so make sure that you take lots of sunblock.

Bonbon

The small fishing town of **BONBON** on Camiguin's west coast has an attractive little plaza and a pretty, whitewashed church; it also lies a few kilometres south of the slopes of the **Old Camiguin Volcano**, which you can climb easily in an hour (entry P5). The path to the summit, from where the views are stunning, is marked by life-size alabaster statues representing the **Stations of the Cross**.

A little southwest of the old volcano you'll see a striking, enormous **white cross** floating on a pontoon in the bay. This marks the site of the **Sunken Cemetery**, which slipped into the sea during a volcanic eruption in 1871 – you can observe reef fish massing around the decaying tombs on a diving or snorkelling trip. The same eruption destroyed the seventeenth-century Spanish **San Roque Church** on the northern fringes of modern Bonbon; its brooding ruins still stand, with a memorial altar inside.

Catarman and around

There are some quiet stretches of sandy beach near the ramshackle little town of **CATARMAN**, 24km south of Mambajao, plus springs and falls, but there's no accommodation in the area. On the southern coast, hidden behind Guinsiliban Elementary School, fifteen minutes east by jeepney from Catarman, is a three-hundred-year-old **Moro Watchtower**.

Santo Niño Cold Springs and Tuasan Falls

Santo Niño Cold Springs daily 8am–8pm, Tuasan Falls daily 9am–5pm • P30 each • A habal-habal round trip to both costs P500–600

Santo Niño Cold Springs lies some 6km north of Catarman, while further north on an island tour will bring you to **Tuasan Falls**. Both have deep pools that are good for swimming, but much to the chagrin of locals, the area surrounding the once-pristine cascades has been blighted by the building of a controversial cross-island highway.

Cantaan Kaliba Giant Clam Sanctuary

Just south of Benoni, at the end of the road past Cabu-an • P25, including mini-tour of the rehabilitation tanks; clams snorkelling fee P125; snorkel hire P200; picnic fee P100

The family-run **Cantaan Kaliba Giant Clam Sanctuary** is home to about three thousand clams. Entry includes a short tour of the rehabilitation tanks, and grants you access to one of the island's most beautiful stretches of white-sand beach, as well as a coral reef that's good for snorkelling. Though the entry fee is reasonable, the extra charges for snorkelling are overpriced.

ARRIVAL AND DEPARTURE   CAMIGUIN ISLAND

By plane The airport, on the coast 1km west of Mambajao, sees daily Cebu Pacific flights to and from Cebu (50min), with a twice a day service on Mon, Fri & Sun. The airport charges a terminal fee of P50.

By boat Ferries leave Balingoan on Mindanao for Benoni

on Camiguin's southeast coast roughly hourly from 5am to 6pm (1hr). Super Shuttle Ferries leave from Benoni for Jagna on Bohol three times a week at 8am (Mon, Wed & Fri, 3–4hr; ☎ 088 387 4034), returning at 1pm.

GETTING AROUND AND INFORMATION

Island transport Transport rates to everywhere on the island are fixed by the tourist office and displayed on a board at the Benoni pier.

Tourist information The tourist office (Mon–Fri 8am–5pm; ☎ 088 387 1097) is in the Provincial Capitol building a short tricycle ride from the centre of

Mambajao. As well as accommodation suggestions, they can advise on activities, including climbing Hibok-Hibok.

Services In Mambajao there are branches of PNB and Landbank and a couple of internet cafés.

ACCOMMODATION

Most of the seaside accommodation in Camiguin is west of Mambajao on the beaches between the small towns of **Bug-ong** and **Naasag**. The standout backpacker resort in this area for a decade was *Camiguin Action Geckos Dive & Adventure Resort*, until it closed in summer 2017. Resorts near the town of **Agoho**, a little west of Bug-ong, remain popular due to their easy access to White Island. East of Mambajao, around the village of **Balgabon**, you'll find more resorts, although the beach here isn't as good as at Agoho, Yumbing or Naasag.

Bahay Bakasyunan sa Camiguin Mambajao ☎ 088 387 0278, ☢ bahaybakasyunan.com. Great for those wanting to be close to town, this villa resort tumbles down from the highway through a landscaped garden, past a spectacular bar to the waterfront. Rooms are either bamboo cottages or newer A-frame huts (P5150), all with private terraces and done out in traditional Filipino design. Ideal for honeymooners. ☏ P3600

Balai sa Babai Agoho ☎ 0918 962 2808, ☢ balaisabaibai.com. The most romantic place on the

island, with plunge pools, private gardens and outdoor Bali-style outdoor bathrooms. Literally meaning "house by the beach", this chichi pad is run on solar power and is straight from the cover of an interior design magazine. The private villa is a stunner (P6900) – as good as Filipino accommodation gets – while the a/c rooms are a lesson in textbook glamour. ☏ P4800

Casa Roca Inn Naasag ☎ 088 387 9500, ☢ casa rocacamiguin.com. Perched on a hillock on the far northwestern tip of the island, this heavenly three-room

9

tranquil resort is a lovely place to wind-down for a few days. There are two standard rooms (P1000, including breakfast), and one veranda room with sweeping sunset views. Good restaurant offering steaks, salmon and crab dishes, too (P300). 🛜 **P1000**

Kurma Yumbing ☎ 0916 469 8912, 🌐 kurmafreedive .com. Formerly known as *Secret Cove Beach Resort*, this place is run by the friendly Diggi and Valerie. There are seven boldly painted fan or a/c rooms (P2300), including two family rooms right on the oceanfront. The resort is the HQ for the couple's highly recommended free-diving and yoga camps (P7000–21,000) as well as the on-site, veg-friendly restaurant that specializes in fusion cuisine using local, organic produce. 🛜 **P1900**

★**Nypa Style Resort** 500m inland from Bug-ong ☎ 0947 181 0196, 🌐 nypastyleresort.jimdo.com. Owned by the hospitable Elena, this gorgeous hilltop resort, centred around a beautiful Indian-almond tree, features six bungalows and a natural swimming pool. The emphasis here is on wellness and massage; the food is superb home-made Italian. Add breakfast for P100. 🛜 **P1600**

Paradiso Hillside Agoho ☎ 088 387 9037, 🌐 hillside. agoho.ph. A little piece of Italy in an unlikely setting. Beyond the sigh-triggering views of White Island from the deck, the advantages of staying at this three-room pad in the hills are twofold: the cooler temperatures and the fabulous welcome from Kalen, the Neapolitan owner who makes the best brick-oven pizzas on the island (P220–380). Accommodation is either in the sole native fan-cooled cottage or the two slightly smarter a/c rooms (P1200). 🛜 **P800**

Paras Beach Resort Yumbing ☎ 088 387 9008, 🌐 parasbeachresort.com. In an enviable position on the shore, this was a private beach house belonging to the Paras family until they decided to add a whole range of a/c rooms with hot showers and cable TV, and open it to the public. Right in the thick of things. Wi-fi in communal areas. 🛜 **P3500**

★**Volcan Beach Eco Retreat & Dive Resort** Naasag ☎ 088 387 9551, 🌐 camiguinvolcanbeach.com. The highlights at this German-run resort are the charming bungalows, the tropical garden strung with hammocks and the excellent dive centre. As if that's not enough, it's got its own reef on the doorstep, a bamboo deck for yoga and a wood-fired oven for home-made breads. It's the perfect place to watch the spectacular sunsets, too. The beach villas (P3500) are among the loveliest on the island. 🛜 **P2000**

EATING

Eating on Camiguin is mostly limited to the **resorts**, but a few new standout **restaurants** have opened in recent years. Like everywhere else in the Philippines, there's an inexplicable number of Italian pizzerias and restaurants, while in Mambajao, there's a cluster of cheap places to eat around the market area.

The BeeHive On the Catibac beach road ☎ 0939 932 0334. With conch shells swinging from the ceiling, driftwood tables, and an idyllic oceanfront setting, this Belgian-run outpost feels more like a castaway's shack than a café. Visitors are spoiled with fresh-brew coffee (P85), honeycomb-shaped pizzas and souvenir pots of organic honey (P330). Worth the journey just to see it. Daily 8am–7pm.

★**Guerrera** Agoho Beach road ☎ 0917 311 9859, 🌐 guerrera.ph. Not even the street-food craze could pass Camiguin by. The location of this first-rate restaurant, set beside a beautiful rice paddy and organic garden, instantly transports you to rural Vietnam or Laos. Dishes such as pad thai (P250), Vietnamese noodle salads (P275) and *bánh xèo* (savoury crispy pancakes; P250) are all knockouts. Also has a couple of rooms. Daily noon–2.30pm & 5–9pm.

J&A Fishpen Taguines Lagoon, Benoni ☎ 088 387 4008. Though it's a trek to get to, this over-the-water seafood shack is an enjoyable place to kill time, particularly if you're getting a ferry to or from Benoni, or fancy trying the nearby zipline over the lagoon (P250). The menu is as straightforward as they come: choose your fish or crabs from the water pens, and they'll cook it how you like. Mains around P200–400. Mon–Thurs 6am–8pm, Fri–Sun 6am–10pm.

La Dolce Vita Opposite the airport ☎ 0999 758 3019. One of Camiguin's many high-quality Italian restaurants, *La Dolce Vita* may not have the ideal hilltop locations of its island rivals, but everything from its al dente pastas and pizzas (P200–250) to pesto is home-made and delicious. Italian owner Alessandro imports much of the ingredients from his homeland. The restaurant also has a pleasant outdoor deck – good for watching the locals buzz between Mambajao and Yumbing. Daily 7am–10pm.

Peninsular Kape Art Next to Paros Beach Hotel, Yumbing ☎ 0977 238 2673, 🌐 facebook.com/ PeninsularKapeArt. This Spanish-run tapas restaurant and handicraft store is a breath of fresh air, providing something entirely different from the usual Italian places. Paellas, spicy mussels or *gambas ajillo* (P200–350) are on offer in the garden, while local Pinikas artwork, jewellery, and woven bags are for sale inside. Free wi-fi. Tues–Sun 8am–10pm.

Butuan

9

The bustling capital of Agusan del Norte province, **BUTUAN** lies around 200km east of Cagayan de Oro. Butuan is thought to have been the first coastal trading settlement in the Philippines; in 1976 a carefully crafted and ornate oceangoing outrigger (*balangay*) was unearthed on the banks of the Agusan River and carbon-dated, astonishingly, to 320 AD. Of nine boats since discovered in the mud, two more have been excavated, dating from 1215 and 1250 and adding to the growing wealth of evidence that the Philippines was actively trading with Asia long before the Spanish arrived. The original "Butuan boat" is now in the small **Balangay Shrine** (Mon–Sat 8.30am–4.30pm; free) around 5km west of the city, along with the remains of a number of other ancient boats and ethnological treasures such as ceramics and coffins.

Butuan National Museum

City Hall compound, 1km north of the city centre • Closed for renovation at time of writing, but usually Mon–Fri 9am–4pm • ⓦ nationalmuseum.gov.ph

Closed for renovation at the time of research, the **Butuan National Museum** is home to a small but intriguing collection including cooking implements and jewellery from pre-Hispanic Butuan. There are two galleries: the Archeological Hall, which exhibits stone crafts, metal objects, pots, gold and burial coffins; and the Ethnological Hall, which focuses on the culture of the Manobo, Mamanua, Higaonon and lowland Butuanons.

ARRIVAL AND INFORMATION

BUTUAN

By plane The airport is 10km west of the city. Flights to Manila are 1hr 25min, served by Philippine Airlines (1 daily) and Cebu Pacific (4 daily). Cebu Pacific also flies here from Cebu City (4 daily; 50min). Taxis (P200–250) and tricycles (P150–180) are on hand to take you into town.
By bus The terminal is 3.5km north of Butuan off Montilla Blvd.
Destinations Cagayan de Oro (hourly; 4hr); Davao (Bachelor Express: daily 1am–5pm, every 20min; 5–6hr); Surigao (hourly; 2hr).
By boat Ferries dock at the port town of Nasipit, 24km

west of Butuan, from where it's a 30min jeepney ride into the city. 2GO has one weekly service on Sunday to Cebu (1.30am; 9hr), while Cokaliong Shipping Lines has a Sunday weekly service to Jagna on Bohol (12pm; 5hr), before returning at midnight every Mon. The same operator also has a route to Cebu, leaving at 7pm four times a week (Mon, Tues, Wed & Fri).
Tourist information The provincial Department of Tourism office is at the Grateful Realty Corp Building, on Pili Drive (Mon–Fri 8am–5pm; ☎ 085 341 8413).

ACCOMMODATION AND EATING

Almont Inland Resort San José St, Rizal Park ☎ 085 3420 5263, ⓦ almont.com.ph. This 56-room resort with pool and man-made lake has a range of spacious rooms and suites (P3000–6000), all with a/c, private bathroom and cable TV. To stay closer to the city bustle, check out its dependable sister, the *Almont City Hotel* next to the Agusan River. 📶 P3000
Café Caliente South Montilla Blvd ☎ 085 342 7496. Near the *Y Hotel* (see p.416) outside the city centre, this fuss-free restaurant serves up Filipino and European classics to a dedicated local crowd who come not just for the sandwiches, burgers, salmon steaks and pork tenderloin, but for the lively karaoke. Mains from P150. Mon–Sat 10am–11pm.
Go Hotels San José St, Rizal Park ☎ 085 341 1568, ⓦ gohotels.com.ph. Value chain hotel with a hundred a/c box-size rooms with hot and cold shower, in-room safe,

and cable TV. Charges for luggage storage. 📶 P990
Ocean Bloom Boutique Beach Resort 5km from Butuan in Manapa ☎ 0918 449 0932, ⓦ facebook.com/OceanBloomPH. This family-run beach hotel is a relaxing place to chill out for a few days. There are a variety of rooms, including deluxe a/c and family rooms (P3000–3500), while the courtyard offers simpler four- and six-bed dorms. The resort accepts no walk-ins, so book in advance. 📶 P1500
★ **Watergate Hotel** Jose Rosales Ave ☎ 085 817 1008, ⓦ watergatehotelbutuan.com. Boutique hotel aimed at the flashpacker and business market, with a design supposedly inspired by the nearby Agusan River. All rooms come with bouncy mattresses, fancy toiletries and power showers, while the excellent service and free pick-ups from the airport underline its status as the best accommodation in the city. 📶 P1790

9

Y Hotel South Montilla Blvd ☎0975 611 5447. Recently given a fresh lick of paint and promising the most modern atmosphere in the city, *Y Hotel*'s a/c rooms are clean and equipped with comfy beds and fridges. The staff couldn't be more personable. There's a coffee shop next door. 🛜 P1175

The Enchanted River

At the end of a 12km dirt road, just beyond the fishing village of Talisay • P30; lifejackets can be rented for P15 • The turning to the river and Talisay is signposted 2km north of Hinatuan on the main coast road, 150km south of Butuan; the main road is served by frequent buses between Butuan and Mangagoy – without your own transport it's a very long walk or habal-habal ride from Hinatuan

Swimming in the **Enchanted River** is one of the highlights of a trip to Mindanao. The accessible part of the river is more like a narrow saltwater lagoon that ends at an underwater cave and ravine crammed with all sorts of tropical fish that get fed every day at noon. The colours are mesmerizing; the water glows like liquid sapphire, surrounded by dense jungle and karst outcrops.

The site is managed as a small park, but it's well off the beaten path, and few foreign tourists make it this far. Crowds of locals descend at weekends, so it's highly recommended to go during the week.

Tinuy-An Falls

15km west of Bislig • P50; bamboo raft P150 • Most people hire a minivan and driver in Butuan (from P3000), but you can take a Bachelor Express bus to Bislig or Mangagoy (5hr) and then a habal-habal to the falls (40min; P400 return)

Around 160km south of Butuan, near the port town of **Bislig**, a dirt road leads some 15km to the astounding **Tinuy-An Falls**, a thunderous, multi-tiered 95m cascade that's like Niagara Falls reimagined in the heart of jungle. Get here early and it's a magical place, with lush foilage, durian trees and giant ferns drooping over the river – you can lounge on the bank and enjoy the views or clamber up to the higher levels and paddle or swim in the pools, where a bamboo raft takes you closer in to get thoroughly soaked. Come in the morning to see the falls' most spectacular rainbows.

Surigao City

The bustling, ramshackle capital of the province of Surigao del Norte, **SURIGAO CITY**, some 120km north of Butuan, is essentially just a place to pass through on the way to the picture-postcard island of Siargao. It's a compact place and easy to get around on foot, but there's just not that much to do here: if you find yourself with time on your hands it's worth a trip up to the pretty pebble beach at **Mabua**, 12km north.

ARRIVAL AND DEPARTURE   SURIGAO CITY

By plane The airport, 5km outside the city on the road to Butuan, sees daily flights to and from Cebu with Cebu Pacific (2 daily; 45min). Tricycles charge P50 into the centre of town.

By bus, jeepney and multicab Buses arrive at the terminal 4km west of the city centre. Jeepneys and multicabs head into town for P10/person (or P30 for a tricycle). To head to Cagayan de Oro or Balingoan (for Camiguin) you'll need to change in Butuan.

Destinations Butuan (hourly; 2hr); Davao (hourly; 8hr).

By boat The Eva M. Macapagal Passenger Terminal is on the harbour; you can walk or take a tricycle from here to the city centre. The terminal fee is P20 for all departures. Coming from the Visayas, Cokaliong Shipping Lines serves Cebu (6 weekly; 9hr 30min, sometimes via Maasin). Heading to Siargao, there are a variety of options, from fast, cramped outriggers (2–3hr) to slower, more spacious and safer RORO boats (3–4hr). Montenegro Lines runs a daily service (12pm; 3hr 30min), as does MV Lines' ferry *Fortune Angel* (3hr). Of the bangkas, MV Lines' daily *LOP* service is the biggest and safest (6am). All of these boats leave Surigao for Dapa on Siargao before noon, so it's best to arrive in town early, or accept that you'll have to spend a night in the city.

INFORMATION

Tourist information Near Luneta Park, City Hall is home to the Department of Tourism (☎ 086 826 8064) and offers information about accommodation and ferries.

ACCOMMODATION

Almont Beach Resort Lipata ☎ 086 826 7544, ⓦ almont.com.ph. For a bit of luxury, 15min drive from the port, the *Almont* offers good rooms with sensational views of the bay. There's also a decent pool and on-site *Café Maharlika* (daily 6am–10pm). Weak wi-fi. 📶 P2500

Hotel Tavern Borromeo St ☎ 086 231 7300, ⓦ hoteltavern.com. Not far from the ferry terminal, this place has smart modern rooms in the newer west wing (P2200) and comfy cheaper rooms in the older east building. Sea views and balconies are available for a little more. Good breakfast buffet and free pick-up both included. 📶 P1900

Le Chard Place 4km south on National Hwy ☎ 0947 890 8891, ⓦ facebook.com/LechardPlace. With a fair amount of designer swagger to it – rooms are painted bold orange, green and purple, and the walls are covered in pop art – this conveniently located B&B manages to squeeze in plenty of goodies. They offer free breakfast and free airport transfers, as well as 24hr security, parking and there's a back-up generator for those all-too-common blackouts. Wi-fi at reception. 📶 P920

One Hive Hotel & Suites Rizal St ☎ 086 232 0065, ⓦ onehivehotel.com. Across the road from the Surigao Provincial Sports Complex, this affordable business hotel has a variety of clean, a/c, bee-themed rooms, such as "queen bee", "bumble bee", "hive room" and so on. Breakfast is included, while downstairs the *Hive Café* serves quick bites and fusion cuisine. 📶 P1200

EATING AND DRINKING

Calda Pizza Blvd Taft ☎ 0932 590 5456, ⓦ caldapizza .com.ph. One of the best pizzerias in Mindanao, serving 28 different varieties of thin-crust New York-style goodness. For meat-lovers, the Etna (chorizo and ham; P195) comes highly recommended, while vegetarians should tuck into a Torinese (pesto, tomatoes and onions; P215). Those feeling brave can try to stomach one of the nationwide chain's monster 40-inch pizzas (from P1290). Daily 9am–midnight.

EJ's Café Borromeo St ☎ 086 826 1881, ⓦ facebook .com/EJsCafeSurigao. In addition to great coffee, milkshakes, frappes, cold-brew teas and beers (P80), *EJ's Café* pulls in the crowds for its imaginative, if scattershot, menu, including the likes of burgers, poutine, empanadas, fettucine and roast-beef sandwiches. If you're waiting for the next ferry, pull up a chair for some people-watching and try the Willy Wonka-esque chocolate bomb frappe (P120). The café is near the *Hotel Tavern* compound. Daily 10am–11.30pm.

Ocean Bounties Seafood Market and Restaurant Boulevard Taft ☎ 086 826 1625. This nautical-themed restaurant – a shrine for seafood lovers – serves up crab, shrimp, abalone and Pacific lobster by the boatload. Previously located on Diez St, it has relocated to the waterfront and since doubled in size. Like similar restaurants around the country, the seafood is served by weight (P80–200/100g); point at what you want, and the chefs will cook it to your liking. Mon–Sat 8am–9pm, Sun 10am–9pm.

Siargao Island

Off the northeastern tip of Mindanao lies the teardrop-shaped island of **SIARGAO**, a largely undeveloped backwater with languid beaches, dramatic coves and lagoons battered by the Pacific Ocean. Some of the first tourists here were **surfers**, who discovered a Pacific reef break at Tuason Point – so good, they called it **Cloud 9**. Though old-timers now dub it "Crowd 9" because of its popularity, there is a friendly, welcoming surfing scene here, and Siargao gives Malapascua and Panglao a run for their money as the backpacker capital of the southern Philippines. The annual **Surfing Cup**, held in late September or early October, has risen in profile over the past few years and attracts international competitors from Australia, the US and Europe, as well as from around the Philippines.

General Luna (GL)

Most visitors arrive at **Sayak Airport**, near Del Carmen, 30km from the surf resorts and honeymoon hideaways around the island's friendly little capital of **GENERAL LUNA**, known as **GL**, on the east coast. Resorts line the coast north from here, and though

9

there are only small patches of decent beach, it's a lush, laidback strip, with swathes of coconut palms, beach bars and surf shops. While surfing has grabbed the headlines in recent years, **kitesurfing** is beginning to make its mark too (see p.420).

Cloud 9 (Tuason Point)

A 30min walk from GL, or quick ride on a habal-habal (P20)

Sleep, eat, surf: that's the mantra 2km further north from GL at **Cloud 9**, the world-renowned break at **Tuason Point**. On most days, from sunrise to sundown, you'll find surfers in action and beach bums watching from the multi-storey **wooden viewing pavilion** in front of the break. The peak **surf season** is September and October, before things slow down at the end of the year; beginners will find the weaker surf in June and July more manageable.

Magpupungko Beach

Entry P50; parking P20; Fri night beach parties P20 • Motorbike from GL takes around 1hr via a bumpy road, or hire a bangka from Cloud 9 (from P900)

Travelling 35km north of GL, mostly via dirt road, brings you to **PILAR**, a village of traditional wooden stilt houses on the edge of the mangroves. It's best known for **Magpupungko Beach**, 2km further north, the site of sporadic Friday night beach parties. The sandy beach is one of the island's best, but the highlight is the giant natural swimming pool that forms to the far left of the beach at low tide. The water is beautifully clear and inviting – assuming the weather cooperates.

Sohoton Cove and Lagoon

Bucas Grande • Cave and lagoon entry P450 • Bangkas from Siargao charge around P2000–3250 per person for an all-day trip for a group of two to four

The enticing island of **Bucas Grande** lies between Siargao and Mindanao proper, with mushroom-shaped limestone rocks sprouting from its shimmering waters. The inland **Sohoton Cove and Lagoon** on the east side of the island is the must-do excursion from Siargao – but it takes two hours each way, so you'll need most of a day to do it justice. The best time to visit is between March and July, when the weather and the sea crossing are at their calmest.

Once at the cove, you'll have to sign in and get a short briefing about the site; you then transfer into another boat that will take you through the cave entrance into the enchanting lagoon, a cavernous space hemmed in by soaring vine-smothered cliffs and home to giant non-stinging jellyfish. It's a phenomenal sight and worth the journey

---

SIARGAO ISLAND-HOPPING

The seas around Siargao are littered with unspoilt and rarely visited **islands**. The easiest to reach are the three islands just off the coast of GL (around 30min by bangka): half-day trips to all three cost from P1200–1600 per person depending on the size of the boat and number of people. Most resorts can fix you up with local bangka operators.

Naked Island is little more than a giant sandbar, and perfect for lounging in the sun. **Dako Island** is the largest of the three, smothered in coconut palms and home to a small fishing community. The villagers will happily serve you fresh coconut (P20) or barbecue chicken (P180), and you can even rent out the basic beach cottages for the day (P200) or overnight (P700–800). Tiny **Guyam Island** comes closest to the stereotype of a classic desert island: a circular clump of sand dotted with palm trees ideal for picnics, swimming or sunbathing. The island caretaker usually charges a fee of P20 per person. **Snorkelling** isn't much good from any of these islands – the best reefs lie in between them, so ask your boat to make an extra stop.

and expense, assuming the weather is good. There are several other caves here that your *banquero* should be able to guide you to with no extra charge: if you are brave and can hold your breath for long enough (unless it's low tide when there is a small gap), you can swim through a short tunnel into **Hagukan Cave** where there are strange fish, stalactites, rock oysters and wild orchids.

ARRIVAL AND DEPARTURE   SIARGAO ISLAND

By plane Cebu Pacific runs flights to Cebu City, and Skyjet Airlines operates flights to Manila. The tiny airport is in the barangay of Sayak on the west coast; minivans will run to GL and Cloud 9 for P300–400/person or P1500–1800/ vehicle – check with your accommodation in advance about free pick-ups. Habal-habals charge P400. The airport charges a P150 terminal fee.
Destinations Cebu (1–2 daily; 1hr); Manila (4 weekly; 1hr 40min).
By bus Siargao is connected to Butuan, on the Mindanao mainland (see p.415), by regular buses (2hr), from where

there are onward connections to Cagayan de Oro and Davao.
By boat A number of companies, including Bretphil, Montenegro Shipping Lines, and MV Lines, operate ferries from Surigao to Dapa, 16km from GL on the south coast. There's a choice of slow ferries (3hr 30min–4hr) or faster outriggers (2hr 30min). All boats from Surigao leave in the morning (5.45am, 11am, 11.45am & noon); boats from Dapa to Surigao leave between 5am and 11am; note that the fastest and most reliable services leave before 6am. You must pay a P20 terminal fee to board the boats.

INFORMATION AND ACTIVITIES

Services There's a post office in Dapa. The ATM doesn't accept all foreign cards, though most places accept credit cards.

Surfing Leading the pack of highly recommended surf schools is *Buddha's Surf Resort* (see p.420), while *Turtle Surf*

9

Camp (🌐 surfcampsiargao.com) and *Kermit Surf Resort* (see below) offer a full range of rentals and classes.

Kitesurfing There are plenty of kitesurfing camps, offering lessons, rental and full beginner courses. Two to try are Sea Breeze Kite Club (🌐 seabreezekiteclub.com) and *Viento Del Mar* (🌐 vientodelmar.com), both located on the beachfront just north of GL.

GETTING AROUND

By habal-habal Choices for getting around the island are fairly limited. Most locals use the habal-habals, good for up to two people and light luggage; the vehicles are customized with retro-fitted carry racks for long- and shortboards. Rates are fixed: Dapa to Cloud 9 is P200, while Dapa to GL is P150. Rides between GL and Cloud 9 should cost P20.

Motorbike rental If you intend to do a lot of roaming around, having your own wheels is definitely recommended. Ask your accommodation about renting a motorcycle (P450–500/day). There is no hospital on the island, so take care if driving: accidents are common, especially at night after the bars close.

Tricycles and minivans Tricycles will charge at least P50/person (P200/vehicle) between Dapa and GL, but sometimes ask for a lot more.

ACCOMMODATION

Siargao accommodation ranges from low-budget surf lodges to upmarket tropical resorts. Most places are a short distance from GL or Cloud 9, and the best can help arrange motorbike rentals, bangka trips and all kinds of tours.

Bravo Beach Resort North of GL ☎ 0905 395 5493, 🌐 bravosiargao.com. If any sign were needed that Siargao is going upmarket, this lovely beach resort is it. Rooms have comfy queen beds, safes, wardrobes and convertible sofas for extra guests. On site is an oceanfront Spanish-fusion restaurant – one of the island's prettiest places to while away a hot afternoon. Despite the frills, it also has a cheapie eight-bed dorm. 📶 Dorms P950, doubles P3200

★ **Buddha's Surf Resort** At the northern edge of GL ☎ 0977 802 2144 🌐 siargaosurf.com. On some nights, this fabulously funky surfers' retreat may resemble an overflowing beer garden, due to its deservedly popular acoustic gigs and burger nights. Run by long-term English expat Ashley Charles, *Buddha's* is the beating heart of GL's surf scene, with thatched-roof a/c privates and suites kitted out with flatscreen TVs, in-room water coolers and inviting balconies. For all manner of lessons and rentals, you really don't need to look further. 📶 P2500

Emerald House 400m before Cloud 9 ☎ 0949 161 9165, 🌐 emeraldhousevillage.com. With open-air villas, this Swiss-run resort is in a quiet tropical garden, just a short walk to the beach and Cloud 9 action. Rooms are stylishly furnished with high ceilings and private bathrooms, plus there is a restaurant and bar on site. A good option for hard-core surfers, as long-term discounts are available. 📶 P1700

Harana Surf Resort Midway between GL and Cloud 9 ☎ 0998 849 5461, 🌐 haranasurf.com. One of the newest surf camps, with a confident open-plan design, beachfront deck and bespoke surf art. The rooms come in a variety of doubles or sprawling family rooms (5800), while the twelve-bed dorm – or community hut – is the nicest on the island. To top it all off, there are appealing hammocks, relaxing beanbags and a great cocktail bar. Wi-fi in the restaurant. 📶 Dorms P700, doubles P2800

Kalinaw Resort Midway between GL and Cloud 9 ☎ 0930 251 5677, 🌐 kalinawresort.com. The most luxurious (and expensive) option on the island, facing the loveliest stretch of beach in the area. The five immaculate wooden villas have gorgeous minimalist interiors, balconies and satellite TV, while the pool villa (P16,400) has its own private infinity tub. There's also a top-notch French restaurant with dishes such as truffle risotto (P490) and croque-monsieurs (P390). 📶 P9900

Kermit Surf Resort 300m off the main GL beach road ☎ 0917 655 0548, 🌐 kermitsiargao.com. In a head-to-head competition with *Buddha's* for the best flashpackers in town, this well-run place has a/c and fan cottages (P2750), as well as dorms with shared bathroom. The real draw is its hangout area, though, with hammocks, ping-pong table, library and sociable bar. 📶 Dorms P950, doubles P1800

Lux Siargao 400m north of Cloud 9 ☎ 0917 620 5643, 🌐 luxsiargao.com. Owned by a couple from LA, this VIP five-room mansion is set on an isolated strip of beach, with a private garden, pool and boat dock, and rooms that wouldn't look out of place in a Malibu beach villa. The whole place is usually booked by wealthy families and used for intimate weddings, but the doubles are definitely splurge-worthy if you can haggle a discount. 📶 P4200

Paglaom Hostel 200m from Kermit Surf Resort Cloud 9 ☎ 0999 990 0000, 🌐 paglaomhostel.com. The last genuine budget deal in town, this sociable hostel is justifiably popular with surfers for its free-to-use kitchen, lockers, and hangout area. The bunk beds have mosquito nets, and all toilet and showers are shared. Minimum three-night stay in high season. 📶 P300

Sagana Resort Cloud 9 ☎ 0947 946 4753, 🌐 cloud9surf.com. Overlooking Cloud 9, Aussie-owned

9

Sagana has six lovely Laotian-inspired cottages – two a/c and four with fan – in a landscaped garden with coconut trees and large, leafy plants. Rates are inclusive of three meals, and the restaurant is one of the island's best, with seafood such as tuna, marlin, and Spanish mackerel, as well as mud crabs and prawns from local fish farms. Rates are for full board per person. ᕙ **P3600**

EATING AND DRINKING

Most of the best places to eat and drink are in the **resorts**, but a number of independent places have opened over the past few years. Everywhere is lively during peak season, particularly during the Surfing Cup, when various places on Cloud 9 put on live music.

The Avocado Tree Off the main Dapa–GL road in town ☎ 0999 339 5060, ⊚ bit.ly/AvocadoTreeGL. This pastel-coloured place is a cross between a boutique emporium, café and juice bar. It sells a variety of locally made products including bracelets, notebooks, sunscreens (P170) and coconut oil (P300), but also has a tasty menu to answer your cravings. There are spring rolls, rice dishes, grilled sandwiches, and the welcome is as warm as the fresh banana bread (P50). Mon–Sat 7am–9pm.

Café Loka Cloud 9 ☎ 0928 960 7745. Overlooking the wooden viewing pavilion and main Cloud 9 surf break, this low-key café draws in an early morning crowd for its top-notch coffees (P80–150), shakes and juices such as calamansi and ginger or apple and guava (P80). Also popular for lunchtime snacks and post-surf mojitos. Daily 6am–6pm.

★ **Kawayan Siarago Resort** Just south of Cloud 9 ☎ 0999 409 6252, ⊚ kawayansiargaoresort.com. Accessed along a leafy garden path, this dimly lit, all-wood bar-restaurant has a Thai lounge feel. There are pool tables, cheap happy-hour beers (P35) and a cracking French-Moroccan-Filipino menu. Choose from the likes of tropical ceviche (P290) and a delicious tagine (P650), accompanied by imported French wines. Also has two lovely cottages for rent out the back. Daily 7am–10pm.

Mama's Grill On the beach road north of GL. This no-nonsense street-side BBQ shack is a hit with surfers and locals alike. Regulars come here nightly for the chicken and seafood kebabs, perfectly cooked on the charcoal-stoked grill, and washed down with a cold San Miguel or two. Daily 6–10pm.

Octopus Beach Bar On the beach road north of GL. This nightclub is very popular with surfers and backpackers, who return night after night. It's dirty, it's a dive bar, and it plays loud, banging music. It's no-frills, and little more than a beach shack, but punters go all out to have a good time. Tues & Wed 9pm–4am.

Rum Bar On the road to Dapa outside GL, near Siargao Divers Club. Like *Octopus*, this late-night dance bar, featuring live bands and DJ parties, plays anything and everything. Make sure you turn up late. Daily 10am–3am.

Shaka Next to Kawayan Siarago Resort ☎ 0929 422 8956. New organic café specializing in healthy shakes, juices and fresh-fruit power bowls made with granola (P250); you can pocket a few raw, vegan energy balls (P50) for the day of surfing ahead. The mini gallery of surf prints for sale on the wall (P2000) adds to the laidback island atmosphere. Daily 6.45am–5.30pm.

Dinagat Island

There are several morning bangkas from Surigao to San José (4hr), from where bangkas (about P1000 for half a day) can take you virtually anywhere along the coast of Dinagat

Just a short bangka ride from Surigao, wild and undeveloped **Dinagat Island**, around 60km from tip to toe, is an adventure paradise-in-waiting. Its rugged coastline has tantalizing **islets**, beautiful sugary-sand **beaches** and sheer cliffs that are attracting an increasing number of **rock climbers**. The main drawback is the lack of **accommodation**: there are basic beach huts on the southwest coast around the town of Dinagat, but not much else. Only a handful of travellers make it this far.

The best way to get an overview of what Dinagat has to offer is to rent a bangka in San José, where ferries arrive from Surigao. On the west-coast islet of **Unib** you'll find unspoilt Bitaug Beach and several immense, largely unexplored caves. The waters of this area are fringed by good coral and deep sea walls, but there's no equipment for rent so you'll have to bring whatever you need, including snorkelling gear. In the same area, the uninhabited islet of **Hagakhak** is another beauty, with scintillating above- and underwater rock formations.

Davao

Known as the **durian** capital of the Philippines and the de facto capital of Mindanao, **DAVAO**, in Mindanao's southeast, is a relaxed city, with a reputation for delicious seafood. There are a couple of things to see in the city itself – and in the barangay of **Lanang**, 6km north along the coast – but mostly Davao makes a good base for exploring the surrounding area. That said, the city's formidable line-up of **annual festivals** is certainly worth attending, especially **Kadayawan**, a harvest festival held annually during the third week of August, which focuses on flamboyant tribal dance parades and a beauty pageant.

Despite the obvious pride locals have for the city, Davao remains caught in a violent tug-of-war between the authorities and terrorist groups such as militant Islamic group Abu Sayyaf (see box, p.405). On September 2, 2016, a bomb rocked a Davao night market, causing at least fifteen deaths and injuring seventy people. President Duterte described the attack as an act of **terrorism**, declaring "a state of lawlessness". Abu Sayyaf initially claimed responsibility for the blast, before apportioning blame to one of its allies.

At the time of research, the region remained under heightened security alert due to an ongoing military offensive against Abu Sayyaf, and any visit to Davao should be **approached with caution.**

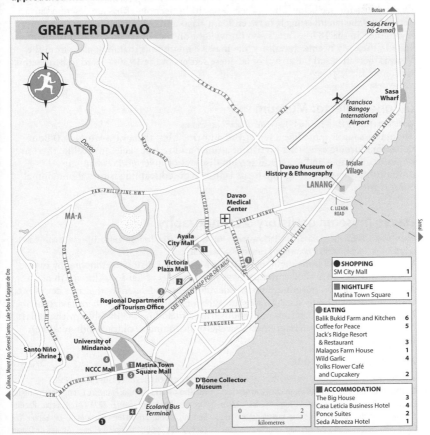

GREATER DAVAO

Butuan

Sasa Ferry
(to Samal)

N

CABANTIAN ROAD

AH26

Francisco
Bangoy
International
Airport

Sasa
Wharf

J. P. LAUREL AVENUE

Davao

MAUDUG ROAD

Davao Museum of
History & Ethnography

Insular
Village

LANANG

PAN-PHILIPPINE HWY

DACUDAO AVENUE

Davao
Medical
Center

C. LIZADA
ROAD

Samal

MA-A

LAUREL AVENUE

CATAGUTAN AVENUE

R. CASTILLO STREET

Ayala
City Mall   1

DON JULIAN RODRIGUEZ SR. AVENUE

Victoria
Plaza Mall   2

SEE DAVAO MAP FOR DETAILS

Regional Department
of Tourism Office   2

SANTA ANA AVE.

UYANGUREN

● SHOPPING	
SM City Mall	1

■ NIGHTLIFE	
Matina Town Square	1

SHRINE HILLS ROAD

University of
Mindanao   4

Santo Niño
Shrine   3

NCCC Mall   3

Matina Town
Square Mall   5

D'Bone Collector
Museum

GEN. MACARTHUR HWY

Ecoland Bus
Terminal   4

0   2
kilometres

● EATING	
Balik Bukid Farm and Kitchen	6
Coffee for Peace	5
Jack's Ridge Resort & Restaurant	3
Malagos Farm House	1
Wild Garlic	4
Yolks Flower Café and Cupcakery	2

■ ACCOMMODATION	
The Big House	3
Casa Leticia Business Hotel	4
Ponce Suites	2
Seda Abreeza Hotel	1

Calinan, Mount Apo, General Santos, Lake Sebu & Cagayan de Oro

9

People's Park

J. Camus St • Mon–Thurs 5.30–10am & 2–11pm, Fri–Sun 5.30–10.30am & 1–11.30pm; fountain show Sat & Sun 7pm (1hr) • Free

A welcome slice of green in the heart of the city, liberally sprinkled with sculptures representing southern Mindanao's indigenous groups, **People's Park** is especially lively at weekends when there's an evening fountain show, and in the early mornings when it's popular with joggers.

San Pedro Cathedral

San Pedro St at C.M. Recto St • Open during Mass only • Free

The bizarre giant concrete bowl that is **San Pedro Cathedral** began life as a simple nipa chapel in 1848. A more solid structure went up in 1886, but the whole thing was rebuilt in the current Modernist style in the 1970s.

Museo Dabawenyo

Pichon St • Mon–Sat 9am–5.45pm • Free • ☎ 082 222 6011

For an overview of Davao's turbulent and complex history and its ethnic make-up, visit the **Museo Dabawenyo**, housed in the restored court building opposite Osmeña Park. It's small but well presented, and though there are fewer objects on display than at the Davao Museum (see below), it is easier to reach. Indigenous tribes are described in detail, as is the fateful struggle between Datu Bago and conquistador Don José Uyanguren in the 1840s. Panels also throw light on the American occupation boom years in the early twentieth century, the massive migrations that took place from the Visayas thereafter and the arrival of Japanese settlers in the 1930s – hard to believe this was once "Little Tokyo".

D'Bone Collector Museum

San Pedro St • Mon–Fri 10am–5pm, Sat 1–5pm • P100 • ⓦ dbonemuseum.com

Though it sounds more like a relic from a horror film, the award-winning **D'Bone Collector Museum** exhibits a myriad of animal and reptile skeletons. While there are bones of all shapes and sizes, and terrific displays of invertebrates hanging ominously from the ceiling, the focus is firmly on **educating** visitors about animal conservation.

Davao Museum of History & Ethnography

Insular Village 1, J.P Laurel Ave, Lanang • Mon–Sat 9am–5pm • P100 • ☎ 082 233 1734 • Lanang is reached via jeepney (marked "Sasa") or by taxi; sign in at the gate and then turn right, from where it's a 5min walk

You'll find the small but enlightening **Davao Museum of History & Ethnography** tucked away at the back of a gated community in the barangay of Lanang, 4km north of Magsaysay Park. On the ground floor, a detailed timeline describes the city's key events, with temporary exhibits such as rare sculptures on display. Upstairs there's a decent introduction to Davao's fifteen indigenous tribes, including the Bagobos, with displays of ancient weaponry, betel nut boxes, jewellery (including a wildcat tooth necklace) and fancy brass work.

ARRIVAL AND DEPARTURE   **DAVAO**

BY PLANE

Davao International Airport The modern and spacious Francisco Bangoy International Airport lies 12km northwest of the city centre. Ignore taxi touts quoting P300–500 for a ride into the city and head for the rank where metered fares cost P150–200.

Airline offices Air Asia, Francisco Bangoy International Airport, Buhangin (☎ 02 722 2742); Cebu Pacific, Summit World, 2/F Victoria Plaza Mall, J.P. Laurel Ave (☎ 082 224 0960); Philippine Airlines, Ateneo de Davao

9

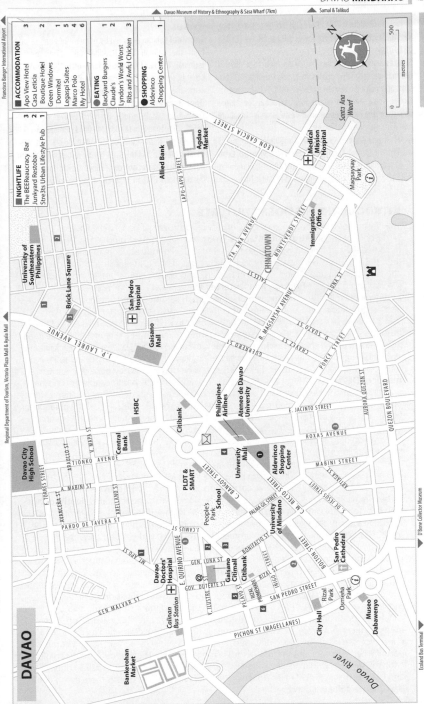

DAVAO

ACCOMMODATION
Apo View Hotel 3
Casa Leticia 2
Boutique Hotel 2
Green Windows 1
Dormitel 5
Legaspi Suites 4
Marco Polo 6
My Hotel

● **EATING**
Backyard Burgers 1
Claude's 2
Lyndon's World Worst
Ribs and Awful Chicken 3

● **SHOPPING**
Aldevinco
Shopping Center 1

■ **NIGHTLIFE**
The BEERreaucracy Bar 3
Junkyard Restoba' 2
Stre3ts Urban Lifestyle Pub 1

Francisco Bangoy International Airport

Davao Museum of History & Ethnography & Sasa Wharf (7km)

Samal & Talikud

Regional Department of Tourism, Victoria Plaza Mall & Ayala Mall

D'Bone Collector Museum

Ecoland Bus Terminal

9

University Building, C.M. Recto St (☎082 221 5513); Silk Air, Suite 056, 5/F Pryce Tower, J.P. Laurel Ave (☎082 221 1039).

Routes Davao airport has handy air links to a host of destinations in the Philippines, including Manila and Cebu, most of which are operated by Cebu Pacific. For all domestic flights, you'll have to pay a P200 terminal fee before departure. The only international destination is Singapore (3hr 35min), served by Silk Air.

Destinations Angeles (3 weekly; 1hr 50min); Bacolod (3 weekly; 1hr 10min); Cagayan de Oro (1–2 daily; 1hr); Cebu (5–7 daily; 1hr); Iloilo (1–2 daily; 1hr 10min); Manila (at least 18 daily; 1hr 50min); Zamboanga (1 daily; 1hr).

BY BUS

Terminal Calinan is served by frequent bus and jeepneys from the Calinan Bus Terminal (aka Annil transport terminal) on San Pedro, just north of E. Quirino Ave. All other buses depart the Ecoland terminal on Quimpo Blvd, across the Davao River from the city centre.

Operators and routes Bus operators, all based at the Ecoland terminal, include Bachelor Express (☎082 244 0654), Mindanao Star (☎082 244 0033), Philtranco (☎082 299 3419), Rural Trans (☎082 244 0637) and Weena Express (☎082 244 0033). A handy resource is Mindanao Bus Traveler ⓦfacebook.com/MindanaoBusTraveler.

Destinations Butuan (Bachelor Express: daily 1am–5pm,

INTRODUCING PRESIDENT DUTERTE

The Philippines has a long and colourful history of controversial leaders. The Ilocos Norte-born politician **Ferdinand Marcos**, who ruled the country from 1965 to 1986, governed the archipelago with an iron fist. Keeping the country under martial law from 1972 until 1981, he ruled as a dictator, before being run out of office after accusations of mass cheating, political turmoil and a series of human rights abuses. Nonetheless, Ferdinand Marcos has nothing on **Rodrigo Roa Duterte**, "The Punisher". The Philippines' current president and military Commander in Chief, Duterte is so ruthless and unpredictable that he's also become known as "Duterte Harry" (after the Clint Eastwood character, Dirty Harry).

At the centre of world debate since he took office in June 2016, Duterte is rarely out of the headlines – from rolling back on a diplomatic promise to China over the territorial dispute of an ocean region off the country's northeastern coast, to calling former US President Barack Obama a "son of a whore". Not only has he has made the extrajudicial killing of drug dealers and – even more controversially – drug users the cornerstone of his domestic policy, but as the former **mayor of Davao** and the first ever Mindanaoan to hold office, he has threatened to impose martial law nationwide if peace and order fails to become the daily norm. That he openly stands up to America, Japan and China, publically swears at press conferences, and has a reputation for frank – and frankly offensive – speechmaking, only adds to his anti-establishment credentials. (While discussing his war on drugs he said, "Hitler massacred three million Jews. Now, there is three million drug addicts – I'd be happy to slaughter them.") This hard-knock reputation and the surrounding mythology has helped him succeed and to swell his grassroots support.

Behind the bluster, Duterte is an ambitious lawyer-turned-politician, with a track record of getting results, even if he splits opinion like an axe. While Mayor of Davao from 2013 to 2016, he vowed to clean up the city's endemic **corruption** and notorious **crime levels** that were the highest in the Philippines. At the time, it was widely alleged that he sanctioned **death squads** who targeted petty criminals, drug dealers and street children. Duterte, many say, appointed himself judge, jury and executioner by rubber-stamping hundreds of extrajudicial killings. The result? Davao's per capita crime rate plummeted to the lowest in the country, and the turnaround helped determine Duterte's political future. Though he is the son of a former provincial governor, he is not a member of the ruling political elite; this has struck a powerful chord with the people of Davao. In 2016, he ran a cleverly marketed election campaign using the slogan Du30 (a shorthand nickname for the politician, which went viral on social media), in which he promised to fight crime and narcotics, and to **eradicate illicit drugs** within six months. Soon after, he was handed the keys to the most important office in the country.

Duterte's brash and abrasive approach continues to divide international opinion. In their human rights report from January 2017, Amnesty International claimed that Filipino police paid officers to kill alleged drug offenders, and planted evidence on vulnerable victims as part of what they call Duterte's "murderous war on the poor". The president shrugged off the criticism, saying it would not dissuade him. "I do not give a shit," he said. "I have a duty to do, and I will do it." Rarely in Manila's House of Representatives, these days, is there ever a dull day when Duterte is around.

every 20min; 5–6hr); Cagayan de Oro (Rural Trans: daily 4am–10.30pm, every 30min; 7hr 30min); Cotabato (Weena Express: daily 4.30am–1.30pm, every 25min; 6hr); General Santos (Weena Express: every 30min; 3hr 15min); Kidapawan, for Mt Apo (Weena Express: daily 4.30am–1.30pm, every 25min; 2hr 30min); Surigao (Bachelor Express: direct, 8am; 9hr).

BY BOAT

Ferries Ferries arrive at and leave from Sasa wharf, 8km northeast along the coast, although aside from bus-ferry connections on the RORO ferry across to Samal, there aren't any destinations of use from here. To take a passenger ferry to Manila, Iloilo, Bacolod, Cebu City or Bohol, you'll need to travel north to Cagayan de Oro.

INFORMATION AND TOURS

Tourist information The tourist office on the south side of Magsaysay Park (Mon–Fri 8am–5pm; ☎ 082 221 6276) offers basic maps and leaflets. The Regional Department of Tourism is on the fifth floor of the Landco Pacific Building, J.P. Laurel Ave, near Victoria Plaza (Mon–Fri 8am–5pm; ☎ 082 221 6955, ⦿ tourism.gov.ph).

GETTING AROUND

By taxi It's cheap and easy to get around Davao by taxi; you can hail them in the street, meters start at P30 and after that it's P3.50/500m. They can also be hired out for day-trips from around P2000, but make sure you clearly establish the price and what it entails.

By jeepney Jeepneys (P8 initial fare for up to 4km; P1/1km thereafter) run back and forth along all major thoroughfares with their destinations pasted on the side – it's just a question of flagging one down and hopping on.

By tricycle Tricycles charge from P8/person for trips within the city – this includes Santa Ana wharf, Ecoland bus terminal, and north as far as Victoria Plaza.

ACCOMMODATION

Apo View Hotel 150 J. Camus St ☎ 082 221 6430, ⦿ apoview.com; map p.425. The oldest upmarket hotel in Davao, with big, comfortable a/c rooms – it can't compete with the *Marco Polo* or *Seda Abreeza* for luxury, but it has a certain old-fashioned charm. You don't always get a view of Mt Apo, although on a clear day you can see it from the top-floor restaurant. 🛜 **P5000**

The Big House 12 Juna Ave, Matina ☎ 082 2285 7665, ⦿ thebighousedavao.com; map p.423. This two-storey, 1950s-era heritage house is one of the oldest in the city and is decorated with family pictures and memorabilia that give it a homely touch. There's a range of eleven rooms, from economy twins (P1500) to queen doubles (P2000), all with wood-frame beds and lamps. The hotel also has a lovely garden and spacious veranda, and breakfast is included. 🛜 **P1500**

Casa Leticia Boutique/Business Hotel Boutique: Near Apo View Hotel, J. Camus St; map p.425. Business: Maya St, Ecoland ☎ 082 224 0501, ⦿ casaleticia.com; map p.423. Don't let the name fool you; these hotels are more business than Spanish homestay, with attractive a/c, en-suite rooms ranging from studios and doubles to smart suites. The boutique hotel also has a reasonable restaurant and a lively music bar, *Toto's*. Patchy wi-fi. 🛜 **P2800**

Green Windows Dormitel 1034 Mt Apo St ☎ 0927 820 1305, ⦿ greenwindowsdormitel.com; map p.425. Davao's best option for shoestring travellers. The value-for-money a/c backpacker dorm comes with personal wardrobes and hot and cold shower, while doubles and triples are a reliable option for those in need of more privacy. 🛜 Dorm **P180**, doubles **P1600**

Legaspi Suites 115 P. Pelayo St, Polbalcion ☎ 082 227 8613, ⦿ legaspisuitesdavao.com; map p.425. In a handy location near bars and restaurants (there are four below the hotel), this place offers high standards for a very reasonable price. Rooms, elegantly furnished in dark wood and decorated in pastel shades, have a/c, LCD TVs and decent bathrooms, and the larger premier superior rooms (P1900) have fridges. Breakfast is included, and there's a P200 discount for single occupancy. Wi-fi in the lobby area. 🛜 **P1700**

Marco Polo C.M. Recto St at Roxas Ave ☎ 082 221 0888, ⦿ marcopolohotels.com; map p.425. Once the city's landmark hotel, the *Marco Polo* has spacious rooms with large bathrooms and flatscreen cable TVs, as well as fine views of either the sea or, on a clear day, Mt Apo. The pool is a lovely place to hang out, with a bar and terrace restaurant facing Apo, and the breakfast buffets (usually included) are excellent. The deluxe suites on the 11–16th floors come with full butler service. 🛜 **P4900**

My Hotel San Pedro St, Polblacion ☎ 082 222 2021, ⦿ myhoteldavao.com; map p.425. The tiny, clean fan rooms here, with communal bathrooms, are among the best bargains in the city, while the a/c rooms are more spacious and have cable TV. Downstairs, there are friendly staff and excellent value at *My Café*. Wi-fi in public areas. 🛜 **P1240**

★ Ponce Suites Rd 3 at Rd 4, Doña Vicenta Village, Bajada; map p.423 ☎ 082 227 9070. You're unlikely to have stayed in a budget hotel like this before – every bit of public wall space is smothered in the exuberant artwork of prolific Mindanaoan artist Kublai Millan, son of the proud owner. The motel-style rooms are far less showy than the communal spaces, but all are en suite and have basic cable TV. *Ponce Suites* also runs professional tours around the city. 🛜 **P975**

9

Seda Abreeza Hotel Abreeza Ayala Business Park ☎ 082 244 3000, ⓦ sedahotels.com; map p.423. Gleaming multi-storey tower overlooking the Ayala Mall, that's home to the most luxurious hotel in the city. The large deluxe rooms come with iPhone dock, radio, mini-bar and big, bouncy beds, as well as eye-popping views of the Davao Gulf. If you fancy an upgrade to a Club Room (P6900) you'll gain access to the Executive Lounge, where you'll be treated to free-flowing wines. 📶 P4720

EATING

Davao's best **restaurants** are scattered all over the city, but the safest bet for a cheap meal are the **food courts** located in or around the shopping malls. Durian fruit is a big deal in Davao, and is available in every form, from durian ice cream to durian-flavoured cappuccino. The best season for the fruit is Sept–Dec.

★ **Backyard Burgers** 88 Quimpo Blvd, Ecoland ☎ 082 295 6935, ⓦ davaoburgers.com; map p.425. Not content to get their burgers from any fast-food joint, locals take great delight in building their own DIY burgers at this appealing open-air diner. Go simple with a yard burger, with caramelized onions and home-made steak sauce (P125) or get creative with a Korean BBQ patty, in a black-sesame bun, with Korean sauce and *kimchi* (P195). Best burger in Mindanao? No contest. Daily noon–9pm.

Balik Bukid Farm and Kitchen Quimpo Blvd, Ecoland ☎ 082 296 4543, ⓦ facebook.com/BalikBukiDako; map p.423. Organic farm-to-fork family restaurant that specializes in wholesome, healthy and fresh food straight from the garden. Vegans are well catered for with salads and rice dishes, while carnivores can go wild over the traditional pork, chicken and river fish. Also makes cheese and delicious home-made chocolate ice cream. Mains from P200. Daily 11am–2pm & 5–10pm.

Claude's 143 Rizal St, Poblacion ☎ 082 222 4287; map p.425. Superb French and Mediterranean restaurant in an elegant 1920s house that was formerly the Mayor's residence and apparently once played host to former president Manuel Roxas. Now owned and operated by a French native Claude Le Neindre, the restaurant serves food that's as exquisite as the architecture. The grilled blue marlin is outstanding, and there are a host of speciality dishes including foie gras, mussels marinière and duck a l'orange (mains from P670). Live music on weekends. Daily 8am–10pm.

Coffee for Peace Frederic Building, MacArthur Hwy ☎ 082 296 1053, ⓦ coffeeforpeace.com; map p.423. As well as serving up the freshest Arabica bean brews in Davao, this collective of big-hearted coffee advocates works closely with farmers, exporters and NGOs for the benefit of the entire community. Well worth a visit to learn more about its backstory. Mon–Sat 8am–11pm.

Jack's Ridge Resort & Restaurant Shrine Hills, Matina ☎ 082 297 8830, ⓦ jacksridgedavao.com; map p.423. Just across from the Santo Niño shrine, this complex is all about the views and cool breezes. The Filipino food in the main *Taklobo Restaurant* is delicious: the *sinigang*, *lechon* (P190), grilled tuna (P90/100g) and BBQ chicken (P110) are all superb. Take a taxi from town (P100). Daily 10am–10pm.

Lyndon's World Worst Ribs and Awful Chicken 740 Roxas Ave ☎ 0922 863 7123; map p.425. Worth including for the name alone, this American-style diner uses reverse psychology to bring in social-media savvy locals. The ribs are finger-lickin' good (P125/200g) and the quarter chicken is as tasty and peppery as anything Colonel Sanders could rustle up (P165). The service isn't five-star, but prices are low and portions belly-filling. Mon–Sat 10.30am–10.30pm.

★ **Malagos Farm House** Bolcan Street, Agdao ☎ 082 226 4446, ⓦ malagosfarmhouse.com; map p.423. Quality cheese in the Philippines – this is a real one-off. Making several delicious varieties of artisan feta, blue and goat cheese, this farm-to-fork fromagerie serves up bite-size pieces, raclette and toasties. It's run by local entrepreneur Olive Puentespina, one of the stars of Davao's food scene, so don't miss her insightful sample tastings, daily at 10am and 5pm. Daily 9am–6pm.

Wild Garlic 497 South St ☎ 082 296 0046, ⓦ facebook .com/WildGarlicDavao; map p.423. Filipino delicacies dominate the menu at this lovely rustic café with a classic deli vibe and wooden tables and chairs. Try the tuna *panga* stewed in *bagoong* (fish paste), a local favourite such as *kinilaw*, or the house speciality of wild garlic chicken (P168). Mon–Sat 11am–10pm, Sun 11am–3pm & 5–10pm.

Yolks Flower Cafe and Cupcakery Bella Vie Building, Circumferential Rd ☎ 0927 488 3528; map p.423. Exquisite pastries, flower-themed cakes and fabulous flower arrangements are the order of the day at this florist-bakery hybrid. They also rustle up budget-friendly set meals from P125 and creative pizzas such as black pepperoni served on a jet-black dough base (P385). Mon–Thurs 8.30am–9pm, Fri–Sat 8.30am–10pm, Sun 11am–9pm.

DRINKING AND NIGHTLIFE

It may not be as avant-garde as Manila, but there's some entertaining **nightlife** in Davao, with cosy live-music venues, karaoke bars and discos. You'll find a cluster of bars and clubs around *Brick Lane Square*, a restaurant and bar quadrangle just south of the University of the Southeastern Philippines.

The BEEReaucracy Bar Brick Lane Square, 29 Polo St ☎0917 718 5560, ⓦfacebook.com/BEEReaucracyBar; map p.425. With dozens of imported beers and craft IPAS, this *Brick Lane Square* joint is heaven for hop-heads and stout-suppers. The beers aren't as cheap as you'd find elsewhere (a pricey P160–290), but the exposed-brick bar is an entertaining place to meet local hipsters. Daily 6pm–1am.

Junkyard Restobar Palma Gil St ☎0927 986 3664; map p.425. In the popular drinking area south of the University of the Southeastern Philippines, this popular pub offers acoustic sessions and karaoke. A motorbike hangs from one of the walls, naturally. Should it get too crowded, you won't be short of other bar options nearby. Daily 5pm–1am.

Matina Town Square MacArthur Hwy ☎082 297 1780; map p.423. Davao's premier cultural hub showcasing a variety of nightclubs, low-key food and drink spots, as well as more refined restaurants. It's a fun place to wander, while on Tues there's a free indigenous music show on the outdoor stage. Daily 8am–2am.

Stre3ts Urban Lifestyle Pub JJ's Commune, Loyala Street ☎0939 658 8471, ⓦfacebook.com/STRE3TS; map p.425. Good-time party place with platters, cheap drink promos and DJ nights. Funky decor, great service and cold draughts (San Miguel P90) make it very popular with Davao's students and office workers. Daily 4pm–2am.

SHOPPING

Aldevinco Shopping Center Opposite the Marco Polo hotel, between C.M. Recto Ave and Roxas Ave; map p.425. For souvenirs and handicrafts, head to this maze of small shops selling tribal artefacts and cheap batik clothes. With a little bargaining, you can grab a sarong for P100 or statues and masks from P400. Daily 10am–7pm.

SM City Mall Quimpo Blvd, Ecoland ☎082 297 6998 ⓦsmsupermalls.com; map p.423. Home to dozens of local and international brands, as well as a multiplex cinema and entertainment centre. The mall was subject to a terrorist bombing in September 2013. Daily 10am–9pm.

DIRECTORY

Hospitals The city's major hospital is the Davao Doctors' Hospital (☎082 221 2101) on General Malvar St.

Post The main post office is on Roxas Ave, close to the junction with C.M. Recto St and Magsaysay Ave (☎082 227 1837).

Around Davao

For many visitors, Davao acts as a springboard for a series of trips beyond the city limits to see southern Mindanao at its finest. Head north to **Calinan** and you'll be in the company of majestic eagles at the **Philippine Eagle Center** and in touching distance of **Mount Apo**, the highest mountain in the archipelago. Venture east and you'll find yourself on the deserted white-sand beaches of **Samal and Talikud Islands**. Both are ripe to be explored.

Samal Island

Just across the narrow Pakiputan Strait from Davao, **Samal Island** is graced with lovely coves, beaches, excellent scuba diving and huge bat caves – there are also plenty of resorts to choose from. Most tourists visit Samal on organized tours but it's also easy to arrange a trip independently. You can spend time at one of the resorts (most of which allow day guests for a fee), or jump on a habal-habal and tour the island by motorbike. Samal is bigger than it seems, with an area of more than 300 square kilometres and nearly 100,000 permanent residents. Of the many beaches, it's worth taking the bumpy, hour-long ride across the island to **Canibad Beach Cove**, a pristine, untouched swathe of sand with little more than a sari-sari store selling soft drinks.

Note that in the past few years Samal has become increasingly prone to **terrorist activity** and **kidnapping**. Alongside a number of locals and other holidaymakers, Canadians John Ridsdel and Robert Hall were abducted and taken by armed Abu Sayyaf gunmen while staying on the island in September 2015. Despite the story going viral around the world, efforts to rescue them failed and they were both beheaded the

9

following year. At the time of going to press, several of the other hostages remained captive, and the Philippines' Armed Forces had stepped up rescue attempts.

Monfort Bat Cave

Sitio Dunggas, Barangay Tambo • Daily 8am–5pm • Night tours 6–7pm • P100 ☎ 082 286 6958 ⓦ monfortbatsanctuary.org

Don't miss the **Monfort Bat Cave** in the northern part of the island, a vast cavern jam-packed with around 1.8 million of the nocturnal creatures – the world's largest known population of Geoffrey's Rousette fruit bats. They usually hang in the cave during the day, but come sundown they flood the skies like a diffusing dark cloud – it's a chilling experience.

ARRIVAL AND DEPARTURE   SAMAL ISLAND

By private boat Getting to Samal from Davao is relatively straightforward. Most resorts on the island have private boats that zip guests across the Pakiputan Strait direct to the hotel grounds, and some of these – notably *Pearl Farm Resort* (see below) – also take day-trippers, for a fee.

By ferry Three main ferry companies make the journey to Samal: Babak, Caliclic and Kaputian ferries.
On a tour Most hotels in Davao will arrange day-tours to the island for around P1000–1200/person.

GETTING AROUND

By habal-habal No matter which port you arrive at, if you want to get beyond the resorts you can choose from the many habal-habal riders offering personalized tours – it's a good idea to hire one for the whole or half-day rather than trying to get separate lifts. Rates vary, but expect to pay

around P300–400 for a half-day.
Tricycles and minivans Tricycles and minivans are available, but unless you have a group, these are much more expensive than habal-habals.

ACCOMMODATION

Most reasonably priced **resorts** on Samal are on the northwest coast, south of the barangay of Caliclic. From the wharf at Babak you can walk to many of these resorts, or hop on a tricycle. All the major resorts have private boats for guests – these depart from piers off R. Castillo St north of the city.

Chema's By The Sea Resort Brgy Limao ☎ 082 286 1352, ⓦ chemasbythesea.com. With a collection of handsome exposed-brick cabanas and bungalows that fuse Balinese and Spanish design, this tropical oasis is only 10min from Davao, yet seems to have stepped out of Boracay. Expect white sands, acres of tropical forest to explore and impressive views of Davao in the distance. Day visitors are charged P250/person. Wi-fi in public areas. 📶 P5625
Paradise Island Park & Beach Resort Caliclic ☎ 082 233 0251, ⓦ paradiseislanddavao.com. This eighty-room resort can get busy at weekends with

day-trippers escaping the city, but has attractive a/c cottages under shady trees in landscaped gardens, a convivial native-style restaurant, and scuba diving. Day guests are charged P200. Wi-fi in public areas. 📶 P5390
★**Pearl Farm Resort** Lizada Village, Lanang ☎ 082 235 1234, ⓦ pearlfarmresort.com. Situated on the west coast, this is the island's classiest and most expensive resort, with more than seventy native-style cottages either on a hillside overlooking the bay or perched on stilts in the sea. For even more luxury, there are also seven secluded villas on beautiful little Malipano Island, a short hop from the main resort. P8500

Talikud

Talikud Island, off the southwest coast of Samal, is even more torpid than its big brother, making it a perfect place to escape Davao's crowds. On the west coast there's good, easy diving and snorkelling in an area known as Coral Gardens, and a couple of more demanding drop-off dives dot the north coast.

ARRIVAL AND DEPARTURE   TALIKUD

By boat Outrigger ferries regularly chug between Santa Ana wharf, near Magsaysay Park in Davao, and Santa Cruz on Talikud (6 daily 10.30am–4pm; 1hr; P60). Boats leave

from the second pier, left of the wharf entrance; just jump on and pay. For day-trippers, the last boat from Santa Cruz wharf to Santa Ana leaves at 3pm.

ACCOMMODATION

La Isla Bonita ☎ 0998 991 2754 82, ⓦ laislabonitaresort .website. For a real budget trip to Talikud, *La Isla Bonita* is your best bet. Rooms are on the palm-fringed, white-sand beach – simple nipa huts and dorms, mostly with no-frills interiors. If you aren't staying here, you can pay P70 for day entry, and its direct Davao-to-resort boat transfers also come in handy (P100 each way). ☞ Dorms P300, doubles P1000

Leticia by the Sea ☎ 082 224 0501, ⓦ leticiabythesearesort.com. Elegant but simple, this is a wonderful escape, visitable from Davao for the day (P1400). A variety of accommodation is available including Bali houses all the way up to deluxe seaside villas (P9800). Rates are per person and include full board and boat transfers. ☞ P4800

Calinan

The small but lively town of **CALINAN**, 45km northwest of Davao on the main highway to Cagayan de Oro, became a major Japanese farming community in the 1930s. Though there's little evidence of this today, the period is commemorated at the **Philippine-Japanese Historical Museum**, and there are a few attractions nearby. It's worth coming here during the week to avoid the crowds, but if you find yourself in Calinan on a Sunday you could head for the *Malagos Garden Resort* free-flight bird show, daily at 10.30am (P225; see p.432). Also responsible for the fabulous *Malagos Farmhouse* in Davao, the resort has recently opened the country's first **chocolate museum** and interactive bean-to-bar laboratory.

Philippine-Japanese Historical Museum

De Lara St, in the Durian Village section of Calinan • Mon–Sat 8am–5.30pm • P20 • ☎ 082 295 0221 • It's hard to find, so take a habal-habal

Calinan's curious and largely forgotten Japanese history is remembered through a collection of old photos and the fascinating written testimonies of Japanese settlers in the **Philippine-Japanese Historical Museum**. Also on display are sepia pictures of the many memorials to Japanese people killed during World War II in the area.

Philippine Eagle Center

Malagos • Daily 8am–5pm • P150 Eagle Center; P6 Philippines Water Authority Park • ☎ 082 224 3021, ⓦ philippineeagle.org • Many hotels in Davao offer day-trips

The **Philippine Eagle Center**, 5km west of Calinan, is known for its excellent work breeding and rehabilitating the Philippine eagle, a majestic creature with a fearsome beak, distinctive frilly head feathers and a 2m wingspan. Sadly, the eagle is now officially on the endangered species list, with only a maximum of four hundred believed to be living in the wilds of Mindanao, Samar and Leyte. While the centre's captive breeding programme focuses on developing a viable gene pool, the goal is to reintroduce the birds into their natural habitat. The first captive-bred bird, Pag-aso (meaning "Hope"), was born here in 1992 and the centre is now home to 36 Philippine eagles, 18 of which are captive-bred.

To get to the centre, you first walk through the Philippines Water Authority Grounds before reaching the entrance proper and a pleasant café overlooking a lily pond. In addition to the large aviaries containing the big eagles, there are plenty of other birds of prey on display, from grass owls and kites to screeching fish eagles. The centre is a bit like an old-fashioned zoo – there are compounds for the Philippine brown deer, warty pig, long-tailed macaques and even a giant crocodile – and some of the cages are very small and dirty. It can be uncomfortably busy at weekends, so try to schedule your visit for a weekday.

ARRIVAL AND DEPARTURE   CALINAN

By jeepney or bus From Davao, take one of the frequent a/c jeepneys (P40) or buses to Calinan (45min) from the Calinan Bus Terminal on San Pedro St, just north of E. Quirino Ave. Once there, a habal-habal trip for the last 5km should cost around P30.

By car You can rent a vehicle from your Davao hotel for the trip, or negotiate directly with a taxi driver – expect to pay P2000 for a day-trip including waiting time. A one-way taxi fare is about P600.

9

ACCOMMODATION

Malagos Garden Resort Brgy Malagos, Baguio District ☎0917 625 2467, ⓦmalagos.com. A hub of activity, this slightly faded garden resort with comfortable, if worn, wood cabins is where Davaoan families come to play at the weekend. It's offers horseriding (P100), has a skate park (P100) and staff can organize a number of outdoor adventures, including the Skywalker high-wires course (P250), while the extensive grounds hide family cottages that can sleep four to six. In addition to all that, there's a pool, an aviary, a butterfly enclosure and the newest attraction in Mindanao – an interactive chocolate museum and laboratory where you can make your own cocoa creation. Day entry P200 (excluding activities). 📶 **P3300**

Mount Apo

Looming over all Davao, **Mount Apo** (2954m) is the highest mountain in the country: the name Apo means "grandfather of all mountains". Apo is actually a volcano, but is certified inactive and has no recorded eruptions. What it does have is enough flora and fauna to make your head spin – the national park has thundering waterfalls, rapids, lakes, geysers, sulphur pillars, primeval trees, endangered plant and animal species and a steaming blue lake. Then there are exotic ferns, carnivorous pitcher plants and the queen of Philippine orchids, the *waling-waling*. The local tribes, the Bagobos, believe the gods Apo and Mandaragan inhabit Apo's upper slopes; they revere it as a sacred mountain, calling it Sandawa or "Mountain of Sulphur".

Although **climbing** Mount Apo has topped many Filipinos' bucket lists in recent years, at the time of research **all hiking trails were indefinitely closed**. On March 26, 2016, 115 hectares of the mountain's grasslands were razed in a **wildfire** believed to have been started by trekkers who left a campfire unattended. The fire started near the peak, and quickly spread down the slopes to Lake Venado and Kidapawan; it took 28 days for firefighters to contain. With government agencies keen to preserve and rehabilitate the area, it may take years rather than months for trekkers to be allowed back.

Climbing Mount Apo

When the trail does reopen, you'll be able to approach the summit via two main routes: the **Kidapawan Trail** on the Cotabato side features hot springs, river crossings and a steep forested trail that leads to the peak via swampy Lake Venado; and the tougher **Kapatagan Trail** on the Davao side that cuts through more stereotypically volcanic terrain, culminating in a boulder-strewn slope up to the crater. Most operators recommend a three- to four-day expedition, but experienced tropical climbers will be able to summit faster.

INFORMATION   MOUNT APO

Tourist offices The Kidapawan Tourist Center (☎0930 620 8602) is next to city hall, while the Kapatagan registration office (no phone) is in the small settlement of Kapatagan.

Tours Mt Apo Adventures (ⓦmtapoadventures.com) is a small-scale trekking organization that can arrange all elements of the climb for P5000–6500 (depending on group size). Another highly recommended outfit is Trail Adventours (ⓦtrailadventours.com), which as well as organizing four-day hikes up the Kapatagan route (P5900), arranges multi-day treks and summit ascents across the Philippines.

ACCOMMODATION

Mt Apo Highland Resort Lake Agko ☎082 275 7955, facebook.com/Mt.ApoHighlandResort. Right on the lake, this place is ideal for whiling away a few days. It has a scattering of rustic cottages on concrete stilts, as well as plenty of pitches for camping. The views of Mt Apo are astounding. Camping **P300**/person, doubles **P2000**

General Santos

Around 140km southwest of Davao on Sarangani Bay, **GENERAL SANTOS** – or "Gensan" – is the Philippines' southernmost city, a dense, noisy metropolis of more than half a million that isn't a significant tourist destination; it's something of a frontier

THE AUTONOMOUS REGION IN MUSLIM MINDANAO

While it is potentially one of the most beguiling areas of the Philippines, the **Autonomous Region in Muslim Mindanao (ARMM)**, a patchwork of several predominantly Muslim provinces in the western part of the island, is not safe to visit. Created in 1989, the regional government (based in Cotabato) has the power to levy taxes and apply Shariah law to Muslims. Despite this autonomy, the region remains extremely poor and the epicentre for anti-government protest.

The US, UK and Australian governments (and most Filipinos) usually advise foreigners to **avoid ARMM** entirely. Especially in light of recent violent incidents (see box, p.405), we recommend that you do not visit this region until the situation has calmed down. Check the latest government travel advice for updates.

town, founded by General Paulino Santos and 62 pioneers from Luzon in 1939. Its recent history has included a series of terrorist bombings, and it remains in the British Foreign and Commonwealth Office's red zone (advising against all travel). Today General Santos is best known as the centre of the tuna industry, and the home town of boxing superstar **Manny Pacquiao**.

ARRIVAL AND DEPARTURE
GENERAL SANTOS

By plane General Santos International Airport is about 25min and 16km southwest of the city, an easy trip by taxi (P300–350), or habal-habal (P100). Despite the name, there are only domestic flights.
Destinations Cebu (1 daily; 1hr 10min); Iloilo (7 weekly; 1hr 25min); Manila (4–5 daily; 1hr 50min).

By boat Ferries arrive at Makar wharf, 10min and 2km west of the centre on P. Acharon Blvd.
By bus Buses arrive at the City Terminal near Bulaong Ave on the western edge of the centre.
Destinations Cotabato (several daily; 5hr); Davao (every 30min; 3hr 15min); Koronodal (hourly; 3hr).

ACCOMMODATION AND EATING

27th Grill Avenue E. Quirino Ave ☎0920 971 4092 ⓦfacebook.com/27thgrillavenue. The rituals at this DIY BBQ joint are simple: each table comes fitted with a personal griller and you can pick and choose the meat or seafood, before cooking it as you like. Try the prawn skewers or glazed pork chops (priced per 100g), or for something cheaper, consider the bargain meat and rice deals (P189). Daily 5.30–10pm.
Hotel San Marco JP Laurel East ☎083 301 1818, ⓦhotelsanmarco.com.ph. Good-value, Italian-influenced boutique hotel with dark-wood and marble finishing that'd look equally at home in Milan or Rome. There's a range of a/c

standard twins, deluxe doubles and superior rooms (P2280), all including cable TV, fridge, safe and beds large enough for Pavarotti. Breakfast is included and served at *Café Verona* on the ground floor. Wi-fi in public areas. ⓦ P1980
Roadhaus Hotel JMP Building 2, Aparente St ☎083 554 2368, ⓦroadhaushotel.com. Also known as the Manny "Pacman" Pacquiao hotel, after its famous boxing-legend owner, this motel pulls no punches in the VIP luxury stakes. Its standard rooms are good value, with free car parking, mini-bar, cable TV and breakfast, and the hotel also throws in a free one-hour session at the local gym, also owned by the boxer. ⓦ P1800

MAP OF MANILA BAY, C.1902

Contexts

History

Philippine history is frequently dismissed as "beginning with the Spanish and ending with the Americans", yet the modern country is a result of many diverse influences – Malay, Chinese, Spanish and American – that have collided in the archipelago down the centuries. While the influence of Spain and the US is significant, recent scholarship has thrown light on the native and Islamic civilizations that flourished here before Magellan's arrival in 1521, and – thanks to new archeological discoveries – their highly developed trade links with the rest of Asia. Today one issue looms over all others: in 1960 the population of the Philippines was just 27 million; in 2014 it was estimated to have topped 100 million. Such explosive growth has meant that real economic gains made in the last fifty years have had a negligible effect on poverty and it remains, along with corruption, one of the country's biggest problems.

Prehistory

Human fossil remains found in Palawan suggest that humans first migrated to the Philippines across land bridges from Borneo during the Ice Age, some fifty thousand years ago. Carbon dating of fossilized human remains discovered at the Tabon Caves in Palawan showed so-called "**Tabon Man**" was living in the cave about 22,000 years ago. Deeper excavations of the caves indicated humans were in the area from 45,000 to 50,000 years ago.

The **Aeta** or Negritos, the country's indigenous people, are said to be descended from these first migrants. Successive migrations populated the islands through the centuries. **Malays** from Indonesia and the Malay peninsula streamed into the archipelago more than two thousand years ago, sailing across the Sulu Sea and settling first in the Visayas and southwestern Luzon. Their outrigger boats, equipped with lateen sails, each carried a family or clans led by a chief. Once ashore, they remained together in villages – known as barangays, after the name for their boats (*balangays*). The bulk of Filipinos today, at least in the Visayas and Mindanao, are descended from these Malay settlers.

Hindu kingdoms and Islamic sultanates

The early Malay communities gradually developed into a complex patchwork of kingdoms such as the Rajahnates of Butuan and Cebu, influenced by the powerful **Hindu empires** in Java and Sumatra. Several archeological finds hint at the sophistication and wealth of these early civilizations: the Laguna Copperplate Inscription, the earliest writing found in the Philippines, dates from around 900 AD and concerns a debt of gold in the Hindu-Malay state of Tondo, around today's Manila

900–1535	1380	1475
So-called "Classical States" period; the archipelago ruled by Hindu-influenced kingdoms	Karim ul' Makdum establishes the Islamic Sultanate of Sulu	Shariff Mohammed Kabungsuwan establishes the Islamic Sultanate of Maguindanao

Bay. Equally enlightening is the Surigao Treasure, a trove of sensational gold objects dug up by accident in Mindanao in 1981 and dating from the tenth to thirteenth centuries. Chinese shipwrecks loaded with porcelain prove that trade ties with **China** and the rest of Asia were extensive by the tenth century.

Contact with Arab traders, which reached its peak in the twelfth century, drew Sufis and missionaries who began the propagation of **Islam** in the Philippines. In 1380, the Arab scholar Karim ul' Makdum arrived in Jolo and established the Sultanate of Sulu. In 1475 Shariff Mohammed Kabungsuwan of Johor (Malaysia), married a native princess and established the Sultanate of Maguindanao, ruling large parts of Mindanao. During the reign of Sultan Bolkiah (1485–1521), the Sultanate of Brunei absorbed Tondo; by the time the Spanish arrived, Islam was established as far north as Luzon, where a great Muslim chief, Rajah Sulaiman II, ruled Manila.

Spanish rule

The archipelago's turbulent relationship with Spain began on April 24, 1521 when **Ferdinand Magellan** arrived in Cebu. Magellan planted a wooden cross to claim the islands for Spain, baptizing a local king, Raja Humabon. **Lapu-Lapu** (1491–1542), a chief on the nearby island of Mactan, and Humabon's traditional enemy, resisted; in the subsequent Battle of Mactan (see box, p.330), Magellan was killed and Spain's conquest of the Philippines was put on hold. Lapu-Lapu is now regarded as a Filipino hero.

Spanish conquistador Ruy López de Villalobos tried once again to claim the islands for Spain in 1543, but was driven out by the natives a year later – though not before naming the islands the Philippines, in honour of the future King Philip II. In 1564 **Miguel López de Legazpi** (1502–72), a minor Basque aristocrat, was chosen to lead a hazardous expedition to establish a permanent base in the Philippines, which the Spanish hoped would act as a wedge between Portugal and China. Legazpi sailed to the Philippines on board the *Capitana*, established a colony in Bohol in 1565 and then moved on to Cebu where he erected the first Spanish fort in the Philippines. But a series of misunderstandings – one involving the gift of a concubine that Legazpi piously refused – made the situation in Cebu perilous, and Legazpi looked for a more solid base.

In 1570 a Spanish expedition defeated Rajah Sulaiman III, and a year later Legazpi occupied his former base; a new Spanish capital – **Manila** – was established on the site of Sulaiman's old Islamic kingdom. Spanish conquistadors and friars zealously set about propagating **Catholicism**, building churches and bringing rural folk *debajo de las compañas* ("under the bells") into organized Spanish *pueblos*, establishing many of the country's towns and cities. They imposed a **feudal system**, concentrating populations under their control into new towns and estates, and resulting in numerous small revolts. Most of the Philippines, however, remained beyond the pale of the colonial authorities.

The Friarocracy

The islands were administered from the Spanish colony of **Mexico**, and its Spanish residents, especially those in Manila, grew prosperous from the galleon trade, exporting Chinese goods from Manila to Mexico. The Church, dreading change, did nothing to improve the subsistence economy, while in the capital, according to an early diarist, "the rich spend ten months of the year with nothing to do".

1485–1521	1521	1565
The Sultanate of Brunei extends Islamic rule as far as modern-day Manila	Ferdinand Magellan arrives in Cebu; killed fighting local chief Lapu-Lapu	Miguel López de Legazpi founds permanent Spanish settlement on Bohol

In theory, the Philippines was ruled by civil and military representatives of the King of Spain, but in practice it was the Catholic **friars** who ran the show. They derived their power from the enormous influence of the monastic orders – Augustinian, Dominican and Franciscan – which spanned the world like global corporations. Secular officials came and went, but the clergy stayed. Many friars ignored their vows of celibacy and sired children with local women. They exercised their power through a number of administrative functions, including setting budgets, conducting the parish census, screening recruits for the military and presiding over the police. There were cosmetic local administrations, but they could not act without the friars' consent.

It wasn't until the late eighteenth century that the ossification of the colonial regime eased in the face of external shocks. Attempts by the Dutch, Portuguese and Chinese to establish a presence in the archipelago were repelled, but the **British** occupied Manila in 1762, in a sideshow to the **Seven Years' War**. They handed it back to Spain under the 1763 Treaty of Paris, but their easy victory served notice that the Philippines was vulnerable. In 1821 Mexico became independent, the galleon trade ended and the Philippines were then administered directly from Madrid, ushering in a period of relatively enlightened colonial rule and prosperity.

The independence movement

The Spanish began to establish a free public school system in the Philippines in 1863, increasing the number of educated and Spanish-speaking Filipinos. The opening of the Suez Canal in 1869 (combined with the increasing use of steam power) cut travel times between Spain and the Philippines to weeks rather than months, and many of this new generation were able to continue their studies in Europe. They frequently returned with liberal ideas and talk of freedom.

A small **revolt** in Cavite in 1872 was quickly put down, but the anger and frustration Filipinos felt about colonial rule would not go away. Intellectuals such as Marcelo H. Del Pilar and Juan Luna were the spiritual founders of the independence movement, but it was the writings of a diminutive young doctor from Laguna province, **José Rizal** (1861–96), that provided the spark for the flame. His novel *Noli Me Tángere* was written while he was studying in Spain in the 1880s, and portrayed colonial rule as a cancer and the Spanish friars as fat, pompous fools. It was promptly banned by the Spanish, but distributed underground along with other inflammatory essays by Rizal and, later, his second novel, *El Filibusterismo*.

In 1892, Rizal returned to Manila and founded the movement La Liga Filipina, which espoused moderate reform, though never revolution. Its members swore oaths and took part in blood rites, and, innocuous as the movement was, the friars smelled sedition. Rizal was arrested and exiled to Dapitan on Mindanao. **Andrés Bonifacio** (1863–97) took over the reins by establishing the secret society known as the Katipunan or KKK (its full name was Kataastaasan, Kagalanggalang na Katipunan nang mga Anak ng Bayan, which means "Honorable, respectable sons and daughters of the nation"). In August 1896, an armed struggle for independence broke out, and Rizal was accused of masterminding it. Rizal had, in fact, called the revolution "absurd and savage" and had earlier turned down an invitation from Bonifacio to participate. His trial lasted a day, one of the seven military judges concluding that Rizal's being a native must be considered "an aggravating factor".

1571	1570–1890s	1762
Legazpi founds Manila; formal Spanish control over the islands begins	The "Friarocracy" controls the Philippines during the colonial Spanish period; the Manila galleon trade links Asia with Spanish Mexico	British occupy Manila during the Seven Years' War

Rizal's Spanish military lawyer did little for him so he finally rose to defend himself. "I have sought political liberty," he said, "but never the freedom to rebel." He was duly found guilty and executed by firing squad in Manila in what is now known as Rizal Park on December 30, 1896. The night before he died he wrote *Mi Último Adiós*, a farewell poem to the country he loved (see p.65).

The Philippine Revolution

News of Rizal's martyrdom inflamed the uprising ignited by Bonifacio. Spanish officials deluded themselves, blaming it on a few troublemakers, but by now Bonifacio had decided violence was the only option and, with his young firebrand general, **Emilio Aguinaldo** (1869–1964), he called openly for a government "like that of the United States". Aguinaldo, a local government official from Cavite, had joined the Katipunan in 1894 and once the fighting started swiftly became the rebels' most successful commander. At the **Tejeros Convention** in 1897 Aguinaldo was elected president of the new Republic of the Philippines by his fellow *katipuneros* – when Bonifacio was offered a far lower position, he declared the election void in a fit of rage. Soon after, Aguinaldo had Bonifacio and his brothers arrested, sentenced in a mock trial and executed. At the end of 1897, the Spanish finalized a truce with Aguinaldo, the **Pact of Biak-na-Bato**: the Spanish would pay the rebels 800,000 pesos, half immediately, a quarter when they laid down their arms and the rest after a Te Deum to mark the armistice was chanted in Manila Cathedral. In exchange Aguinaldo agreed to go abroad. A cheque in his pocket, he sailed for Hong Kong, disavowing his rebellion.

However, in 1898, as a result of a dispute over Cuba, war broke out between the **United States** and Spain, and as an extension of it the US decided to expel Spain from the Philippines. The Spanish fleet was soundly beaten in Manila Bay by ships under the command of George Dewey, who on the morning of April 30, 1898, gave the famous order to his captain, "You may fire when you are ready, Gridley." The Filipinos fought on the side of the US, and when the battle was over General Aguinaldo, now back from Hong Kong having disavowed his disavowal of the rebellion, declared the Philippines independent; the First **Philippine Republic** was formally established by the **Malolos Constitution** in January 1899, with Aguinaldo as first president. The US, however, had other ideas and paid Spain US$20 million for its former possession. Having got rid of one colonizing power, Filipinos were now answerable to another.

American rule

After the Spanish left the country, the Filipinos continued to fight for independence in what's known as the **Philippine–American War**, a savage conflict that is virtually forgotten in the US today. Fighting began in early 1899 and lasted for three years, although skirmishes continued for another seven years, especially in Mindanao. US troops used tactics to pacify locals that they would later employ in Vietnam, such as strategic hamleting and scorched earth, and by the end of February, Manila was ablaze as American troops took charge of the city. But crushing the Filipinos was not easy. The US forces, for all their superior firepower, were nagged by relentless heat, torrential rain and pervasive disease. Aguinaldo still commanded Filipino forces, though the intensity of the Manila assault had shocked him. Malolos, to the north of Manila, the seat of his

1821	1872	1887	1892
Mexico becomes independent; the Manila galleon trade ends	Cavite Revolt	José Rizal's novel *Noli Me Tángere* published in Berlin	Andrés Bonifacio founds the Katipunan to fight for independence from Spain

revolutionary government, was overrun, but by June 1899 the Americans had become bogged down and controlled territory no more than 40km from Manila. The war degenerated into a **manhunt** for Aguinaldo, and when he was finally captured in March 1902 in Palanan on Luzon's east coast, the war ended officially three months later. After a brief internment, the wily general took an oath of allegiance to the US, was granted a pension from the US government and retired from public life until 1935 (see below). The war had resulted in the death of at least 600,000 Filipinos and 4234 Americans; exact records were not kept of Filipino casualties.

Benevolent assimilation

When the Philippine–American War ended, American teachers fanned out across the country to begin President McKinley's policy of "**benevolent assimilation**". They were known as Thomasites, as the first group arrived on a ship called the *Thomas*. The Thomasites took to their task with apostolic fervour and Filipinos quickly achieved the highest literacy rate in Southeast Asia.

The American administration in the Philippines sought to inculcate Filipinos with American ethics, to turn the Philippines into a stable, prosperous democracy. Filipinos learned to behave, dress and eat like Americans, sing American songs and speak American English. American educators decided that teaching Filipinos in their many local languages would require too many textbooks, so English became the lingua franca. Meanwhile in Washington, debate raged over what form of government the Philippines should have. It wasn't until 1935 that a bill was passed in Washington allowing President Roosevelt to recognize a new Philippine constitution and the ten-year transition status of "**Commonwealth of the Philippines**" – autonomous but not completely independent. Presidential elections were held in September of that year and won by **Manuel Quezon** (1878–1944), leading light among a new breed of postwar politicians, beating Aguinaldo, who had come out of retirement. (Aguinaldo was to cooperate with the Japanese in World War II, but after briefly being jailed by the Americans a second time, lived to see Philippine independence.)

World War II

Quezon realized how vulnerable the archipelago was and invited the US commander of the country, **General Douglas MacArthur**, to become military adviser to the autonomous regime. MacArthur accepted, demanding US$33,000 a year and an air-conditioned suite in the *Manila Hotel*.

Within minutes of the December 1941 attack on **Pearl Harbor**, Japanese bombers hit military bases in Cavite and at Clark. MacArthur appealed for help from Washington, but it never came. He declared Manila an open city in order to save its population and prepared for a tactical retreat to Corregidor, the island at the mouth of Manila Bay, from where he would supervise the defence of the strategic Bataan peninsula. Quezon, now increasingly frail from tuberculosis, went with him.

The Philippines underwent heavy **bombardment** during World War II and casualties were high. Japanese troops occupied Manila on January 2, 1942. MacArthur and Quezon abandoned Corregidor when it became clear that the situation was hopeless, but arriving in Darwin, Australia, MacArthur promised Filipinos, "I shall return."

1896	1897	1898
José Rizal executed by the Spanish in Manila; the Philippine Revolution breaks out	Bonifacio is executed by rival rebel leader Emilio Aguinaldo	Spanish–American War; the US navy destroys the Spanish fleet in Manila Bay

MacArthur left behind soldiers engaged in a protracted and bloody struggle for **Bataan**. When it fell to Japanese forces, they then launched an all-out assault on Corregidor. The island, defended by starving and demoralized troops huddled in damp tunnels, capitulated in days. On the notorious **Bataan Death March** that followed, some ten thousand Americans and Filipinos died from disease, malnutrition and wanton brutality.

Two years of **Japanese military rule** followed. Unable to quell popular opposition and a nascent guerrilla movement, the Japanese turned increasingly to brutality, beheading innocent victims and displaying their bodies as an example. The guerrillas multiplied, however, until their various movements comprised two hundred thousand men. The strongest force was the People's Anti-Japanese Army, the Hukbalahap in Tagalog or the **Huks** for short, most of them poor sharecroppers and farm workers. MacArthur, meanwhile, kept his promise to return. On October 19, 1944, with Quezon at his side, he waded ashore at Leyte, forcing a showdown with the Japanese and driving across the island to the port of Ormoc. The Huks helped the US liberate Luzon, acting as guides in the push towards Manila and freeing Americans from Japanese prison camps. None exploited their wartime adventures more than **Ferdinand Marcos**, an ambitious young lawyer from Ilocos who now set his sights on entering politics.

The Marcos years

The Philippines received full **independence** from the US on July 4, 1946, when **Manuel Roxas**, an experienced politician from Panay, was sworn in as the first President of the Republic. His government marred by corruption and conflict with the now outlawed Huks, Roxas died of a heart attack in 1948 and was replaced by his Ilocano vice president Elpidio Quirino. The 1950s were something of a golden age for the Philippines, with the presidency of Ramón Magsaysay (1953–57) considered a high point: politics was largely corruption-free, trade and industry boomed and the country was ranked Asia's second cleanest and best governed after Japan. In the early 1960s, however, the Liberal government of Diosdado Macapagal was crippled by Nacionalista Party opposition in Congress. It was in these years that **Ferdinand Marcos** came to power, promoting himself as a force for unification and reform.

Marcos (1917–89) was born in Sarrat, Ilocos Norte. A brilliant young lawyer who had successfully defended himself against a murder charge, he was elected to the Philippine House of Representatives in 1949, to the Senate in 1959 and became president in 1965 on the Nacionalista Party ticket, defeating incumbent Macapagal. Marcos's first term as president was innovative and inspirational. He invigorated both populace and bureaucracy, embarking on a huge **infrastructure** programme and unifying scattered islands with a network of roads, bridges, railways and ports. During these early years of the Marcos presidency, before the madness of martial law, **First Lady Imelda** (see box opposite) busied herself with social welfare and cultural projects that complemented Marcos's work in economics and foreign affairs.

Martial law

In 1969 Marcos became the first Filipino president to be re-elected for a **second term**. The country's problems, however, were grave. Poverty, social inequality and rural

1899	1899–1902	1935
Philippine Republic proclaimed with Emilio Aguinaldo president, but Spain cedes the Philippines to the US	Philippine–American War; US introduces "benevolent assimilation"	The Commonwealth of the Philippines is established: Manuel Quezon is the first president

THE IRON BUTTERFLY

Imelda Remedios Visitación was born on July 2, 1929, in the little town of Tolosa in Leyte. Her youth was troubled, her father jobless. At 23 she left Leyte for Manila with just five pesos in her purse, seeking her fortune. Her break came in 1953, when a magazine editor featured her face on his cover; she then entered a beauty contest and won the title of **Miss Manila**. Ferdinand Marcos later recounted that he saw the magazine picture and told friends, "I'm getting married." He arranged an introduction and, after an eleven-day courtship, proposed.

Following his 1965 election victory, Marcos said of Imelda, "She was worth a million votes." In fact, Imelda had cleverly cajoled tycoon Fernando Lopez into standing as Marcos's vice president, bringing with him his family's immeasurable fortune. Once the election was won, Imelda announced she would be "more than a mere decorative figure", and in 1966 made her international debut when she sang to Lyndon Johnson at a White House dinner. "A blessing not only to her country, but also to the world", gushed a US newspaper columnist.

Imelda laid on lavish fiestas for every visiting dignitary. She posed as a patron of the arts, flying in international stars such as Margot Fonteyn. Her husband later made her **governor of Manila** with a brief to turn the city into a showpiece. She set about the task with gusto, spending P37 million on the Coconut Palace (see p.70) and at least P100 million on the Manila Film Center (see box, p.70). As well as a patron of the arts, the First Lady also appointed herself the country's roving envoy, relentlessly roaming the world on jumbo jets "borrowed" from Philippine Airlines to meet the likes of Fidel Castro, Emperor Hirohito and Chairman Mao. A prodigious social climber, she pursued Rockefellers and Fords, and dreamed of betrothing her daughter Imee to Prince Charles.

Throughout much of the 1980s Imelda went on notoriously profligate **shopping binges** to New York and Los Angeles, spending millions of dollars on grotesque art, jewellery and the occasional apartment. In Geneva, another favourite haunt, she spent US$12 million in jewellery in a single day. After her husband's downfall in 1986, Imelda became deeply upset at reports that three thousand pairs of **shoes** had been found inside the Malacañang Palace, claiming that she had only accumulated them in order to promote the Philippine shoe industry in her trips abroad. The shoes became the most potent symbol of her mad spending.

Imelda returned to Manila in 1991, still popular in some quarters. In 1995 she was elected **Congresswoman** for her home province of Leyte, and in 2010 she was elected to represent the second district of Ilocos Norte, replacing her son Ferdinand Marcos, Jr (who was elected to the Senate). She was re-elected to the same post three years later. Various corruption cases against Imelda have dragged on over the years, but her nickname – the **Iron Butterfly**, for her thick-skinned bravura – is surely well deserved.

stagnation were rife. Marcos was trapped between the entrenched oligarchy, which controlled Congress, and a rising communist insurgency that traced its roots back to the Huks (see opposite), fuelled mostly by landless, frustrated peasants led by the articulate and patriarchal José Maria Sison (b.1939), who lives today in exile in the Netherlands. The country was roiled by student, labour and peasant unrest, much of it stoked by communists and their fledgling military wing, the **New People's Army**. On September 21, 1972, Marcos declared **martial law**, arresting **Benigno "Ninoy" Aquino** (1932–83) and other opposition leaders. A curfew was imposed and Congress suspended. Marcos announced he was pioneering a Third World approach to democracy through his "New Society" and his new political party the New Society Movement. His regime became a byword for profligacy, corruption and repression.

1942	1944	1946
Japan defeats US forces in the Philippines in World War II	US forces retake the Philippines	Republic of the Philippines becomes fully independent; Manuel Roxas first president

The **Mindanao** problem also festered. After the Jabidah Massacre in 1968, when Filipino troops executed 28 Muslim recruits who refused to take part in a hopelessly misconceived invasion of Sabah, Muslims took up arms against the government, forming the **Moro National Liberation Front** (MNLF; see box, p.405). Marcos made few real efforts to quell the insurgency, knowing it would give him another excuse for martial law. The US worried that the longer Marcos's excesses continued the faster the communist insurgency would spread, threatening their military bases in the islands.

The People Power Revolution (EDSA)

Ninoy Aquino, who by the spring of 1980 had been languishing in jail for seven years, was released on condition that he went into exile in the US. In 1983 he decided to return, but when he emerged from his plane at Manila airport on August 21, 1983, he was assassinated. The country was outraged. In a snap election called in panic by Marcos on February 7, 1986, the opposition united behind Aquino's widow, **Corazón Aquino** (1933–2009), and her running mate Salvador Laurel. On February 25, both Marcos and Aquino claimed victory and were sworn in at separate ceremonies. Aquino, known by the people as Cory, became a rallying point for change and was backed by the Catholic Church in the form of **Archbishop Cardinal Jaime Sin** (1928–2005), who urged people to take to the streets in a **People Power Revolution**, known as the EDSA Revolution.

When Marcos's key allies saw which way the wind was blowing and deserted him, the game was up. Defence Minister Juan Ponce Enrile and Deputy Chief of Staff of the Armed Forces, General **Fidel Ramos** (b.1928), later to become president, announced a coup d'état. The US prevaricated, but eventually told Marcos to "cut and cut cleanly". Ferdinand and Imelda fled into exile in Hawaii, where Ferdinand died in 1989. Conservative estimates of their plunder put the figure at US$10 billion, US$600 million of it spirited into Swiss bank accounts – rumours persist that Marcos had also appropriated a hoard of Japanese war loot dubbed "Yamashita's Gold", though this has never been proven.

The return of democracy

Hopes were high for the presidency of **Cory Aquino**, but she never managed to bring the powerful feudal families or the armed forces under her control. **Land reform** was eagerly awaited by the country's landless masses, but when Aquino realized that reform would also involve her own family's haciendas in Tarlac, she quietly shelved the idea: most of the country's farmers remain beholden to landlords today. Aquino survived seven coup attempts and made little headway in improving life for most Filipinos, who remained below the poverty line. The communist New People's Army (NPA) emerged once again as a threat, and human rights abuses continued.

Aquino also had to deal with another thorny issue: the presence of **US military bases** in the country, Clark Air Base and Subic Naval Base. Public opinion had been turning against the bases for some time, with many seeing them as a colonial imposition. In 1987 Congress voted not to renew the bases treaty and the US withdrawal, set for 1991, was hastened by the portentous eruption of **Mount Pinatubo** (see box, p.120), which scattered ash over both Clark and Subic, causing millions of dollars of damage to

1965	1969	1972	1981
Ferdinand Marcos becomes president	Marcos is re-elected amid allegations of electoral fraud	Marcos declares martial law	Martial law is lifted; Marcos wins presidential elections again

US aircraft and ships. The withdrawal made jobless six hundred thousand Filipinos who had depended on the bases for employment either directly or indirectly.

In **Mindanao**, the **Moro National Liberation Front** had started a war for independence in the 1970s that dragged on until 1987, when it accepted the offer of autonomy. The Autonomous Region in Muslim Mindanao, or ARMM, was created in 1990 (see box, p.405), but the more radical **Moro Islamic Liberation Front** (MILF) refused to accept the 1987 accord and continued fighting.

Ultimately, Aquino's only legacy was that she maintained some semblance of a democracy, which was something for her successor, **Fidel Ramos**, to build on. Ramos took office on July 1, 1992, announcing plans to create jobs, revitalize the economy and reduce the US$32 billion foreign debt. First, he had to establish a reliable electricity supply: the country was being paralysed for hours every day by **power cuts**, and no multinational companies wanted to invest under such conditions. Ramos's success in sorting this out – at least in Manila and many cities – led to a moderate influx of foreign investment, for industrial parks and new manufacturing facilities. The economy picked up, but foreign debt was crippling and tax collection was so lax that the government had nothing in the coffers to fall back on. Infrastructure improved marginally and new roads and transit systems began to take shape. Ramos also liberalized the banking sector and travelled extensively to promote the Philippines abroad. Most Filipinos view his years in office as a success, although when he stepped down at the end of his six-year term, poverty and crime were still rife.

Erap

Ramos's successor, former vice president **Joseph Estrada** (b.1937), was a former tough-guy film actor with pomaded hair and a cowboy swagger, known universally as **Erap**, a play on the slang word *pare*, which means friend or buddy. Estrada's folksy, macho charm appealed to the masses and in 1998 he was elected president against politicians of greater stature on a **pro-poor** platform. His rallying cry was *Erap para sa mahirap*, or "Erap for the poor". He promised food security, jobs, mass housing, education and health for all, but the media was soon accusing him of lacking direction and of returning to the **cronyism** of the Marcos years. The **economy** floundered, and every day there was some new allegation of mismanagement, favours for friends or plain incompetence.

In 2000, the Philippine Center for Investigative Journalism (PCIJ) began to research Estrada's wealth. Its report listed seventeen pieces of **real estate** worth P2 billion acquired by Estrada and his family members since 1998. Some, it was alleged, were for his favourite mistress, former actress Laarni Enriquez. Later in 2000, Luis Singson, governor of Ilocos Sur, alleged that Estrada had received P500 million in **gambling payoffs** from an illegal numbers game known as *jueteng* (pronounced "wet-eng"). On November 13, 2000, Estrada became the first president to be **impeached**, setting the stage for a Senate trial that would grip the nation for weeks. When the Senate let him off, people gathered in the streets to demand his resignation. The Church and its leader, Cardinal Jaime Sin, again became involved and urged Estrada to step down. Half a million people gathered at the EDSA shrine in Ortigas in scenes reminiscent of those before the downfall of Marcos – the four-day demonstrations were later dubbed

1983	1986	1989
Benigno Aquino returns to the Philippines, but is assassinated as he leaves his plane	People Power Revolution (aka EDSA Revolution) sees Marcos flee the country; Corazón Aquino becomes president	Ferdinand Marcos dies in exile in Hawaii

EDSA II. On the evening of Friday January 19, 2001, cabinet members saw that the cause was lost and began to defect.

The decisive blow came when the **military** announced it had withdrawn its support for Estrada. The next morning he was ushered ignominiously from the Malacañang Palace and vice president Gloria Macapagal-Arroyo was promptly sworn in as the fourteenth President of the Republic of the Philippines. Anti-Erap forces hailed what they deemed a noble moral victory. But a nagging question remained: Estrada had been voted into office by a landslide of 10.7 million people and removed by a predominantly middle-class movement of five hundred thousand who took to the streets. His impeachment trial had been aborted and he had been found guilty of nothing.

Macapagal-Arroyo

Gloria Macapagal-Arroyo (b.1947) proved slightly less dramatic as president than her predecessors, but just as divisive. The first years of her presidency were solid if unspectacular, her main priority simply to survive and bring some level of stability. The House of Representatives and Senate were bitterly divided along pro- and anti-Estrada lines. In 2007, Estrada was finally found guilty of plunder; a month later, he was pardoned by the president.

After winning her second term in 2004, things started to unravel for Macapagal-Arroyo; she was accused of vote rigging, though two attempts to impeach her failed. In 2006 an army plot led to a state of emergency across the country. On the economy, the president had some success, with GDP growth rates the strongest in decades, though critics disputed the figures, which in any case failed to improve the lives of the poor.

In Mindanao, things looked even worse. A new terrorist organization, **Abu Sayyaf**, emerged on Basilan Island, thought to be responsible for the February 2004 bombing of *Superferry 14*, which sank with 116 dead. The Moro Islamic Liberation Front launched new attacks on government troops in 2008 after the Supreme Court ruled unconstitutional a deal offering them large areas of the south. In 2009, 57 people (including 34 journalists) were murdered in the **Maguindanao Massacre**, part of a local election-time "clan" war.

Macapagal-Arroyo's term finished in 2010, marred by claims of cronyism, extrajudicial killings, torture and illegal arrests; corruption still ran unchecked, and the gap between the impoverished and a thin layer of super-wealthy had grown ever wider, with the dirt-poor growing in numbers and wretchedness, accounting probably for sixty percent of the population of nearly one hundred million. After standing down as president, Macapagal-Arroyo defied convention and stayed in politics, and she still sits in the House of Representatives today.

The return of the Aquinos

The presidential election of 2010 was typically dramatic. In 2009, Cory Aquino died from colon cancer, aged 76, sending the country into a five-day period of deep mourning – the former president was genuinely loved. Following her funeral many voters appealed to Cory's son, senator **Benigno Aquino III** ("Noynoy Aquino" or just "PNoy"; b.1960), to stand for president; the "Noynoy Phenomenon" posed a special dilemma because

1991	1992	1996	1998
The US abandons Clark Air Base after the Mount Pinatubo eruption smothers it with ash; Imelda Marcos returns to the Philippines	Fidel Ramos becomes president; US naval base at Subic Bay closed	Peace agreement reached with Muslim separatist group, the Moro National Liberation Front	Joseph Estrada elected president

THE GREATEST AND THE PACMAN

Boxing has been a Filipino passion for over one hundred years. Ferdinand Marcos capitalized on the nation's love of the sport by using government money to finance the "**Thrilla in Manila**" in 1975, a notoriously brutal encounter between Muhammad Ali and Joe Frazier often ranked as one of the greatest fights of twentieth-century boxing. Fought at the Araneta Coliseum in Quezon City, Ali won in the 15th and final round. The beneficent Marcos even stumped up the cash for the fight's multimillion-dollar purse.

Filipinos have never made it in the high-profile heavyweight game, but in the lighter divisions they've excelled. In recent years, one name stands out in particular: **Manny "the Pacman" Pacquiao** (b.1978), the poor boy from Mindanao who became world super featherweight champion, made a movie, made millions, and was the first boxer in history to win ten world titles in eight different weight divisions (he's current super welterweight champ). In probably his most famous bout, he defeated Oscar De La Hoya in Las Vegas in 2008, in what was dubbed the "Dream Match". In 2010 Pacquiao was elected to the House of Representatives, representing the province of Sarangani, fuelling rumours about his **political ambition**; it's conceivable that he could stand for higher office once he retires from boxing.

Aquino's Liberal Party had already chosen a candidate for the presidency, Manuel "Mar" Roxas (grandson of the first president), and the former leader's son had until then not been expected to run. Driven by nostalgia as much as politics, support for Benigno Aquino grew so fierce that Roxas withdrew from the race. Aquino's rival in the election was none other than ex-president Joseph Estrada. After a keenly fought campaign Aquino won with 42.08 percent of the vote to Estrada's 26.25 percent.

Benigno Aquino, respected for his family connections and obsessed over in the tabloids for his love life, was a teetaller and self-styled fighter of corruption. He abolished lunchtime closing in government offices, and his "no *wang-wang*" policy cut the use of sirens by official vehicles to get through traffic. He made some progress in Mindanao – generally peaceful since 2010 – and signed a **peace deal** with the MILF in 2014, promising a new Muslim autonomous entity called **Bangsamoro** to replace the Autonomous Region of Muslim Mindanao.

Aquino was heavily criticized for his administration's slow reaction to November 2013's Typhoon Haiyan (known as **Yolanda** in the Philippines), which particularly devastated the Visayas, killing at least 6268 people. He also took a lot of flak for the January 2015 **Mamasapano massacre**, when an operation to capture two jihadist bomb-makers in Mindanao was successful but cost the lives of 44 police officers; in the aftermath, Congress halted passage of the Bangsamoro autonomy bill.

Aquino's opponents accused him of laziness, and coined the term **noynoying** to describe his supposed indolence. One big success he had was to push through a 2012 **Reproductive Health Act** in the teeth of strong clerical opposition, guaranteeing free access to contraception for everybody.

Rodrigo Duterte

Having served six years, Aquino was ineligible to run in the 2016 election, which was won for the PDP–Laban by Davao's outspoken and controversial mayor, **Rodrigo**

2001	2005	2009	2010
EDSA II: Estrada is replaced by his vice president, Gloria Macapagal-Arroyo	The influential cardinal Jaime Sin dies	Maguindanao massacre; 57 people killed in Mindanao	Benigno "Noynoy" Aquino becomes president; Imelda Marcos is elected to Congress

Duterte (see box p.426), running on a law-and-order ticket. Duterte's vice-presidential running mate, however, was defeated by the Liberal Party's **Leni Robredo** – unsurprisingly, he and Dutetrte do not always see eye to eye.

The first Filipino president to hail from Mindanao, Duterte took office promising to transform the Philippines into a **federal country**, in which Bangsamoro would gain its promised autonomy. As he did in Davao, Duterte has instituted a policy of **killing suspected drug dealers** extrajudicially, which has met with condemnation from human rights groups, but has much support domestically. In **foreign policy**, Duterte distanced himself from the US (in typical style, he called US president Barrack Obama a "son of a whore", although he seems to more comfortable with Obama's successor, Donald Trump), but has moved closer to China and Russia. In particular, he has backed off from territorial disputes with China over islands in the South China Sea.

Duterte has also been conciliatory over Muslim autonomy in **Mindanao**, promising federal statehood for Bangsamoro, and creation of the Bangsamoro Autonomous Region in any event, even if his aim of federalism nationwide is not achieved. As a sign of his commitment, in November 2016, he expanded the Bangsamoro Transition Commission and made a speech reiterating his support for the peace process. However, after Islamist militants and government forces clashed in Marawi City in May 2017, Duterte introduced **martial law** on Mindanao for sixty days.

Despite criticism from human rights organizations and notwithstanding his willingness to court controversy and to ignore convention, Duterte remains extremely popular. *Shabu* (methamphetamine) addiction was undoubtedly a serious problem in the Philippines, and the president's policy of extrajudicial killing has certainly reduced it, whatever the collateral damage and killings of the innocent that may have accompanied this strategy. His 2016 decision to allow Ferdinand Marcos's burial in Manila's Heroes' Cemetery shocked many, and appeared to suggest some endorsement of the former president's contempt for democracy. The February 2017 arrest of his staunchest critic, Liberal senator Leila de Lima, for supposed involvement in drug trafficking, also sounded alarm bells – Amnesty International called it "a blatant attempt ... to silence criticism." However, in other fields Duterte has been keen to expand democratic rights, and to tackle corruption. His July 2016 **Freedom of Information Order**, for example, has increased government transparency, guaranteeing citizens the right to examine all official transactions except for those affecting national security. In typical Duterte style, he has threatened to throw corrupt officials out of helicopters.

Whether the president can continue to enjoy popular support probably depends on whether he can do anything to tackle **poverty**, and also possibly on how successful his policy of **federalism** will turn out to be. Yet, for the moment, Duterte looks well entrenched, and – unperturbed by strong opposition from liberals – the majority of Filipinos are happy to endorse his rule.

2012	2012	2013	2016
Peace plan signed with the Muslim rebel Moro Islamic Liberation Front	Congress votes for state-funded contraception	Typhoon Yolanda devastates the central part of the country, killing over six thousand	Rodrigo Duterte elected sixteenth president of the Philippines

Religious beliefs

Religious belief – among Muslims as well as Christians – is genuine and deeply held all over the Philippines. Though the nation remains predominantly Roman Catholic, parts of Mindanao are one hundred percent Islamic, and even traditional Catholic communities have been shaken up by new Catholic movements such as El Shaddai. Perhaps most surprising has been the success of Protestant churches such as Iglesia ni Cristo, which has branches all over the archipelago.

Catholicism

The Philippines is one of only two **predominantly Catholic** nations in Asia (the other being East Timor) – more than eighty percent of the population is Roman Catholic, with around ten percent Protestant. In addition to the Christian majority, there is a Muslim minority of between five and ten percent, concentrated on the southern islands of Mindanao and Sulu.

Yet to describe the Philippines as a Roman Catholic country is an over-simplification. Elements of tribal belief absorbed into Catholicism have resulted in a form of "**folk Catholicism**" that manifests itself in various homespun observances – a folk healer might use Catholic liturgy mixed with native rituals, or suited entrepreneurs might be seen scattering rice around their premises to ensure that their ventures are profitable. And the infamous **re-enactments of the Crucifixion** held near San Fernando, Pampanga, every year (see box, p.117) are frowned upon by the official Church. Even the **Chinese** minority has been influential in colouring Filipino Catholicism with the beliefs and practices of Buddhism, Confucianism and Taoism; many Catholic Filipinos believe in the balance of *yin* and *yang*, and that time is cyclical in nature.

The new Catholic movements

Today, the supremacy of the Catholic Church in the Philippines is being challenged by a variety of Christian sects. The largest of these is **El Shaddai**, established by lay preacher Mike Velarde on his weekly Bible-quoting radio show in the 1980s. Known to his followers as Brother Mike, Velarde has captured the imagination of poor Catholics, many of whom feel isolated from the mainstream Church. Velarde started preaching in colloquial and heavily accented Tagalog at huge open-air gatherings every weekend on Roxas Boulevard – the movement moved into a purpose-built P1 billion "House of Prayer" in Paranaque, Metro Manila, in 2009. Velarde tends to wear screamingly loud, made-to-measure suits and outrageous bow ties, but his message is straightforward: give to the Lord and He will return it to you tenfold. He now has over eight million followers, most of whom suffer from *sakit sa bulsa*, or "ailment of the pocket", but are nevertheless happy to pay ten percent of their income to become card-carrying members of the flock. Brother Mike's relationship with the mainstream Catholic Church is uneasy. His relationship with politicians is not. With so many followers hanging on his every word, Brother Mike is a potent political ally and few candidates for high office are willing to upset him. In the 1998 elections, Brother Mike backed Joseph Estrada, which was a significant factor in the former movie actor's initial success. The **Neocatechumenal Way**, a Catholic movement that started in Spain in the 1960s, also has a very large and expanding presence in the Philippines.

THE ASWANG WHO CAME TO DINNER

Heard the one about the pretty young housewife in a remote Visayan village who was possessed by the spirit of a jealous witch? Or the poor woman from a Manila shanty town who had taken to flying through the barangay, terrorizing her neighbours? These are stories from the pages of Manila's daily tabloid newspapers, reported as if they actually happened. Foreign visitors greet news of the latest barangay haunting with healthy cynicism, but when you are lying in your creaking nipa hut in the pitch dark of a moonless evening, it's not hard to see why so many Filipinos grow up embracing strange stories about creatures that inhabit the night. Even urbane professionals, when returning to the barangay of their childhood on holiday, can be heard muttering the incantation *tabi tabi lang-po* as they walk through paddy field or forest. Meaning "please let us pass safely", it's a request to the spirits and dwarves that might be lying in wait.

Most Filipino **spirits** are not the abstract souls of Western folklore who live in a netherworld; they are corporeal entities who live in trees or hang around the jeepney station, waiting to inflict unspeakable horrors on those who offend them. The most feared and widely talked about creature of Philippine folklore is the **aswang**; hundreds of cheesy films have been made about the havoc they wreak and hundreds of *aswang* sightings have been carried by the tabloid press. By day the *aswang* is a beautiful woman. The only way to identify her is by looking into her eyes at night, when they turn red. The *aswang* kills her victims as they sleep; threading her long tongue through the gaps in the floor or walls and inserting it into one of the body's orifices to suck out the internal organs.

Other creatures on the bogeyman list include the arboreal *tikbalang*, which has the head of a nag and the body of a man, and specializes in the abduction of virgins. Then there's the *duwende*, an elderly, grizzled dwarf who lurks in the forest and can predict the future, and the *engkanto*, who hides in trees and throws dust in the faces of passers-by, giving them permanently twisted lips.

Protestantism and the new religious movements

Some of the fastest-growing religious movements in the Philippines are actually Protestant. Eddie Villanueva, one of the candidates in the 2004 and 2010 presidential elections (he came last both times), established the charismatic **Jesus is Lord Church** in 1978, which he claims has some six million members, with branches in Asia, Europe and North America.

You'll see the distinctive fairy-tale spires of **Iglesia ni Cristo** churches throughout the Philippines, an independent, purely Filipino movement founded by Felix Manalo in 1914 (the movement is currently run by his grandson, Eduardo V. Manalo). Iglesia ni Cristo is explicitly anti-Catholic in its beliefs (the doctrine of the Trinity is rejected, for example) and is very influential during elections. Membership is estimated to be over three million but is probably much higher.

One of the churches most successful at expanding overseas is the **Pentecostal Missionary Church of Christ**, founded in 1973 and based in Marikina City. **The United Methodist Church** in the Philippines is an umbrella group for around one million Methodists in the country, while there are about twenty different **Baptist** groups in the islands, at least half a million **Mormons**, and half a million **Seventh-Day Adventists**.

Another well-known loose affiliation of groups, the **Rizalistas**, have only a tenuous connection with standard Christian doctrine. All regard José Rizal (see p.437) as the second son of God and a reincarnation of Christ, and some hold Mount Banahaw (see p.194) in Quezon province to be sacred, regularly attending pilgrimages to the mountain.

Islam

Islam spread north to the Philippines from Indonesia and Malaysia in the fourteenth century, and by the time the Spanish arrived it was firmly established on Mindanao and

Sulu, with outposts on Cebu and Luzon.

Islam remains a very dominant influence in the southern Philippines (25 percent of Mindanao's population is Muslim), and Muslims have added cultural character to the nation, with Filipino Christians expressing admiration over their warlike defiance of colonization. However, many Muslims feel they have become strangers in their own country, ignored by the Manila-centric government and marginalized by people resettled in Mindanao from Luzon; the **Autonomous Region in Muslim Mindanao** was established in 1990, the only region that has its own government (see boxes, p.405 & p.433).

While all Filipino Muslims follow the basic tenets of Islam, their religion has absorbed a number of indigenous elements, such as making offerings to spirits which are known as **diwatas**. Many Muslim tribes believe in a spirit known as **Bal-Bal**; with the body of a man and the wings of a bird, Bal-Bal is credited with the habit of eating out the livers of unburied bodies. In Jolo and Tawi-Tawi, Muslims use mediums to contact the dead, while many Muslim groups trade amulets, wearing them as necklaces to ward off ill fortune.

Muslim **women** are freer in the Philippines than in many Islamic countries, and have traditionally played a prominent role in everything from war to ceremonies. "The women of Jolo", wrote a Spanish infantryman in the eighteenth century, "prepare for combat in the same manner as their husbands and brothers and are more desperate and determined than the men. With her child suspended to her breast or slung across her back, the Moro woman enters the fight with the ferocity of a panther."

Filipino arts and culture

In *El Filibusterismo*, José Rizal worried that Filipinos would become "a people without a soul". It's a theme that has been much developed by travel writers ever since, from Pico Iyer's description of "lush sentimentality" and Filipina "obsession" with high-school romance and pageants in *Video Night in Kathmandu*, to Michael Palin observing that American interest in the country is "unashamedly obvious" in *Full Circle*. Yet there is a lot more to Philippine culture than cover bands, girlie bars and endless beauty pageants. Over the years Filipino writers, rappers, film-makers and artists have developed distinctive styles that incorporate elements of all the nation's disparate cultural elements.

Fine arts

Classical painting in the Philippines goes back to the Spanish period, but there are two acknowledged Filipino masters: **Juan Luna** (1859–99) and **Félix Hidalgo** (1855–1913). Both artists helped shine attention on the Philippines after submitting paintings to the 1884 Exposición General de Bellas Artes in Madrid. Luna's huge and drama-laced *Spolarium* (1884) is perhaps the most famous painting in the Philippines (on display at the National Art Gallery; see p.66), while his equally admired *The Blood Compact* graces the Malacañang Palace. Luna spent most of his career in Europe and died in Hong Kong, and he's best known today for painting literary and historical scenes. Hidalgo also spent much of his career in Europe and died in Spain, creating haunting works such *Las Virgenes Cristianas Expuestas al Populacho* ("The Christian Virgins Exposed to the Populace") and *Laguna Estigia* ("The Styx").

With the end of Spanish rule and a growing sense of independence in the twentieth century, Filipino painters were more content to develop their craft at home. **Fernando Amorsolo** (1892–1972) studied at the University of the Philippines' School of Fine Arts and gained prominence during the 1920s and 1930s for popularizing images of Philippine landscapes and demure rural Filipinas; his *Rice Planting* (1922) became one of the most popular images of the American period, and he became the first "National Artist" in 1972. Meanwhile, **Victorio Edades** (1895–1985) introduced Modernism to the Philippines with *The Builders* (1928), a style he'd developed in the US in direct contrast to Amorsolo. He went on to establish the UST College of Fine Arts in the 1930s, a bastion of avant-garde art.

World War II changed the way artists saw the world: Amorsolo's pastoral scenes gave way to the grimmer, urban images of **Vicente Manansala** (1910–82), as portrayed in works like *Jeepneys* (1951). Other notable late twentieth-century painters include **José T. Joya** (1931–95), the Filipino abstract artist, and **Fernando Zóbel de Ayala y Montojo** (1924–84), a Modernist painter who also developed his craft in the US.

The **contemporary art scene** in the Philippines is dynamic and eclectic, fed in part by exceptionally good art schools in the capital, with popular current forms and styles covering everything from installation art and video to realism and street art. One of the most highly acclaimed contemporary artists is **Ronald Ventura**, whose *Grayground Painting* fetched almost P47 million at auction in 2011, making it the most expensive Philippine painting ever sold. Pilipinas Street Plan (ⓦpilipinastreetplan.blogspot.com) and the Juju Bag (ⓦthejujubag.wordpress.com) are **art communities** that showcase street art, graffiti, posters, stickers and installations, while **Rocking Society through**

Alternative Education (Rock Ed; ⓦrockedphilippines.org) has produced some cutting-edge art through its work with schools and prisons. One of the hottest visual artists today is **Maya Muñoz**, whose work is often displayed in Manila's galleries.

Film

Although film-making has a distinguished history in the Philippines, and locally made movies (and their stars) remain popular, they remain a long way behind their Hollywood counterparts in terms of audience and income.

Early movies arrived in the Philippines in the late 1890s, but the first genuinely Filipino film is credited to **Jose Nepumuceno**, the "Father of Philippine Movies", who made a version of a popular play, *Dalagang Bukid* (Country Maiden), in 1919. The domestic film industry didn't really get going until the 1950s, when four big studios (Sampaguita, LVN, Premiere and Lebran) churned out hundreds of movies such as Gerardo de Leon's *Ifugao* (1954) and Manuel Conde's *Genghis Khan* (1952). Despite Gerardo de Leon's lauded adaptations of the Rizal novels *Noli Me Tángere* (1961) and *El Filibusterismo* (1962), the following decade was much poorer creatively and all four studios eventually closed.

Despite censorship during the Marcos years, **avant-garde** movie-making flourished in the 1970s, with Lino Brocka's *The Claws of Light* (1975) considered by many critics to be the greatest Philippine film ever made, and Kidlat Tahimik's *Mababangong Bangungot* (Perfumed Nightmare) winning the International Critic's Prize at the Berlin Film Festival of 1977. Brocka's *This Is My Country*, which tackles the issue of labour union control under Marcos, was entered into the 1984 Cannes Film Festival.

The late 1980s and 1990s is regarded as a weaker period, but since the turn of the century **independent Filipino movies** have been undergoing something of a renaissance, in part thanks to digital technology. In 2003 Mark Meily scored a big hit with the comedy *Crying Ladies*, about three Filipinas working as professional mourners in Manila's Chinatown, while *Ang Pagdadalaga ni Maximo Oliveros* (The Blossoming of Maximo Oliveros; 2005) by Auraeus Solito and *Kubrador* (The Bet Collector; 2006) by Jeffrey Jeturian were internationally acclaimed. Filipinos have also excelled in other formats: Carlo Ledesma won best short film at the Cannes Film Festival in 2007 for *The Haircut*. In 2008, Brillante Mendoza's *Serbis* (Service) became the first full-length Filipino film to compete at Cannes since 1984; the account of a day in the life of a family running a porno film theatre in Angeles City is bawdy and brutally realistic. Mendoza's *Kinatay* (Butchered) competed at Cannes the following year.

Lavish historical drama *El Presidente* (2012), another film directed by Mark Meily, is the nation's most expensive movie to date, starring several acting heavyweights and exploring the life of Emilio Aguinaldo. The **Metro Manila Film Festival** showcases the latest Filipino films over the Christmas period every year, not all of them arthouse material. To get a feel for what Filipinos like to watch today – from kitsch and campy romantic comedies to fantasy romps – see *Enteng Ng Ina Mo* (Your Monther Enteng; 2011), a fantasy parody; *Sisterakas* (2012), a contemporary slapstick comedy starring vet Vice Ganda (the name is a play on Sister Act); and blockbuster *The Unkabogable: Praybeyt Benjamin* (Private Benjamin; 2011), an action comedy also starring Ganda as a reluctant soldier – the name is a loose reference to the 1980 Goldie Hawn movie, but the slapstick and sexual themes are very different.

Music

Any Friday night in Manila (and all over Asia), countless Filipino **showbands** can be seen in countless hotel lobbies performing accomplished cover versions of Western classics. While there's no doubt that when Filipinos mimic they do it exceedingly well, **indigenous music** does survive. Tagalog pop and rap artists and to a lesser extent rock groups have all been making a comeback in recent years, part of a slow but discernible trend away from the adulation of solely American pop stars and celebrities. A useful website for general information about Filipino music is ⓦphilmusic.com.

Traditional tribal music

Folk songs and stories, handed down orally, are still sung at tribal gatherings and ceremonies among indigenous peoples. Among the ethnic and tribal groups of Mindanao and the Sulu archipelago there's a sophisticated musical genre called **kulintang**, in which the main instruments are bossed gongs similar to the Indonesian gamelan. *Kulintang* is commonly performed by small ensembles playing instruments that include the *kulintang* itself (a series of small gongs for the melody), the *agung* (large gongs for the lower tones) and the *gandingan* (four large vertical gongs used as a secondary melodic instrument). *Kulintang* music serves as a means of entertainment and a demonstration of hospitality; it's used at weddings, festivals, coronations, to entertain visiting dignitaries and to honour those heading off on or coming back from a pilgrimage. It is also used to accompany healing ceremonies and, up to the beginning of the twentieth century, was a form of communication, using goatskin drums to beat messages across the valleys.

The Manila Sound

The "**Manila Sound**" was the sound of the 1970s in the Philippines. Against a backdrop of student riots and martial law, some audiences found comfort with bell-bottom-wearing bands, like **The Hotdogs** and **The Boyfriends**, who set romantic novelty lyrics to catchy melodic hooks. Some sneered at the frivolity of it all, but the Manila Sound was as big as disco. Today it's effectively extinct, but it gave rise to a number of major stars who evolved and are still going strong. The most well known is indefatigable diva **Sharon Cuneta**, who is known throughout the country by the modest moniker "The Megastar". She first appeared in the Philippine pop charts at the age of 12 singing the disco tune *Mr. D.J.* and has since released numerous albums including one of duets with other apparently ageless Filipina singers such as Pops Fernandez (the "Concert Queen") and Sunshine Cruz.

The folkies

In the 1970s the only truly original artists performing in Manila were folksy beatniks such as singer-songwriters **Joey Ayala** and **Freddie Aguilar**. In the 1980s, Aguilar wrote a popular ballad called **Anak** and found himself a fan in First Lady Imelda Marcos who, ever eager to bathe herself in the reflected glory of Manila's celebs, invited him to Malacañang Palace so they could sing the song together at banquets. Aguilar was appalled by the excesses he saw inside the palace and never went back.

As the anti-Marcos movement grew, so did the popularity of *Anak*. Aguilar, by now something of a talisman for left-wing groups opposing martial law, took the opportunity to become even more political, recording a heartfelt version of *Bayan Ko* (My Country), a patriotic anthem that now took on extraordinary political significance.

One of the most well-known groups of the new generation was **APO Hiking Society**, a foursome from Ateneo University whose anthem *Handog ng Pilipino sa Mundo* (A New And Better Way) has been covered by numerous Filipino artists. Its lyrics are carved on the wall of Manila's Our Lady of EDSA Shrine, traditionally a focal point of protests and revolutions.

Tribal-pop and OPM (Original Pilipino Music)

In the 1990s – largely as a reaction to the decline of the protest movement and the creeping Americanization of Filipino music – a roots movement emerged that took the traditional rhythms and chants of tribal music such as *kulintang* and merged them with contemporary instruments and production techniques. One of the chief exponents of so-called tribal-pop (the term **Original Pilipino Music** or Original Pinoy Music was coined in the late 1980s) was **Grace Nono**. She never quite cracked the big time, but cleared the path for others, including **Pinikpikan**, the most successful tribal-pop band in the country (the band reformed as **Kalayo** in 2007). Over the last few years the term OPM has become diluted, and now encompasses the young stars of the twenty-first century, most of whom have modelled themselves on Celine Dion and Michael Bublé, not the revolutionary Manila singers of the Marcos years. This new generation includes **Kyla**, **Erik Santos**, **Sarah Geronimo** and **Christian Bautista**.

The mainstream: Filipino pop, rock and alternative music

Any consideration of mainstream popular **rock music** in the Philippines won't get off the ground without reference to the irreverent **Eraserheads**. After more than a decade at the top they disbanded in 2003 but remain the most popular Filipino band ever. Many current popular groups have been inspired by their infectious blend of irony and irresistibly melodic pop, including **Rivermaya**, still producing platinum-selling albums at a rate of knots, and **Parokya ni Edgar**, one of the few bands that have come close to equalling the Eraserheads; their 1996 debut album, *Khangkhungkherrnitz*, features a tribute to the nation's favourite food: instant noodles. Today Filipino pop, rock and alternative music is flourishing, with bands such as **6cyclemind**, **Kamikazee**, **Chicosci**, **Sponge Cola** and **Sandwich**.

But despite the proliferation of progressive acts, the popular Philippine music scene has become dominated in recent years by comely solo performers singing plaintive **ballads** in the style of Whitney Houston or Mariah Carey. In the hierarchy of balladeers, Regine Velasquez and Martin Nievera are at the top. **Regine Velasquez**'s story is the quintessential Tagalog movie script: a beautiful girl from the sticks – she grew up in Leyte in the 1970s – wins a singing contest in 1989 (with a performance of *You'll Never Walk Alone* in Hong Kong) and heads off to Manila. Her repertoire is typical of the Filipina diva canon, comprising misty-eyed love songs such as *Could It Be?*, *What You Are to Me* and *Long For Him*. Velasquez follows in the tradition of Sharon Cuneta, Pops Fernandez and Kuh Ledesma, who at one time or another have all been dubbed the country's "concert queen" by the media. **Martin Nievera** puts his success – he's been recording since 1982 – down to the fact that Filipinos love a good drama. His songs are indeed melodramatic, his album *Forever, Forever* being an open book about his high-profile marital break-up with singer-actress Pops Fernandez.

Filipino hip-hop

Filipino hip-hop or **Pinoy rap** emerged in the 1980s, with tracks by **Dyords Javier** and **Vincent Dafalong**. The genre hit the mainstream with **Francis Magalona**'s debut album, *Yo!* in 1990, which included the nationalistic hit *Mga Kababayan* ("My Countrymen"), a call to political arms that bore the hallmarks of Freddie Aguilar. In 1994, Death Threat released the first Filipino gangsta rap album *Gusto Kong Bumaet* ("I Want to be Good"). Since 2004 the **Philippine Hip-Hop Music Awards** has been held annually in Metro Manila and the genre remains incredibly popular throughout the country; current stars include **Gloc-9** (former member of Death Threat), **Abra** and **Pikaso**. The most successful Filipino-American rapper is the Black Eyed Peas' **apl.de.ap**, who was born in Angeles City in 1974 and moved to Los Angeles at the age of 14.

DISCOGRAPHY

FOLK

Freddie Aguilar *Collection* (1985). A mixture of studio and live recordings featuring most of the folk hero's greatest songs, including *Trabaho* and a cover version of Joey Ayala's *Mindanao*. *Pinoy* is a dark, but melodic exposition of the average Filipino's lot, while the lyrical *Magdalena* was based on conversations Aguilar had with Manila prostitutes, all of whom desperately wanted to escape the life. There's no *Anak*, but there are plenty of other Freddie Aguilar collections that feature it.

TRIBAL-POP

Cynthia Alexander *Insomnia and Other Lullabyes* (1996). Introspective but affecting collection of progressive/tribal ballads from Joey Ayala's talented little sister. The navel-gazing becomes wearisome at times, but there are also some memorable moments, including *No Umbrella*, a pleading love song with sonorous strings and plaintive fretless bass.

Barbie's Cradle *Music from the Buffet Table* (1999). Their semi-acoustic sound dominated by the frail but evocative voice of Barbie Almalbis, Barbie's Cradle injected a new note of realism into OPM songwriting, with lyrics – in both English and Tagalog – that spoke not of love and happiness, but of vulnerability and dysfunction. Highlights include *Money for Food*, a musical poem about poverty, and *It's Dark and I Am Lonely*, a personal and frank assessment of modern life for young people.

Grace Nono *Isang Buhay* (1997). Quintessential Nono, this is an album of sometimes strident but hypnotic tribal rhythms and original tribal songs blended with additional lyrics drawing attention to the plight of the tribes, the environment and the avarice of the country's rulers. *Isang Buhay* means one house; the title track is Nono's plea for unity.

Pinikpikan *Kaamulan* (2003). Psychedelia meets tribal tradition on this, Pinikpikan's third album, released in 2003. The band's influences are eclectic and worn on the sleeve, from the Hindu overtones on *Child* to the flute solos – inspired by the wooden-flute music of the Manobo tribe of Mindanao – on *Butanding*, a haunting stream-of-consciousness piece about the endangered whale shark.

ROCK, POP AND HIP-HOP

6cyclemind *Project 6 Cyclemind* (2009). The last album by the popular alt-rockers before the controversial departure of lead singer Ney Dimaculangan is primarily a collection of thoughtful tunes and ballads, though the band still gets to rock out on tracks such as *Mahiwagang Pag-ibig*.

Abra *Abra* (2012). First solo album from the gifted rapper of Pinoy hip-hop group, Lyrically Deranged Poets, his trademark lyrical style and humorous raps in full effect – the smooth R&B-inspired hit *Gayuma* (featuring the son of Freddie Aguilar) has over 27 million hits on YouTube, a record in the Philippines.

Bamboo *Tomorrow Becomes Yesterday* (2008). Bamboo's fourth, final and best album: intelligent and thoughtful indie rock in Tagalog and English, with everything from acoustic ballads to hard rock anthems.

Eraserheads *Ultraelectromagneticpop* (1993). Thoroughly enjoyable debut album featuring spirited Beatles-inspired pop, novelty pieces that poke fun at everyone and everything, and the brilliant *Pare Ko* ("My Friend"), which

had the establishment in a spin because it contained a couple of swear words and gay references. The band matured after this and even got better – their second album, *Circus*, includes the track *Butterscotch* which takes a not so gentle dig at the Catholic Church ("Father Markus said to me/Just confess and you'll be free/Sit yer down upon me lap/And tell me all yer sins") – but *Ultraelectromagneticpop* will always be special because it blazed a trail.

Gloc-9 *Liham at Lihim* (2013). The seventh album ("Letter and Secret") from current godfather of Tagalog rap sees speed-rapper Gloc-9 collaborating with Rico Blanco and even veteran chanteuse Regine Velasquez.

Kamikazee *Romantico* (2012). If you want to get a taste of current Tagalog indie rock this is for you, with the catchy riffs and jangling guitars on the Manila punk band's fourth album reminiscent of Green Day.

Kitchie Nadal *Kitchie Nadal* (2004). The debut album of the soulful Filipino singer-songwriter Nadal, featuring the award-winning *Wag na Wag Mong Sasabihin*, an indie anthem worthy of Coldplay.

Martin Nievera *Live with the Philippine Philharmonic Orchestra* (2000). Two-disc set recorded in Manila that captures some of the energy of Nievera live, when he's a much greater force than on many of his overly sentimental studio recordings. A master of patter and performance, Nievera sings in English, in Tagalog, on his own, and with guests including the popular Filipina singing sisters Dessa and Cris Villonco – and his dad, Bert. The highlight is a mammoth montage of Broadway hits from *Carousel*, *West Side Story* and *Evita*, the nadir a self-indulgent spoken preamble to one of his signature songs, *Before You Say Goodbye*.

Rivermaya *It's Not Easy Being Green* (1999). Rivermaya's audience is unashamedly middle of the road and so is their music, an amiable blend of guitar-driven pop and laidback love songs for twenty-somethings. This album is typical, suffused with British influences ranging from the Beatles to Belle and Sebastian. The highpoint, however, is Pure Pinoy, the ironic ballad *Grounded ang Girlfriend Ko* ("My Girlfriend's Grounded Me"), which owes more to Eraserheads than Britpop.

Sponge Cola *Ultrablessed* (2014). Fifth studio album of the award-winning Pinoy rock band and the much-awaited follow up to 2011's bestselling *Araw Oras Tagpuan*. It includes the single *Anting-Anting*, featuring Gloc-9, and plenty of the band's trademark smooth pop-rock.

Regine Velasquez *Unsolo* (2000). This was the album that marked the beginning of Velasquez's attempts to become an international star, or at least a pan-Asian one, raising her profile with duets featuring the likes of David Hasselhoff – for a syrupy rendition of *More Than Words Can Say* – and Jacky Cheung. There's only one song in Tagalog.

Books

The Philippines hasn't been as well documented in fiction or non-fiction as many of its Asian neighbours. There are, however, a number of good investigative accounts of two subjects – American involvement in the Philippines and the excesses of the Marcoses. Some of the books reviewed below are published in the Philippines, and are unlikely to be on sale in bookshops outside the country; you should have more luck online.

HISTORY AND POLITICS

Alan Berlow *Dead Season: A Story of Murder and Revenge*. This brilliantly atmospheric work is the story of three murders that took place in the 1970s on Negros, against the backdrop of communist guerrilla activity and appeals for land reform. It's impossible to read without feeling intense despair for a country where humble, peaceful people have often become pawns in a game of power and money played out around them. Cory Aquino comes out of it badly – the Church asked her to investigate the murders but she refused, fearful that this might entail treading on too many toes.

Raymond Bonner *Waltzing with a Dictator*. Former *New York Times* correspondent Bonner reports on the complex twenty-year US relationship with the Marcos regime and how Washington kept Marcos in power long after his sell-by date: US bases in the country needed a patron and Marcos was the right man. Marcos cleverly played up the threat of a communist insurgency in the Philippines, making it seem to Washington that he was their only hope of stability.

Luis Francia *History of the Philippines: From Indios Bravos to Filipinos*. A welcome history of the archipelago offering the perfect introduction to the country and plenty of new insights about the Spanish and American periods in particular.

★**James Hamilton-Paterson** *America's Boy: The Rise and Fall of Ferdinand Marcos and Other Misadventures of US Colonialism in the Philippines*. A controversial narrative history of the US-supported dictatorship that came to define the Philippines. The author makes the very plausible claim that the Marcoses were merely the latest in a long line of corrupt Filipino leaders in a country which had historically been ruled by oligarchies, and gathers first-hand information from senators, cronies, rivals and Marcos family members, including Imelda.

★**James D. Hornfischer** *The Last Stand of the Tin Can Sailors*. Gripping and in parts harrowing narrative of the battle between the Americans and Japanese off Samar in October 1944, and the larger battle of Leyte Gulf that followed, the beginning of the American liberation of the Philippines. Hornfischer also intelligently provides a Japanese perspective to the battle. Well written and easy to read.

★**Stanley Karnow** *In Our Image: America's Empire in the Philippines*. This Pulitzer Prize-winning effort is really a book about America, not about the Philippines. The Philippines is the landscape, but the story is of America going abroad for the first time in its history at the turn of the last century. The book examines how the US sought to remake the Philippines as a clone of itself, an experiment marked from the outset by blundering, ignorance and mutual misunderstanding.

Eric Morris *Corregidor*. Intimate account of the defence of the island fortress, based on interviews with more than forty Filipinos and Americans who battled hunger, dysentery and malaria in the run-up to the critical battle with Japanese forces. As the book explains, the poorly equipped Allied troops, abandoned by General MacArthur and almost forgotten by military strategists in Washington, had little chance of winning, though against all the odds Corregidor held out for six months.

Ambeth Ocampo *Rizal without the Overcoat*. This collection of essays and musings (originally a column in the *Philippine Daily Globe*) offers entertaining and easily digested insights into the great Filipino hero. It's become almost as common in schools as Rizal's *Noli* (see p.457).

Beth Day Romulo *Inside the Palace: The Rise and Fall of Ferdinand and Imelda Marcos*. Beth Day Romulo, wife of Ferdinand Marcos's foreign minister Carlos Romulo, was among those who enjoyed the privileges of being a Malacañang insider, something she feels the need to excuse and justify on almost every page. Her book borders on being a Marcos hagiography – she clearly didn't want to upset her old friend Imelda too much – and is gossipy more than investigative, but does nevertheless offer some insight into Imelda's lavish and frivolous lifestyle, and the disintegration of the regime.

William Henry Scott *Barangay: Sixteenth-Century Philippine Culture and Society*. This lucid account of life in the Philippines during the century the Spanish arrived is the best there is of the period. The author's love for the Philippines and his deep knowledge of its customs are reflected in this scholarly but accessible investigation into Hispanic-era society, the country's elite, its tribes and their customs – everything from that most quotidian of rituals, taking a bath, to the once common practice of penis piercing.

Hampton Sides *Ghost Soldiers: The Epic Account of World War II's Greatest Rescue Mission*. Recounts the astonishing and mostly forgotten story of the combined US Ranger and Filipino guerrilla force that managed to free hundreds of POWs from behind Japanese lines in 1944.

CULTURE AND SOCIETY

Sheila Coronel (ed) *Pork and Other Perks*. Comprising nine case studies by some of the country's foremost investigative journalists, this pioneering work uncovers the many forms corruption takes in the Philippines and points fingers at those responsible. The book is concerned mainly with what happens to "pork", the budget allocated annually to every senator and congressman. It's thought that much of the money goes towards hiring corrupt contractors who use below-par materials on infrastructure projects, with the politicians themselves benefiting from the discrepancy between the official and actual cost of the projects concerned.

★**James Hamilton-Paterson** *Playing With Water: Passion and Solitude on a Philippine Island*. "No money, no honey," says one of the characters in Hamilton-Paterson's lyrical account of several seasons spent among the impoverished fishermen of Marinduque. This is a rich and original book, which by turns warms you and disturbs you. The author's love of the Philippine landscape and the people – many of whom think he must be related to US actor George Hamilton – is stunningly rendered. The diving accounts will stay with you forever, as will the episode in which H-P discovers he has worms.

★**F. Sionil José** *We Filipinos: Our Moral Malaise, Our Heroic Heritage*. Deeply cynical and incredibly patriotic in equal measure, this collection of essays from the nation's pre-eminent writer is required reading for anyone wanting to get under the skin of Philippine culture.

★**Manny Pacquiao** *Pacman: My Story of Hope, Resilience, and Never-Say-Never Determination*. Ghost-written? Certainly. Full of corny sentiment? Perhaps. But Pacquiao's story is so remarkable that it's hard to put this "autobiography" down, charting the tenacious fighter's rise from the backstreets of Mindanao to boxing champion of the world and multimillionaire. Inspirational stuff.

Earl K. Wilkinson *The Philippines: Damaged Culture?* Written by a long-time expat, this book explores the underlying reasons for the many maladies affecting the country. *Damaged Culture* is never pontificating or presumptuous, but it is sometimes shocking in its revelations of corruption in high places, highlighting a number of travesties of justice which the author campaigned to put right. He also offers solutions, arguing that the nation's entrenched elite could start the recovery ball rolling by abandoning its traditional antipathy towards free-market competition.

ARCHITECTURE

Pedro Galende *San Agustin*. An evocative tribute to the first Spanish stone church to be built in the Philippines, San Agustin in Intramuros. The first part of the book is a detailed account of the church's history, while the second is a walking tour, illustrated with photographs, through the church and the neighbouring monastery.

Pedro Galende & Rene Javelana *Great Churches of the Philippines*. Coffee-table book full of beautiful colour photographs of most of the country's notable Spanish-era churches. The accompanying text explains the evolution of the unique "earthquake Baroque" style developed to protect stone structures against earthquakes. The style typifies Philippine churches and provides a reminder that many of these stunning buildings are in a perilous state, with little money available to guarantee their upkeep and survival.

THE ENVIRONMENT

Robin Broad et al. *Plundering Paradise: The Struggle for the Environment in the Philippines*. Disturbing but often inspiring account of how livelihoods and habitats are disappearing throughout the Philippines as big business harvests everything from fish to trees, turned into packaging for multinational companies and chopsticks for restaurants. The authors travelled through the Philippines, recording the experiences of people who are fighting back by working alongside NGOs and environmental groups to police the environment and report illegal logging, poaching and fishing, much of which is allowed to take place through the bribing of local officials.

Gutsy Tuason and Eduardo Cu *Anilao*. Winner of the Palme d'Or at the World Festival of Underwater Images in Antibes, France, this hard-to-get but stunning coffee-table collection of colour photographs were all taken around Anilao, Batangas, one of the country's most popular diving areas. What's remarkable about the book is the way it makes you take notice of the small marine life many divers ignore; the images of bobbit worms, ghost pipefish and sea fans are terrific.

FOOD

Reynaldo Alejandro et al. *The Food of the Philippines*. Proof that there's so much more to Filipino cuisine than adobo and rice. The recipes range from classics such as chilli crab simmered in coconut milk to a fail-safe method for that

trickiest of desserts, *leche* flan. Every recipe details how to find the right ingredients and what to use as a substitute if you can't. There's also a revealing history of Filipino food.
Glenda Rosales-Barretto *Flavors of the Philippines*. Rosales-Barretto is chief executive officer of the popular *Via Mare* restaurant chain in Manila, and what she doesn't

know about Filipino food isn't worth knowing. This lavishly illustrated hardback highlights recipes region by region. There's a classic Bicol Express, with lots of spices and fish paste, but many of the recipes here are far from standard – instead, modern variations feature, such as fresh vegetarian pancake rolls with peanut sauce and roast chicken with passionfruit.

FICTION

Cecilia Manguerra Brainard *When the Rainbow Goddess Wept*. The moving story of Yvonne Macaraig, a young Filipina during the Japanese invasion of the Philippines in World War II; the myths and legends of Philippine folklore sustain her despite the carnage all around. Though some of Brainard's character development and language is uneven, it's this connection with the rural, pre-Hispanic Philippines that makes the book so memorable. Brainard was born in Cebu but emigrated to the US in 1968.

Jessica Hagedorn (ed) *Manila Noir*. Hagedorn's latest project forms part of New York-based Akashic Books' *Noir* series, a collection of compelling short stories with Manila as a focus for Gothic, supernatural and crime genres. The plots might be fictional but up-and-coming writers such as Gina Apostol and Budjette Tan portray the city with uncanny realism.

F. Sionil José *Dusk*. This is the fifth book in the author's acclaimed saga of the landowning Rosales family at the end of the nineteenth century. It wouldn't be a quintessential Filipino novel if it didn't touch on the themes of poverty, corruption, tyranny and love; all are on display here, presented through the tale of one man, a common peasant, and his search for contentment. *Dusk* has been published in the US in paperback, though you can always buy it from

José's bookshop, Solidaridad, in Manila (see p.97).
★**F. Sionil José** *Ermita*. Eminently readable novella that atmospherically evokes the Philippines from World War II until the 1960s and stands as a potent allegory of the nation's ills. The Ermita of the title, apart from being the *mise en scène*, is also a girl, the unwanted child of a rich Filipina raped in her own home by a drunken Japanese soldier. The story follows young Ermita, abandoned in an orphanage, as she tries to trace her mother and then sets about exacting revenge on those she feels have wronged her.
★**José Rizal** *Noli Me Tángere*. Published in 1886 (and banned by the Spanish), this is a passionate exposure of the double standards and the rank injustice of colonial rule; it's still required reading for every Filipino schoolchild. It tells the story of Crisostomo Ibarra's love for the beautiful Maria Clara, infusing it with tragedy and significance of almost Shakespearean proportions. Rizal's second novel *El Filibusterismo* takes up Ibarra's story thirteen years later, but the conclusion is just as bitter.
Miguel Syjuco *Ilustrado*. Winner of the 2008 Man Asian Literary Prize, this gripping saga takes over 150 years of Philippine history, as well as offering a scathing indictment of corruption and inequity among the Filipino ruling classes. Syjuco is a Filipino writer now based in Montreal.

THE PHILIPPINES IN FOREIGN LITERATURE

William Boyd *The Blue Afternoon*. Boyd has never been to the Philippines, but spent hours researching the country from England. In flashbacks, the novel moves from 1930s Hollywood to the exotic, violent world of the Philippines in 1902, recounting a tale of medicine, the murder of American soldiers and the creation of a magical flying machine.

Alex Garland *The Tesseract*. Alex Garland loves the Philippines, so it's hardly surprising that the follow-up to *The Beach* is set there. Garland may get most of his Tagalog wrong, but his prose captures perfectly the marginal existence of his characters. The story involves a foreigner abroad, a villainous tycoon called Don Pepe, some urchins and a beautiful girl. The characters may be clichéd, but Garland's plot is so intriguing that it's impossible not to be swept along by the baleful atmosphere the book creates.

Jessica Hagedorn *Dogeaters*. Filipino-American Jessica Hagedorn assembles a cast of diverse and dubious characters that comes as close to encapsulating the mania of life in Manila as any writer has ever come. Urchins, pimps, seedy tycoons and corpulent politicos are brought

together in a brutal but beautiful narrative that serves as a jolting reminder of all the country's frailties and woes.
★**James Hamilton-Paterson** *Ghosts of Manila*. Hamilton-Paterson's excoriating novel is haunting, powerful and for the most part alarmingly accurate. Much of it is taken from real life: the extrajudicial "salvagings" (a local word for liquidation) of suspected criminals, the corruption and the abhorrent saga of Imelda Marcos's infamous film centre. From the despair and detritus, the author conjures up a lucid story that is thriller, morality play and documentary in one.
Timothy Mo *Brownout on Breadfruit Boulevard*. Mo wrote this blunt satire of cultural and imperial domination in 1995 when he'd fallen out with his publisher (the book is still self-published), and his career subsequently fell off a cliff; the novel starts with a now infamous sex scene involving excrement. This story is much better than its sales (and the first page) suggested, though, set in the fictional town of Gobernador de Leon and following a motley bunch of locals and foreigners attending a conference.

Language

English is widely spoken in the Philippines, a legacy of the country's time under US rule. Most everyday transactions – checking into a hotel, ordering a meal, buying a ferry ticket – can be carried out in English, and most people working in tourism speak it reasonably well. Even off the beaten track, many Filipinos understand enough to help with basics such as accommodation and directions. However, it's worth learning a few words of Tagalog, the official language of the islands. You will be a source of amusement if you try, even though the response will most likely come in English. Tagalog has assimilated many Spanish words, such as *mesa* (table) and *cuarto* (bedroom, written *kuwarto* in Tagalog), though few Filipinos can speak Spanish today. Cebuano (or "Visayan") spoken in the south of the archipelago uses even more Spanish – including all the numbers. This section focuses on Tagalog; Cebuano is covered in the Visayas chapter (see box, p.315).

Tagalog

Tagalog, also known as Filipino or Pilipino, is spoken as a first language by seventeen million people, mostly on Luzon, and was made the official language in 1947. The structure of Tagalog is simple, though the **word order** is different from English; as an example, take *kumain ng mangga ang bata*, which literally translates as "ate a mango the child". Another key difference between the two languages is the lack of the verb "to be" in Tagalog, which means that a simple sentence such as "the woman is kind" is rendered *mabait ang babae*, literally "kind the woman". For **plurals**, the word *mga* is used – hence *bahay/mga bahay* for house/houses – although in many cases Filipinos simply state the actual number of objects or use *marami* (several) before the noun.

Consonants and vowels

Tagalog sounds staccato to the foreign ear, with clipped vowels and **consonants**. The p, t and k sounds are never aspirated and sound a little gentler than in English. The g is always hard, as in **g**et. The letter **c** seldom crops up in Tagalog and where it does – in names such as Boracay and Bulacan, for example – it's pronounced like *k*. The hardest sound to master for most beginners is the **ng** sound as in the English word "si**nging**"

TAGLISH: FILIPINO ENGLISH

Educated Filipinos move seamlessly between English and Tagalog, often in the space of the same sentence, and many English words have been adopted by Filipinos, giving rise to a small canon of patois known affectionately as **Taglish**. Many of these peculiarities stem from the habit of translating something literally from Tagalog, resulting in Filipinos "closing" or "opening" the light, or "getting down" from a taxi. Among those who don't speak English so well, an inability to pronounce the f-sound is common, simply because it doesn't exist in any Philippine tongue. Filipinos are well aware of this trait and often make self-deprecating jokes about it, referring to forks as porks and vice versa. Other ear-catching Taglish phrases include "I'll be the one to" – as in "I'll be the one to buy lunch" instead of "I'll buy lunch" – and "for a while", meaning "wait a moment" or "hang on".

(with the *g* gently nasalized, not hard); in Tagalog this sound can occur at the beginning of a word, eg in **ng***ayon* (now). The **mg** combination in words such as *mga* looks tricky but is in fact straightforward to pronounce, as *mang*.

As for **vowels and diphthongs** (vowel combinations):

a is pronounced as in apple	iw is a sound that simply doesn't exist in English; it's close to the *ieu* sound in "lieu", but with greater separation between the vowels (almost as in "lee-you")
e as in mess	
i as in ditto, though a little more elongated than in English	
o as in bore	oy as in noise
u as in put	uw as in quarter
ay as in buy	uy produced making the sound oo and continuing it to the i sound in "ditto".
aw in mount	

Vowels that fall consecutively in a word are always pronounced individually, as is every syllable, adding to the choppy nature of the language; for example, *tao* meaning person or people is pronounced "ta-o", while *oo* for yes is pronounced "o-o" (with each vowel closer to the *o* in "show" than in "bore").

Stress
Most words are spoken as they are written, though working out which syllable to **stress** is tricky. In words of two syllables the first syllable tends to be stressed, while in words of three or more syllables the stress is almost always on the final or penultimate syllable. In the vocabulary lists that follow, stressed syllables are indicated in **bold** text except where the term in question is obviously an English loan word. Note that English loan words may be rendered a little differently in Tagalog, in line with the rules mentioned above; thus "bus" for instance has the vowel sound of the English word "put".

USEFUL WORDS AND PHRASES

GREETINGS AND CIVILITIES

hello/how are you?	kamusta	what's your name?	anong pangalan mo?
Fine, thanks	mabuti, salamat (*formal*) okay lang (*informal*)	my name is ...	ang pangalan ko ay ...
		do you speak English?	marunong ka bang mag-**Ingles**?
goodbye	bye		
good morning	magan**dang** umaga	I (don't) understand	(hindi) ko naiintindihan
good afternoon	magan**dang** hapon	could you repeat that?	paki-ulit?
good evening/good night	magan**dang** gabi	where are you from?	taga saan ka?
please ...	pa**ki** ...	I am from ...	taga ... ako
(before a request)		(most countries are rendered as in English)	
thank you	salamat	I don't know	ewan
excuse me (to say sorry)	ipagpau**man**hin mo **ak**	(used to avoid confrontation)	
excuse me (to get past)	makiki**raan** lang po/ pasensiya ka na	okay?/is that okay?	puwe**de**?/puwe**de ba**? (*informal*)
sorry	sorry	mate, buddy	pare

FORMAL LANGUAGE: THE USE OF "PO"

Tagalog has formal and informal **forms of address**, the formal usually reserved for people who are significantly older. The "po" suffix indicates respect and can be added to almost any word or phrase: *o-po* is a respectful "yes" and it's common to hear Filipinos say *sorry-po* for "sorry". Even the lowliest beggar is given esteem by language: the standard reply to beggars is *patawarin-po*, literally, "forgive me, sir". First names are fine for people of your own generation; for your elders, use Mr or Mrs (if you know a woman is married) before the surname. It's common to use *manong/manang* (uncle/aunt) and *kuya* (brother/sister) to address superiors informally, even if they are not blood relatives (eg *manong* Jun, *kuya* Beth).

COMMON TERMS

yes	oo
no	hindi
maybe	siguro
good/bad	magaling/masama
big/small	malaki/maliit
easy/difficult	madali/mahirap
open/closed	bukas/sarado
hot/cold	mainit/malamig
cheap/expensive	mura/mahal
a lot/a little	madami/konti
one more/another...	isa pa ...
beautiful	maganda
hungry	gutom
thirsty	nauuhaw
very ... (followed by adjective)	tunay ...
with/without ...	meron/wala ...
watch out!	ingat!
who?	sino?
what?	ano?
why?	bakit?
when?	kailan?
how?	paano?

GETTING AROUND

airport	airport
bus/train station	istasyon ng bus/tren
pier	pier
aeroplane	eroplano
ferry	barco (*for large vessels – "ferry" will also do*)
boat (outrigger)	bangka
taxi	taxi
bicycle	bisikleta
car	kotse
where do I/we catch the ...to ... ?	saan puwedeng kumuha ng ... papuntang ...?
when does the ... for ... leave?	kailan aalis ang ... papuntang ...?
when does the next ... leave?	anong oras ho aalis ang ...?
ticket	tiket
can I/we book a seat	puwedeng bumili kaagad ng ticket para i-reserba ang upuan
I'd/we'd like to go to the ... please	gusto naming pumunta sa ...
[I'd like to] pay (*to a jeepney or tricycle driver*)	bayad po
how long does it take?	gaano katagal?
how many kilometres is it to ...?	ilang kilometro papunta sa ...?

please stop here	paki-tigil ditto or para
I'm in a hurry	nagmamadali ako

DIRECTIONS

where is the ...?	saan ang ...?
bank	banko
beach	beach
church	simbahan
cinema	sinehan
filling station	gasolinahan
hotel	hotel
market	palengke
moneychanger	taga-palit ng pera (*or just "money-changer"*)
pharmacy	botika
post office	koreo (*or post office*)
town hall	town hall
left	kaliwa
right	kanan
straight on	derecho/diretso
opposite	katapat ng
in front of	sa harap ng
behind	sa likod ng
near/far	malapit/malayo
north	hilaga
south	timog
east	silangan
west	kanluran

ACCOMMODATION

do you have any rooms?	meron pa kayong kuwarto?
could I have the bill please?	puwedeng kunin ang check?
bathroom	CR (*comfort room*) or banyo
room with a private bathroom	kuwarto na may sariling banyo
single room	kuwarto para sa isa
double room	kuwarto para sa dalawang tao

EMERGENCIES

fire!	sunog!
help!	saklolo!
there's been an accident	may aksidente
please call a doctor	paki-tawag ng duktor
ill	may sakit
hospital	ospital
police station	istasyon ng pulis

clean/dirty	malinis/marumi	60	animnapu	sesenta
air-conditioner	aircon	70	pitumpu	setenta
fan	elektrik fan	80	walampu	otsenta
key	susi	90	siyamnapu	nobenta
telephone	telepono	100	sandaan	syen
mobile phone/cellphone	cellphone or cell	1000	isang libo	mil
laundry	labahan	1,000,000	isang milyun	un miyon
passport	pasaporte	a half	kalahati	medio/a

SHOPPING

do you have …?	meron kang …?
[we have] none	wala
money	pera
how much?	magkano?
it's too expensive	masyadong mahal or sobra (*too much*)
I'll take this one	kukunin ko ito
cigarettes	sigarilyo
matches	posporo
soap	sabon
toilet paper	tisyu

NUMBERS

Filipinos often resort to Spanish numbers, spelt as they are pronounced, especially when telling the time.

	Tagalog	Filipino Spanish
0	zero	sero
1	isa	uno
2	dalawa	dos
3	tatlo	tres
4	apat	kuwatro
5	lima	singko
6	anim	seis
7	pito	siyete
8	walo	otso
9	siyam	nuwebe
10	sampu	dyis
11	labing isa	onse
12	labing dalawa	dose
13	labing tatlo	trese
20	dalawampu	bente
21	dalawampu't	benteuno isa
22	dalawampu't dalawa	bentedos
30	tatlumpu	trenta
40	apatnapu	kwarenta
50	limampu	singkwenta

TIMES AND DATES

Days of the week and months of the year are mostly derived from Spanish.

what's the time?	anong oras na?
9 o'clock	alas nuwebe
10.30	alas diyes y media
morning	umaga
noon	tanghali
afternoon	hapon
evening/night	gabi
midnight	hating-gabi
minute	minuto
hour	oras
day	araw
week	linggo
month	buwan
year	taon
today/now	ngayon
tomorrow	bukas
yesterday	kahapon
Monday	Lunes
Tuesday	Martes
Wednesday	Miyerkoles
Thursday	Huwebes
Friday	Biyernes
Saturday	Sabado
Sunday	Linggo
January	Enero
February	Pebrero
March	Marso
April	Abril
May	Mayo
June	Hunyo
July	Hulyo
August	Agosto
September	Setyembre
October	Oktubre
November	Nobyembre
December	Disyembre

FOOD AND DRINK TERMS

Most menus in the Philippines are in English, although in places that specialize in Filipino cuisine you'll see Tagalog on the menu, usually with an explanation in English below. For foods that arrived in the Philippines comparatively recently there often isn't an equivalent Filipino word, so to have cake, for example, you ask for cake. Even in the provinces waiters and waitresses tend to speak enough English to understand what you're after.

GENERAL TERMS

can I see the menu?	patingin ng menu?
I would like …	gusto ko …
delicious	sarap
hot (spicy)	maanghang
can I have the bill please?	puwede kunin ang check?
I'm vegetarian	vegetarian ako or gulay lang ang kinakain ko (literally "I only eat vegetables")
breakfast	almusal
lunch	tanghalian
dinner	hapunan (rare) or dinner
fork	tinidor
knife	kutsilyo
plate	plato
spoon	kutsara
glass	baso

STAPLES AND COMMON INGREDIENTS

bread	tinapay
bread rolls	pan de sal
butter	mantikilya
cheese	keso
chillies	sili
coconut milk	gata
egg	itlog
fermented fish/ shrimp paste	bagoong
fish sauce	patis
garlic	bawang
ginger	luya
noodles	pancit
onion	sibuyas
pepper	paminta
rice	bigas (the uncooked grain) or kanin (cooked rice)
salt	asin
soy sauce	toyo
sugar	asukal
tomato	kamatis
vegetables	gulay

MEAT (*KARNE*) AND POULTRY

baboy	pork
baka	beef
crispy pata	deep-fried pig's knuckle
kambing	goat
kordero/karnero	lamb
lengua	tongue
manok	chicken
pato	duck
pugo	quail
tenga ng baboy	pig's ears

COMMON MEAT DISHES

asado	roast meat
adobo	chicken and/or pork simmered in soy sauce and vinegar with pepper and garlic
beef tapa	beef marinated in vinegar, sugar and garlic, then dried in the sun and fried
Bicol Express	fiery dish of pork ribs cooked in coconut milk, soy sauce, vinegar, *bagoong* and hot chillies
bistek tagalog	beef tenderloin with lime and onion
bulalo	beef shank in onion broth
dinuguan	pork cubes simmered in pig's blood with garlic, onion and laurel leaves
ginisang monggo	any combination of pork, vegetables or shrimp sautéed with mung beans
kaldereta	spicy mutton stew
kare-kare	rich oxtail stew with aubergine, peanut and *puso ng saging* (banana flower)
lechon (de leche)	roast whole (suckling) pig, dipped in a liver paste sauce
longganisa/longganiza	small beef or pork sausages, with a lot of garlic
longsilog	longganisa with garlic rice and fried egg
mechado	braised beef
pochero	boiled beef and vegetables
sinigang	Sour fish, pork, beef, shrimp or chicken soup or stew flavoured with tamarind
sisig	fried chopped pork (usually including pig's head), liver and onions
tapsilog	beef tapa with garlic rice and fried egg
tinola	tangy soup with chicken, papaya and ginger
tocino	marinated fried pork
tosilog	marinated fried pork with garlic rice and fried egg

FISH (*ISDA*) AND SEAFOOD

alimango	crab
bangus	milkfish
hipon	shrimps
hito	catfish
lapu-lapu	grouper
panga ng tuna	tuna jaw
pusit	squid
sugpo	prawns
tahong	mussels
talaba	oysters
tanguingue	popular and affordable sea fish, not unlike tuna in flavour

COMMON SEAFOOD DISHES

daing na bangus	milkfish marinated in vinegar and spices, then fried
gambas	shrimps sautéed in chilli and garlic sauce
pinaksiw na lapu-lapu	grouper marinated in vinegar and spices, served cold
rellenong bangus	stuffed milkfish

SNACKS (MERIENDA) AND STREET FOOD

adidas	chicken feet served on a stick with a choice of sauces for dipping
arroz caldo	rice porridge with chicken
balut	raw, half-formed duck embryo
camote	sweet potato fried with brown sugar, or boiled and served with a pat of butter
chicharon	fried pork skin, served with a vinegar dip
dilis	dried anchovies, eaten whole and dipped in vinegar as a bar snack or added to vegetable stews
ensaimada	sweet cheese rolls
fishballs, squidballs	mashed fish or squid blended with wheat flour and deep-fried; served on a stick with a sweet sauce

A glossary of **Filipino fruits** is given in Basics (see box, p.33).

goto	rice porridge often containing pork and garlic
isaw	grilled chicken or pig's intestines served with a cup of vinegar for dipping
lugaw	plain rice porridge
lumpia	fried spring rolls (from Hokkien)
mami	noodle soup
mais -cob	steamed corn-on-the
pugo	hard-boiled quail's eggs, sold in packets of fifteen to twenty
pulutan	general term for snacks or finger food
puto	rice muffins
sinangag	garlic fried rice
siopao	Chinese buns filled with spicy pork
sorbetes	ice cream

DESSERTS

bibingka	cake made of ground rice, sugar and coconut milk, baked in a clay stove and served hot with fresh, salted duck's eggs on top
bilo-bilo	glutinous rice and small pieces of tapioca in coconut milk
brazos	meringues, often with cashew-nut filling
cassava cake	dark, sticky cake with a fudge-like consistency
champorado	chocolate rice pudding
guinatan	chocolate pudding served with lashings of coconut cream
halo-halo	sweet concoction made from ice cream, shaved ice, jelly, beans and tinned milk; the name literally means "mix-mix"
kutsinta	brown rice cake with coconut shavings
leche flan	caramel custard
maja blanca	blancmange of corn and coconut cream

polvoron	sweets made from butter, sugar and toasted flour, pale in colour with a crumbly texture
puto bumbong	glutinous rice steamed in a bamboo tube, infusing it with a delicate, woody taste
sago at nata de coco	blend of sago and coconut served cold in a glass
suman	sweet and sticky rice cake served inside a banana leaf
turon	banana and jackfruit in a fried spring roll

DRINKS (*INUMIN*)

(merong/walang) yelo	(with/without) ice
(merong/walang) asukal	(with/without) sugar
alak	wine (in practice, everyone just says "wine")
beer	beer
buko juice	coconut water
calamansi juice/soda	calamansi juice (see box, p.33), made into a cold drink by adding soda or a hot one with boiled water and a touch of honey
chocolate-eh	thick hot chocolate
gatas	milk
ginebra	gin
juice	juice
kape	coffee
lambanog	alcoholic drink made from fermented fruit and available in a range of flavours
mineral	mineral water
rum	rum (the popular Tanduay brand has become almost synonymous with rum)
tapuy	rice wine
tsa	tea
tubig	water
tubo juice	sugar-cane juice

Glossary

amihan the northwest monsoon from November to April (dry season)

bahay house

bahay kubo wooden house

bahay na bato house built of stone

bangka boat carved from wood, with stabilizing outriggers made from bamboo; the so-called "big bangkas" are used as ferries and often feature cabins

barangay the smallest political voting unit, whose residents elect "barangay captains" to represent their views to the mayor; barangays take different forms, ranging from part of a village through a whole village to a district of a town or city. In the Guide barangay is used more generally to mean "village".

barong or **barong tagalog** formal shirt worn by men, woven from fine fabric such as *piña* and worn hanging outside the trousers

barrio village

bulol rice god carved from wood, used by many northern hill tribes in religious rituals

buri type of palm used to make mats and rugs

butanding whale shark

capiz a white seashell that's almost translucent when flattened and is used to make windows and screens

carabao water buffalo

carinderia canteen where food is presented in pots on a counter-top

chinito a Filipino/Filipina who looks Chinese

chinoy slang for Filipino/Filipina Chinese

cogon/kogon wild grass that is often used as thatch on provincial homes and beach cottages

CR toilet ("comfort room")

DoT Department of Tourism

earthquake Baroque style of church architecture typical of Spanish churches in the Philippines, which were built with thick buttresses to protect them from earthquakes and a separate bell tower that wouldn't hit the main church if the tower collapsed

GRO guest relations officer; waitress or hostess in a bar who receives a cut of the payment for the drinks a customer buys her; often a euphemism for sex worker

habagat southwest monsoon from May to October (wet season)

ilustrado the wealthy elite

isla island

kalesa or **calesa** horse-drawn carriage, still seen in some areas including Chinatown in Manila and Vigan

kalye street

kuweba cave

mabuhay literally, "long live". Used most often at toasts, at rallies, or to welcome guests (and in tourism campaigns)

malong tube-like woven garment worn by many Muslims in Mindanao, similar to a sarong

Moro Muslim

narra the national tree, whose wood is considered best for furniture

nipa short, sturdy palm that is dried and used for building houses

nito native vine woven into hats, mats and decorative items such as lampshades

pasalubong The (almost mandatory) Filipino tradition of bringing back gifts, usually food items, for friends and family from abroad – one which serves tourist shops well

Pilipino Filipino; also means Tagalog

piña fibre taken from the outside of the pineapple and woven into fine, shiny cloth

Pinoy/Pinay slang for Filipino/Filipina

poblacion town centre

rugby boys street children, named after the "Rugby" brand of glue they are often addicted to sniffing

sabong cockfighting

sala living room

santo saint; also small statues of the saints found in churches and sold in antique shops

Santo Niño the Christ Child; patron of many communities, revered by Christian Filipinos

sari-sari store small store, often no more than a hut, selling essentials such as matches, snacks, shampoo and toothpaste

sikat native grass woven into various items, especially rugs

sitio small village or outpost, often consisting of no more than a few houses

tamaraw dwarf water buffalo, an endangered species found only on Mindoro

terno classic Filipino formal gown popularized by Imelda Marcos, with high butterfly sleeves and low, square-cut neckline

tinikling folk dance in which participants hop adeptly between heavy bamboo poles as they are struck together at shin height, at increasing speed

Tsinoy slang for Filipino/Filipina Chinese

Small print and index

A ROUGH GUIDE TO ROUGH GUIDES

Published in 1982, the first Rough Guide – to Greece – was a student scheme that became a publishing phenomenon. Mark Ellingham, a recent graduate in English from Bristol University, had been travelling in Greece the previous summer and couldn't find the right guidebook. With a small group of friends he wrote his own guide, combining a contemporary, journalistic style with a thoroughly practical approach to travellers' needs.

The immediate success of the book spawned a series that rapidly covered dozens of destinations. And, in addition to impecunious backpackers, Rough Guides soon acquired a much broader readership that relished the guides' wit and inquisitiveness as much as their enthusiastic, critical approach and value-for-money ethos. These days, Rough Guides include recommendations from budget to luxury and cover more than 120 destinations around the globe, from Amsterdam to Zanzibar, all regularly updated by our team of roaming writers.

Browse all our latest guides, read inspirational features and book your trip at **roughguides.com**.

ABOUT THE AUTHORS

Nick Edwards has written Rough Guides to Greece, India and the USA. He really enjoyed his time travelling around the beautiful Visayas and meeting the welcoming inhabitants. An Oxford University classicist, Nick has resided in Athens and Pittsburgh, and now lives with spouse Maria back in his native southeast London, from where he makes regular forays across the river to watch his beloved and mighty Spurs. Nick's other abiding passions are obscure psychedelic music and Universal Oneness.

Esme Fox has contributed to various travel guidebooks, magazines and websites, and has been a travel writer since 2009. She has lived in five different countries on four different continents, including the Philippines when she was a teenager. She loves snorkelling, and some of her favourite places in the Philippines can be found under the waves around Palawan, the Calamian Islands, and Ticao ⓦesmefox.com.

Daniel Jacobs has worked on Rough Guides to West Africa, Morocco, Tunisia, Egypt, Israel/Palestine, Kenya, India, Bolivia, Mexico, Brazil and Colombia.

Mike MacEacheran is a travel writer and guidebook author who has worked for publications including *Conde Nast Traveller*, *Sunday Times Travel*, *BBC Travel*, CNN, *The Wall Street Journal*, *The Independent* and *Esquire*. Although he has explored 106 countries, this was Mike's first visit to the Philippines. He found beach paradise on Malapascua Island and swears that to really understand the country you need to travel at least as far south as Camiguin and Siargao in Mindanao. Follow Mike on Twitter @MikeMacEacheran and see more of his work at ⓦmike-maceacheran.co.uk.

Rough Guide credits

Editors: Helen Abramson, Tim Locke and Polly Thomas
Layout: Pradeep Thapliyal
Cartography: Rajesh Chhibber
Picture editor: Aude Vauconsant
Proofreader: Susanne Hillen
Managing editor: Andy Turner
Assistant editor: Payal Sharotri

Production: Jimmy Lao
Cover photo research: Sarah Stewart-Richardson
Editorial assistant: Aimee White
Senior DTP coordinator: Dan May
Programme manager: Gareth Lowe
Publishing director: Georgina Dee

Publishing information

This fifth edition published October 2017 by
Rough Guides Ltd,
80 Strand, London WC2R 0RL
11, Community Centre, Panchsheel Park,
New Delhi 110017, India
Distributed by Penguin Random House
Penguin Books Ltd, 80 Strand, London WC2R 0RL
Penguin Group (USA), 345 Hudson Street, NY 10014, USA
Penguin Group (Australia), 250 Camberwell Road,
Camberwell, Victoria 3124, Australia
Penguin Group (NZ), 67 Apollo Drive, Mairangi Bay,
Auckland 1310, New Zealand
Penguin Group (South Africa), Block D, Rosebank Office
Park, 181 Jan Smuts Avenue, Parktown North, Gauteng,
South Africa 2193
Rough Guides is represented in Canada by DK Canada, 320
Front Street West, Suite 1400, Toronto, Ontario M5V 3B6
Printed in Singapore
© Rough Guides, 2017
Maps © Rough Guides

480pp includes index
A catalogue record for this book is available from the
British Library
ISBN: 978-0-24127-937-3
The publishers and authors have done their best to
ensure the accuracy and currency of all the information
in **The Rough Guide to the Philippines**, however,
they can accept no responsibility for any loss, injury, or
inconvenience sustained by any traveller as a result of
information or advice contained in the guide.
1 3 5 7 9 8 6 4 2

MIX
Paper from
responsible sources
FSC
www.fsc.org FSC™ C018179

Acknowledgements

Nick Edwards: In London, thanks to Gerry Panga and
Richard de Villa of the DoT; on Boracay, Charley Magabo,
Jane Santiago and the staff of *Discovery Shores*, and Archie
at *W Hostel*; on Romblon, Carlos of *Stone Creek House*, David
of *Romblon Deli* and Dennis of *Anchor Bay*; on Negros, Kaila
Ledesma in Bacolod and Dave Albao on Danjugan Island,
Peter and Daisy of *Driftwood Village* on Sugar Beach, and Zoe
at *Liquid Dumaguete*; on Siquijor, Camille and Mike Butler at
Coco Grove Beach Resort; and to Julia Crowley. Thanks also to
fellow Rough Guiders Kiki Deere, Simon Foster and Stephen
Keeling, co-authors Daniel (mind the gap!), Esme and Mike,
and to Andy and Helen for setting up and seeing through
the project. Last but not least, thanks to Maria for top work
back home, especially arranging the great do.

Esme Fox: Thanks to Rahul Aggarwal from Travel The
Unknown; Bryan Ocampo for all his invaluable knowledge
and contacts; Philippine Tourism Attaché Gerard O. Panga
for his contacts; Andrew Zuniga for his help in Bicol;
Carmel Garcia and Marjorie Avila for their assistance in
Catanduanes; blogger Apple Allison from Sole Searching
Soul for her insider tips on Naga; Francisco Correia at
Misibis Bay; tourism officer Dennis Jardin in Lucban;
tour guide Donna Gunn from Corazon Travel for her
help in Palawan; Butch F. Tan Jr. in Puerto Princesa and
Sabang; Chin Fernandez in Coron; Al and Mae Linsangan
from Calamianes Expeditions & Ecotours in Coron;
and Gemma, Simon, Sarah and Ander for their help
discovering the best bars and restaurants in Coron. A
special thanks to editors Andy Turner, Helen Abramson,

and particularly Polly Thomas. Lastly, thank you to Dan
Convey for being a fun and patient travel companion.

Daniel Jacobs: Big thanks to Jane Manibog, Gabby de Leon,
Iryn Camtan and everyone at Pension Natividad in Manila,
Sally Vitug and her team at Cagayan Provinical Tourism in
Tuguegarao, Imelda Garduque at Region 2 Department of
Tourism in Tuguegarao, Trevor and Jocelyn at Jotay Resort in
Santa Ana, Buonna at the DoT office in Vigan, Imee Awichen
and Jovi Lopez at Bontoc Municipal Tourism, Jake at
Banaue Tourism, Maribel Eugenio at Cauayan City Tourism,
Emerita B. Albas at the Mount Pulag DENR Visitors' Center in
Ambangeg, Ronette Masferré at Pines Kitchenette in Bontoc.

Mike MacEacheran: Thanks to all those who helped out
and provided assistance along the way, in particular: Jason
Keall at KLM; Princes Marie-France Anderle at *Radisson Blu
Cebu*; Frances Alfafara at *Marriott Cebu*; Katalene Agmata
and Luisa Luz F. Estanislao Eastlaw at *Amorita Resort*; Juliet
Fallowfield, Cassandra Cuevas and Lesley Tan at *Shangri-La*;
David Joyce and Matt Reed at *Evolution* on Malapascua;
Ashley Charles at *Buddha's Surf Camp* on Siargao; Bianca
Espinos on Siargao; Becky Smith and Catalina Michelle
Tina at *Hale Manna* on White Beach; and everyone at
Bohol Tourism who went out of their way to help. Thanks
to my fellow authors and ever-patient senior editor Helen
Abramson who did a stellar job in London, turning my text
into guidebook gold. Finally, to Katalin and Kyle, my official
Explorers No.2 and No.3, without whose love and support
none of this would have been possible.

Help us update

We've gone to a lot of effort to ensure that the fifth edition of **The Rough Guide to the Philippines** is accurate and up-to-date. However, things change – places get "discovered", opening hours are notoriously fickle, restaurants and rooms raise prices or lower standards. If you feel we've got it wrong or left something out, we'd like to know, and if you can remember the address, the price,

the hours, the phone number, so much the better. Please send your comments with the subject line "**Rough Guide Philippines Update**" to mail@uk.roughguides.com. We'll credit all contributions and send a copy of the next edition (or any other Rough Guide if you prefer) for the very best emails.

Readers' updates

Thanks to all the readers who have taken the time to write in with comments and suggestions (and apologies if we've inadvertently omitted or misspelt anyone's name):

Derycke Jean Baptiste, Maria Gotzner, François Longpré, Monica Mackaness & John Garratt, Jure Mesec, Michiel Ouvry, Gavin Parnaby, Dan Michael Suezo.

Photo credits

All photos © Rough Guides, except the following:
(Key: t-top; c-centre; b-bottom; l-left; r-right)
1 Robert Harding Picture Library: Aurora / Jason Langley
2 Alamy Stock Photo: Hemis / Ducept Pascal
4 Alamy Stock Photo: imagegallery2
7 AWL Images: Christian Kober (t); Danita Delimont / Karen Su (bl). **Robert Harding Picture Library:** Jose Fuste Raga (br)
8 Alamy Stock Photo: Thomas Cockrem
9 Alamy Stock Photo: Julio Etchart
10 Alamy Stock Photo: WaterFrame
11 Alamy Stock Photo: WaterFrame (t). **AWL Images:** Michele Falzone (c). **Getty Images:** Moment Open / Ferdz Decena (b)
12 Getty Images: Topic Images Inc.
13 Alamy Stock Photo: Michele Falzone (b); LOOK Die Bildagentur der Fotografen GmbH (t). **Robert Harding Picture Library:** Andre Seale (c)
14 Alamy Stock Photo: John Warburton-Lee Photography (bl); Steve Bloom Images (tr). **Getty Images:** Laurie Noble (tl); Ahmad Syukaery (br)
15 Alamy Stock Photo: Charly Iataste (b); Maximilian Weinzierl (c). **Corbis:** National Geographic Society / Mike Theiss (t)
16 Alamy Stock Photo: imageBROKER (t). **AWL Images:** Michele Falzone (b). **Getty Images:** AFP / NOEL CELIS (c)
17 Alamy Stock Photo: nobleIMAGES (tr, br); ZUMA Press, Inc. (bl). **Corbis:** Bruno Morandi (tl)
18 AWL Images: Michele Falzone
21 Corbis: Design Pics / Deddeda / www.deddeda.com
54–55 Robert Harding Picture Library: Jose Fuste Raga
57 Alamy Stock Photo: Hemis
75 Alamy Stock Photo: Prisma Bildagentur AG (t). **AWL Images:** Danita Delimont / Karen Su (br)
87 Alamy Stock Photo: Marc F. Henning (tr). **AWL Images:** Travel Pix Collection (tl). **Robert Harding Picture Library:** Jose Fuste Raga (br). Top of the Citi: William Urbano (bl)
100–101 Alamy Stock Photo: LOOK Die Bildagentur der Fotografen GmbH

103 Alamy Stock Photo: David Fleetham
113 Alamy Stock Photo: imageBROKER (t); John Warburton-Lee Photography (br). **Robert Harding Picture Library:** Oriental Touch / Hugo D. Yonzon III (bl)
126–127 Alamy Stock Photo: imagebroker
129 Getty Images: TED ALJIBE / AFP
149 Alamy Stock Photo: Hemis (t). **Getty Images:** Laurie Noble (b)
169 Alamy Stock Photo: Design Pics Inc. (b); nobleIMAGES (tr). Kiki Deere: (tl)
186–187 AWL Images: Christian Kober
189 Robert Harding Picture Library: Alain Evrard
207 Getty Images: Alex Robinson (t). **iStockphoto.com:** GoodOlga (b)
223 Alamy Stock Photo: Romero Blanco (bl); Quincy (br). **AWL Images:** Christian Kober (t)
232–233 Alamy Stock Photo: Prisma Bildagentur AG
235 Alamy Stock Photo: WaterFrame
249 Alamy Stock Photo: Thomas Cockrem (b). **Robert Harding Picture Library:** Christoffer Askman (t)
256–257 Alamy Stock Photo: Design Pics Inc.
259 Alamy Stock Photo: LOOK Die Bildagentur der Fotografen GmbH / Per-Andre Hoffmann
310–311 AWL Images: Michele Falzone
313 Robert Harding Picture Library: LOOK / Per-Andre Hoffmann
325 Getty Images: Moment Open / NICK
373 Corbis: AWL Images / Michele Falzone
385 Alamy Stock Photo: John Warburton-Lee Photography (tl); Emmanuel LATTES (tr)
400–401 Corbis: NurPhoto / Eli Ritchie Tongo
403 Dreamstime.com: Junpinzon
421 Corbis: Hironobu Takeuch (b). **iStockphoto.com:** Osborne (t)
434 Alamy Stock Photo: Universal Images Group Limited

Cover: El Nido, Palawan **Getty Images:** Tuul and Bruno Morandi

Index

Maps are marked in grey

Map symbols

The symbols below are used on maps throughout the book

International boundary	Telephone office	Chinese temple	Cliff
State/province boundary	Internet café/access	Monastery	Reef
Chapter-division boundary	Tourist office	Dive site	Beach
Road	Hospital/clinic	Monument	Lighthouse
Unpaved road	Post office	Spring/spa	Fuel station
Railway	Parking	Gardens	Market
Steps	Embassy/consulate	Waterfall	Building
Ferry route	Gate	Museum	Church (town maps)
Footpath	Point of interest	Bridge	Stadium
Airport	Ruin	Mountain peak	Beach
Transport stop	Golf course	Mountain range	Park
LRT	Statue	Cave	Cemetery
MRT	Church (regional)	Turtle nesting site	
Philippines national railway	Mosque	Shipwreck	

Listings key

- Accommodation
- Eating
- Drinking and nightlife
- Shopping

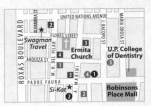

TRAVEL THE UNKNOWN